# BLIGH

## *William Bligh in the South Seas*

# ANNE SALMOND

University of California Press | *Berkeley Los Angeles London*

University of California Press, one of the most distinguished university presses in the United States, enriches lives around the world by advancing scholarship in the humanities, social sciences, and natural sciences. Its activities are supported by the UC Press Foundation and by philanthropic contributions from individuals and institutions. For more information, visit www.ucpress.edu.

First published by Penguin Group (NZ), 2011

First University of California Press edition, 2011

1 3 5 7 9 10 8 6 4 2

Designed and typeset by Anna Egan-Reid, © Penguin Group (NZ)
Maps by Outline Drafting and Graphics Ltd
Printed in Australia by McPherson's Printing Group

Library of Congress Control Number: 2011926790
ISBN 978-0-520-27056-5 (cloth : alk. paper)

# Contents

| | | |
|---|---|---:|
| | List of Illustrations | 8 |
| | List of Maps | 11 |
| | Acknowledgements | 13 |
| Introduction | The Paradise of the World | 17 |
| Chapter 1 | The Death of Captain Cook | 22 |
| Chapter 2 | The *Resolution*'s Master | 45 |
| Chapter 3 | Island of the Blest | 69 |
| Chapter 4 | The Old Boy Tips a *Heiva* | 85 |
| Chapter 5 | *Bounty* | 98 |
| Chapter 6 | The Finest Sea Boat | 122 |
| Chapter 7 | Captain Cook's 'Son' | 138 |
| Chapter 8 | Bligh / Parai | 149 |
| Chapter 9 | Mr Bligh's Bad Luck | 171 |
| Chapter 10 | These Happy Islanders | 184 |
| Chapter 11 | Huzza for Otaheiti! | 202 |
| Chapter 12 | I Have Been Run Down by My Own Dogs | 219 |
| Chapter 13 | An Island Fort | 241 |
| Chapter 14 | Murder and Mayhem | 258 |
| Chapter 15 | Pandora's Box | 279 |
| Chapter 16 | Wreck of the *Pandora* | 299 |
| Chapter 17 | The Mutineers' Babies | 312 |

| | | |
|---|---|---|
| Chapter 18 | *Providence* | 331 |
| Chapter 19 | This Modern Cyprus | 349 |
| Chapter 20 | Belle of the Isle | 367 |
| Chapter 21 | Paradise Lost | 383 |
| Chapter 22 | The Awful Day of Trial | 397 |
| Chapter 23 | A Floating Forest | 419 |
| Epilogue | Death of 'the Don' | 442 |
| | Selected Bibliography | 474 |
| | Notes | 479 |
| | Index | 515 |

*For my darling mother Joyce,*
*in her 95th year*

# List of Illustrations

1. 'An Offering before Captain Cook', by John Webber, in Cook and King (1784), IV, pl.60 — 24
2. 'Tereboo, King of Owhhee, bringing presents to Capt. Cook', by John Webber (Dixson Library, State Library of New South Wales, Sydney, PXX 2, 35) — 26
3. 'A Boxing Match before Captain Cook', by John Webber (Bernice Bishop Museum, Honolulu, Acc.no. 1922.129) — 28
4. 'Sketch of the Sandwich Islands; Sketch of Karakakooa Bay', in Cook and King (1784), IV, pl.59 — 30
5. 'Omai', portrait by Sir Joshua Reynolds (Castle Howard Collection) — 48
6. 'Ice Islands', by William Hodges (Mitchell Library, State Library of New South Wales, Sydney. PXD11 N.27) — 52
7. Chart of Van Diemen's Land by William Bligh, in Cook and King (1784), IV, pl. 5 — 56
8. 'Portrait of the Chief Kahoura', by John Webber (Dixson Library, State Library of New South Wales, Sydney. Pe 214) — 58
9. 'A Night Dance by Men at Hapaee', by John Webber (Dixson Library, State Library of New South Wales, Sydney, Pf.54) — 63
10. 'The Natche, a Ceremony in Honour of the King's Son, in Tongataboo', engraving by John Webber in Cook and King (1784), IV, pl.22 — 67
11. 'Omai's Public Entry on his First Landing at Otahelte', engraving after Daniel Rood by Royce in Rickman, John (1781), *Journal of Captain Cook's Last Voyage in the Pacific Ocean* (London) — 73
12. 'Oedidee, Otaheite', by William Hodges (National Library of Australia, Canberra, R742) — 76
13. 'Omiah, the Indian from Otaheite, presented to their Majesties at Kew, by Mr. Banks and Dr. Solander, 17 July 1774' (Rex Nan Kivell Collection, National Library of Australia) — 77
14. 'A Human Sacrifice, in a Morai, in Otaheite', by John Webber in Cook and King (1784), IV, pl. 25 — 80

15. 'War Boats of Otaheite', by William Hodges (National Maritime
Museum, Greenwich)                                                                 82
16. 'Portrait of James Cook', by John Webber (National Portrait Gallery,
London)                                                                            83
17. 'A View of Aimeo Harbour', by John Webber (British Library, London,
Add. Ms. 15513, f.20)                                                              86
18. 'A View of the Inside of a House in the Island of Ulietea', engraving by
Giovanni Battista Cipriani after drawings by Sydney Parkinson (Dixson
Library, State Library of New South Wales, Sydney, PXX2, 14)                        89
19. 'A Portrait of Poedua', by John Webber (National Maritime Museum,
Greenwich)                                                                         92
20. 'The Apotheosis of Captain Cook', engraving by Philippe Jacques de
Loutherbourg after and John Webber (Art Gallery of New South Wales,
15.1992)                                                                           99
21. 'Portrait of Joseph Banks', by Benjamin West (National Maritime Museum,
Greenwich)                                                                        106
22. '*Bounty* Decks, November 1787' (National Maritime Museum, Greenwich,
J2031)                                                                            111
23. 'Portrait of Captain John Fryer', by Gurtano Calleja (State Library of
New South Wales, Sydney, ML 413)                                                  115
24. 'A survey of Matavai Bay', by William Bligh (National Archives, UK,
MPI/1/69)                                                                         139
25. 'A Young Woman of Otaheite, bringing a present', by John Webber
(Dixson Library, State Library of New South Wales)                                142
26. "Arioi dancer', engraving by R.B. Godfrey from Sydney Parkinson, pl VII,
Parkinson (1773)                                                                  150
27. 'A Portrait of a Chief of Oporapora', by John Webber (British Library,
London, Add MS 15513, f.24)                                                       177
28. 'Dress of the Chief Mourner', by Herman Sporing (British Library,
London, Add. MS. 23921, f.32)                                                     199
29. The bullet used by Lt. Bligh to weigh rations on board the *Bounty*'s launch
(National Maritime Museum, Greenwich, F3144)                                      220
30. 'Lt. Bligh and his crew of the ship *Bounty* hospitably received by the
governor of Timor', by Charles Benazech (National Library of Australia,
Rex Nan Kivell Collection, NK5516)                                                227
31. 'The Death of Captain James Cook', by Johann Zoffany (National Maritime
Museum, Greenwich, BHC0424)                                                       260
32. 'Engraving of George Hamilton', in Hamilton (1793), frontispiece             290
33. 'The *Pandora* in the act of going down', in Barrow (1831), facing p.187     306
34. 'Portrait of Captain George Vancouver' (National Portrait Gallery,
London)                                                                           313
35. 'Figures called Ettee, Island of Otahytey. Carved on a tree' (Mitchell
Library, State Library of New South Wales, PXA563/50)                             378

36. 'Portrait of Nessy Heywood' (Manx National Heritage Library) 399
37. 'Portrait of Peter Heywood' (Manx National Heritage Library) 399
38. 'Portrait of Samuel Hood' (National Portrait Gallery) 406
39. 'North West side of Whytootackay' (Mitchell Library, State Library of New South Wales, PXA563/64) 421
40. 'Transplanting of the bread-fruit trees from Otaheite', by Thomas Gosse, engraved mezzotint (National Library of Australia, NLA pic-an6016209) 430
41. 'The arrest of Governor Bligh', 1808 (Mitchell Library, State Library of New South Wales, Safe 4/5) 464
42. 'Landing in Bounty Bay', engraving by E. Finden after F.W. Beechey, in Beechey (1831), facing p. 97 467
43. 'John Adams, aetat 65', engraving by E. Finden after F.W. Beechey, in ibid, facing p. 67 467

# Colour Plates

1. 'Portrait of William Bligh', by John Webber (private collection) PLATE 1
2. 'Portrait of Captain James Cook', by John Webber (Museum of New Zealand Te Papa Tongarewa, E10396) PLATE 2
3. 'A View taken in the Bay of Oaite Peha Bay', by William Hodges (National Maritime Museum, Greenwich) PLATE 3
4. 'The Mutineers turning Lieut. Bligh and part of the officers and crew adrift from his Majesty's Ship the *Bounty*', painted and engraved by Robert Dodd (Mitchell Library, State Library of New South Wales, Sydney, DL Pf 137) PLATE 4
5. 'A View of Kealakekua Bay', by John Webber (Dixson Library, State Library of New South Wales, Sydney, PXX 2, 39) PLATE 5
6. 'The Death of Captain James Cook', by John Webber (Dixson Library, State Library of New South Wales, Sydney, PXD59, f.1) PLATE 6
7. 'Portrait of Elizabeth Bligh', by John Webber (private collection, Australia) PLATE 7
8. 'Portrait of Captain Charles Clerke', by Nathaniel Dance (Government House, Wellington, New Zealand) PLATE 8
9. 'The *Resolution* and *Adventure* in Matavai Bay, Tahiti', by William Hodges (National Maritime Museum, Greenwich) PLATE 9
10. 'View of Morea, one of the Friendly Islands, 1787', drawn on the spot by Jas. Clevely (Mitchell Library, State Library of New South Wales, Sydney, DGD 27) PLATE 10
11. 'Otoo, King of Otaheite', by William Hodges (National Library of Australia, Canberra. R755) PLATE 11

12. 'The Bread Fruit of Otahytey' (Mitchell Library, State Library of New South Wales, Sydney, PXA 563/2)     PLATE 12

13. 'Avattarow, or Great Altar', by William Bligh (Mitchell Library, Sydney, PXA565/19)     PLATE 13

14. 'Portrait of William Bligh' (Captain Cook Memorial Museum, Whitby)     PLATE 14

15. 'Portrait of Elizabeth Bligh' (Captain Cook Memorial Museum, Whitby)     PLATE 15

16. 'The attempt by Capt. Bligh of the *Bounty* who with 18 sailors had been set adrift in an open boat on April 28th, 1789, to land on Tofoa Island', by Robert Clevely (Mitchell Library, State Library of New South Wales, Sydney, N6)     PLATE 16

17. 'The *Providence* and (her Tender) the *Assistant* 1791', by George Tobin (Mitchell Library, State Library of New South Wales, PXA563/1)     PLATE 17

18. 'Native Hut of Adventure Bay', by George Tobin (Mitchell Library, State Library of New South Wales, PXA563/16)     PLATE 18

19. 'Point Venus, Island of Otahyty', by George Tobin (Mitchell Library, State Library of New South Wales, PXA563/24)     PLATE 19

20. 'On Matavai River - Island of Otahytey 1792, from recollection', by George Tobin (Mitchell Library, State Library of New South Wales, PXA563/32)     PLATE 20

21. 'A Toopapow, with the Corpse on it', by George Tobin (Mitchell Library, State Library of New South Wales, PXA563/31)     PLATE 21

22. 'A double Canoe – Island of Otahytey', by George Tobin (Mitchell Library, State Library of New South Wales, PXA563/41)     PLATE 22

23. 'In the district of Whapiano, Island of Otahytey', by George Tobin (Mitchell Library, State Library of New South Wales, PXA563/38)     PLATE 23

24. 'Morai Point, at Oparrey – Island of Otahytey', by George Tobin (Mitchell Library, State Library of New South Wales, PXA563/42)     PLATE 24

25. 'The Morai at Oparrey, Island of Otahytey', by George Tobin (Mitchell Library, State Library of New South Wales, PXA563/39)     PLATE 25

# List of Maps

1. The Three Voyages of Bligh     endpapers

2. William Bligh at Tahiti     70

3. Tupua'i Island in 1759     247

# Acknowledgements

Writing a book about William Bligh in the South Seas has been an odyssey in its own way, with a series of discoveries and surprises.

Firstly, there is the book itself, which emerged from a wider project about the early contact period in Tahiti. In the course of the research, I did not expect to become riveted by William Bligh, that most notorious of all Pacific explorers, but that is exactly what happened. Although Bligh's role as the *Resolution*'s young master during Cook's third and last Pacific voyage has been obscured by the loss of his journal, as I studied that expedition in depth, particularly his outspoken comments on a copy of the official publication of the voyage, he began to emerge in vivid, if fragmentary, detail. The *Bounty* expedition, with its mutiny followed by an extraordinary voyage across the Pacific in the ship's launch, has always been one of the great sagas of maritime adventure, but as I read Bligh's letter to his wife from Batavia, telling her about the loss of his ship, with its raw, unguarded emotion, I became fascinated by their relationship. The letters between William and Betsy Bligh have been one of the revelations of the research, with their ardent expressions of devotion from Bligh and staunch, loving loyalty from his wife, casting shafts of light on the triumphs and disasters of his life and career.

Secondly, there is the enigma of Bligh's paradoxical character – the generous, genial patron who could turn into an overbearing, vitriolic bully, as his former protégé Fletcher Christian and his nephew Frank Bond found to their cost and consternation. If an immediate subordinate failed to live up to Bligh's exacting standards, putting the outcome of a voyage or a project at risk, they were punished with virtuoso displays of invective; although at the next moment, he might invite them to dinner. The contrasts between Bligh's tender domestic life and his public disputations and rages; his sense of injury after Cook's third voyage and his willingness to inflict almost identical insults upon others; his unwillingness to use physical violence, coupled with extreme verbal aggression; his long-standing relationship with Sir Joseph Banks alongside an almost complete lack of political sagacity, leading to a series of disasters, offer lessons in the complexity of 'human nature', and the fragility and dangers (as well as the rewards) of relationships with others.

Thirdly, as I examined each of William Bligh's three Pacific expeditions in turn – on board the *Resolution* with Captain Cook; during his first breadfruit voyage on the *Bounty*; and on the second breadfruit voyage with the *Providence*, it became clear that although he is famed as a practical seaman and hydrographer, Bligh was also a pioneering ethnographer, who made major contributions to our knowledge of life in Polynesia during the early contact period, especially in the Society Islands. Assisted by the high priest Ha'amanimani, his adopted 'uncle' from Ra'iatea, Bligh made a particular study of Tahiti; and in his charts and sketches, as well as the surviving logs and journals, made many irreplaceable observations, fostered by a close relationship with his 'family', the Pomare clan, and a confidence that Sir Joseph Banks, his patron back in Britain, would cherish any detail he could glean about life in those islands. The study of the Pacific contexts for each of these expeditions in turn illuminates the narrative, with the friendships forged by Bligh or the conflicts in which he and his shipmates engaged during successive visits helping to shape what happened later, including the fatal attack in Tonga just after the mutiny on the *Bounty*.

Finally, there is the sheer excitement and terror of these voyages, sailing in uncharted waters, through storms, frozen mazes of inlets and islands, and around coral reefs and outcrops; the intensity of relationships on board those ships, where men lived in close confinement for months and years at a time, far from their families, poorly fed and clothed, working in dank, dirty, demanding and hazardous conditions; and the perils of traversing unfamiliar 'worlds' in the Pacific and elsewhere, where people spoke unknown languages and lived by different assumptions about reality, leading to unpredictable clashes and misunderstandings. There are some terrible tales in this book – not just of the killing of Captain Cook and the mutiny on the *Bounty*, but also the lesser-known stories of the *Pandora* and her shipwreck on the Barrier Reef, the bloody affrays in which the *Bounty* sailors were involved during their time in Tupua'i, Tahiti and Pitcairn's Island, and the small boat voyages of Edwards and Oliver to the East Indies.

Following in the wake of William Bligh, I became indebted to many people. I would like to acknowledge the Royal Society of New Zealand and the Marsden

Fund for the grant, 'Cross-cultural Voyaging in the Pacific', which made the research possible. My collaborator Professor Serge Tcherkézoff of the CREDO Research Institute in Marseilles, with the support of the French Embassy in Wellington, New Zealand, helped to secure a grant from the Pacific Fund for fieldwork in France and Tahiti, and to fund the transcription and translation of documents recording early European visits to that island. In Tahiti, our friend and colleague Professor Bruno Saura of the Université de Polynésie Française, along with the Académie Tahitienne Fare Vāna'a generously checked and corrected a number of details in the manuscript; while Robert and Denise Koenig, Raanui Daunassans and Francis and Jacquie Mortimer provided hospitality and encouragement. I am grateful to Ari'ihau and Karine Tuheiava, who arranged a series of workshops in the Society Islands to foster the preservation of *marae* Taputapuatea in Ra'iatea; and the government of French Polynesia for an invitation to join the Experts' Committee for the nomination of that *marae* as a World Heritage site. In Hawai'i, I would like to pay tribute to Herb Kane, trailblazing Hawai'ian voyager and artist, whose expert knowledge of early life in Hawai'i and a memorable visit we made together to Kealakekua Bay enriched my understanding of William Bligh's visits with Captain Cook to that harbour.

I would also like to acknowledge and thank those who helped to locate the documents and books on which this narrative is based, especially the Interloans section of the University of Auckland library, and its head Christine Jackson, who tracked down a number of sources in obscure and unlikely places. This account would not have been possible without their indefatigable efforts, and those of Alan Franklin, the Librarian at the Manx National Heritage Library on the Isle of Man; my research assistant Merilyn Savill, who printed out microfilms, transcribed journals and laid them out ready for reconstructive interpretation; and Kororia Netana, who kindly assisted by tracking down and copying many published sources.

More, perhaps, than any other book that I have written, *Bligh* has been enhanced by the suggestions of a number of generous and erudite individuals. I am indebted to the Bligh scholar Rolf Du Rietz in Uppsala, Sweden, who devoted endless hours to the arduous task of commenting on the manuscript, correcting a number of errors, making insightful remarks and challenging some of my interpretations. As an unrivalled expert on the records from Bligh's voyages, he persevered with unflagging good humour and attention to detail, despite my biblio-textual lapses. We do not always agree about William Bligh, but it has been a pleasure and privilege to work with him, debating the life and career of this controversial, myth-ridden figure. Glyndwr Williams, professor emeritus in history from the University of London, brought to bear his expertise as a writer and international authority on British maritime exploration, and made a number of suggestions that transformed the manuscript; as did my friend and colleague, the historian Professor Raewyn Dalziel at the University of Auckland. Glynn Christian, authority on the mutiny of the *Bounty* and descendant of Fletcher Christian, gave helpful feedback; N.A.M. Rodger, the great authority on the British Navy at the University of Oxford, and Nigel Rigby at the National Maritime Museum in Greenwich, answered detailed questions about the role and promotion of masters; while Cassandra Pybus at the University of Sydney offered insights into the Rum Rebellion in Sydney towards the end of Bligh's career. I would also like to pay tribute to the stellar publishing team at Penguin New Zealand: my long-time friend and literary advisor Geoff Walker, doyen of New Zealand publishers, for his advocacy and support over many years; Jeremy Sherlock and Debra Millar for their invaluable advice; and Mike Wagg, astute, meticulous editor of this Pacific trilogy – *The Trial of the Cannibal Dog*, *Aphrodite's Island*, and now *Bligh*. This book owes so much to these good-hearted individuals that, in many ways, it is a collective effort.

Last and first, there is my family. Jeremy and I travelled together to Tahiti, Hawai'i and the Isle of Man, retracing the footsteps of Bligh and his wife, Elizabeth (née Betham). The joys and tribulations of research make life at once rich and demanding, and in both, Jem is the best of companions. Our daughter Amiria, until recently a Fellow at Gonville and Caius College and Senior Curator at the Museum of Archaeology and Anthropology at the University of Cambridge, and my collaborator, sparked off a strand of philosophical musing that underlies the pages that follow. This book is dedicated to my mother, Joyce Thorpe, in her ninety-fifth year of *aroha* for others.

My gratitude and thanks to all these people.

> E paru i te tinana, e mā i te wai
> E paru i te aroha, ka mau tonu e!
>
> If you're touched with mud, you can wash it off
> If you're touched with aroha (loving kindness), it lasts forever.

# Introduction

## The Paradise of the World

When William Bligh first arrived in the South Seas in 1777, the *Resolution*'s master was just twenty-two years old. A portrait painted at that time by John Webber, the expedition's artist, shows Bligh as a short, stocky, black-haired man with piercing blue eyes, a rounded face, dimpled chin and a porcelain complexion [PLATE I]. He looks quizzical and very young, in striking contrast to Webber's portrait of Captain James Cook, their tall, weather-beaten commander, with his look of determination and air of resolute authority, imposing in his post-captain's uniform [PLATE 2].[1] At this time Cook's two ships, *Resolution* and *Discovery*, were on a voyage of exploration, crossing the Pacific Ocean to search for the fabled Northwest Passage; and on his way to the west coast of America, Cook had been ordered to return Ma'i (or Omai, as he was known in Britain), a young man from Ra'iatea, home to the Society Islands.

On 12 August 1777 when the ships entered Vaitepiha Bay on the south coast of Tahiti, they were sailing into a European dream. High jagged mountains soared above a grassy plain, shaded by groves of breadfruit trees and coconut palms and carved by a winding river. During his visit in 1768, the French explorer Louis-Antoine de Bougainville had named the island 'New Cythera' after the birthplace of Aphrodite, the Greek goddess of love; while Commerson, his naturalist, described Tahiti as a Utopia where love was innocent and free:

> Born under the most beautiful of skies, fed on the fruits of a land that is fertile and requires no cultivation, ruled by the fathers of families rather than by kings, they know no other Gods than Love. Every day is dedicated to it, the entire island is its temple, every woman is its altar, every man its priest. And what sort of women? you will ask. The rivals of Georgian women in beauty, and the sisters of the unclothed Graces.

There, neither shame nor modesty enforces their tyranny: the action of creating one's fellow creature is a religious act . . . Strangers are all welcome to share in those happy mysteries, it is even a rule of hospitality to invite them: so that the fortunate Utopian continually enjoys both his own feelings of pleasure and the spectacle of those of others.[2]

At the same time in Britain, the news of an island Paradise in the South Seas was greeted with scepticism. When Captain Cook arrived at Tahiti in 1769, anchoring in Matavai Bay, Joseph Banks (the wealthy young naturalist who led the Royal Society party of artists and scientists on board the *Endeavour*) also drew on classical mythology to describe his first impressions, exulting: '[The] groves of Cocoa nut and bread fruit trees [were] loaded with a profusion of fruit and giving the most gratefull shade I have ever experienced, under these were the habitations of the people: in short the scene we saw was the truest picture of an Arcadia of which we were going to be kings that the imagination can form.'[3] When Banks returned to London, however, and James Boswell repeated his idyllic tales about Tahiti to Samuel Johnson, the great poet and essayist was scathing:

> *Boswell*: I am well assured that the people of Otaheite who have the bread tree, the fruit of which serves them for bread, laughed heartily when they were informed of the tedious process necessary with us to have bread – plowing, sowing, harrowing, reaping, thrashing, grinding, baking.

> *Johnson*: Why, Sir, all ignorant savages will laugh when they are told of the advantages of civilised life. Were you to tell men who live without houses, how we pile brick upon brick, and rafter upon rafter, and that after a house is raised to a certain height, a man tumbles off a scaffold, and breaks his neck, he would laugh heartily at our folly in building; but it does not follow that men are better without houses. No, Sir (holding up a slice of a good loaf), this is better than the bread tree.[4]

Many educated Englishmen took a similar line, and when Banks boasted about his amorous exploits in Tahiti (including a brief interlude with 'Oberea' [Purea], the 'Queen of Otaheite'), the satirists had a field day with the young botanist, mocking him in a flurry of salacious cartoons and poems.[5]

Despite these sardonic reactions, when Cook returned to Tahiti in 1773, Johann Reinhold Forster, the German naturalist on board the *Resolution*, was also moved to pay tribute to this spectacular island, quoting Virgil's description of the Elysian Fields (a vision later immortalised by John Webber in his painting of Vaitepiha Bay):

> They reached the places of joy and the grassy groves of the Happy Ones, and the homes of the Blessed. Here a more wholesome air clothes the plains in a brilliant light, and they have their very own sun and stars to enjoy.
>
> Some were exercising themselves in the grassy fields of sport, playing games and wrestling on the yellow sand; some beat out rhythms with their feet and sang songs. [Aeneas] saw others to left and right feasting on the grass, and singing a joyful hymn in chorus, amid a scented grove of laurel, whence the mighty stream of Erydanus rolls through the woodland in the upper world.[6]

As James Cook sailed away from Tahiti, even this matter-of-fact Yorkshireman lamented his departure from 'these happy isles on which Benevolent Nature, with a bountiful and lavishing hand hath bestowed every blessing a man can wish'.[7]

By the time that William Bligh, Cook's young master, arrived at the island for the first time on Captain Cook's third and last Pacific voyage, the idea of an island Paradise in the South Seas was a part of shipboard lore. During the long nights at sea, the *Resolution*'s men listened enthralled as the old Pacific hands spun yarns about their exploits, including sexual idylls with Tahitian women, while their more educated comrades drew on authors from antiquity (Virgil, Horace, Pliny and Lucian as well as Homer) and images such as the 'Islands of the Blessed' to describe their experiences.[8]

Captain Cook was now a legendary figure in the Pacific; and when he arrived in Tahiti for the last time in August 1777, landing at Vaitepiha Bay, the people cried out 'Tute!' (his Tahitian name), greeting him with joy. Although William Bligh was overshadowed by his illustrious captain, during this voyage he worked closely with Cook, surveying and charting Desolation Island (where Cook had named the first landmark 'Bligh's Cap'), the south coast of Tasmania and the Tongan archipelago; and later, the north-west coast of America and the Hawai'ian islands; taking him as his model of a naval commander. Later, when James Cook was killed at Kealakekua Bay in Hawai'i, outraged by the conduct of several of his senior officers, Bligh spoke his mind. By the time the ships arrived back in England, he had lost their patronage and support.

It was not until 1787 that William Bligh was finally given the command of a small naval armed ship, *Bounty*, and sent to collect breadfruit plants from Tahiti, and carry these to the West Indies. When they arrived in the Society Islands, David Nelson, the naturalist who had also sailed on Cook's third Pacific expedition, told the Tahitians that Bligh was Captain Cook's 'son'; and in his turn Bligh was adopted as the *taio* or bond friend of Tu, the paramount chief of the island. Standing beside Webber's portrait of Captain Cook (a gift from Cook to Tu), he was showered with gifts and hailed as a high chief. Like Cook, Bligh adored his time in Tahiti, exclaiming in his journal: '[T]his is certainly the Paradise of the World, and if happiness could result from situation and convenience, here it is to be found in the highest perfection. I have seen many parts of the World, but Otaheite is capable of being preferable to them all.'[9]

After this idyllic visit, however, when the *Bounty* headed off again into the Pacific and Bligh tried to reassert shipboard discipline, the men resisted. Although he was surprisingly lenient with the lash, Bligh had a vicious tongue; and he did not hesitate to humiliate those who failed to meet his exacting standards. When he raged at his acting lieutenant, Fletcher Christian, in front of the crew, accusing him of cowardice and theft, Christian snapped. At dawn the next morning while William Bligh was still asleep, Christian and several armed sailors burst into his cabin, taking him prisoner. Along with a number of 'loyalists' among the crew, Bligh was forced into the ship's longboat with a little food and water and set adrift off the coast of Tofua in the Tongan islands [PLATE 4]. During his extraordinary 3618-mile voyage to the East Indies in this small open boat, Bligh led the men through trials and dangers; and when he arrived back in England, he was hailed as a hero.

For the rest of his life, Bligh would blame the mutiny on Tahiti, 'the Paradise of the World', and the allure of the island's women. At first, his account – evoking as it did the trials of Odysseus, as well as Adam's seduction in the Garden of Eden – was widely accepted in Britain. In its report of the loss of the *Bounty*, for instance, the *General Evening Post* invoked the episode in Homer's epic in which Odysseus, bewitched by Circe, remained enthralled for a year on her magical isle:

> With regard to the conduct of the conspirators, the most probable conjecture is, that, being principally young men, they were so greatly fascinated by the Circean blandishments of the Otaheitean women, they took this desperate method of returning to scenes of voluptuousness unknown, perhaps, in any other country.[10]

Later, after Bligh had left England on a second voyage to fetch the breadfruit from Tahiti, and some of the mutineers were captured and court-martialled in Britain, their friends and relatives tried to save them by depicting William Bligh as a cruel and despotic captain – a classical villain. In this way, the mutiny on the *Bounty* raised questions in Britain about the legitimacy of naval authority, just as the Tuileries Palace was being stormed by the Parisian mob. According to some scholars, 'the mutiny of 28 April 1789 came to be regarded as a British equivalent of the Fall of the Bastille'.[11]

Over the past 220 years, the story of the mutiny on the *Bounty* has been told and retold in poems, pantomimes, popular journalism, films and novels as well as in scholarly studies. Typically, the tale (in parallel with the *Odyssey*) hinges upon the shipboard dynamics of the 'wooden world' of the *Bounty*, or the mutiny as a pivotal episode in Bligh's own career; while the people whom he met in Tahiti, New Zealand, Tonga, Hawai'i and other islands, and the volatile dynamics of island histories at this time, are sketched as peripheral to the main story. In these accounts, Bligh's reputation as a brutal, rapacious commander is either dramatised or revised in various ways. While I share their fascination with Bligh's complex, contradictory personality and the floating societies on board his ships, however, this book also seeks to illuminate the island world, its key players and their relationships with William Bligh, his 'father' Captain Cook and their sailors during each of Bligh's three voyages to the Pacific islands – on board *Resolution* with Cook in 1776–80, on the *Bounty* in 1787–90, and aboard the *Providence* in 1791–93.

Why? Because the tale of the mutiny on the *Bounty* and its aftermath is not just a Western story. At its heart, the historical and mythic trajectories of Britain and the South Seas intersect, transforming lives on the islands as well as on board the ships and back in Europe. This is an episode in the history of the world, not simply the history of the West; and the Pacific protagonists were as real as their British counterparts, helping to shape what happened. If in its retelling, the islanders are marginalised, this is not adequate history (although it may be powerful mythography). Rather, as those fine scholars Natalie Zemon Davis, Greg Dening and Marshall Sahlins have shown, the challenge is to work across disciplines and cultural traditions as far as possible in order to illuminate the full humanity of the past.[12]

# 1

# The Death of Captain Cook

The morning of 6 January 1779 dawned bright and clear, with light sea breezes. Over the past seven weeks Captain Cook's two ships had been sailing around the Hawai'ian islands, looking for a sheltered harbour. Day after day William Bligh, the *Resolution*'s young master, and his men had been sent out in the boats, but failed to find a safe haven. The ships had been battered by terrible storms, and their crews were weary and disgruntled. The supplies were getting low, and when Cook (who was also the expedition's purser) tried to force his men to drink sugar-cane beer instead of grog, the sailors wrote him a 'mutinous' letter.[1] As the *Discovery*'s first lieutenant, John Rickman, lamented, 'Nothing could be more toilsome or distressing than our present situation; within sight of land, yet unable to reach it; driven out to sea by one storm, and in danger of being wrecked on the breakers by another.'[2] As they headed towards the west coast of Hawai'i, where a high black lava cliff loomed up behind a low green point, Cook ordered Bligh to take in two armed boats to examine the harbour. When he returned in the pinnace that evening, having found a safe channel, Bligh reported to Captain Cook that he had found 'a tolerable shelterd bay, a good beach to land & behind it a pool of indifferent water, [and was] treat'd with great kindness on shore'.[3] As Rickman remarked: 'This was 'joyful news, and . . . the harbour promised fair to answer all that had been said of it.'[4]

On shore, too, the Hawai'ians were elated. During his visit ashore, Bligh had landed at Hikiau, one of the most important ceremonial sites on the island, where a priest's village lay beside a sacred pool at the head of the harbour. Near the pool, a stone temple (or *heiau*) stood on the black, rocky beach, shaded by a grove of trees. At dawn the next morning when Bligh guided the ships into Kealakekua Bay ('the pathway of the gods'), they were given an unprecedented welcome.[5] [PLATE 5] Huge crowds stood along the cliff tops and on the beaches, gazing at the *Resolution* and *Discovery*, and a thousand canoes paddled out to greet them. As John Ledyard, one of the marines, rejoiced:

> There were at least 15,000 men, women and children in the canoes, besides those that were on floats, swimming without floats, and actually on board and hanging round the outside of the ships. The crouds on shore were still more numerous. The beach, the surrounding rocks, the tops of houses, the branches of trees and the adjacent hills were all covered, and the shouts of joy, and admiration proceeding from the sonorous voices of the men confused with the shriller exclamations of the women dancing and clapping their hands, the overseting of canoes, cries of the children, goods on float, and hogs that were brought to market squealing formed one of the most tumultuous and the most curious prospects that can be imagined.'[6]

When the wind died and Bligh's boats took the ships under tow, hundreds of men, women and children swam 'like shoals of fish' around them.[7] So many girls clung to the side of the *Discovery* that the ship heeled over; and when the islanders swarmed on board, singing, dancing, and climbing up the rigging, women went below and offered themselves to the sailors. According to one of the sailors, 'It was with the greatest difficulty that we could move or stir on board, for the ships were thronged with them in every part, the men having taken possession of the upper-decks, and the women being nearly as numerous below.'[8] Bligh had to guide the boats through the milling canoes to get the ships safely moored. On board the *Resolution*, the deck was so crowded that they were forced to send some of the Hawai'ians overboard: 'We could not come at the ropes without first driving the greatest part of them overboard; which they bore with the utmost cheerfullness and good nature, jumping from every part of her into the water, as fast as they could, appearing to be much diverted at it.'[9]

As the ships' anchors rattled down into the bay, a fine-looking young chief named Palea boarded the *Discovery*; while Kanina, a tall, handsome man 'with lively dark eyes and [an] easy, firm and graceful carriage', climbed up the side of the *Resolution*. He was followed by a small, wizened old priest, Ko'a'a, who presented Captain Cook with a small pig and two coconuts and wrapped a length of red bark cloth around him, a gesture that acknowledged and intensified his *mana* or ancestral power. Cook invited these men to dinner, and afterwards they boarded his pinnace, escorted by William Bligh, who guided them through the throng of canoes to Hikiau, the sacred site that he had visited the previous evening. As they crossed the bay, the old priest and his companion held up long

*Captain Cook is honoured at the House of Lono in Kealakekua Bay, Hawai'i.*

white poles tipped with dog's hair, announcing the presence of the gods, and the crews of the canoes bowed their heads and covered their faces until the pinnace had passed.

On the beach, the bargemen took Captain Cook on their shoulders, and the crowd of spectators prostrated themselves, arms outstretched and faces to the ground, while the chiefs escorted Cook to the *heiau*, holding up white poles and crying out, 'The great Orono is coming!' In Hawai'i, Lono was the god of fertility, a legendary ancestor who had sailed away to the island of Kahiki (Tahiti). Every year at this time when he returned home again, bringing fertility and prosperity in his wake, the Makahiki festival was held in his honour, an exuberant affair with ceremonies at the *heiau*, feasting, dancing, singing, and boxing and wrestling matches. When Captain Cook's strange vessels arrived from Tahiti just at this moment in the ritual cycle, the priests decided that this must be Lono, sailing home, heralded by his messenger (William Bligh); and he was given an uproarious welcome.[10]

At the temple, Bligh and his crew watched as the old priest led Captain Cook to the summit, where he introduced him to a semicircle of god-images, and then holding him by the hand, climbed up a wooden scaffold. On this rickety perch, Ko'a'a wrapped Cook in red bark cloth. When they descended, the priest led the commander to a small image, Ku the god of war, asking him to salute it. Cook did so, and after this ceremony, he and his companions were regaled with a feast and *kava*, a chiefly beverage; and the priests set aside a sweet potato field beside the temple for the shore camp, erecting white rods on the stone wall around the site to make it sacred. As the islanders showered Cook with gifts, Bligh and his shipmates were in raptures. As David Samwell, the *Discovery*'s Irish surgeon, noted: 'We live now in the greatest Luxury, and as to the Choice & number of fine women there is hardly one among us that may not vie with the grand Turk himself.'[11]

Over the weeks that followed, Captain Cook was treated with reverence. When he visited the 'House of Lono', for example, the dwelling of the head priest to the west of Hikiau temple, thousands of people prostrated themselves, covering their faces. According to Ledyard, the House of Lono stood at the end of the row of priests' dwellings, interspersed with their own private baths and standing around the sacred pool, shaded by coconut palms and other trees.[12] At this idyllic spot the old priest held up Cook's arms, wrapping him in red bark cloth and anointing his head with coconut oil, chanting, although on this occasion he was introduced to an image of Lono, the god of peace and plenty. At the end of the ritual, the priests gave Cook more *kava* and a delicious meal of baked pig and sweet potatoes, feeding him by hand, a sign that he was *kapu* or sacred.

At the time of Cook's arrival, Kalani'opu'u, the high chief of the island, was away from Hawai'i, waging a successful campaign on the neighbouring island of Maui. On 24 January, however, the heralds placed a *kapu* restriction on Kealakekua Bay, proclaiming, 'The Lono Lahi is coming!' ('Great Lono', one of Kalani'opu'u's ancestral titles). When some of Cook's men went ashore, an elderly woman greeted them with a graceful *hula*, a ceremonial dance. At dawn the next morning as a fleet of 150 canoes sailed into the bay, a large double canoe approached the *Resolution*. To their surprise, Bligh and his comrades recognised Kalani'opu'u, a tall, emaciated man about sixty years old with flaking skin, inflamed eyes and trembling limbs (the marks of an inveterate *kava* drinker), as an old chief who had visited them off Maui several weeks earlier.[13] Kalani'opu'u was accompanied by his wife, his twin sons, his nephew Kamehameha (a robust, wild-looking young warrior dressed in black, the colour of war), and a powerful, agile chief named Nu'a. When Captain Cook invited them into the Great Cabin and gave them gifts, the high chief exchanged names with Cook, taking him as his bond friend. According to Ledyard, '[F]rom that moment [they seemed] to conceive an uncommon attachment to each other.'[14] In Polynesia, the ceremony

*Kalani'opu'u visits Captain Cook, with his priests and ancestral gods.*

of name exchange brought about a mingling of identities, in which bond friends acquired each other's titles and lineages, and were obliged to support each other and share their possessions. After this ritual the islanders always addressed Cook as 'Kalani'opu'u' or 'Lono', and the high chief as 'Kuki', acknowledging their special relationship.[15]

After supper Bligh escorted the high chief and his family across to the *Discovery*, the bargemen dressed in white shirts and black caps, a French horn playing. Captain Clerke presented his guests with gifts, and Bligh took them to Ka'awaloa, a chiefly village of about 300 houses on the north point of the bay. At noon the next day, he watched as a stately procession of double canoes approached the ships, their crews chanting. The first canoe brought out Kalani'opu'u and his twin sons, accompanied by Kamehameha and other warrior-chiefs, resplendent in red and yellow helmets and feather cloaks and armed with long spears and daggers. The second canoe, crewed by priests, carried Ka'u'u, the high priest of Ku, the god of war, and his son (the high priest of Lono, who was also addressed by that name),[16] and four tall wickerwork god-images covered in bright feathers, their eyes made of mother-of-pearl and their mouths bristling with dog's teeth; while the third canoe was laden with gifts of pigs and vegetables. After circling the ships, the canoes landed in front of Hikiau *heiau*, where their crews laid down their gifts, including a pile of coconuts that almost covered the beach.

When Captain Cook returned ashore in the pinnace, the people prostrated themselves. During these excursions, Cook was usually escorted by Bligh and a priest whom the sailors dubbed 'The Taboo-man', who stood in the bow, holding up a tall white rod and crying out, 'The great Orono is coming!'[17] As they landed in front of the observatory, Kalani'opu'u flung his own feather cloak around Cook's shoulders, placed a fly whisk in his hand and laid six glorious feather cloaks at his feet, the regalia of a high chief in Hawai'i. In return Cook presented his bond friend with his own naval sword, a quantity of red feathers and other gifts, and showed him around the observatory. Kalani'opu'u was enthralled by the astronomical instruments, especially the telescopes, which Cook told him were used to gaze at the stars and to guide his ships across the ocean.

Over the days that followed, the high chief showered Captain Cook and his herald William Bligh, Captain Clerke and the other officers with gifts and entertainments. On 28 January an ensign announcing the Makahiki festival, decorated with the skins of two wild geese, bark cloth and bunches of red and yellow feathers, was erected on a pole near the *heiau*, where the islanders sat in a large circle, watching the warriors compete in wrestling, boxing and other athletic matches. Bligh and his comrades revelled in this joyous interlude. When one of the *Discovery*'s officers played his violin to entertain the crowd, the islanders found this hilarious, collapsing in 'immoderate laughter';[18] although they liked the German flute played by one of the *Resolution*'s men, and a cotillion performed by some of the sailors. The mood was affable and merry; and when three midshipmen, returning to their ships, capsized their canoe in the surf, a group of children ran to fetch their parents while others pulled the officers up on the rocks and out of danger.

At the same time, however, there were clashes with local people. As David Samwell, the *Discovery*'s surgeon, confessed:

These people behave to us on all occasions when we are rambling on shore and entirely in their Power, with the utmost kindness and Hospitality, [but] it must hurt every benevolent Mind to be informed that notwithstanding all this, some among the lower Class of our People often behave in a brutal Manner towards them.

A poor Indian to day for some trifling offence on board the *Discovery*, such as not moving quick enough out of the way, had a blow given to him by one of the Captain's servants which made a large Wound on his forehead. Had any of our Men received such Treatment from the Indians we should have a number of Epithets to bestow on them such as savage, barbarous &c.[19]

*Captain Cook is honoured with a boxing match, with the Makahiki standards flying.*

When Lieutenant James King and the astronomer, William Bayly, who were in charge of the shore camp, frustrated by the *kapu* restrictions, began to bring women into their tents, the sailors followed their example, desecrating the sacred precinct. Aghast, the priests decided to remove the *kapu*. As soon as the white rods were taken down, people crowded into the tents, watching the British at work and play and marvelling at their weird behaviour.[20]

Although the Hawai'ians regarded Captain Cook with awe, they were unsure about his companions; and on 1 February when an old marine, William Watman, died on board the *Resolution*, they realised that the strangers were mortal. Keli'ikea, the bearded young leader of the Hikiau priests, gave his permission for the marine to be buried on the *heiau*, and the coffin was carried ashore, draped in a flag, and taken to the temple, led by a guard of armed marines dressed in scarlet jackets, playing the Funeral March and followed by Captain Cook, accompanied by his young master and the other officers, marching gravely in procession. As Cook read the funeral prayers, Keli'ikea threw a small pig into Watman's grave, and would have sacrificed more if Cook had not stopped him. Later that afternoon the Makahiki festival resumed with more boxing and wrestling matches; and that night the priests went to the *heiau* where they erected a funeral bier over Watman's grave, offering further sacrifices.[21]

After Watman's death, Captain Cook decided that the time had come to leave the island. His men had strained local resources to the limit, and according to King, the Hawai'ians had begun to suggest, 'stroking the sides, and patting the bellies of the sailors (who were certainly much improved in the sleekness of their looks, during our short stay in the island), and telling them, partly by signs, and partly by words, that it was time for them to go'.[22] The ships were short of firewood, however, and there were no timber trees in Kealakekua Bay. An old wooden palisade stood on top of the stone temple, topped by skulls and other human bones,[23] and early the next morning when Bligh took his commander ashore, Captain Cook offered Ka'u'u, the high priest of Ku, the god of war, two hatchets in exchange for his permission to dismantle this ramshackle structure. When he refused, Cook thrust three hatchets at Keli'ikea, the young priest of Hikiau, and ordered his men to demolish the palisade. As they did so, however, they grabbed the semicircle of wooden god-images, tossing them into the boats. When King, Cook's second lieutenant, saw this, he hurried to the high priest to apologise, although Ka'u'u seemed unconcerned, asking only that the image of Ku should be returned to him.[24]

That afternoon a Hawai'ian man performed a comic dance, entertaining the assembled crowds, followed by more boxing and wrestling matches. As Captain Cook approached, people prostrated themselves, murmuring 'Lono', and sang a song in his honour. The heralds went round the bay, calling the people to bring pigs, bark cloth, breadfruit, taro, coconuts, sweet potatoes, stone hatchets, and red and yellow feathers as gifts for 'Lono'. Assuming that this tribute, which was piled outside the priests' houses, was for him, Cook showed his gratitude that evening by firing off sky and water rockets, scattering the terrified crowd in all directions.

The next morning when the priests, led by the old high priest Ka'u'u, presented all of the pigs, feathers, bark cloth and other treasures to Kalani'opu'u (who had inherited the title of Lono from one of his ancestors), Cook was mortified. Noting his chagrin, the high chief set aside some of the gifts for his bond friend. Shortly afterwards the sailors, supervised by Bligh and Edgar, the *Discovery*'s master, dismantled the tents, loaded the sails, stores and instruments on board the boats, and carried them out to the ships. When the crew of the launch tried to haul the *Resolution*'s rudder to their boat, they found it too heavy, and asked some Hawai'ian bystanders to help them. Grabbing the rope, these men began to mock the sailors, groaning loudly as they heaved and obstructing their efforts. Thinking them insolent, Bligh's mate William Lanyon struck a Hawai'ian, and when his companions, 'shewing their disregard and scorn, which had long been growing towards us, laughed at him, hooted him, and hove stones', Ledyard, the corporal of marines, asked Captain Cook for permission to arm his men with muskets loaded with small shot. According to Ledyard, on such occasions

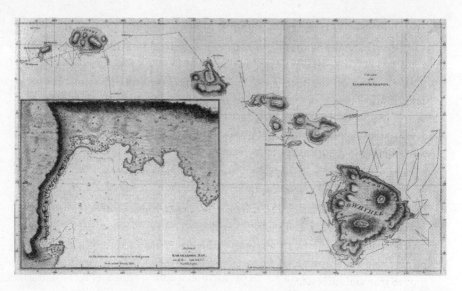

*William Bligh's survey of Kealakekua Bay.*

both Cook and Kalani'opu'u acted as peacemakers, 'and as there was really a reciprocal disinterested regard between him and this good old man it tended much to facilitate these amicable negotiations'.[25]

About the same time on board the *Discovery*, her commander Charles Clerke was told that one of the ship's cutters was missing – a wide-hulled sailing boat, used for surveying work and to ferry passengers and stores ashore. When Clerke accused Palea (who had kept the islanders in order on board the *Discovery*) of stealing the boat, the chief bared his chest, saying that it would be better for the captain to run him through with his sword than to accuse him of so dishonourable an action. Soon afterwards the carpenter's mate, who had taken the cutter ashore, returned with the boat, and Palea left the ship, fuming at this unmerited insult. That night Bligh and his shipmates watched from the *Resolution*'s deck as the houses beside the temple in which the sailmakers had slept were burned to the ground, no doubt to cleanse the broken *kapu*. At dawn the next morning when the ships sailed out of the bay, Ko'a'a, the old priest who had first boarded the *Resolution*, offered to pilot the ship to Maui. Although Kalani'opu'u and the other chiefs at Ka'awaloa village seemed relieved, according to Lieutenant King, the priests at Hikiau, the sacred precinct, lamented their departure.

During their visit to Hawai'i, William Bligh had drafted a chart of the island, showing the high mountains inland, and made a meticulous survey of Kealakekua Bay. As one of the officers remarked, Captain Cook was 'now growing exceedingly fond of this discovery, and never would think enough of his good fortune';[26] and he was eager to survey the rest of the Hawai'ian islands. On 7 February, while the ships were tacking off Maui, Cook sent Bligh in the pinnace to survey a bay on that island and look for fresh water, escorted by Ko'a'a (who was now calling himself 'Peretane' or 'Britannee' – 'Britain'). As Bligh reported when he returned to the *Resolution*:

> Instead of meeting with safe anchorage, as Britannee had taught him to expect, he found the shores low and rocky, and a flat bed of coral rocks running along the coast; and that, in the mean time, Britannee had contrived to slip away, being afraid of returning, as we imagined, because his information had not proved true and successful.[27]

A storm was blowing up, and during Bligh's absence a sudden gale hit the ships, damaging the *Resolution*'s foremast. Cursing, not for the first time, the shoddy work carried out in the naval dockyards in Britain, Cook was forced to return to Kealakekua Bay, since he knew of no other sheltered harbour nearby. When Bligh returned to the ship, having rescued an old woman and two men whose canoe had capsized in the storm, Cook sent him across to the *Discovery* to tell Captain Clerke that the *Resolution* was badly damaged, and they headed back to Hawai'i, 'all hands much chagrin'd & damning the Foremast'.[28]

On 10 February as the ships approached the big island, guided by the boats, several canoes came out to meet them. Later that day Kamehameha, the young warrior chief, boarded the *Discovery* where he bartered a feather cloak for nine iron daggers that had been forged on board the ship, each as long as his arm. As Samwell observed, over recent days the Hawa'ians had preferred these iron daggers to any other trade goods. That night Kamehameha slept on board with his male lover, shocking the sailors. The weather was wet and squally, and early the next morning the *Resolution* almost grounded on a reef. Cook hastily signalled to the *Discovery*, warning them of their danger.

At dawn when Bligh in the pinnace led the *Resolution* into Kealakekua Bay, Cook and his men were astounded to find the harbour deserted. No canoes came out to greet them, and the villages were almost empty. After the ecstatic welcome they had received just a month earlier, this was a sobering sight. As Ledyard observed:

Our return to this bay was as disagreeable to us as it was to the inhabitants, for we were reciprocally tired of each other. They had been oppressed and were weary of our prostituted alliance, and we were agrieved by the consideration of wanting the provisions and refreshments of the country, which we had every reason to suppose . . . would now be withheld from us.

What we anticipated was true. When we entered the bay where before we had the shouts of thousands of people to welcome our arrival, we had the mortification to see not a single canoe, and hardly any inhabitants in the towns. Cook was chagrined, and his people were soured.[29]

Mortified by this sombre reception, Captain Cook sent Bligh ashore to find out what was happening, who was told that Kalani'opu'u had gone away, leaving the bay under a *kapu* (or sacred restriction). During their previous visit, Cook's men had depleted the local food supplies and committed many outrages. When the sailors had sex in the sacred precinct, for example, or images of the gods were taken for firewood, many of the Hawai'ians shuddered in fear, dreading the anger of their gods. The British had not expected to be so utterly ignored, however, and Cook was dismayed and disconcerted.

Nevertheless, his first priority was to repair the *Resolution*'s foremast. By dusk, the crew had cleared the forehatch and unrigged the mast, ready to lower it into the water. That evening, to Cook's relief, some canoes straggled out bringing pigs, breadfruit, bananas, coconuts and a few women. Early the next morning, 12 February, the sailors erected the tents on their old site by the stone temple, and the sailmakers began to mend the ships' tattered sails. Although Keli'ikea, the young head priest at Hikiau, seemed glad to see the British, again setting up white rods to protect the shore camp, the atmosphere was uneasy. Later that day when Kalani'opu'u returned to the bay, accompanied by a fleet of canoes, although the high chief presented Captain Cook with gifts he seemed suspicious, asking his bond friend why he had returned to the island. According to one of the sailors:

> The King ask'd Capt Cook what brought him back again. Cook said his mast was broken. The King told the Capt. that he had amused him with lies – that when he [Cook] went away he took his farewell of him and said that he did not know he should ever come again.[30]

Kalani'opu'u must have been afraid that Captain Cook had returned to settle on the island, taking over his role as high chief; and the British were no longer welcome. Later that afternoon, Bligh and his comrades saw a large canoe filled with warriors paddle past the ships, and Clerke posted sentinels on the *Discovery*'s gangway, ordering the ship's guns to be loaded with ball. From the decks they could see a crowd of warriors on a high hill piling up heaps of stones, although they soon dispersed in the darkness. All that night, large fires flared up on shore.

Early the next morning as Bligh and his men towed the *Resolution*'s foremast to the beach, another large fleet of canoes landed at Ka'awaloa. When a group of warriors harassed the watering party, rolling lava rocks down the hill, Cook went ashore in the pinnace, where he ordered Ledyard's marines to load their muskets with ball. On board the *Discovery*, where the armourer (whom the Hawai'ians associated with Pele, the goddess of volcanoes) was working at his forge, a chief grabbed the tongs, dived overboard and swam for the shore. Clerke's men chased after the thief and captured him, bringing him back to the ship, where he was tied to the gratings and given a severe flogging. Soon afterwards when Palea, who had kept his people in order on the *Discovery* during their previous visit, boarded the ship, Captain Clerke was glad to see him, and invited him to dinner. While they were below, however, one of Palea's companions grabbed a chisel and the same pair of tongs, and leaped down into the canoe, which raced ashore. The ship's cutter set off in hot pursuit, but in their haste Thomas Edgar, the *Discovery*'s master, and his crew had grabbed only two oars and no muskets. When Captain Clerke and Palea were called on deck, Clerke ordered his men to fire at the fleeing canoe while Palea jumped into another craft and paddled off to retrieve the stolen articles.

Meanwhile at the shore camp, hearing the shots, Captain Cook ran along the beach to intercept the fleeing canoe, ordering Lieutenant King and a marine to accompany him. According to King:

> It was with great difficulty I could at all join him; on coming up to him I askd him if he had heard any tidings of the thief or thing stolen, he said no, but that they point'd a little farther.
>
> We kept running on till dark & I believe more than 3 miles from the tent, sometimes stopping & enquiring after the thief, the Captn threatening to make the Centry fire, if they did not bring the man. Whenever the Marine made any motion of presenting the Croud would recoil back, but it was observable enough that they began to laugh at our threat.[31]

While Cook and King were off on this wild goose chase, armed warriors gathered behind the beach, led by the high priest of Lono (the son of the high priest of Ku), a man who like Cook and Kalani'opu'u also carried the title of

Lono, whom the Hawai'ians 'revered almost to adoration'. Out in the bay, a canoe brought the tongs and chisel out to the cutter and gave them to Edgar, along with the lid of a water cask that no one on board had realised was missing.

Just as Edgar was about to return to the *Discovery* with the stolen items, however, the crew of the *Resolution*'s pinnace, which lay just off the beach, decided to go to his assistance. Since William Bligh usually commanded the pinnace and he and Edgar had a close working relationship, it is likely that the young master led this impetuous foray. Seeing that he was about to be reinforced, Edgar resolved to capture the canoe that had rescued the thief, which was now hauled up on the beach. When George Vancouver, one of the *Discovery*'s midshipmen, jumped ashore, grabbed this craft and began to shove it into the water, however, Palea tried to stop him, protesting that this was his canoe. As the chief seized the paddle, Edgar rushed to help the midshipman; and although Palea repeated that this was his canoe, the master ignored his protest, trying to wrest the paddle from him. In response, Palea pinioned Edgar's arms behind his back, grabbing him by the hair; but when the chief turned towards the canoe, one of the crew of the pinnace hit him on the back of the head with an oar, knocking him down. In a rage, Palea seized the oar and smashed it over his knee, while about 300 infuriated warriors standing on a rise behind the beach whirled their slings, hurling a volley of rocks at the sailors.

As the pinnace's crew brandished their swords, they were hit by a withering barrage of stones, and were forced to abandon their boat and swim out to the cutter, which had stayed at a safe distance offshore. While the warriors plundered the pinnace, which had grounded, stripping her of oars and sails, Edgar and Vancouver, who could not swim, waded out to a rock in the tide where they were pelted with stones. Just as a warrior attacked Edgar with a broken oar, the midshipman stepped forward and intercepted the blow. Fortunately at that moment Palea stopped the attack, urging Edgar and Vancouver to return to the *Discovery*. When they said that they could not do this because the warriors had taken their oars, Palea went to retrieve them, and Edgar headed along the beach to the shore camp to fetch help, while Vancouver climbed into the pinnace.

As soon as Palea was out of sight, however, the warriors attacked again, knocking Vancouver down, and taking his cap. Fortunately for the young midshipman, Palea had met Edgar on his way to the shore camp, and giving him a pair of oars, sent him back to rescue his comrade. Pushing off the pinnace, Edgar helped Vancouver to row out to the cutter, and as they headed back to the shore camp, Palea met them in his canoe, returning Vancouver's cap and asking anxiously whether 'Kuki' would kill him for what had happened. Back at the camp, Captain Cook rebuked his men for taking his pinnace without permission, and for confronting the Hawai'ians while they were unarmed, exclaiming, 'The behaviour of the Indians would at last oblige him to use force; for that they must not . . . imagine that they have gained an advantage over us.'[32] That night, Bligh and his shipmates watched uneasily as fires flared up along the cliff tops, and warriors crept behind the stone walls around the tents, trying to find a way into the shore camp. Although the sentry fired at one of these men, the musket flashed in the pan and the warrior escaped unharmed. During the rest of the night, as Lieutenant King remarked, 'we remained unmolested'.[33]

At dawn the next morning, 14 February, Lieutenant Burney, the officer on watch on board the *Discovery*, realised that the ship's great cutter was missing. Overnight, the boat had been sunk to stop its planks from warping, and in the dark, warriors had cut it loose from the buoy and towed it away, no doubt in retribution for the attack on Palea. This was a serious loss, and when Burney reported the theft, Charles Clerke boarded his pinnace and rowed across to the *Resolution* to inform his commander. Upon hearing Clerke's report, Captain Cook suggested that his consort captain should go ashore, invite Kalani'opu'u on board the *Discovery* and take him hostage until the Hawai'ians had returned the cutter. At this time, however, Clerke was very ill with tuberculosis, and he begged to be excused, pleading that the 'least rough useage from the Natives would shake him to pieces'.[34] Hearing this, Cook decided to go ashore himself and bring the high chief out to the *Resolution*; or if that failed, to seize the large canoes in the bay and burn down the houses at Ka'awaloa.

Having made this decision, Cook began to fire off orders, telling Clerke to despatch the *Discovery*'s launch and small cutter, their crews armed with muskets loaded with ball, to the south-east point of the bay, to search for the great cutter and stop the canoes from escaping. As soon as Clerke left, Cook sent William Bligh with the *Resolution*'s great cutter to intercept a big sailing canoe that was heading out to sea, and John Williamson, the ship's Irish third lieutenant, to take the launch with a crew of forty armed men, accompanied by the small cutter (commanded by William Lanyon, one of Bligh's mates), to the north-west point to seal the blockade. When James King, who was in charge of the shore camp, arrived on board to check his timepiece and inform his commander of the attempted attack the previous night, he found Cook loading his double-barrelled musket, with ball in one barrel and small shot in the other. Captain Cook told King to return to the camp by the temple and to keep the people quiet, by assuring them that they would not be molested.

As the boats set off, Bligh in the *Resolution*'s great cutter chased the sailing canoe, which fled along the eastern coastline. When they caught up with it, his crew fired their muskets, driving the great canoe ashore at the east point of the bay, where its occupants scrambled ashore. Afterwards, Bligh learned that this canoe had been carrying 'Lono', the sacred high priest who had commanded the warriors the previous day. On board the *Resolution*, Captain Cook stood watching the pursuit; and when one of his men asked what would happen if the warriors in the fleeing canoe fought back, he replied confidently, 'There could be no great difficulty, for he was very positive the Indians would not stand the Fire of a single Musket.'[35] At 7 a.m. when all of the boats were at their stations, Cook boarded the *Resolution*'s pinnace, accompanied by Molesworth Phillips (the Lieutenant of Marines), a sergeant, a corporal, seven privates and a crew of six armed men led by Henry Roberts, another of Bligh's mates, and headed off to Ka'awaloa.

As they approached the chiefs' village, Cook hailed Lieutenant Williamson in the launch, ordering him to come in closer to the beach and lay on the oars, keeping his eye on the pinnace. When they landed, Lieutenant Phillips ordered the marines to line up along the beach, and Cook sent a messenger to fetch Kalani'opu'u's twin sons, who had often stayed with him on board the *Resolution*. Upon their arrival, the boys told Captain Cook that their father was asleep in a nearby house and led him to Ka'awaloa, escorted by the marines in their scarlet jackets. As this procession marched through the paved streets of the village, the Hawai'ians prostrated themselves, but the men were wearing black, the colour of war; and behind the houses, women and children were fleeing to the mountains. Kalani'opu'u's sons entered the house where their father was sleeping, which stood about 100 yards from the beach, and although several attendants came out with gifts of pigs and red bark cloth, there was no sign of the high chief. Fearing that he had been tricked, Cook sent Lieutenant Phillips in to the house, who found that the high chief was just stirring. When Phillips took Kalani'opu'u by the hand, telling him that Captain Cook had come to see him, the high chief seemed disconcerted. No doubt he was surprised to have been woken in this way, because in Hawai'i it was considered dangerous to startle a sleeping person, because their spirit was wandering and might not be able to return to their body.

As soon as Kalani'opu'u appeared, Captain Cook invited the high chief to share his dinner on board the *Resolution*. After talking with him, Cook was convinced that Kalani'opu'u knew nothing about the theft of the *Discovery*'s cutter, but was still determined to take him hostage (a terrible breach of his obligations to a bond friend). They linked arms, and as they walked towards the beach, one of Kalani'opu'u's sons ran ahead and jumped into the pinnace, eager to go out to the ship. By this time the beach was crowded with people, and when a canoe raced ashore, bringing a man who yelled that Lieutenant Rickman (who commanded the *Discovery*'s launch) had shot a chief named Kalimu on the east side of the bay, the crowd began to mutter in anger. According to the oral traditions, the messenger cried out to Kalani'opu'u, 'Oh heavenly one! Stop! It is not safe on the sea; Kalimu is dead. Go back to the house.'[36] When she heard this, Kanekapolei, the mother of the boys, burst into tears and threw her arms around her husband's neck, begging him to stay ashore; and two chiefs took the high chief's arms, tugging him away from Cook and forcing him down on the beach, where he sat looking 'dejected and frightened', telling Captain Cook that he could not go with him out to the *Resolution*.

By this time, about 2000 warriors were milling about on the beach. Anxious to secure his line of retreat, Lieutenant Phillips suggested that the marines should line up along the shore; and Cook agreed, remarking, 'We can never think of compelling him [Kalani'opu'u] to go onboard without killing a number of these People.'[37] As the marines marched to the rocks, the people let them through although, at the back of the crowd, men were arming themselves with clubs and iron daggers. When an old priest approached Cook and Phillips, chanting at the top of his voice and offering them a coconut, Captain Cook shouted, 'Get away, get away!' Just at that moment, however, a warrior hurled a piece of breadfruit in his face, and Koho, the chief of the Kona district, dressed in a thick war mat and brandishing a dagger, threatened him with a stone, calling him a traitor. Incensed, Cook fired his musket at the chief, using the barrel loaded with bird shot. As one of his midshipmen, Watts, later remarked: 'This piece of ill-timed humanity in the Capt. only exaggerated the difficulty & encreased the Audacity of the Chiefs.' When he realised that he was not hurt, Koho yelled out in triumph, saying that his mat was not 'burnt';[38] and another man began to advance on Lieutenant Phillips, who fended him off with the butt of his musket.

As a warrior whirled his sling, hurling a stone and knocking down a marine, Captain Cook fired a musket ball at him but missed, shooting another warrior through the thighs. When the sergeant told him that he'd killed the wrong man, Cook ordered him to shoot the right man instead; and the sergeant did so, although this man was standing next to Kalani'opu'u. Enraged, the warriors hurled a furious volley of stones; and as the barrage struck, the sailors in the *Resolution*'s launch and pinnace opened fire with their muskets. According to Watts, Cook was angry with his men for firing without permission: 'The Captain perceiving this done without Orders turned to the Boats, waved his hand & ordered with much warmth a cessation; in the mean time the marines with the same undisciplined infatuation began to fire also.'[39] As soon as Cook ordered the marines to cease fire, however, they dropped their muskets and fled into the sea. In the confusion Lieutenant Phillips was hit by a stone; and as he fell, a warrior stabbed him in the shoulder with an iron dagger. Phillips managed to shoot his assailant, who fell dead at his feet; and seeing that 'all my people were totally vanquished', he also dived into the ocean.

Captain Cook, who could not swim, was left alone on the beach. After fending off some warriors with the butt of his musket, he aimed the gun at them, which made them pause for a moment. When he turned to wade out to the pinnace, however, commanded by Bligh's mate Henry Roberts, one of the Hawai'ians struck Cook on the back of the head with a club. Crying out 'My God!,' he fell to one knee, dropping his musket; and as he staggered, Nu'a, the powerful, agile chief who had visited him on board the *Resolution*, stabbed him in the base of the neck with one of his own iron daggers.[40] As Cook toppled face forwards into a channel in the reef, a warrior held his head underwater. According to Samwell, 'One man sat on his Shoulders & beat his head with a stone while others beat him with Clubs & Stones, they then hauled him up dead on the Rocks where they stuck him with their Daggers, dashed his head against the rock & beat him with Clubs and Stones.'[41] [PLATE 6]

When Roberts ordered his crew to row in and rescue their captain, the pinnace grounded on a rock. As the fleeing marines scrambled into the boat, jostling her crew, who were unable to aim their muskets, they were forced to watch in horror as many of their shipmates were slaughtered. Four marines, who like Cook could not swim, waded into the sea, where they were struck down. Although one of these men, John Allen, cried out to the men in the launch, begging them to save him, John Williamson, the *Resolution*'s third lieutenant, ordered the crew to row away from the beach, threatening them at gunpoint when they begged to go in and rescue their shipmates. Later, Williamson protested that when Captain Cook waved out to him, he thought that he was ordering him to return to his station, although no one believed this improbable story.

Back on board the *Resolution*, where Lieutenant Gore had taken over the command, the sailors fired their cannons into the crowd of warriors on the beach, dispersing them. Despite this lull in the fighting, Williamson ordered his men to retreat to the *Resolution*, although not before directing William Lanyon (another of Bligh's mates) in the *Resolution*'s small cutter, with his crew of four midshipmen, to go in to the beach and shoot any remaining warriors. After

Lanyon's men had fired only a few shots, however, Williamson ordered them to retreat, and they were unable to retrieve the bodies of their commander and their fallen comrades. Lieutenant Phillips, who had dived from the overcrowded pinnace, swam across to the launch; and as soon as he was pulled on board, accused Williamson of cowardice, and later said that he had thought of shooting him on the spot.

When the launch reached the *Resolution*, the sailors saw that Williamson's men had barely fired their muskets, and that their cartridge boxes were still full. Upon hearing that Captain Cook had been killed, they 'cry'd out with Tears in their Eyes that they had lost their Father!'[42] As George Gilbert, one of the *Resolution*'s midshipmen remarked:

On the return of the boats informing us of the Captains Death, a general silence ensued throughout the ship for the space of near half an hour: it appearing to us somewhat like a Dream that we could not reconcile ourselves to for some time. Greif was visible in every Countenance; some expressing it by tears and others by a kind of gloomy dejection, for as all our hopes centred in him, our loss became irreparable and the sense of it was so deeply impressed upon our minds as not to be forgot.[43]

After hearing Lieutenant Williamson's report of what had happened, Gore sent the third lieutenant to tell Captain Clerke that Captain Cook was dead, and that he was now in command of the expedition.

By the time that Williamson boarded the *Discovery*, the news about his role in Cook's killing had spread. According to one of the eyewitnesses, as the launch came alongside 'a great Clamour arose immediately', and one of the mates shouted, 'Did not our Irishman make a notable retreat?'[44] James Trevenen, a midshipman who had been on board the *Resolution*'s small cutter that morning, spoke for many of his shipmates when he wrote later: '[Williamson] is a wretch, feared and hated by his inferiors, detested by his equals and despised by his superiors; a very devil to whom none of the midshipmen spoke for above a year.'[45] Although the *Discovery*'s midshipmen urged Captain Clerke to arrest Williamson, saying that he had deserted Cook and their comrades, his men were so afraid of the lieutenant, a notorious bully, that they stood 'as mute as blocks'; and only one of them was brave enough to testify against him. No doubt for the same reason, Roberts and Lanyon, Bligh's two mates who had been at the scene and blamed Williamson for abandoning Cook, changed their story when they were questioned by the captain.[46]

Without a formal complaint, Charles Clerke could not act. As the men clamoured for revenge, he tried to calm them, saying, 'Yes damn me boys you shall
and by God I'll head you myself, but in the meantime we must get our foremast
and boats off, that's the first thing boys, for by God we are ruined if we don't
get our foremast!'[47] Boarding his boat, Clerke rowed across to the *Resolution*,
where he found William Bligh waiting alongside in the great cutter. Ordering
the master to go to the shore camp, he instructed him to tell Lieutenant King
to get the mast in the water as quickly as possible, pack up the tents and return
with his men to the *Resolution*.[48]

At the shore camp, which was guarded by only seven marines, Lieutenant
King and William Bayly (the astronomer) had been startled to hear cannon fire
at Ka'awaloa. When the priests asked King what was happening, and a canoe
crossed the bay to report that Captain Cook had been killed, King assured them
that this could not be true, because Cook was still on board the *Resolution*.
Nevertheless, he told Keli'ikea to bring his grandfather, the high priest Ka'u'u,
and the other priests into a large house by the *heiau* for their own safety. When
Bligh arrived at the shore camp and told King that he was ordered to evacuate
the camp at once and tow the mast back to the ship, the second lieutenant ignored
Clerke's instructions. Posting the marines on the summit of the *heiau*, he handed
over the command to Bligh, and taking the cutter, hurried back to the *Resolution*.
Warriors were already arriving from the other side of the bay, and as the cutter
rowed away they began to hurl stones at Bligh's small party, although the young
priest tried to stop them. Fortunately Lieutenant Rickman in the *Discovery*'s
launch, noticing their plight, landed to reinforce Bligh and his men. The warriors continued their attack, and when some of them were shot, the sailors were
amazed to see how bravely their companions faced the muskets, trying to drag
their wounded back to safety. One man in particular made several attempts to
rescue his injured comrade, although he was badly wounded on each occasion,
until finally he fell dead beside the *heiau*.

As soon as Lieutenant King arrived on board the *Resolution*, he asked Clerke
to fire the ship's cannons at the warriors who were attacking the shore camp.
Although the cannonballs missed the warriors, one ball hit a rock and shivered it
to pieces while another smashed a coconut tree in half, terrifying the Hawai'ians.
At 10 a.m. when King returned to the shore camp, accompanied by the rest of the
ship's boats and a large contingent of armed men, he spoke to Keli'ikea, saying
that if he told the warriors to stop hurling rocks at the marines, he would order
his men to stop firing. The young priest agreed, and the warriors stopped their
barrage. By this time, about eight or nine Hawai'ians had been shot. According

to John Watts, who arrived with the boats, 'It was however manifest that they never would Attempt a close fight & we only acted upon the defensive till the Tents were put in the Boats & our Carpenters had rolled the Mast into the Water in order to carry it on Board.'[49] At about 1 p.m. as the boats rowed away, with Bligh in the great cutter, the warriors hurled a few desultory stones with their slings, and then the bay was quiet.

Stunned by the death of their commander, Captain Cook's men looked around for a scapegoat. Although some blamed Lieutenant Rickman for shooting Kalimu, whose death had infuriated the Hawai'ian warriors, most accused John Williamson, the *Resolution*'s third lieutenant, of deserting their commander. William Bligh saw it differently, however. That night before he went to sleep, he wrote a detailed account of everything he had heard about Captain Cook's death, although this narrative has not survived. Years later when he was working at the Hydrographic Office and a copy of King's account of the voyage came into his hands, Bligh picked up a pencil and savagely annotated it in the margins.[50] In his view, King was a dilettante who had avoided the worst of the fighting, and Bligh never forgave him for abandoning him and his small party at the shore camp.[51] He thought that the marines, led by King's friend Molesworth Phillips, were ill-disciplined and badly led, and that their cowardice was largely responsible for the death of their commander; and that King's account of Cook's death was inaccurate and self-serving.

Beside King's account of the attack on Cook, for instance, Bligh scrawled, 'The Marines fired & ran which occasioned all that followed, for had they fixed their bayonets & not run, so frightened as they were, they might have drove all before them.'[52] He added caustically, 'The whole affair from the Opening to the End did not last 10 minutes, or was their a spark of courage or Conduct shown in the whole busyness.'[53] King's comment that Cook's temper might have led to his death provoked an infuriated riposte: 'Mr. King is fully of p . . . y in this.'[54] Beside King's glowing tribute to Phillips for saving a marine from drowning after the attack, Bligh noted with venom, 'This person [Phillips], who never was of any real service the whole Voyage, or did any thing but eat and Sleep, was a great Croney of C. King's. The Man was close to the Boat & swam nearly as well as the Lieut, [who] was only near him.'[55]

To Bligh's indignation, in his account of Cook's death, Lieutenant King wrote that 'having placed the marines on top of the Morai, which formed a strong and advantageous post, and left the command with Mr. Bligh, giving

him the most positive directions to act entirely on the defensive, I went on
board the *Discovery*, in order to represent to Captain Clerke the dangerous
situation of our affairs,'[56] but that despite his instructions, the master had
allowed the marines to open fire on the Hawai'ians. Incensed that King, who
had ignored Clerke's orders to immediately evacuate the shore camp, was
trying to shift the blame for the shootings onto his shoulders, Bligh wrote a
comment so incendiary in the margin that somebody (probably Bligh himself)
later erased it. Later, beside King's account of the retaliatory attack on the
Hawai'ians, which he claimed to have missed because he was unwell, Bligh
retorted, 'Whenever any dangerous situation should be taking place he [was]
allways being ill.' Beside a passage in which King deplored this raid, when a
village had been burned, some Hawai'ians shot, and the heads of two warriors
brought back to the ship, remarking, 'I am sorry to [say], that our people were
hurried into acts of unnecessary cruelty and devastation,' Bligh exclaimed, 'A
pretty Old Woman's story . . . If this had not been done they would never have
been brought to submission.'[57] On the subject of John Williamson's conduct at
Kealakekua Bay, he remained silent.

Although Bligh's own journal of the voyage has not survived, his views of
Cook's death, inscribed in these scribbled marginalia, say as much about Bligh
as they do about Lieutenants King and Phillips. William Bayly, the astronomer,
for instance, who was at the shore camp with Lieutenant King, gave an account
of the events at the *heiau* which closely mirrors that of King; while Trevenen,
the young midshipman who loathed Lieutenant Williamson, regarded King as
a hero (although he also admired William Bligh, remarking that after Cook's
death, both he and King 'reached & saved me from the gulph; & offered me the
use of their cabins & advice').[58] In his own report on what happened on the beach
at Kealakekua Bay, although Lieutenant Phillips made no mention of saving one
of his men from drowning, many of his shipmates mentioned this brave act; and
only Bligh ever denied that it happened.

While some of Bligh's accusations are overheated, however, he owed a great
deal to Captain Cook, and his commander's death at Kealakekua Bay left him
with a burning sense of injustice. Cook had given Bligh his first great chance, and
during this voyage of discovery they had worked closely together. Like Bligh,
James Cook was a skilled hydrographer and cartographer, who had struggled
for advancement in the Royal Navy. By sheer competence and courage, however,
Cook had risen to command the *Endeavour* and *Resolution*, winning a reputation
as one of the Navy's greatest commanders. As a Member of Parliament, William
Windham, later exclaimed to James Burney (formerly first lieutenant of the

*Discovery*) at a turning point in Bligh's own career, 'What officers you are! *You men of Captain Cook!* You rise upon us in every trial!'[59]

And yet despite Captain Cook's brilliant reputation, after his untimely death none of the officers whose conduct had been questioned were held to account, either during or after the voyage. When Charles Clerke took over the command of the expedition, Lieutenants King and Williamson were both promoted, although Clerke collected affidavits about Williamson's actions for a possible court martial back in England; while Bligh's mate William Harvey, whom Captain Cook had earlier disrated and sent into the *Discovery* for letting a prisoner escape, was brought back to the *Resolution* as her third lieutenant. According to Bligh, neither King nor Williamson were good practical sailors; and when the ships sailed from Hawai'i and Captain Clerke was so weak that he could not come on deck, 'he publickly gave me the Power solely of conducting the Ships & moving as I thought proper. His orders were "You are to explore the Isles as much as you can & from thence carry the Ships to Kamschatka & thence do your utmost endeavours to discover the NW Passage."'[60] Bligh often exaggerated his own role in events, however; and it is unlikely that Clerke would have ignored his two senior officers in this way. No doubt he had been outspoken about the events at Kealakekua Bay; and after Clerke's death in Kamchatka on the east coast of Russia, there were no more signs of confidence in the *Resolution*'s master.

In the flurry of promotions that followed Clerke's death, William Lanyon, another of Bligh's mates, was made second lieutenant of the *Discovery*. Although Bligh had worked well with Lanyon, this must have been galling. This was the second of his mates who had been made an acting lieutenant during the voyage; while Bligh himself, having passed his lieutenant's exam before leaving England, was eager for a commission.[61] The affidavits that Clerke had collected (which may have included Bligh's account of Cook's death) were destroyed;[62] and the last instalment of Captain Cook's journal describing his final visit to Hawai'i is also missing.[63] Many years later, Lieutenant Phillips wrote that 'Williamson most certainly would have been broke had Capt. Clarke lived, depositions were taken, but when Clarke died Williamson broke open the Captain's bureau, and procured the papers';[64] while according to the midshipman Alexander Home, Williamson took other precautions, forming a kind of 'mason's lodge' on board the *Resolution* by 'bribing [the sailors] with brandy, and got them to promise as brothers, they would say nothing of his cowardice when they came back to England'.[65] Perhaps Bligh joined this 'lodge', because he always kept silent about his comrade's conduct at Kealakekua Bay. Williamson was right to be afraid, because the Articles of War that were read out to the crew on board every

British naval vessel declared: 'Every person in the fleet, who through cowardice, negligence, or disaffection, shall in time of action withdraw or keep back, or not come into the fight or engagement, . . . and being convicted thereof by . . . a court-martial, shall suffer death.'[66]

When the *Resolution* and *Discovery* returned home, it is likely that Bligh's willingness to speak his mind about some of his senior officers put their careers at risk. Both Phillips and King had influential friends, however, and when the ships limped back to England, King and Phillips were both promoted (as was Williamson), while King was commissioned to write the third volume of the official *Voyage*, using Bligh's charts without permission or acknowledgement. To make matters worse, King attributed these charts to Henry Roberts, Bligh's mate who had worked under his supervision, and was now promoted to lieutenant. In the *Voyage*, King failed to mention that Captain Cook had been left to die alone on the beach at Kealakekua Bay, suggesting instead that his commander had caused his own death by provoking the Hawai'ians.[67] Almost alone among Cook's officers, William Bligh was not promoted.[68]

If Cook's death in Hawai'i was shocking, the way that it was dealt with was shabby. While Captain Cook's own reputation had been sullied, those who had abandoned him on the beach were rewarded. As for Bligh, despite the long hours in the boats and his meticulous surveys and charts, he was denied any recognition for his contributions to the voyage. It is not surprising that when he read King's account of what had happened in Hawai'i, he burned with rage. Although the great Cook scholar J.C. Beaglehole once asked, 'Why was Bligh so rancorous? I confess I do not know,'[69] it seems that the answer lies here, in the circumstances surrounding Captain Cook's death in Kealakekua Bay, and its aftermath back in Britain.

# The *Resolution*'s Master

Since he was a boy, William Bligh had been destined for a naval career. Born on 9 September 1754 at Tinten Manor, his grandfather's stone farmhouse in Cornwall in the parish of St Tudy, he belonged to a family that had produced Admiral Sir Richard Rodney Bligh (1737–1821), General Edward Bligh (1685–1775), the Earls of Darnley, and five mayors of Bodmin.[1] According to family records, a month after his birth William was baptised at St Andrew's Church in Plymouth, where his father Francis worked as a customs officer. Both of his parents had been married before, and his mother, Jane Pearce, who was forty-one years old when he was born, already had a grown-up daughter who was married to John Bond, a naval surgeon.[2] Given these links with the Navy, it is not surprising that in July 1762, when William was just seven years old, he was listed as a 'captain's servant' on the muster roll of a 64-gun warship, HMS *Monmouth*.

Instead of sailing on the *Monmouth*, however, it is likely that young William remained safely on shore. At this time in the Navy, when midshipmen had to serve six years at sea before they could be promoted to lieutenant, parents with influence often asked a ship's captain to register their son as a servant, allowing him to put in 'sea time' while still living on land. In any case, over the next seven months before the old warship was decommissioned, the *Monmouth* spent most of her time tied up in Plymouth Sound, apart from an occasional cruise in the Channel.[3]

Little is known about William Bligh's upbringing. He once told a friend that when he was introduced to George III after his *Bounty* voyage, and the King asked him about a scar on his face, he had to confess to his monarch 'that his father, in throwing a hatchet to turn a horse which they were both trying to catch in an orchard, accidentally struck him on the cheek'.[4] As the only son of older parents, Bligh's childhood must have been lonely, although he was devoted to his half-sister Catherine and her husband. During his education, he learned to write vividly and well, and became an excellent mathematician. In 1769 when he was fifteen years old, his mother Jane died, and the following year his father married for the third time.[5]

Two months later Bligh enlisted as an able-bodied seaman on board the *Hunter*, a 10-gun sloop commanded by John Henshaw, on patrol in the Irish Channel. It seems likely that William joined up as an AB while waiting for a midshipman's berth to become vacant; and six months later, his hopes were rewarded when he was promoted to midshipman.[6] In 1771 Bligh transferred to HMS *Crescent* as a midshipman, a 32-gun frigate and former French privateer commanded by Captain Corner, who sailed to the Leeward Islands in the Caribbean. It is possible that he began to study surveying at this time, although none of his early charts have survived.[7] Captain Corner was a harsh disciplinarian; and in 1774 when the *Crescent* returned to England, seventeen of Bligh's shipmates were flogged for attempted desertion.

Back in England, Bligh was appointed as the second mate of the *Ranger*, a leaky 8-gun sloop commanded by his former captain, John Henshaw, who promoted him back to midshipman the following year.[8] Once again Bligh was on patrol in the Irish Sea, sailing between Holyhead, Liverpool and the Isle of Man, a notorious haven for smugglers. During this tour of duty, he completed the six years at sea that was required for a naval commission. When the War of Independence with the American colonies broke out in 1775, the *Ranger* was ordered to intercept and search ships suspected of carrying intelligence to the rebels. During these patrols the *Ranger* often anchored in Douglas Harbour, the main port on the Isle of Man, and during one of these visits it seems that Bligh met Elizabeth Betham [PLATE 7], the vivacious, attractive daughter of a prosperous family on the island. Elizabeth's father, Dr Richard Betham LLD, was Receiver-General of Customs at Douglas; her maternal grandfather Dr Neil Campbell was Principal of Glasgow University and Chaplain to the King, a friend of Adam Smith and David Hume, leading figures in the Scottish Enlightenment; while her uncle, Duncan Campbell, was a wealthy merchant who owned convict hulks on the Thames and a fleet of merchant vessels trading with the West Indies. Elizabeth (or Betsy, as Bligh always called her) was a charming and cultivated young woman, who spoke both French and Italian. Through his links with Elizabeth's family, Bligh began to acquire powerful patrons.

During his service on the *Ranger*, Bligh passed his master's examination for fifth- or sixth-rate ships. He was still a midshipman, however, and there must have been raised eyebrows when, at the age of twenty-one, he was appointed as the *Resolution*'s master, a role that would require him to work closely with Captain Cook, famed for his two voyages of Pacific discovery.[9] A master was the senior warrant officer on a vessel, appointed by Trinity House, who worked alongside his captain in navigating the ship, surveying coastlines, bays and harbours, taking care of the rigging, sails and provisions, and drawing up charts and coastal profiles; and these officers were usually experienced navigators.[10] On this expedition this role would be vital, because the ships were being sent to explore and chart the northern coast of America, and search for the Northwest Passage. Cook was now forty-seven years old, however, an advanced age for a sailor in the eighteenth-century Navy, and perhaps with his long experience at sea and Bligh's youthful vigour and enthusiasm, it was felt that they would be a good combination. As George Forster, the young German naturalist who sailed with Captain Cook on his second Pacific voyage, remarked, Cook liked to choose sailors 'distinguished above all by their skills, their strong and healthy bodies, and their youth'; and Bligh fitted that description.[11] In any case, he was due to be appointed a master, and perhaps the *Resolution* was the only ship available.

The voyage would be long and arduous, because as well as searching for the Northwest Passage along the icebound coasts of North America, Cook had orders to examine several islands recently discovered by Marion du Fresne and Kerguelen in the Indian Ocean; to drop off a variety of European animals in New Zealand and Tahiti; and to take Ma'i (known in Britain as 'Omai', a young Ra'iatean who had sailed from Tahiti on board the *Adventure* during Cook's second Pacific voyage, and subsequently spent two years in England) home to the Society Islands. At twenty-one years old, however, Captain Cook's new master had never fought at sea or sailed on a voyage of discovery, although on 1 May 1776 Bligh sat and passed his lieutenant's examination (a signal that he did not wish to end his days as a warrant officer, but hoped for a commission, and ultimately to win his own command).[12]

How did William Bligh rise to these formidable challenges? It is difficult to say. Although his expedition with Cook was formative for the young master, both as a sailor and a person, his log, journal and charts from the voyage are all missing, gone with the *Bounty*. For this reason, we do not have Bligh's own account of his time with Captain Cook, the survey work he carried out during the voyage, and his adventures in places like the Tongan islands, Tahiti and Hawai'i, although these were crucial to relationships that he later forged in the South Seas, first on board the *Bounty*, and then the *Providence*. The glimpses of Bligh from this voyage are fleeting – references in the journals of others; comments by Cook about tasks that he had given his master; or the work carried

*Ma'i, by Sir Joshua Reynolds.*

out by the boats that Bligh often commanded – the pinnace for inshore work; and the great cutter for transporting supplies or surveying in open waters. To make matters more frustrating, evidence of his arduous and skilful work in the boats was obscured when, after the expedition's return to England, the credit for many of his charts and surveys was taken by others. In order to do justice to the young master, it has been necessary to take a forensic approach, reconstructing his activities from these fragmentary traces.

Only one letter from the Cape of Good Hope from Bligh to his brother-in-law, John Bond, and the notes that he later scrawled in the margins of the official *Voyage*, survive as direct testimony of his experiences on board the *Resolution*

– enough to indicate that these were often passionately felt, but no substitute for the detailed entries of a daily log or journal. For this reason, in many accounts of Bligh's life and career, his service with Captain Cook is passed over in haste; and yet this is fundamentally misleading. In his later shipboard routines, his skill in surveying and hydrography, his affection for Pacific peoples, his style of command, and his reactions to Cook's death and its aftermath, William Bligh was forged by his experiences on board the *Resolution*. If he sometimes seems elusive, almost absent from the record of the voyage, this is due solely to these documentary lacunae. We know that Bligh was there, often beside his commander, near the heart of the story.

As it happened, the Admiralty did not originally intend that Captain Cook should lead the third Pacific expedition. At the end of Cook's previous voyage, during which he had almost died from an intestinal obstruction off the icy edges of Antarctica, Lord Sandwich, the First Lord of the Admiralty, offered him a sinecure as a captain at Greenwich Hospital.[13] Cook was dubious about this arrangement, however, writing to his friend and mentor in Whitby, the Quaker ship-owner Captain John Walker:

> The *Resolution* . . . will soon be sent out again, but I shall not command her, my fate drives me from one extream to a nother a few Months ago the whole Southern hemisphere was hardly big enough for me and now I am going to be confined within the limits of Greenwich Hospital, which are far too small for an active mind like mine, I must however confess it is a fine retreat and a pretty income, but whether I can bring my self to like ease and retirement, time will shew.[14]

At the same time, Lord Sandwich promised the command of this expedition to Cook's first lieutenant, Charles Clerke [PLATE 8], who had sailed with him on his first two Pacific voyages. During the *Endeavour* voyage, Clerke, an engaging man with a 'happy, convivial Turn & humorous Conversation; [which], joined to an open generous Disposition, made him universally caressed and engaged him in excesses', became friendly with Joseph Banks, the wealthy young naturalist (and close friend of Lord Sandwich) who led the Royal Society party of scientists and artists on board the ship. Although Clerke 'did not possess that degree of Firmness & Resolution necessary to constitute the Character of a great Commander',[15] Banks was loyal to his friend, ensuring that he was offered the command of the third Pacific expedition. Soon afterwards, however, Clerke found himself in desperate straits, having acted as a guarantor for his brother, Sir John Clerke, who had absconded to India without settling his debts. Pursued by loan sharks and lawyers, he was unable to concentrate upon organising the voyage.

When the bailiffs descended, Cook stepped into the breach. At a dinner early in February 1776 hosted by Lord Sandwich and attended by his friend Sir Hugh Palliser, who impressed the importance of the expedition upon him, he volunteered to lead it.[16] Concerned about Clerke's tangled affairs, the Admiralty accepted with alacrity. When Cook wrote to the Admiralty Secretary on 10 February, formally offering himself for the command, they accepted at once; and Clerke was given the consort ship *Discovery* instead. On that same day, the appointments of several other officers were announced, including John Gore, who took over Clerke's role as the *Resolution*'s first lieutenant, an American and a close friend of Clerke's who had clashed with Cook during their voyage on the *Endeavour*,[17] and then sailed with Banks on a voyage to Iceland;[18] James King, the *Resolution*'s second lieutenant, a clever, thoughtful man who had studied science at Paris and Oxford; and James Burney, the *Discovery*'s first lieutenant, who through his well-connected father enjoyed the patronage of Lord Sandwich. Given their personal histories, it is likely that Lord Sandwich, Joseph Banks and Charles Clerke had a hand in these appointments. In addition there was David Nelson, a 'gardener' or botanist employed by Banks, who sailed on board the *Discovery*. Although Molesworth Phillips, the second lieutenant of marines on board the *Resolution*, was a later appointment, he was a close friend of Burney's and, later, his brother-in-law. Each of these men would have a lasting impact on Bligh's life and career.

This flurry of appointments also included three, slightly older, master's mates, all of whom had previously sailed in the Pacific with Cook and Clerke, and would work under Bligh's direct supervision. William Harvey, aged twenty-four, from London, had served as a midshipman with Cook during his two previous voyages; William Lanyon, twenty-nine and Cornishman, had sailed on the *Adventure* as an able-bodied seaman; and Henry Roberts from Sussex, also twenty-nine, was a fine draughtsman and artist who had been an AB on the *Resolution*. Unlike these men, William Bligh was appointed as the *Resolution*'s master some weeks after Captain Cook had taken over the command. Without doubt, he hoped to impress the great navigator and win further promotion, perhaps that coveted commission. From the outset, Bligh set his sights on proving his capabilities as a practical seaman, hydrographer and journal-keeper; and at some point, he decided to keep his own private account, with the idea of publishing it after the voyage. Perhaps Betsy Betham's family (or Betsy herself), with their close links with the Scottish Enlightenment, helped to inspire this ambition, along with Bligh's enthusiasm for scientific exploration as an avenue for professional and social advancement.

At the same time, Bligh was anxious to make a good impression on Charles Clerke and his patrons, Joseph Banks and Lord Sandwich. The relationship between Clerke and Cook was not straightforward, however. After the *Endeavour* voyage, while the second expedition was being planned, Clerke had made disloyal remarks about Cook to Banks; and at the outset of their third voyage to the Pacific, it seems that Clerke resented his demotion. Although their roles had been carefully outlined when he and Cook were appointed to their ships, Clerke had to be sent an explicit order by the Admiralty 'to put himself under the command of Cook'; and in early June when he wrote to the Secretary of the Admiralty, asking for permission to go to London to attend to 'my own private affairs', he did not tell Captain Cook, who had ordered him to take the *Discovery* to Plymouth, and get the ship ready to sail.[19]

One can imagine that Clerke, who had been summoned to appear before the King's Bench in London, was ashamed to confess his difficulties to his austere, upright commander. As he wrote to Banks: 'I am very sorry to inform you that now I am fairly cast away – the damnation Bench of Justices fell out among themselves . . . I'm resolv'd to decamp without beat of drum, and if I can out sail the Israelites get to Sea and make every return in my power.'[20] Before Clerke could escape to Plymouth, however, the bailiffs threw him into the King's Bench debtors' prison, delaying the *Discovery*'s departure until Banks and Lord Sandwich, once again First Lord of the Admiralty, could get him released. By that time, Clerke had contracted tuberculosis, an illness that would gravely affect the outcome of the voyage.

Because of Clerke's ill-timed defection, Captain Cook was left to make the final arrangements for the third Pacific expedition. Although it was his job to assist his commander in refitting, provisioning and equipping the *Resolution*, William Bligh was an inexperienced master; and because war with the American colonies was imminent, the naval dockyard at Plymouth was preoccupied with preparing a fleet of fighting ships for battle. Under these circumstances, the work on Cook's vessels was skimped, and when the *Resolution* sailed alone from Plymouth on 12 July 1776, it soon became apparent that the ship had not been properly caulked. The weather turned rough, and water poured into cabins and storerooms, drenching books, clothing and supplies. Lieutenant Gore wrote

*HMS* Resolution.

sardonically to Joseph Banks: 'If I return in the *Resolution* the next trip I may safely venture in a Ship built of Ginger Bread.'[21]

Despite the *Resolution*'s defects, however, they had a good run to the Equator, where according to Bligh, 'We had the vile practice of ducking put in execution to afford some fun.'[22] Although Captain Cook allowed his men to carry out the ceremonies that celebrated 'crossing the line', including the custom of blindfolding those men who had not crossed the Equator before, putting them on a ducking stool and dropping them into the sea from the yardarm, his young master thought this custom brutal and outmoded. On 18 October when the *Resolution* arrived at the Cape of Good Hope and Bligh went to check that the deck was clear, the stopper rope struck him in the leg as the anchor was lowered, bruising him badly. Despite this injury, which left him bedridden for days, Bligh was content, writing to his stepsister's husband John Bond, who had warned him about one of his messmates (no doubt John Williamson, the unpopular third lieutenant): 'We are very happy in our Mess and have no doubt but will continue so. _____ is all that you told me of him, but I'll keep friends with him if it lies in my power . . . Omai [Ma'i] is very well and in high spirits.'[23]

When Charles Clerke finally sailed from Plymouth on 1 August, he sent an ebullient message to Banks: 'Huzza my Boys heave away – away we go – adieu my best friend I wont pretend to tell you how much I am your Gratefull and Devoted C. Clerke.'[24] Anchoring the *Discovery* at the Cape of Good Hope on 19 November, Clerke sent Banks another missive: 'Here I am hard and fast moor'd alongside my old Friend Capt. Cook so that our battles with the Israelites cannot now have any ill effects upon our intended attack on the North Pole.'[25] Glad to have his consort captain beside him at last, Cook was also in high spirits, writing to Banks: '[W]e are now ready to proceed on our Voyage, and nothing is wanting but a few females of our own species to make the *Resolution* a Compleate ark. Omai consented with Raptures to give up his Cabbin to make Room for four Horses. He desires his best respects to you, Dr. Solander and to a great many more, Ladies as well as Gentlemen; I can only say that he does not forget any who have shewed him the least kindness.'[26]


On 30 November 1776 the *Resolution* and *Discovery* left the Cape together, heading south-east across the Indian Ocean. As a novice, it cannot have been easy for Bligh to work with Cook as his sailing master. As George Forster remarked, James Cook was a brilliant navigator and practical seaman:

[As soon as] he mounted the deck, [he would notice] that in the tangle of ropes and lines aloft, one or the other were hauled too taut or paid out too much, preventing the ship from travelling more rapidly; and yet the officer of the watch, an experienced seaman, had been watching for many hours and not spotted the problem.

When it was a question of visually estimating distance from the shore, the heights of mountains, rocks and similar objects, Cook's guess [was] always closest, just as his sure eye did not deceive him when it was a matter of finding the narrow entrance to a harbour, or even . . . tacking in against the wind.[27]

At the same time, Cook was a superb, if demanding, teacher, who saw great promise in several of his junior officers, including William Bligh and his mate, Henry Roberts:

I had several young men amongst my sea-officers who, under my direction, could be usefully employed in constructing charts, in taking views of the coasts and headlands nearly which we should pass, and in drawing plans of the bays and harbours in which we should anchor.[28]

On 24 December, when the two ships were sailing in thick fog, searching for land that had been previously sighted by Kerguelen, the French navigator, in the southern latitudes of the Indian Ocean, a rugged coastline emerged from the mist, and Captain Cook sent Bligh off in the boats to survey 'Desolation Island', as he called it. As an islet loomed up out of the fog, Cook just managed to avoid this obstacle, naming it 'Bligh's Cap' after his master, perhaps in thanks for a timely warning. When the weather cleared that afternoon, Cook sent Bligh to survey and sound 'Christmas Harbour'. Upon his return, Bligh reported that the bay was 'safe and commodious with good anchorage, and great plenty of fresh Water, Seals, Penguins . . . but not a stick of Wood'.[29] According to James Burney, the penguins stood in serried ranks along the shore, greeting their arrival with 'melancholy croakings . . . Nature seems to have designed this Spot solely for the use of Sea Lions, Seals, penguins and Sea Fowls.'[30]

Two days later, when the sailors had filled the ships' barrels with fresh water, Cook allowed each of his men to take a quart bottle of rum ashore, and celebrate the Yuletide season. By 28 December, Cook and Bligh were conducting a running survey of the coast of Desolation Island, picking their way through rocky outcrops and kelp-lined channels.[31] When another harbour was sighted, a strong wind blew up, and the ships took shelter in this bay, which Captain Cook named

'Port Palliser' in honour of his patron, Admiral Sir Hugh Palliser. Once again, Bligh was despatched to survey the upper reaches of this harbour, which proved to be rocky and barren. The surviving charts of these two harbours, later attributed to Henry Roberts (an accomplished draughtsman, who may have produced the final sketches), were based on surveys by Bligh and Edgar (the *Discovery*'s master); along with a superb chart of the north-east coast of Desolation Island that was later attributed to Cook and Roberts.[32]

During Cook's previous voyage, George Forster gave a vivid description of the kind of work in which Cook and Bligh were engaged during this passage:

> Close to the shore, particularly when there appeared to be a harbour or when shallows with a beach bordered the sea, the sounding lead was used frequently to determine whether there was any holding ground [for an anchorage].
>
> The ships changed direction, following the inlets and points of the coast, often trying to complete their charts before casting anchor. Wherever it was not advisable to enter the apparent entrance immediately, a boat was lowered and sent to explore. Where it was easy to miss the true entrance, the boats would anchor in the shoals on both sides, and even despite this precaution a rock often remained concealed under the surface, and was only spotted when the ship was in danger of being lost.
>
> Cook selected the anchorage, the anchor was cast at the predetermined spot, the sails were furled and the boats were once again manned to try and find out what the land would yield.[33]

After heading away from this 'Cold Blustering Wet Country of Islands, Bays and Harbours',[34] in late January 1777 the ships put into Adventure Bay on Bruny Island, off the south coast of Tasmania, where Captain Cook sent Bligh in the boats to make a running survey of the south coastline, which both he and Cook mistook for part of the mainland of Australia. This is one of the few surviving charts from the expedition to be titled with Bligh's name, although his authorship was not acknowledged when it was engraved and published with a series of coastal profiles in the official *Voyage* (some of which Bligh had also drafted).[35] Scornful of the Aborigines in Adventure Bay who walked about naked and urinated where they stood, Ma'i terrified them by firing his musket. After leaving Tasmania, Cook headed east to the luxuriant fiords of Queen Charlotte Sound in New Zealand, where he knew he could obtain grass for the cargo of animals that he had brought to the Pacific, and fish and scurvy grass for his men. During Cook's previous voyage, when his two ships had been separated by

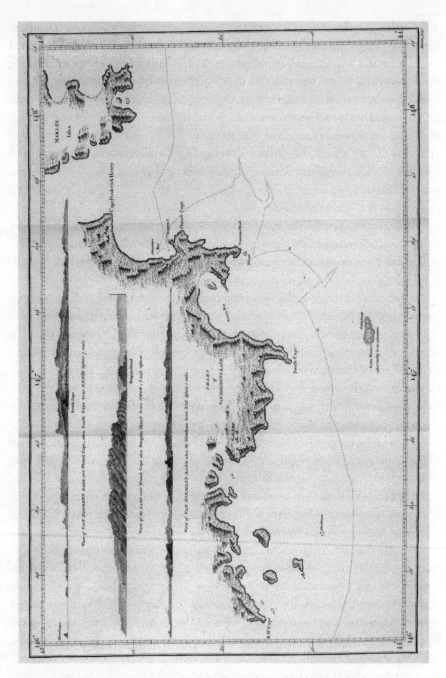

*Chart and coastal profiles of Van Diemen's Land by William Bligh.*

a ferocious storm off the east coast of New Zealand, the *Adventure* had taken refuge in Tolaga Bay. By the time that Captain Furneaux reached the appointed rendezvous in Queen Charlotte Sound, the *Resolution* had already sailed. During their stay in the sound, some of Furneaux's men quarrelled with local Māori, and a few days later when the crew of the cutter were sent out to cut grass, the boat failed to return. When Furneaux despatched the ship's launch, commanded by his second lieutenant, James Burney, to search for their shipmates, they landed at Grass Cove, where they made a horrifying discovery. On the beach, the butchered bodies of their comrades lay trussed up in flax baskets, while a head, several hands, feet and entrails were scattered on the sand. After shooting at a crowd that had gathered for the ritual sacrifice, 'the Lieutenant not thinking it safe to trust the crew in the dark, in an open boat, within reach of such cruel barbarians, ordered the canoes to be broken up and destroyed, and after carefully collecting the remains of our mangled companions, they made the best of their way from this polluted place'.[36]

The crew of the *Adventure*'s launch never forgot that shocking sight, and for the rest of his life James Burney could only speak about it in a whisper. Now Burney and four of his *Adventure* shipmates (including Maʻi, and one of Bligh's mates, William Lanyon) were returning to Queen Charlotte Sound for the first time since that harrowing episode, eager to avenge their fallen comrades. Captain Cook, however, was still reserving his judgement about the death of the *Adventure*'s men. During his previous voyage he had often been frustrated by the poor discipline on board the consort ship, and when Furneaux's sailors had raped several women in Tahiti, he was infuriated. Thinking that the killings in Grass Cove may have been due to a similar provocation, he wrote:

> I shall make no reflections on this Melancholy affair untill I hear more about it. I must however observe in favour of the New Zealanders that I have allways found them of a Brave, Noble, Open and benevolent disposition, but they are a people that will never put up with an insult if they have an opportunity to resent it.[37]

In February 1777 when the *Resolution* and *Discovery* entered Queen Charlotte Sound, guided by Bligh in the boats, Kahura, the warrior who had led the attack on the *Adventure*'s men, came on board the *Resolution*. Impressed by his bravery, Cook questioned the chief, who told him that while the *Adventure*'s men had been ashore, a local man had stolen a jacket from the boat, but before he could escape a black sailor struck him on the head, killing him outright. Seeing this,

*Kahura.*

his warriors had attacked the sailors, killing them all, although during the skirmish two of them were shot, and Kahura himself was slashed on the arm with
a sword.[38] Although many local Māori urged him to kill Kahura, Captain Cook
refused to take any action against him, remarking: 'I admired his courage and
was not a little pleased at the confidence he put in me.'[39] On 16 February when
Cook, accompanied by Clerke, Bligh and Maʻi, took the ships' boats to collect
grass for the shipboard menagerie, they landed at Grass Cove, where the killings
had taken place. Several local men met Cook on the beach, where they gave him
another account of the attack on the *Adventure*'s men, saying that it had happened
when a local man snatched bread from one of the sailors, and was shot. When
his companions retaliated, another Māori had been shot, and the sailors were
killed in revenge for these shootings.[40] Although these men identified Kahura as
the leader of the attack, Cook still refused to punish him.

No doubt Bligh was impressed by Cook's restraint, because later, when he got
his own command, he would also be reluctant to punish islanders, even in the face

of severe provocation. From a Polynesian point of view, however, Cook's failure to avenge his men was a sign of weakness. By ritually eating the *Adventure* sailors, Kahura and his people had attacked Captain Cook's mana (ancestral power); and unless he took utu (equivalent return), it would be fatally weakened. Given the overwhelming power of his weapons, the local people could not understand why Cook did not retaliate, concluding that he must either be a fool or a coward. Ma'i understood this, and when Kahura paid a second visit to the *Resolution*, and Captain Cook invited him into the Great Cabin where he asked John Webber to paint his portrait, the young Ra'iatean was aghast, crying out, 'Why do you not kill him? You tell me that if a man kills an other in England he is hanged for it, this Man has killed ten and yet you will not kill him, tho a great many of his countrymen desire it and it would be very good!'[41]

James Burney, now the first lieutenant of the *Discovery*, and his other former shipmates from the *Adventure*, were also outraged. As Burney protested, '[I]t seemed evident that many of them held us in great contempt and I believe chiefly on account of our not revenging the affair of Grass Cove, so contrary to the principles by which they would have been actuated in the like case. As an instance of how little they stood in fear of us, one man did not scruple to acknowledge his being present and assisting at the killing and eating the *Adventure*'s people.'[42] There were angry murmurings on board both ships, and when some of the *Discovery*'s midshipmen took a Māori dog acquired by Edward Riou, one of their comrades, and put it on trial for cannibalism, they declared it guilty of the crime, killed it, cooked and ate it, using this 'rough humour' to show Captain Cook how Māori cannibals ought to be treated.

Although Clerke must have known about this mock trial, he turned a blind eye, no doubt finding it amusing; and Captain Cook ignored it, angering the sailors. Almost as soon as the ships sailed from Queen Charlotte Sound in February 1777, accompanied by two young Māori who sailed as Ma'i's attendants, there was 'a general disobedience among the people'. Some meat was stolen on board the *Resolution*, and when Cook tried to get his men to name the culprits, they refused. When he punished the crew by reducing their daily allowance, they would not eat anything at all, which as Lieutenant King remarked, was 'a very mutinous proceeding'[43] – the first use of that ominous word in the logs and journals from any of Captain Cook's voyages.

As the *Resolution*'s master, Bligh was acutely aware of the sailors' defiant mood; and their reactions when, angry and frustrated, Cook turned to the cat-o'-nine-tails to reassert his authority. From this time onwards, the number of lashes meted out to the sailors on board the *Resolution* soared to a level about twice that of his two previous voyages. During this expedition, forty-four of Cook's crew would be punished with 684 lashes in all, compared with twenty-one men on board the *Endeavour* (with 354 lashes) during his first Pacific expedition, and twenty men on board the *Adventure* (with 288 lashes) during the second.[44] Indeed, the marines bore the brunt of this new regime, although it was their task to uphold shipboard discipline – perhaps a reason why on the beach in Kealakekua Bay they ran away, rather than standing their ground to save their commander.

As they sailed north from New Zealand, Bligh and his shipmates were heading into the heart of the Pacific, known to Māori as Te Moana-nui-a-Kiwa, and at that time in Europe as 'the South Sea'. Across this vast ocean, which covers a third of the earth's surface, the ancestors of the Polynesians had sailed their fast voyaging canoes out of island South-East Asia, heading east into the prevailing winds, orienting themselves by the stars, sun, winds and currents, searching for new groups of islands and inventing blue-water sailing. If no land appeared on the horizon, they turned around and headed home again with the wind in their sails. After discovering the islands of western Polynesia, Tonga and Samoa by about 950 BC, these intrepid explorers had stayed for a while, before venturing on the long, dangerous voyages to the archipelagos of east Polynesia – the Society Islands, the Tuamotus, the Marquesas and the Cook Islands; New Zealand to the south; Hawai'i to the north; and far to the east, the remote little speck of Easter Island. According to recent archaeological findings, by about AD 1000 some canoes had reached the west coast of South America, where they collected sweet potatoes to take back to their home islands, leaving behind Polynesian chickens and perhaps other animals.[45] These star navigators were at home in this wide, watery world, and in their far-reaching explorations had a great deal in common with Captain Cook and his men.

On 28 March 1777 when the *Resolution* and *Discovery* reached the island of Mangaia in the Cook Islands, Cook sent Bligh and Edgar to search for an anchorage. A man in a canoe came alongside to challenge the ships, brandishing his weapon and chanting loudly, and while others swam around the boats, Bligh sketched the coastline of their island. Because surf was running high on the reef, Cook decided not to attempt a landing. When they arrived at Atiu, he sent the boats ashore to look for a safe anchorage; and when some islanders boarded the *Resolution*, Ma'i presented them with a pet dog that he had brought from England. The next day when Cook ordered Lieutenants Gore and Burney to take Ma'i ashore with an armed party, Bligh sketched and surveyed the coastline of Atiu.[46] After being ferried across the reef by canoe, Ma'i and his companions landed on the beach, where a priest asked the young Ra'iatean, 'Are you the glorious sons of Tetumu?' – an echo of a prophecy made at Taputapuatea, the headquarters of the war god 'Oro on Ra'iatea, Ma'i's home island in about 1760, when a fleet of warriors from the neighbouring island of Porapora had attacked Ra'iatea, desecrating the sacred temple. When the priest Vaita had visited the ravaged *marae*, distraught at the devastation, he entered a trance, speaking with the voice of the god:

> The glorious children of Tetumu
> will come and see this forest at Taputapuatea.
> Their body is different, our body is different
> We are one species only from Tetumu.
>
> And this land will be taken by them
> The old rules will be destroyed
> And sacred birds of the land and the sea
> Will also arrive here, will come and lament
> Over that which this lopped tree has to teach
> They are coming up on a canoe without an outrigger.[47]

Afterwards, when canoes from the Society Islands were driven by a storm south to Atiu, they carried news of this ominous prophecy. When the *Resolution* and *Discovery* arrived off the coast of the island, the Atiu people wondered whether these were the 'canoes without outriggers' about which Vaita had spoken, come to take over their land. Men crowded around Ma'i and his companions, jostling and threatening, until the young islander managed to divert them by performing a Tahitian war dance, telling them fantastic stories about his adventures and exploding a musket cartridge with a flaming coal. Ma'i and the officers were relieved when they were eventually allowed to return to the boats, leaving these intimidating warriors behind them.

At Manuae, where men threatened them from the beach, others came out in canoes, snatching some salt beef that was being towed behind the *Discovery*, and tried to kidnap a boy from her cutter. When Bligh and his shipmates landed on Palmerston Island, an uninhabited atoll where the sailors collected coconuts, palm hearts and scurvy grass, Ma'i caught fish in scoop nets and trapped birds, cooking a meal for his shipmates in an earth oven. As Burney noted, the young Ra'iatean was 'a keen Sportsman an excellent Cook and never idle – without him we might have made a tolerable Shift, but with him we fared Sumptuously'.[48] The winds had shifted, however, and instead of heading for Tahiti, Cook decided to head west to the Tongan archipelago, giving up all thought of visiting the north-west coast of America that year.

Upon arriving at Nomuka early on 29 April 1777, they were greeted by the local chief, a man named Tupoulagi; and Cook sent Bligh at dawn to take soundings off the south-west coast of the island, where there seemed to be a sheltered harbour, and trade with the local people. Upon his return, Bligh reported that although the bay was well protected from the winds, there was no fresh water ashore.[49] After hearing his report, Cook decided to return to an anchorage on the northern coast that he had visited during his previous voyage, and to spend some time in the Tongan archipelago, exploring and charting the surrounding islands.

Over the next three months, Captain Cook kept William Bligh busy in the boats, guiding the ships through labyrinths of coral reefs, shoals and islets, sounding passages and shallows, and surveying harbours and coastlines. This was intricate work. In charting a harbour, for instance, Bligh had to sketch the shoreline and take soundings in the bay, locating rocks, shoals and channels. Next, a baseline was measured on level ground ashore, at least half a mile long, while his men erected tall poles at intervals around the harbour. The survey was completed by taking the bearings of each pole from one end of the baseline, and then from the other, fixing their positions.[50] Because he was often away from the ship, working in small boats and surrounded by canoes, Bligh met many of the islanders, gaining some familiarity with Tongan customs and leaders. No doubt many dramatic episodes were recorded in his journal; and he became increasingly confident in his dealings with these people.

At this time there were three ruling chiefs in the archipelago – the Tu'i Tonga, a sacred chief directly descended from the gods; the Tu'i Ha'atakalaua, a secular leader appointed by the Tu'i Tonga; and the Tu'i Kanokupolu, to whom much of his secular power had been delegated. The Tu'i Kanokupolu at that time, a man named Finau, was a skilled navigator. When he escorted them to Nomuka, preceded by a canoe carrying musicians who sang and played their instruments, the local chiefs knelt, touching their foreheads to Finau's feet; and Ma'i adopted him as a bond friend. Finau, who worked closely with Bligh, piloting the ships through the Tongan islands in his fast sailing canoe, was described by one of the sailors as 'one of the most graceful men I ever saw in the Pacific ocean. He was about 5 feet 11 inches high, fleshy but not fat: He was open and free in his disposition, full of vivacity, enterprizing and bold, expert in all the acquirements of his country, particularly in their art of navigation, over which he presided;

*The night dances in Lifuka.*

was possessed of uncommon strength and agility; he was besides extremely handsome, and the idol of the fair.'[51]

One day off Nomuka, one of Finau's chiefly companions stole an iron bolt on board the *Resolution*, and Captain Cook had this man flogged with a dozen lashes and confined with his hands tied behind his back. That night there was a torrential downpour, with thunder like cannon fire, and flashes of lightning. On 7 May, the *Discovery* shifted her anchorage, and during this manoeuvre Clerke lost his best bower anchor, and almost dropped another anchor through the *Resolution*'s deck, tangling her cable. Several days later, after pouring oil on the surface of the sea, Edgar and Bligh managed to find and raise the missing anchor.

On 11 May, Finau guided the ships to the northern end of Lifuka in the Ha'apai Islands, where Bligh was sent to look for an anchorage. Soon afterwards, the son of a chief named Tapa (whom the sailors nicknamed 'Lord North' after the Prime Minister), who had been acting as their orator and advisor, was put in irons for stealing a cat. Infuriated by this insult, the local warriors plotted to ambush Captain Cook and his officers (including Bligh) after the night dances, performed in unison by men and women accompanied by an orchestra of slit drums. Although Cook knew nothing about this plan, he sent the marines ashore to perform their drill, where they fired several volleys. That evening he mounted a fireworks display that terrified the islanders, who called off the ambush. As Lieutenant King remarked:

Such roaring, jumping, & shouting . . . made us perfectly satisfied that we had gaind a compleat victory in their own mind. Sky & water rockets were what affected them most, the water rocket exercis'd their inquisitive faculties, for they could not conceive how fire shoud burn under water. Omai who was always very ready to magnify our country, told them, they might now see how easy it was for us to destroy not only the earth, but the water & the Sky; & some of our sailors were seriously perswading their hearers, that by means of the sky rockets we had made stars.[52]

After sailing from Lifuka, the ships headed south, guided by Bligh in the great cutter. When the *Discovery* ran onto a shoal near the southern end of the island, he was sent to sound and survey a nearby bay, which proved to be full of coral outcrops. After hearing Bligh's report, Cook decided to return to Nomuka, sending his master ahead in the cutter to examine the channel. Having picked his way through a treacherous maze of coral islets, shoals and breakers, Bligh persuaded Cook to retrace their previous track to Nomuka. During this passage a large sailing canoe approached the *Resolution*, bringing out the Tu'i Tonga, a corpulent, amiable man who was the highest-ranking chief in the archipelago. When Ma'i realised that this man was senior to his bond friend Finau, he was bitterly chagrined.

On 31 May, the ships headed past the island of Kotu, wending their way past reefs and islands. After staying on deck until midnight during this intricate, dangerous passage, Cook handed the wheel to his young master, 'with such direction as I thought would keep the Ships clear of the dangers that lay round us'. When the wind abruptly shifted, however, the *Resolution* 'very near ran plump on a low Sandy isle [Putuputua] surrounded by breakers'.[53] Fortunately most of the sailors were already on deck, and hastily ordering the sails to be hauled aback, Bligh narrowly avoided disaster, firing a cannon to warn the *Discovery* of the danger. Although Cook was philosophical, writing in his journal that 'the necessary movements were not only executed with judgement but with alertness and this alone saved the Ship. Such resks as thise are the inevitable Companions of the Man who goes on Discoveries',[54] Bligh was mortified. Annoyed by the account of this episode in the *Voyage* – 'the Master whose watch it was (one of the officers being sick) immediately threw all aback . . . otherwise we might have ended our discoveries here' – Bligh later copied what he claimed to be Cook's own journal entry into the margins of the book (although his version does not correspond with any of the surviving copies of Cook's journal).

The next morning when Cook anchored off Kotu, Bligh was sent ahead to cut grass for the cattle, and sound the passages between the nearby islands. Over the next few days, he was kept busy getting greenery for the livestock, and bartering with local people. On 9 June as they approached Tongatapu, guided by Bligh and Edgar, both ships scraped on the rocks, although neither grounded. Later that afternoon, Bligh made the signal for a good anchorage; and as the ships entered Nuku'alofa Harbour, the Tu'i Tonga and Finau came out in large double canoes, running over several small craft that got in their way and ignoring their crews, who were left floundering in the water. According to the Tu'i Tonga, his great-great-grandfather had previously met two European ships, which the British thought must have been Tasman's vessels.[55]

The Tongan chiefs often treated the commoners harshly, beating them and sometimes killing them for trivial offences; and during his visit to the archipelago, Cook followed their example, meting out floggings of two dozen, four dozen and six dozen lashes to islanders who stole from the ships, although he strictly forbade the sailors to shoot them. Bligh and his comrades were astounded, because until this time Captain Cook had always prohibited any violence towards local people. As George Gilbert, one of his midshipmen, remarked, during this visit Cook punished the Tongans 'in a manner rather unbecoming of a European, viz by cutting off their ears; fireing at them with small shot; or ball as they were swimming or paddling to the shore; and suffering the people to beat them with the oars; and stick the boat hook into them; whereever they could hit them'.[56]

Intimidated and impressed by these brutal displays, on 15 June the Tu'i Tonga organised a ceremony on Tongatapu during which his son Fatafehi and Captain Cook became ritual friends, followed by a feast and displays of dancing and weapon-handling. When Captain Cook responded by ordering the marines to perform their drill, flags flying and a band playing French horns, fifes and drums, according to William Anderson (the ship's surgeon), 'our soldiers were by no means examples of the best discipline'.[57] Bligh agreed, remarking tartly that this was 'a most ludicrous performance for the Marine Officer [was as] incapable of making his men go through their Exercise as C. Cook's musicians or Musick was ill adapted'.[58] Fortunately, however, a haka (war dance) performed by Ma'i's young Māori attendants made a better impression, and when Cook ordered another display of fireworks, the Tongans were awestruck.

In his instructions, Captain Cook had been ordered to leave European animals at various Pacific islands, and on 20 June when a kid and two turkeys were stolen from the shore camp, he took the Tu'i Tonga and Finau hostage in a house until these animals were returned. The high chiefs were revered by their people, and as hundreds of Tongans gathered around the house, weeping loudly, a crowd of warriors surrounded the building. In reply Cook ordered the marines to encircle the Tu'i Tonga, bared bayonets aimed at his chest, until the warriors retreated. When the stolen animals were returned, Cook released his aristocratic captives, who presented him with vast quantities of pigs, turtles, large fish and other foodstuffs, carried by their people as a gesture of propitiation, although they were furious about the way that they had been treated.

By this stage in their journey, William Bligh and the third lieutenant, John Williamson, had become friends; and on 23 June they went inland on a hunting expedition. Incensed by the way that their chiefs had been treated, the people refused to provide Bligh and Williamson with food, so after taking provisions at gunpoint they went on their way, crossing the lagoon and heading west. When Bligh stopped to put a new flint in his musket, however, three men attacked, knocking him flat and grabbing his weapon and ammunition, while the boy who was carrying Lieutenant Williamson's musket ran off into the forest. Upon returning to the shore camp, Williamson reported their losses to Lieutenant King, and asked Ma'i to help them retrieve their weapons. Delighted to help, Ma'i went off and threatened the Tu'i Tonga, who fled with Finau, although Finau had already found and returned Bligh's musket. Captain Cook was forced to send a message to the chiefs, assuring them that they would not be punished for the thefts, and when they returned, they reproached him for letting his men wander about the island, saying that they could not protect them under such circumstances. Irate with Williamson and Bligh, Cook decided not to pursue the matter with the chiefs; and when he reprimanded his officers for going inland without permission, Williamson was bitterly resentful:

> I cannot pass over the strange conduct of Captn. Cook upon this occasion
> . . . If a small nail was stolen from Captn Cook, the thief if taken was most
> severely punished, if of a little more consequence than a nail, then the Chiefs
> were immediately seized until the things stolen were return'd; I was much more
> affected by such arbitrary proceedings, than with the loss of my gun, although
> it was great, as I could have no redress.[59]

Despite these clashes, the Tu'i Tonga was about to install his son Fatafehi as his successor, and Captain Cook was a powerful ally. As the Tu'i Tonga informed the astronomer William Bayly, despite his status as the most sacred chief in the

*The* 'inasi *ritual.*

Tongan islands, he was outranked by his father's sister, who had married a great chief in Fiji, five days' sail from Tongatapu.[60] When he invited Cook, Captain Clerke and Ma'i to witness the *'inasi* ceremony, the Tu'i Tonga's attendants insisted that if the visitors were to be present, they would have to strip to the waist and untie their hair. Cook resisted at first but eventually his curiosity got the better of him; and Bligh and his comrades were astonished and dismayed to see their commander walking in the procession, chest bared and his hair flying. As Williamson wrote: 'I do not pretend to dispute the propriety of Capt. Cook's conduct, but I cannot help thinking he rather let himself down.'[61] Along with Cook's violent outbursts of rage and his refusal to punish the 'cannibals' in Queen Charlotte Sound, these lapses of dignity baffled his men. They began to call Cook 'Tute', his Tahitian name, hinting that he was behaving more like a Polynesian high chief than a Royal Navy captain.

During their stay at Tongatapu, Bligh completed a survey of their anchorage. When the winds changed at last and Cook decided to leave the island, sending him to look for a better passage, the master found a safe channel between Makaha'a and Monuafe islands. On 5 July, Cook invited Bligh to join him, Captain Clerke, Lieutenant King and William Bayly, the astronomer, in observing an eclipse of the sun, although the master was unable to get the sun into the field of his telescope.[62] Bligh was very proud of the surveys that he carried out en route from New Zealand and in the Tongan archipelago, and later, when he found that these had been attributed to Henry Roberts, his own mate, he was incensed. In the copy of the official account of the voyage in the Hydrographic Office, he wrote in pencil below a chart of the 'Friendly Islands' (the Tongan archipelago): 'This is a Copy of my Chart, which was an entire Survey of my own except the South side of Amsterdam & the Isld. Eeoa [Eua] which C. Cook laid down'; while below the chart of Tongatapu Harbour, he remarked: 'This Plan is an exact Coppy from the original one done by me.'[63]

During their passage to Tahiti, Captain Cook continued to instruct Bligh in the finer arts of navigation. Four days after leaving the Tongan islands, the two men observed an eclipse of the moon with their sextants, while Lieutenant King watched it with a night telescope.[64] When a fierce gale split the *Resolution*'s sails, snapping the *Discovery*'s topmast, Cook sent Bligh across in the cutter to get news of the damage. After Clerke's men had rigged a jury-mast, the two ships sailed to Tupua'i, one of the Austral archipelago, where Cook despatched Bligh and Edgar in the boats to survey and chart the coastline. Later, this small island would play a key role in the mutiny on the *Bounty*. When two small canoes came out, their crews brandishing weapons, blowing conch-shell trumpets and beckoning the strangers ashore, however, Cook decided not to land and sailed away, heading for the Society Islands.

# 3

# Island of the Blest

On 12 August 1777 when the high peaks of southern Tahiti appeared on the horizon, William Bligh and his shipmates were wild with delight. In the Royal Navy, Tahiti was legendary as a Paradise on earth, with its warm, scented nights, delicious food and glorious, beguiling women. Apart from Captain Cook himself, Charles Clerke was the Pacific veteran among them, having visited the island on three occasions during Cook's previous two expeditions; although John Gore, Cook's first lieutenant, had visited Tahiti with Captain Wallis on board the *Dolphin* (the first European ship to arrive at the island) before sailing there with Cook on the *Endeavour*. Samuel Gibson, a sergeant of marines who had also sailed on Cook's first two voyages, was reputed to be the best speaker of Tahitian among the sailors. Altogether, twenty-four of Cook's crew had spent varying lengths of time in the Society Islands, and they were eager to be reunited with their old friends and lovers. As the ships headed for the coastline of Tahiti-iti (southern Tahiti), the men were agog, waiting for canoes to flock out from the beaches, and shoals of bare-breasted young girls to swim out to greet them.

By the time of Bligh's first visit to the island, however, Tahiti was no untouched Utopia. As Horace Walpole once remarked: 'Not even that little speck could escape European restlessness!'[1] During the previous decade, no fewer than eight European ships from three European nations – Britain, France and Spain – had anchored off the Tahitian coastline, bringing with them guns and muskets, iron tools and strange clothing, and venereal and epidemic diseases. These visits by European ships, with their high masts, rigging and billowing white sails, had transformed local life; and each of the leading chiefs in the various districts had forged alliances with their commanders, transforming the political landscapes of the island. Eleven Tahitian men had sailed away on these ships, although

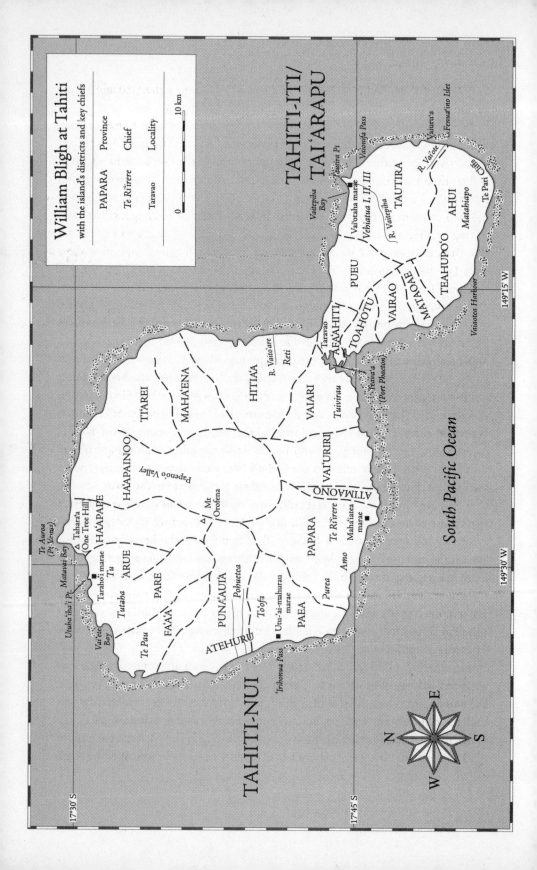

## William Bligh at Tahiti

with the island's districts and key chiefs

PAPARA — Province
*Te Ri'irere* — Chief
Taravao — Locality

0 ___ 10 km

### TAHITI-ITI/ TAI'ARAPU

Vaionīfa Pass
Fenuaʻino Islet
Tautira Pt
Vaitepiha Bay
Vaiʻotaha marae
Vehiatua I, II, III
R. Vaitepiha
R. Vaiote
TAUTIRA
PUEU
TOAHOTU
ARA'AHITI
VAIRAO
MATAOAE
TEAHUPO'O
AHUI
Matahiapo
Te Pari
Cliffs
Vaiaotea Harbour
Taravao
ʻĀRAʻAHITI
Teuvaʻa
(Port Phaeton)

### TAHITI-NUI

Te Aurau
(Pt. Venus)
Matavai Bay
Utuʻhaʻihaʻi Pt.
Taharaʻa
(One Tree Hill)
Taharaʻa
Tarahoi marae
Tu
ʻARUE
HAʻAPAPE
Vaiʻete Bay
Tutaha
PARE
HAʻAPAINOO
TIAREI
MAHAʻENA
HITIAʻA
R. Vaitoʻare
Reti
Papenoʻo Valley
Mt Orofena
VAIARI
Tuivirau
Te Pau
FAAʻA
PUNAʻAUIA
Pohuetea
Toʻofa
Utu-ʻai-mahurau marae
ATEHURU
PAEA
VAIʻURIRI
ATTIMAONO
PAPARA
Te Riʻirere
Mahaʻiatea marae
Purea
Amo
ʻTribonua Pass

### South Pacific Ocean

N E W S

17°30′ S
17°45′ S
149°30′ W
149°15′ W

only four of them had returned home again to tell tales of their extraordinary adventures.

During the most recent of these visits, in November 1774, after an exploratory foray, two Spanish ships from Peru commanded by Don Domingo Boenechea had arrived in southern Tahiti, setting up a portable mission in Vaitepiha Bay and landing two friars, a sailor and a young Peruvian marine named Máximo Rodríguez. Boenechea, who had died before his ships set sail again, was buried below a cross in front of the mission. Máximo could already speak Tahitian, having studied the language with some young men in Lima, and during the year that he spent on the island had a marvellous time, forging bond friendships with Tu, the paramount chief of the island, and Vehiatua II, the high chief of southern Tahiti, drinking 'ava (a chiefly beverage) and having affairs with local women. When the ships returned from Peru in November 1775 they picked up the missionary party, leaving the portable mission, the cross and Boenechea's grave behind on the beach at Tautira.

Not surprisingly, in 1777 when the masts and sails of *Resolution* and *Discovery* appeared on the horizon, heading for Vaitepiha Bay, the inhabitants of southern Tahiti thought that these must be Spanish ships, returning to their district. Upon seeing the British flags, however, they were troubled and uneasy. Máximo (or 'Matimo', as they called him) had warned them against Captain Cook and his countrymen, saying that Spain and Britain were enemies; and during his visit they had adopted the Spanish as their allies. The *Resolution* and *Discovery* were virtually becalmed, and when Bligh and Edgar went ahead in the boats, towing the ships into Vaitepiha Bay, to their dismay only two canoes came out to greet them, one carrying the brother-in-law of Ma'i, the young Ra'iatean whom Cook was bringing back to the Society Islands, and several other acquaintances. According to Cook, when they saw Ma'i, 'there seemed to be a perfect indifferency on both sides', and the crews of the canoes gave the British a desultory welcome.[2] Bligh and his shipmates were devastated, because contrary to their expectations, there were no women on board these canoes, let alone flocks of naked girls; and as Lieutenant King lamented, there were 'no remarkable bursts of surprise, applause or pleasure'.[3]

Fortunately, however, during their recent visit to Tonga, Cook's men had acquired rich supplies of red feathers, which they had been told were used in the worship of 'Oro, the god of fertility and war in the Society Islands. When Ma'i took his brother-in-law below and showed him his stock of these treasured items, this man hastened to inform his companions, who now clamoured to adopt Ma'i as their *taio*. Instead of snubbing Captain Cook, they welcomed him and his people, saying that since his last visit to their district, Vehiatua II had died and been succeeded by his younger brother, Vehiatua III. Ships from 'Rema' (Lima) had twice visited the district; and during their stay, the Spanish had planted a small vineyard, brought ashore many European animals, built a house and erected a tall cross beneath which their commander was buried. They told Captain Cook about 'Matimo', saying that he had 'conformed to their customs & manners and indulged himself with those plesures which the island afforded, particularly among the Girls, which last Circumstance was so agreeable to the Genius of these People that they looked upon him to be the best Fellow among his countrymen'.[4] According to these men (and to Captain Cook's intense annoyance), Matimo had told them that the Spanish King had invaded Britain, killed King George and enslaved his people; and that after meeting Tute's ship at sea, they had sunk it with their cannons. The Tahitians spoke contemptuously about the Spanish friars, however, ridiculing the way that they blessed their food and counted their beads, and mocking their refusal to sleep with local women.

Like his shipmates, William Bligh was enchanted by his first sight of southern Tahiti, with its soaring, sharp-edged volcanic mountains, green hillsides and wide, sunlit bay. Although the Season of Scarcity was under way and food supplies were scanty, when these men returned ashore with news of Captain Cook's cargo of red feathers, the local people were eager to acquire these powerful relics. As the ships sailed into Vaitepiha Bay, canoes flocked out, laden with large pigs, breadfruit, 'curiosities' (artefacts) and lovely young women. By this time, most girls on the island were aware that sex with visiting Europeans was often followed by terrible illnesses, but the lure of red feathers overcame their scruples. As the astronomer William Bayly remarked: '[N]umbers of fine women have come on board the ship . . . As soon as they had obtained a small Quantity [of red feathers] by cohabiting once – have disappeared & not been seen after by us either on board or on Shore.'[5] According to Cook, however, the value of the red feathers quickly plummeted: 'Not more feathers than might be got from a Tom tit would purchase a hog of 40 or 50 pound weight, but they fell in their value above five hundred per cent before night.'[6]

At dawn the next day, determined to impress the local people, Cook sent the horses ashore. When Lieutenant Burney and Ma'i rode along the beach, Ma'i fired his pistol, creating a sensation, although when he fell off his horse, the other islanders laughed in derision. Ma'i was not an aristocrat, and he and his family had been exiled from Ra'iatea. He was regarded as an upstart, and despite his new-found wealth the Tahitians mocked his pretensions. During the passage from Tonga, Ma'i had woven a *maro 'ura* or red feather girdle for Tu, decorated

*Ma'i on horseback.*

with red and yellow feathers. In the Society Islands, where Ta'aroa, the creator, was a feathered god, birds with red and yellow feathers were the messengers of 'Oro, the god of fertility and war; and when a high chief donned his red feather girdle, he became a living embodiment of 'Oro. When Ma'i showed this powerful insignia to a local prophet, the priest urged him to present it to Vehiatua III, the high chief of southern Tahiti, although Captain Cook tried to persuade him to keep it for Tu, his own bond friend and ally on the north coast of the island.

On 16 August, Cook, Clerke and Ma'i went ashore in the pinnace with Bligh to pay a ceremonial visit to Vehiatua III, a boy about eleven years old. During this encounter, Ma'i ignored Cook's advice, presenting the red feather girdle to the young high chief and asking him to send it on to Tu, now widely recognised as the paramount chief of the island. Tu already had two red feather girdles or *maro 'ura*, however – one inherited from his mother, the eldest daughter of the paramount chief of Ra'iatea, and the other, Te Ra'i-puatata, a famous relic brought from Taputapuatea *marae*, the headquarters of 'Oro on that island. During this meeting Vehiatua III and his mother Purahi, who were longing for a red feather girdle of their own, decided to keep this prized regalia. When Captain Cook presented the young *ari'i* (high chief) with a sword, a cotton gown and a bunch of red feathers, Vehiatua was delighted, exchanging names with the British commander and taking him as his bond friend, while Purahi adopted Captain Clerke as her *taio*. Despite these friendly overtures, however, Vehiatua and his mother lauded the Spaniards, saying that they had treated them kindly, giving them many presents without expecting any return.

Annoyed by their praise of the Dons, the following evening Captain Cook organised a fireworks display, which Bligh and his shipmates attended. The Tahitians were terrified and amazed, and when Cook heard them exclaim that 'the Lima ships had neither red feathers, nor fireworks!' he was pleased. The next day, Lieutenant Williamson was invited to an *'arioi* performance during which two little girls and a young woman exposed their genitals as they danced, seeking to arouse 'Oro, the god of fertility and war. Since Williamson and Bligh were friends, it is likely that Bligh was also present on this occasion; and from this time onwards, he was treated as an initiate in the *'arioi* society.

Among the *'arioi*, a graded cult of artists, musicians, warriors, navigators and priests dedicated to the worship of 'Oro, the younger initiates often exposed themselves or had sex during their rituals, to activate the power of the god. Although the sailors saw such performances as erotic enticements, like those in brothels back home in England, in fact these were sacred rituals, usually carried out in secret. During the creation of the cosmos in Tahiti, when male and female powers came together, new kinds of beings were created. Spirits passed from Te Po, the dark world of the ancestors, into Te Ao, the everyday world of light, through the genitals of women (in the birth of children, for example); or from Te Ao to Te Po in death, where they were greeted by an old, blind woman; while male genitals embodied Tetumu, the phallus of Ta'aroa, the creator god on the island. In Tahiti, sex was a sacred power, associated with life and death; and ensuring the fertility of land, people, plants and animals. While men and women were active in the *'arioi* society, and their sexuality was dedicated to the god, they were not permitted to have any living children.

At the same time, the *'arioi* were regarded as sacred people. As a former chief *'arioi* explained to John Orsmond, an early missionary on the island:

There were many ranks among the 'arioi. The avae parae [black-leg] or head
'arioi sat on the high platform and had his legs blackened by tattoo. He was
the head man of the party. Bark-cloth was heaped up before him, and heaps
of pigs. He wore a red loin girdle. He had a fleet of canoes at his disposal. He
pronounced the names of those who shared in the distribution of gifts.

The 'arioi were a company of fine-bodied people, separate from others.
They were set apart, with their scented oil, flowers and scarlet bark-cloth . . .
They had long houses, surrounded by bread-fruit fences . . . If an outsider
trespassed in their ceremonies, he was struck down with a club . . . No-one
could step on the places where they slept. They were sacred.[7]

After this 'arioi celebration, the ships carried on to Matavai Bay [PLATE 9],
Cook's favourite port in the Pacific.

On 23 August when the Resolution and Discovery arrived off Point Venus, Bligh
and his comrades were thrilled. At last, they received the kind of welcome that
they had been anticipating. Hundreds of canoes crowded around the ships, laden
with 'curiosities' and provisions, and crowded with beautiful young girls. Crying
out frantically for Tute (Cook), Pane (Banks) and Tate (Clerke), the islanders
boarded the ships, weeping and slashing themselves, searching for old friends
and lovers and embracing them fervently when they found them. According to
Ledyard:

> Capt. Cook and Lieut. Gore were particularly recognized, and found more
> old acquaintance than they knew how to dispose with; in short the ship was so
> crouded and confused that we could attend to no duty the remaining part of the
> day, Cook fairly gave it up as a day of festivity, not only to the Otaheiteeans
> but to his own people particularly those who had been there before who were
> as much and perhaps more pleased than if they had been moored in any part
> of Great-Britain.[8]

Others approached those sailors who were new to the island, particularly
the officers, offering to adopt them as taio. As master of the Resolution, William
Bligh was a desirable bond friend, and must have acquired his first taio on this
occasion (along with his Tahitian name, 'Parai'). When Hitihiti, a young 'arioi
from Porapora who had sailed with Captain Cook during his second Pacific
voyage, boarded the Resolution, however, Samwell noted with disappointment

*Hitihiti.*

that he was 'one of the most stupid Fellows on the Island, with a clumsy awkward Person and a remarkably heavy look; he is married to a pretty woman who lives at Matavai; he frequently came on board to see us along with his Wife & was almost constantly drunk with Kava'.[9] Captain Clerke failed in his first attempt to tack the *Discovery* into the bay, and that evening Cook sent Bligh in a boat with a light to mark the point of the reef, so that the consort ship could avoid this hazard.[10] The following day when Tu, the paramount chief of the island, arrived in Matavai Bay, accompanied by a fleet of canoes, Captain Cook decided to outdo the Spanish. Led by a guard of honour made up of armed marines in their scarlet jackets, he and Captain Clerke went ashore in a stately procession, followed by Bligh and his officers, dressed in their best uniforms. Tu [PLATE 11], a very tall, robust young man in his late twenties, about 6 feet 3 inches tall with a conspicuous mop of curly hair, was sitting on the beach, surrounded by a huge crowd. At this time Tu was a high priest and leading figure in the *'arioi* society, who had no living children. He was accompanied by his younger brothers Ari'ipaea and

*Ma'i at Court in England.*

Vaetua; and their three sisters (Ari'ipaea Vahine, Tetua-te-ahama'i and Auo), all of whom were also devotees of 'Oro. Their father Teu, a thin old man with a white beard, and their mother Tetupaia, a high-ranking *'arioi* from Ra'iatea, had left the society in order to have these children. Later, when William Bligh inherited Captain Cook's friendship with Tu and his family, this alliance took him into the heart of the cult of 'Oro, shaping his experiences on the island.

When Cook introduced Ma'i to Tu, the young Ra'iatean knelt, embracing the paramount chief around the legs and presenting him with a piece of red-feathered cloth and some gold cloth from Britain. In England, Ma'i had enjoyed himself immensely, learning to ice-skate and play chess, attending the opera, having his portrait painted by Sir Joshua Reynolds, meeting King George III and Queen Charlotte at Richmond Palace, and having affairs with English women; and he had returned home laden with treasures. After presenting his gifts to Tu, Ma'i addressed the crowd, boasting about his travels and lauding the power of the King of England. When Tu realised that Ma'i had given a red feather girdle to Vehiatua, however, he was incensed, regarding the young Ra'iatean with suspicion.

Although Captain Cook had intended to leave Ma'i with Tu, hoping that he would help Tu's people to care for the animals that he had brought from Britain, the young man behaved so foolishly that Cook's plans were thwarted. As he remarked in frustration:

> I expected that with the property he was master of he would have had prudence enough to have made himself respected and even courted by the first persons in the island, but instead of that he rejected the advice of those who wished him well and suffered himself to be duped by every designing knave.[11]

Despite Ma'i's antics, however, Cook's relationship with Tu flourished during this visit. When the young paramount chief boarded the *Resolution* with his stout, dignified, warm-hearted mother Tetupaia, the eldest daughter of the paramount chief of Ra'iatea, and his brothers and sisters, Cook gave them rich gifts and ordered his bagpiper to play for them. Ari'ipaea, Tu's younger brother and a leading fighting sailor, adopted Captain Clerke ('Tate') as his bond friend; and when Tu offered his youngest sister Auo to Captain Cook as a bedmate, Cook ('Tute') declined as gracefully as possible. Several days later he sent Bligh with a pair of peacocks, two geese, two turkeys, some ducks, a bull and two cows, a ram and two ewes, and a billy goat with two nanny goats to Pare for Tu and his family, and ordered his men to plant pineapples, potatoes, melons and some shaddock trees in a nearby garden for the young paramount chief.

On 30 August messengers from the neighbouring island of Mo'orea arrived to report that Mahine, the former high chief of the island, had led an uprising against Mahau, his successor, who had many close relatives in northern Tahiti. War seemed imminent; and that night when a group of women, dressed in short, ruffled skirts over bark-cloth petticoats, performed a sultry dance beside the Tuauru River, Bligh and his fellow officers watched in amazement as these young women lifted up their garments, exposing their genitals. According to the surgeon David Samwell:

> [The dance] bespoke an excess of joy and licentiousness, though perhaps it might be their usual custom. Most of these were young women, who put themselves into several lascivious postures, clapp'd their hands and repeated a kind of Stanzas.
>
> At certain parts they put their garments aside and exposd with seemingly very little sense of shame those parts which most nations have thought it modest to conceal, & a woman more advanc'd in years stood in front, held her cloaths continually up with one hand and danced with uncommon vigour and effrontery, as if to raise in the spectators the most libidinous desires . . .

The men flock'd eagerly round them in great numbers to see their performance and express'd the most anxious curiosity to see that part just mentioned,
at which they seem'd to feel a sort of rapture that could only be express'd by
the extreme joy that appear'd in their countenances.[12]

Although the British saw this performance as 'licentious' and 'libidinous', the
women were dancing to excite 'Oro, the god of war, encouraging him to support
their district in the coming war, and their menfolk watched with reverence and
pride.

The next morning, a close kinsman of Mahau, a man named Teto'ofa (a
fighting sailor whom the British nicknamed the 'Admiral'), sent a message to
Tu, saying that he intended to offer a human sacrifice to 'Oro for the forthcoming battle; and that as *ari'i maro 'ura* of the island (paramount chief of the red
feather girdle), his presence was required. Eager to witness this 'extraordinary
and barbarous custom', Cook asked Tu if he could attend the ceremony, and his
bond friend agreed. Escorted by Bligh and Pohuetea, the powerful warrior chief
of the Pa'ea district, they travelled in the pinnace to 'Utu-'ai-mahurau *marae*, a
stone temple on the west coast of the island where the famous red feather girdle,
Te Ra'i-puatata, was held. When Captain Cook met Teto'ofa on a small offshore
islet and the 'Admiral' pleaded with him to join the attack on Mahine, Cook
refused, and the old man tartly rebuked him for refusing to support his friends
and allies; although Ma'i agreed to go and fight with him, taking one musket to
terrify the enemy warriors.

As they approached the site of the great temple, shaded by its grove of sacred
trees, Tu asked Cook to tell Bligh and his crew to stay behind with the pinnace.
Cook and his *taio* walked together to the *marae*, followed by a crowd of men
and boys (since women were not allowed to attend these ritual occasions). Soon,
they saw a great tiered stone platform adorned with carved wooden boards,
and sacrificial platforms laden with rotting fruit and hogs. Nearby, the human
sacrifice lay in a small canoe, with a priest standing on the *marae* holding up two
bark-cloth bundles – one containing the red feather girdle, Te Ra'i-puatata, and
the other a feathered image of 'Oro. As other priests chanted, the high priest
plucked an eye from the human sacrifice, and placing it on a green leaf, offered it
to Tu who opened his mouth without touching it, allowing the spirit of the dead
man to enter his body. During this ceremony, Tu became the living embodiment
of 'Oro; and as the *varua* or spirit of the sacrifice entered his body as an offering
to the god, a kingfisher cried out from the trees, bringing a message from 'Oro.
Tu looked pleased, remarking to Cook, 'That's the Eatua [*atua* (god)].'[13]

*A human sacrifice in Tahiti.*

Early the next morning when Tu and Captain Cook returned to the *marae*, they stood side by side between two tall sacred drums. As the bundle holding Te Ra'i-puatata was unwrapped, the red feather girdle (or *maro 'ura*) was unrolled on the pavement, releasing its *mana* (ancestral power). During a later visit to the island, William Bligh would sketch this famous object, the cause of so many wars. Cook described the girdle as a sash about 5 yards long and 15 inches wide, decorated with squares of bright yellow feathers with some red and green ones pasted onto bark cloth, and stitched to a red flag from the *Dolphin*, the first European ship to visit the island. In the Society Islands, every time a new *ari'i maro 'ura* (high chief of the red feather girdle) was installed, a new section was stitched to the sash; and at each stage in this process, a human sacrifice was offered. In 1767 when the *Dolphin* had arrived in Tahiti, Purea, the 'Queen of Otaheite', and her husband Amo had been planning to install their son, Teri'irere, as the paramount chief of the island. Purea had forged a bond friendship with Captain Wallis, the *Dolphin*'s commander, and afterwards, her high priest, Tupaia, stitched a section of the *Dolphin*'s red pennant to the red feather girdle, joining the power of the British gods to the *mana* of 'Oro. Before Teri'irere's installation could take place, however, Tu's supporters had attacked, capturing the girdle and carrying it off to their own *marae* in the Pa'ea district. Later, when Captain Cook arrived on board the *Endeavour*, Purea renewed her alliance with the British, taking Cook as her bond friend. It was thus fitting that Captain Cook and Tu should stand side by side during this ceremony – just as later, during his *Bounty* visit, William Bligh would take Captain Cook's place in similar rituals. As the great drums sounded, the high priest opened one end of the other bundle, which held the feathered image of 'Oro. Taking some red feathers from 'Oro's body, the priest handed these to the paramount chief, who tucked them into the red feather girdle, renewing its power, and the sacred relics were wrapped up, returning their *mana* to Te Po and ending the ceremony.

By this time, Tu's elderly father Teu had shifted to a house on Point Venus, where he appointed guards to protect the British and their possessions. Every morning these guards gathered tribute from the girls who had spent the night on board the ships – a lucrative traffic. Bligh's friend, Lieutenant Williamson, was on good terms with Molesworth Phillips, the commander of the marines, but after a quarrel over one of these girls, they fought a duel with pistols, narrowly missing each other with their shots; although later, they made peace with one another.[14] One of the sailors remarked bitterly: 'Many persons would have rejoyced if Mr. Williamson our third Leutenant had fell, as he was a very bad man & a great Tyrant.'[15] Although in their journals and letters, a number of Cook's crew expressed hearty dislike of their third lieutenant, it is notable that none of them criticised Bligh. Despite later speculations to the contrary, there is no evidence that the young master was unpopular with the sailors during this voyage.

Cook's men loved their time in Tahiti, where their red feathers granted them free access to the women. As Lieutenant Rickman exulted: 'We had not a vacant hour between business and pleasure, that was unemployed. We wanted no coffee-houses to kill time, nor Ranelaghs or Vauxhaulls [pleasure gardens in London] for our evening entertainments . . . In these Elysian fields, immortality alone is wanting to the enjoyment of all those pleasures which the poet's fancy has conferred on the shades of departed heroes, as the highest rewards of heroic virtue.' Some of the men took these pleasures to excess, however, as Rickman noted primly: 'Several of the [seamen] were severely punished for indecency in surpassing the vice of the natives by their shameless manner of indulging their sensual appetites.'[16]

On 21 September, the day of the spring equinox, Tu came out to the *Resolution* to invite Captain Cook to inspect the Matavai fleet, which was ready to sail to Pare. When Bligh escorted Cook ashore in the pinnace, they found a fleet of about 70 large canoes drawn up on the beach, carved prows curving up into the sky, decorated with banners and feather pennants and packed with at least a thousand warriors, who stood in the hulls and on the fighting stages, brandishing

*The Tahitian fleet.*

their weapons. As Cook landed, dressed in his best uniform and accompanied by a party of marines in scarlet jackets, carrying an English Jack, Tu invited him and Lieutenant King to board one of these canoes, while Ma'i (who had returned from Mo'orea) joined Po'e'eno, the fighting chief of Matavai Bay, on board his vessel. As Bligh watched, the two canoes engaged in a sham fight, advancing and retreating, and when they charged headlong at each other, Ma'i's warriors swarmed on board Tu's canoe and tipped it over, forcing its occupants to jump overboard. After this performance Ma'i donned a suit of armour that King George had given him and climbed on board the platform of another canoe which paddled around the bay, although most of the warriors ignored this glittering spectacle.

Later that day, Moana, the *ari'i* (high chief) of Matavai Bay, entertained a party of officers, proudly escorting them to a table with benches – the first European-style furniture that they had seen in a Tahitian dwelling. After a lavish meal, Moana presented them with women as bedfellows, and before the officers returned to their ships they gave him red feathers. It is likely that Bligh was present on this occasion, because later, during his *Bounty* visit, Moana and his son Po'e'eno always treated him as a close friend and ally. Although Moana and Po'e'eno, the chiefs of the Ha'apape district, were friendly with Tu, they were eager to become independent of Pare, and to forge their own alliances with British officers.

Tu's naval review proved to be another delaying tactic. On 22 September another messenger arrived to report that despite Ma'i and his musket, after

*Captain James Cook, by John Webber.*

burning houses and canoes on Mo'orea, Teto'ofa had been defeated in a great
sea battle. When the 'Admiral' returned to Tahiti, incensed with Tu and 'irritated
to a Degree of Madness, [he] Abused of him Every where and was very glad to
get any of us to Listen to him. He would curse Ottou for an Hour together and
Foam At the Mouth with rage.'[17] When Cook, who had 'a mighty Friendship'
for Tu, heard that the 'Admiral' had threatened to kill his bond friend after the
British ships sailed from the island, he made an impassioned speech, vowing
to return and destroy any chief who dared to attack the paramount chief in his
absence. Teto'ofa was angry because he had been forced to make peace with
his enemy on unfavourable terms, and offer up more human sacrifices for the
peacemaking rituals.

By this time, Tahiti had almost been drained of pigs and ripe breadfruit,
and Captain Cook decided that it was time to leave the island. According to
James Burney, during this visit, Charles Clerke (who was now very ill) and the
*Resolution*'s surgeon William Anderson, both of whom were suffering from
tuberculosis, asked Captain Cook for his permission to 'resign their situations,
that they might remain where they were, and trust themselves to the care of the

natives, as the only hope left them of being restored to health'.[18] Cook did not welcome this request, which would have set a precedent, encouraging many of his men to desert the ships. Unwilling to refuse them outright, he told Clerke that he could not leave the expedition until all of his papers and accounts were in order; but as a consolation prize, when some of the Tahitian women begged to accompany their 'husbands' to Ra'iatea, he allowed them to do so.

On 28 September while the sailors were packing up the shore camp, Tu came out to the *Resolution* with a small carved canoe as a gift for the King of England, although it was too large to bring on board; and urged Cook to tell King George to send him red feathers, axes, horses and half a dozen muskets with powder and shot. In exchange, Cook presented his *taio* with a large locked chest containing a portrait of himself that the ship's artist, John Webber, had painted at Tu's request, handing him the key to the locker. This portrait of Cook must have been similar to others painted by John Webber during the voyage, perhaps a head-and-shoulders image of Captain Cook in uniform, his jaw set, gazing steadily out of a black background reminiscent of Te Po – the dark realm of ancestral presence and power. As Bligh watched this presentation, he had no way of knowing that in future he would stand alongside this portrait on a number of ritual occasions. Afterwards the 'Admiral', who had taken Ma'i as his *taio*, presented him with a fine sailing canoe, which the young Ra'iatean immediately boarded.

Early the next morning, 29 September 1777, when the ships set sail from Tahiti, Captain Cook fired a salute of eight guns for Tu as he boarded the *Resolution* with his mother Tetupaia, the young paramount chief weeping as he farewelled his *taio*. During this visit, Cook's men felt that he had done well in upholding his *mana* in the face of the Spanish challenge. As David Samwell, one of the surgeons, remarked: '[N]o Man could be more esteemed & dreaded than Capt. Cook was among them, who upon all Occasions preserved his Consequence with an admirable address, & the name of Toottee will be handed down to Posterity as the greatest Chief & a man of the greatest Power that ever visited their Island.'[19]

More than a decade later, during his visit on board the *Bounty*, the *mana* that Captain Cook had acquired would fall upon the shoulders of William Bligh.

# 4

## The Old Boy Tips a *Heiva*

During his previous visits to Tahiti, Captain Cook had not yet charted Mo'orea, off the west coast. Guided by Ma'i in his canoe, the ships headed to the island; and when they arrived, Cook sent Bligh ahead in the boats to sound and survey Papeto'ai Bay.[1] According to Samwell, this spectacular inlet was 'one of the best Harbours we have met with among the South Sea Islands';[2] while Gilbert remarked: 'At the head of this Harbour is a very fertile and delightful valley, with a large rivulet of excellent water running thro' it. It is entirely surrounded with hills, and high steep cliffs affording a great variety of the most pleasing and romantic prospects I ever beheld.'[3] The devastation caused by the 'Admiral' and his warriors was obvious, however – trees stripped of their fruit, ruined gardens, and houses charred by fire or lying in ruins. As Alexander Home remarked: 'All things relating to them bears the Melancoly Marks of Slavery and Opression.'[4] The ships were crawling with rats, so Cook ordered the vessels to be moored by ropes to the trees, allowing these vermin to escape ashore.

Captain Cook was anxious to meet Mahine, but when this famous warrior came alongside the *Resolution* the next day, he proved to be a bald, fat, one-eyed man about forty-five years old. As Alexander Home exclaimed, 'We were much disappointed in Our Notions of this Champion of Liberty. We Expected to see A youthfull Sprightly Active fellow But Instead of that He Turned out An Infirm Old man more than half blind.'[5] Mahine refused to board the *Resolution*, although when Cook presented him with some red feathers and a cotton gown, he exchanged names with the British commander, returning soon afterwards with a large pig that he presented to his new *taio*. Well aware of the conflict between Mahine and Mahau, and Mahine's anger against Tu, Captain Cook decided to ensure that the high chief of Mo'orea would not try to attack his *taio* after the ships sailed from the Society Islands.

*Papeto'ai Bay, Mo'orea.*

Throughout this voyage, Cook's temper had been uncertain. As James Trevenen, one of his midshipmen, wrote in his journal, Cook was stern with the men:

> O day of hard labour! O Day of good living!
> When TOOTE was seized with the humour of giving –
> When he cloathed in good nature his looks of authority
> And shook from his eyebrows their stern superiority.[6]

He added: '*Heiva*: the name of the dances of the southern islanders which bore so great a resemblance to the violent motions and stampings on the Deck of Capt Cook in the paroxysms of passion, into which he frequently threw himself upon the slightest occasion that they were universally known by the same name, & it was a common saying, both among officers & people, "The old boy has been tipping a *heiva* to such or such a one."'[7] Cook was suffering from rheumatic pains, and on 6 October 1777 when a kid that had been left to graze ashore disappeared, he flew into one of these tantrums.

The next day Captain Cook sent Bligh in the cutter with a threatening message to Mahine, saying that if he did not return the kid, he and his people would be punished. The goats were sent ashore again to graze; and during the afternoon, Bligh returned with the kid, and the man who had taken it, delivering them to his commander. Although the islander told Cook that he had seized the kid in return for some breadfruit and plantains that the goats' keeper had taken without permission, Cook had him thrown into irons. When the animals were collected that evening, it was found that a nanny goat in kid was missing. In his rage, Cook stamped on the deck, threatening death and destruction to Mahine and his people.

On 7 October, after sending Williamson and Bligh with the *Resolution*'s three boats to the west coast of the island, Captain Cook set off with 35 armed men, including all of his midshipmen and marines. Although Ma'i urged him to shoot anyone that they met, Cook forbade him to fire his musket. When they arrived at the place where the goat was supposedly hidden, a group of warriors pelted them with stones. These men denied any knowledge of the goat, and angered by their temerity, Cook told the sailors to burn the houses in their village and three large canoes. During their rampage across the island, Ma'i and his Tahitian companions plundered and burned twelve more houses and thirteen war canoes, some of which were big enough to carry 120 paddlers, and confiscated their domestic animals, ignoring the lamentations of their owners; although out of respect to Tu, they did not harm any of the houses or canoes in the district of his kinsman and ally, Mahau.

There was still no sign of the goats, however, and the next morning Cook sent Bligh in the pinnace with another threatening message for Mahine, saying that unless the stolen animals were returned, he would destroy every canoe on the island. When he received no reply, Cook sent another armed party ashore to demolish more houses and smash and burn more canoes, killing pigs and dogs as they marched across the island. Finally that evening, the nanny goat was returned to the *Resolution*. The men were troubled by Cook's uncharacteristic fury. As the young midshipman George Gilbert wrote in his journal:

> Where ever Capt. Cook met with any Houses or Canoes, that belonged to the party (which he was informed) that had stolen the goat, he ordered them to be be burnt and seemed to be very rigid in the performance of His orders, which every one executed with the greatest reluctance except Omai [Ma'i], who was very officious and wanted to fire upon the Natives . . .
>
> Several women and old men, still remained by the houses whose lamentations were very great, but all their entreaties could not move Capt Cook to desist in the smallest degree from those cruel ravages . . . and all about such a trifle as a small goat . . . I can't well account for Capt. Cook's proceedings on

this occasion as they were so very different from his conduct in like cases on his former voyages.[8]

No doubt Bligh shared their puzzlement. Even Lieutenant Williamson thought that Cook was too severe, remarking, 'I cannot help thinking the man totally destitute of humanity, and I must confess this once I obey'd my Orders with reluctance. I doubt not but Captn. Cook had good reasons for carrying His punishment of these people to so great a length, but what his reasons were are yet a secret.'[9] Cook had become fond of his *taio* Tu, however, and this demonstration of force was at once a show of support for Mahau, and intended to deter any attacks upon Tu and his family, after he sailed from the Society Islands.

After devastating Mo'orea, on 11 October Captain Cook headed for Huahine, where Ma'i had decided to settle. As they entered Fare Harbour on the lee side of the island, led by Bligh in the boats, a man from Mo'orea was found with stolen goods in his possession and Captain Cook flew into another rage, instructing the ship's barber to shave this man's head and cut off his ears. The barber was in the midst of carrying out this order when one of the ship's officers, thinking that Cook could not be serious, stopped the punishment and told the man to swim ashore.

When they landed, Cook (who was still unwell) learned that his old friend Ori, the high chief of the island, had been succeeded by his son, Teri'itaria. Instructing Ma'i to put on his best suit, he went to pay a visit to the new high chief, a boy just nine years old, and his mother, who was acting as his regent. During their meeting, Cook hastened to reassure the gathering that if Ma'i went to Ra'iatea, it would be as a friend and not an enemy to the Porapora people; and when he heard this, a chief from Porapora stood up and declared that Huahine and everything in it was now Tute's, and he could give any part of the island that he liked to Ma'i, promising to protect the young Ra'iatean and his possessions.

Over the next few days Ma'i's attendants (including two Māori boys who had accompanied him from Queen Charlotte Sound) dug a deep ditch around 'Peretane' (Britain), as the Huahine people called the site, and a garden was prepared where the sailors planted vines, shaddock trees, pineapples, melons and other European plants. When the carpenters began to build Ma'i's small house, Bligh and his men landed the wood from the captured canoes to use in its construction, and a menagerie of strange animals – the horse and a mare, a cow and a calf, a pair of rabbits, sheep, cats, goats, chickens, ducks and a monkey, which the Huahine people thought was a kind of person. Cook also instructed his master to fumigate the bread room, and to condemn and destroy any pieces

'Arioi *dancers.*

that had been badly damaged by rats, weevils and cockroaches.[10] While Bligh
was engaged in this unglamorous task, shifting the bread to a house near the
shore camp, girls flocked out to the ships, attracted by the red feathers, and every
time the officers rode the horses, 'they were followed by Thousands of Indians
running & shouting like mad People'.[11]

On 22 October, this joyous mood was shattered when a man stole a quadrant
from the observatory, which the sailors had erected in the bay. It was the time
of the spring festival, and a visiting troupe of *'arioi* had arrived from Ra'iatea.
That night the *'arioi* house of the district was lit with fires and candlenut tapers,
and crowded with spectators. As Bligh and his comrades gazed in fascination,
the 'black leg' *'arioi* of both sexes sat on a high platform, one foot up on the
opposite thigh, wiggling their toes and cooling themselves with fans decorated
with white dog-tail hairs. When the visiting head *'arioi* entered the house, his face
painted bright red and his body glistening with *monoi* (scented oil), he strutted
like a peacock, crossing his arms over his chest as he recited the names of his
mountain, the *'arioi* house, the main *marae*, the high chief, and the river of his
home district, presenting a *rahiri* or bunch of braided coconut leaves and other
gifts to the high chief of the island to thank him for his hospitality. For the rest
of the evening, this man acted as the master of ceremonies, joking and clowning
as he guided his troupe through the *heiva*.

These *'arioi* performances included dancing, skits and music; and Bligh and his shipmates watched spellbound as a girl 'as beautiful as Venus' danced before them, bark-cloth petticoats shimmering as her hips swayed seductively, and a group of male *'arioi* performed a riotous satire. When Captain Cook was told that the astronomical quadrant had been stolen, however, he stormed ashore, interrupting this performance and berating the local chiefs, demanding that they hand over the culprit. Ma'i was with him, and noticing a Porapora man in the audience, he accused this man of stealing the quadrant, and drawing his sword, took him captive, to the astonishment of the local chiefs. The man was carried on board the *Resolution* where Cook had him clapped in irons, and Ma'i forced him to confess where he had hidden the quadrant, which was retrieved the next morning.

Determined to make an example of the thief, Captain Cook ordered the barber to shave his head and eyebrows and cut off both his ears, and the boatswain's mate gave him a flogging that flayed the skin from his back, although he remained resolutely silent. As soon as he was released, however, the Porapora man stormed ashore and destroyed Ma'i's garden, ripping up plants, smashing the fences and releasing the European animals. When he was captured again and brought back on board, Cook had him clapped in irons on the quarterdeck. Many of the sailors thought this punishment too severe, and several nights later when the man escaped overboard, Cook flew into another fury, accusing the sailors of releasing him. Sending the midshipman on duty before the mast, he also demoted Bligh's mate, William Harvey, who had been on watch that night, discharging him into the *Discovery*. As Bayly, the astronomer, remarked soberly: 'It is an unfortunate stroke for both these Gentlemen as their preferment soly depended on Captain Cook's Interest.'[12] Each of the sentries on watch was given three dozen lashes. In addition, Cook ordered his first lieutenant, John Gore, whom he had excused from keeping watch while they were in harbour, to return to duty and keep an eye on the men at all times, trying to restore shipboard discipline.

On 26 October, Ma'i's dwelling, complete with a loft and a door with a lock, was finished. Bligh and his men loaded the gifts that the young man had received in Britain into the boats, including a bed, a table and chairs, portraits of the King and Queen, Joseph Banks and Lord Sandwich, a jack-in-a-box, and an 'electrifying machine'; and ferried them ashore. Cook gave Ma'i a saddle for his horse, swords and cutlasses, a musket and a bayonet, a brace of pistols, a fowling piece and plenty of powder and ammunition which were stored in canisters on the shelves. To celebrate the occasion, the young Ra'iatean gave a feast for Cook and his officers and the high chief and his family, serving them with wine and grog, playing his hand organ and demonstrating the electrifying machine, although Captain Clerke was too ill to be present. As Bligh and his fellow officers watched in amusement, Ma'i tricked his countrymen into receiving electric shocks, just as Banks and Lord Sandwich had fooled him in England. When the chiefs were a little drunk, Cook ended the feast with a display of fireworks, terrifying them in an effort to ensure that they would take care of Ma'i after he had departed.

On 2 November 1777 when Cook decided to leave Huahine, two more of the sailors on board the *Resolution* were flogged, one for sleeping on duty. As they said goodbye, Ma'i embraced Captain Cook, weeping bitterly, and Cook was visibly affected. As he remarked in his journal: '[W]hatever faults this Indian had they were more than over ballanced by his great good Nature and docile disposition. His gratifull heart always retained the highest sence of the favours he received in England nor will he ever forget those who honoured him with their protection and friendship during his stay there.'[13]

On 3 November when the ships arrived at Ha'amanino Bay in Ra'iatea, Tupaia's birthplace, Bligh guided them into this calm, sheltered harbour. Reo, the leading chief on the island and Cook's *taio*, came out to greet them, accompanied by his beautiful young daughter, Poiatua. By this time, Captain Cook was feeling better, but after his recent brutal outbursts, his men had begun to imitate his behaviour. When one of the sentries was insulted by a local man, the marine ran him through with his sword, and the corpse was hastily carried away.[14] On 13 November a Ra'iatean who had been caught taking a nail from a sailor's pocket was brought on board the *Resolution*, and as he lay trussed up on the deck, Lieutenant Williamson tried to jump on his head; and when the man rolled away, Williamson stamped on the side of his face, knocking out some of his teeth.

Later that night, William Bligh had his first experience of desertion in the Society Islands. John Harrison, one of the *Resolution*'s marines who had been flogged after the escape of the thief from Porapora, slipped into a canoe at midnight, taking his musket with him, and ran ashore. When he was told, Captain Cook took his young master and set off in hot pursuit in the boats. They finally found Harrison two days later, sleeping blissfully between two women, garlanded with red and white flowers. Although his older lover, who belonged to one of the aristocratic families on the island, summoned a party of warriors to rescue him, the armed boats rowed away before they could attack. When Harrison was brought back to the ship, he was put in irons and given two dozen lashes.

*Poiatua.*

Encouraged by this relatively lenient treatment, ten days later as the Season of Plenty began, two more sailors bolted from the *Discovery*. One of these men, Thomas Shaw, was a gunner's mate; while the other, Alexander Mouat, was a midshipman and the son of a naval captain, a friend of Captain Clerke's. Shaw had a girlfriend ashore, and when Mouat, who had fallen in love with a high-born young woman from Huahine, asked Captain Cook for permission to stay on the island, Cook had refused. Determined to retrieve the deserters, Cook set off again with Bligh in the pinnace to search the east side of the island, and then the coastline of the adjoining island of Taha'a, but the two sailors had already fled to Porapora. After inviting Reo's beautiful young daughter Poiatua and her brother, leading members of the 'arioi society, on board the *Discovery* to receive some gifts, Captain Clerke locked them in his cabin, its windows barred, while Cook's men captured all the large canoes in the harbour. Poiatua was distraught, weeping inconsolably during her captivity. Alongside the *Discovery*, their friends and relatives sat in fishing canoes and lamented, slashing their heads with shark's teeth until the sea ran red with their blood.

At first Reo was unwilling to believe that his bond friend Captain Cook was aware that Captain Clerke had imprisoned his children; but when Cook assured him that unless the deserters were returned, he would carry his son and daughter away from the island, Reo was enraged by his *taio*'s treachery and decided to kill the two captains. Every evening during their visit to Ha'amanino Bay, Cook and Clerke bathed in the local river, but that afternoon when Reo urged Clerke to take a swim, a young girl from Huahine, 'a Fat, Jolly girl [who] expressed great Horror at Fighting and Bloodshed',[15] warned her sailor lover that there were warriors hiding in the bushes, waiting to kill him. Captain Cook hastily sent 100 armed men ashore in two boats, with Bligh in the great cutter; and when they saw them approaching, the warriors fled before the sailors could fire their muskets.

Meanwhile the two deserters had been carried by canoe to Porapora, the headquarters of the old warrior chief Puni. Determined to retrieve them, Cook decided upon a ruse. Telling the chiefs that he was going to release the prisoners, he invited them on board the *Resolution* to celebrate the occasion. They greeted their offspring with joy, weeping, but while they were dining, Cook sent his officers, including Bligh, in the boats to blockade the bay and capture their canoes. Afterwards, Cook took the chiefs prisoner, including Reo, who sent an urgent message to Puni, imploring him to return the deserters to Ra'iatea – a rehearsal of the ploy that later led to Captain Cook's death in Kealakekua Bay. When the old chief of Porapora made no reply, on 29 November Cook allowed Reo to leave the ship to retrieve the deserters. He chased them as far as Tupua'i in the Austral Islands, which William Bligh had earlier charted; and when he brought them back to the ships, trussed up in ropes, Captain Cook freed Reo's children and put the deserters in irons; although Reo and his people were appalled at his treachery.

No doubt Bligh learned a great deal from this episode. Later, he would refuse to take hostages among the chiefs, even when trying to retrieve men who ran from his ships. He also became acutely aware of the allure of these islands to British sailors. As Alexander Home explained: 'The Natives were Constantly Inviting us to Stay Amongst them. Their promise was a Large Estate and a Handsome Wife, and Every thing that was fine and Agreeable that their Country Afforded. It was not to be Wondered at that Such proposals were listened to by many and some of good Sense too, for it was by No Means Visionary Dreams of Happyness but absolutely real . . . It seemed Exactly the paradise of Mahomet in Every thing but Immortality.'[16]

Aware that his men were seduced by these promises, Cook used his personal authority to dissuade them. Mustering them on deck, he made a rousing speech, promising that if they deserted, he would always get them back, because no matter how much the islanders liked them, they liked their chiefs better. He assured the sailors that if any of them ran from the ships, he would take the local chiefs hostage until they were returned, 'and dead or Alive, he'd have them!' His eloquence impressed Bligh and his comrades, leaving no doubt about their captain's determination to retrieve any deserter. Despite his lurid threats, Captain Cook was lenient with Mouat, however, stripping him of his midshipman's status and sending him before the mast, although he ordered his accomplice to be given two dozen lashes. As Lieutenant Williamson remarked: 'Captn Cook had on this occasion all ye feelings of a parent, & often with great tenderness & concern us'd to say, how soon a young man, even without ye least propensity to Vice (and such was this young man) might by one boyish Action, make a worthy family miserable forever.'[17] Three days later Cook turned all of the girls out of the ships, dismaying the sailors, although by this time more than thirty of his men were suffering from venereal infections.

Curious to meet Puni, the old warrior chief from Porapora (which at this time was the headquarters of the 'arioi society) who had conquered Ra'iatea and Taha'a and dominated Huahine, on 7 December 1777 Captain Cook set off from Ra'iatea, accompanied by Reo and heading for Porapora. According to James Burney, Cook had promised Captain Clerke that as long as his papers were in order, he could go ashore at this island, and stay there. Off Avanui Bay, a large, sheltered harbour on the west side of Porapora, Captain Cook sent Bligh ahead in the great cutter to find a safe anchorage. When Bligh reported that there was a good channel through the reef, wide enough to turn the ships, Cook followed in the pinnace, landing on the beach where they were greeted by Puni, the high chief of the island. Although Cook presented this blind old warrior with a linen nightgown, a shirt, a mirror and six large axes, the winds were contrary, preventing the ships from sailing into the harbour; and Clerke and Anderson were unable to go ashore. After farewelling Reo and Puni, Cook returned to the *Resolution*, and the ships set sail together, heading for the west coast of America to search for the Northwest Passage.

During his first visit to the Society Islands, William Bligh had met many of the islanders who would later shape his life and career. As Captain Cook's master, he was often at his side, watching Cook dealing with Tongans and Tahitians, enjoying his friendship with Tu and his family, impressed by his easy authority, and no doubt puzzled and troubled, like his shipmates, by their commander's uncharacteristic fits of violence. Bligh also gained his first understandings of Tahitian society; and through his friendship with Williamson, was initiated into the *'arioi* rituals and their approach to sexuality, which he later described with greater insight than any other European. It was not just the management of a ship, surveying and charting that William Bligh learned from James Cook, but also a deep interest in local customs and beliefs. Eventually, he became one of the finest ethnographers among the European explorers, rivalling Máximo Rodríguez in his knowledge of life in the islands; and for that reason, too, it is deeply frustrating that his *Resolution* journal is missing.

As William Ellis, the *Discovery*'s surgeon, remarked of the *'arioi*:

> The society of the areeois is esteemed the most polite establishment in these islands; the members of which are always people of rank and fortune, and are distinguished by being tattooed in a peculiar manner, particularly those who are natives of Porapora . . .
>
> They generally go in companies of ten or twelve sail of canoes, and let them direct their course to whatever island they please, they are always certain of being well received; nay, if they have even been at war but a few days before the visit, all animosity is laid aside, and they are as perfect friends as if nothing had happened.
>
> One of their privileges is to keep two, three, or more women at once, who however must be members. They always wear the best cloth the islands produce, and eat many peculiar things, which others, even if arees [*ari'i*: high chief], are not permitted to do. They are generally distinguished for their prowess, valor and activity in battle, and if any of them shew the least signs of cowardice, he is excluded from the society, and no one will associate or speak to him.
>
> Their amusements during their meetings consist of boxing, wrestling, dancing, and making feasts and entertainments, at which crowds of female spectators attend, the fairest of whom are always made choice of by the conquerors. In general, they continue in this society to the age of thirty or thirty-five, when by suffering one of their children to survive, they debar themselves of the privileges of an arreoi.[18]

Bligh and his comrades had been treated like travelling *'arioi*; and as George Gilbert, one of Cook's midshipmen, observed, if their commander had not been so determined to retrieve the deserters, most of the sailors would have run ashore. According to Thomas Edgar, the *Discovery*'s master, the local girls were 'Angels'. He added: 'I can without vanity affirm it was the happiest 3 months I ever spent.'[19] John Rickman, a lieutenant on board the *Discovery*, praised these women for their loyalty: 'When once they have made their choice, it must be owing to the sailor himself if his mistress ever proves false to him. No women upon earth are more faithful.'[20] Alexander Home, a *Discovery* midshipman, added: '[A]lmost Every man had a girl that Eat as much as himself and we lived in the Utmost Affluence. The Over flowing plenty, the Ease in which men live and the Softness and Delightfulness of the Clime, the women are Extremely Handsome and fond of the Europeans, prodigiously insisting and Constantly Importuning them to stay, and their Insinuations are Backed by the Courtesy of the Chiefs and the admiration of the people in general. It is Infinately too much for sailors to withstand.'[21]

As they sailed away towards the icy shores of north-west America, many of Cook's men must have felt that the happiest part of their voyage was over. Perhaps William Bligh saw it differently. Over the months that followed, he would distinguish himself in the boats, surveying Christmas Island (where his shipmates caught 220 turtles), and Kaua'i and Ni'ihau in the Hawai'ian Islands, excelling himself in the freezing, arduous task of charting Nootka Sound, Prince William Sound, Cook Inlet and Norton Sound on the north-west coast of America. When they crossed the Arctic Circle, where the weather was so cold that according to Rickman, 'icicles hung at our hair, our noses, and even at the men's finger ends', and their food froze solid,[22] Bligh's meticulous work, along with that of Thomas Edgar, resulted in a remarkable series of large charts of the North Pacific coast from Nootka to Kamchatka, complete with coastal views sketched by Bligh, and proudly signed with his name.[23]

By February 1779, however, Captain Cook lay mangled on a rocky beach in Kealakekua Bay, battered to death by infuriated warriors; while in August of that year, Charles Clerke, who was dying of consumption, wrote Joseph Banks a poignant letter of farewell, off Kamchatka on the icy coast of Russia:

> My ever honoured friend
> The disorder I was attacked with in the King's Bench prison has prov'd con-
> sumptive . . . it has now so far got the better of me that I am not able to turn
> myself in my bed, so that my stay in this world must be of a short duration;
> however I hope my friends will have no occasion to blush in owning themselves
> such, for I have most perfectly and justly done my duty to my country as far
> as my abilities would allow me . . .
>   Now my dear & honoured friend I must bid you a final adieu; may you enjoy
> many happy years in this world, & in the end attain that fame your indefatigable

industry so richly deserves. These are the warmest and sincerest wishes of your devoted, affectionate and departing servant, Charles Clerke.[24]

With the death of Captain Clerke, Bligh had lost both of his shipboard patrons. John Gore, that 'old conceited American who never conformed to any scheme of which he was not the proposer, who never took advice in life, and consequently never took a right step in his life',[25] took over the command of the expedition, while John King replaced him as commander of the *Discovery*. Neither of these men had any sympathy for William Bligh.

# 5

## *Bounty*

In January 1780, when a posthumous letter from Charles Clerke arrived in England, announcing Captain Cook's death in Hawai'i, there was an outpouring of grief at the loss of the great navigator. As soon as he heard the news, Lord Sandwich wrote to Joseph Banks:

> What is uppermost in our minds allways must come first, poor Captain Cooke is no more. He was massacred with four of his people by the Natives of an Island where he had been treated if possible with more hospitality than at Otaheite.[1]

As Fanny Burney, James Burney's novelist sister, lamented:

> How hard, after so many dangers, so much toil, – to die in so shocking a manner – in an island he had himself discovered – among savages he had himself rendered kind and hospitable. He was, besides, the most moderate, humane and gentle circumnavigator who ever went out upon discoveries; agreed the best with all the Indians, and, till this fatal time, never failed, however hostile they met, to leave them his friends.[2]

Captain Cook was hailed as a hero – a man of peace, killed by unruly barbarians. When a pantomime about Cook's voyages was performed in London, one of the backdrops depicted Cook in uniform, floating above Hawai'i on a cloud, heralded by an angel blowing a trumpet and leaning against Britannia (although her headdress looks Tahitian), holding his sextant in one hand while reaching out in an imploring gesture with the other.

*The Apotheosis of Captain Cook.*

On 30 September 1780 when the *Resolution* and *Discovery* anchored off Yarmouth, there must have been gossip about the unhappy circumstances of Captain Cook's death, and the conduct of some of his officers. The Admiralty played down these rumours, however, and Lord Sandwich and Joseph Banks organised a flurry of promotions for the survivors. As John King, now commander of the *Discovery* (whom Charles Clerke had recommended to Joseph Banks as 'my very dear & particular friend'), noted with satisfaction in the official account: 'Captains

Gore and King were made post, Mr. Burney and Mr. Williamson, masters and commanders; and every mate and midshipman that had served their time [including Bligh's two mates, William Harvey and William Lanyon] were made Lieutenants and several of the men warrant officers.'[3] At first William Bligh hoped that he would also be given a lieutenant's commission, especially when he was kept on full pay for several months to complete his charts of Desolation (Kerguelen) Island, Tasmania, the Tongan and Hawai'ian islands, and his meticulous surveys of the north-west coast of America.

Although Bligh had a high regard for John Gore, however, who had succeeded Clerke as the commander of the expedition, Gore did not return the compliment. On their arrival in Britain, when Gore sent Captain King and Henry Roberts, Bligh's mate, to the Admiralty with the *Resolution*'s journals, logs and charts, he described Roberts in an accompanying note as 'principal assistant Hydrographer to Capt. Cook, and certainly a verry Deserving young man'.[4] In fact, however, this was the role that William Bligh had played during the voyage, while Roberts had worked under his direct supervision. On 4 November, when Captain King attended the Board of Longitude, he produced the 'logs, books of astronomical observations, charts etc. kept and made by him in the course of the late voyage', and was given a reward of £500.[5] In this way, the credit for the surveying and charting work carried out by Captain Cook, Bligh and Edgar (the master of the *Discovery*) was claimed by King and Roberts.[6] When Roberts, who had produced the fair versions of many of their charts, was promoted to lieutenant, Bligh must have felt humiliated, although he was not the only officer who suffered. When he and Edgar (who had passed his lieutenant's examination in 1768) made personal applications for lieutenant's commissions to Lord Sandwich, the First Lord of the Admiralty, neither of them received his new captain's support. Bligh's role as Cook's primary hydrographic assistant, and Edgar's role as Clerke's assistant, were ignored, and both of these men remained masters.[7]

According to John King in a letter to Joseph Banks, Bligh had threatened to publish his own journal:

> I have just received the inclosed letter [which does not survive], which as it is proper to acquaint you with its contents I have sent the whole to you. Should Mr. Bligh put his threats of printing, which as I judge from the inclosed he has thrown out, into practice, I think with deference to your judgement it may not be amiss . . . to put in an advertisement of the intention of the Admiralty with regard to publication.[8]

Whether or not Bligh had indeed made such a threat, King's letter was intended to scupper his chances of promotion. Unauthorised accounts of the voyage were a direct affront to Banks, who with Lord Sandwich was in charge of the official publication of Cook's journal from his last voyage. Indeed, when John Rickman (first lieutenant of the *Discovery*, now King's ship) and Heinrich Zimmerman (a coxswain from the same vessel) published accounts of the voyage in 1781, followed by William Ellis, a surgeon's mate from the same ship, who published an account under his own name, it cost them any chance of preferment. Although Cook's men had been ordered to hand in their logs and journals upon arriving in England, so that the Admiralty could authorise and control the publication of the official record of the voyage, discipline on board the *Discovery* under King's command had lapsed, and a number of his men held on to their own charts and journals.

In the midst of these trials, William Bligh's father died, just three months after his son's return to England, and was buried in Plymouth. Shortly after the funeral, Bligh visited the Isle of Man, where he was reunited with Betsy Betham. After a whirlwind courtship, they were married in Onchan church on 4 February 1781, a love match that would survive the triumphs and disasters of Bligh's turbulent career. When they heard his tales about Captain Cook's last voyage, Betsy's family were indignant about how he had been treated. Her uncle Duncan Campbell, a shipowner and kinsman of Vice-Admiral John Campbell, interceded on Bligh's behalf; and ten days after their marriage, Bligh was appointed the master of *Belle Poule*, a 32-gun frigate captured from the French.

In April 1781 the *Belle Poule* captured a French privateer in the English Channel, and took her as a prize. Soon afterwards, Bligh wrote to Betsy in London, assuring her that he was fit and well, but in a letter to his cousin (who promptly told Betsy) confessed that the conditions were so damp and foggy that he and many of his shipmates had colds and rheumatism, although 'they were very happy amongst themselves'. As Betsy remarked to Bligh's brother-in-law, the ship's surgeon John Bond, 'I hope they have no old Growls amongst them.'[9] In August while the *Belle Poule* and other warships were escorting a large merchant fleet from the Baltic to England, commanded by Admiral Hyde Parker, they met a fleet of Dutch ships at the Dogger Bank and fought a bloody battle. During this engagement many of the British sailors were killed or wounded, and Bligh's ship was badly battered.[10]

In September 1781 when the *Belle Poule* was declared unfit for sea, Bligh was finally given an acting commission, transferring as fifth lieutenant to the *Berwick*, a 74-gun ship that had fought in the same action. Their squadron was now commanded by Commodore the Honourable Keith Stewart, a relative of Elizabeth Bligh's, who gave him this promotion.[11] During his time on the *Berwick*, Stewart confirmed Bligh's commission, although 'not with Sandwiches goodwill', according to one contemporary.[12] Unfortunately, Lord Sandwich disapproved of losing good masters by having them turned into junior lieutenants.[13] In November of that year, Bligh had another disappointment. Although he had been nominated (perhaps by one of Betsy's relatives) for election as a Fellow of the Royal Society on the basis of his journal and charts from his voyage around the world, this did not succeed.[14] He was delighted, however, when Betsy bore him a daughter, Harriet, a little more than nine months after their wedding.

Soon after his transfer to the *Berwick*, Bligh was sent to the 80-gun *Princess Amelia*, which had also fought in the battle on the Dogger Bank.[15] After only ten weeks, the ship's entire company was transferred to HMS *Cambridge*, a first-class ship of the line, and Bligh became a sixth lieutenant. As a newly married man with a child, Bligh was eager to capture an enemy vessel and claim his share of the prize money. While the *Cambridge* was being repaired in the naval dockyard, however, the fleet captured an enemy convoy, and Bligh missed out on his share of the proceeds. By this time, Betsy had returned to the Isle of Man. As she confessed to Bligh's brother-in-law, John Bond, she was missing her husband: 'I try to make myself contented here, as I imagine I can live at less expence to Mr. Bligh than anywhere else, but whenever I hear of his being at times in England, I cannot help wishing myself there . . . My little girl is a mighty pretty black-eyed baby, but not a Giantess. She is so like Mr. B. I'm sure you would be surprised to see her.'[16] Through her connections, Betsy kept a close eye on Bligh's naval career, reporting to Bond that her friend, Lady Selkirk, had informed her about several good opportunities for more senior appointments for her husband, but because he owed so much to Keith Stewart, 'Mr. B.' was unable to take them.

In September 1782 the *Cambridge* joined a fleet of 183 warships commanded by Lord Howe, which sailed to relieve the besieged island fortress of Gibraltar. After an inconclusive battle with the combined French and Spanish fleets, Lord Howe provisioned the garrison and captured some enemy ships; and Bligh, who received a small share of the prize money, was promoted to fourth lieutenant.[17] Upon hearing that Lord Howe had relieved Gibraltar, Betsy wrote to Bond: 'One of Mr. Bligh's last injunctions to me was desiring me to write to you, and as I am a very obedient Wife, especially when I like the commands imposed, I now sit down with pleasure to obey him.' Despite her anxiety for her husband, she assured Bond:

I do my best to keep up my spirits, and trust that Providence who has been so kind to me hitherto in preserving Mr. Bligh will continue his goodness. I have great pleasure and comfort in my little Girl, she turns out a very fine thriving Child, and considering I made her a very bad Nurse, is wonderfully forward.

I hope you will soon have the pleasure of seeing [Bligh and his shipmates] all return safe to Portsmouth; how happy should I be were I there to welcome my dear Mr. Bligh upon his safe return home, but I console myself for being deprived of that pleasure by thinking that I cost him less here than I could do any where else, however I still hope that fortune will favour us soon, and that we shall all meet and be happy together at Plymouth.[18]

Unaccustomed to poverty, Betsy hated their enforced separations, and found the uncertainties of war at sea a torment.

When the Peace of Paris was signed and the American states won their independence from Britain, the Navy was rapidly reduced in size, and many officers, including Bligh, were discharged and put on half pay. In 1783 a junior lieutenant on half pay received only 2 shillings a day, too small a sum to support a man with a wife and child. To try and save money, William Bligh joined his wife on the Isle of Man – a picturesque island about half the size of Tahiti, with stony beaches and sunken, tree-lined lanes – where they lived in cramped, miserable lodgings. Betsy's marriage had reduced her to penury. As the cynics during this period warned, 'Love in a cottage? Give me indifference and a coach and six!'[19]

Bligh also found their straitened circumstances difficult to bear. Restless and frustrated, he wrote to his brother-in-law:

> Upon the whole I can never be brought to believe or think that the Isle of Man is so cheap or desirable a place and the only advantage a person in but low circumstances can have is that there is nothing here to lead him to expence . . . Bread is of a very great price and a sixpenny loaf is full one third smaller than in England – one does not last the Child three Days. However with all the carping and caring imaginable my living here will amount to just 20 Shillings pr. week totally exclusive of ware and tare.
>
> – You will be surprised to hear all this, but it is really so and I do not taste a spoonful of Spirits from one end of the week to the other . . . I remain at home and as I can get plenty of Books, improve myself this way.[20]

As the young couple struggled to make ends meet, Betsy placed great faith in her uncle Duncan Campbell, a wealthy merchant who owned a fleet of trading ships that sailed between the Caribbean and Britain, to relieve them. True to her expectations, in May that year Campbell loaned Bligh £40 to lease and furnish a house, promising him the command of a ship. Bligh was delighted, planning to decorate the new house with some of his souvenirs from his voyage with Captain Cook: 'I have at my Cousin's a large Dining Room Mat and several others of an inferior quality and small size made of grass that I brought from the South Sea, also a long Spear and some other curiosities that I intend to send for.'[21]

After giving Bligh this loan, Duncan Campbell urged him to apply for leave to join the merchant service. In July 1783 Bligh wrote back, saying the Admiralty had granted their permission:

> I am glad to hear you think it likely I may soon be wanted in Town as I am anxious to show you that whatever my services may be, my endeavours in every respect will not be wanting either in exercise or care. – I shall be ready at an hour's notice and nothing can stop me now but a contrary wind, which at this season of the year is not likely to happen.[22]

Soon afterwards, Campbell appointed Bligh the captain of the *Lynx*, one of his West Indiamen, at £500 a year, placing his son John under his command. John enjoyed his time on the *Lynx*, telling his father that Bligh 'behaved to me very kindly, and instructed during my leisure in navigation, all in his power'.[23] As John Trevenen, one of the young midshipmen on the *Resolution*, had noted, Bligh was a generous and attentive mentor, doing his best to pass on his knowledge and skills.

Over the next four years as Bligh sailed back and forth between England and the West Indies, in command of various of Campbell's trading ships (the *Lynx* and the *Britannia* in particular), Betsy stayed at the Isle of Man before shifting to Broad Street in Wapping, London, to be near her husband during his visits to England.[24] When their second daughter, Mary, was born, fearful that Harriet might catch smallpox, Betsy left her little girl on the Isle of Man with her father, confessing, '[It] was very distressing to me, as she had never been from me, and is a very engaging and dear child.' Bligh was enjoying his new life in the merchant marine, however, and their domestic situation was far more comfortable. As Betsy wrote to John Bond: 'Mr. B's ship will soon be out of dock. She is now fitted up for passengers and he tells me is in every respect a very fine one. I flatter myself this voyage will be successful and should a long peace take place, a Rum and Sugar Captain may be as well off as any other.'[25]

In addition to his friendship with Duncan Campbell, Bligh had a warm relationship with his father-in-law, Dr Betham, often visiting him on the Isle of Man. Betsy had many friends and acquaintances on the island, and after hearing about John Campbell's sojourn on board the *Lynx*, some of these families asked Bligh to take their sons or relatives to sea. Fletcher Christian, an athletic, bow-legged midshipman, was one of these young men. When Bligh turned down a request to take him to the West Indies, saying that he had a full complement of officers, Christian sent him a personal plea, explaining that wages were no object, and that he only wished to learn his profession: 'We Midshipmen are gentlemen; we never pull at a rope; I should be even glad to go one voyage in that situation, for there may be occasions, when officers may be called upon to do the duties of a common man.'[26]

After receiving this letter Bligh relented, appointing Christian as mate on another of Campbell's ships, the *Britannia*. They got on well, and after the voyage Christian told his brother Edward, a professor of law at Cambridge, that Bligh had been kind to him, showing him the use of his charts and instruments; and that although Bligh was a 'very passionate' man, he knew how to humour him. On his next voyage to the West Indies, when Fletcher sailed as a gunner, Bligh urged the warrant officers to treat him as an officer. After the mutiny on the *Bounty*, the chief mate of the *Britannia*, Edward Lamb, would write to Bligh, remarking that during this voyage, he had been too indulgent to Christian:

> When we got to sea and I saw your partiality for the young man, I gave him every advice and information in my power, though he went about every point of duty with a degree of indifference that to me was truly unpleasant; but you were blind to his faults and had him to dine and sup every other day in the cabin; and treated him like a brother in giving him every information.[27]

This was a happy time for William Bligh. When the official record of Captain Cook's last Pacific voyage was published in 1784, however, his equanimity was shattered. Overseen by a committee including Lord Sandwich and Joseph Banks, this sumptuous edition of Cook's journal (edited for publication by Dr Douglas, and augmented by James King's account of the voyage after his death) portrayed him as a wise, humane commander. Cook's complaints about the shoddy work carried out on the *Resolution* had been excised; and King gave no hint of Lieutenant Williamson's conduct in Kealakekua Bay. To his fury, Bligh found that engravings of many of his charts, used without permission or acknowledgement, had been credited to Henry Roberts, his master's mate.[28]

*Joseph Banks, South Sea explorer.*

As he later wrote indignantly in the margins of the copy of the *Voyage* in the Hydrographic Office: 'None of the Maps and Charts in this publication are from the original drawings of Lieut. Henry Roberts, he did no more than copy the original ones from Captain Cook who besides myself was the only person that surveyed & laid the Coast down . . . Every Plan & Chart from C. Cook's death are exact Copies of my Works. Wm. Bligh.'[29]

When he read King's account in the official *Voyage* about the survey of the north-west coast of America, which included an editor's footnote: 'Captain King has been so good as to communicate his instructions on this occasion, and the particulars of the fatigue he underwent, in carrying them into execution', Bligh exploded, writing in the margin of the volume:

C. King might well say it was fatigues he underwent for he never bore any nor was he capable – His whole account if he had been a seaman he would have been ashamed to have related.[30]

Bligh also wrote to James Burney, who had sailed with him on Cook's last expedition, fulminating about a non-existent island that Roberts had inserted in his chart of the North Pacific: 'This unaccountable error arose only from sheer ignorance not knowing how to investigate the fact, & it is a disgrace to us as Navigators to lay down what does not exist.'[31] He added:

> The Sandwich islands published wth. Cook's Voyage are entirely my survey – the Friendly Islands the same, except the part of Amsterdam seen before by Capt. Cook. The Surveys of the parts we saw of the East part of Asia to the southward of Behring's streights, Kamschatka & Japan – Karrakakooa [Kealakekau] Bay – Macao & Typa are likewise my productions.
>
> Unfortunately by way of describing Mountains & making flourishes Roberts has mortified me by his plan of the Sandwich Islds, for in my Plan which he coppied from, the situations of the remarkable Mountains were accurately shown, but in the present they are lost. The Parts of America from our first making the Coast to the time of C. Cook's death was surveyed by himself and were coppied by Mr. Roberts.[32]

The *Voyage* was a runaway success, and copies were sold as fast almost as they could be printed, fuelling Bligh's bitterness. Overall, these accounts of Cook's Pacific expeditions served to reinforce the image of the South Seas as a Paradise, irresistible to seamen.

Fortunately for Bligh, however, as a prominent shipowner and merchant, Duncan Campbell had a number of contacts with Sir Joseph Banks. Upon his return from his voyage around the world with Captain Cook on board the *Endeavour*, this wealthy, well-connected young botanist had been brimming with ideas and schemes, many of which involved the Pacific. Despite his amorous escapades in Tahiti, and the ribald satires that these had inspired, Banks had become a pillar of British society – a friend of King George III, and patron of Kew Gardens. Described by James King as the 'common center of us discoverers', in 1779 Banks was elected President of the Royal Society, and in 1781 he was made a baronet. Two years later, Erasmus Darwin, the grandfather of Charles Darwin, dedicated a translation of Linnaeus's botanical writings to Banks, exulting:

> The rare and excellent example you have given, so honourable to science, of forgoing the more brilliant advantages of birth and fortune, to seek for knowledge through difficulties and dangers, at a period of life when the allurements of pleasure are the least resistable, and in an age when the general effeminacy

of manners seemed beyond that of former times to discourage every virtuous exertion, justly entitles you to the preeminence you enjoy in the philosophical world.[33]

With the enthusiastic connivance of King George, Banks was now sending plant collectors around the world to bring back a stream of new species to Kew Gardens and the Chelsea Physic Garden in London, where they were transplanted, grown and studied. Under his guidance, species that seemed likely to be useful or decorative were transported to other parts of Britain and her colonies – as one can see in those English gardens where New Zealand flax plants, kōwhai trees and cabbage trees, for instance, have flourished since the eighteenth century.[34]

One of Banks's favourite projects at this time was a voyage to bring bread-fruit plants [PLATE 12] from Tahiti to the West Indies, to feed the black slaves on the British plantations. As a plantation owner and shipowner, with a fleet of merchant vessels plying to and from the West Indies, Duncan Campbell had an interest in this scheme, which dated back to the *Endeavour*'s visit to Tahiti in 1769. At that time, Banks had written: 'In the article of food these happy people may almost be said to be exempt from the curse of our forefathers. Scarcely can it be said that they earn their bread with the sweat of their brow when their chiefest substance, Breadfruit, is procured with no more trouble than that of climbing a tree and bringing it down.'[35] Almost as soon as they returned to England, he and Dr Solander, his scientific companion on board the *Endeavour*, had begun to promote the idea of transporting this invaluable fruit to British colonies in the tropics. As Solander wrote to John Ellis, the naturalist and linen merchant:

> The breadfruit of the South Sea Islands within the Tropics, which was by us during several months, dayly eaten as a substitute for Bread, was universally esteemed as palatable and nourishing as Bread itself; no one of the whole ship's company complained when served with Breadfruit in lieu of Biscuit; and from the health & strength of whole nations, whose principal food it is, I didn't scruple to call it one of the most usefull vegetables in the world . . . I am sure no expense ought to be spared in an undertaking so interesting to the public.[36]

Their advocacy was persuasive, and in 1776 the Royal Society of Arts (of which Banks was a member) offered a gold medal for the successful introduction of living breadfruit plants to the West Indies; while during the following year the West Indies merchants posted a reward. When the War of Independence broke out, however, the Navy was put on a combat footing, and no breadfruit voyage was undertaken. In the meantime, American ships that had formerly carried provisions to the West Indies were prohibited from sailing to the British colonies; and when hurricanes were followed by severe famines, approximately 20,000 black slaves died of starvation.[37]

During the War of Independence, too, it was no longer possible to expel British convicts to the North American plantations; and before long, the prisons in Britain were full and overflowing. When an attempt to establish a penal colony in Africa failed, Joseph Banks suggested the remote, vast continent of Australia – especially Botany Bay, which he had briefly visited with Captain Cook – as an alternative.[38] In addition to his West Indian plantation and ships, Duncan Campbell was the Superintendent of Convicts on the River Thames, owning many of the hulks used as temporary penal accommodation (and popularly known as 'Campbell's Academies' for that reason),[39] and he must also have met Banks in connection with this scheme.

During one of their meetings, Campbell spoke to Banks about the way that William Bligh had been treated after Cook's last voyage, pricking his conscience. Banks belonged to a committee headed by Lord Sandwich that had handled the publication of the official account of Cook's third voyage; and no doubt he made further enquiries, perhaps asking Bligh to produce his *Resolution* journal, surveys and charts for his inspection. In July 1785 when Lord Sandwich finalised the plan to distribute the royalties from these handsome volumes, the lion's share went to Mrs Cook, James Cook's widow, but one-eighth of the royalties were dedicated to Mr Bligh, 'who was Master of the *Resolution* during the Voyage and did much of the surveying';[40] while Henry Roberts, to whom the charts had been credited, received nothing.

By this time, Bligh's *bête noire* John King had died of tuberculosis, no doubt contracted from Clerke or Anderson during their expedition with Captain Cook. As Fanny Burney remarked: 'Tis very strange that all the Circumnavigators, though they seemed well at first, are now apparently broken in their constitutions. There are now <u>eight</u> others falling into the same premature decay.'[41] Fortunately for Bligh and his family, he escaped this affliction, and in April 1786 he wrote gratefully to Campbell, thanking him for securing his share of the royalties, which over the next fifteen years amounted to almost £1000.[42] A month later, Betsy bore him their third daughter, Elizabeth ('Betsy'), at Lambeth, in London.[43]

In early 1787, when a report arrived in London that a cargo of breadfruit plants had been delivered to the French West Indies, the British government was galvanised into action at last, asking Sir Joseph Banks to assist the Admiralty in organising an expedition to carry breadfruit to feed the starving slaves in the British plantations. At first, Banks thought that his two pet projects might be usefully combined – a ship transporting convicts to Botany Bay might pick up a cargo of breadfruit plants in Tahiti during its return voyage, and carry these plants to the West Indies before returning to England. Accordingly, in early 1787 he drew up a plan for such a voyage for the Prime Minister, William Pitt the Younger, which included a foray to pick up flax plants from New Zealand. The British government agreed to this proposal, but as he became involved in the practical details, including the need to transform the ship's Great Cabin into a greenhouse with tubs for the plants, a stove to heat it in cold weather and a large supply of fresh water to wash salt water off the plants, Banks realised how difficult it would be to execute such a design in a new penal colony, where supplies of timber, clay and skilled labour would be scarce.[44]

Just as the First Fleet carrying the first group of convicts to Botany Bay was about to set sail, Banks had a change of heart. On 30 March 1787 he wrote to the government, pointing out the disadvantages of using a convict transport to carry breadfruit plants; arguing that it would be better to fit out and crew the ship in England; and suggesting that the Admiralty should purchase a 200-ton brig with a crew of forty and six 4-pounder carriage guns, and entrust it to a commander who had sailed to the Pacific with Captain Cook. The ship should leave England no later than July of that year to avoid the easterly monsoons; and after sailing to Tahiti to collect the breadfruit plants, proceed via the Friendly Islands (Tonga) and the strait between Australia and New Guinea to the East Indies, where more plants could be collected. Afterwards the ship should head for the West Indies, where the breadfruit plants would be distributed. Impressed by Banks's mastery of these complex logistics, King George suggested that he should be asked to organise the voyage.

On 16 May, only three days after the First Fleet of convict transports had sailed from England, the Navy Board invited Banks to choose one of five ships that they had nominated for the breadfruit expedition. Banks had already appointed David Nelson, the botanist who sailed with Captain Cook on his third voyage, to propagate the breadfruit plants and look after them during the voyage.[45] He and Nelson selected a 230-ton coastal trader, the *Bethia*, just three and a half years old, built at Hull and owned by Wellbank, Sharp & Brown of London, purchasing this little ship for £1,950 and renaming her the *Bounty*.[46]

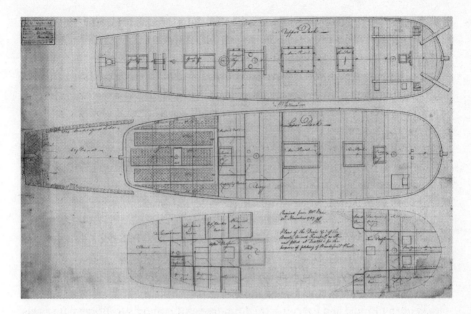

Bounty *deck plans.*

While David Nelson was organising the *Bounty*'s provisions and supplies, Banks turned his attention to the appointment of her commander. After the controversy over the charts from Captain Cook's last voyage, he was familiar with William Bligh, and his skills as a hydrographer. Bligh had sailed to Tahiti on the *Resolution* with Captain Cook; and to the West Indies in command of Campbell's merchant vessels. Moreover, since his naval career had stalled, Bligh would not be insulted to be invited to command so small and strange a ship on such a quirky voyage. Rather, with the prospect of a promotion, the promise of Banks's patronage, and the prize money put up by the West Indies merchants and plantation owners, it might be an attractive proposition. An invitation from someone as eminent and powerful as Sir Joseph Banks was as good as an instruction; and when a message was sent to Bligh, he replied in a grateful letter on 6 August 1787,[47] and his official commission arrived from the Admiralty ten days later. At the age of thirty-two, William Bligh had won his first naval command.

Ever since his circumnavigation with Captain Cook, Joseph Banks had been dying to fit out a ship for a voyage of Pacific exploration. At the outset of Cook's second voyage, when the Navy Board asked Cook to select the vessel, he had selected another Whitby collier, the *Resolution*. Considering the ship too small, Banks had demanded that an upper deck be added, but when the *Resolution* sailed on her first sea trial, she was so top-heavy that she almost capsized. As Charles Clerke wrote to Banks: 'By God, I'll go to sea in a grog-tub if required, or in the *Resolution* as soon as you please, but I must say that I think her the most unsafe ship I ever saw or heard of!'[48] Banks had been obdurate, however, and when he visited the ship and discovered that the upper deck had been removed, he 'swore and Stamped on the wharfe, like a Mad Man, and instantly ordered his Servants and all of his things out of the ship'.[49] After resigning from the expedition, Banks made a public attack on Captain Cook, infuriating Lord Sandwich, who wrote him a searing letter.[50] With the *Bounty*, Banks had been given another ship to play with, and he was determined to spare no effort or expense (although once again, the Navy Board was footing the bill).

The *Bounty*, adorned with a figurehead of a lady in a green riding habit, had sweet, elegant lines, but she was small, only 84 feet long. Rated a cutter or 'HM Armed Vessel', this little ship was entitled to a crew of forty-five men, with one servant for the captain, and no marines. During the alterations, the masts were shortened for stability (at Bligh's suggestion); her hull was sheathed with copper, with bronze fittings; and four short 4-pounder cannons and 10 half-pound swivel guns were brought on board. By the time that the Great Cabin had been refitted with skylights, lead floors and water runways for drainage, a stove for heat and scuttles for ventilation, the Navy Board had spent £6,000, three times more than they intended.[51] Despite this, years later, Banks, still smarting about Lord Pitt's insistence that he should use 'every possible degree of Economy' in equipping the *Bounty* for the voyage, blamed the mutiny on this 'niggardly arrangement'.[52]

With these alterations, Banks had transformed the *Bounty* into a floating greenhouse, leaving little room for her crew and captain. The commander's tiny cabin lay amidships on the lower deck, on the starboard side, opposite the master's cabin at the foot of the rear stairway. Between them and the fo'c'sle lay the captain's dining room and pantry; and a small, cramped space for the master's mates and the midshipmen aft of the fore stairway, beside the main arms chest. The rest of the crew – thirty-three men – were crammed together with the galley in the fo'c'sle on the same deck, a dark, unventilated space near the bow which measured only 22 feet wide by 36 feet long, beside the pens in which the goats, pigs and sheep were confined. The dark, airless cubbyholes for the boatswain and carpenter, the steward, surgeon, captain's clerk, botanist and gunner had been shifted below to new mezzanine decks perched on either end of the hold. The officers and gentlemen had headroom of 7 feet in their living spaces, while the ordinary sailors had just 6 feet 3 inches. Even by naval standards, these were cramped, difficult living conditions. Usually the captain's sanctum and symbol of his authority, the Great Cabin had been taken over as a greenhouse, lined with lead and furnished with raised racks for the earthenware pots, leaving the captain with little privacy. During their voyage around the world, the *Bounty*'s commander and his men lived cheek by jowl.

Because the *Bounty* was rated a cutter or 'HM Armed Vessel', she was commanded by a lieutenant, with no other commissioned officers and only a master and two midshipmen to support him.[53] Like Cook on board the *Endeavour*, Bligh would lead the *Bounty* expedition as a junior officer; and he was determined to make as brilliant a voyage. After the debacle of Cook's death and its aftermath, Bligh had everything to prove. As Duncan Campbell wrote to a relative in the West Indies, his promotion would depend upon the success of the expedition: 'Bligh is now fitting out a small ship in the King's service which I helped to procure him the command of, he is going to Ottaheetee to bring the breadfruit plant to your island and St. Vincent. Tho he goes out only as a Lieutenant yet if his conduct is approved it is the sure road to being made a Capt. on his return, this Lord Howe has absolutely promised.'[54]

In so small a ship, the sailors had to work well together, and Bligh was eager to appoint his own men, who would regard him as their patron. During their two voyages together on the *Britannia*, as we have seen, Bligh had become a friend and mentor to Fletcher Christian, a tall, commanding, bright-faced young man of twenty-three years old who had close links to Elizabeth Bligh's family on the Isle of Man. The seventh of ten children, born in a farmstead outside Cockermouth, Christian had attended primary school with the poet William Wordsworth (although Wordsworth was six years younger), being raised as a gentleman and given a good education. His father Charles was an attorney, and his family had been among the most powerful and prosperous on the Isle of Man, with mining and shipping interests, a tradition of serving as Deemsters (judges) on the island, and a fine mansion on the mainland. Many of Christian's cousins, who included two bishops and a chief justice of England, were also wealthy, influential men. Although his father had died when he was young, two of his elder brothers had attended the University of Cambridge.

At school, Fletcher Christian had been a promising student. According to his brother Edward, he 'staid at school longer than young men generally do who enter into the navy, and being allowed by all who knew him to possess extraordinary abilities, is an excellent scholar'.[55] When his mother became bankrupt because of his elder brothers' extravagances, however, she could not afford to send him to Cambridge. In 1783 at the age of eighteen, Christian enlisted in the Navy as a midshipman, serving on board the *Eurydice* and sailing to India, where he wrote to a kinsman: 'It was very easy to make one's self beloved on board a ship; one has only to be always ready to obey one's superior officers, and to be kind to the common men.'[56] Later, when his brother Edward met some of the *Eurydice*'s officers, they assured him that Fletcher had performed exceptionally well: 'They said he was strict, yet as it were, played while he wrought with the Men – he made a Toil a pleasure and ruled over them in a superior, pleasant Manner to any young Officer they had seen.'[57] After only a year on the *Eurydice*, he was promoted to acting lieutenant – a significant achievement, at a time when young officers were required to serve six years in the Navy before being eligible to apply for a lieutenant's commission.[58] When peace broke out and Christian found himself on half pay, one of his Manx relatives, who knew Bligh, asked him to take the young man as a mate on board the *Britannia*. After some persuasion, Bligh agreed, later promoting him to gunner, and then to master's mate on board the *Bounty*. From the *Britannia*, Bligh also recruited quartermaster John Norton, a big, beefy 34-year-old from Liverpool; the sailmaker Lawrence Lebogue, aged forty and from Nova Scotia; and one of the able-bodied sailors, Thomas Ellison, just fifteen years old and from Deptford.

The two midshipmen's berths on board the *Bounty* went to young men who, like Fletcher Christian, knew Bligh's wife's family well. John Hallett, fifteen years old and from London, was the son of a wealthy architect, while his sister was a lifelong friend of Betsy's; and Thomas Hayward, nineteen years old and with five years of naval experience, had been recommended by William Wales, the astronomer who had sailed on Cook's last two expeditions. Three other young men, also well connected, were rated as able seamen but treated as midshipmen during the voyage. The family of George Stewart (already, at twenty-one years old, a firm disciplinarian) had entertained Bligh in the Orkneys during the *Resolution*'s return voyage to England. They must have kept in touch, because just two weeks after being given the command, Bligh appointed Stewart to the *Bounty*. Edward Young, the short, stocky, dark-skinned 'nephew' of Sir George Young (a distinguished naval captain whom Bligh had met in the West Indies, and who with Joseph Banks had urged the establishment of the penal colony at Botany Bay), had been born in the West Indies, and was reputed to have a 'touch of the tar brush'.[59] Like Stewart, Young was appointed as an AB, but treated as a midshipman. So was Peter Heywood, a fair-headed youth of fifteen who had never been to sea before, another friend of Bligh's wife's family on the Isle of Man (indeed, Bligh had rented their house), and a distant relative of Fletcher Christian. Heywood's family had formerly lived at the Nunnery, a fine house near Douglas, and his father had been a Deemster and Seneschal to the Duke of

*John Fryer, master of the* Bounty.

Atholl. When Heywood's father became embroiled in business difficulties, Dr Betham, Bligh's father-in-law, urged the young man's appointment:

> He is an ingenious young Lad & has always been a favorite of mine & indeed every body here. And indeed the Reason of my insisting so strenuously upon his going the Voyage with you is that after I had mentioned the matter to Mrs. Bligh, his Family have fallen into a great deal of Distress, on account of their Father's losing the Duke of Atholl's Business, and I thought it would not appear well in me to drop this matter.[60]

No doubt at Sir Joseph's insistence, Bligh was also joined by a number of Pacific veterans. David Nelson, the *Bounty*'s botanist, had sailed with Bligh on board the *Resolution* during Cook's last voyage, and worked closely with Banks to organise the breadfruit expedition. The *Bounty*'s warrant officers included

Joseph Coleman, the armourer, a responsible, highly skilled man, strong and grey-headed and with a heart tattooed on his arm, who had been on board the *Discovery*; while William Peckover, the *Bounty*'s gunner, had sailed on each of Cook's three Pacific voyages.[61] Each of these men had visited Tahiti before, and they knew Bligh well. Thomas Huggan, his obese, drunken surgeon, had no previous Pacific experience, however. When Bligh protested his appointment, Banks managed to get a young surgeon's mate, Thomas Ledward, to assist him. As Ledward (who came from a distinguished family of surgeons and apothecaries) remarked: 'The captain, though a passionate man, is, I believe, a good hearted Man, and has behaved very handsomely to me.'[62]

John Fryer, the *Bounty*'s master, a Norfolk man who had been captured by a French privateer and spent eighteen months in a French prison, had served only seven years in the Navy and had not previously sailed in the Pacific, although he had qualified as a master of the third rate, and at first Bligh considered him very able.[63] The other warrant officers included William Purcell, the carpenter; William Elphinstone, master's mate, from the Orkneys; his close friend Peter Linkletter, quartermaster, also from the Orkneys; and William Cole, boatswain, who came from a fireship, the *Alecto*. James Morrison, a well-educated man from Stornoway off the Isle of Lewis who had served in the West Indies, fighting the French, and later passed his master gunner's examination, was appointed as the *Bounty*'s boatswain's mate, responsible for floggings with the cat-o'-nine-tails. Later, he would write a brilliant if searing account of the voyage.[64] Crucially, with so many midshipmen, master's mates, warrant officers and petty officers on board the *Bounty*, there were only thirteen able-bodied seamen to work the ship, along with Michael Byrne, the half-blind Irish fiddler. None of these men were pressed, however – unusually, the *Bounty* was manned entirely by volunteers (although eight men, including two who had been caught by the press, deserted from the ship at Deptford before she set sail).[65]

When Bligh requested three well-built boats to be supplied to the *Bounty*, Banks made sure that he got them – a 23-foot launch with copper fastenings; a 20-foot, six-oared cutter; and a 16-foot cutter or 'jolly-boat'.[66] Banks also ordered a lavish assortment of items to barter with the Tahitians – 234 dozen 'toeys' (*toʻi*) especially made of iron in the shape of traditional Tahitian adzes, and an array of other iron tools; 24 dozen looking glasses; 80 pounds of red, white and blue beads; and 22 dozen stained-glass earrings. In addition there were pens, ink, paper, watercolours, fly traps, an insect box, journals, guns and gunpowder;

arsenic to kill rats and cockroaches; watering pots, a camp forge and a copper oven; while David Nelson acquired hundreds of differently sized clay pots for the breadfruit plants. The ship was provisioned for eighteen months at sea, with extra supplies of sauerkraut, dried malt, sugar, juice of wort, and salt for salting fresh meat and fish. In addition, they were given five hundredweight of portable soup (a kind of meat extract), thought to keep the men healthy during long sea voyages. When Bligh asked for his log, journal and charts from the *Resolution* to be handed over by the Admiralty, they were released; and in fact he largely followed Cook's track on his third Pacific voyage during this expedition.

While the ship was being refitted, Bligh kept in close touch with Banks. When several well-intentioned gentlemen quizzed him about the expedition, however, he vented his frustrations. Upon being asked by Sir George Yonge about the arrangements for the voyage, for instance, he remarked that he knew less about it than David Nelson, the gardener. Offering to have Bligh instructed in botany, Yonge scolded Banks in a letter:

> You will Excuse me for saying that unless you do interest the Captain himself
> & instruct him and inspire him with the Spirit of the undertaking it is to very
> little Purpose the Vessell would sail. It is not enough to inform a Gardiner. A
> Captain in the King's service can not & ought not to be contented with doing
> as a gardiner bids.

Annoyed by this gratuitous advice, Banks retorted: 'As for his attempting to Learn any part of the Gardiners trade I must heartily wish he may Forbear the attempt I have seen so much mischief happen from dablers in a science (who generally think they know more of it than professors).'[67]

Bligh also confided concerns about his own rank and the scale of the expedition to Betsy's family friend Lord Selkirk, who wrote a letter to Banks criticising the arrangements for the voyage, and arguing that Bligh should be made a master and commander. This letter reflects the depth of Bligh's resentment that Lord Sandwich had refused to promote him to lieutenant after his voyage with Captain Cook, especially now that his contemporary Hunter, who had recently sailed with the First Fleet to Botany Bay with Governor Phillip, had been made a post-captain. According to Lord Selkirk:

> Mr. Bligh himself is but very indifferently used, for he seems to have lost hopes
> of getting any preferment. It would have been strictly Justice to him, to have
> made him Master & Commander before sailing: nay considering that he was,

I believe, the only person that was not in some way or other preferrd at their return of all who went last out with Capt Cook, it would be no unreasonable thing to make him Post Captain now, more especially as Ld. How made Captain Hunter Post when he went out lately to Botany Bay.

Hunter and Bligh were in very similar situations, they had both been Masters, & both were refused by Sandwich to be made Lieuts, and it happened that both of them were made Acting Lieutenants by Keith Stewart, & afterwards confirmed, not with Sandwich's good will. I have wrote to Keith Stewart, wishing him to help his friend Bligh, if he can, with How.

An Officer of the Navy who happens to be here just now on a visit, tells me that this Establishment of Bligh's vessel is that of a Cutter, & says it is highly improper for so long a Voyage; only 24 able Seamen, & 21 of all others, without a Lieutenant, or any Marines, with only a Surgeon without a Surgeon's Mate, but if Bligh's Surgeon meets with any Accident they must want all Medical assistance God knows how long.

This is the good of adhering without judgement to the Etiquette of an Establishment, without following the common sense of what is requisite for the particular circumstances.[68]

Lord Selkirk's letter proved to be prophetic. As George Forster pointed out after Cook's last voyage, the size and type of ships taken on voyages of Pacific exploration were crucial to the success of these expeditions. Byron, Wallis and Bougainville had all sailed in frigates, fighting ships with larger crews, but not enough storage space to carry sufficient provisions for a long voyage. These vessels were difficult, if not impossible, to careen (i.e. haul on shore for repairs), and the size of their crews meant that they could not stay long at an island without draining it of supplies. For that reason, their commanders had to hasten across the Pacific, without the leisure to explore and survey new coastlines. By contrast, Captain Cook's colliers had been smaller, but sturdy, with good storage space for provisions and supplies. They could be careened, and because their crews were smaller, they could stay longer at an island. At the same time, colliers were large enough to carry a full complement of officers and marines – three lieutenants and three master's mates in the case of the *Resolution*.[69] This had proved to be a highly successful model for voyages of Pacific exploration. As Lord Selkirk's naval friend warned him, however, the *Bounty* was a small ship, with a very small crew, no marines and only one medical man among them, and Bligh would be the only commissioned officer on board. For an experienced naval officer, the risks were obvious, and formidable.

Irritated by these admonitions, Banks filed this letter under 'Plan for the Voyage, with letters from various persons who interferd in the management of it', and did nothing to secure Bligh a promotion. All the same, when Bligh wrote to him soon afterwards, pleading with him to ask Lord Howe to promote him to master and commander, Banks answered kindly enough, sending him two fine instruments – a Ramsden sextant and Kendall's second chronometer – along with other navigational instruments for the voyage.[70] Worried that he had pressed him too hard, Bligh wrote back: 'I trust nothing can prevent me from completing my Voyage much to your satisfaction, difficulties I laugh at while I have your countenance and shall always be sufficiently repaid whilst I am admitted to subscribe myself your Affectionate Humble Servant Wm. Bligh.'[71]

By 15 October 1787, the *Bounty* was ready for sea. War with the Netherlands seemed imminent, and before the *Bounty* sailed to Spithead, arriving there on 4 November, Joseph Banks had already left London for Revesby Abbey, his estate in Lincolnshire.[72] At first Bligh was happy and excited, writing gratefully to Duncan Campbell:

I shall take care My Dear Sir, & allow me to call you my best of Friends, to get you some good wine when I leave Tenariff, & I hope to pass once more many happy evenings with you & and your worthy Dear Family. I beg you will present to Mrs. Campbell my most Affectionate respects & thanks for all her great kindness & civility to me & my little Family.[73]

Distracted by the war preparations and without Banks to harass them, however, the Admiralty kept Bligh waiting for his orders; and if Stewart spoke to Lord Howe, he failed to secure Bligh a promotion. When a number of his peers won senior commissions and Bligh repeated his plea to Banks that he should be made a master and commander, explaining that 'one step would make a material difference to Mrs. Bligh and her children in case of any accident to me', Banks wrote back that all of these men had been promoted to fighting vessels.[74] Forced to anchor off the Isle of Wight, incensed by the Admiralty's refusal to promote him and fuming with impatience, on 10 December Bligh fired off two indignant letters. To Joseph Banks, he wrote:

I had supposed from the polite manner Lord Howe behaved to me when I took leave of him that I stood a fair chance of promotion the first time there was any.

[This] is certainly a violation of all justice with respect to me, who they have now kept, to pass a remote part of the Globe at an unseasonable time of the year from mere neglect, and myself may be subject to blame for what no Man can accomplish. This is a glaring circumstance to every one.[75]

To his wife's uncle, Duncan Campbell, he exclaimed: 'If there is any punishment that ought to be inflicted on a set of Men for neglect I am sure it ought on the Admiralty, for my three weeks detention at this place during a fine fair wind which carried all outward bound ships clear of the channel but me, who wanted it most. This has made my task a very arduous one indeed for to get round Cape Horn at the time I shall be there I know not how to promise myself any success and yet I must do it if the Ship will stand it at all or I suppose my character will be at stake.'[76]

His father-in-law Dr Betham sympathised with Bligh's predicament, considering the ship too small and the crew too few for such a long and arduous journey around the world, and tried to console him:

I own I have a different Idea of [the voyage] from what I had conceived before I was acquainted with the Circumstances of the Vessel, & the way in which it is fitted out. Government I think have gone too frugally to work: Both the Ship and the Complement of Men are too small in my opinion for such a voyage. Lord Howe may understand Navy matters very well, but I suppose mercantile Projects are treated by him with Contempt.'[77]

While Bligh shared Dr Betham's reservations, he was raring to go. As he assured Duncan Campbell: 'My little Ship is in the best of order and my Men & officers all good & feel happy under my directions.'[78]

During their enforced stay off the Isle of Wight, Fletcher Christian's brother Charles, a ship's surgeon on an East Indiaman, paid him a visit. During Charles's most recent voyage, the captain, a brutal, capricious man, had ordered a sailor to be 'flogged to death', and when the sailor threatened him with a loaded pistol and the first officer intervened, the captain had his lieutenant locked in his cabin. When Charles Christian protested, the captain also accused him of mutinous conduct. The East India Company directors were now deciding his fate, and during this visit Charles must have poured out his woes to his brother, and his fury against his despotic commander. Despite his own woes, Charles was impressed by his brother's high spirits, remarking that Fletcher was 'full of professional Ambition and of Hope. He bared his Arm, and I was amazed at its Brawniness.

"This," says he, had been "acquired by hard labour." He said, "I delight to set the Men an Example. I not only can do every part of a common Sailor's Duty, but am upon a par with a principal part of the Officers."[79] During this interval Bligh, a tender husband and father, frequently visited his wife and three little daughters who had come to the Isle of Wight to be near him, the youngest of whom contracted smallpox; and his commander Lord Hood winked at these absences, which were 'quite a secret to Sir J. Banks'.[80] On at least one of these occasions, Bligh took Fletcher Christian to meet his 'dear little Family'.

Before he sailed from England, Bligh gave Betsy a power of attorney to act for him in his affairs, which included an entangled inheritance from his father; although she must have regretted his decision to rejoin the Navy, which left them financially embarrassed. After resigning from Campbell's employment, Bligh had suffered a major drop in income, from £500 a year as a merchant captain to £73 a year as a naval lieutenant. As she wrote to Bligh's nephew Frank Bond, Betsy felt guilty about having taken all of her children to the Isle of Wight to be near him: 'I begin to be ashamed of myself for having been so extravagant, all my own relations abuse me for it and say that such a wife is enough to ruin a poor man. I think the fate of you poor officers resembles the poor Curates, but I do my best to moderate the expense I put my husband to, and am now a mere nurse, who passes the whole day with one child in her arms, and another hanging upon her.'[81] In the eighteenth-century Navy, the lot of a naval wife was far from easy, with a small income, long absences, and the worry of never knowing whether her husband was alive or dead; and from her letters, it seems that Betsy had no servants to assist her, not even a nursemaid. For a young woman raised in comfort, these were challenging circumstances, and throughout their lives together, William Bligh would be acutely aware of the hardships that Betsy suffered as his wife.

# The Finest Sea Boat

On 23 December 1787 the *Bounty* sailed from England at last, heading for South America. On Christmas Day, Bligh ordered beef and plum pudding to be served as a Yuletide celebration. Two days later, high waves crashed into the *Bounty*, ripping planks from the large cutter and stoving in the ship's stern, washing away barrels of beer, splitting two casks of rum, smashing an azimuth compass in the Great Cabin and drenching the bread in the store. After carrying out temporary repairs, in January 1788 Bligh arrived at Tenerife, where he sent Fletcher Christian ashore as his representative, to meet the Spanish governor. He also purchased beef, potatoes and pumpkins (which he considered very dear), 800 gallons of wine, and two hogsheads of the very finest Canary wine on commission for Sir Joseph Banks.

Upon sailing from Tenerife, Bligh was delighted to be on his way, noting in his journal that he had 'a Chearful & happy Ships Company all in good health and Spirits'.[1] To Duncan Campbell, he wrote: 'I have the happyness to tell you my little Ship does wonderfully well. I have her now the completest ship I believe that ever swam.'[2] Most of the 'beef' that he had bought at Tenerife had to be thrown overboard, however. It tasted so rank that his men, convinced that it was the flesh of an ass or a mule, refused to eat it. In order to ensure that the crew had enough rest, Bligh put them into three watches (with only four men in each), as Captain Cook had done at a similar stage in his third Pacific voyage, appointing Fletcher Christian the officer of the third watch; but at the same time, reduced their allowance of bread to ensure that it would last throughout the voyage. Like Cook, he was determined to keep his men healthy, ensuring that they cleaned out the ship, fumigated below decks with gunpowder and vinegar, washed their clothes with hot water and aired their clothes and bedding; and served them anti-scorbutics, consulting his copies of James Lind's *A Treatise on*

*Scurvy* and *On the Most Effectual Means of Preserving the Health of Seamen in the Royal Navy* at regular intervals.

In his determination to make a perfect voyage, Bligh even managed to exceed Captain Cook's solicitude for his men. Every Sunday, following Cook's example, he ordered the sailors to clean the ship below, mustered the crew and inspected their clothes and persons, read the Articles of War with its sombre roll call of offences and punishments, and performed divine service (a ritual that Captain Cook had often neglected).[3] Every fine afternoon at sea, he ordered his men to dance on deck for a couple of hours to the music of Michael Byrne, the Irish fiddler – his own innovation. In the tropics, he ordered awnings to be rigged to protect the men from the sun. As Bligh had suspected, however, the surgeon Huggan proved to be a liability: 'I now find my Doctor to be a Drunken Sot he is constantly in liquor, having a private Stock by him which I assured him shall be taken away if he does not desist from making himself such a Beast.'[4] When the *Bounty* crossed the Equator, two sailors dressed as 'Neptune' and 'Amphritite' took over the ship, lathering the novices (27 men and officers) with a disgusting mixture of tar and slops and 'shaving' them with a jagged iron blade, although Bligh would not allow them to duck their shipmates from the yardarm, paying a penalty of two bottles of rum for an officer and one bottle for a sailor, and serving each of the crew half a pint of wine when the ceremony was over.[5]

On 17 February 1788 they met a whaler, *British Queen*, headed for Cape Hope, and Bligh sent letters to the Lords of the Admiralty and buoyant missives to Joseph Banks and Duncan Campbell. As he exclaimed to Banks: 'I am happy and satisfyed in my little Ship and we are now fit to go round half a score of worlds, both Men & Officers tractable and well disposed & chearfulness & content in the countenance of every one. I have no cause to inflict punishments for I have no offenders and every thing turns out to my most sanguine expectations.'[6] To Duncan Campbell, he wrote: 'My Men all active good fellows, & what has given me much pleasure is that I have not yet been obliged to punish anyone. With fine Sour Krout, Pumpkins and dryed Greens and a fresh Meal five times a week, I think is no bad living. My Men are not badly off either as they share in all but the Poultry, and with much content and chearfullness, dancing always from 4 untill eight at Night I am happy to hope I shall bring them all home well.'[7]

As his men later noted, however, Bligh's reports of high spirits on board the *Bounty* were exaggerated. Because the ship was so small, he had taken on the role of purser, and no doubt saw this appointment as a chance to recoup some of his financial losses. After a period on half pay, he was not happy to be poor again; and now he had a wife and three daughters to support. As he confessed in a letter to Campbell, however, being a purser was a demanding job: 'As my pursing depends on much circumspection & being ignorant in it with a worthless clerk, I have some embarrassment, but as I trust nothing to anyone and keep my accounts clear, if I fail in rules of office I do not doubt of getting the better of it.'[8]

Perhaps because of his inexperience, Bligh's handling of the supplies led to constant friction with the men. According to the boatswain's mate James Morrison, when a cask of cheese was opened for airing, Bligh declared that several of the cheeses had been stolen; and when the cooper protested that these cheeses along with a cask of vinegar had been delivered to Bligh's home before the ship had sailed, Bligh refused to listen, stopping the men's cheese ration as a punishment. In protest, the sailors refused to eat their butter as well, until the cheese ration was reinstated.[9] Near the Equator when the pumpkins began to spoil, and Bligh ordered them to be served to the men instead of their bread ration, they refused to accept this substitution.[10] According to Morrison, Bligh abused them roundly, yelling, 'You damn'd Infernal scoundrels, I'll make you eat Grass before I have done with you!'[11] Later, when a sheep died of malnutrition, Bligh ordered it to be served to the men instead of their normal meat rations, although 'it was no other then Skin & Bone'.

Both Morrison and the master John Fryer later claimed that throughout the voyage the best meat was taken to Bligh's dining room while the sailors' meat was served in short measure; and that when the crew protested, he threatened to flog the next man who complained about his rations. When the butter and cheese ran out, oil was served at the rate of a half pint of oil for one pound of butter, and one ounce of sugar for an allowance of cheese; while the wheat and barley that were boiled for breakfast were served in such short measure that there were fights around the copper. During one of these brawls the ship's corporal, Charles Churchill, scalded his hand; while in another, two of the cook's ribs were broken.[12] Although Morrison and Fryer were far from dispassionate, and Bligh later vehemently denied these accusations, even David Nelson, Banks's gardener and 'the mildest man in Nature', later complained about Bligh's 'Damnd Oeconomy', remarking that it had ruined their voyage.[13]

Like Bligh, Captain Cook had acted as his own purser, and during his last expedition when his relationships with his men became strained, Cook's crew had also quarrelled with their commander over their provisions. When Cook refused to punish a Māori chief who had killed and eaten some of their *Adventure* shipmates, his men expressed their displeasure by refusing to name some sailors who had stolen meat from the messes; and when he reduced their daily allowance of salted meat as a punishment, they refused to eat any meat at all.[14] During that voyage, too, Captain Cook had often exploded with rage, stamping his feet on the deck and cursing and swearing at the sailors. Although Bligh modelled himself upon Cook, giving himself similar liberties, this was unwise, because their circumstances were very different.

To begin with, James Cook was a tall, imposing man, almost six feet tall, with a commanding presence. In Polynesian terms, he had *mana*, or power. The sailors admired him, and he knew how to win them over. On board the *Resolution*, too, Cook had a full complement of commissioned officers and marines, and he lived in the Great Cabin, apart from the officers and crew. During his last voyage when Cook became increasingly violent, doubling the floggings of his sailors and handing out savage punishments to islanders who stole from his vessels, there was little that they could do about it. William Bligh had few of these advantages. A short, slightly chubby man, only about five feet tall, he lacked Cook's air of resolute authority. On board the *Bounty*, Bligh was the only commissioned officer, with no marines to support him; and the peculiar layout of his ship meant that he had no privacy and few of the privileges of other captains. It was difficult to maintain discipline when he and his men were living cheek-by-jowl in conditions that were extremely cramped, even by naval standards. To make matters worse, the boatswain's cabin (which formerly stood opposite the galley) had been shifted below, away from the sailors, although it was his job to help keep the men in order.

Even the usual recourse of flogging offenders did not work when there were only thirteen able-bodied seamen on board, and a flogging might leave a man unable to work, endangering the safety of the vessel. In an effort to shore up his command, on 2 March 1788 Bligh promoted Fletcher Christian to Acting Lieutenant, although the *Bounty*'s complement did not include a second lieutenant. While Bligh needed another watch-keeper and this was only an acting appointment, it is possible that this decision annoyed the *Bounty*'s master. John Fryer, a warrant officer who had not passed the lieutenant's examination, would not have expected this promotion himself, but until Christian's appointment, apart from Bligh, he had been the senior sailing officer on board the *Bounty*; and in the eighteenth-century Navy, the relationships between masters and lieutenants were often difficult. Given his own bitter experiences on board the *Resolution*, when three of his master's mates had been promoted over his head, one might have expected Bligh to have had some sympathy for Fryer, but he was tough on his direct subordinates.[15] A week later, to Bligh's fury, Fryer reported Matthew Quintal for 'insolence and contempt', spoiling his perfect record of no punishments up until that stage of the voyage. Quintal was stripped to the waist, spread-eagled against the deck grating and given a dozen lashes, a sentence which was repeated soon afterwards. As Bligh noted: 'Upon a complaint made to me by the master, I found it necessary to punish Mathew Quintal, one of the seamen, with two dozen lashes . . . Before this, I had not had occasion to punish any person on board.'[16]

As the *Bounty* sailed down the east coast of South America, pods of whales swam around the ship, spouting water over the decks, while the sailors fired at them with muskets loaded with ball. When they approached Cape Horn, Bligh suffered another severe disappointment. As he feared, he had missed the season for a fair passage. Near the Cape, the *Bounty* was battered by screaming winds, sleet and sharp hail. As George Forster, who had experienced such storms during his voyage with Captain Cook, noted:

> If the force of the wind increases, some of the sails must be reefed, and others struck. It is terrible to watch this dangerous work. As soon as the lower sheets have been released, the wind catches the sail and dashes it against the yard and the mast, making the whole ship tremble. With admirable agility and . . . courage, the seamen immediately climb up to the second or third extension of the mast.
>
> A fluttering rope . . . serves as a support for the feet of the brave sailor. On this rope tread [the] sailors, despite the wind tossing the flapping sail to and fro with great force and plucking at the rope under their feet; this despite the rolling of the ship, which is much stronger at this height than it is on the deck. Every wave . . . swings a sailor on a yard arm some fifty yards up through an arc of fifty to sixty feet. One moment he seems to be hurled into the sea, the next to touch the stars.[17]

On 2 April when the storm reached its climax, the *Bounty* was tossed in mountainous seas, the worst any of them had ever experienced, with huge foaming crests running in all directions. During the storm the surgeon Huggan was flung down a ladder, and two of the able-bodied sailors were hurt as the ship lurched wildly in the wind. Two weeks later when the sails were heavy with snow, and the waves stood between him and the horizon 'like a wall', blocking out the sun, Bligh had himself lashed to the mast to take his noon sights. As he wrote in his log, the men suffered terribly in these conditions:

The Sails & Ropes were worked with much difficulty, and the few Men who were obliged to be aloft felt the Snow Squalls so severe as to render them almost incapable of getting below, and some of them sometimes for a while lost their Speech.[18]

During this passage Bligh was magnificent in his care of the men, ensuring that they had a hot breakfast every morning (as Cook had also done in the far southern ocean) and dry clothes when they went below; and making them wash and dry their clothes and hammocks at every opportunity. Although he was strict, punishing the young midshipman Peter Heywood for an infraction by 'mastheading' him (i.e. forcing him to stay up the masthead for a long period) in the midst of a violent storm,[19] this was an accepted punishment for 'young gentlemen' in the Navy.

As his men faced these dangers, their irritations receded. Bligh was impressed by the way that they handled the ship: 'Upon the whole I may be bold to say that few Ships could have gone through it as we have done, but I cannot expect my Men and Officers to bear it much longer, or will the object of my Voyage allow me to persist in it.'[20] He formally thanked the crew for their courage and endurance, and on 17 April when he announced that he had decided to give up the attempt to round Cape Horn and turned for Africa instead, the sailors gave him three cheers. Two days later, however, when Bligh turned again for Cape Horn, they were less impressed, and on 22 April when he changed course again for the Cape of Good Hope, they wondered what he was doing.

On 24 May 1788 when the *Bounty* anchored off the Cape of Good Hope, Bligh confided his frustrations to his journal: 'I am thoroughly convinced that had I been a fortnight sooner there I could have made my passage round Cape [Horn] into the South Sea with the greatest ease.'[21] At the same time, he revelled in their epic attempt to round the Horn. As he boasted to Sir Joseph Banks: 'I have suffered much fatigue but I always thrive best when I have the most to do and I was never better in my life', adding:

Perhaps a Voyage of five Months which I have now performed without touching at any one place but at Tenarif, has never been accomplished with so few accidents, and such health among Seamen in a like continuance of bade Weather . . . Having never had a symptom of either Scurvy, Flux or Fever, and as such a fortunate event may be supposed to have been derived from some peculiar Mode of Management it is proper I should point out what I think has been the cause of it.

Seamen seldom attend to themselves in any particular and simply to give directions that they are to keep themselves clean and dry as circumstances will allow, is of little avail, they must be watched like Children, as the most recent danger has little effect. The Mode I have adopted has been a Strict adherence to the first grand point, cleanliness in their persons and bedding. Keeping them in dry Cloaths & by constant cleaning and drying the Ship with Fires.

After all that can be done perhaps Ships may be subject to Fevers and Fluxes; but the Scurvy is rarely a disgrace to a Ship, provided they have it in their power to be supplied with Dryed Malt, Sour Krout, and Portable Soup. When these articles are properly issued, I am firmly convinced no Scurvy will appear. Chearfullness with exercise, and a sufficiency of rest are powerful preventatives to this dreadful disease.[22]

His men were also proud of their hardiness. In a letter to his family in the Isle of Man that was published in the local newspaper, Peter Heywood (who had survived his mastheading) declared: 'I suppose there were never seas, in any part of the known world, to compare with those we met off Cape Horn, for height, and length of swell; the oldest seamen on board never saw anything to equal that, yet Mr. Peckover (our gunner) was all the three voyages with Captain Cook. I have the happiness of telling you that the *Bounty* is as fine a sea boat as ever swam.'[23]

Just a day after mooring the ship off the Cape, however, Bligh was forced to order his second flogging – six lashes for John Williams, a seaman, for neglect of duty in heaving the lead. In a letter to Duncan Campbell, he wrote: 'Upon the whole, no People could live better. I fed them with hot breakfasts of ground Wheat and Sugar – Portable Soup and Krout equal to cabbage made a valuable meal . . . I supplied half their allowance of salt meat by giving them Flour & Raisins in lieu. I assure you I have not acted the Purser with them, for profits was trifling to me while I had so much at Stake.'[24] He was still worried about money, however, and after lending Fletcher Christian some cash, sent the bill of credit to Campbell with a demand that Christian's brother should repay it with interest. Afterwards, Bligh often reproached Christian about the debt, which the young man bitterly resented. As one of the sailors reported: 'Mr. Christian . . . was under some obligations to him of a pecuniary nature, of which Bligh frequently reminded him when any difference arose. Christian, excessively annoyed at the share of blame which repeatedly fell to his lot, in common with the rest of the officers, could ill endure the additional taunt of private obligations: and in a moment of excitation told his commander that soon or later a day of reckoning would arrive.'[25]

At the Cape, Bligh also told his men who had been keeping journals that they would have to hand them in before returning to England. After his mortifying experience with the publication of Cook's third *Voyage*, Bligh was determined to take no risks with his account of the breadfruit expedition. As Ledward, the surgeon's mate, remarked ruefully: 'I have hitherto kept a Journal of the Voyage; but I believe I shall not carry it on any further. The reason of this is that a very accurate account will be published by the Captain under the Auspices of the Admiralty, & to enhance the value of the publication. All care will be taken that no other account can come out before it.'[26]

By 2 July 1788, the *Bounty* had been repaired, refitted, and supplied with fresh provisions. When Bligh set sail from the Cape of Good Hope, heading for the south coast of Australia, the weather was often rough and cold, punctuated with gales and squalls of hail. Their passage was uneventful, however, dominated by the regular routine of cleaning ship, washing and airing clothes, and serving out the anti-scorbutics recommended by Cook – sweet wort, fine old rum, sauerkraut, mustard, vinegar, malt essence and portable soup, which unfortunately were almost useless as remedies against scurvy. On 21 August the *Bounty* anchored at Adventure Bay on Bruny Island off the coast of Tasmania, which Bligh had charted eleven years earlier. When Thomas Hayward found an inscription carved on a tree by one of Furneaux's men in 1773, Bligh sighed, 'I cannot help paying this humble tribute to Captain Cook's memory . . . as his remarkable circumspection in many other things shows how little he was wrong.'[27]

At Adventure Bay, however, Bligh's relationships with his men began to unravel. When he reproached the carpenter, William Purcell, for cutting firewood into lengths that were too long for easy stowage, Purcell retorted that Bligh had come ashore only to find fault. They had a blazing row, but because the carpenter was a warrant officer, Bligh could not have him flogged, sending him instead to unload the water barrels. Although he could have had Purcell locked in his cabin, Bligh seemed irresolute, and reluctant to give the order. Several days later when the carpenter refused to unload the barrels and the master John Fryer reported him for insubordination, Bligh was forced to punish him, saying that until he had done his duty, Purcell would have no provisions. He was furious with everyone involved in this incident – with Fryer for reporting the carpenter; with Christian who had been in command of the wooding party, and with Purcell himself for his defiant behaviour.

As George Tobin, who sailed with Bligh on a later voyage, would remark,

Bligh had 'violent tornados of temper when he lost himself, yet when all in his opinion, was right, when could a man be more placid and interesting?'[28] In his tempestuous rages, Bligh struck out indiscriminately, often causing lasting offence; and from that time on, he and Fryer stopped dining together, and avoided each other as much as possible. At the same time, the men were beginning to make alliances, Fletcher Christian taking Peter Heywood under his wing, while Heywood and George Stewart became close friends. Christian, who was very fit and agile, able to balance a musket on his outstretched hand and jump from inside one barrel to another, was widely admired on board the *Bounty*.

On 29 August, Bligh consoled himself by accompanying David Nelson to the east side of Adventure Bay, where they planted three apple trees, nine grapevines, six plantain trees and two sorts of corn, along with cherry, apricot, peach and pear stones. After a fleeting encounter with a group of Tasmanians, whom Bligh described as 'the most wretched & stupid People existing, yet . . . the most inoffensive',[29] the *Bounty* sailed from the island on 5 September. Two weeks later when they sighted a cluster of rocky uncharted islands south of New Zealand, Bligh surveyed them, naming them after his ship, the Bounty Isles. Although he had intended to visit Dusky Bay in the South Island, reluctant to risk any encounters with Māori man-eaters, Bligh sailed around the southern end of New Zealand instead, heading for Tahiti. On 3 October they crossed a sea covered with luminous plankton, which gave off 'a light like the blaze of a Candle'.[30] Three days later, when Bligh was told that James Valentine, one of the most robust of his men, was dying from a wound that had become infected after a blood-letting, he was enraged with his drunken surgeon. On 9 October when the sailor died and Huggan blamed his death on scurvy, Bligh was beside himself, railing at the master and the surgeon for this blot on the voyage. Again, however, he took no decisive action to stop Huggan from drinking.

That same day, Bligh's relationship with Fryer hit a new low. When the boatswain and the carpenter presented their expense books, he signed them, asking the master to add his signature. Still angry with Bligh, Fryer refused to sign these books until his captain signed a certificate that the master had acted properly throughout the voyage. In retaliation, Bligh called his bluff. Mustering the crew, he read out the Articles of War, emphasising Article XI: 'Every person in the fleet, who shall not duly observe the orders of . . . his superior officers to the best of his power, and being convicted thereof by the sentence of a court martial, shall suffer death.' According to James Morrison, when he said to Fryer, 'Now Sir Sign them Books,' the master did so, muttering under his breath, 'I sign in obedience to your orders, but this may be Cancelled hereafter.'[31] Bligh had humiliated his master in front of the men, and feelings were running high. On 19 October when two of the men refused to dance, complaining that their joints were aching (symptoms that Huggan also attributed to scurvy), Bligh cut off their allowance of grog and threatened them with a flogging. The men began to mock him in the ditties they sang as they danced on deck, brooding over their grievances.

In his letter from the Cape of Good Hope, Bligh had assured Sir Joseph Banks that as long as the men were provided with anti-scorbutics, and plenty of rest and exercise, 'I am firmly convinced no Scurvy will appear.'[32] Not surprisingly, given such an unequivocal declaration, Bligh was reluctant to admit that any of his men might be suffering from this affliction. When other sailors began to complain of aches and pains, which Huggan diagnosed as signs of scurvy, he complained that the surgeon was too drunk to give a reliable opinion. Insisting that the symptoms were caused by rheumatism or prickly heat instead, he wrote in his journal that these men had 'no eruptions or swellings, [which] convinced me that the complaint is not scorbutic. Their Gums are as sound as any can be expected, and their breath is not offensive neither is their teeth loose.'[33] On 24 October when Huggan put himself on the sick list as suffering from a 'Paralytic affliction', Bligh accused him of being blind drunk (another offence under the Articles of War),[34] ordering his foetid cabin to be cleaned and searched, and finally confiscating his liquor.

The following day when the high island of Me'eti'a, east of Tahiti, was sighted, the men were overjoyed, knowing that they would soon have access to plenty of fresh fruit and vegetables, and island women. As far as Bligh was aware, no ships had visited Tahiti since Cook's last voyage, and he hoped that in the meantime the islanders might have cured themselves of venereal diseases. When he ordered Huggan (who was back on duty) to examine the men, the surgeon reported that they were all free of venereal infections; although he had treated at least two of the sailors for these diseases during the voyage.[35] About twenty people ran along the beach at Me'eti'a, waving and displaying large pieces of bark cloth, hoping to entice them ashore, but Bligh was bound for Tahiti, and had no intention of stopping at this small island.

As they headed west towards Tahiti, Bligh appointed William Peckover, the gunner and veteran of all three of Cook's Pacific voyages, and the best speaker of Tahitian on board the *Bounty*, to control the trade with local people. At the same time, he had a set of instructions nailed to the mizzenmast, laying out his orders for the conduct of his men when they reached the island. Eager to capitalise on Captain Cook's *mana* among the Tahitians, he wrote:

1st. At the Society . . . Islands, no person whatsoever is to intimate that Captain Cook was killed by Indians or that he is dead.

2nd. No person is ever to speak, or give the least hint, that we have come on purpose to get the breadfruit plant, until I have made my plan known to the chiefs.

3rd. Every person is to study to gain the good will and esteem of the natives; to treat them with all kindness; and not to take from them, by violent means, any thing that that may have been stolen; and no one is ever to fire, but in defence of his life.

4th. Every person employed on service, is to take care that no arms or implements of any kind under their charge, are stolen; the value of such thing, being lost, shall be charged against their wages.

5th. No man is to embezzle, or offer to sale, directly, or indirectly, any part of the King's stores, of what nature soever.

6th. A proper person or persons will be appointed to regulate trade, and barter with the natives; and no officer or seaman, or other person belonging to the ship, is to trade for any kind of provisions, or curiosities; but if such officer or seaman wishes to purchase any particular thing, he is to apply to the provider to do it for him.[36]

Ashore in Tahiti, after Captain Cook sailed away from the island in December 1777, the people had been relieved when no more tall ships appeared over the horizon. The War of Independence had distracted Britain, France and Spain from their jousting in the Pacific, stretching their navies to the limit. At first, many Tahitians, weary of the conflicts and diseases that accompanied these European incursions, were glad to be left in peace; but after a while they began to wonder what had happened to those strange ships, with their towering masts, curving sails and cargos of treasure. As their iron tools, weapons and nails rusted, and the red cloth and red feathers became tattered and faded, they began to long for replacements; while those kin groups who had relied on their European allies felt increasingly vulnerable. Vehiatua and the people of southern Tahiti waited in vain for the Spaniards to return to their harbour, while Tu and his people at

Pare-'Arue, who had come to rely on Captain Cook's formidable reputation to protect them, were exposed to the jealousies of their neighbours.

As it happened, it was more than a decade before another European ship anchored off the coast of Tahiti. This was a convict transport, the *Lady Penrhyn*, commanded by Captain William Sever, which had set sail from Britain with the First Fleet on 13 May 1787, carrying 103 female convicts and 32 sailors and marines to Botany Bay. Although Joseph Banks had abandoned his scheme of sending a convict transport from Australia to Tahiti to pick up breadfruit plants, the plan had been discussed with the First Fleet captains, and the idea of a stopover in the Society Islands was in the air.[37] Lieutenant John Watts, who had sailed as a midshipman in the *Resolution* with William Bligh and Captain Cook during the third Pacific voyage, had been appointed by the owners of the *Lady Penrhyn* to keep an eye on their brand-new vessel. After a three-month stay in Port Jackson, where they unloaded the female convicts, the ship sailed for China to collect a cargo of tea. Fresh fruit and vegetables were scarce in the new penal colony, however, and by the time they reached the Kermadec Islands, a number of the sailors were so ill with scurvy that they were unable to get out of their hammocks, while many of the others had 'swelled gums, the flesh exceeding black and hard, a contraction of the sinews, with a total debility',[38] symptoms of this awful affliction. Knowing that they would find plentiful supplies of fruit, vegetables, pork and fish in the Society Islands, Watts decided to head to Tahiti. Their brief visit heralded the return of the British, and Bligh's arrival at the island on board the *Bounty* soon afterwards.

On 10 July 1788 when the *Lady Penrhyn* sailed into Matavai Bay, Tu's people were ecstatic. Along the beaches of Port Venus, hundreds of islanders waved plantain branches and pieces of white bark cloth; and the sailors gazed, rejoicing, at the groves of coconut, breadfruit and plantain trees ashore and the crowds of friendly people. Watts ordered the Union Jack to be hoisted, and as soon as they realised that this ship came from Peretane [Britain], canoes flocked out to the *Lady Penrhyn*, their crews crying out '*Taio! Taio!*' and '*Pahi no Tute!*' ('Cook's ship!'), bringing out loads of coconuts, breadfruit, plantains, taro and *vi* (Tahitian apples), with a few pigs and chickens. Knowing that the islanders revered Captain Cook, Watts and Sever had agreed to conceal the fact of his death at the hands of Hawai'ian warriors, although Watts had been present in Kealakekua Bay when Cook was killed. When their visitors asked him about 'Tute', Watts assured them that his former commander was still alive in England, although he was now an old man.

At nightfall when Moana, the *ari'i* of Matavai Bay, came out to the ship, he recognised Lieutenant Watts, greeting him warmly and telling his companions that this was one of Tute's people. After adopting Watts as his *taio*, Moana told his new bond friend that Tu, the paramount chief of the island, was alive and well, although he was away on a visit to the east side of the island. He also told Watts that some years after the *Resolution* and *Discovery* had sailed away from the Society Islands, Mahine, the *ari'i rahi* (high chief) of Mo'orea, had gathered a large army. Joined by a contingent led by the 'Admiral' Teto'ofa, they landed at night in Tu's district, killing every animal that they could find to avenge Captain Cook's rampage across Mo'orea. As Captain Cook's *taio*, Tu was held responsible for the damage that Cook and Ma'i and their men had inflicted, and during this attack he and his family fled into the mountains. That night, Captain Sever, acutely aware of the vulnerability of his ship, posted sentries armed with cutlasses and muskets on watch, hoping to deter Tu's enemies from attempting an ambush.

When Hitihiti, the high-born young Porapora *'arioi* who had sailed with Cook during his second voyage, arrived on board the *Lady Penrhyn* several days later, he asked Lieutenant Watts about his friends from the *Resolution*, and told him that since Captain Cook's departure, this was the first European ship to arrive at the Society Islands. During their meeting, Watts kept up the pretence that Cook was still alive, presenting Hitihiti with a gift from the great commander. According to Hitihiti, all of the cattle and other animals that Cook had given to Tu had been slaughtered by Mahine, the high chief of Mo'orea; and Ma'i and his young Māori attendants had died of illness long ago, although one of Ma'i's horses was still alive on Huahine. That night, young girls danced the *heiva* on the quarterdeck and spent the night with the sailors. The ship's surgeon Bowes Smyth remarked primly: '[T]he greater part of their action during the Dance wd. in England be thought the height of indecency, & indeed they seem calculated to excite Venereal desires to a great degree, as we have reason also to think their Songs are.'[39]

After dawn on 14 July, a messenger came out to invite Lieutenant Watts and Captain Sever ashore, where Tu was waiting to greet them. A joyous crowd of about 10,000 people had gathered, and so many single and double canoes swarmed in the bay that as they rowed to the beach, they could barely see the water. Tu, a tall, muscular man wearing thick layers of bark cloth around his waist, his hair plaited and decorated with fragrant flowers, stood on the black sand, waiting for them, attended by a number of *ari'i*. Beside him a man held up Webber's portrait of Captain Cook, presented to Tu before Cook had sailed away from Tahiti. Even during the raids on his district, Tu had managed to hold on to this precious talisman. In Tahiti, portraits were not understood as images, but as embodiments of the person depicted, imbued with their *varua* or spirit; and this portrait invoked Cook's presence. As he greeted Captain Sever, adopting him as his *taio*, Tu sent the portrait into the boat before he would come on board, repeating the same procedure when they arrived alongside the *Lady Penrhyn*.

In the Great Cabin, Tu had Captain Cook's portrait fixed to the wall, and his attendants draped the entire ship with bark cloth, hanging it down the sides of the vessel and laying it over the quarterdeck, turning the transport into a great altar piled high with gifts – four large pigs, great piles of breadfruit, coconuts, chickens, bananas, *mahi* (fermented breadfruit) and mangoes. In Tahiti, sacred objects and people were often wrapped in layers of bark cloth, intensifying their *mana*, and when they were unwrapped, the *mana* was released, summoning the gods. Upon visiting the between-decks, Tu and his companions were astonished to see so small a crew – and many of them ill and confined to their hammocks. This must have been a moment of acute temptation, because the ship was full of iron and other prized goods and it would have been easy for Tu's warriors to seize it from the enfeebled sailors. Fortunately for the British, however, Tu was a peaceable man, not given to fighting.

On this occasion, Tu was accompanied by a woman whose advice he often sought, although the British considered her neither pretty nor charming. This was his wife 'Itia, the high-born, strong-willed niece of Mahine, whose brother Mahau had hoped to succeed Mahine as the paramount chief of Mo'orea. After Mahine's attack on Pare, Tu's district, however, some years after Captain Cook's departure, his rival Mahau had taken refuge with Tu, and his sister 'Itia married Tu, while Mahau had married Tu's sister Auo. Incensed by this provocative exchange of marriages, Mahine attacked Tu's forces, this time at Matavai Bay. In the battle, Tu's younger brother Vaetua killed the great warrior, driving his fleet back to Mo'orea. Although Tu's marriage to 'Itia was a political match, he seemed very much attached to this bold, enterprising woman. 'Itia was not beautiful, but she was impressive – a fine sportswoman, famous as a surfer, wrestler and archer; a fearless warrior; a benevolent, astute 'Great Woman' who was fiercely loyal to her family, and helped to shape the fortunes of the Pomare dynasty.[40] Although 'Itia and Tu both begged Captain Sever to take them to Mo'orea and punish Mahine for his depredations, as Captain Cook had promised, Sever refused, knowing that he had too few men for such an excursion.

During this brief stay at Matavai Bay, whenever the British went ashore, the islanders crowded around them so closely that they could scarcely breathe, until one of the chiefs came out with a long rod and laid about him, forcing the people to make room. Although Tu urged Captain Sever to shift the *Lady Penrhyn* to the *Resolution*'s old berth, closer to the beach, Sever decided against allowing the Tahitians to help his men work the ship, in case they tried to capture it. He posted sailors armed with muskets and cutlasses on deck every night, and did not establish a shore camp. None of his officers ventured far inland, and throughout their stay the sailors stayed on board the *Lady Penrhyn*. Lieutenant Watts vividly remembered the trouble that had been caused when two of Cook's men deserted from the *Resolution*; and Sever could ill afford to lose any of his sailors, since his crew numbered barely enough to work the vessel.

Although Tu and his people often remarked how easy it would be for them to capture the *Lady Penrhyn*, they remain faithful and friendly, showering the British with presents. They bartered eagerly for iron – hatchets, knives, nails, gimlets, files and scissors, along with looking glasses. Surprisingly, red feathers were no longer prized, although they accepted them as presents. Cats (which according to the islanders had brought fleas to the island)[41] and goats had multiplied in Tahiti, along with pumpkins and chilli peppers, and Watts noticed that the Tahitians were now applying new patterns to their bark cloth, copied from the printed cloth that they had received from Captain Cook and other European visitors. Every evening the local girls danced on the quarterdeck, and according to Bowes Smyth, they were 'total strangers to every idea of Shame in their Amours',[42] although many people had died from venereal diseases since the *Resolution*'s visit in 1777. As the sailors feasted on fresh fruit, meat and fish and slept with the young women, their symptoms of scurvy retreated with remarkable speed and they quickly regained their health and high spirits.

On 19 July when an *'arioi* tattooist came on board, most of the sailors had their arms marked, including Captain Sever, Bowes Smyth and Lieutenant Watts (who by now was tattooed over most of his body). Now that the ship was fully provisioned, the officers decided to carry on to China, and on 24 July 1788 before dawn, Captain Sever and Lieutenant Watts set sail from Matavai Bay without warning, fearing that the ship's departure might provoke an attack. Contrary to their fears, however, Tu and his people flocked out in their canoes, following their *taio* seven or eight miles out to sea, weeping and farewelling them affectionately. Hitihiti, who came out with his two wives, begged to sail with them to England; and when Tu told Captain Sever that he did not approve of this request, and Sever refused to allow it, Hitihiti wept bitterly. The Tahitians exchanged locks of hair with their *taio*, and Tu 'expressed great sorrow at their departure, mentioned how much time had elapsed since the *Resolution* and *Discovery* were at Otaheite, begged they would not be so long absent any more, and desired very much to have some horses brought to him'.[43] As he boarded his canoe, Tu asked to hear the great guns, and two of the cannons were fired, astonishing and terrifying the islanders. He wept as he farewelled them, prompting Bowes Smyth to exclaim as they sailed away, 'There cannot be a more affectionate people than the Otaheiteans!'[44]

# Captain Cook's 'Son'

As it happened, Tu's plea that the British 'would not be so long absent any more' would be quickly answered. On 26 October 1788, just three months after the *Lady Penrhyn*'s departure, William Bligh in the *Bounty* arrived at the island, sailing up the east coast of Tahiti, and in brilliant sunshine hauled around Point Venus into Matavai Bay. As canoes flocked around the ship, bringing out large quantities of pigs, breadfruit and coconuts, the sailors, who had heard vivid tales about the glories of Tahiti from their shipmates, were ecstatic. Alongside, the crews of the canoes asked eagerly whether the sailors were *taio* (friends) and whether they came from Peretane (Britain) or Rima (Lima). When Bligh assured them that they were British, the islanders clambered on board, making it difficult to work the ship. As he remarked plaintively: '[I]n ten minutes I could scarce find my own people.'[1] Distracted by this enraptured welcome, the sailors failed to clear the anchor or reef the sails, and the ship drifted towards the rocks. When the wind died, Bligh was unable to reach the *Resolution*'s old anchorage, and had to anchor the *Bounty* a mile offshore from One Tree Hill (Tahara'a). As they gazed inland, her crew could see jagged mountains soaring high into the sky, their ridges covered with reeds and the tops of the hills with trees; and waterfalls tumbled down into the valleys, glittering in the sunlight. They had arrived at the promised land.

When the *Bounty*'s anchors rattled down into the lagoon at Matavai Bay, several 'inferior chiefs' came on board, bearing gifts. By late October the Season of Scarcity was under way, and they had few breadfruit to offer. Overjoyed to recognise Bligh and David Nelson (Banks's gardener), William Peckover (the gunner) and Joseph Coleman (the armourer), all of whom had previously visited

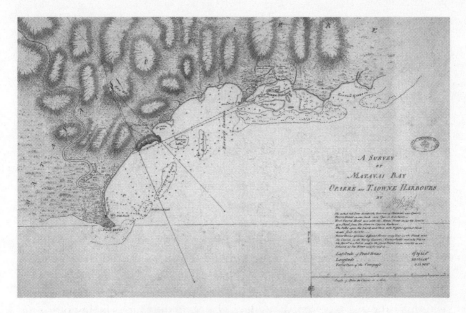

*William Bligh's survey of Matavai Bay.*

Tahiti with Captain Cook, these men asked about 'Tute', remarking that a ship commanded by 'Tona' (John Watts) had visited the bay three months earlier, whose sailors had told them that Captain Cook had died in Hawai'i. Although Sever and Watts had agreed not to tell the Tahitians that Captain Cook had been killed, some of the crew (perhaps the *Lady Penrhyn*'s steward, who had also sailed on board the *Resolution*) had told the Tahitians about the death of the great navigator; and they were anxious to establish the truth of this matter.

When David Nelson, obedient to Bligh's instructions, told the chiefs that Captain Cook was not dead, but alive and well in 'Peretane' (Britain), and that William Bligh was Cook's 'son', these men were elated. Although stature was a mark of rank in the Society Islands, and Bligh was a short man (in contrast to Banks and Cook, who were both about six feet tall), his complexion was pale, a sign of high status; and as Cook's 'son', he was treated with reverence. Eagerly asking after 'Pane' (Banks) and 'Tolano' (Dr Solander, Banks's scientific companion) from the *Endeavour*, Lieutenant Williamson from the *Resolution* and Cook's sergeant of marines Samuel Gibson, the chiefs told Bligh that Ma'i had died from an illness sent by the *atua* (ancestor gods). When Bligh asked after Tu, as far as he could understand them, these men told him that Tu was absent from the Pare-'Arue district, but would return in three or four days' time.

Contrary to Bligh's expectations, none of their visitors tried to steal from the ship on this occasion. Instead, using sign language, they quickly adopted *taio* among the sailors who had not previously visited the island. According to James Morrison, the boatswain's mate, 'some of the Weomen who came on board became very Intiligent in a short time and soon brought their quondum husbands into a method of discourse by which everything was transacted'.[2] As the sailors quickly discovered during these exchanges, despite Captain Cook's best attempts to control the spread of sexually transmitted diseases and Bligh's hope that the Tahitians might have discovered a cure for these maladies, venereal infections were now widespread on the island.

Early the next morning when Bligh shifted the *Bounty* to Cook's old mooring in Matavai Bay,[3] Po'e'eno (the son of Moana, the *ari'i* or high chief of the Ha'apape district, who had befriended Bligh during his previous visit) came on board with Ari'ipaea (the younger brother of Tu), a tall, stately man, more formally known as Teari'ifa'atau. Ari'ipaea, renowned as a sailor and naval commander, had taken Captain Clerke as his *taio* during Cook's last voyage; and Bligh had met him on board the *Resolution*. When he boarded the *Bounty* with gifts of small pigs, breadfruit, coconuts, plantains and *vi* or Tahitian apples, Ari'ipaea was accompanied by his father Teu, a tall, mild-mannered man about seventy years old with a long, white beard, weak eyes, and skin scurfed from drinking *'ava*. Soon afterwards, two messengers despatched by Tu arrived with two small pigs and plantain branches, welcoming Bligh back to Tahiti.

Soon afterwards when a man boarded the *Bounty* and stole a tin pot, Ari'ipaea flew into a violent rage, belabouring the culprit with clubs and driving him overboard. When Ari'ipaea urged him to flog anyone who stole from the ship, Bligh remarked in astonishment, 'This was a mode of conduct I never saw in any Otaheite Cheif Before.'[4] After asking the chiefs about the cattle, horses, sheep, goats and other animals that Captain Cook had left behind on the island, Bligh was given many different answers, all of them unfavourable; and Ari'ipaea told him that Teto'ofa, the famous 'Admiral', had died since Cook's departure. By this time the Tahitians had adopted iron axes for woodworking, and they asked eagerly for these tools, but unfortunately Banks had provided Bligh with adzes (manufactured especially from iron, but in the shape of their traditional tools), which they no longer wanted. They were also very keen to obtain files, gimlets, knives, combs and looking glasses.

When he escorted Bligh ashore, Po'e'eno indicated the site on Point Venus where 'our Tent was fixt in 1777', asking him to place his shore camp on this hallowed spot. Afterwards they walked together through a shady breadfruit grove to Po'e'eno's house, where Bligh was seated on a fine mat. The chief's wife and sister were painting bark cloth with red dye; and as the people crowded around, crushing him, Bligh asked Po'e'eno to tell them to stand back. Among the crowd, Bligh saw a man whose arm had been amputated just above the elbow, although the wound seemed perfectly healed, and when he asked Po'e'eno what had happened, the chief told him that the man had fallen from a coconut tree and smashed his elbow. Bligh's Tahitian was imperfect, however, and he could not understand Po'e'eno's explanation of how the amputation had been performed. During this visit Po'e'eno exchanged names with Bligh, ratifying their friendship by adopting him as a *taio*, and when Bligh returned to the ship for dinner, Po'e'eno's wife and sister clothed him in red bark cloth and a fine mat before escorting him back to the *Bounty*.

Later that day, an envoy from Tu brought John Webber's portrait of Captain Cook out to the *Bounty*, explaining that this sacred relic was '*Tute ari'i no Tahiti*' ('Cook, the high chief of Tahiti'), and that Tu had sent it to Captain Bligh. According to this man, when he presented Tu with this portrait, Captain Cook had told him that when his son arrived in Tahiti, Tu must show it to him, and they would always be friends. As Captain Cook gazed sombrely out from the canvas, Bligh must have felt that his old commander was beside him. A chiefly woman who had accompanied the envoys was wearing a calico shirt which she said had been given to her by an *ari'i* on board 'Tona's ship'; and when Bligh inspected it he saw that the shirt was marked with Lieutenant Watts's name. Later that afternoon, Tu's younger brother Vaetua, who was now about twenty-five years old, came on board, so drunk with *'ava* that he was almost stupefied. At nightfall Bligh sent all of the islanders ashore, except for the women who spent the night on board, carousing with the sailors.

Early the next morning Bligh despatched David Nelson and his assistant William Brown to look for breadfruit plants. The fruit that the islanders brought to the tent included red peppers and shaddocks (which they called '*uru no Peretane*' or 'breadfruit from Britain'),[5] planted by Cook's men during their previous visits. Impatient to meet Tu, Bligh despatched his acting lieutenant, Fletcher Christian, to fetch him. Later that afternoon, the high chief, with his mild expression and conspicuous mop of curly hair, who at six feet four inches tall towered over Bligh, boarded the *Bounty* with his wife 'Itia and his thin, white-bearded father Teu (or 'Tu Po'e'eno', as the old man was addressed on this occasion). When Tu asked Bligh whether he was a *taio* of Tute's (or Captain Cook's), whose name he still carried, and Bligh agreed that he was, Tu gestured towards 'Itia, saying, 'Here is my Wife, take care of her.'[6] As a *taio* of Captain

*Presentation of bark cloth.*

Cook's, Bligh was also a bond friend of Tu's, and entitled to share 'Itia's sexual favours (since *taio* were bound to offer their wives, along with their other treasured possessions, to each other).

After this exchange Bligh invited Tu, 'Itia and their retinue to dine in his cabin. Tu asked him to wait, however, and wrapping a large quantity of bark cloth around him, pressed noses and exchanged names with him, calling himself 'Parai' and addressing Bligh as 'Tina' (one of the names that Tu was using at this time), ratifying their relationship by formally adopting him as a bond friend. From this time on, his bond friendship with Tu meant that Bligh became a part of Tu's family, sharing his name, his lineage and ancestors, and his network of enmities and alliances on the island.

After Tu and Bligh exchanged names, a woman approached Bligh wrapped in a huge quantity of bark cloth, which she slowly unwound from her body, spinning around before him until she stood naked. This was a graceful way of

presenting bark cloth to an honoured guest in Tahiti, with no necessary implica-
tion of sexual availability. Bligh was also presented with a large pig and some
breadfruit; and in exchange, he gave Tu hatchets, adzes or *to'i*, files, knives,
gimlets, a saw, looking glasses, two shirts and two red flamingo wings that he had
acquired at the Cape of Good Hope, since during his previous visit red feathers
had been treasured as offerings to 'Oro, the god of war and fertility (although
to his surprise, red feathers were no longer greatly prized). When he presented
'Itia with earrings, necklaces and beads, this powerful, rather masculine-looking
'Great Woman' showed a strong preference for iron tools. Tu and 'Itia were
eager to visit Bligh's cabin, which was very small, and although he was reluctant
to show them this dark, dank cubbyhole, he invited them in; and when they
pointed to objects that they liked, he gave them everything that they wanted.

Back on deck, Tu asked for one of the 4-pounders to be fired. When Bligh
gave the order, the paramount chief and his companions (except 'Itia) were so
frightened that they fell to the deck, stopping their ears. Nevertheless, Tu had
the presence of mind to track the flight of the cannonball across the sea. As a
young man, Tu had been present when Captain Wallis bombarded the Tahitian
naval fleet, raking the crowds on the beach with the *Dolphin*'s guns, and since
that time he had been terrified of firearms. He told Bligh that some years after
Cook's last departure, the Mo'orea people led by Mahine had attacked his people
and defeated them, driving them into the mountains; and that they had seized
the sheep, cattle, ducks and geese that Cook had given him and carried them
off to Mo'orea.

As Bligh now learned, during his previous visit to the island Tu and 'Itia had
both been leading *'arioi*, and their first child (a girl) had been strangled at birth
so that they could remain active in the *'arioi* society. When Tu's eldest son was
born, however, Tu left the *'arioi* society; and his son had inherited his sacred
title, taking the name 'Tu-nui-a'a-i-te-atua' from his father while Tu became
known as 'Tina' or 'Mate'. Later when his eldest daughter became ill with a chest
infection that gave her a racking cough, Tu had taken the name 'Pomare' ('*Po
mare*', lit. 'night cough'), the name now associated with his lineage on the island.[7]

Tu also talked with Bligh about 'Tonah' (John Watts) and his ship, saying that
the sailors had bartered plenty of red feathers before sailing away to Tongatapu
three months earlier (evidently the Tahitians had decided that because the *Lady
Penrhyn* headed north-west upon leaving the Society Islands, they were heading
for the Tongan archipelago). After asking endless questions about Captain Cook,
Tu enquired whether anyone on board the *Bounty* could paint his portrait, and
Teu's (presumably so that their images could be displayed alongside that of

Captain Cook on ritual occasions), and was dismayed when Bligh confessed that there was no one on board with that talent. By way of consolation, Bligh offered Tu an English sow and boar that he had admired, and gave him a fine dinner. The high chief was fed by his servant or *teuteu* while the women waited apart; and he would only drink coconut milk, avoiding all alcohol.

Afterwards, Tu asked Bligh to take him to his dining room where he and 'Itia shared a meal, breaking the food *tapu* (sacred restriction) which forbade men and women to eat together – one of the fundamental rules in Tahitian society. 'Itia was so aristocratic, however, that she escaped this prohibition. That afternoon, in spite of the Season of Scarcity, more large pigs were brought out to the ship, along with piles of coconuts and breadfruit, plantains and a few yams. Delighted by these supplies of fresh food, Bligh exulted, 'I believe no Men ever lived in such abundance as we do at present.'[8] At the same time Tu asked Bligh to look after the most prized gifts that he had been presented on board the ship, assuring him that otherwise they would be stolen. He explained that since Mahine's attack on Pare-'Arue, he had been exiled to his mother's lands in Vaitepiha Bay in southern Tahiti, and no longer lived at Pare. According to Bligh, since Tu had been succeeded by his son as paramount chief of the island, he was 'only nominally possessed of power, as the Cheifs revile him upon all occasions'.[9]

The following morning when Bligh went to visit his bond friend Tu, he found him resting under a canoe awning about a quarter of a mile east of Point Venus with his wife and three children. Afterwards, he went to see his other friends Po'e'eno and his father Moana, the chiefs of Matavai Bay, and had his men sow melon, cucumber and salad seeds in their gardens. Noticing large patches of tobacco and pumpkins growing nearby, planted during Captain Cook's visits, Bligh observed that the breadfruit and coconut trees were laden with fruit, and that harvest time was approaching. When he returned to the *Bounty*, he found Ari'ipaea and Vaetua, Tu's younger brothers, both active *'arioi*, waiting on board, accompanied by a girl whom Bligh recognised from her visits to the *Resolution* during his previous visit. This young woman shocked him with her graphic tales of the ravages caused by venereal diseases on the island, which she assured him had killed many 'fine Girls' after the British ships departed.

After dinner, Tu sent a messenger to invite Bligh to meet him at Ari'ipaea's house, a long thatched roof on pillars, its sides open to the tropical breezes. When he arrived, a piece of bark cloth 41 yards long and 2 yards wide was laid on the ground and Bligh was draped with a length of red bark cloth, the costume of a high-ranking *'arioi*, and presented with two very large pigs that weighed about 200 pounds each, and a large quantity of baked breadfruit and coconuts.

A vast crowd had gathered, and when Tu asked Bligh to walk along the bark-cloth runner and back again, the spectators were gratified, especially when they exchanged the word '*taio*' several times, ratifying their bond friendship. When Tu returned on board the *Bounty*, Bligh presented him with more gifts, some of which he immediately redistributed to his supporters, including Moana, the high chief of Matavai Bay. After this visit Bligh remarked that among other changes on the island, only European breeds of pigs were now seen, displacing the smaller Polynesian pigs which had been common during his previous visit; and that goats were well established, a goat and a kid having been bartered to William Peckover that morning.

At daybreak the next day, 30 October, Tu and 'Itia came out to the ship, where they were joined for dinner by two chiefs of the Hitia'a district, on the east coast of the island. On this occasion, 'Itia ate apart from the men; and one of their visitors was fed by an attendant, a custom observed by those chiefs whose children had not yet had the birth *tapu* raised from them by a cycle of ceremonies. Afterwards when Bligh was told that parts of the gun tackles had been stolen, Ari'ipaea hurried ashore to retrieve them, while Bligh cleared the ship of all visitors. One warrior, who resented his exclusion, struck at the sentinel with a club, and when the sentry called out for Bligh, he ordered him not to fire his musket. Although Bligh raised his gun, he decided to show restraint, and did not shoot the offender. At sundown when the chiefs went ashore, Bligh raced his five-oared cutter against a sailing canoe with four paddlers, beating them to the beach; and as Ari'ipaea disembarked from the cutter, he took some white bark cloth and stuck it on the bow as a sign of victory, to the loud applause of the spectators. Tu also sent a small box which had been a gift from Captain Cook out to the ship, asking for the carpenter to repair it. The box had been broken open by his enemies, and now contained only two large axes.

At sunrise the next morning, Moana came out to the *Bounty* with a message from Tu, saying that he was afraid and could not come out to the ship that morning, although he had sent Ari'ipaea in search of a thief who had stolen from the British. Soon afterwards, Bligh was informed that the buoy from the best bower anchor was missing, and sent a message to Tu and 'Itia, urging them to come on board and reassuring them that despite the theft, he was still their friend. Captain Cook had been accustomed to punish thefts of this kind by capturing canoes and taking chiefs hostage, and in the past, Tu had always fled from the British on such occasions. In Tahiti, the ancestor Hiro, revered as a trickster god and associated with the '*arioi*, was the patron of thieves; and if a man could steal a prized object (like the buoy of the *Bounty*, for example) without being intercepted, this was a great coup, showing that the power of the god had made him invisible. If he was caught, however, the thief was severely punished – tied to a large stone and dropped into the sea from a canoe, for instance, and drowned.[10] According to the missionary William Ellis, the man who stole the *Bounty*'s buoy on this occasion was named Tareu, and his feat was commemorated in a ditty:

| | |
|---|---|
| *'O me eia e Tareu eia* | Such a one a thief, and Tareu |
| *Eia te poito a Bligh* | Stole the buoy of Bligh.[11] |

After receiving Bligh's friendly message, Tu and 'Itia returned to the *Bounty* where he gave them a fine dinner and more gifts, and refrained from taking them hostage. This restraint marked a new step in the relationships between visiting captains and their chiefly friends in Tahiti, because it seemed that here at last was a high-ranking European who understood how a *taio* should behave, honouring his bond friends as members of his own family.

In response to Bligh's kindness, Tu invited him to go with him that afternoon to Pare to meet his son, Pomare II, who had succeeded him as the paramount chief of the island. Bligh gathered rich presents and when they set out, invited Tu to join him in the cutter. As they sailed down to Pare, Tu told Bligh about the war with Mo'orea that had broken out since Captain Cook's departure. According to Tu, Cook's dire warning that he would return and destroy anyone who dared to attack his *taio* had acted as a deterrent for five years and three months; but finally his enemy Mahine had decided that Captain Cook would not return. After forging an alliance with Teto'ofa (the 'Admiral'), the old *ari'i* of the Fa'a'a district, he attacked Pare with their combined fleet. As soon as the enemy fleet was sighted, Tu and his people fled to the mountains; and when they landed, the enemy warriors ravaged the district, destroying houses, canoes and gardens and chopping down fruit trees.

Bligh had noticed that there were now only two or three large canoes left in the northern districts, and no large houses, and that everyone was sleeping in little light shelters. According to Tu, all of the cattle (including eight calves), sheep (including ten lambs), ducks, geese, turkeys and peacocks that Captain Cook had given him had been slaughtered or carried away by the marauding warriors, who also plundered the rest of Cook's gifts except for the small tool box and three axes, which he had managed to hide away. When Tu begged Bligh to tell Captain Cook about this attack, asking him to come in a big ship and avenge him, Bligh replied that not only Tute but King George would be furious with Mahine, and that when the next British ship arrived, they would send him many presents. Thrilled by these assurances, Tu implored Bligh to stay on the island as long as possible to protect him and his people from his enemies. When Bligh remarked that King George had been generous, sending Tu so many gifts, Tu mentioned breadfruit as a possible return gift, and Bligh replied casually that the King would be delighted.

When Bligh and Tu landed at Pare, Ari'ipaea greeted them, presenting Bligh with a scraper and a small iron hoop that had been stolen from the *Bounty*. Tu had warned Bligh that no one (including himself and his wife) could visit his son without stripping to the waist, asking his *taio* to respect this custom. According to the local people, the god Tane had visited 'Itia in the night and made her pregnant; and as the child of the union with the god of peace and beauty, Pomare II was exceptionally *ra'a* or sacred. Bligh was about to comply with Tu's request when, thinking of the blazing sun, he replied that he preferred to dress as he would do in the presence of King George, the greatest *ari'i* in the world. As he took off his hat, Tu threw bark cloth around his shoulders and they walked together through shady groves of breadfruit trees, followed by a vast, curious crowd.

On the opposite bank of the river (probably the Vaipo'opo'o), Bligh saw a house set in a beautifully picturesque spot. The young paramount chief (*ari'i rahi*), a boy about six years old, soon emerged, carried on the shoulders of a man, clothed in fine white bark cloth and followed by two other children who were also 'flying' on the shoulders of their attendants. Pomare II was so sacred that no one could touch his body or pass a hand over his head; nor could his feet touch the ground. As the missionary Ellis wrote about the paramount chief of the island: 'His houses were called the *aorai*, the clouds of heaven; *anuanua*, the rainbow, was the name of the canoe in which he voyaged; his voice was called thunder; the glare of the torches in his dwelling was denominated lightning; and . . . when he passed from one district to another on the shoulders of his bearers, instead of speaking of his passage from one place to another, they always used the word *mahuta*, which signifies to fly.'[12] During his lifetime, it was also forbidden to pronounce any words that contained a syllable of his name.

Escorting Bligh to the riverbank, Tu instructed his *taio* to greet his son as '*Tu ari'i rahi*' (Tu, the paramount chief), and how to address the other *tama aitu* or sacred children. Following his advice, Bligh divided his gifts into three parts, one for each of the children; presenting the first part to a messenger, saying that this was for the *ari'i rahi* from his friend, who hated thieves and came from Britain; and repeating the same message with his gifts to each of the other two children.

Tu told Bligh that he and 'Itia had another child living at Matavai Bay, and four living children altogether, two sons and two daughters, all born since they had left the *'arioi* society.[13]

After his long voyage, Bligh was delighted to be back in Tahiti. Like Captain Cook during his third Pacific expedition, Bligh often felt more at home with Tu and his family than he did with his own men, with their sniping at his authority and rancorous quarrels. When the presentations to Pomare II were over, Bligh replaced his hat; and Tu took the bark cloth from his shoulders, escorting him past several *marae* and asking him to remove his hat again as they passed a *ti'i* or carved image about 14 feet high, which he identified as the god of the bark-cloth plant. Five minutes later, they passed another smaller *ti'i* before arriving at a house where four male *'arioi* entertained them, playing a drum and three nose flutes. As Bligh remarked: 'By the form of their Flutes they are confined to a few Notes, Yet are they harmonious and the Cadences musical and pleasing.'[14]

After this performance they carried on to Ari'ipaea's house where Tu presented Bligh with a large pig and some coconuts, introducing him to his elderly uncle Mou'aroa (also known as Teri'i-hinoi-atua), the leading *'arioi* of the Porionu'u people and his father Teu's younger brother.[15] When Tu asked Bligh to fire his pocket pistol, he did so, and the spectators threw themselves on the ground in abject terror.

Ari'ipaea, Tu's younger brother who had taken Captain Clerke as his *taio* during Cook's last visit, a tall powerful 'black leg' or senior *'arioi*, was Pomare II's naval commander. As a senior *'arioi*, Ari'ipaea was married, but had no living children. While they were rowed back to the ship, he asked Bligh about Britain, and how many ships and guns King George had at his disposal. When Bligh assured him that the King had ships with 100 guns, he could hardly believe it until Bligh drew a sketch of one of these ships on a sheet of paper. When Ari'ipaea saw this sketch he asked incredulously whether this ship was as high as a mountain; and Tu begged Bligh to bring one of these big ships to Tahiti with himself or Tute on board, packed with clothing, hats, spyglasses, hatchets, high-backed chairs, beds, guns, muskets and ammunition. Tu also asked if King George would send him a five-oared cutter with sails; and Bligh told him as soon as he returned to England, he would send him one of these boats. As the representative of King George and the son of Captain Cook, Bligh was treated with the utmost deference by Tu and his family during this visit, and he invited them and their friends to dine with him every day; whereas on board the *Bounty* at sea, since his quarrel with Fryer, Bligh usually dined alone.

# Bligh / Parai

On 31 October 1788 after his meeting with Pomare II, William Bligh decided to set up the shore camp on Point Venus in Matavai Bay – 'the Paradise of the World', as he called it.[1] Shifting the *Bounty* to a new mooring with its guns covering the camp, he ordered his men to erect two tents on the black, sandy point. In a fateful decision, Bligh put Fletcher Christian in charge of the shore camp, with the midshipman Peter Heywood, the gunner William Peckover, the two gardeners David Nelson and William Brown, and a guard of four armed sailors. At sunrise the next morning, Moana and his son Po'e'eno, the high chiefs of the Ha'apape district, who regarded themselves as his friends and allies, came out to the ship; and later that afternoon, Bligh went to visit Tu's father Teu. The old, grey-bearded man seemed afraid at first, but soon gave him a warm welcome.

According to Bligh, all of the men in Tu's family were avid consumers of the chiefly beverage 'ava, taking it four or five times a day. Their attendants chewed 'ava roots which were placed in a coconut shell, mixed with water and squeezed through fibres, and then handed the 'ava to the principal chiefs, who each drank about a pint. After this visit, Tu escorted Bligh to an 'arioi performance, where musicians playing two drums accompanied a young girl who danced for them, twisting her mouth awry (a gesture greatly appreciated by the Tahitians, although the Europeans found it grotesque); wearing a ruff of feathers on her head and a costume made with layers of pleated white bark cloth. Between the dances, two male 'arioi entertained them with a burlesque skit, greeted with hilarious applause.

Early the next morning when Bligh went ashore, Tu, Moana and Po'e'eno marked a boundary around the shore camp. None of the islanders could cross this line without permission; and Moana offered to stand guard over the tents.

'Arioi *dancer with mouth awry.*

After fixing the boundary, the chiefs accompanied Bligh on board the *Bounty* for dinner. The sailors were served fresh pork, breadfruit and coconuts, which gave some of them indigestion; and later one of these men was diagnosed as suffering from 'cholera morbus', an acute form of gastroenteritis with extreme stomach cramps; while another had 'peripneumonia notha', in which the lungs were severely congested. Both disorders were infectious; and in Tahiti, illness was understood as a sign of the anger of the gods. It seems likely that these disorders were spreading, making the Tahitians afraid that 'Oro was angry that the British had returned to the island.

That afternoon, fleets of *'arioi* canoes began to arrive at Matavai Bay from the other districts of Tahiti, and from the islands of Ra'iatea and Huahine for the ceremonies that heralded the Season of Plenty (*Matari'i-i-ni'a*). When the Pleiades (*Matari'i*) sparkled at twilight above the horizon near Orion's Belt,[2] the breadfruit trees began to flower; and the gods and the *'arioi* returned to Tahiti, bringing with them prosperity and pleasure. According to Pomare II in later years, this event began on about 20 November; although the breadfruit trees cropped at different times in different districts, no doubt affecting the timing of the rituals that were performed to ensure an abundant harvest.[3] After dinner, Tu invited Bligh to accompany him to a presentation of gifts to two leading *'arioi* who had arrived from other islands, a ceremony known as *fa'amu'a* or 'feeding', in which large quantities of food and bark cloth were given to visiting black leg *'arioi*.[4]

In preparation for this ceremony, Bligh was invited to sit in a canoe which was dragged along the banks of the Vaipo'opo'o River by eight men, a gesture to honour an *ari'i* or high chief.[5] When he landed, he was taken to a place where a large quantity of breadfruit and some roasted pigs had been delivered in baskets and piled up with bales of bark cloth. About 40 yards away, a leading *'arioi* on the riverbank was being welcomed by one of Tu's men (no doubt his orator), who stood in a canoe, chanting in short bursts. As the crowd parted, a piece of bark cloth about 6 yards long was laid down, and Bligh was instructed to hold one end before placing it carefully on the ground. Accompanied by four men carrying baskets of food and a small sucking pig, the sacred pig of the *'arioi*, Bligh walked to the end of the bark-cloth runner where these offerings were laid at the feet of the visiting black leg *'arioi*, repeating short sentences dictated to him by Tu, 'which as I did not pronounce them very exact, created great mirth, and I retired'.[6] This ceremony was repeated three times, and a fourth time for another black leg *'arioi* who had just arrived from Ra'iatea. A long strip of bark cloth laid on the ground was often used during Tahitian rituals – for instance, during the marriage ceremony when gifts were presented to the young couple, or a woman was taken onto a *marae*, to prevent her feet from touching the sacred pavement. Tu had often asked Bligh about his children in Britain, and knowing that his friend had four girls, he now instructed his *taio* to take three baskets of breadfruit and another sacred pig, walk along another strip of bark cloth laid on the ground, and present these gifts to the first black leg *'arioi* in order to obtain his blessing for each of his children. In these rituals, Bligh was being treated with distinction, and he was deeply gratified.

Since the *Bounty*'s arrival in Matavai Bay there had been sporadic thefts from the boats and the shore camp, which Bligh blamed upon the 'negligence and inattention of the Petty Officers and Men',[7] although Ari'ipaea usually managed to retrieve the stolen items. On 3 November 1788 when the gudgeon from the large cutter was stolen, however, Bligh decided to make an example of Alexander

Smith, the man in charge, ordering him to be punished with a dozen lashes for allowing the theft to occur. Although the chiefs' wives wept and begged for the flogging to stop, Smith was given his full sentence. Smith, nicknamed 'Reckless Jack' by his shipmates, was a brown-haired Cockney, heavily scarred with smallpox, who had deserted his last ship and joined the *Bounty* under an alias (his true name was John Adams);[8] and he would not forget this punishment. Later that afternoon, Bligh instructed the gardeners to make a garden for Tu at Matavai Bay with seeds and plants from the Cape of Good Hope, telling him that King George had sent these good things to his *taio*; and in return Tu promised to provide him with a large quantity of breadfruit and other plants. When Bligh showed him the Great Cabin, which was now being set up as a greenhouse, Tu seemed very pleased, asking again that in exchange for the plants, the King would send him large axes, files, saws, cloth, hats, chairs, bedsteads, guns, ammunition and a large boat with sails on the next British ship that visited the island.

The following day Tu introduced Bligh to another black leg *'arioi*, an elderly chief from Ra'iatea named Ha'amanimani (the brother of Tu's mother Tetupaia, and the inheritor of the Tamatoa title, the most senior in the islands, also known as 'Tutaha' or 'Mauri'). As the guardian of Taputapuatea, the sacred site on Ra'iatea which served as the headquarters of the *'arioi* and the worship of 'Oro, Ha'amanimani was intensely *tapu*, an *ari'i* who was entitled to wear the *maro 'ura* or red feather girdle and to offer human sacrifices to the god, although he had been exiled by the Porapora invaders. He was accompanied by his close relative Hitihiti (the young *'arioi* who had sailed with Cook on board the *Resolution*), who told Bligh that Ma'i and his Māori attendant Te Weherua had both died on Huahine, Ma'i about thirty months after Cook's departure from the Society Islands, although the young Māori boy Koa who had accompanied him from New Zealand was still living. Ma'i's house had accidentally burnt down; and Poiatua of Ra'iatea, Ori's beautiful daughter whose portrait Webber had painted, had also died since Cook's last visit. Hitihiti still remembered some English, and Bligh admired the elegance of his manners.

Later that day the *Bounty*'s barber, who had a hairdresser's dummy, styled its hair, put the head on a stick and adorned it with a kind of dress. When Bligh showed this dummy to his visitors, they cried out in ecstasy '*Vahine no Peretane!*' ('An English lady!'). Half convinced that it was real, they asked Bligh whether this was his wife; and one of the women ran off, bringing back a basket of breadfruit which she offered to this 'English woman'. The chiefs were so delighted with this dummy that some pressed noses with it and kissed it; and they begged Bligh to bring English women with him during his next visit to Tahiti.

Soon afterwards, Tu's people delivered a variety of plants out to the *Bounty*, including a very fine sugar cane that measured six inches in circumference (*to*, or *Saccharum officinarum*); the *'ahi'a* or Malay apple (*Eugenia malaccensis*); the *vi* or native apple (*Spondias dulcis*); the *ti* (a species of *Cordyline*); *'ape* (*Alocasia macrorrhiʒa*), a close relative of the taro; and a particularly fine plantain known as *raia*.

Over the days that followed, Bligh and his men settled down in Matavai Bay. At Bligh's request, Nelson planted a fig tree and two pineapple plants with some melons beside Po'e'eno's house, and some rose seeds, which as he remarked, would delight the Tahitians, who loved the sweet-smelling *tiare* flowers. When the garden that he had planted at Matavai Bay was trampled by the visiting crowds, however, the botanist was furious. Every morning Nelson and William Brown went off to collect suckers and shoots from breadfruit trees, transplanting these into the clay pots from England. The rising of the *Matari'i* (Pleiades) and the opening of the Season of Plenty was approaching, when the gods would return to the island; and it is probable that the Tahitians thought the British were collecting these trees for some kind of fertility ritual. When the pigs that were bartered or presented to them as gifts were butchered and the chunks of pork salted, the sailors were allowed to eat the left-over pieces. The men refilled the water barrels and cut firewood while the carpenters refitted the Great Cabin to accommodate the potted breadfruit plants.

At this time Bligh was becoming immersed in island customs, and developing his ethnographic expertise. He noted that each of the chiefs had many names, adopting perhaps a dozen different ones over a thirty-year period, each commemorating some ancestor or event; and that as soon as a chief's first son was born, his names (in fact his titles) passed to that child. He wrote down the names of Tu's four living children; and as his Tahitian improved, chatted with 'Itia about all kinds of topics. One day when he asked her about how island women gave birth, 'Itia demonstrated by sitting on her heels between an attendant's legs, his arms clasped on the top of her belly and pressing downwards; and when Bligh described the sufferings of English women in childbirth, she laughed heartily, placing herself back in this posture and exclaiming, 'Here, let them do this & not fear and the Child will be safe.'⁹ When she asked Bligh whether English women sometimes had more than one child at a time, and he said that they had two, and sometimes three, 'Itia remarked that when Tahitian women had triplets they usually died, along with the babies. She and Tu explained that their first child (or *mua*) had been killed because they were *'arioi* at the time, but that they had left the *'arioi* society because they wanted to keep their second child alive. Bligh's growing intimacy with Tu and 'Itia consoled him for his difficulties with his men; and while the sailors and their Tahitian helpers gathered breadfruit plants and refitted the ship, he found contentment in the rhythms of chiefly life on the island.

The other leaders on the island, however, were becoming worried about Tu's friendship with Bligh (now known to the Tahitians as 'Teina' or 'Mate', the names by which Tu was known at this time; while Tu was addressed as 'Parai', Bligh's name in Tahitian). By monopolising the influx of iron tools and other new forms of wealth, Tu was regaining his lost *mana*. In their turn, they tried to recruit Captain Bligh as a friend and ally. Pohuetea of Pa'ea, for instance, the great warrior chief who had joined Mahine in the attack on Pare, sent his second wife with a message that he was eager to visit the British; while others came out of curiosity – for instance, 'the man from Lima' (probably the navigator Puhoro), who had visited Peru with Boenechea and still could speak some Spanish. Even Tu's brother Ari'ipaea was jealous of Tu, presenting Bligh with so many rich gifts that finally Tu asked his *taio* not to accept any more of his presents. In addition, when Tu's younger brother Vaetua (a leading warrior who had adopted the midshipman Thomas Hayward as his *taio*) visited the ship, once again so inebriated with *'ava* that he was almost insensible, Tu called him a drunkard and would not talk to him.

On 8 November when Tu brought his *tahu'a* or priest to dinner, the priest explained to Bligh that their 'Great God was called Oro and that they had many others of lesser consequence',[10] prompting a theological discussion. The Tahitians were intensely curious about life in Britain, and when Tu and his companions quizzed him, asking whether he had a god, Bligh assured them that he did; and when they asked whether his god had a son and the name of his wife, he tried to explain that his god had a son but was not married. This amused the Tahitians, who asked about the god's father and mother, and when Bligh tried to explain that his god had no parents and a child but no wife, they 'laughed exceedingly' and asked how the god could have a child without sleeping with a woman. Given their ideas about fertility and the creator god Te Tumu, the idea of a god having a child without sleeping with a woman struck them as ridiculous. Bligh's Tahitian was too limited to explain the intricacies of Christian doctrine, however, and in the end he had to give up his efforts to illuminate these difficult questions.

That afternoon the celebrations that heralded the rising of the Pleiades (*Matari'i*) got under way in Matavai Bay. A crowd of at least 1500 people had gathered in the shade of the breadfruit trees, forming a circle, and before the wrestling matches began, two children and four men danced for about half an hour in this arena. Afterwards Tu produced a long length of bark cloth, giving one end to Bligh and the other to 'Itia to carry. Helped by many others, they presented this gift to the *arioi* dancers; and when the other chiefs brought out their bark cloth, Bligh was invited to make similar ritual presentations, six times in succession. After these presentations, the *arioi* began to run through the crowd, stripping fine bark cloth from the female spectators and dragging along any woman who resisted (one of the privileges enjoyed by the devotees of 'Oro). When the ring re-formed, many wrestlers stepped inside, each one hitting a cupped hand into the inner bend of his opposite elbow, making a loud sound like an axe chopping wood as a challenge to their opponent, and striking so hard that the skin tore and the flesh bruised and bled. These challenges lasted for about half an hour, and when one wrestler finally accepted, touching his fingertips with those of his or her adversary, they closed on each other, seizing the body or hair of their opponent and struggling to toss each other on their backs. 'Itia, herself a famous wrestler, presided over the ring, with Tu staying at a distance. There were a number of strangers present, and Tu and 'Itia kept a close eye on Bligh, and seemed worried whenever he disappeared into the crowd.

During these festivities Bligh was given an arrowroot (*pia*) pudding, watching with fascination as the dish was prepared. The roots were peeled and grated with a coral file, steeped in water and then strained and squeezed through fibres in a wooden trough, where the fluid was allowed to settle. After an old coconut or two was grated, the coconut milk was squeezed into the mixture and the water was quickly poured off, leaving a thick white milky paste into which red-hot stones were dropped. These were rolled for about five minutes in the paste, which was cooled with coconut milk to stop it burning, forming jellied lumps of baked pudding, which Bligh found delicious.[11] He also watched as the breadfruit were baked, the pitted green skin scraped off, the fruit cut in half and wrapped in their own leaves in an earth oven, where they were cooked for about two hours.

In response to their hospitality, on 13 November Bligh invited Tu's family and Hitihiti to dine with him on board the *Bounty*. During this meal, Hitihiti told Bligh that Puni, the paramount chief of Porapora who had conquered Ra'iatea, and whom Cook and Bligh had visited, had died two and a half years earlier. He also told him more about Ma'i, saying that after Captain Cook had left the young Ra'iatean behind at Huahine, Ma'i and others had fought a battle against the combined armies of Ra'iatea and Porapora, winning a great victory with the aid of his muskets, which were fired with a glowing stick. After peace was made, however, Ma'i had died of natural causes, and his Māori attendant Te Weherua died soon after. He explained that Ma'i was not a *teuteu* or servant, but a *manahune* (commoner) or *ra'atira* (freeholder). According to his account, the *teuteu* or servants were the lowest-ranking people on the island. Above them were the *manahune*, the freeholders and commoners, the *ta'ata mauri* or 'esquires', the *ta'ata tu'au* (?) or 'barons' and then the *ari'i* ('lords' or high chiefs); with the *ari'i rahi* ('King', or literally, great high chief) at the pinnacle of Tahitian society.[12] Again, this was intricate ethnographic detail, which Bligh may have collected out of sheer curiosity, or in order to share it with Sir Joseph Banks after the voyage, knowing of his avid interest in Tahitian life and customs.

After dinner that afternoon, Bligh became ill, suffering acute pains (perhaps an attack of the 'cholera morbus'). He was astonished when the chiefs gathered around and Tu and 'Itia sat on either side of him, massaging his arms, legs and body. When they asked him whether this disorder might prove fatal, and he answered that it might, they wept bitterly. Bligh found their concern endearing. As he mused in his journal:

> From this circumstance I may be allowed to conceive every favorable idea of these people, surely they may be supposed to possess every degree of sensitivity and Affection.[13]

Over the days that followed, as Bligh recovered, Tu and his family often dined with him, discussing all kinds of topics. Tu told him, for instance, about an island called Uru-pou (which also appears on the island lists dictated to Captain Cook by the high priest-navigator, Tupaia), assuring him that there were eight-legged *pua* or pigs on this island; and when Bligh told him that this could not possibly be true, Tu took no notice. On another occasion after Tu had left the table, Ari'ipaea and Hitihiti regaled Bligh with a juicy bit of gossip, saying that 'Itia was having an affair with her *teuteu* or servant, a man named Taieri, and that not only did Tu know about it, but he often slept with her in this man's presence. Tu and 'Itia were devoted to each other, however, and they were tender friends to Bligh.

Two days later when Bligh decided that he wanted to look at an English cow that was being kept in the Fa'a'a district, they escorted him to Ta'apuna in the district of Pa'ea, although this was enemy territory. As far as he understood them, they said that Te Pau (the *ari'i* of Fa'a'a) and his people had joined with the Pa'ea people and their allies from Mo'orea to fight against Tu's Pare people and their allies from Matavai Bay; and this animal had been part of their share of the plunder (although probably they were talking about Te Pau's brother, who was hostile to Tu, rather than Te Pau, his close friend and ally).

When they arrived at Ta'apuna, Bligh was carried ashore on a man's shoulders, and as he landed, he was surrounded by a curious crowd, some of whom tried to pick his pockets. Ari'ipaea hurried off to find the cow, returning with the animal, which proved to be a fine brown heifer. When they returned to Pare the sun had already set, and as they passed To'aroa Harbour, Tu and his companions hastened to strip to the waist, explaining that since this harbour belonged to Pomare II, the *ari'i rahi*, it was sacred. That night Tu, Ari'ipaea and Hitihiti drank a great deal of wine, and as Bligh remarked, 'were as fine a Bacchanalian set as I had seen for a long time'.[14] The next morning they all complained bitterly that they were *mate 'ava* or hung over from drinking *'ava Peretane* (or 'British kava', as they called all types of alcohol). Although *'ava*, the chiefly beverage on the island, produced a kind of euphoria, it didn't give them a hangover.

On 20 November when the Pleiades sparkled above the horizon, marking the beginning of the Season of Plenty, Moana and his son Po'e'eno, the chiefs of Matavai Bay, escorted Bligh to Farero'i, their own *marae*. Tu had already left for 'Utu-'ai-mahurau *marae* for the ceremonies to welcome the return of the gods, without inviting Bligh to accompany him on this occasion. *Marae*, the stone temples on the island, served as portals between Te Ao and Te Po (the bright world of people and the dark world of the ancestors), and were dark, fearsome places, shaded by sacred trees. Here the chiefs and priests spoke with their ancestors; and since Bligh was Po'e'eno's bond friend, the gods at Farero'i *marae* were also a part of his lineage. During their visit to this *marae*, Moana and Po'e'eno did their best to explain the various parts of the sacred complex. According to these men, it was only those *marae* with stone walls and pavements that served as 'repositories for the Dead'. On or near the paved forecourt, platforms were erected to carry the offerings of food for the gods. On a *marae* belonging to the *ari'i*, or high chief, there were stone platforms or *turu'i* that were not burial grounds, but places where the priests or *tahu'a* stood during the rituals. Only those killed in battle were buried on *marae*, while those who had died a natural death were placed on funerary biers or *tupapa'u*, whose size and decorations reflected the rank of the dead person. Each *marae* had its own *tahu'a* or priest, who spoke with the gods. These chiefs added that when the corpse of an *ari'i rahi* was embalmed, after extracting the viscera the body was massaged with scented oil; and although the bodies of commoners remained on display for about a month, the bodies of high chiefs might be kept for several years.[15] In times of war, a man was placed in charge of the embalmed body and carried it off into the mountains, so that the enemy could not seize it.[16] During this mourning period, the body of the *ari'i rahi* was carried in state to each of the *marae* upon which he could claim an upright stone with its associated title, so that the people and spirits of that *marae* could farewell him.[17] Again, this information was much more detailed and insightful than any previous account of Tahitian *marae* and funerary customs.

Ever since his visit to the Fa'a'a district, Bligh had been eager to obtain the English heifer that Te Pau (the high chief of the district) had in his possession, although this *ari'i* had been absent when Bligh visited. When Bligh sent a messenger offering rich gifts in exchange for the beast, Te Pau accepted with alacrity; and on 21 November he arrived in Matavai Bay with the animal and its owner, a young man who was given a hatchet, a file, a rasp, a gimlet, a knife, a spike nail and a shirt for the heifer. It must have been during this visit that Te Pau's younger brother and heir took the young midshipman Peter Heywood as his bond friend. These exchanges evidently worried Tu, who feared that Bligh might also forge an alliance with Te Pau; because later that afternoon he invited Bligh to a special *heiva*, asking him to bring the portrait of Captain Cook from the *Bounty*.

In an innovative move, Tu had decided to place Captain Bligh and Captain Cook at the heart of this ceremony. Like other sacred objects belonging to the Pomare dynasty, including the skulls of their ancestors, Cook's portrait had been hidden during the recent fighting, and Tu had managed to preserve it from his enemies.[18] Since this portrait was regarded not only as an image of Cook, but as his living presence, it was intensely sacred. When Bligh arrived ashore from the *Bounty* with the portrait, accompanied by some of his men, the crowd formed themselves into a large ring, with armed sailors standing inside the circle to keep back the spectators. As Bligh sat at the head of this arena beside Webber's portrait of Captain Cook, his mentor and 'father', accompanied by Tu, 'Itia and several other leading women, and faced by twelve *arioi* arranged in four rows of three sitting on their heels, headed by two women, the black leg *arioi* of Ha'apape stood behind these men, uttering the chant for his district:

> My mountain above is Orohena, the highest on Tahiti
> My courtyard below is Fa'aria
> My point outside is Fauroa [on the east side of Point Venus]
> My river is Faiai
> My *arioi* house is Te Atita
> It is I, the head *arioi* Teaau,

Confused by the cannon balls that whistle through our skies [referring to Wallis's attack on the Tahitian fleet].[19]

When the portrait of Captain Cook was held up beside Bligh, the priest declaimed:

Hail, all hail Cook,
Chief of Air, Earth and Water,
We acknowledge you Chief from the beach to the Mountains,
Over Men, Trees & Cattle
Over the Birds of the Air and Fishes of the Sea![20]

After this oration another priest wrapped the portrait in a short length of white bark cloth, while a larger piece was wrapped around Bligh, intensifying his *mana*.

While another speech was being delivered, a one-eyed old priest rushed up and placed a piece of plaited coconut leaf at Bligh's feet, and others in front of Tu and Captain Cook's portrait. These plaited coconut leaves, used in a number of ceremonies, were twisted into patterns that carried messages to the gods.[21] After this presentation, the male *'arioi* sitting in front of Bligh and Tu stood up and performed the *heiva*, throwing their arms and legs in violent gestures, holding up one leg to expose their genitals and 'giving themselves the most lascivious and wanton motions'.[22] Next, the female *'arioi* advanced with their garments held up, and performing 'the same Wanton gestures' in the *'upa* dance, exposed themselves to Tu and his *taio*.

In this remarkable ceremony, the combined *mana* of Tu, Captain Cook and Captain Bligh was being used to summon the presence of 'Oro, the god of fertility and life. Just as Tu and Captain Cook had stood shoulder to shoulder in rituals during Captain Cook's last visit to the island, invoking the god, now Tu, Cook's portrait and his 'son' William Bligh stood side by side for the same purpose. In their dancing, the male *'arioi* invoked Tetumu, while the women sought to excite him. When the Season of Plenty was imminent, 'Oro's acolytes, the *'arioi*, danced, inciting him to unleash his potency and bring fertility and prosperity to the island.

Stunned by this graphic display, Bligh took his cue from Tu, who reacted with dignified pleasure. 'Itia and the other chiefly women were also thrilled by this performance, proudly asking Bligh whether they had this kind of *heiva* in England.[23] As Bligh insisted, however, 'no people, unless in these dances, are more cautious and guard their persons with greater decency'.[24] Contrary to European understandings, which likened these sexually explicit dances to the bacchanals seen in brothels or below decks in port, these were sacred performances, similar in intent to ceremonies in cathedrals, for instance. Although the significance of such displays had eluded previous European visitors to the island, Bligh was beginning to glimpse their meaning; and while other Europeans (except for William Monkhouse, the *Endeavour*'s surgeon; Máximo Rodríguez; and Lieutenant Williamson) had been excluded from these performances, during this visit to the island the *'arioi* invited William Bligh to a series of such rituals.

On this occasion, Tu was taking no chances. In order to ensure that the gods would return to the island for the Season of Plenty, he supported his son in playing his role on 'Utu-'ai-mahurau *marae* as the paramount chief (*ari'i maro 'ura*) of Tahiti. At the same time, on this occasion he appealed to the power of the gods of the British, using the portrait of Captain Cook, the most impressive of the European commanders, and Captain Bligh, Cook's 'son' and successor, to summon their ancestors. William Bligh was being treated with extreme veneration as a high chief and, after all his trials, as Captain Cook had also found, this was a gratifying experience.

During the next day, Bligh ordered the *Bounty*'s figurehead, an image of a woman dressed in riding costume, to be painted in bright colours. No doubt the Tahitians understood this as a tribute to the fertility ritual. Like the portrait of Cook, the figurehead was taken to be a living object, possessed by the spirit of the individual portrayed; and the Tahitians were delighted, exclaiming '*Maita'i vahine no Peretane!*' ('What a fine woman from Britain!'). He also decided to set up his observatory at this time, and Tu ordered his men to carry a house to Matavai Bay for the purpose. When Bligh began his lunar observations that evening, it seemed to confirm his interest in the Matahiti (First Fruits) ceremonies, whose timing was signalled by the stars. On 24 November a cooked turtle – the food of high chiefs, and a symbol of 'Oro – was brought on board the *Bounty*, where Tu, his family and a large group of chiefs dined with Bligh before attending the climax of the Matahiti rituals. Tu's mother Tetupaia was about to return to Matavai Bay from Teti'aroa, the atoll belonging to Tu's family where she had been staying. Tu did not intend to take Bligh to this sacred ritual, but instead asked his *taio* to take care of his mother.

When Tetupaia arrived at Pare that afternoon with two elderly female attendants, Bligh sent his boat ashore to collect them. Tu's mother, a very corpulent, stately aristocrat from Ra'iatea in her late fifties, with very fine teeth, was a dignified, warm-hearted person. When they returned to the ship, it was a struggle to get her on deck; although when she finally arrived on board the *Bounty*, Tetupaia greeted Bligh like a long-lost son, saluting him with floods of tears. When she asked him about Captain Cook, Bligh assured her that if he had not died in the meantime, Cook would return to Tahiti in ten months' time. Tetupaia was delighted by this assurance, since the crew of the *Lady Penrhyn* had told her that Captain Cook had been killed in Hawai'i. After her attendants wrapped Bligh in three lengths of bark cloth, she presented him with a large pig, breadfruit, coconuts and plantains; and when she went below, Tetupaia was accompanied by her attendants and a favourite cat, bred from one that Cook had given her. During this meeting she told Bligh about the troubles which had dogged her family since Cook's departure, saying that the people of Mo'orea, Pa'ea and Tai'arapu had joined forces and attacked them, forcing them to fly to the mountains and taking their cattle and everything else that Cook had given them. Since the British ships had always anchored at Matavai Bay, however, the people of Pare and Matavai regarded them as their best friends. As she put it, '[Y]ou have many sincere friends here whose love and regard for you is not from the tongue but from the heart.'[25]

Moved by Tetupaia's affectionate assurances, when Ti'itorea, the regent of southern Tahiti, no doubt taking advantage of Tu's absence, arrived with gifts soon afterwards, Bligh took her advice and ignored this old enemy of the Pomare lineage. Moana and his son Po'e'eno, the *ari'i* of the Ha'apape district and his old friends, were also on board, and they told Bligh that Tu and his brother Ari'ipaea were on bad terms, and would fight each other as soon as he sailed, because their wives had had a serious disagreement. When Tu's mother left the ship the following morning, Bligh presented her with gifts to seal their friendship, although she asked him to keep them for her on board the *Bounty* so that they would not be stolen.

By the last days of November, Bligh already had a full cargo of breadfruit plants in pots at the shore camp. In this part of the Pacific, however, where the hurricane season runs from November to April, bad weather was approaching. Bligh had been ordered to explore the straits between Australia and New Guinea during his return voyage to England; and if he set sail at this time, he would be forced to battle westerly winds all the way across the Pacific, with the prospect of being caught in a series of terrible storms. He had to wait, and as the winds rose, the weather became rough and waves crashed on the reef at Matavai Bay; and during one of these gales, Bligh watched the islanders surfing on their paddles. Placing the blades under their bellies, they held the handles with outstretched hands, and catching a wave, raced ashore at breakneck speed.

At about this time, Bligh noted in his journal that many of the islanders had ulcerated arms and legs, some having lost their toes and fingers. Although the surgeon Thomas Huggan was convinced that these were the symptoms of venereal diseases, Bligh doubted this explanation. He was right, for in many cases these symptoms must have been caused by yaws, a related (but not sexually transmitted) disease that was endemic in the Society Islands. Tu's younger sister Auo was one of the sufferers; and when the surgeon's mate dressed the sores, the symptoms were greatly relieved, to her intense gratitude. Bligh was intrigued when a blind boy and an albino man also visited the shore camp. On 30 November when Tu returned from the Matahiti rituals, he asked Bligh to have a large locked chest made for him in which he could store his gifts, saying that otherwise they would be stolen.

On 1 December 1788, 'by the remissness of my Officers & People at the Tent', a boat's rudder was stolen – another demonstration of Hiro's (the trickster god's) power. When they heard about the theft, Tu, Teu, Tetupaia and their family were afraid and stayed away from the shore camp. 'Itia came to see him, however, and asked Bligh whether he was angry. When he assured her that he was only angry with the thief, who would be severely punished, 'Itia promised him that Tu's people would catch the culprit. Bligh was inclined to blame the theft on visitors from Huahine and Ra'iatea who had arrived for the Matahiti rituals, rather than Tu and his followers, who up until that time had protected his possessions. Afterwards, when Tu dined on board the *Bounty*, Bligh promised to help him build a house with a door and a lock, in which he could keep his new possessions. On this occasion Tu was accompanied by Moana and his son Po'e'eno, and his younger brothers Ari'ipaea and Vaetua. Vaetua had given up drinking 'ava and now seemed a fine active young man, handsome and elegantly dressed. As Bligh noted, he was reputed to be a great warrior, having killed Mahine, the paramount chief of Mo'orea, during the attack on Pare. When Ari'ipaea assured Bligh that one of Tu's own people had stolen the rudder, given Tu and 'Iti'a's sheepish demeanour, he was inclined to believe him.

Over the next few days, each evening at about an hour before sunset the 'arioi gathered on the beach, celebrating the imminent return of the gods. The men staged wrestling matches, grabbing the hair, leg or any other part of their opponent to try to throw him onto his back, and laughing heartily if they were tossed; while the women danced in teams, chanting, stamping their feet and clapping their hands 'with many wanton odd motions'. One woman would put a breadfruit on her foot and flick it to the other team, and if they dropped the fruit her team danced, exposing their genitals in derision to their rivals. Other people played flutes and danced to soft drumming, while men and boys competed to throw light lances at a stump at about 30 yards' distance.

Although these were ancestral amusements, life on the island was rapidly changing. Whereas Polynesian rats had formerly swarmed around the houses, now hardly any of these little fruit-eating animals were seen, which Bligh attributed to the introduction of European cats. Bligh also remarked that the Tahitians had become skilled with iron axes, preferring these for woodwork over their traditional stone adzes; and that as soon as they had a sufficient supply of iron knives and drills, they gave up using bamboo knives and stone drills. They disliked using saws, but prized needles and scissors and loved wearing odd bits of European clothing.

In addition, despite Bligh's hope that the Tahitians might have discovered a cure for venereal disease, these illnesses (including syphilis) were now prevalent on the island. During this visit to Tahiti, according to the muster roll, more than a third of the *Bounty*'s crew received treatment for venereal infections. These men included the acting lieutenant Fletcher Christian; one of the midshipmen, Peter Heywood; William Cole, the boatswain; William Purcell, the carpenter; Lawrence Lebogue, the sailmaker; John Norton, the quartermaster; William Brown, the assistant gardener; and twelve of the able-bodied sailors (Quintal, Heildbrandt, Hall, Skinner, Alexander Smith, John Smith, Burkett, Millward, Muspratt, Valentine, Lamb and Byrne, the fiddler). Since syphilis, for instance, can be latent for long periods, with no visible symptoms, it was often not diagnosed during the eighteenth century; and it is possible that other members of the crew (or indeed some of these men) were already infected with this malady when they arrived at Tahiti; while the rest contracted this or other venereal infections during their time on the island.[26]

Now that the islanders had adopted iron tools, they were eager to keep them sharp; and on 5 December, Hitihiti brought a large stone, asking to have it cut as a grindstone. Although Bligh agreed, the carpenter William Purcell (one of the men with a venereal disease) refused to do this, remarking unpleasantly, 'I will not cut the stone for it will spoil my Chisel, and there is [no] law to take away my Tools.'[27] Incensed by this return of Purcell's earlier 'mutinous' behaviour, Bligh ordered the carpenter to be locked up in his cabin. Purcell's defiance proved infectious, however, and later that afternoon one of the sailors, Matthew Thompson, was punished with twelve lashes for 'insolence and disobedience of orders'.[28]

This was the first time in weeks that Bligh had mentioned any of his crew in his journal, and his tone was one of violent irritation. Although he could be verbally abusive, however, Bligh rarely flogged his men. In fact, and in sharp contrast with his later reputation, he flogged the sailors less often than almost any other British commander in the Pacific during this period – for instance, only 10 per cent of the crew on board the *Bounty* were flogged, compared with 25 per cent on Captain Cook's *Resolution*.[29] Bligh's account gives the clear impression that during this time on the island, he largely gave up the effort to discipline his men, leaving them to their own devices unless they directly challenged his authority, and spending most of his time with Tu and his family.

For most of the year, Matavai Bay was well sheltered from the prevailing south-east winds, but during November, December and January, strong westerlies blew directly into the harbour. This was *te tau miti rahi*, the season of high seas, when the Tahitians used the westerly winds to sail back home from Tonga and Samoa,[30] and people from Huahine, Ra'iatea and the other Leeward Society Islands used the same winds to sail to Tahiti.[31] On 6 December when a violent storm blew up, huge waves rolled over the Dolphin Bank, crashing over the *Bounty*. Releasing Purcell, Bligh ordered the carpenter to batten down the hatches, and as the sea hurtled over Point Venus, drenching the sailors, the ship lurched and rolled. As he remarked: 'In this state we remained the whole Night with all hands up in the midst of torrents of Rain, the Ship sending and rolling in a most tremendous manner, and the Sea foaming all round us so as to threaten instant destruction.'[32] At daybreak as Bligh ordered the yards and topmasts to be struck, he saw that the shore camp was now marooned on a small island surrounded by water, with the Tuauru River raging right around it.

Later that morning when Tu, 'Itia and Moana braved the storm and came out to the *Bounty*, paddling their canoe through the boiling surf, they embraced Bligh, weeping and saying that they had offered many prayers to the *atua* (god) for his safety. Although the old man Moana, convinced that the ship would be wrecked, wept inconsolably, saying that the *pahi rahi* (great canoe) would soon be on the shore, Tu and 'Itia were quickly reassured, asking Bligh if he was hungry and giving him coconuts and breadfruit for breakfast. When they warned him that the stormy season was approaching, he had taken no notice, and now he was desperate to shift his ship into a safer harbour. That afternoon the friends of the crew came out in their canoes or swam through the surf to the *Bounty*, bringing bunches of coconuts and other fruit for their *taio*.

On 7 December 'Itia came out to the *Bounty* in a double canoe, bringing a large pig and fruit and refusing to accept any return gifts, insisting that this presentation was purely for friendship. When Bligh's *taio* Po'e'eno and his wife came on board soon afterwards, his wife slashed her scalp with a shark's tooth, bleeding profusely, a sign of her distress at their predicament. Asking Bligh whether he was anxious about the safety of his ship, Po'e'eno offered to give him a home in his district if the *Bounty* was wrecked, assuring him, 'You shall live with me if the Ship is lost, and we will cut down Trees to build another to carry you to Pretanee.'[33]

Early the next morning the winds had died, and when Bligh came ashore, bringing two men with him to saw planks for the chest he was making for Tu, Tetupaia and several other women greeted him joyfully, congratulating him on his escape from the tempest. Tu, Po'e'eno and his father Moana joined them, escorting Bligh to a house where women were dyeing bark cloth scarlet, yellow, black and brown, or mending it by pasting patches onto it and beating these into place as the children played happily around them. During this visit, Bligh collected the Tahitian words for the different colours, and remarked that the local bark cloth and fine mats had improved immeasurably since his last visit to the island, which he attributed to their close examination of the bark cloth and mats that Cook's people had brought to Tahiti from Tonga.

The next day while the sailors were hauling the launch ashore, watched by a curious crowd, a boy slipped and fell under the rollers, and was crushed, although none of his limbs were broken. When Bligh sent for the surgeon, he was told that Huggan was dead drunk, and later that evening when the surgeon's assistant asked whether Huggan could be carried up on deck because he was finding it difficult to breathe, Bligh, still furious, delayed sending for the master. By the time Fryer arrived, the surgeon had collapsed, and died shortly afterwards. When the master reported this to Bligh, he railed against his surgeon, saying that he had become 'so filthy in his person that he was latterly a nuisance'; and had killed himself with drink and indolence.

When they heard the news the next morning, according to Bligh, the chiefs expressed similar sentiments, remarking that Huggan (or 'Teronu' as they called him) had died from 'not working and drinking too much Ava no Pretanee [British *kava*]'.[34] Bligh asked Tu's permission for Huggan to be buried ashore, and the paramount chief agreed, although he told Bligh that he should also seek his father's permission. After returning from this errand, Bligh discovered that two of Tu's men had already started digging the grave, a custom first introduced to the island with the burial of Boenechea, the Spanish commander. Tu asked him anxiously whether they were doing this properly, pointing out that the grave was aligned east and west to the rising and setting of the sun, which he evidently considered to be a European custom. Later that afternoon, Huggan's funeral was held on shore with all of the chiefs in attendance; and at dinner the next day they refused to drink wine, saying that this was the drink that had killed Teronu. Tu and his family also told Bligh not to be angry with his own men for the accident with the young boy, blaming their own people and saying that 'they were always crouding round us & that they therefore deserved anything that befell them'.[35]

On 12 December the chiefs, who were always intensely curious about British customs, asked Bligh what he intended to do about the surgeon's cabin. At first he did not understand them, but eventually they managed to explain that in Tahiti, when a man died and was carried to the funerary bier or *tupapa'u*, his body was surrounded by ancestral spirits at night, and that if anyone went by himself to the place where the man had perished, these spirits would devour him. When Bligh asked them about the *'arioi* in his turn, they explained that the most senior *'arioi* (whom they termed the *'arioi rahi*)[36] never married. When a male or female *'arioi* married and had a child, the baby was killed at birth, and they lost some of their *mana*; but if they kept the child alive, although they kept the title of *'arioi* they lost all of their privileges, and were known as *'arioi fanaunau*. If the baby remained alive, their sacred qualities passed to the child, and the parents became relatively *noa* (common or profane). As chiefly priests later told the missionary John Orsmond:

> Players who became parents [were] a distinct class of *'arioi*. They were dis-
> enfranchised. They entered no more into the company of black legs, but
> associated with those other *'arioi* who had become parents. He had been in the
> high rank but was now defamed. His red loin girdle was taken away, [and] the
> sacred pig. He went no more on the high scaffold from which was pronounced
> the names of those to whom the sacred hog and loin girdle [belonged]. On
> being told to go no more up, he wept, the [mucus] streamed from his nose, he
> fell behind, ashamed, washed off his scented oil and red dye and went to dwell
> with players of old who had also been put out for having families.[37]

That afternoon, Huggan's effects were auctioned among his shipmates, with Tu and Moana watching curiously. Afterwards, Tu asked Bligh how canoe builders, for example, were rewarded for their work in England – with pigs, clothes or coconuts? Showing him a coin, Bligh explained that everyone in Britain was paid for their labour with money, which they used to buy things. Entranced by this novel idea, Tu said that in that case he would take this coin and buy a shirt from Peckover, the gunner.

Later that day Bligh had the pleasure of discharging the boy who had been crushed by the ship's boat from the *Bounty*'s sickbay, since he had fully recovered. Afterwards, Tu asked whether he and his family could attend divine service, and because the next day was a Sunday, Bligh invited him and his relatives to join his crew on board the *Bounty*. Generally the chiefs behaved well during the service, although when some of the women giggled at the ritual responses and Bligh scolded them, they were shocked, because in Tahiti, people talked and laughed freely during rituals on the *marae*.

On 15 December early in the morning, Tu came out to the *Resolution* to invite Bligh ashore for a special *heiva*, or entertainment. When he landed, he found the chiefs and a large crowd gathered on the beach for a *heiva parae* (*parae* ritual). Eleven men, each dressed in a *parae* or 'Chief Mourner's costume', as it is sometimes called – in fact, the ritual costume of a senior *'arioi*[38] – holding pearl-shell clappers in their hands, were arranged in three rows in front of him, squatting on their heels. These were the 'black leg' *'arioi* (or *avae parae*), the leaders of the *'arioi* lodges. They were a remarkable sight, with each man's face hidden behind a *parae* – a mask made of four polished discs of pearl shell, three black discs evoking Te Po, the dark world of the ancestors, and a white disc invoking Te Ao, the bright world of people. Below the mask hung a curved wooden board, decorated with pearl shells – the moon goddess – and a shimmering array of little rectangles of pearl shell, stitched together in rows to represent the Pleiades, the eyes of chiefs turned into stars. Dressed in these costumes, each of the black leg *'arioi* embodied the Tahitian cosmos.

As a priest recited a long chant, a man ran towards Bligh, sometimes stopping abruptly and performing peculiar movements before placing two sacred twisted coconut plaits at his feet. As he did this, Bligh was wrapped in bark cloth and the chief *'arioi* stood up and performed a few steps in unison, clacking their pearl shells together. After the priest chanted again, the man who had placed the plaited coconut leaves at Bligh's feet picked up one of these emblems and carried it to the priest. As a man standing in front of the performers spoke a few words, they all leaned in unison to one side with their arms outstretched towards the ground; and when he spoke a few more words, they repeated the same gesture in the opposite direction. Finally, they all sprang up, clacking their pearl shells in unison and ending the ritual.

Tu explained to Bligh that this ceremony recognised him as an *ari'i* of Matavai Bay, since the insignia of twisted coconut plait was a token given only to principal chiefs. Drawing as it did upon the collective *mana* of the *'arioi* lodges, this was a potent ritual. Bligh was delighted, thinking that Matavai Bay had been presented to him, but in fact this was an honorific gesture, often made as a compliment to a distinguished visitor. In any case, he was the *taio* of Po'e'eno, the son of the high chief of Matavai Bay, a relationship that already gave him rights in that district.[39] In return, Bligh presented each of the performers with an adze and a nail, and invited the chiefs to dine with him on board the *Bounty*.

While Bligh was being showered with honours by the Tahitians, his relationship with his men continued to sour. At about this time, the supply of pigs began to dwindle; and according to James Morrison, Bligh began to play his 'purser's tricks' again, claiming all of the pigs, dead or alive, that were brought out to the *Bounty*, including those belonging to the master, John Fryer. When Bligh served out the pork as rations at the rate of one pound a day for each man, although he had more than forty pigs of his own on board for this purpose, Fryer protested. According to Morrison, Bligh retorted 'he would convince him that evry thing was *his*, as soon as it was on board, and that He would take nine tenths of any mans property and let him see who dared to say anything to the contrary'.[40] When the Tahitians heard about this, they tried to bring their pigs on board in Bligh's absence; and when he ordered the mate of the watch to keep a register of every pig that was brought on board the ship, they cut up the pork and hid it under breadfruit in baskets which they gave to their *taio*, a ruse which according to Morrison, Bligh never suspected. In Bligh's defence, however, the rules that he had nailed to the *Bounty*'s mast strictly forbade the men from trading for food on their account, and making private transactions with the local people.

Eager to escape his disgruntled crew, on 17 December Bligh accompanied Moana and David Nelson on an excursion up the Tuauru Valley. The scenery was glorious, with shady groves of breadfruit and coconut trees on the plains, and higher up the valley, small gardens of taro, bark cloth and 'ava plants. The bark-cloth plants were grown on banks ditched around and protected by stone fences, and carefully weeded; while the taro were in irrigated gardens and the yams on high plateaus that had been cleared by fire.[41] The yams were large, sometimes 6 feet long, but because it took so much effort to dig them up, Bligh was told that they were only used when breadfruit were scarce.

Near the head of the valley, they came to a *marae* where about fifteen men sat on their heels, listening to a priest chanting to herald the Season of Plenty, while others cooked a pig and some breadfruit. Each of these men had several small plaits of coconut leaf at his feet, very like those that had been presented to Bligh during the *parae* ceremony; and a plaited band of coconut leaf around his wrist. When the priest chanted again, these men responded, and picking up their plaited coconut leaves, placed them at the foot of a pole which stood before them, covered with a plaited coconut branch. Afterwards, they explained to Bligh that the god would eat their offerings of plantains and coconuts and be grateful. The summer solstice on 21 December was approaching, and they were preparing for the *Para'a Matahiti* ceremonies that would follow, when the first fruits of the breadfruit would be harvested and the gods would return to the island.

Although these men invited Bligh and his companions to breakfast, Bligh was eager to carry on with his journey. Climbing higher up the valley until it narrowed, they came to a stupendous waterfall, cascading over a perpendicular cliff 200 feet high, formed of square pillars of stone. His companions told him that this cascade, with its deep bathing pool at the base, was called Pi'aroa; and when they walked back down the river, they were entertained by a Tahitian friend of David Nelson's who welcomed them to his house, showing them two fine shaddock trees that Nelson had planted during Captain Cook's 1777 visit. Further downstream, the people were driving fish into bag nets, catching fish of all sizes.[42] On each of the two days after this expedition, Bligh was entertained by a *heiva* performed by *'arioi* dancers; and in the interval some male performers gave an hilarious burlesque of the British rowing their boats, with the officer bawling out the sailors every time that something went wrong.

During this interlude in Matavai Bay, Bligh enjoyed an unparalleled exposure to *'arioi* rituals and amusements. As a curious inquirer into Tahitian customs, he was following in the footsteps of Joseph Banks, James Cook and Máximo Rodríguez. Although Joseph Banks has sometimes been called the father of Pacific ethnography, William Bligh's accounts of life in Tahiti are more detailed and astute than anything Banks was able to accomplish – no doubt because of his repeated visits to the island. As his understanding of the language became more fluent and subtle, his reports grew more accurate and insightful. Since Bligh was able to converse quite freely with the Tahitians, he shared more experiences with them; and because Po'e'eno and his father Moana, and Tu and his wife 'Itia, were his bond friends, they were obliged to answer his questions and share their knowledge (even sacred information) with him.

On 19 December the weather turned nasty again, with a long swell breaking over the Dolphin Bank; and the flying spray threatened to damage the bread-fruit plants at the shore camp. Although Bligh thought about taking the *Bounty* to Mo'orea, where he could anchor in one of the deep, safe harbours on the north coast of that island, when he told Tu about this plan, his friend became extremely agitated, begging him to remain in Matavai Bay for at least another month. Although Bligh invited his *taio* to go with him to Mo'orea, Tu replied that this was impossible, because the Mo'orea warriors would kill him. When 'Itia went ashore that evening to look after her smallest child, Bligh asked her to bring back any iron tools that needed sharpening or mending; and ordered the carpenters to finish Tu's chest, a large box 7 feet long by 3 feet wide with a kind of 'barrow' beneath it (like a *fare atua* or god-house, in which the bound gods were kept in seclusion) which could be placed on his sailing canoe, and was big enough for him to sleep on. Bligh also had a carved wooden board with the date of Huggan's death erected at the foot of the surgeon's grave, and the grave covered with stones.

When he went ashore at Matavai Bay on 20 December, the day before the summer solstice, Bligh found Tu, Tetupaia, Moana and their families lamenting his intended departure. They assured him that the Mo'orea warriors were his ene- mies, and would kill him in revenge for Cook's rampage across their island. After listening to their warnings, Bligh sent Fryer in the launch to Pare to check the depth of the water inside the lagoon between One Tree Hill and the easternmost harbour there, just west of Taraho'i *marae*. When Fryer returned to report that there was a safe passage, Bligh decided at the last minute not to go to Mo'orea, but to take the *Bounty* instead to To'aroa Harbour. This sheltered bay, which Fryer had explored and sounded, was protected by reefs and surrounded by a fertile countryside; and as Bligh remarked: 'Great joy is among the People here on this Account altho they cannot help complaining at my leaving Matavai.'[43]

# 9

# Mr Bligh's Bad Luck

On 24 December 1788, the sailors loaded 774 breadfruit plants into the *Bounty*'s Great Cabin, and packed up the tents of the shore camp. Although they had completed the task for which they had been sent to Tahiti, the hurricane season had arrived, making it too dangerous to leave the island. Once again, the Admiralty's delay in sending Bligh his orders was putting the voyage at risk. The launch was loaded with spars, and when Christmas Day dawned dark and cloudy, Bligh sent the boat ahead with orders to meet the ship at the entrance to the harbour. The *Bounty*'s anchors were raised and they sailed outside the reef to the mouth of To'aroa Harbour, where they found the launch partly blocking the narrow passage.

As the *Bounty* sailed in to the bay, Bligh had to steer around the launch, and in the overcast conditions, it was difficult for the lookout, the master John Fryer, to see the underwater outcrops in the lagoon. While the anchors were being lowered, the ship grounded on the coral. Bligh was furious, ordering the boats to take a couple of anchors ahead so that the sailors could haul the ship off the rocks. They did this by hand, tangling two anchors and cables in the process. Concerned for the safety of his ship, Bligh was angry that Tu and his family had witnessed this inept performance: 'I had the Company of all the Royal Family on board and they were exceedingly distressed at the Accident.'[1]

Later that afternoon, Bligh's men managed to retrieve the anchors. When they landed at Pare the next morning, Tu presented Bligh with a large house for the use of his people. A huge crowd had gathered, and Tu invited Bligh to attend a ceremony of thanksgiving (or *otai*) for his safe arrival. During this ritual Bligh was seated next to Moana, the high chief of Matavai Bay, his 'father' and until now his host, on a carved wooden stool (the prerogative of a senior *'arioi*), while Tu and around twenty men sat opposite about 30 yards away. As a priest standing behind Tu prayed to 'Oro, his companions answering at regular intervals, a man carrying a small pig and a plantain branch laid these at Bligh's feet, saying that this was an offering for the god of Peretane (Britain). Afterwards, another small pig and a plantain branch were presented to King George, and then another small pig and a plantain branch to Bligh. When these presentations were over, Tu told him that an offering had already been made to 'Oro in thanksgiving for the *Bounty*'s safe arrival, presumably at Taraho'i *marae*. At the end of the ceremony, Moana stood and spoke on Bligh's behalf, thanking the Pare people as his friends and warning them not to steal from the British:

> Bring your Pigs, your Cocoanutts and Breadfruit, and you will have Toeys [*to'i* or adzes], knives and Nails in return, they take nothing from you without your Consent, and then give many good things for whatever it is. Every Man therefore is to quit this place at Night, for if you come here when it is dark you will be killed.[2]

After these exchanges, those Tahitians who had *taio* on board the ship went out in their canoes with pigs, dogs and cats as gifts for their friends, and a similar ceremony was performed on board the *Bounty*.

In his journal, Bligh explained that while Tu was his *taio* or bond friend, Moana, the *ari'i* of Matavai Bay, was his *ari'i*, his champion and protector, and that Po'e'eno, Moana's son, was also his *taio*. When he was in Matavai Bay, therefore, Bligh had been addressed as 'Po'e'eno', while in the Pare-'Arue district he was addressed as 'Teina' or 'Mate', suggesting that *taio* relationships could be restricted to particular districts on the island. Bligh added that when Captain Cook had last visited Matavai Bay, Tu had been his *taio* or bond friend while Moana's son Po'e'eno was his *ari'i* or 'champion' (in fact, 'high chief'), which explains why, since that time, Po'e'eno had been the guardian of Cook's portrait. Po'e'eno and his father Moana, the *ari'i* of the Ha'apape district and Matavai Bay where the British ships traditionally anchored, had befriended Bligh during his previous visit to the island with Captain Cook, and they had a measure of independence from Pare-'Arue; although Tu himself and his son Pomare II played the main ceremonial roles on the island. Thus while the *Bounty* (and Cook's ships) were anchored at Matavai Bay, Moana and Po'e'eno were their guardians and protectors, except on ceremonial occasions, when Tu and Pomare II took over. Now that the *Bounty* had left Matavai Bay, however, and was anchored in Pare, Tu's family held the *mana* over Bligh and his vessel. These fascinating insights, recorded in Bligh's journal, are more subtle and complex than any of Cook's or the Forsters' understandings of life on the island.

At noon Bligh invited the chiefs to dine on board the *Bounty*, and later that afternoon he ordered William Muspratt, the cook's assistant, to be flogged for 'neglect of duty'. His men had worked hard, moving the ship, retrieving the anchors and cables and unloading the breadfruit plants, and Bligh was relieved to have arrived in this large, sheltered harbour:

> The Plants are much better situated than at Point Venus; being shaded with the Trees they want no covering untill near Mid-day, and we find very happy dews, a circumstance much to their advantage, which at Matavai they never had the benefit of.
>
> This is a delightful situation in every respect. I lye perfectly sheltered by the Reefs, with smooth Water and close to a fine Beach without the least surf on it, and I have therefore directed the Ship to be laid up and everything put below for the remainder of the time I stay in this Country.[3]

On 28 December, after dividing the crew into two divisions and firing the great guns and muskets to impress the Tahitians, Bligh ordered the men to be served a double ration of grog as a belated Christmas Day celebration. The sailors had a marvellous time, taking their extra rations and grog ashore to share with their girlfriends, while Bligh invited Tu and the other chiefs to join him for dinner on board the *Bounty*. After this festivity when Bligh ordered the men to go on to a half ration of rum, they did not complain. While they were at Tahiti they drank their rum with coconut milk, making a delicious cocktail (which is drunk in the islands to this day).

The next day when Bligh sent one of the sailors to dive down to inspect the *Bounty*'s hull to see whether it had been harmed by the collision with the reef, he reported that only a small piece of the copper sheathing near the bow had been damaged. After their hapless display off Pare, however, Bligh was eager to reassert his authority; and when the butcher Robert Lamb (his former crew member from the *Britannia*, and another sufferer from venereal disease) allowed his cleaver to be stolen, he had him flogged, assuring Tu and the other chiefs that he would likewise flog any of their people who were caught stealing from the ship or the shore camp. Captain Cook had always stringently forbidden any man who had a venereal disease to sleep with island women, on pain of a flogging (a rule that the sailors bitterly resented), and it is possible that Bligh was following Cook's example, using the loss of a cleaver as a pretext.

Breadfruit and the fine plantain known as *raia* were scarce at this time, although the *fe'i* or mountain plantains were cropping profusely. This season was known as Teta'i, or 'weeping', when the weather was wet and the people had to rely on wild foods while they waited for the new crop of breadfruit to ripen. It was a good time for fishing, however, and over the next few days Tu brought his *taio* gifts of tuna, shark and dolphins. The dolphins were caught several miles offshore with lines trailed behind a sailing canoe, baited with flying fish (which had been caught with tall rods weighted with stones and carrying a short line and hook that were dragged behind the canoes); while the sharks were lassoed with a noose over their heads.[4] On moonless nights the islanders fished with seine nets, which the fish could not see in the dark; and when it was moonlit they went torch-fishing, spearing fish in the lagoon or from the reef or catching them with small hand nets. On fine nights, so many people went fishing in the harbour that the sea gleamed with the flames reflected from their torches.[5]

According to Bligh, the Tahitian women were allowed to eat fish but not meat, although they eagerly ate meat when they dined with the Europeans. Even the men rarely ate meat, perhaps only one day in ten. The islanders lived mainly on root crops and fruit, with some fish that they ate raw or baked in earth ovens. A favourite food was baked breadfruit, pounded with a little water into the consistency of thick custard, using a stone pestle while sitting on a four-legged stool. Although the Tahitians kept themselves meticulously clean, washing their hands before touching food and bathing twice a day, he noticed that many of them had ulcerated arms and legs, visiting the surgeon's assistant to have them treated. When these sores were regularly cleaned and dressed, however, they quickly healed, again suggesting to Bligh that they were not of venereal origin. Even when the sufferers were horribly disfigured, he saw that their families and friends showed no revulsion, inviting them to join in their dances and festivities. Bligh must have learned a little Tahitian during his previous visit, and he was now studying the language more seriously, recording the key kinship terms in his journal.

During this visit to Pare, Ari'ipaea, now Pomare II's regent and the leading fighting sailor in Pare-'Arue, was clearly unhappy that Tu was still living in his district, rather than returning to Tahiti-iti where he had been living in exile since Mahine's attack on Pare-'Arue. At that time, Tu had been despatched to his mother's lands in the south of the island, although his brothers Ari'ipaea and Vaetua (who had killed Mahine in battle) had gained considerable *mana* from their roles in the battle. Tu's bond friendships with Captain Cook and Cook's 'son' William Bligh, however, gave him the freedom to return to the Pare-'Arue district, where he was regaining much of his old prestige and power. Tu's children also lived nearby, although according to Bligh they were not allowed to visit the ship or have contact with the Europeans, but stayed on the other side of the river. Fearful of offending Tu, he ordered his men not to go there. Although the young high chief, Pomare II, was often paddled around the *Bounty*, sitting on the shoulders of his attendant who sat in the bow of the sacred canoe (which according to Morrison was the position of honour), he never boarded the British vessel.

On 5 January 1789, three of Bligh's small crew – the ship's corporal Charles Churchill, John Millward and William Muspratt (who had recently been flogged) – ran from the *Bounty*. Interestingly, both Millward and Muspratt were among the venereal sufferers, which might have affected their behaviour. That night while Millward was on sentry duty, the mate of the watch (the midshipman Thomas Hayward) fell asleep on deck, lying on an arms chest that stood between the guns. On board the ship's small cutter were eight muskets and eight cartouche boxes of ammunition in a small arms chest, and seizing these arms, Churchill and his comrades rowed silently away in the boat, guided by Tapairu, Moana's enterprising son from Matavai Bay.[6] As soon as their desertion was reported, Bligh ordered Hayward to be clapped in irons for sleeping on duty. This was a serious offence in the Navy, punishable by death on a fighting ship in times of war (Article of War xxvii: 'No person in or belonging to the fleet shall sleep upon his watch, or negligently perform the duty imposed on him, or forsake his station, upon pain of death'). He also took the large cutter ashore and alerted the chiefs, who told him that these men had taken the arms chest into a canoe and gone to Matavai Bay; and from Matavai had sailed by canoe to Teti'aroa, the coral islets owned by Tu's family, which they used as a resort.

Anxious to retrieve the cutter, Bligh sent Fryer accompanied by Tu, Ari'ipaea and Moana in the darkness to retrieve it (although Vaetua, Hayward's *taio*, furious that his bond friend had been put in irons, refused to assist on this occasion). Arriving at One Tree Hill in the middle of the night, they saw the small cutter being rowed by five islanders who were bringing it back to the *Bounty*. After presenting the chiefs with gifts, Bligh told them that he relied upon them to retrieve any deserters, warning them: 'I would not quit the Country without them, and that as they had always been my Friends I expected they would show it in this instance, and that unless they did I should proceed with such violence as would make them repent it.'[7] Although they were afraid that the deserters might shoot them with their muskets, the chiefs agreed that at daybreak, Ari'ipaea and Moana would set off in two canoes to capture the runaways. Despite their anxiety that Bligh might take them hostage, as Captain Cook had invariably done on similar occasions, when he assured them that they could leave the ship whenever they liked, they took him at his word. As Bligh remarked:

> As I have never shown any Violence or Anger at the trifling Thefts that have been committed, because it was our own faults, and having lived among them with so much harmony and good will, they place every confidence in my word, and are faithfull in return to me. I have therefore no doubt but that they will bring the Deserters back, but in case of failure I shall proceed to no extremities untill I have the Plants on board.[8]

In contrast with his tolerance towards the chiefs, however, Bligh showed no mercy to his own men, raging against them for their lack of vigilance. After releasing Thomas Hayward from irons, he stripped him of his midshipman's rank, sending him before the mast. As he fumed in his journal: 'Such neglectfull and worthless petty Officers I believe never was in a Ship as are in this. No Orders for a few hours together are Obeyed by them, and their conduct in general is so bad, that no confidence or trust can be reposed in them, in short they have drove me to every thing but Corporal punishment and that must follow if they do not improve.'[9] It is likely that John Hallett protested about Hayward's punishment, because in the index to a missing section of his personal log, Bligh referred to 'Mr. Hallett's contumacy' and 'Mr. Hallett's behaviour'.[10] To make matters worse, when he searched Churchill's sea chest, Bligh found a list of names, including that of Churchill himself, along with Christian, Heywood and several others of the shore party (presumably Peckover, the gunner, or several of the sailors); and stormed ashore where he accused these men of complicity in the desertions.[11] At sea, when sailors swore themselves to desertion or mutiny, it was customary to take a piece of paper and sign their names; and Bligh took this list as a sign that these men intended to betray him.

He may have been right. Later, when some of the sailors who had refused to take part in the mutiny told their story to a correspondent for *Walker's Hibernian Magazine*, they claimed that Christian, who had delighted in his 'female connections' in Tahiti, had decided that he could lead a happier life on the island:

> Three others, who were midshipmen, Heywood, Young, and Stewart, were equally enamoured with the women at Otaheite, who being possessed of great

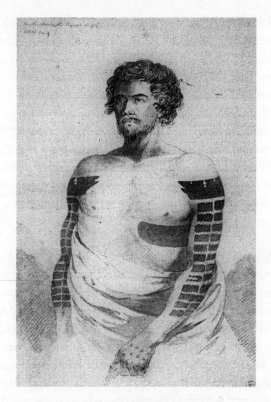

'Arioi *warrior from Borabora.*

sensibility and delicacy are exceedingly engaging, and withal remarkably handsome. . . . These four had privately imparted to each other their wish of abiding in the island . . . Christian artfully prevailed upon Charles Churchill, who was master at arms; John Mills, the gunner's mate; and James Morrison, the boatswain's mate, to join him in his intended projects.[12]

Although Heywood always vehemently denied that he was involved in the mutiny, and his later accounts were supported by the testimony of some of his shipmates, he was trying to avoid being hanged at that time. In any case, after finding the list of names, Bligh became wary of Christian and Heywood, making it much more difficult for them to desert from the *Bounty.*

Indeed, it is likely that Christian, Stewart and Morrison, and perhaps others, had made some kind of pact during their time on the island. During Cook's second Pacific voyage, a number of the sailors formed themselves into a secret society inspired by the black leg *'arioi* (whom they called the 'Knights of Porapora'), calling themselves the 'Knights of Otaheite'. Accordingly, they had a star tattooed on their left chest representing the star of St George, one of the insignia for the Order of the Garter, the highest honour in Britain, but at the same time, evoking the large spot or bar tattooed on the left chests of senior *'arioi*.[13] Apart from Bligh, three other men on the *Bounty* had sailed with Captain Cook, and they must have passed on this tradition to their shipmates. During this visit, the midshipmen Fletcher Christian and George Stewart, and one of the sailors, the American Isaac Martin, each had a star tattooed on their left chest; while James Morrison, the boatswain's mate, had a star tattooed on his left chest and a garter around his left leg with the inscription, 'Honi Soit Qui Mal Y Pense', the motto of the Order of the Garter. It is quite likely that others (including Heywood and Young, who were both heavily tattooed) also had stars on their chests, but not realising its significance, Bligh did not specify this detail when he later described their appearances. The list that Bligh discovered in Churchill's chest may have recorded the names of the members of the 'Knights of Otaheite' on board the *Bounty* – although this does not mean that they had decided to desert the ship, or mutiny against their captain.

By this time, Bligh had quarrelled with almost all of his officers, and most of the *Bounty*'s sailors. Apart from the 'purser's tricks' that outraged his men, he had begun to flog any of the crew who allowed naval property to be stolen, while Tahitian thieves went unpunished. To make matters worse, he praised the chiefs who had helped their shipmates to escape, while accusing Christian and the shore party of complicity in their desertion, and clapping one of his own midshipmen in irons. In *Mr Bligh's Bad Language*, his fine study of the mutiny on the *Bounty*, Greg Dening has argued that Bligh's intemperate tirades were the main reason for the collapse of his command.[14] The causes are more complex, however. As noted earlier, during his last visit to the Society Islands, Captain Cook had also been given to violent rages, stamping on the deck and cursing his men – or 'tipping a *heiva*', as they called it; and as Dening has pointed out, during that voyage Cook was far more severe than Bligh in the lashes meted out to sailors and islanders alike, and how the chiefs were treated. When three of Cook's men deserted at Ra'iatea, one of them after a flogging, for instance, Cook responded by capturing members of the paramount chief's family and holding them hostage until his men were returned, and in revenge the Ra'iateans had plotted to kill him.

With so small a crew, no marines or other commissioned officers on board the *Bounty*, however, Bligh could not adopt such strategies without risking his ship; although on this occasion, he threatened the chiefs that unless his men were returned, 'I should make the whole Country Suffer for it.'[15] While his verbal abuse was galling, Bligh was not a violent man; and if his command began to unravel, this was largely because of the decisions made by Joseph Banks and the Admiralty in planning the voyage – the selection of so small a ship for an expedition around the world, and the decision to transform the Great Cabin (traditionally the captain's private domain) into a greenhouse for the breadfruit plants. In consequence, he had only a handful of able-bodied seamen to sail the ship, no Great Cabin to bolster his authority, no other commissioned officers and no marines to back his orders; and he and his men had to live cheek-by-jowl during the voyage. Furthermore, although some of the offences committed by his men (sleeping on watch, and desertion) were taken very seriously in the Navy, as a lieutenant Bligh could not order the appropriate punishments, but had to wait for a court martial back in England.

In addition, the Admiralty's delay in finalising his orders meant that the *Bounty* had been caught by the Pacific hurricane season, and was forced to stay in Tahiti much longer than Banks and Bligh had intended. During the five months that they spent on the island, his men had become lax, forging intimate relationships with local families and lovers. In addition, during each of Captain Cook's earlier voyages to the Society Islands, sailors had attempted to desert the ships; and some of Cook's crew were now on board the *Bounty*. Bligh also had the living memory of those desertions to contend with, both on the ship and on shore among the Tahitians.

To make Bligh's situation worse, by this time the Tahitian chiefs were desperate to recruit Europeans for their skills in musket-fighting, ironworking and carpentry. No doubt Churchill, Muspratt and Millward had seductive visions dangled before them by Tapairu and the other chiefs from Matavai Bay. Given their long stay in Tahiti, the relationships they had forged with some of the islanders and the promise of sensual bliss, coupled with the tensions between Bligh and his men, the likely conditions on board during the voyage back to England and the kind of life that they might expect back at home, it is little wonder that these men ran from the *Bounty*.

The next morning when Ari'ipaea and Moana set off for Teti'aroa to capture the 'Villains who had left me', the weather turned foul and they were forced to return to Pare. Several days later, his bond friend Po'e'eno visited Bligh and confessed that he had stayed away from the camp and the ship for fear of being taken hostage (for although Bligh did not know this, Tapairu, who had recruited the deserters, was Po'e'eno's brother).

On 9 January 1789 one of the officers picked a branch from a candlenut tree growing on a *marae* (probably Taraho'i) and took it into the large house that Tu had set aside for Bligh's men, where he tied the branch to one of the house posts, thinking to keep it free of thieves. As soon as he had done this, however, all of the Tahitians hastily left the premises. Afterwards, none of them would return, saying that the house was now *ra'a* (sacred, prohibited) and that they could not go inside until Tu had raised the sacred restriction. When Bligh asked his *taio* to do this, Tu arrived soon afterwards with a plantain branch, chanted a prayer, and took the branch to Taraho'i *marae* as an offering to 'Oro, raising the *tapu*.

Although Bligh was impressed by the power of the gods on the island, he noted that whenever he attended a ritual in Tahiti, the people laughed and chatted, apparently paying little attention. They seemed to look upon 'Oro as a powerful being, capable of violent passions, who might either help them or strike them down; and sought to win his support with offerings, but otherwise thought little about him. During this interval, hoping that Bligh and Tu were now estranged, the great warrior Pohuetea sent messengers urgently inviting him to visit him in the Pa'ea district.

Finally, on 13 January when the weather cleared, Ari'ipaea set off for Teti'aroa, promising to bring back the deserters. Moana was supposed to accompany him, but as the father of Tapairu, who had lured them away, he was in a difficult position and delayed his departure until the following morning. Bligh could only wait, and in the meantime he recorded a little more about Tahitian customs. He noted that infidelity was punished on the island, and that during his visit one woman thrashed another who slept with the coxswain, her 'husband'; while a man who was caught sleeping with another man's wife was stabbed in the belly with an iron knife by the enraged husband. Another day when 'Itia visited Bligh, she was accompanied by a *mahu*, a man who lived as a woman and slept with men, an accepted role in Tahitian society. At first Bligh thought that this man had been castrated, because he spoke in a high voice, but after inspecting his privates he discovered that this was not the case, although his genitals, which had atrophied, were kept drawn up between his thighs.

According to Tu, although *mahu* were selected in boyhood and raised with the girls 'solely for the caresses of the men', they did not commit sodomy, but instead gratified their partners between their thighs.[16] As Bligh remarked of 'Itia's attendant: '[T]he Women treat him as one of their Sex, and he observed every restriction that they do, and is equally respected and esteemed.'[17] In the eighteenth-century British Navy, however, homosexuality was a capital offence, and Bligh and his companions were amazed to discover that a man could live as a woman in Tahiti without being stigmatised. Bligh also remarked upon the lives of the children, who lived in a state of cheerful activity:

> It is delightful to see the swarms of little Children which are in every part of the Country at the different amusements, some flying Kites, some swinging from the bough of a Tree in a Rope, Wrestling, [playing what] in some places of England is called a Cats cradle and a variety of other little tricks which I believe are not to be found with a less docile and inoffensive set of People.[18]

On 16 January the *heiva parae* was performed for Bligh as it had been in Matavai Bay. Dressed in the senior *'arioi*'s costume (or *parae*), the men chanted and clacked their pearl-shell clappers, and once again, twists of knotted coconut leaves were laid at Bligh's feet. According to his *taio* Tu, this ritual recognised the British commander as an *ari'i* of the Pare district as well as Matavai Bay, although it may also have been part of the seasonal festivities. The *Para'a Matahiti* ceremony, held in December or January to celebrate the 'ripening of the year' when the new breadfruit crop was ready, was fast approaching, when new canoes, mats, bark cloth and vast quantities of first fruits would be brought to the *marae* by visiting groups, and the people would celebrate with dancing, wrestling, boxing and *'arioi* performances.

While Bligh was immersed in this ritual, the man who had taken the deserters by canoe to Teti'aroa arrived on board the *Bounty*, but instead of taking him prisoner, the master John Fryer sent a message to Bligh, asking him what he should do. As Bligh exclaimed in disgust:

> As he knew perfectly my determination in punishing this Man if ever he could be caught, it was an unnecessary delay in confining him, but what was still worse, while the Messenger was absent, which was about 10 Minutes, he suffered this Offender to jump overboard and escape without hoisting the Cutter out which was on deck, so that I now lost an Opportunity of securing the return of the Deserters without disturbing my friendly intercourse with the Cheifs.[19]

To aggravate matters, early the next morning when the spare sails were laid out on the beach to air, Bligh discovered that the canvas was mildewed and had rotted in many places. In his frustration he raged at his petty officers, berating Fryer and the boatswain William Cole in particular:

If I had any Officers to supercede the Master and Boatswain, or was capable of doing without them, considering them as common Seamen, they should no longer occupy their respective Stations. Scarce any neglect of duty can equal the criminality of this, for it appears that altho the Sails have been taken out twice since I have been in the Island, which I thought fully sufficient and I had trusted to their reports, Yet these New Sails were never brought out![20]

Trying to console himself, over the next few days Bligh used Po'e'eno to negotiate for possession of a bull that Cook had left behind in Tahiti in 1777, now held in Hitia'a on the east coast by a prophet known as 'Ama no Parai' (Ama, belonging to 'Parai' [Bligh]); no doubt hoping to breed the bull with the heifers to establish a supply of cattle on the island. It is intriguing that both the British and Spanish bulls were in the possession of men who were regarded as *ata* or incarnations of 'Oro, perhaps because the virility of these animals evoked the potency of the god. On this occasion Po'e'eno acted as the negotiator, and some days later the bull was delivered to Bligh, who sent it to Matavai Bay under Po'e'eno's protection.

On 23 January the weather was wet and wild. As thunder boomed and lightning flashed in the mountains, Hitihiti came out to the *Bounty* to tell Bligh that the deserters had just sailed past Pare to Fa'a'a, five miles away. Although it was almost dark and they could barely see the reef, Bligh and Hitihiti boarded the boat and chased after them. When they landed on a beach some distance from Te Pau's house, drenched and battered by the storm, they lost sight of the boat; and soon afterwards they were ambushed by some men who tried to strip them of their possessions. Brandishing his pistols, Bligh threatened to shoot the warriors, driving them away, and afterwards abused Hitihiti for leading him into an ambush. At Te Pau's house, they were warmly welcomed, and Te Pau (who as a *taio* of Tu's, was friendly towards Bligh) told him that the deserters were sheltering in a house nearby. Bligh, Hitihiti and Te Pau set off in the darkness, and as they approached this house, the three deserters came out unarmed and surrendered. The weather was still wild and miserable, so Bligh asked Te Pau for a canoe awning. While the rest of his men slept comfortably in the boat that night, Bligh and two armed sailors guarded the deserters under this small shelter. Early next morning when Bligh went to Te Pau's house, the chief gave him the muskets, bayonets and scabbards that the deserters had taken, except for a musket, two bayonets and some scabbards and belts that had been lost when their canoe capsized en route from Teti'aroa.

Although Churchill, Muspratt and Millward assured him that after Ari'ipaea and Moana had tried to capture them on Teti'aroa, they had decided to give themselves up, Bligh did not believe them. Rather, he was certain that they had been trying to escape to Mo'orea when they were caught by the storm and forced to land at Fa'a'a, where their canoe had capsized, tossing a musket into the surf. Back on board the *Bounty*, he had the deserters thrown in irons, discovering to his annoyance that during his absence the chronometer had been allowed to run down. In the morning Bligh mustered the crew and read out the Articles of War, reciting its ominous roll call of punishments, especially Article xvi: 'Every person in or belonging to the fleet, who shall desert or entice others so to do, shall suffer death, or such other punishment as the circumstances of the offence shall deserve, and a court martial shall judge fit.' Afterwards Churchill was given a flogging of a dozen lashes while each of the others was given two dozen lashes – a lenient punishment, under the circumstances. When the flogging was over, Bligh again berated his petty officers, especially the midshipman Thomas Hayward who had been asleep on duty when the men had deserted. As he remarked despondently in his journal afterwards, however: 'It is unpleasant to remark that no feelings of honor, or sense of shame is to be Observed in such an Offender.'[21]

During his search for the deserters, Bligh had twice passed Taone Harbour (a little further to the north of their anchorage) in stormy weather, noting that on the east side of the bay, the water seemed calm and still. Now that the deserters were confined on board the *Bounty*, Tu's people relaxed again (although Vaetua was still very angry about the way his *taio* Hayward had been treated). The breadfruit crop was ripe and the *Para'a Matahiti* festivities finally got under way, celebrating the first fruits of the harvest and the return of the gods to the island. Each morning, the men entertained themselves with cockfighting, and when one district challenged another they staged a feast, followed by fights with as many as 200 cocks in the cockpit.[22] Before sundown every evening the people drifted to the beach opposite the anchorage, where the women played the game of tossing a breadfruit with their feet while the men threw lances and the boys jumped with skipping ropes, walked on stilts or tried their skill at wrestling. When one of the young men dislocated his elbow one evening in a wrestling match, three strong men grabbed him and placing their feet against his chest, pulled on his arm until the joint popped back into place. As the musicians played and little girls danced, Bligh remarked contentedly: 'I believe no Ship was ever in so happy a situation . . . At these times we see an Assembly of three or four hundred people, happily diverted and good humoured and Affectionate to one another without ever a Single circumstance happening to counteract it. These are things I am spectator of every fair evening.'[23]

# 10

# These Happy Islanders

During this visit to Tahiti, Tu and his family and Te Pau often visited Bligh, and one day Te Pau complained that he was ill. When the surgeon's mate examined Te Pau he found cancerous holes in the roof of his mouth (perhaps syphilitic lesions, or yaws), which seemed to be healing. On one of these occasions, Tu and 'Itia assured Bligh that their first-born son Pomare II had been conceived when Tane, the god of beauty, had visited 'Itia in the night, although it was to 'Oro that they offered their food and prayers. Their son was so sacred that he had to stay away from the British, although occasionally Bligh hailed him at his house, which stood about 400 yards away from the British post across the river. Tu and 'Itia also told Bligh that 'Oro was the offspring of Ta'aroa (the creator god), and that while he literally ate the offerings that were presented to him, including the human sacrifices, he was invisible, hovering about them and living in Te Po, the suprasensible dimension of ancestors, darkness and spirits. According to Bligh, the carved figures of *ti'i* were not idols, but 'more for Ornament than anything else'.[1] This was true, except during ritual occasions, when they were possessed by ancestor gods.

Bligh had a great admiration for 'Itia, Tu's senior wife, describing her as a very 'quick and sensible' woman who enjoyed firing the sentinel's musket. By way of contrast, Tu, a timorous man who was terrified of firearms, periodically stupefied himself with *'ava*. Tu and 'Itia both often pleaded with Bligh to take them to England, saying that they would only take two attendants with them; and Bligh only dissuaded Tu by telling him that his wife would die of seasickness, and that he would return later with a larger ship, and King George's permission to take them to his court. Tu was extremely eager for information about other countries, especially other islands in the Pacific, asking about these places and memorising their names. Bligh enjoyed Tu's company, and dined with him almost every day, commenting, 'Nothing can exceed the Mirth and jollity of these People when they meet on board.'[2]

Tu's alliance with the British brought him and his family many enemies, however, which put them in grave danger. As Bligh noted with concern:

There is a great deal due from England to this Man and his Family; by our connections with him and them we have brought him numberless Enemies. Their elligible situation for our Ships has brought us intimately connected with them, and by this perhaps we have not only sown the seeds of discord but of revolution. On one side he has Attahooroo [Atehuru, now the Pa'ea district] disposed to attack him, and on the other Tiaraboo [Tai'arapu, southern Tahiti] ready for a total extirpation of his Authority, while he has an Enemy equal to the other in Morea, who will venture anything buoyed up by their former Successes.

All those I am confident will on my leaving this Place make a joint Attack on this part of the Island, and these poor people will have no recourse but to fly to the Mountains and defend themselves there . . . I hope, however . . . that they will never be forgot by us, because it will . . . be justifiable in England to support the Otow [Tu] family, and they have shown that faith and Affection to the Erree no Pretanee [Ari'i no Peretane – the King of Britain] as demands all our Assistance and utmost efforts to defend them . . . If therefore these good and friendly people are to be destroyed from our intercourse with them, unless they have timely assistance, I think it is the business of any of his Majesty's Ships that may come here to punish any such attempt.[3]

By threatening Tu's enemies with revenge if they attacked his *taio*, Captain Cook had adopted such a policy, demonstrating his determination by his ferocious attack on Mo'orea. This had kept Tu safe for some years, but not indefinitely, and now Bligh was urging the King of England to adopt the Pomare dynasty (and especially Tu) as his allies on a permanent basis.

Eager to entertain his *taio*, on 29 January 1789 Tu took Bligh to watch a fleet of double canoes fishing outside the reef, catching bonitos with bamboo rods and lines with unbaited hooks. Before leaving the beach the fishermen prayed to the sea god, and each canoe was equipped with a square woven basket carrying coconuts, breadfruit and plantains as an offering. On the canoes, a long curved pole (or *tira*) fixed in the prow worked like a crane, lowered and raised by two men who stood in the stern, hauling on two ropes tied about halfway up the pole. This pole had a forked end with a fishing line baited with baked breadfruit tied to each prong of the fork, and a bunch of black feathers that attracted the fish when it was lowered close to the water. When the fish were drawn towards the feathers, the breadfruit baits jiggled and jumped in the water; and when a large fish was hooked, this device made it easy for the fishermen to pull the fish up into the canoe.[4]

On 30 January Bligh ordered the American sailor, Isaac Martin, to be punished with two dozen lashes for striking an islander, although at Tu's request he reduced the sentence to nineteen lashes. Soon afterwards, he told the deserters that he had decided not to court-martial them. During their confinement they wrote Bligh an abject letter (which he probably dictated), begging for clemency:

> Sir,
> We should think ourselves wholly inexcusable if we omitted taking this earliest opportunity of returning our thanks for your goodness in delivering us from a trial by Court-Martial, the fatal consequences of which are obvious; and although we cannot possibly lay any claim to so great a favour, yet we humbly beg you will be pleased to remit any farther punishment; and we trust our future conduct will fully demonstrate our deep sense of your clemency, and our stedfast resolution to behave better hereafter.
>
> We are, Sir
> Your most obedient, most humble servants,
> C. Churchill, Wm. Muspratt, John Millward.[5]

Bligh was not prepared to forgo any further punishments, however, and on 4 February he had the deserters released from irons and given their final floggings – twelve lashes for Churchill and two dozen lashes for Muspratt and Millward.

Bligh also threatened Thomas Hayward with a flogging or court martial for sleeping on watch, a threat that ensured his obedience. Two days later during a tropical downpour, when the *Bounty*'s bower cable was cut underwater near to the beach, Bligh threatened the chiefs with retaliation unless the culprit was identified. No one confessed, although as he later confided to some of the *Bounty* sailors, Tu's younger brother Vaetua, Hayward's *taio*, had cut the cable, intending to rescue his bond friend from Bligh's wrath when the ship was wrecked on the coral.[6] Tu, 'Itia, Te Pau and their families all fled to the hills, although before he left, Tu assured Bligh that he knew nothing about what had happened. When Ari'ipaea returned from Teti'aroa that afternoon, he told Bligh that his canoe had almost been wrecked in the storm, and that Moana had been forced to head for Mo'orea. According to Ari'ipaea, after capturing the deserters he had tied them up; but when these men begged to be untied, promising good behaviour, he had released them. As soon as he did so, however, the deserters grabbed their muskets, threatening him with these weapons. According to Churchill, Muspratt and Millward, on the other hand, the chiefs had been having a wonderful time at Teti'aroa, enjoying the *Para'a Matahiti* celebrations. Almost a hundred canoes were drawn up on the beaches at the islets, where Ari'ipaea had been entertained with feasting and merriment.

Although it was customary for the Pomare chiefs and their followers to go fishing at Teti'aroa at this time of the year, where the chiefs and *'arioi* entertained themselves, being ritually fed with *po'e* (a sweet pudding made of bananas mashed with manioc or *taro* and coconut cream) and becoming fat, sleek and pale as a sign of the prosperity of their people (the custom known as *ha'apori*)[7], Bligh was livid to hear that Ari'ipaea had been waylaid by these festivities. When Tu and 'Itia finally returned to Pare on 8 February, still denying any knowledge about the attempt to wreck the *Bounty*, Bligh 'reviled them and their Country at large, at which they felt much inward distress that at last gave vent by tears'.[8] Mollified by their misery, Bligh invited them to dinner, accompanied by a relative of Vehiatua's who was urging Bligh to go to southern Tahiti. Upon Tu's advice, Bligh gave this messenger gifts of a shirt and some iron tools, but told him that he had decided not to visit any other harbour on the island. Over the next few days, Tu persuaded Bligh that although he had made every effort to discover who had cut the *Bounty*'s cable, he had been unsuccessful (unlikely, since the culprit was his younger brother). As Bligh remarked: 'His readiness to serve me and his good disposition convinces me he has no knowledge of the person who has done it, and it has given no small degree of happiness to the whole Family that I have acquitted them of their having any hand in the Affair.'[9]

According to John Turnbull, a later visitor to the island, whenever one of the greater chiefs returned from a sojourn on Teti'aroa:

> They never fail to make the circuit of the whole island. Their retinue is then numerous, for they are not without a taste for pomp . . . The same merriment and diversion continues wherever they stop; add to this, they are every where loaded with presents; so that by the time they have made the circuit of the island, a peregrination which usually occupies them three months, their canoes return as rich as a fleet of galleons.[10]

As the missionary William Ellis reported, for these journeys to Teti'aroa, or the '*motu*', the chiefs used *va'a motu*, large single outrigger canoes with high washboards and a strong plank that extended across the hull out to the outrigger, on which the men stood to counterbalance the vessel in high winds. These canoes had a single, mobile mast, a sail with a straight inner seam and a curved outer edge, and were steered with a steering paddle (or sometimes two or three in very strong winds).[11] On this occasion Ari'ipaea and his companions used the wind known as *to'erau maeha'a*, the Westerly Twins, which blew from the north-west for several days, veered around the compass and then returned to the west, a cycle which was often repeated over eight or ten days at a time during this season.[12]

Now that Ari'ipaea had returned to Tahiti, on 11 February Te Pau and his family farewelled Bligh and returned to their own district (Pa'ea) for a grand *heiva*, which would be staged by an *'arioi* troupe that was touring around the island, showered with food and bark cloth each time they performed in a district. As the ethnologist Teuira Henry later noted, in addition to celebrating the first fruits, these festivities also announced the passage of the spirits of those who had died to Rohutu-no'ano'a, the perfumed *'arioi* paradise, where they became *'oromatua* or ancestors.[13] That afternoon when the *'arioi* arrived at Pare, Bligh asked them to perform their *heiva*. This troupe was comprised of four men and two girls, the youngest girl a 'mere child', and when they danced for Bligh, they were accompanied by two types of drums, skin-headed drums and the much rarer slit drum, which was beaten with two sticks. The girls were wrapped up in layers of bark cloth, and as they danced, a long plaited string attached by a feathered ring to a finger on each hand swayed gracefully, accentuating their gestures. At the end of the dance each of these girls dropped their bark-cloth garments as a gift before Bligh, standing naked before him; and afterwards the four male *'arioi* danced, making the most extraordinary distortions with their genitals, using twine and small cloth bandages for this purpose.[14] In Tahiti, bindings were often applied to *to'o* or god-images, sacred tools and weapons, war canoes, *'arioi* houses or human sacrifices to intensify the sacred power of the gods; but on this occasion the *'arioi* dancers used them to intensify the generative power of the penis (an *ata* or incarnation of Tetumu, the source of life in the cosmos).[15]

Although this was a ritual performance, Bligh found these phallic distortions so disconcerting that he could scarcely bear to watch, and after a few minutes he begged the *'arioi* to stop, to the hilarity of the spectators. Later that morning, Tu accompanied Bligh on a ceremonial visit to the widow of Teto'ofa (the 'Admiral'), who was waiting for them on the beach. As Bligh and Tu, accompanied by three men and a priest who carried a small puppy, a chicken and two young plantain suckers, approached and seated themselves at a distance, this high-born old lady addressed them in short sentences while her male attendant presented them with gifts, which were identical to those carried by Tu's priest. Upon receiving this presentation, the priest gave a short prayer and, handing over Tu's gifts one by one, made a short statement to accompany each presentation. Afterwards Tu and the old lady embraced each other affectionately, and she wept for almost half an hour, although as soon as Tu escorted her to a small shed she quickly recovered her good humour; and Tu and Bligh farewelled her and went out to the *Bounty* for dinner.

During the preparations for the Matahiti festivities, *pia* or arrowroot had been prepared. The roots were washed, scraped very clean and grated into a small wicker basket about six inches deep lined with layers of fibres to serve as a strainer, which was placed over a wooden trough. The *pia* was rubbed over the fibres, and the strained liquid left to settle in the trough. Two days later when the water was poured off, the *pia* was rolled into large balls which were left in the sun to dry. Afterwards, the dried mixture was scraped off and mixed with boiling water or coconut milk into a paste, another dish that Bligh found delicious.[16]

On 13 February Tu invited Bligh to attend a ceremony to acknowledge him as an *ari'i* in Pare in front of the Pa'ea people. When Bligh arrived, escorted by 'Itia, they found that almost 2000 people had gathered; and at her suggestion, armed sailors were posted to keep the crowd back from the arena. They were met by Tu and several chiefs, and a wooden stool was brought upon which Bligh was seated alongside Tu and his companions. As three lengths of coarse bark cloth were produced, each carried by an 'inferior chief' and laid on the ground before him, each of these chiefs made a speech acknowledging Bligh as an *ari'i* in Pare, exclaiming '*Ia Ora Teina! 'Ia Ora Mate! 'Ia Ora Ari'ipaea!*' ('Long live Teina, Mate and Ari'ipaea!' – the names Bligh had acquired by his name exchanges with Tu and Ari'ipaea). On this occasion, the black leg *'arioi* from Pare-'Arue recited the chant for his district, hailing Pomare II or Tu-nui-a'a-i-te-atua (also known as 'Tu') as their high chief, and Ari'ipaea as his subordinate:

> The mountain above is Mahue
> The assembly ground below is Vai-rota
> The water inland is Pu-'o-'Oro
> The point outside is Ahu-roa
> The *marae* are Taraho'i and Rai-a-mau
> The high chief is Tu-nui-a'a-i-teatua

The under chiefs are Ari'i-pue and Ari'i-pa'ea
The chief messenger is Turuhe-mana
The *'arioi* house is Na-nu'u
The schools of learning are Va-uri, Utu-mea and Fare-fatu
The principal teacher is Matau.[17]

As 'Itia helped Bligh to take up the lengths of bark cloth one by one, they presented them along with other gifts to the Pa'ea women who were about to dance, who received them with pleasure. These women performed on a large, fine mat, and as a finale they unwound their bark-cloth garments, leaving them at Bligh's feet. Afterwards, about twenty men carried in two long pieces of patterned red bark cloth which they referred to as *maro* (after the *maro 'ura* or red feather girdles of the paramount chiefs of the island), laying one of these at Tu's feet and the other at Bligh's, along with a *taumi* or warrior's breastplate. Tu directed Bligh to present one of these *maro* to Ari'ipaea, and the other to the god 'Oro, but to keep the breastplate and the women's bark-cloth costumes for himself.

After these presentations, a wrestling match was staged, but because the men from Pa'ea (who had often fought against Tu's army) took part, it threatened to get out of control; and Teu (Tu and Ari'ipaea's father) asked Bligh to get his men to put a stop to the combat. In an instant, however, all of the warriors took up their weapons and began to fight. 'Itia, who was wrapped up in thick layers of bark cloth tied around with a rope, came to check that Bligh was safe, and then left, saying that she was off to join the battle. Although Bligh had nine armed men with him, and a boat with seven armed sailors lying off the beach, he did not take any immediate action. However, just as he was about to signal for the ship's guns to be fired (without shot) to disperse the fighting men, Tu and 'Itia came to tell him that everything had been settled. Afterwards they took Bligh with them to visit some elderly relatives of Tu's from Pa'ea as part of the peacemaking process; and Bligh told Tu and 'Itia that after this fracas, he would not permit any more wrestling matches to be held near the shore camp.

The next morning Tu brought three large pigs with a quantity of breadfruit to Bligh, asking him to present one pig and a pile of breadfruit to the chiefs of Pa'ea; another to the *'arioi* from that district; and the last to the chiefly women who had danced in the *heiva*. Tu's guests seemed delighted with these gifts, which were part of the peacemaking rituals between Tu and the chiefs of the Pa'ea district. Bligh was very impressed with Tu's generosity, remarking how often he gave food and hospitality to others, yet 'it is all done without any ostentation, like a man actuated solely with a desire to do good, and altho he has no pomp, yet his good nature and manners rise him above the level of all the Cheifs I have yet seen'.[18]

The next morning, a Sunday, Bligh performed divine service with Hitihiti, Te Pau and other chiefs in attendance. At dinner, they talked about the world. According to Bligh, the Tahitians could measure distance only in terms of time travelled, and supposed that the horizon ended at a certain point. Because they knew that it took a ship nine months to sail to England, a very large land-mass, they thought that this must be the place where the horizon ended. The islanders were familiar with the rising and setting of particular stars, and believed that the sky was inhabited by ancestors. They saw the world as a vast plain with the sun, moon and stars circling around it, and often asked Bligh whether he had been to the sun and moon, supposing that as a great traveller, he must have visited those places.

As Bligh remarked, almost all of the island's chiefs and the *'arioi* were now gathered at Pare; and on 17 February a wrestling match was held between the women of Pare and those of Pa'ea. Although Bligh had often heard about these contests, he had never before attended one of these bouts. The women grappled with no holds barred, gouging eyes and yanking each other's hair, and sometimes wrestling with the men; but when Bligh expressed his dismay to 'Itia (herself a famous wrestler), saying that it was a disgrace to see women fighting, she laughed and retorted that it was very good in Tahiti.

The next day, Tu took Bligh to visit his 'country residence' in the hills, which had a glorious view of Pare, Matavai Bay and Teti'aroa. Bligh noted that the soil was very rich, and that the house was surrounded by large plantations of coconut trees and groves of breadfruit trees that Tu had planted, with stands of sugar cane and extensive gardens of yams and sweet potatoes, although the plants were not yet in flower. The *'ava* and bark-cloth plants grew in meticulously tended gardens at the bottom of the valley, drained by deep trenches, where Bligh sowed ten ears of corn. As he noted, the inland mountains were covered with forest and criss-crossed by paths. Over the next few days, Tu and 'Itia went off to visit other chiefs, returning with large gifts of food for Bligh which included delicious puddings made of scraped and grated taro mixed with coconut cream and cooked for about five minutes in a wooden trough with hot stones from a fire, stirred constantly to prevent it from burning. The mixture was then made into rolls, wrapped with leaves and baked in an earth oven for about twenty minutes. Another type of pudding was made of ripe plaintain and grated taro mixed with coconut cream and baked in an earth oven for twenty-four hours.

One day when Tu dined with Bligh, teasing him for not filling his wine glass to the brim, Bligh asked him why someone always had to serve him. Tu explained that when a married chief had a child, the midwife handed the baby first to the father, who passed it to the mother; and from that time on until his son was a man, the father was so sacred that he had to be fed by another person. He added that each time 'Itia had a child, she had to be fed for about ten months before an *amo'a* ceremony was performed, when she presented some coconut, sugar cane and two small sacred branches to the baby, raising the *tapu* (sacred restrictions) of birth from them both. The length of the ritual prohibition varied with the *mana* of the couple concerned, and he and 'Itia had to be fed longer than any other couple on the island. Since babies came from Te Po, the realm of ancestors and spirits, they were imbued with the *mana* of the gods; the blood spilled during the process of childbirth made the baby doubly *ra'a* or sacred; and a long series of these rituals were required to raise at least some of these restrictions from a high-ranking child.[19] Commoners (who were *noa* or ordinary and unrestricted) were never present when a chief's child was born; and if a chief had a child by a commoner, it had to be killed as soon as it left the mother's body. *Manahune* (commoners) and *teuteu* (servants) did not perform these rituals, since like them, their children were *noa*.

Bligh was now being treated as a part of Tu's family, although one day when 'Itia's youngest child was ill and he offered her the surgeon's assistance, she called in a local healer instead. By this time many of the islanders were infected with tuberculosis (probably introduced by Charles Clerke and William Anderson, the commander and surgeon of the *Discovery* during Cook's last voyage), and when a man died of this disease, Bligh went to see the corpse, which was laid out straight on his back, eyes closed, wearing a loincloth with a piece of cloth around his neck. His right hand lay on his stomach and his left hand on its chest; and one finger on each hand was decorated with a coconut fibre ring decorated with a tuft of red feathers, allowing the man's spirit to ascend to Rohutu-no'ano'a, the perfumed paradise of chiefs and *'arioi*, instead of descending to the stinking, excremental underworld of commoners.[20] Below the funeral bier lay the grave in which the corpse would be buried a month later. Some Tahitians were now being buried in coffins, and while 'Itia told Bligh that they had adopted this practice from the Europeans, others claimed that this was an ancient custom.

Over the days that followed, Bligh spent a great deal of time with his 'uncles', the Ra'iatean high priest Ha'amanimani (Tu's mother's brother, also known as

'Mauri' and 'Tutaha'), and Mou'aroa (Tu's father's elder brother, whose title was Teri'i-hinoi-atua). An unmarried black leg *'arioi* notorious for his many affairs, Ha'amanimani had been the highest-ranking titleholder of Ra'iatea before he was exiled from his home island. Like Tupaia, the Ra'iatean high priest who under similar circumstances had supported the claims of Te Ri'irere (the son of Purea, the 'Queen of Tahiti' and Great Woman of Papara) to paramount status, before leaving the island with Captain Cook, Ha'amanimani was deeply involved in Tahitian politics, supporting Pomare II's claim as the paramount chief of the island. According to the oral histories, when he arrived at Tahiti, Ha'amanimani had brought with him various sacred relics from Taputapuatea that he presented to his great-nephew – the *maro 'ura* named Teraipu Tata, the bonnet or *taumata* named Te Ata o Tu, and the fan or *tairu* named Hotu, strengthening his ritual status and access to 'Oro's power.[21]

Just like Tupaia, Ha'amanimani was fascinated by the strangers, and during his sessions with Bligh, he began a serious study of English, memorising the names of many objects and common actions.[22] At the same time, he and Mou'aroa (another black leg *'arioi*) began to teach Bligh about Tahitian ways of life, instructing him about Tahitian and Ra'iatean notions of time, dictating the names of the six breadfruit seasons during which different varieties of breadfruit cropped, the thirteen lunar months, and the thirty days of the month in the Society Islands; and how to count up to 200,000 in Tahitian.

Despite Bligh's relationship with these senior chiefs, on 2 March 1789 a water cask, some bedding and part of an azimuth compass vanished from the shore tent. In a fury, he blamed George Stewart for allowing the theft to occur. Suspecting that Tu's people were responsible for the thefts, he sent a messenger to Tu, saying that he would no longer be his friend unless the thief was surrendered. Startled by his anger, Tu, 'Itia, Teu, Tetupaia and Ha'amanimani fled to the mountains, although later that morning Tu and Ari'ipaea set off with some armed men in search of the culprit. About an hour later, Tu returned with the thief, assuring Bligh that this man was not from the Pare-'Arue district or Matavai Bay, but from the windward side of the island. According to Bligh, Tu declared:

"There is the Theif – kill him." I now told him that he had acted very properly and that he had secured my friendship and good Will, and explained with much Success how unjust it was and unfriendly to Steal any thing from us, and the risk which they run in the Attempt; that I punished my people for the most trifling Offence against them, and that I would therefore insist on like punishment, on their side.

Tynah [Tu] now stopt me from saying any more by embracing me and the Whole Croud calling out Tyo Myty [*taio maita 'i* – good friend]. The Glass and Card of the Compass were found useless and Tynah left me to go in search of the bedding, which was said to be taken away by another person.[23]

Bligh ordered the thief to be taken on board the *Bounty*, where he was given a flogging of 100 lashes that shredded the flesh from his back, and was clapped in irons. The wind was blowing strongly from the north-west, and in the afternoon Bligh sent a man to Taone Harbour further along the coast, to see whether it was still sheltered in these boisterous conditions. Upon his return, the sailor reported that in both Matavai Bay and Taone Harbour, high waves were crashing over the reef and on the beaches. As Bligh remarked with satisfaction, however, in To'aroa Harbour 'we lye as smooth as in a Mill-pond'.[24]

The following day was dark and gloomy, with downpours of rain, thunder and lightning. By this time, Te Pau was very ill. Distressed by his *taio*'s sickness, Tu told Bligh that since Te Pau had no children, when he died he would be succeeded by his brother, who was Tu's enemy. Under his leadership the people of the Fa'a'a district would ally themselves with the Pa'ea people and attack the Pare-'Arue district. Perhaps because they were so apprehensive about what would happen when Bligh left the island, Tu and 'Itia pleaded with him to take them to England, although when they realised that he was adamantly opposed to this proposal, they pleaded for a brace of pistols and ammunition instead, so that they could defend themselves after his departure. Tu assured Bligh that 'Itia, a great warrior, would fight with one pistol while Hitihiti would fight with the other, since they were both expert marksmen. Apparently Tu and 'Itia ('as great a Heroine as can be found existing')[25] led the land army of Pare-'Arue, while Ari'ipaea and Vaetua led their navy.

On 4 March, another young man died of tuberculosis. He was one of the 'middling class' (or *ta'ata mauri*), and when Bligh went to visit the corpse, he found the father sitting on the ground, massaging his son's legs which lay across his lap, while the mother slashed her head with a shark's tooth, the blood streaming down. The body lay on a mat with several twists of coconut leaves placed beside its head, and others beside a small heap of breadfruit. There was also a bunch of coconut leaves tied up like a bouquet nearby, which they called the *marae* of the dead man, presumably the place where the spirits alighted during the mourning rituals. The next morning the father made a wooden coffin for his son, lashing planks together and fastening a stick on each corner to hold up a light roof covered with white bark cloth and ornamented with black feathers, while the mother and two young children sat by her son's body, weeping bitterly. Early the next morning the dead man's father went to the hills to gather reeds and sticks to fence in the grave, while another male relative dug the hole. When the father returned, he and this man made the fence, and at noon they carried the coffin to the grave, where it was propped up on four small posts, one at each corner. Now that the coffin was in place, the grieving father sat by his wife, both slashing their heads with shark's teeth. The coconut insignia or *marae* was placed inside the railing, and just outside it a pole was erected carrying a basket of breadfruit and coconuts as an offering to the god. Bligh was now assured that using a coffin was a new custom, adopted from the Spanish after Boenechea's burial.

These deaths were yet another sign of how the Tahitian world was changing. Although in 1772 Johann Reinhold Forster had estimated the local population to be at least 200,000 people,[26] during the *Bounty*'s visit sixteen years later, Morrison guessed that there were only 30,000 inhabitants left on the island.[27] The venereal and epidemic diseases introduced by successive ships, and now tuberculosis, were ravaging the island, causing its population to plummet. This had provoked a crisis of faith in the gods; for in Tahiti, people often cast off a god who failed to protect them and illness was a sign of weakness, not just of the individual concerned but of the ancestors who were supposed to look after them. There must have been many kin groups who cast off their *atua* at this time. According to Teuira Henry, in such a circumstance a chief would declare: 'This god is no longer helping us; he is a man-devouring god. Let us cast him off!'; and his priests went to the *marae* and chanted: 'I am casting you off. Do not possess me again. I am tired of you, you terrify me. Look at the family, they are stricken with illness; you are taking them, you man-devouring god!'[28] Faced with these strange maladies, the islanders were trying to draw upon the *mana* of the European god, burying their dead in coffins, asking for European medicines and adopting European symbols of power; acts foreshadowing the destruction of 'Oro and the *'arioi* cult and the adoption of Christianity several decades later.[29] Perhaps this was a reason why at this time in Tahiti, red feathers (used in the worship of 'Oro) had lost much of their power.

At dawn on 7 March the thief who had been flogged with 100 lashes escaped from his chains, and vanished from the *Bounty*. This escape was similar to one that had occurred during Cook's third voyage, when a Porapora man whose ears had been cropped for theft escaped from the *Resolution*. Like Captain Cook on that occasion, Bligh was convinced that the mate of the watch, the midshipman George Stewart, considering the penalty too severe, had set the offender free. As he fumed in his journal:

I have such a neglectfull set about me that I beleive nothing but condign punishment can alter their conduct. Verbal orders in the course of a Month were
so forgot that they would impudently assert no such thing or directions were
given, and I have been at last under the necessity to trouble myself with writing
what by decent Young Officers would be complied with as the common Rules
of the Service.[30]

According to Morrison, however, after watching the yeoman put some marlin
spikes by the foremast, the prisoner had managed to grab one of these spikes and
twist the lock to pieces, jumping overboard and swimming ashore. Although
Stewart vehemently protested his innocence, Bligh threatened him with a court
martial for this offence when they returned to Britain. Bligh's relationship with
his officers was now at rock bottom, eroded by his incessant accusations of
incompetence and disloyalty; and in so small a ship, with no marines and on the
other side of the world from the Admiralty, there was little that he could do to
shore up his authority.

On the other hand, the Tahitians were still honouring Bligh as a high chief
at every opportunity. The autumn harvest festival, always a brilliant affair, was
held at this time of year, and on 13 March a large party of 'arioi including Vahine
Metua, Ari'ipaea's wife and a senior 'arioi, returned from Teti'aroa for the 'ihi
ari'i ceremony, a presentation to the paramount chief of the island. An envoy
had been sent around the district, warning the ra'atira or landowners to tell
their tenants, the manahune, to collect food for the ceremony.[31] When the ritual
began, Vahine Metua approached Bligh and 'Itia with two female 'arioi, each of
whom was dressed in a short bark-cloth petticoat, with long lengths of very fine
cloth wrapped around their torsos; and six men wearing loincloths decorated
with long strips of multicoloured bark cloth that hung almost to the ground.
The faces and bodies of these male 'arioi were smeared with scarlet dye or mati
(the sacred colour), and as they walked two by two in a stately procession to
the house where Bligh and 'Itia were waiting, they held up plantain branches.
After their stay at Teti'aroa, where they had been fattening themselves, resting
and staying in the shade, the 'arioi looked plump and fair-skinned; and this was
a huapipi ceremony such as Máximo Rodríguez, the young Peruvian marine,
had also witnessed during his visit to the island. The men presented Bligh with
two pieces of white bark cloth, and then walked to Ari'ipaea's house where they
gave Tu's brother a similar present.

Back at the house where Bligh was waiting with 'Itia, the two women who
had been wrapped in bark cloth approached him and slowly spun around,

unwinding the bark cloth from their bodies and leaving it at Bligh's feet, stripping themselves naked; but as they did so, a crowd of 'arioi grabbed the bark cloth, tearing it into pieces as they struggled over it, and taking these away. 'Itia sent three large pieces of cloth, a large pig and a heap of breadfruit to Bligh, and helped him to carry the lengths of bark cloth one by one to Vahine Metua. As they presented the pig and the breadfruit to the 'arioi, the crowd shouted in admiration. Finally, 'Itia assisted Bligh in presenting a baked pig to the envoys from each of the principal ari'i from the different districts (although the ari'i themselves were not present), and in return as the representative of the ari'i maro 'ura (paramount chief of the red feather girdle), her son, 'Itia received five baked pigs. Afterwards, twenty-four men walked in a procession, each carrying two woven baskets on a pole bearing breadfruit, taro, coconuts or different kinds of puddings which they also presented to 'Itia, gifts which she despatched to her son Pomare II at his sacred dwelling.

As Bligh remarked on this occasion, although during his visit to Pare he saw Pomare II about once a week, this young boy (who was about six years old) was so sacred that they always stood at least 30 yards apart. He invariably brought gifts for the chiefly children, who were delighted to see him for this reason. They lived on the opposite side of the sacred stream which sprang from a rock near Tu's house in the mountains, the two boys (Tu and his younger brother Teri'itapunui, who was about three years old) in one house and the two girls (Teri'i-na-vaho-roa, who was about four years old, and a baby girl, Tahamaitua) in another. At night Tu and 'Itia slept in the girls' house, although they were away from their children for most of the day. The two daughters of Auo, Tu's sister, also lived with these girls, and were treated with the same veneration. Commenting upon the way that the Tahitians lived, Bligh noted that men and women lived in different dwellings, the women's houses being called fare noa (profane, or unrestricted houses). Of the women, only 'Itia could eat with him and Tu, and when Bligh complained about this custom the women laughed, saying that when he came back to Tahiti he should bring a pahi noa (profane ship) and then he could have all the women he liked to eat and drink with him.

Bligh also noted that every now and then one of the women would inform his crew that she had caught a venereal infection, and absent herself, but before long she would be back, apparently cured. According to 'Itia, all these women had to do was abstain from intercourse for about ten days, and when the symptoms disappeared, they were no longer infectious. As mentioned earlier, although many of the people had ulcers or sores in the groin or at the sites of other glands, these were not always of venereal origin but were rather classic symptoms of yaws, a highly contagious, non-venereal disease which was often contracted during childhood and passed from child to mother, leaving horribly deforming lesions of the skin and bones. The agent that causes syphilis is very difficult to distinguish from the one that causes yaws, and someone who has suffered from yaws acquires immunity to syphilis,[32] perhaps helping to account for those mild cases of venereal infection observed by the Europeans, that were so quickly cured.

Bligh was now preparing to sail from Tahiti, and shortly after the presentation to the 'arioi, Tu's mother and father Teu and Tetupaia also returned to Pare, bringing Bligh a gift of a large pig with breadfruit and coconuts. An uncle of Tupaia (the high priest-navigator from Ra'iatea who had brought Te Ra'i-puatata, the famous red feather girdle, from Taputapuatea in Ra'iatea; and later sailed away with Captain Cook), a man about sixty-five years old, boarded the ship, where he begged Bligh to bring him a lock of his nephew's hair when he returned to the island; and Bligh presented him with a couple of nails. When another elderly chief, a close kinsman of Teto'ofa from Pa'ea, arrived, carrying a fly flap with a handle made out of the rib of a young bullock, Tu greeted this chief with reverence, and Bligh gave him a rich present. At this time pigs were scarce (although the vi or Tahitian apples were now in season), and on 17 March 1789 Te Pau was forced to place a rahui or ritual restriction on the pigs from the Fa'a'a district.

At this time, there was also a rash of petty thieving from the ship and the shore camp, although as Bligh remarked philosophically: 'I am perfectly certain that had the Ship been lying in the River Thames, a hundred times as much would have been Stolen in the Same Time.'[33] The following day, Bligh's clerk, John Samuel, returned from an excursion to the summit of Orohena Mountain, which had taken him two days of clambering through thick forest and over difficult terrain. He had seen blue parakeets and green doves, along with white-bellied petrels, and from the mountaintop sighted the islands of Me'eti'a and Huahine.

On 20 March Tu invited Bligh to attend a heiva that was being performed for a warrior from Porionu'u who had been ill-treated at Mo'orea, provoking a war. Two young girls wrapped in long lengths of bark cloth chanted in unison for about a quarter of an hour, accompanied by two drums. They wore long split feathers fastened to rings of coconut fibres on their fingers, which they gave to the warrior before unwinding the bark cloth around their torsos and presenting this to Bligh. At about this time, Tu had begun to prepare parae or

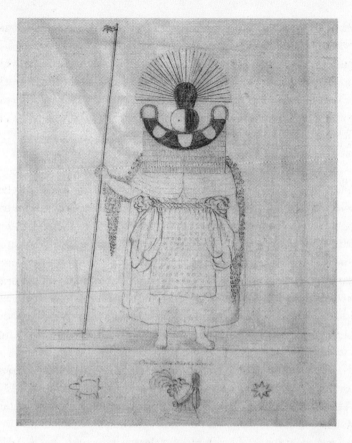

Parae *costume*.

black leg *'arioi*'s costumes as a gift to King George, finally accepting that he and 'Itia would not be sailing with Bligh to England. He begged Bligh to return as soon as possible, bringing a large ship with plenty of room to accommodate him and 'Itia, and then they would make the voyage, asking him to tell King George to send this ship in thirty months' time, when he would have collected plenty of pigs and provisions. Ma'i had spoken so glowingly about his time in England that as Bligh remarked: 'I could, if I had occasion for it, man the ship with Otaheiteans, and even with Cheifs.'[34]

On 24 March, Tu went into the interior to fetch tropic bird tail feathers for the *parae* costumes, returning the next morning. According to Morrison, these sacred birds (*ata* or incarnations of 'Oro) nested in burrows on the face of high cliffs, and the men, sitting on crossbars slung at the end of long ropes, were lowered down to these burrows where they reached into the nests and grabbed the birds' tail feathers before being hauled up again.[35] Soon after Tu's return, Bligh gave gifts to many of the chiefs, and ordered his men to remove all of the cats and dogs from the ship (as Banks had ordered, for the safety of the breadfruit plants) and search the *Bounty* for stowaways, telling them that they could only take as many 'curiosities' with them as would fit into their sea chests.

On 27 March the *parae* costumes were finished, and hung up in Tu's house for the people to admire. Later that day the priest recited a long prayer, and the costumes were presented to Bligh as gifts for the King of England. Afterwards Tu wept, begging Bligh to return to the island and take him and 'Itia to London; and then left for Pa'ea, no doubt for some kind of ritual associated with these sacred garments. As the sailors' *taio* showered them with farewell gifts, Bligh remarked: '[T]here appears such a universal kindness and Attention among these friendly people as exceeds any account I can give of them.'[36] Two days later when Tu returned to Pare, Hitihiti warned Bligh that many strangers had arrived in the district who hoped to steal something from the *Bounty* before she sailed. Tu and Ari'ipaea dined on board the following day, bringing more gifts of coconuts, plantains and pigs, and Bligh gave them more presents, including some he intended for Te Pau.

Finally, on 1 April 1789 the *Bounty* was unmoored, and the last breadfruit plants were loaded into the Great Cabin and onto the quarterdeck, along with special varieties of plantain, *vi*, *rata* or Tahitian chestnuts, *raia* or plantains and a variety of other useful plants that David Nelson had collected for Sir Joseph Banks and Kew Gardens. The wind was contrary, however, and that night Tu and 'Itia slept on board the *Bounty*. Early the next morning, Hitihiti came out to the ship, hoping to accompany Bligh to England. Although Hitihiti was born in Porapora, he had attached himself to Tu's family, to whom he was related by marriage, his wife being Tu's aunt and Te Pau's wife's sister. Although Bligh refused to take Hitihiti with him, he gave him rich farewell presents. That night the mood was sombre, and no dances or celebrations were held on the beach. Tu and 'Itia slept on board again the next night, and at last, on 4 April, buoys were placed in the channel and the boats towed the *Bounty* out to sea, followed by a flock of canoes headed by a sailing canoe carrying Bligh's 'parents' Teu and Tetupaia, who wept inconsolably as they farewelled him.

When they reached Matavai Bay, Bligh ordered the small cutter to be lowered; and as Tu and 'Itia boarded the cutter, Tu asked to have the ship's cannons fired. Although Bligh refused, saying that the salute might damage his precious cargo of breadfruit plants, he ordered his men to farewell Tu and 'Itia with three cheers. Before they left the ship, Bligh inscribed the back of Webber's portrait of Captain Cook with the date of his ship's arrival at and departure from Tahiti (26 October 1788 / 4 April 1789), and the number of breadfruit plants carried on board the *Bounty*, thus adding his own *mana* to the power of the icon. He presented it to Tu with gifts of shirts, looking glasses, fish-hooks, knives, a musket, the coveted brace of pistols, some powder and ball flints and about a thousand rounds of ammunition, and a treasure trove of iron tools in a wooden chest, while the carpenter, William Purcell, gave Tu an American musket. When they reached the beach Tu ordered the cutter to be loaded with coconuts for the voyage; and he and 'Itia stood there weeping as they watched the *Bounty* sail away, heading for Huahine.

Apart from his marriage to Betsy, and the birth of his daughters, this was one of the happiest moments in Bligh's life. The *Bounty* was laden with a flourishing cargo of breadfruit and other exotic plants, ready for transport to the West Indies and Kew Gardens; and he could already taste the triumph of his homecoming. As he later exulted: 'I left Otaheite all well with 1015 Bread Fruit Plants in Pots and many more in Tubs & Boxes in a most flourishing condition, [and] Sailed with my expectations raised to the highest pitch, of the great success I was likely to meet with. The Ship in the most perfect order and every soul well.'[37] In Tahiti, Bligh had been regarded as Captain Cook's heir and successor, and honoured as a high chief; and Tu and his family had treated him with affection. After his humiliations following Captain Cook's death, which had left him battered and embittered, and the acrimonious struggles with his men on board the *Bounty*, this was heart-warming consolation. As Bligh wrote of the Tahitians: 'They are kind and humane to one the other beyond a doubt and are tender parents. What then have we need of more to prove, that in their natural civilization they have the leading virtues of a happy life?'[38]

# 11

# Huzza for Otaheiti!

As the *Bounty* sailed away from Tahiti, Bligh ordered a double ration of grog to be served to the men. According to James Morrison, 'Evry body seemd In high spirits and began already to talk of Home, affixing the length of the Passage and Count up their Wages and One would readily have Imagined that we had Just left Jamaica instead of Taheite so far onward did their flattering fancies waft them.'[1] That night Bligh wrote a detailed account of how a ship might safely anchor in To'aroa Harbour, along with a list of the names of the members of the 'royal family' in Tahiti. He remarked that despite the attacks on Pare, Pomare II was now widely recognised as the paramount chief of the island, the other chiefs acknowledging his superior *ra'a* or sacred status by stripping to the waist in his presence. According to Bligh, the young paramount chief had the sole right to wear the *maro 'ura* at 'Utu-'ai-mahurau *marae* on the east coast of the island (the temple that Bligh always called 'Taputapuatea', the name given to any *marae* where the image of 'Oro was held). When the people of the Pare-'Arue and Pa'ea districts were at war, however, Pomare II had no access to the *maro 'ura*, and peace had to be made so that the rituals ensuring the fertility of the island could be carried out on this *marae*.

After spending so much of his time during this five-month visit to the island with Tu's family, all of whom were either former or current senior '*arioi*, Bligh had learned a great deal about the '*arioi* society and its practices. According to his account:

> The Erreeoys from leading an Idle and gay life have among them the finest Women of the Island. They have luxuriant and fine situations where they have their Meetings and live with all the disipation imaginable, and they vary the enjoyments of their lives with the Seasons of the Year. For Example the Island

of Teturoah [Teti'aroa], they resort to in Crouds in the Season when the Fish is plenty, and at other times to some Charming places in the Mountains to enjoy other peculiar dainties. They are always in large Parties. Always drest with the greatest profusion of the best Cloth and are generally fat and Saucy.[2]

The 'arioi men were all warriors. Although in times of war they avoided women, at other times they were virile lovers, having many affairs. Brothers were permitted to sleep with each other's wives, and as Bligh commented: 'It is considered no infidelity, for I have known a Man to have done the Act in the presence of his own Wife, and it is a common thing for the Wife to assist the Husband in these Amours.'[3] Adultery outside these relationships provoked violent reactions, however, the offended husband or wife taking their revenge on the lover, sometimes killing him or her. Although husbands and wives were not particularly demonstrative, they were 'very affectionate and fond of their children'. While the girls began to have intercourse when they were still very young, perhaps just seven years old, the largest family Bligh encountered on the island had only six children. In order to remain active in the society, the 'arioi had to kill any children that were born to them; and Teu's sister (who was married to Te Pau, the ari'i of Fa'a'a) for instance, had killed eight children in succession, although she then adopted her nephew, of whom she seemed very fond.

On 6 April 1789 when the Bounty arrived off Fare Harbour at Huahine, Bligh raised the red ensign, 'which all the Islanders know perfectly well to be English'.[4] A double canoe came out, paddled by ten men; and a handsome youth, one of Ma'i's Huahine friends who saluted Bligh by name, reported that Te Weherua and Koa (Ma'i's two Māori attendants) had fallen ill and died, and Ma'i had died of natural causes about thirty months after the Resolution's departure from the island. Ma'i's monkey, which the Huahine people always referred to as a 'hairy man', had also died after falling out of a coconut tree. After Ma'i's death, his house had been torn to pieces and the planks plundered, and his muskets were taken to Ra'iatea. According to this young man, whenever he and Ma'i rode on horseback, Ma'i wore his riding boots; and Bligh noticed that a number of the Huahine people had a man on horseback tattooed on their legs.[5] The envoy also brought a message from the high chief of the island, urging Bligh to bring the Bounty into Fare Harbour, but Bligh declined his invitation, saying that he did not have time for an extended visit. When more canoes came out bringing out a few coconuts and plantains, and large quantities of yams, Bligh speculated that Ma'i might have encouraged them to grow these root crops to barter with visiting ships. As they tacked away from Huahine, a man who had fallen overboard from one of the visiting canoes was seen swimming in the sea, and when Bligh's sailors rescued him and another canoe took him on board, the crew remarked that this man was insane. Soon after the *Bounty* sailed away from Huahine a large waterspout rose up close to the ship, which swayed as it approached them, rustling and swerving towards the *Bounty*, missing the stern by only about 10 yards and almost spinning the ship right around.

After this visit to Huahine, until the fresh supplies ran out, the sailors were served plantains and taro instead of bread, with one pound of fresh pork a day. On 11 April in dark, stormy weather they sighted Aitutaki, one of the southern Cook Islands, an island with brilliantly white beaches and a high conical hill, another new 'discovery' for Europe. Although they saw no signs of inhabitants, Bligh remarked: 'It is scarcely to be imagined that so charming a little spot is without them.' He found this island beguiling, with its fringe of flat land dotted 'with innumerable Cocoa Nutt and other Trees, and the higher Grounds beautifully interspersed with Lawns'.[6] The following day one of the sailors, John Sumner, was given a flogging of twelve lashes for 'neglect of duty'; and when an outrigger canoe braved the high surf and came alongside the *Bounty*, the crew of four tattooed fishermen boarded the ship without signs of fear or astonishment.

Two of these men wore large pearl-shell breastplates hung on plaited collars of human hair, and when their leader pressed noses with Bligh, he placed his shell ornament around his neck. Upon being offered a meal of pork and boiled plantains, they ate it eagerly; and told Bligh the island's name, and that their high chief was called 'Lomack Kaiah'. After they added wistfully that they had no pigs, dogs, goats, yams or taro on Aitutaki, Bligh presented these men with a pair of young pigs, yams, taro and some knives, hatchets, nails, beads and looking glasses, although they were already familiar with iron. When their leader took all of these treasures into his possession, only one of his companions seemed uneasy. Although two of these men volunteered to remain on board that night, Bligh found that his crew had asked the other two men to bring women on board the following morning, and quickly sent all four islanders ashore.

On 17 April they passed Niue or 'Savage Island', as Captain Cook had named it, but Bligh did not risk a landing on this island, where Cook's sailors had come under violent attack during a brief visit in 1774. Two days later after exercising the crew in the middle of the night in squally, wet weather, Bligh accused Fletcher Christian of failing to take proper care of the ship's sails. According to John Fryer, the master, since leaving Tahiti Christian had found Bligh's tirades insufferable, exclaiming, 'Sir your abuse is so bad that I cannot do my Duty with any Pleasure. I have been in hell for weeks with you.'[7] After five months ashore in the 'Paradise of the World', Christian and many of his shipmates were finding it almost intolerable to be back at sea. Crammed below decks and cooped up with a commander whom they no longer respected, it was a torment to recall the joys of island life – the freedom to dance and feast on shore; their kind-hearted, generous *taio*; the delicious puddings, pork, fish and fresh fruit; and the warm, scented nights with their island lovers. Likewise, Bligh was suffering from a sense of loss, after the ease and affection that had surrounded him on the island; and as his temper frayed, the relationship between him and his officers became increasingly tense and bitter.

On 21 April 1789 the lookout sighted Kao, the most northwesterly island in the Tongan archipelago, with its high mountain, an active volcano; and the next day the *Bounty* anchored off Nomuka, which Bligh had previously visited with Captain Cook in 1777. When the canoes came out bringing a few coconuts and yams, Bligh asked eagerly after Paulaho, Finau and Tupoulagi, high chiefs whom he had got to know when he was charting the Tongan islands as the *Resolution*'s master. During Captain Cook's last visit to Nomuka, however, a chief had been flogged for stealing an iron bolt, and during that third voyage Cook had been at his most violent, ordering Tongans who stole from the ships to be severely flogged (with up to seventy-two lashes), allowing his men to gouge them with boathooks or shoot them with small shot and ball, and slashing the arms of a man who had stolen from the ship. Not surprisingly, the local people had few fond memories of the *Resolution*'s visit.

It was not until the next morning that a lame, scarred old man named Tapa came on board, who asked after Captain Cook, Mr Gore and several of their shipmates. Although Bligh recognised this chief, whom Cook's sailors had nicknamed 'Lord North', he did not know that during their 1777 visit, when Tapa's son had been flogged for killing a cat, the old warrior had instigated a plan to attack and kill Cook and his men in revenge for the insult after the night dances on Lifuka. Tapa assured Bligh that Paulaho and Finau (the Tu'i Tonga and the Tu'i Kanokupolu, whom Bligh also remembered) were at Tongatapu and would soon visit the ship, and that the cattle left by Captain Cook were breeding on that island.

On 24 April, to Bligh's fury, while the *Bounty* was being anchored close to the *Resolution*'s former mooring, the master's mate William Elphinstone allowed the bower anchor buoy to sink 'for want of a little exertion'. When Bligh went ashore, escorted by Tapa who offered him a canoe house for his men, he saw a number of fine pineapple plants left there by Captain Cook, and was told that these were now flourishing on many of the Tongan islands. A number of the local people were in mourning, their foreheads scarified, most of their hair cut off and some of their fingers amputated; and both men and women had dreadful sores over their bodies, either yaws or the symptoms of venereal diseases. The next morning, a fleet of sailing canoes surrounded the *Bounty*, bringing out a few pigs, breadfruit, coconuts and plantains, some dogs, birds and chickens and plenty of yams and shaddocks to barter. That afternoon, when Bligh went ashore with David Nelson, Tapa and Tupoulagi, the high chief of Nomuka showed him a small cove where his men could obtain firewood.

At daybreak on 26 April when Bligh sent a watering party of eleven men ashore under Fletcher Christian, and a party of four men commanded by William Elphinstone, he allowed the waterers to take their muskets but ordered them to leave their weapons in the boats. The Tongan chiefs had still not forgiven Captain Cook and the British for the flogging of Tapa's son, however. The watering hole was a quarter of a mile inland, and as they walked there, their people mingled with the sailors, managing to steal an axe and an adze; and when Christian and Elphinstone aimed their muskets (which they had taken ashore, contrary to Bligh's instructions) at the offenders, the warriors seemed unimpressed, using spears and clubs to mimic their menacing gestures. Because they had orders not to shoot, there was nothing these officers could do to check the warriors' defiance. Bligh made no allowances for these difficulties, however, lamenting in his journal: 'As to the Officers I have no resource, or do I ever feel myself safe in the few instances I trust them.'[8]

Back on board the *Bounty*, when Christian tried to explain to Bligh what had happened on shore, 'Bligh dam'd him for a Cowardly rascal, asking him if he was afraid of a set of Naked Savages while He had arms; to which Mr. Christian answer'd "the Arms are no use while your orders prevent them from being used"'.[9] This was unwarranted abuse from his captain, and Christian was bitterly distressed by this tirade in front of the sailors. As Bligh later noted, 'He is subject to a violent perspiration in his hands so that he soils any thing he handles';[10] an affliction aggravated by the contemptuous way in which he was being treated. In his refusal to let the men shoot at the islanders who robbed or threatened them, Bligh was following the precedent set by Captain Cook, which Cook himself had fatally breached at Kealakekua Bay. Even in his most violent outbursts, however, Cook did not humiliate his officers in front of the sailors. By calling Fletcher Christian a coward, Bligh was using the worst insult that one fighting man could throw at another, while hiding behind his status as the *Bounty*'s commander. In civilian life, such an insult would have led to a duel.

During the morning as a number of large sailing canoes arrived off Nomuka, Bligh inspected them carefully, impressed by their design and the skilful way in which they were handled. Some of these double canoes could be sailed in either direction by swivelling the large lateen sail and shifting it from one end of the craft to the other; and according to Morrison, 'sail at an amazing rate in smooth Water, but in a rough sea they can never answer'.[11] A large platform was lashed between the two hulls of these canoes, carrying a hut in which the crew kept their provisions and supplies; and each canoe was steered by two long steering paddles. Some of these craft carried ninety passengers, and the different sections of their hulls were neatly lashed together on the inside.

That afternoon Bligh sent Nelson ashore to collect plants, and Fryer with the watering party. At the watering place, a large, unruly crowd surrounded the sailors as they bartered for yams and coconuts for their own use, and quantities of mats, spears and other curiosities which they hoped to sell at a profit upon their return to England. Tapa's people were waiting for an opportunity to avenge themselves on the British, and when they began to steal, there was nothing that the sailors could do to stop them. As a warrior brandished his club above Fryer's head and was about to strike, Matthew Quintal shouted out a warning. Back at the watering place, Christian had been surrounded by warriors who were pelting him with stones, while a chief threatened him with a long spear. At the same time, Nelson was jostled, losing a spade. While the casks were being loaded into the cutter, the islanders distracted the sailors by sending children to play tricks around the boat, muddying the water, and managed to steal the grapnel.

When Fryer returned to the *Bounty* and reported what had happened, Bligh was furious about the theft of the grapnel; and when Fryer tried to minimise the incident, saying that as there were several spare grapnels on board, 'our loss was not very great', Bligh retorted furiously, 'Not very great Sir by God! Sir if it is not great to you it is great to me!'[12] Although Tapa had promised that he would send for Paulaho and Finau, Bligh noticed that no canoes had set off from Nomuka to Tongatapu; and decided to take four of the chiefs on board hostage (including Tapa himself and a young chief named Nagiti) until the grapnel was returned. Arming the crew, he told the chiefs on board that they would be held until the grapnel was brought back to the *Bounty*.

Outraged at being taken prisoner, the chiefs despatched canoes to chase the thief, although they assured Bligh that the grapnel was not on Nomuka but had been carried to another island. Infuriated by the sloppy way that the sailors mustered when he summoned them to guard the chiefs, Bligh dismissed them, except for two whom he kept as sentries, abusing his men as a 'parcel of lubberly rascals and [saying] that he would be one of five who with good sticks would disarm the whole of them',[13] and threatening William McCoy with his pistol. When the chiefs were sent down into the messroom, Bligh ordered them to peel shells from the coconuts (a task usually performed by servants) – a terrible insult. At sunset some women came alongside in a canoe, weeping bitterly and slashing their faces and shoulders with shark's teeth, and the men in other canoes began to strike their skulls with their paddles, making a dull, thudding sound. One man would have cut off his finger, if he had not been stopped. When Tapa wept in reply, beating himself with his fists around the eyes and cutting his cheekbones, appalled by this bloody display, Bligh decided to set him and his companions free and sent them ashore with gifts of iron tools, assuring them that the English were their friends, although they would never tolerate the theft of their property. As they parted, according to Bligh the chiefs embraced him 'with a flood of Tears';[14] although as Morrison remarked: '[T]hey only smotherd their resentment, seeing that they could not avenge the insult.'[15] Predictably, Tapa and the other Nomuka chiefs, who were already incensed with the British, would not forget Bligh, and the humiliations he had inflicted upon them.

The next night as the *Bounty* approached Tofua, the volcano belched up fiery columns of smoke and flame. The deck and the boats were laden with yams and curiosities, and when Bligh came up and inspected his own pile of coconuts between the guns, he thought that some were missing. In a rage, he mustered the officers and interrogated them. Although they assured him that none of them had taken any coconuts, Bligh cursed them, saying that when the *Bounty* reached the Endeavour Straits, they could all go to hell and he would drop them ashore. After sending Elphinstone to fetch the coconuts from the stern, Bligh asked each of his officers to say in turn how many coconuts he had purchased at Nomuka. According to John Fryer:

> After all the nuts was on deck that was found below . . . Mr. Bligh began, whose are these; when the owner Answerd which was Mr Young – how many Nuts did you bye. So many Sir. And how many did you eat? he did not know but there was the remainder which he had not counted – then all the other Gentlemen were called and likewise the People.[16]

Although Fletcher Christian, who had kept the morning watch (which started at 4 a.m.), was asleep in his hammock, Bligh had him summoned on deck where he asked him the same question. Christian replied, 'I do not know Sir, but I hope you don't think me so mean as to be Guilty of Stealing yours.' According to Morrison, Bligh screamed at him in a rage, 'Yes you dam'd Hound I do – You must have stolen them from me or you could give a better account of them – God dam you, you Scoundrels, you are all thieves alike, and combine with the men to rob me. – I suppose you'll Steal my Yams next, but I'll sweat you for it you rascals, I'll make half of you Jump overboard before you get through Endeavour's Streights!'[17]

Summoning his clerk John Samuel, who also acted as the *Bounty*'s steward, Bligh yelled, 'Stop these Villains Grog, and Give them but half a Pound of Yams tomorrow, and if they steal then, I'll reduce them to a quarter.'[18] Confiscating all of the coconuts, he had them carried aft, as the men began to mutter that soon the captain would also seize all their yams. Setting his course west, Bligh ordered Fryer to take the first watch, Peckover to take the middle watch, and Fletcher Christian to take the morning watch again. This was harsh, because Christian was exhausted, and under the three-watch system, an officer was supposed to keep this watch (from 4 a.m. to 8 a.m.) only one night in three, to ensure that he got enough sleep.[19]

Having accused his acting lieutenant of theft as well as cowardice, and punished him, Bligh tried to make his peace by inviting him to dinner. Christian sent his excuses, however, saying that he was unwell. When Thomas Hayward (who despite being put in irons in Tahiti for sleeping on duty, had remained loyal to his captain) agreed to dine with Bligh, the other sailors hissed him. That evening, Fletcher Christian was beside himself. After keeping the morning watch, he had been woken on Bligh's orders and called a thief as well as a coward. Brooding over these insults and unable to go back to sleep, he approached Purcell, tears 'running fast from his eyes in big drops' and complaining of his treatment. When the carpenter commented that he also suffered at the hands of their captain, Christian retorted that as a warrant officer, at least Purcell could not be flogged, 'but if I should speak to him as you do, he would probably break me, turn me before the mast, and perhaps flog me; and if he did, it would be the death of us both, for I am sure I should take him in my arms, and jump overboard with him'. As a master's mate, Christian was still a midshipman, whose captain could send him before the mast and have him punished with the cat-o'-nine-tails, an unbearable indignity for a gentleman. Although Purcell tried to calm him, saying that 'it is but for a short time longer', Christian was inconsolable, exclaiming, 'In going through Endeavour Straits, I am sure the ship will be a hell!'[20]

In his desperation, Christian decided to make a raft and leave the ship that night. After speaking with Purcell, he went to the fore-chains where he tore up his letters and personal papers, throwing them overboard and giving away all the 'curiosities' that he had collected in the islands. When he told Purcell and his friends George Stewart and Peter Heywood what he intended to do, they were sympathetic, giving him some nails, beads and pork which he put into a bag and hid in a sailor's hammock. It was a fine moonlit night with a fresh breeze. At 10.30 p.m. as the volcano on Tofua flared up in the darkness, and Bligh came on deck to give his orders for the night watches, Fryer remarked that it was lucky that the new moon had risen and would shine upon the Barrier Reef when they arrived off the coast of Australia. Bligh answered, 'Yes Mr. Fryer it will be very lucky for us to get on the coast with a good moon.'[21] After Bligh had retired to his cabin, Christian lashed two masts from the ship's launch to a plank, took two staves to use as paddles, wrapped a roasted pig and put it in a bag, waiting for his opportunity to go ashore.

At midnight when William Peckover took over the watch, Fryer went to his cabin. There were always men on deck, however, and eventually Fletcher Christian went below and fell asleep. At 4 a.m. the next morning, 28 April 1789, when George Stewart woke his friend to take the next watch, he warned Christian against leaving the ship on a raft, considering the scheme suicidal. According to Morrison, Stewart remarked that 'the People are ripe for anything' – a provocative statement under the circumstances.[22] In Tahiti, Bligh had threatened Stewart with a court martial for allowing a prisoner to escape, and like Christian, he was angry with his captain.

Exhausted and desperate, and brooding over what Stewart had said, Christian decided to take over the ship. Determined not to be captured if he failed, he tied an iron lead around his neck, hiding it under his shirt, planning to jump overboard and drop into the ocean if it seemed that he might be detained. When he approached Matthew Quintal (who had formed an attachment to a Tahitian woman), suggesting that they might take Bligh as a prisoner, send him and Fryer ashore at Tofua and return to Tahiti, Quintal hesitated, saying that this was a very dangerous scheme. Accusing him of cowardice, Christian then spoke to Isaac Martin, the American sailor, one of the 'Knights of Tahiti', who had been flogged in Tahiti. When Martin slapped his thigh, declaring, 'By God, I am for it!', Quintal changed his mind and decided to join them; and they summoned Charles Churchill (the ship's corporal, a high-spirited young man and another of the 'Knights', who also had a lover in Tahiti and had earlier tried to desert from the *Bounty* to join her).

Although the two midshipmen, John Hallett and Thomas Hayward, were on watch that night, Hallett was sleeping below (a dereliction of duty), while Hayward was alternately dozing and watching a shark that was swimming in the ship's wake, leaving young Tom Ellison at the wheel. Taking advantage of their inattention, Christian went below and demanded the keys to the arms chest from the armourer Joseph Coleman (who was holding them for John Fryer, the master), saying that he wanted to shoot the shark. Finding Hallett asleep on the arms chest, Christian ordered him up on deck. In guilty haste, the young midshipman climbed up the foreladder and ordered one of the sailors to pluck and clean a chicken for their dinner. After taking the muskets from the arms chest, Christian was joined by Churchill, Martin and Quintal, and giving each of them a weapon, ordered them to stand guard below in strategic locations. They were followed by Alexander Smith and Matthew Thompson (both of whom had been flogged in Tahiti), Burkett and Mills, Sumner (who had been flogged off Aitutaki), Williams and McCoy. After arming themselves, several of these men went up on deck where they took Hayward and Hallett prisoner, sending them back to their berths under guard. In addition to Charles Churchill, the ship's corporal, nine of the thirteen able-bodied sailors who carried out the heavy work of sailing the *Bounty* had now joined the mutiny.

At 5 a.m., Christian ordered Quintal and Sumner to stand guard by the stairway at the rear of the ship, outside the cabins of Fryer and Bligh; and posted Matthew Thompson, armed with a cutlass, beside the arms chest, guarding the fore stairway. When they were in place, Christian, armed with a cutlass, accompanied by Churchill, Burkett and Mills, who brandished muskets and bayonets, burst into Bligh's cabin. Bligh was asleep, and when he was jolted awake, it must have seemed like a nightmare. Fletcher Christian, his hair flying loose, shirt undone, eyes red-rimmed and glaring, stood over his bunk, holding a cutlass to his throat, while Charles Churchill, the master-at-arms and one of the tallest men on board, loomed up behind him, armed with a loaded musket. Hauling him from his bed, these men trussed Bligh's hands behind his back, ordering him not to make a sound, or they would kill him.[23] Despite their threats, Bligh yelled out 'Murder!' at the top of his voice, waking John Fryer, the master, who was asleep in his cabin on the opposite side of the rear stairway. When Fryer tried to leave his cabin, however, Quintal and Sumner pushed him back inside, saying, 'Sir, you are a prisoner.' These two men stood guard on the aft companionway which led down to the mezzanine deck, preventing the men in the cabins below from joining their captain – Bligh's clerk John Samuel, the botanist David Nelson, the acting surgeon Thomas Ledward, and the gunner William Peckover; while Thompson guarded the fore stairway, keeping an eye on the mates' and the midshipmen's berths.

By this time, Smith, McCoy and Williams had been joined by Robert Lamb, one of the sailors, William Brown the assistant gardener, and Henry Heildbrandt, their Hanoverian shipmate, who guarded the foreladder, preventing the petty officers in the fore cabins on the mezzanine deck from coming to Bligh's assistance – the sensible, experienced boatswain William Cole, the old sailmaker Lawrence Lebogue, the carpenter William Purcell, and the armourer Joseph Coleman. At the fore part of the quarterdeck, Burkett now stood armed, while Isaac Martin was posted by the hen coop. Soon afterwards, young Tom Ellison, who had been on the helm that morning, also picked up a musket.

When Matthew Quintal reported that the ship had been secured, Christian led Captain Bligh up on deck, bare-arsed in his nightshirt, followed by Churchill, Smith and Burkett, their bayonets pointing at his back. As they passed John Fryer's cabin, Bligh caught the master's eye, hoping that Fryer would remember that he had a brace of pistols in his cabin. There was no love lost between Fryer and his captain, however, and Fryer (who later protested that he had no ammunition for the pistols, although Bligh vehemently denied this) ignored this exchange of glances.[24]

After checking the fore companionway, Quintal told William Purcell that the ship had been taken from Bligh. Overhearing this exchange, the boatswain William Cole said to Purcell, who had often quarrelled with their captain, 'For God's sake I hope you know nothing about this,' and the carpenter denied any involvement. Poking his head through the fore hatchway, Cole could see Bligh standing beside the mizzenmast (near the stern of the ship), his hands tied behind his back, guarded by several armed mutineers. Hastening down the foreladder, he woke up Morrison, McIntosh, Simpson and Millward, who were asleep in the forecastle, and told them what had happened. When Millward heard about the mutiny, he was horrified, saying that after his earlier desertion, Churchill was bound to force him to join the uprising. As he had predicted, soon afterwards Churchill called him up on deck and ordered him to take a musket. When Millward obeyed, fifteen of his men had taken up arms against William Bligh.

Seeing that they were outnumbered, Cole, Morrison and Purcell went on deck to ask Christian about his intentions. Threatening them with his cutlass, the acting lieutenant ordered them to lower the small cutter, saying that he intended to set Bligh, his clerk John Samuel and the two midshipmen, Hayward and

Hallett, adrift off the coast of Tofua. When they examined the cutter, however, and found that the bottom was rotten, they urged him to choose another boat. After much hesitation Christian agreed, telling them to clear out the large cutter, which was packed with yams, and lower it into the ocean. As soon as the cutter was alongside, Cole told Michael Byrne to stand in the boat and fend it off the *Bounty*'s hull. When Christian ordered some of the armed men to fetch the two midshipmen (Hayward and Hallett), and the captain's clerk John Samuel from below, and Bligh demanded upon what authority he gave these orders, Christian, 'his eyes flaming with revenge', yelled at him to be quiet.[25]

Fortunately for Bligh, his clerk had managed to enter the captain's cabin where he grabbed a compass, the *Bounty*'s muster roll, Bligh's jacket and trousers, his purser's records and his commission (the proof of his command, which gave him authority to buy supplies on the Admiralty's credit), although the guards would not let Samuel take any of Bligh's charts, journals or navigational instruments. When Christian allowed Fryer to come on deck, and the master tried to persuade him to release Bligh, Christian roared, 'Hold your tongue, Sir, it is too late,' and sent him back below, guarded by John Millward, a sturdy, dark-haired sailor with a *taumi* (Tahitian breastplate) tattooed on his belly.[26] As the ship's master, Fryer still had some authority, however, and ordering Millward to let him go below to the mezzanine deck, he found David Nelson and William Peckover, the gunner, sitting disconsolately in Peckover's cabin. When they asked Fryer what he thought they should do, he urged them to stay on board so that they could try to take over the ship, although Peckover disagreed, saying that in that case, they would all be treated as pirates if they were captured.

Cole (the boatswain) and Purcell now decided to go with Bligh in the boat. Finding that the bottom of the large cutter was also leaking (a sign that, as Bligh often complained, Purcell had neglected his duties), they protested about its condition; and eventually, Christian allowed them to lower the launch, the largest boat on board, which was 23 feet long and 6 feet 9 inches wide, with two masts and six oars. As they did so, Isaac Martin protested, saying, 'If you give [Bligh] the Launch, I'll go with him; you may as well give him the Ship.'[27] As soon as the launch was lowered, Christian told Hayward and Hallett to go on board, ignoring their desperate pleas to stay on the *Bounty*; and as Hallett climbed into the boat, he wept bitterly. When Bligh tried to reason with Christian, the acting lieutenant, looking almost demented, ordered him to be quiet, screaming: 'Mamoo, Sir, not a word, or you are dead this Instant!' (*Mamu* means 'Be quiet' in Tahitian.) Although William Cole tried to calm him, Christian shouted, ''Tis too late, I have been in Hell for this Fortnight passd and am determined to bear it no longer, and you know Mr. Cole that I have been used like a Dog all the voyage!'[28]

Holding the rope that tied Bligh's hands, Christian now ordered John Smith, Bligh's servant, to serve each of the armed men a dram of rum; and as he named various men to be sent into the launch, the mutineers swore and cursed at their shipmates, brandishing their muskets. When the armourer Coleman and the carpenter's mates Norman and McIntosh asked to go with their captain, however, Christian refused, not wanting to lose their skills, and ordered them stay on board the *Bounty*.

In the chaos of the uprising, the boatswain William Cole and several other 'loyal' sailors had managed to gather 150 pounds of ship's biscuit, 28 gallons of water and some coconuts; a small quantity of rum and wine, twine, canvas, sails and line, nails and saws; and an old quadrant and compass, loading these into the launch – although Christian forbade them to take any maps, charts, the chronometer or other navigational instruments. As the carpenter climbed into the boat, carrying his tool chest, one of the mutineers swore, 'Damn my Eyes he will have a Vessel built in a Month.'[29] At this time Bligh was still under guard by the mizzenmast, his hands tied behind his back, with armed men aiming their muskets at his chest. When he dared them to fire, although their shipmates yelled out 'Shoot the Buggar!' and 'Blow his brains out!',[30] these men uncocked their muskets. Taking pity on Bligh, whose mouth was cracked and dry, the American sailor Isaac Martin gave him a shaddock to suck; but when Martin tried to climb into the launch, Quintal quickly ordered him back on board, holding a gun to his head.[31]

Heartened by Martin's kindly gesture, Bligh pleaded with Christian, promising that if he relented, all would be forgiven; and reminded him that he had dandled Bligh's own children on his knee. According to Bligh, Christian exclaimed, 'I know it, captain – hold your tongue – say no more – I am a villain – I am – but – it can't be helped. Oh, God – I am in hell.'[32] Exchanging his cutlass for a bayonet, he grabbed the cord that tied Bligh's hands and threatened to kill him at once if he did not keep quiet. Christian now ordered Fryer into the launch, and when the master begged to stay on board, he threatened him with his bayonet. As Fryer turned to his captain to ask his permission to leave the ship, Bligh whispered that Martin was a friend, telling him to knock Christian down. According to Bligh, Fryer did nothing, however, climbing reluctantly into the launch which was already very low in the water, with only seven inches of freeboard.[33]

As soon as he was on board, Fryer begged Christian to allow his young brother-in-law, John Tinkler, to join them; and although Churchill had intended to keep Tinkler as his servant, Christian finally agreed. Tinkler was sent into the boat, where he was joined by the sailor Robert Lamb, who had now repented of his role in the mutiny. By this time, there were eighteen sailors in the launch, which had been built for short journeys with a crew of no more than fifteen.

Grabbing Bligh by the cord around his hands and jabbing the bayonet into his side, Christian shoved him across the deck and forced him to join the men in the launch. As he did so, one of the mutineers yelled out, 'Damn his eyes, put him into the Boat, and let the bugger see if he can live upon three-quarters of a Pound of Yams per day!'[34] A few pieces of clothing and some cuts of pork were tossed down, and according to Morrison, at Bligh's request Christian handed him the captain's pocketbook and private journal, his own sextant along with a copy of the *Practical Navigator, and Seaman's New Daily Assistant*, and four cutlasses, although he refused to give Bligh the Kendall chronometer that Joseph Banks had loaned him, or a musket.[35] Instead, the mutineers jeered at their captain, informing him that he 'was well acquainted with where [he] was going and therefore did not want them'.[36]

As the mutineers hauled the launch along by a rope to the stern, the carpenter's mates McIntosh and Norman leaned over the rail, weeping. Michael Byrne was sobbing in the cutter; and Joseph Coleman, the armourer, called out to Bligh from the stern, saying that he had no part in this business. While the mutineers – this 'Tribe of Armed Ruffians', as Bligh called them – mocked and jeered at their shipmates, Norton begged for his jacket, and Sumner yelled at him, 'If I had my will you bugger, I would blow your brains out.'[37] Fearing that the mutineers were about to start firing their muskets, Cole urged Bligh to cast off; and the sailors took the oars and pulled away from the *Bounty*. As they did so, George Stewart, the dark-skinned midshipman, came on deck and danced 'in the Otahitean manner'.[38] Bligh cried out to Coleman, McIntosh and Norman, 'Never fear, my lads you cant all go with me . . . I'll do you justice if ever I reach England!'[39] As the *Bounty* sailed away, all that could be heard were the cheers of 'Huzza for Otaheite!' fading in the distance.[40]

Stunned by this turn of events, as the launch headed for Tofua Bligh tried to understand what had happened, and why Christian and his comrades had betrayed him. Hayward had a signal book with him, and Bligh took it in order to keep a journal, and a running survey of the islands they passed. He wrote in this notebook, 'I can only conjecture that they had Idealy assured themselves of a more happy life among the Otaheitans than they could possibly have in England, which joined to some Female connections has most likely been the leading cause of the Whole business . . . The Secrecy of this Mutiny is beyond all conception, and surprizing it is that out of thirteen of the party who were sent with me and lived always forward among the People, no one could discover some symptoms of bad intentions among them.'[41] After deciding that his conscience was clear, however, he felt strangely calm, even buoyant:

> Here we may observe to what a height the baseness of human Nature may arrive at, not only ingratitude in its blackest die, but eternal criminality against their Country and connections.
>
> In the midst of all I felt an inward happiness which prevented any depression of my spirits, conscious of my own integrity and anxious solicitude for the good of the Service I was on. I found my mind wonderfully Supported, and began to conceive hopes notwithstanding so heavy a Calamity, to be able to recount to my King and Country my misfortune.[42]

Having thus exonerated himself from all blame, Bligh decided to land at Tofua to collect breadfruit and water, and then sail to Tongatapu, where he intended to ask Paulaho, the Tu'i Tonga (sacred paramount chief) and Finau (the secular high chief), whom he had met during his voyage with Captain Cook, for provisions.

As they rowed towards the high volcanic island, a very large shark struck at one of the oars. When they reached the barren, rugged coast of Tofua that afternoon, George Simpson swam through the high surf but failed to find a safe place to land [PLATE 16]. That night as the volcano flared in the sky, Bligh served grog to his men, and they slept in the boat. The next morning they went ashore at a stony cove on the island's north-west coast, where Bligh rested beside a fire and Fryer guarded the launch while their companions went in search of food, returning with just a few quarts of water. That afternoon as they rowed along the coast, they sighted coconut palms on top of a high cliff, and some of the men hauled themselves up the precipice on vines, returning with about twenty coconuts.

The following day, 30 April 1789,[43] Bligh led another expedition up the cliff to hunt for food, although they found only three small bunches of plantains. In the heat, Bligh became dizzy, and had to be helped back down. There was a cave at the back of the little bay, where Bligh decided to sleep that night while some of his men kept guard and the others slept in the boat. Early the next morning, John Norton, the quartermaster, came down to the beach, calling out to Fryer in the launch, 'Good news, good news, here is a Man and Woman – they came down to the cove where Captain Bligh was – he made friends with those people.'[44] After giving Bligh and his companions water and fruit, the couple were soon joined by a number of others, so that before long about thirty men and women were bartering with the British. According to local oral traditions, the sailors slept with several of these women that night.[45]

On 2 May, 200 warriors crossed to Tofua from the island of Nomuka, led by two chiefs, an elderly high chief named Ikaifou and his companion. They were followed by two canoes bringing a younger man called Nagiti, one of the chiefs whom Bligh had taken hostage during his last visit to the island, after the grapnel had been stolen.[46] When these men asked Bligh what had happened to the *Bounty*, and he told them that it had sunk, and that only he and his companions had survived, they must have been delighted to find Bligh so vulnerable; and when he asked about Paulaho and Finau, they assured him that the high chiefs were away at Tongatapu.

Although Bligh was glad to see these people, they were still bitterly angry about the earlier affronts by Captain Cook, and Bligh's treatment of their chiefs during his recent visit to Nomuka. After asking more questions about Captain Cook and Captain Clerke, they decided that no one was going to come to Bligh's rescue. Grabbing the rope, the men tried to pull the launch ashore, and when Bligh brandished his cutlass, they clacked their sling-stones (a vivid reminder of Bligh's ordeal on the *heiau* after Cook's death, when the Hawai'ian warriors had pelted his party of marines with a barrage of rocks). Ignoring these hostile gestures, Bligh carried on bartering for breadfruit, water and spears. After giving food to the sailors, he shared his meal with the chiefs before retiring to the cave to write up his journal.

When the senior chief, Ikaifou, asked whether he intended to sleep on shore that night, however, and Bligh replied that he always slept in the boat, the old man said grimly, 'You will not sleep on shore – *mate* [you will be dead].' Hearing this, Bligh called out to Fryer, asking him to bring the launch ashore, and quietly told John Tinkler to load their possessions on board. When this was done, with 'every one [watching] in a silent kind of horror', Bligh took Nagiti by the hand, holding his cutlass in the other, and walked with him to the boat. As soon as the captain boarded the launch, helped by Purcell who had followed him across the beach, armed with a stick, Nagiti shook his hand loose. One of the warriors grabbed the carpenter's legs, although the sailors managed to haul him back into the launch, and as they frantically began to row away, the big, clumsy quartermaster John Norton, who had gone to cast off the stern rope, was knocked down and battered to death, while other warriors hurled sling-stones at the launch 'like a shower of shot'.[47] As one man grabbed the stern rope and began to haul the launch back to the shore, Bligh managed to cut the painter.

As they rowed frantically away from the beach, the grapnel snagged on a rock, and for a few terrifying moments the launch held fast. According to Fryer, Bligh yelled out, 'Heave away Lads, if they come up with us they will cut us all to peeces', and the old sailmaker Lawrence Lebogue retorted, 'God damn my eyes Sir you frighten us all out of our wits – let the theifs come and be damned if they will, we will fight as long as we can.'[48] Desperately hauling on the rope, they managed to break the fluke of the grapnel and rowed away, chased by two canoes whose crews pelted them with stones, battering the sailors. After throwing some clothing overboard as a diversion, they finally escaped, rowing away into the darkness. Raising the foremast and getting the rudder in place, they set sail and headed south. As Bligh recorded in his journal: 'The poor Man I lost was called Jno. Norton, this was the Second Voyage with me as Quarter Master [the first had been on the *Britannia*], and his worthy character made me feel his loss very severly. He has left an Aged Parent I am told who he supported.'[49]

# 12

## I Have Been Run Down by My Own Dogs

After fleeing from Tofua, at first Bligh was eager to return to Tahiti. According to Fryer, however, when they pointed out that the mutineers might have gone there, and that Tu might not welcome their return, Bligh changed his mind and resolved to head for Timor, almost directly west of their position, via Australia. After calculating the likely length of their journey, he made a set of scales out of two coconut shells and a musket ball, and taking a quarter-of-a-pint horn mug to measure the water (artefacts later handed down to his children, which are now held in the National Maritime Museum in Greenwich),[1] said to the sailors, 'Well my lads, are you all agreeable to live on two ounces of Bread and a Gill of water per day?' When they assented, Bligh divided up five coconuts into equal pieces and strictly rationed the water, rum and pork, serving each man one twenty-fourth of a piece of bread twice a day and a quarter of a pint of water daily, with an occasional sip of rum and an ounce of salted pork; and eating his own meals from a bowl made out of a gourd.

Although several of the sailors later accused their captain of dropping bits of bread when he served out the rations, and eating these pieces himself, Bligh adamantly denied this accusation.[2] As he noted in his log:

> After examining what our real Stock of provisions was and recommending this as a sacred promise forever to their memory, [I] bore away across a Sea where the Navigation is dangerous and but little known, and in a Small Boat 23 feet long from Stem to Stern, deep loaded with 18 Souls, without a Single Map, and nothing but my own recollection and general knowledge of the situation of places assisted by an old Book of latitudes and longitude to guide me, in which particular I was happy to see every one better satisfied than myself.
>
> Our Stock of Provisions consisted of about 150lbs of Bread, 28 Gallons of

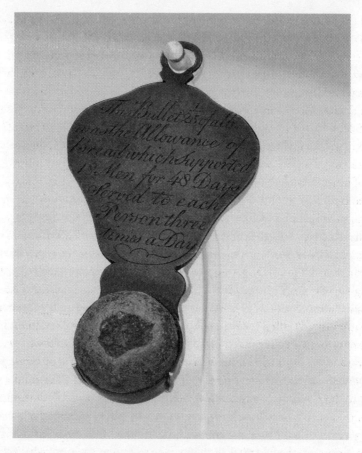

*The bullet with which Bligh rationed the food and drink on board the* Bounty's *launch.*

Water, 20 lbs of Pork, 3 Bottles of Wine and 5 Quarts of Rum, a few Cocoa Nutts and some Breadfruit, but the latter useless.[3]

While Fryer and William Cole, the boatswain, took turns to steer the launch, that night Bligh led the men in prayers, and '[returning] God thanks for our miraculous preservation, and fully confident of his gracious support, I had a mind more at ease than I had before felt'.[4]

At dawn the next morning, 3 May 1789, the sky and sea were both fiery red, signs that a storm was brewing. When the gale struck, waves crashed over the launch's stern, forcing the sailors to bail for their lives and threatening to capsize the boat. The bread was soaked, and Bligh put it in the carpenter's chest; and to lighten the launch, ordered the men to throw any spare sails, rope and clothing overboard. The storm lasted for two days, exhausting the sailors with the need for incessant bailing. During the wet, cold nights they were drenched, numb and shivering; and because there was not enough room to stretch out, their legs became painfully cramped. In the mornings Bligh served each man a teaspoon of rum, and when the storm finally died down, led them in prayers of thanksgiving.

On 5 May 1789 they sighted eight islands in succession, the Windward Islands in the Fijian archipelago, and Bligh surveyed their coastlines. The next morning, two large, high islands came into sight, Ngau and Nairai, followed by a series of other smaller islands. Off Viti Levu on 7 May, they were chased by two large canoes packed with warriors, but managed to escape. Bligh had made an impromptu log and line which allowed him to reckon the launch's speed during their passage. His apprenticeship with Captain Cook and his arduous survey work in the *Resolution*'s boats were serving him well. According to the British hydrographer A.C.F. David, despite these unpropitious circumstances, Bligh's running survey through the southern Fijian islands was remarkably accurate. Supposing himself the discoverer of these islands (which Abel Tasman had previously visited), Bligh now named the archipelago 'Bligh's Islands'.[5]

The next night the men sang before going to sleep; and the following morning they drank coconut milk for breakfast. During this part of their passage they caught only one fish, and a few birds that incautiously landed on their little vessel. To add to their distress, the sailors became severely constipated, with agonising cramps in their bowels. When the stormy weather returned on 9 May, forcing them to bail by day and night and soaking their ragged garments, Bligh told them to wring out their clothes in the sea and put them back on, which warmed them for a while. In the cold, wet conditions, which made them shiver and shake, there was plenty of water, and they did not get dehydrated.

Sometimes at night there were no stars, and in the intense darkness Bligh had to steer by the wind. On 13 May they sighted a high conical hill, the island of Mota in the Banks group, and two days later another high mountain came into view, probably Toga in the Torres Islands. The weather was still wet and miserably rough, and on 17 May a waterspout narrowly missed the launch. Three days later Bligh wrote: 'We are [so] covered with Rain and Sea that we can scarce see or make use of our Eyes. Sleep, altho we long for it, is horrible, for my part I seem to live without it. We suffer extreme cold and every one dreads the approach of Night.' That evening there was a violent downpour of rain, and on 22 May Bligh made a sombre entry:

The Misery of this day has exceeded the preceeding. The Night was dreadfull. The Sea flew over us with great force and kept us bailing with horror and anxiety. At Dawn of day I found every one in a most distressed Situation, and I now began to fear that another such Night would produce the End of several who were no longer able to bear it.

Every one complained of Severe Bone Achs which was cured in some Measure by about two Spoonfulls of Rum, and having wrung our Cloaths and taken our breakfast of Bread and Water we became a little refreshed. Towards Noon it came fair but very little abatement of the Gale and the Sea equally high. With great difficulty I got an observation.[6]

As heavy seas battered the launch, Bligh composed a prayer for deliverance, which he recorded in his journal:

Continue O Lord we beseech thee, through the mediation of our blessed Saviour Jesus Christ, this thy goodness towards us, – strengthen my mind & guide our Steps – Grant unto us health and strength to continue our Voyage, & so bless our miserable Morsel of Bread, that it may be sufficient to our undertaking.

O Almighty God relieve us from our extreme distress, such as men never felt, – conduct us through thy mercy to a Safe Haven, and in the End restore us to our disconsolate Families and Friends. We promise to renew our unfeigned thanks at thy Divine Altar & amend our lives according to thy holy word.[7]

Two days later the sun came out, warming the men, and the next day a noddy landed on the launch, which they caught and ate raw. The following day they caught two boobies, and the next day two more. Taking this as an answer to his prayers, Bligh wrote gratefully in his notebook: 'Providence seems to supply us with food we are now in great want and distress – Killed the Bird for Dinner & with the other gave us great refreshment.'[8]

Finally, on 28 May, just after midnight, John Fryer, the master, hearing the sound of surf crashing on a reef, woke his shipmates, who were delirious with joy to realise that they were close to land. An hour later as they rowed away from the waves, which were pounding on the Great Barrier Reef off the coast of Australia, Bligh called out, 'Pull my lads we shall all be swamped!' Thinking that he was panicking, Fryer shouted, 'My lads Pull! There is no danger.'[9] After thirty-one days at sea, Bligh still had an accurate fix on their position, having used Christian's sextant, the old quadrant, compass, Peckover's watch, the *Practical*

*Navigator* and a set of navigational tables for this purpose. In his journal, he also recorded a detailed description of each of the mutineers during their passage, although he refused to give John Fryer, the master, a pencil and paper to keep his own narrative of their ordeal.

That morning they found a pass through the reef, and after rowing through the gap, found themselves in smooth water, 'one of the finest Harbour mouths that Possibly could be'.[10] When they went ashore on Restoration Island on 28 May in the afternoon, staggering like drunks, Fryer was so weak that he fell down on the sand. Crazed with hunger, the sailors gathered oysters and periwinkles from the reef, voraciously eating them raw. The next morning Bligh used his magnifying glass to make a fire, and they found fresh water, which they dug from a hollow hidden among the wire grass. Fortunately one of the men had taken a copper pot into the launch, although when Bligh cooked an oyster stew with a little bread and pork, Fryer complained that he had not added enough water. The men were dizzy, weak and cramped with starvation, and as they ate oysters, along with fernroot, berries and the hearts of palms (which David Nelson told them were safe), they began to feel better. Discovering the skeleton of a snake 8 feet long draped over the branch of a tree, two shelters and a pointed stick used by the Aborigines as a weapon, however, they wondered what other perils might confront them.[11] Although there were the fresh tracks of kangaroo on the sand, they did not see any of these animals.

The next day to his dismay Bligh discovered that, once again, some of the pork had been stolen. When he refused to add bread to the stew, saying that they must save some for the passage to Timor, Fryer and the carpenter William Purcell were 'troublesomely ignorant, tending to create a disorder among those if any were weak enough to listen'.[12] As Bligh exclaimed in his notebook: 'Kind providence protects us wonderfully but it is a most unhappy situation to be in a Boat among such discontented People who don't know what to be at or what is best for them.'[13] After his deliverance from death and shipwreck, he had experienced a religious awakening. According to Fryer, during their stay on this island, while the men were gathering food, Bligh sat under a tree all day, writing, and 'Mr Hallett told me that he was correcting the prayer Book — after we sailed from this Isle we had a new prayer night and morning'.[14]

On 31 May after mustering the men, Bligh conducted divine service. Towards the end of the prayers, a group of twenty Aborigines armed with spears gathered on the opposite shore, shouting out in protest at this intrusion. Bligh embarked his men on the launch. In the daylight the coast seemed less fertile, with many white sand hills, and as they passed between an islet and the mainland, a group of seven Aborigines, two armed with weapons, waved green branches, beckoning them ashore. Bligh could see a larger group approaching in the distance and, determined not to risk a confrontation, headed for another island further from the shore, which he named Sunday Island.

When they landed on this island the next morning, they found water in a hollow and a canoe with a carved prow, 33 feet long, hauled up on shore. Bligh ordered the sailors to search the islet for food, saying that each man could eat the oysters that he gathered. Afterwards, however, when he tried to take Purcell's oysters from him, the carpenter defied him, again testing Bligh's authority:

> The Carpenter began to be insolent to a high degree. He told me with a mutinous aspect he was as good a Man as I was. I did not just now see where this was to end. I therefore determined to strike a final blow at it, and either to preserve my Command or die in the attempt, and taking hold of a Cutlass I ordered the Rascal to take hold of another and defend himself, when he called out that I was going to kill him and began to make concessions.
>
> I was now only assisted by Mr. Nelson, and the Master very deliberately called out to the Boatswain to put me under arrest and was stirring up a great disturbance, when I declared if he interfered when I was in the execution of my duty to preserve Order and regularity I would certainly put him to death . . .
>
> This had a proper effect on this man and he now assured me that on the Contrary I might rely on him to support my Orders and directions for the future. I saw there was no carrying command with any certainty and order but by power, for some had totally forgot every degree of obedience.[15]

According to Fryer, however, 'I could not help laughing to see Captain Bligh swagering with a cutless over the carpenter's head', and his call to arrest Bligh enraged his captain.[16] Bligh wrote in his journal: 'Notwithstanding he held an ostensible place as the next officer in command, not a person but considered him a mean & ignorant fellow, ever disposed to be troublesome & then ready to beg pardon.'[17] After this confrontation, Bligh always kept his cutlass close at hand.

Upon setting off from Sunday Island the following day, Bligh headed the launch up the east coast of Australia inside the Barrier Reef, conducting a running survey and stopping every now and then to replenish their supplies of clams and oysters. Matthew Flinders, a fine cartographer who later sailed with Bligh and subsequently repeated his survey, would praise his accuracy, comparing his chart favourably with that of Captain Cook, and paying tribute to the hydrographic skills of his old teacher, William Bligh:

> It has been to me a cause of much surprise, that under such distress of hunger and fatigue, and of anxiety still greater than these, and whilst running before a strong breeze in an open boat, Captain Bligh should have been able to gather materials for a chart; but that this chart should possess a considerable share of accuracy, is a subject for admiration.
>
> [I] pride myself in being, in some sort, [Captain Cook's] disciple; my first acquirements in nautical science having been made under one who mostly gained his from that great master himself: untoward circumstances shall not prevent me repeating the name of Bligh.[18]

As Lieutenant-Commander A.C.F. David has noted: 'Bligh has carried his longitude over a distance of over 2,000 miles in an open boat and is still within 60 miles of his true easting. This is an astonishing[ly] accurate judgement of the correct allowance to be made for leeway, effect of currents and the speed made good through the water . . . This means that Bligh's chart is considerably more accurate for scale and orientation than Cook's.'[19]

By this time Nelson, Purcell and several others were ill, poisoned by the berries they had eaten. At Turtle Island, where they captured some turtles and a number of birds, Fryer lit a fire to keep warm and inadvertently set alight the grass, infuriating Bligh, who feared that this would betray their position to the Aborigines. Passing Booby Key, Bligh assured the sailors that they could reach Timor in only eight or ten days' time. Praying 'to God for a continuance of his most gracious protection', on 4 June 1789 they headed into the rough waters of Torres Straits. By this stage of the journey, he remarked, he felt neither hunger nor thirst, and he marvelled at the tales of cannibalism among castaway sailors:

> My allowance satisfies me, knowing I can have no more. This perhaps does not admitt me to be a proper judge on a story of miserable people like us being at last drove to the necessity of destroying one another for food, but if I may be allowed, I deny the fact in its greatest extent. I say I do not believe that among us such a thing could happen.[20]

As they crossed the Torres Straits, the weather became stormy again, and they found themselves 'constantly bailing the Boat in all this dreadfull Weather, being continually wet and never having a Dry Rag about us'.[21] The men were near the limits of their endurance, and on 10 June Bligh wrote in his journal: 'An extreme Weakness, Swell'd legs, Hollow and Ghastly countenances, great propensity to sleep and an apparent debility of Understanding, give me melancholy proofs of an approaching disolution.'[22] Two days later when they sighted land at last, the launch had been forty-eight days at sea, and Bligh's men were almost dead from thirst and starvation, their bodies emaciated and their limbs livid with sores.

As Bligh exclaimed: 'It is not possible for me to describe the pleasure which the blessing of the sight of land diffused among us.'[23] Unsure that this was Timor, however, Bligh steered away towards a coastline that proved to be a group of islands. Convinced that they were heading away from Timor, Fryer kept his counsel until it was clear that Bligh was mistaken. As he reported later:

I was forward in the Boat looking out – the Gentlemen and people said to me several times Mr Fryer them are Islands, we are running off from the land – after all our sufferings we shall get no where . . .

At last Captain Bligh said Mr Fryer what do you think of that land ahead. – I said Sir what I first thought it was – Islands. Why did you not give your Oppinion before – you must have heard me say Sir that they were Islands when we first saw them, but as you did not ask my oppinion I did not think it proper to give it.

Captain Bligh was in a great Passion about my saying that my oppinion had not been ask[ed] – he said Sir I suppose that you will take the boat from me – I said no Sir I Dispise your Ideas – far from my intentions to take the boat from you. – O no Sir I am not afraid that you would take the Boat from me I would soon cut you to peices . . . It was then blowing very strong out at sea.[24]

On 14 July they finally approached Coupang (Kupang), a settlement in the Dutch East Indies. Waves crashed on the reef, and a powerful current almost swamped the boat. With Fryer steering the launch, Bligh celebrated the end of his 3618-mile odyssey by hoisting a home-made Union Jack on the main shrouds, and preparing his papers for a meeting with the Dutch governor. When he went ashore, Bligh left Fryer and a sailor, John Smith, in charge of the boat, although they were both perishing with hunger. Although the governor, Van Este, was very ill, he ordered Bligh to be given a house and meals; and his deputy, Mr Wanjon, was extremely kind to the castaway sailors. The commander of one of the Dutch ships in port, Captain Spikerman, invited them to dinner; and when he realised to his horror that Fryer and Smith were still on board the launch, Spikerman immediately sent them a pot of tea with some cakes. As Fryer

*The arrival of Bligh and his men at Timor.*

commented bitterly: 'All this time I might have gone to the Devil for my good friend Captain Bligh.'[25]

When the launch was finally at anchor and Fryer and Smith, having shaved, were brought to Spikerman's house where they were offered a meal, the master sat and wept instead of eating, then drank a glass of wine and went to sleep. That night Bligh thanked God for his miraculous deliverance:

> Instead of rest, I found my mind more disposed to reflect on the sufferings I had gone through, of the failure of my expedition, but above all of the thanks due to Almighty God who had given me power to support and bear such heavy Calamities, and to enable me at last to be the means of Saving 18 Lives which would never otherwise have been thought of.
>
> When I reflect how providentially our lives were saved at Tofua by the Indians delaying their Attack, and that with scarce any thing for forty Eight Days to support life we have crossed a Sea of more than 1200 Leagues without shelter or protection from the Evils of the Climates, besides the great probability of foundering at Sea, and when I view the great good fortune we had to pass the unfriendly Natives of other Countries without accident, and at last happily to meet with the most friendly and best of People to releive our distresses, it

calls up a distracted mind of astonishment, and most humble gratitude and reverence to Almighty God.

Thus happily ended through the assistance of Divine Providence without accident a Voyage of the most extraordinary Nature that ever happened in the World.[26]

Over the days that followed, Bligh and many of his men fell ill with fevers and other disorders. When he recovered, Bligh presented a short account of the mutiny to Van Este along with a detailed description of each of the mutineers, asking him to circulate this to each of the ports in the Dutch East Indies with an order that if the *Bounty* landed, the mutineers should be arrested as pirates. According to British common law, if a vessel with its cargo and equipment was violently seized from its commander, this was piracy and robbery as well as mutiny; and the Dutch had no love of pirates.[27]

Bligh also purchased a small schooner for 1000 rix-dollars (in Dutch currency), named it HMS *Resource*; and asked the governor to pay his accounts in Kupang in exchange for bills on the Commissioners of His Majesty's Navy. By this time the botanist David Nelson was very ill, suffering from blindness and burning pains in his stomach; and on 20 July he died, to the sorrow of Bligh, who greatly valued this quiet, dedicated man. The day before setting off to Surabaya, Bligh wrote a heartfelt letter to his wife, telling her about the mutiny:

> My Dear Dear Betsy
>
> I am now in a part of the world that I never expected, it is however a place that has afforded me relief and saved my life, and I have the happyness to assure you I am now in perfect health . . . What an emotion does my heart & soul feel that I have once more an opportunity of writing to you and my little Angels, and particularly as you have all been so near losing the best of Friends . . .
>
> Know then my own Dear Betsy, I have lost the *Bounty*!

In this unguarded account, Bligh raged against the Admiralty: 'I had not sufficient officers, and had they granted me marines, most likely the affair would never have happened.' He told her how proud he had been when he set off on his journey, and confessed that the mutiny had taken him completely by surprise. Bligh blamed Fletcher Christian, Peter Heywood and George Stewart for the disaster:

Christian I had assured of promotion when he came home, & with the other two I was every day rendering them some service. It is incredible! these very young Men I placed every confidence in, yet these great Villains joined with the most able Men in the Ship got possession of the Arms and took the *Bounty* from me, with huzza's for Otaheite.

I have now reason to curse the day I ever knew a Christian or a Heywood, or indeed a Manks man . . . Even Mr. Tom Ellison took such a liking to Otaheite that he also turned Pirate, so that I have been run down by my own Dogs.

He also railed against his two midshipmen:

I had not a Spirited & brave fellow about me & the Mutineers treated them as such. Hayward & Hallet were Mate & midshipmen of Christian's Watch, but they alarmed no one, & I found them on Deck seemingly unconcerned untill they were ordered into the Boat. The latter has turned out a worthless, impudent scoundrel.

Although Elizabeth Bligh was devoted to her husband, the Isle of Man was her home, and her father was very fond of Peter Heywood. In addition, Hallett's sister was her lifelong friend; Tom Ellison was a protégé of her uncle's, Duncan Campbell; while Fletcher Christian's family was highly regarded on the island. Six months after her husband's departure, she had borne twin daughters who died three weeks later; and her health had suffered. This letter, with its revelations about the loss of the *Bounty* and its imprecations against these young men, must have tested her faith in her husband to the limit.

William Bligh had been through many dangers, however; and he adored his wife and children. As he exclaimed in his letter:

Thus happily ended through the assistance of divine providence, without accident a Voyage of the most extraordinary nature that ever happened in the world, let it be taken either in its extent, duration or so much want of the necessaries of life . . .

I know how shocked you will be at this affair but I request of you My Dear Betsy to think nothing of it all is now past & we will again look forward to future happiness. Give my blessing to my Dear Harriet, my Dear Mary, my dear Betsy & to my Dear little stranger & tell them I shall soon be home. I give all that an Affectionate Husband can give Love Respect & all that is or ever will be in [my] power.[28]

During the passage to Surabaya on the *Resource*, Bligh used a Dutch map, which he considered highly inaccurate.[29] When they arrived on 16 September 1789 and Bligh went ashore to meet the governor, he was invited to dinner, and left his men on board the schooner. Returning to the *Resource* the next day in the commandant's launch, he sent some provisions to put on board the pinnace, but the crew refused to row out to the ship. In a fury, Thomas Hayward threatened to leave them behind, although his shipmates abused him, calling him 'a Lackay'. When they eventually followed Bligh out to the schooner, the midshipman John Hallett and the master's mate William Elphinstone were so angry with their captain that they refused to go on duty. After the commandant left the ship, and Bligh asked the master, 'Are they drunk or Ill or what is the matter with them?' Fryer retorted, 'Am I a Doctor? Ask them what is the matter with them.' Incensed by this reply, Bligh exclaimed angrily, 'What do you mean by this insolence?' Fryer replied, 'It is no insolence. You not only use me Ill but every Man in the Vessel and every Man will say the same.' According to Bligh, the other men muttered, 'Yes, By God, we are usd damn ill, nor have we any right to be usd so.' William Purcell also spoke up, complaining that when Bligh had sent provisions to the pinnace, he had left his men to pay for their carriage. After their terrible sufferings, they found it intolerable that Bligh would abandon them while he was being entertained ashore, and that when he returned to the *Resource*, they were expected to pay his purser's bills.

Another mutiny seemed imminent. Seizing a bayonet, Bligh ordered Fryer and Purcell to go below; and hailing the commandant's launch, asked him to return to the *Resource*. When the commandant, a man named de Bose, came on board with an escort of armed men, he told Bligh that some of his men had spread a report ashore that 'I should be hanged or blown from the Mouth of a Cannon as soon as I got home', identifying William Purcell as the culprit. When he heard this, Thomas Hayward protested his loyalty, weeping and throwing himself into his captain's arms. According to Bligh, 'The Honor and integrity of this young Man made the Wretches about him tremble and having gained my good wishes his grief subsided.' Taking Fryer and Purcell as prisoners, Bligh asked the commandant to hold an inquiry, saying that any of his men who had complaints against him should go ashore to testify before that tribunal. Only the acting surgeon Thomas Ledward, John Hallett and William Cole were willing to give evidence, and when they were examined the following day, Hallett complained that Bligh had beaten him for not getting into the boat at Tahiti; Ledward stated that Bligh would not allow him to go ashore at Surabaya; while William Cole made no particular accusation. John Fryer, however, who was being held in prison, presented a document signed by Van Este, the governor at Kupang, saying that Bligh had inflated the sums in his bills from that place against the Commissioners of the Navy, and accused Bligh of giving his men short allowance throughout the voyage, profiting at their expense. Later, Bligh angrily retorted:

> I had nothing more to do to show the Villainy of this Man and the improper and Unwarrantable conduct of Van Este in laying a plot with an inferior officer to entrap his Commander, than to show my papers in which were receipts and vouchers for all my transactions in Timor Signed by the Master and Boatswain and Witness'd by two respectable Residanters.[30]

As soon as Bligh returned to the schooner, however, Fryer lost his nerve, apologising in an abject letter. On 17 September when Bligh interviewed Fryer in the presence of the Commandant, according to Bligh the master 'trembled, look'd pale and humbly asked to be forgiven, declairing he would make every concession & disavowal of the infamous reports that he spread. That he would give every reparation I pleased to Ask.'[31] Bligh was unrelenting, sending Fryer and Purcell under arrest into a *prau* (canoe) that would accompany the schooner on the journey to Samarang (Semarang), en route to Batavia.

After the *Resource* arrived at Semarang on 23 September 1789, Bligh met the Dutch governor, who invited him to dinner. At Semarang Fryer sent a letter from the *prau*, begging to be released and once again apologising for the things that he had said at Surabaya. He also forwarded the note signed by Van Este, saying that he had not met the governor at Kupang and that the note had been sent to him by Captain Spikerman, asking that it should be withdrawn.[32] Upon arriving at Batavia (now Jakarta) on 1 October, Bligh fell ill with a high fever and violent headaches, during which 'my temples throbed with great Violence, and a pain across my forehead was so severe that I thought my Head would burst asunder',[33] and was sent to the Convalescent Hospital. At the same time Thomas Hall suffered from a flux, dying on 11 October.

When Bligh recovered, he sold the *Resource* for only 295 rix-dollars; and when he advanced the men money for their living costs, demanded onerous securities for these loans, forcing each of them to sign a formal affidavit that the mutiny had been unprovoked, and that the loss of the *Bounty* was not of his making. As Thomas Ledward, the acting surgeon, wrote to his uncle from Batavia:

> When I arrived at Timor, I was so weak, I could not walk, so that had we been at sea two or three Days longer I should certainly have perished; & it was full

six Weeks before I gained any tolerable firmness. The sad affair happened early in the Morning Watch; as soon as I was informed fully how the matter stood, I instantly declared I would go with the Captain, let the consequence be what it would, & not stay among Mutineers.

But I have been at great & unavoidable expenses; first at Timor, where I arrived among the Dutch naked, who I must say behaved extremely well to us; & secondly at this place which is extremely dear. I am now at the only Inn, where strangers are entertained, along with the rest of the Officers, & one would not wish to appear like an Outcast or a Beggar.

There is one thing I must mention which is of consequence: the Captain denied me, as well as the rest of the Gentlemen, who had not Agents, any Money unless I would give him my power of Attorney & also my Will, in which I was to bequeath him all my property; this he called by the name of *proper security*. This unless I did, I should have got no money, though I shewed him a letter of Credit from my Uncle & offered to give him a Bill of Exchange upon him. In case of my Death I hope this matter will be clearly pointed out to my Relations.[34]

While Bligh was demanding this kind of 'security' from his men, he also drafted reports of the mutiny to Sir Joseph Banks and the Admiralty, accompanied by a self-righteous letter to Banks, protesting that he was innocent of any blame for the uprising, which he described as 'one of the most atrocious and consumate acts of Piracy ever committed'.[35] He added: 'My health has been much impaired but conscious of my honor and integrity with a self acquitted of every particle of disgrace, It has buoyed my spirits in a most amazing degree.' Of his men, he noted: 'I have saved their lives most miraculously & now to save my own I am obliged to fly from Batavia . . . I have been since here almost dead with a fever, but it seems to be at present tolerably removed.'[36] At the same time Bligh reproached himself for his failure to justify Banks's faith in him: 'When I think that it was through you Sir who undertook to assert that I was fully capable, and the eyes of every one regarding the progress of the Voyage, and perhaps more with envy than with delight, I cannot say but it affects me considerably.'[37] Knowing that as a young man, Banks himself had spent three idyllic months in Tahiti, he added:

It may be asked what could be the cause for such a Revolution. In Answer to which I have only to give a description of Otaheite, which has every allurement both to luxury and ease, and is the Paradise of the World.

The Women are handsome, mild in their Manners and conversation, possessed of great sensibility, with sufficient delicacy to make them admired and loved. What a temptation it is to such Wretches when they find it in their power (however illegally it can be got at) to fix themselves in the midst of Plenty in the finest Island in the World, where they need not labour, and where the allurements of disipation are more than equal to any thing that can be conceived . . .

I can only conjecture that the Pirates (among whom is poor Nelson's assistant) have Ideally assured themselves of a more happy life among the Otaheiteans than they could possibly have in England, which joined to some female connections, has most likely been the leading cause of the whole busyness.[38]

Unlike Captain Cook, however, who had shown a fatherly concern for Alexander Mouat, the young midshipman who had deserted from the *Resolution* in Ra'iatea, Bligh was relentless in his condemnation of the mutineers, railing against them as 'villains' and 'pirates'. In this and later reports, Bligh suggested that the mutiny was a well-organised plot that had been laid in Tahiti (rather than a spontaneous, chaotic uprising, as the evidence suggests); glossing over the fact that although the mutineers were a minority of the crew, those men who were 'loyal' to him had made no real effort to resist – although to be fair, Christian and his fellows had taken them by surprise, quickly seizing all of the muskets and pistols on board the *Bounty*. He also failed to mention any of his clashes with his officers during the voyage.

Intent upon vengeance, Bligh sent a list of physical descriptions of those who had remained on board the *Bounty* to the Admiralty, beginning with the officers – Fletcher Christian ('master's mate, aged twenty-four years, five feet nine inches high, blackish, or very dark brown complexion, dark brown hair, strong made, a star tattooed on his left breast; tattooed on his backside; his knees stand a little out, and he may be called rather bow-legged. He is subject to violent perspirations, and particularly in his hands, so that he soils anything he handles'); George Stewart ('midshipman, aged twenty-three years, five feet seven inches high, good complexion, dark hair, slender made, narrow chested; tattooed on the left breast with a star, and on the left arm with a heart and darts, is also tattooed on the backside'); Peter Heywood ('midshipman, aged seventeen years, five feet seven inches high, fair complexion, light brown hair, well proportioned, very much tattooed; and on the right leg is tattooed the three legs of Man. At this time he has not done growing, and speaks with the Manx accent'); and Edward

Young ('midshipman, aged seventeen years, five feet eight inches high, strong made, has lost several of his fore teeth, and those that remain are all rotten; and on the right arm is tattooed a heart and dart through it').[39]

While vilifying 'the pirates', Bligh wrote warmly about Tu and his family in Tahiti. As he wrote to Sir Joseph Banks:

> I left these happy Islanders in much distress, for the utmost affection, regard and good fellowship remained among us during my Stay. The King and all the Royal Family were allways my guests, and their good sense and Observations, joined with the most engaging dispositions in the World, will ever make them beloved by all who become acquainted with them as Freinds.[40]

When he heard that a Dutch ship (the *Vlydt*) was about to sail for the Cape of Good Hope with room for only three passengers on board, Bligh claimed these berths for himself, his servant and his clerk on the grounds of ill health, leaving the rest of the crew behind in Batavia with a month's pay and orders to return to England as soon as possible. During this passage, Bligh criticised the Dutch captain and his seamanship, remarking, 'I am certain that if I had the Command of this Vessel I could run 1½ knot pr Hour more than this man'; and complaining bitterly about the conditions on board:

> The Men are stinking and dirty with long beards, and their Bedding a nuisance, as may be conceived when they have not washed Hammocks since they have been from Europe. The Capt. in his person and bedding equally dirty. Some of the people [have] not a second shift of Cloaths. Cookery so bad I cannot make a Meal: such nasty beasts.[41]

At the Cape of Good Hope, Bligh just missed Edward Riou, who had also sailed with Captain Cook in 1777. Riou (whose pet Polynesian dog had been tried for cannibalism in Queen Charlotte Sound) was now the commander of the *Guardian*, a convict transport bound for New South Wales. Twelve days after leaving the Cape of Good Hope, the *Guardian* hit an iceberg and began to sink, and Riou was forced to order his men to abandon ship and take to the boats, while he stayed with the listing vessel. Unlike Bligh, however, Riou was popular with his men, and three of the midshipmen and twenty-two sailors refused to leave him. They managed to patch up the *Guardian*'s hull, and by pumping for their lives, got the ship back to the Cape, arriving there in February 1790, although only one of her four boats made it back into port.[42] There Riou met and detained

John Fryer, who was being taken as a prisoner back to England; and Fryer helped him to refit the battered vessel. During this period Fryer must have told Riou about Bligh's behaviour on board the *Bounty*, the mutiny and their sufferings on the *Bounty*'s launch.[43]

As soon as Bligh arrived in England, landing at the Isle of Wight on 13 March 1790, he hastened ashore; and four days later was presented to George III, presenting the King with a copy of his account of the mutiny and its aftermath that created a sensation when it was published later that year. While a mutiny on board a Royal Navy ship was always newsworthy, the tale of an uprising provoked by the temptations of a life of sensuous bliss on an island Utopia captured the popular imagination. The French Revolution was unfolding, and the political elite in Britain were anxiously watching events across the Channel. In April 1789, when the mutiny on the *Bounty* took place, riots in Paris caused by low wages and food shortages had been forcibly suppressed by the army. The French royal government was insolvent, and when Louis XVI tried to force the nobility to pay taxes and share some of their power, they intransigently resisted. The third estate representing the commoners declared itself the National Assembly, and was locked out of meeting houses by royal decree, until some nobles and clergymen declared their support, and Louis was forced to recognise the Assembly's legitimacy. Aristocrats' houses were attacked and ransacked, and on 14 July the Bastille was stormed in Paris. In August 1789 the Assembly adopted *The Declaration of the Rights of Man and of the Citizen*, and in October the palace at Versailles was ransacked. While the pillars of the Ancien Régime were toppling in France, a debate about human rights was raging in Britain. Although some – especially the ruling elite, decried the Revolution as a return to a savage state, and the rule of the mob, others – especially the Dissenters and others excluded from parliamentary power – heralded the Revolution as the dawn of a new age of 'liberty, equality and fraternity'.

In November 1789, for instance, the Welsh Unitarian minister Dr Richard Price delivered an exalted sermon, hailing the uprisings in France:

> And now, methinks, I see the ardour for liberty catching and spreading; . . . the dominion of kings changed for the dominion of laws, and the dominion of priests giving way to the dominion of reason and conscience. Behold the light you have struck out, after setting America free, reflected to France and there kindled into a blaze that lays despotism in ashes and warms and illuminates Europe.[44]

The poet William Wordsworth (Fletcher Christian's former schoolmate at Cockermouth, who owed the return of his family fortune to Fletcher's brother, Edward), inspired by the early stages of the French Revolution, wrote an ecstatic ode suggesting that the Utopias hitherto imagined in 'secreted islands' were being realised across the Channel:

> Bliss was it in that dawn to be alive,
> But to be young was very heaven! – Oh! times,
> In which the meagre, stale forbidding ways
> Of custom, law and statute took, at once
> The attraction of a country in romance! . . .
> Now was it that both found, the meek and lofty . . .
> Were called upon to exercise their skill,
> Not in Utopia, subterranean fields,
> Or some secreted island, Heaven knows where!
> But in the very world, which is the world
> Of all of us, – the place where, in the end
> We find our happiness, or not at all![45]

In response to these idealists, in January 1790 the statesman Edmund Burke, appalled by the attack on Versailles, penned a blistering attack on Dr Price's sermon, defending the constitutional monarchy in Britain. Blaming the French Revolution on the Utopian dreams of Rousseau and Voltaire, Burke argued that respect for authority was at the heart of British tradition; and that defiance of authority led to licentiousness and slavery to the passions:

> We still bear the stamp of our forefathers. We have not yet subtilised ourselves into savages. We are not the converts of Rousseau; we are not the disciples of Voltaire; Helvetius has made no progress among us. Atheists are not our preachers; madmen are not our law-givers.
>
> We have real hearts of flesh and blood beating in our bosoms. We fear God; we look up with awe to kings; with affection to parliaments; with duty to magistrates; with reverence to priests; and with respect to nobility. Why?
>
> Because when such ideas are brought before our minds, it is *natural* to be so affected; because all other feelings are false and spurious, and tend to corrupt our minds, to vitiate our primary morals; and by teaching us a servile, licentious and abandoned insolence, make us fit for, and justly deserving of, slavery, through the whole course of our lives.[46]

In this volatile political climate, while some hailed the *Bounty* mutineers for having struck a blow for freedom and the rights of man, others saw them as exemplars of 'licentious and abandoned insolence'.

Eager to avoid public sympathy for Fletcher Christian and his followers, the British authorities treated Bligh as a hero. News of another mutiny against the merchant captain John Meares at Nootka (during which almost all of the crew had signed a paper that bound them to join the uprising, intending to sail for the 'voluptuous abodes' of Hawai'i) had arrived in London – another clash of personal freedom against British authority in the Pacific.[47] When Bligh arrived back in England in March 1790, the newspapers were full of his extraordinary feat in safely navigating the launch to Timor; and the story flew to India and the West Indies, where the newspapers breathlessly recounted tales of the mutiny on the *Bounty*. In Kingston, for example, the *Daily Advertiser* marvelled:

> The escape of the Lieutenant and the companions of his miserable misfortune, cannot be accounted less than a miracle of miracles, which baffles all human wisdom in the bare contemplation, and sets all reasoning at defiance.[48]

According to the *Madras Courier*, although good order had prevailed on the *Bounty*, at daybreak on 27 April 1789, off the 'Friendly Islands' (i.e. Tonga), 'the Officer of the Watch, assisted by three others, dragged [Bligh] on the deck, menacing his life, if he attempted to speak. His endeavours to exhort and bring back the *Conspirators* to their duty, proved of no avail. Each of these desperadoes was armed with a drawn cutlass, or fixed bayonet, and all their muskets were avowed to be charged!'[49]

Back in England, only weeks after Bligh's arrival, an anonymous account of the mutiny was advertised in the press, with 'secret Anecdotes of the Otaheitean Women, whose charms, it is thought, influenced the pirates in the commission of the daring conspiracy';[50] and a theatrical performance was staged at the Royalty Theatre entitled 'The Pirates, or, the Calamities of Capt. Bligh'. The advertisements of this play promised:

> A Fact, told in action, Exhibiting a full Account of his Voyage . . . The Captain's reception at Otaheite, and exchanging the British Manufactures for the Bread Fruit – with an Otaheitean Dance – the Attachment of the Otaheitan Women to, and their Distress at parting from, the British Sailors – an exact representation of the Seizure of Capt. Bligh, in the cabin of the Bounty by the Pirates, with the affecting scene of forcing the Captain and his faithful followers into

the Boat – their Distress at Sea, and Repulse by the Natives of Timur . . . and their happy arrival in England.[51]

Given this sort of publicity, popular opinion was firmly on Bligh's side; and the Admiralty gave him paid leave, although they refused to reimburse him for his possessions that had vanished with the *Bounty*, including 'a valuable collection of books, maps, and drawings with all my remarks and observations for fifteen years past'.[52] This was indeed a great loss, since these papers included his *Resolution* and *Bounty* logs and charts; and Bligh was an accomplished cartographer, observer and artist (in a naive style).

James Matra, who sailed with Cook on the *Endeavour*, echoed public sentiment when he wrote to Joseph Banks: 'The escape of poor Bligh by his companions is a miracle that has not been equalled these 1700 years.'[53] According to Fanny Burney, one day when she and her brother James were on their way to witness Warren Hastings's impeachment at the House of Lords they met William Windham, an MP, who exclaimed, 'But what officers you are! *you men of Captain Cook*; you rise upon us in every trial! This Captain Bligh – what feats, what wonders he has performed! (What difficulties got through! What dangers defied! And with such cool, manly skill!)'[54] At that time, too, Bligh's wife's family friend, George Keate, published a poem welcoming him home to England, and castigating Christian as 'a first-born wretch, who 'gainst a brother raised his murd'rous hand', exhorting Bligh:

> O gallant Sailor! Urge thy bold career.
> If the prophetic Muse aright forsee
> Throu' seas untry'd thou still thy course may'st steer,
> And what *Cook* was, thereafter *Bligh* may be.[55]

In his triumph, however, Bligh was ruthless. Fletcher Christian's family, who loved him dearly, had been devastated by news of the mutiny. As his brother Charles, the surgeon, wrote: 'I was struck with horror and weighed down with a Sorrow to so extreme a pitch that I became stupefied . . . I have in bed perspired with agony of mind till I thought my nostrils were impressed with a smell of Death – such was the peculiar sensation I experienced.'[56] In his desperation, he wrote to Dr Betham, Bligh's brother-in-law, pleading for his brother: 'Fletcher when a Boy was slow to be moved . . . [But] when Men are cooped up for a long Time in the Interior of a Ship, there oft prevails such jarring Discordancy of Tempers and Conduct that it is enough on many Occasions by repeated Acts of Irritation and

Offence to change the Disposition of a Lamb into that of an Animal fierce and resentful.' Predicting that 'it would be found that there had been some Cause not then known that had driven Fletcher to this desperate Step . . . My feelings were so harrowed up with this unlooked for and unhappy intelligence that I would have him consider that instead of Ink, it was my Heart's Blood I wrote with.'[57] When Dr Betham showed this letter to his son-in-law, however, Bligh declared that Fletcher must have been insane. And when Peter Heywood's recently widowed mother wrote him an imploring letter, Bligh responded with a brutal note:

London, April 2 1790

Madam,

I received your Letter this Day & feel for you very much, being perfectly sensible of the extreme Distress you must suffer from the Conduct of your Son Peter. His Baseness is beyond all Description but I hope you will endeavour to prevent the Loss of him, heavy as the misfortune is, from afflicting you too severely. – I imagine he is with the rest of the Mutineers return'd to Otaheite.

To one of Peter's uncles, Colonel James Holwell, Bligh wrote even more harshly:

SIR,

I have just this Instant received your Letter – with much Concern I inform you that your Nephew, Peter Heywood is among the Mutineers: his Ingratitude to me is of the blackest Dye for I was a Father to him in every Respect & he never once had an angry Word from me thro' the whole Course of the Voyage, as his conduct always gave me much pleasure & Satisfaction. I very much regret that so much Baseness form'd the Character of a young Man I had a real regard for & it will give me much Pleasure to hear his Friends can bear the Loss of him without much Concern.[58]

Like Christian's family, Peter Heywood's relatives were distraught, and his mother and his sisters flatly refused to believe that he was capable of mutiny. Begged by Peter's sister Nessy to inquire further, J.M. Heywood, a cousin of Peter's father, met with Bligh, who assured him that 'the Cause of this horrid Transaction [was] the Attachments unfortunately form'd to the Women of Otaheite'. It is probable that Bligh also told Heywood that Peter was among those who had received treatment for venereal infections during their time on the island. When Heywood tried to comfort Nessy, saying that with his excellent record and good character, 'and some Allowance for the unbridled passion of Youth', Peter might still be pardoned, he urged her not to tell her mother 'the true Cause of your Brother's not returning'.[59]

While Bligh was being hailed for his extraordinary journey, two of his companions in the launch (his master's mate William Elphinstone and Peter Linkletter, a quartermaster) died in Batavia, and the butcher Robert Lamb also perished during his voyage back to England. According to Arthur Denman, the young surgeon Thomas Ledward died on the homeward journey when his ship foundered and, as he had feared, it is likely that Bligh inherited his estate.[60] As the *Calcutta Gazette* lamented: '[We] bring the unpleasing intelligence that most of the hands, who endured so much hardship in an open boat through the Pacific Ocean were so exhausted that it was feared nature would never be recruited in them. Four of the unfortunate sufferers are dead, and all the rest were left in a very languishing state.'[61] Of the eighteen men who accompanied William Bligh on the launch, only twelve survived the ordeal.

When the last of these men arrived back in England, and Bligh's court martial was finally held on board the *Royal William* on 22 October 1790, his men did not repeat the accusations that they had made in the East Indies. Although Fryer had earlier made serious allegations about Bligh's conduct as a purser, and his transactions in the Cape of Good Hope and Kupang, Bligh had damning evidence about his master's disloyalty during the voyage. Each of them had too much at stake in the court martial, and in the event made a pact to keep quiet.[62] After expunging his hostile comments about Fryer from the official version of the ship's log, Bligh told the court martial that he had no complaints to make about any of his men except for William Purcell, the carpenter, who had flouted his orders at the Great Barrier Reef; while Fryer kept silent about his commander's financial transactions. His men corroborated Bligh's account that the mutiny was unexpected and that Christian had captured him while he was asleep, holding him under armed guard before forcing him into the launch. As a result, Bligh and all of the sailors except Purcell, who was reprimanded, were honourably acquitted and discharged.[63]

Under these circumstances, it is not surprising that Joseph Banks remained loyal to Bligh; and after the court martial when Bligh was promoted to commander and given the 14-gun sloop *Falcon*, Banks regarded this as a niggardly return for his sufferings. He argued his case with the Admiralty until, on 15 December 1790, William Bligh was promoted to post-captain on half pay, awaiting a new command.

PLATE I: *William Bligh, by John Webber.*

PLATE 2: *James Cook, by John Webber.*

PLATE 3: *Vaitepiha Bay in southern Tahiti (Tahiti-iti)*.

PLATE 4: *The mutiny on the* Bounty.

PLATE 5: *Kealakekua Bay.*

PLATE 6: *The death of Captain Cook.*

PLATE 7: *Elizabeth (Betsy) Betham, by John Webber.*

PLATE 8: *Charles Clerke.*

PLATE 9: *Matavai Bay, Tahiti.*

PLATE 10: *A view in Moʻorea, by James Cleveley.*

PLATE 11: *Tu*.

# 13

## An Island Fort

In the chaos and confusion of the mutiny on the *Bounty*, it was difficult to know who were in fact 'loyalists' or 'mutineers', and who were simply caught up in the mayhem and found themselves on one side or another. Those who were sent into the launch included most of the men who had previously sailed with Bligh – William Peckover the gunner, who had sailed on all three of Cook's voyages; David Nelson, the botanist, who had sailed with them on Cook's third expedition (although Joseph Coleman the armourer, another of their shipmates, had been forced to stay on board the *Bounty*); and Lawrence Lebogue the sailmaker and John Norton, quartermaster, who had sailed with Bligh on the *Britannia*, although their shipmate Thomas Ellison joined the mutineers. Christian also sent the master, John Fryer; the boatswain, William Cole; and the two midshipmen, Hayward and Hallett, down into the launch. Almost all of the able-bodied seamen and all of the 'young gentlemen' who had enlisted as ordinary sailors but were treated as midshipmen – Fletcher Christian, George Stewart (who had forged a close relationship with a woman in Tahiti), Peter Heywood and Edward Young – remained on board the *Bounty*. One way or another, nineteen men including Bligh were sent down into the launch, while twenty-four of their shipmates stayed on board with Fletcher Christian.

As the launch disappeared in the distance, Christian told the men who had remained on board about what had happened the previous night – how he had decided to make a raft and leave the ship, and why he had changed his mind and decided to try and take over the *Bounty*. Although he offered the command of the ship to George Stewart, as a strict disciplinarian Stewart was not popular with the men, who quickly assured Christian that they wanted him to act as their captain. After talking together, they decided to head for Tahiti via Tupua'i in the Austral Islands, which William Bligh had charted during Cook's third voyage.

Taking command of one of the watches, Christian put George Stewart in charge of the other, while James Morrison (the sallow, black-haired boatswain's mate) was promoted to boatswain; Thomas McIntosh (the carpenter's mate, his face scarred by smallpox) to carpenter; and John Mills (a tall, fair man who at forty years old was still a gunner's mate) to gunner. At 9 a.m. when a breeze sprang up, the sailors trimmed the sails; and most of the breadfruit plants that Bligh had collected with such pains were thrown overboard. When the Great Cabin was cleared, the bark cloth and curiosities obtained in Tahiti and Tonga were stored there with the officers' effects, while Christian took over Bligh's own cabin. Although the armourer Joseph Coleman and some others talked about trying to recapture the ship, they were overheard; and when Christian was told, he threatened to leave them at Tupua'i, and taking the keys to the arms chest from Coleman, gave them to the ship's corporal Charles Churchill. Determined that his shipmates should adopt some semblance of naval discipline, Christian also ordered the studding sails to be cut up into uniforms, edged with cloth from his own lieutenant's uniform; and the mizzen and staysails were cut up for this purpose.

On 28 May 1789 when they finally arrived off Tupua'i, a small island encircled by dazzling strips of white sand, Christian sent George Stewart in the small cutter, armed only with a brace of pistols, to examine the reef and Tearamoana Pass on the northern coast, which William Bligh had charted during Cook's last voyage. When the cutter entered the pass, a war canoe came out, packed with men armed with long spears who attacked the little boat, wounding one of the sailors, boarding the boat and seizing a jacket. Stewart was taken by surprise, but when he fired one of his pistols (the other having misfired), the warriors retreated. During Cook's last voyage, two of his men had deserted from the *Resolution* at Ra'iatea and been taken by canoe to Tupua'i, where they became the first white men to stay on the island. When Reo's men came to capture them, however, there had been killings, and the Tupua'i warriors had no love for the white strangers.

The next morning the cutter was sent off again to mark the pass. When the *Bounty* entered the lagoon, anchoring off a sandy bay, warriors boarded a fleet of canoes and surrounded the ship, blowing conch-shell trumpets; while other warriors dressed in red and white stood on the beach, armed with clubs and shining black wood spears, and blowing conch shells to challenge the mutineers. Although the sailors spoke in Tahitian to the men alongside in the canoes, who seemed to understand them, they refused to board the ship, making threatening gestures before returning to their island.

By dawn the next morning, 31 May, many more canoes and warriors had assembled. When an old man came out in a canoe and boarded the *Bounty*, gazing about him in astonishment and starting in alarm when any of the pigs, goats or dogs looked at him, Christian gave him gifts; and although the old man promised to visit him again, the sailors noticed that he was carefully counting their numbers. During the afternoon a double canoe paddled by six men came out, carrying eighteen beautiful young women, neatly dressed with flower and pearl-shell headdresses and necklaces and with black wavy hair down to their waists. These girls stood up and sang as they approached the ship, beating time, led by a chief's daughter. Christian ordered the men to arm themselves, and as the women boarded the ship, hoping to distract the strangers, about fifty canoes, each carrying between fifteen and twenty warriors, approached the other side of the *Bounty*. The sailors were on the alert, however, and as soon as the warriors realised that their ploy had failed, they blew conch-shell trumpets and followed the girls on board where they grabbed everything that they could lay their hands on, just as the Tahitians had done during their first encounters with the *Dolphin*.

When one man stole the card from the ship's compass, Christian decided to make an example of him. Seizing the thief, he flogged him with a knotted rope and sent him down into his canoe, followed by his companions, including all of the women. Seeing this, the crews of the other canoes brandished their weapons, which they had previously hidden, threatening the sailors; and when one man cut the rope from the anchor buoy and began to paddle the buoy back to land, Christian fired his musket and ordered a 4-pounder loaded with grape shot to be fired into the milling canoes, which hastily fled ashore. The boats were lowered and the sailors chased the canoes to the beach, where the warriors pelted them with barrages of stones, retreating only when some of their number were shot and fell dead into the water. Upon examining the abandoned canoes, the sailors found a number of ropes on board, carried to tie up any of the strangers who were captured. Christian ordered the men to tow the canoes out to the *Bounty*, but during the night these craft broke loose and drifted back to the island.

Thinking that the population of Tupua'i was so small that it could readily be subdued with firearms, and that no European ship was likely to visit this isolated island (which had no safe port), Christian decided that this was a good place to settle. The next morning he led two armed boats to the eastern point, one flying a white flag and the other a Union Jack, landing close to several groups of houses where they left a gift of hatchets, although the inhabitants hid in a swamp. According to Morrison, 'for want of their usual bedding, the [islanders] caught Colds, Agues and Sore Eyes, running at the Noses'. This illness must have been contracted on board the *Bounty*, however, and the Tupua'i people blamed it on the gods of the strangers.[1] The next morning several men came down to the beach who retrieved the floating canoes, and afterwards Christian sent a boat ashore with a young goat and two pigs, which were ailing. When the boat returned to the *Bounty* they set sail for Tahiti, where Christian planned to collect a supply of pigs, goats and chickens for their new settlement, since they had seen none of these animals on Tupua'i. During their passage back to Tahiti, Christian told the men to draw lots for the clothes and effects of those who had been sent into the launch with Captain Bligh, saying that when they returned to Tahiti, any deserters would be shot, and that none of them was to mention the name of Tupua'i or to say anything about their plans to settle on that island.

On 6 June 1789 when the *Bounty* arrived back in Matavai Bay, their friends flocked on board, greeting them warmly and asking what had happened to the breadfruit plants and the rest of the crew. When Tu asked Christian what had happened to Mr Bligh and the breadfruit plants, Christian told him that after leaving Tahiti, they had discovered to their astonishment that Captain Cook was still alive and living on Aitutaki. After taking Mr Bligh and the others on board his ship with the breadfruit plants and the longboat, Captain Cook had sent Christian and his companions back to Tahiti to fetch pigs, goats and other animals for a new settlement on Aitutaki. Tu was sceptical, however, asking repeatedly why Bligh had not returned with him, or indeed, Captain Cook, to whom his people were devoted. As Coleman later reported, Tu's wife 'Itia, who had been remarkably attached to Captain Bligh, became exceedingly melancholy at his seeming indifference, and his failure to return with the *Bounty*. On this account she entertained an aversion to Christian and his accomplices, and seldom or ever accompanied her husband in his visits.[2] Their Tahitian girlfriends were thrilled to see the sailors, however, preparing a feast and a *heiva* for Christian and his men; and Stewart and Churchill, who had forged attachments to particular women, were reunited with their lovers. Morrison was sent ashore to barter for pigs, goats and other animals, while Joseph Coleman was put to work making trade goods out of iron.

Meanwhile, Christian entertained the chiefs, plying them with wine and arrack, of which they were very fond. According to Morrison, while none of the chiefs truly liked Bligh, whom they flattered for his riches, 'Mr. Christian was beloved by the whole of them'[3] (although Morrison was hardly dispassionate). As the consequences of his impulsive uprising sank in, however, Christian became moody and sullen. During his previous visit, he had become attached to a tall, aristocratic woman called Mauatua, whom he called 'Isabella' and the sailors nicknamed 'Mainmast' for her upright posture; and he now turned to sex as a consolation. According to Coleman, 'he gave a loose to passion, which served in a great measure to dispel those gloomy thoughts which occasionally stole in to the great annoyance of his rest'.⁴ It proved to be very difficult for Christian to control his shipmates, however, and there were several clashes with the Tahitians. On 10 June, for instance, William McCoy, who was standing sentry duty, fired at islanders who were crowding on the gangway, although no one was hurt; and on 14 June, when Churchill hailed a canoe that was approaching the ship and received no answer, he fired at its crew.

On 16 June after a cargo of 460 pigs, fifty goats, many chickens, a few dogs and cats had been loaded on board the *Bounty*, along with a bull and cow that had been bartered for red feathers, the mutineers set sail for Tupua'i, accompanied by a number of Tahitians. These included Christian's lover Mauatua or 'Mainmast'; George Stewart's 'Peggy' (Teria, the daughter of Te Pau, the high chief of Fa'a'a); Te'ehuteatuaonoa or 'Jenny', the good-looking partner of Alexander Smith (who had tattooed her left arm with an inscription, 'AS 1789'); and William McCoy's lover Te'o, or 'Mary'.⁵

As they sailed out of Matavai Bay, the *Bounty* briefly grounded on the Dolphin Bank, and when they reached the open sea, a number of stowaways emerged from their hiding places, including several of the sailors' *taio* (among them Tupairu, Coleman's bond friend from Matavai Bay), and Hitihiti, the high-born young *'arioi* from Porapora who had sailed with Captain Cook in 1773–74 to Tonga, New Zealand, the Antarctic, Easter Island and the Marquesas. In all, nine Tahitian women, eight men, seven boys and one female child had boarded the *Bounty*. Christian agreed to take these people to Tupua'i, and although he warned them that they would never see Tahiti again, none of them seemed upset at this prospect.

During the passage to Tupua'i the weather was rough, and after falling down several times, the bull collapsed and died. It was hot and the carcass soon turned putrid, and had to be thrown overboard. Otherwise only four of the pigs and one goat were lost during this passage, and on 23 June 1789 when they finally anchored in 'Bloody Bay' on Tupua'i (as they had dubbed the harbour west of Mata'ura village), they found that the islanders were now friendly, boarding the ship without further warlike challenges. The epidemic that had followed their previous visit had been blamed upon the gods, who were said to have been angered by the attack on the strangers by the chief Tinarou and his warriors. Over the next few days, the boats rowed back and forth through Tearamoana Pass, ferrying the cow and 200 pigs and landing some on the islets and some on shore, these strange animals startling the local people more than the sailors' firearms had done. According to the Tahitians, who readily understood the Tupua'i dialect, during the attack at the end of May, eleven men and one woman had been killed. The local people were unconcerned, however, since the victims had come from the south-eastern district of Paorani; while they were now in Toerauetoru (now called Mata'ura), the north-western district opposite the lagoon entrance, the largest in the island, led by a chief named Hiterire, now succeeded by his son Tamatoa. Tamatoa, who was at war with Tinarou, was delighted that he and his warriors had been vanquished. Some of his people had collected musket balls after the battle, and wore them as trophies on strings around their necks.

After welcoming Christian ashore, Tamatoa adopted him as his bond friend. Leading the young man to his *marae*, he seated him on a large bale of bark cloth, surrounded by the leading men of the district. After making a long speech, the high chief presented Christian with a plantain shoot, the emblem of peace, and an *'ava* root, saluting him as 'Tamatoa', a sign that they had exchanged names and were now bond friends. He was followed by the other chiefs, each of whom presented Christian with a piece of bark cloth, a plantain branch and *'ava* root; and they in turn were followed by fifty 'landed men', each accompanied by an attendant who carried a piece of bark cloth and two baskets of provisions, including raw and dressed fish, breadfruit, taro, plantains, coconuts and other food; and the women of the chief's family, who also brought bark cloth and gifts of food, placing these before the young lieutenant. When the ceremonial presentations were over, the piles of food were loaded into the boats; and that night Tamatoa stayed on board the *Bounty*, reciting incantations at Christian's bedside. In the morning Christian presented him with hatchets, red feathers, bark cloth and fine mats, which the chief received with delight, especially the red feathers.

The next day, Christian accompanied his friend to look for a place to settle. Finding no suitable site in Tamatoa's district, he carried on to the Natieva district at the north-east end of the island. Natieva was led by a chief named Tahuhuatama, now succeeded by his son Ta'aroatohoa, an enemy of Tamatoa's who invited him to stay there. When Christian agreed to settle in Ta'aroatohoa's district, however, also exchanging names with this chief, Tamatoa was infuriated by this betrayal of their bond friendship. Smarting at Christian's desertion, he and the chief of the eastern districts, Tinarou, formed an alliance against the mutineers, forbidding their people to visit the ship or to have anything to do with Fletcher Christian. This was in spite of the fact that Tinarou was married

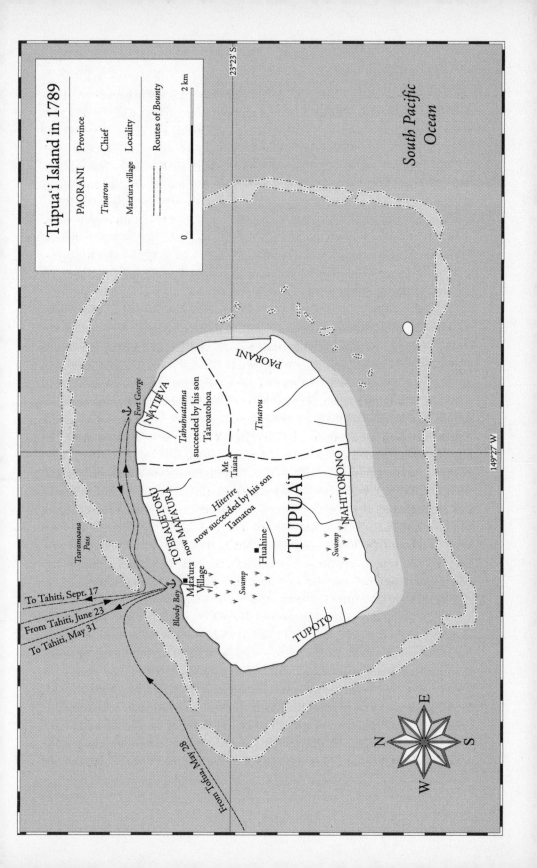

Tupua'i Island in 1789

PAORANI    Province

Timarou    Chief

Matarura village    Locality

—·—·—·—    Routes of *Bounty*

0           2 km

South Pacific
Ocean

23°23′ S

149°27′ W

Fort George

NATIEVA

PAORANI

*Tahuhuatama*
succeeded by his son
*Taaroatohoa*

*Timarou*

Mt
Taiata

*Hiterire*
now succeeded by his son
*Tamatoa*

TO'ERAUETORU
now MATAURA

Teatamoana
Pass

To Tahiti, Sept. 17

From Tahiti, June 23

To Tahiti, May 31

Bloody Bay

Matarura
Village

*Swamp*

*Huahine*

*Swamp*

TUPUA'I

NAHITORONO

*Swamp*

TUPOTO

From Tongataboo May 28

N
E
S
W

to Tahuhuatama's sister. The supplies of food dried up, and when Ta'aroatohoa's district proved to be too small to feed the strangers, Christian tried to make peace with his former friend, but he and his people ran away. Christian had betrayed his friendship with Tamatoa, who would never forgive him.

On 5 July, according to Peter Heywood, some of their shipmates refused to take orders from Fletcher Christian; and the following day two men were put in irons after a vote among their shipmates. Over the days that followed, 'drunkenness fighting and threatening each others life was so common that those abaft were obliged to Arm themselves with pistols'.[6] Despite these difficulties, Christian was determined to settle on Tupua'i, and on 7 July he and Churchill drew up a set of Articles in which each man formally forgave the others for any past offences, asking each of their shipmates to sign it (although Matthew Thompson refused to do this). The next day, Christian selected a site with a spring for a fort four miles east of Tearamoana Pass, which Ta'aroatohoa gave him in exchange for red feathers. After lightening the *Bounty* by pumping out its water ballast and offloading the booms and spars, the sailors warped the ship inside the lagoon opposite the site, a difficult and dangerous job because of the numerous coral outcrops. Although the booms and spars floated away on the tide, Christian was not upset by their loss, because he did not intend to leave the island. On 10 July when he went ashore to see Ta'aroatohoa, Quintal and Sumner landed without permission. As soon as they returned on board the next morning and Christian rebuked them, they retorted, 'The Ship is Moord and we are now our own Masters!' Taking a pistol from his pocket Christian clapped it against Quintal's head, shouting, 'I'll let you know who is Master!'[7] and had them put in irons. When Quintal and Sumner were brought back on deck the next day they begged his pardon and promised to behave in future, and he freed them.

In order to prevent further incidents of this kind, Christian gave permission for two of the men to sleep ashore each night; and for anyone who wished to go ashore on Sundays. He distributed red feathers among the men, but when he found that a number of these prized objects were missing from his cabin, accusing Thomas Ellison, the dark-haired seventeen-year-old who had been appointed as his servant, of theft, he had had him stripped and tied up on the gangway, although the young man vehemently protested his innocence. When no evidence against him was produced, Ellison was released. Christian had the forge erected ashore and put the armourer Joseph Coleman, assisted by William McCoy, to work making iron rammers for the muskets and turning the trade axes into spades, hoes, mattocks and adzes for felling trees. The assistant gardener William Brown was put in charge of making a yam garden, helped by one of the Tahitian men; Heildbrandt the Hanoverian cooper acted as the cook; Michael Byrne and Thomas Ellison with some of the Tahitian boys were put in charge of the boats; while the rest of their shipmates worked ashore, clearing land for gardens.

On 18 July, Ta'aroatohoa and several other chiefs presented Christian with two young plantain trees and two 'ava roots as a peace offering. The ground was measured for a fort, the sailors turned the first sod and raised the Union Jack on a flagstaff. During this ceremony, Christian named the place 'Fort George' after the King of England, ordering an extra allowance of grog for all hands to celebrate the occasion. Afterwards, they began to build a long house and two smaller ones to live in, before starting work on the fort.[8] Although some of the men, anxious that they might be seen by a passing ship, wanted to burn the *Bounty*, Christian and others disagreed, saying, 'If the vessel might be the means of their detection, she might also be the means of their escape.'[9] Finding the place overrun with Polynesian rats, they brought several cats ashore from the ship and let them loose. By this time, too, the pigs and goats from Tahiti were running wild, causing damage to fruit trees and gardens and angering the local people. Later that day, hearing shrieks and yells, they were alarmed, thinking that an attack was imminent. Instead, they found that one of the local chiefs had died (another victim of the epidemic?), and while his body was being buried, the priest chanted as the mourners screamed and cried out, cutting their heads and chests with sharp shells and smearing their bodies with blood.

Over the next few days the mutineers laid out Fort George, a fortification with walls 100 yards long on each outer side of a ditch 18 feet wide and 20 feet deep; an inner wall 18 feet thick; and a drawbridge to the north facing the beach.[10] As the fort began to take shape, the sailors set up a 4-pound cannon on each corner with two swivels at each side, keeping two swivels in reserve in order to repel any attack. Christian worked alongside the men, and twice every day had half a pint of porter served to the labouring sailors.[11] During the month of August as the work continued, the islanders visited the mutineers every day, bringing provisions in exchange for red feathers, rather than cloth or iron. The Tupua'i people did not covet the iron tools that the sailors had brought, preferring their own stone adzes, and liked fine Tahitian bark cloth or their own water-repellent glazed bark cloth better than European fabric.

On 20 August, Christian and some others sailed around the island in the large cutter, landing on the southern coast where they were welcomed by a chief named Hiterire. When they came to the eastern coast, although Tinarou sent out a peace offering of a young plantain and an 'ava root, inviting Christian ashore, he declined. Ta'aroatohoa's people had tried to keep their women away from the strangers, at least at night, but did not always succeed, and tensions were rising. On 25 August several of the Tahitian men who had been sent to gather coconuts were attacked by local warriors, and one was almost killed by a flying stone. As soon as he was informed, Christian armed a party of men and marched to the site of the attack, where they found the assembled warriors and fired two muskets at them, killing one of these men by shooting him in the back.[12]

Several days later when a number of Tupua'i women decoyed several sailors into Tinarou's district, they were stripped, and Alexander Smith was taken to the chief's house as a hostage. As Christian marched with an armed party of sailors into his district, guided by Smith's Tupua'i mistress, the chief fled before them and Smith was freed, dressed only in his shirt. Although Christian sent messages to Tinarou, asking him to return the rest of Smith's possessions, the chief refused, so Christian burned his house, taking some clubs and spears and seizing two carved household gods, decorated with pearl shells, human hair, teeth and nails cut in a curious pattern, surrounded by a crescent of red tropic bird tail feathers. When one of Tinarou's men tried to resist, he was run through with a bayonet.[13] As the house collapsed in flames, Smith's Tupua'i mistress accompanied the mutineers back to the fort, lamenting that her fellow islanders would punish her for her friendship with the strangers.

On 1 September the gates were erected in the gateway of the fort, and three-quarters of the walls had been finished. The following day, Tinarou arrived with a party of his people, laden with provisions that he presented to Christian with a peace offering, and begged for the return of his household gods. Christian agreed, on the condition that Tinarou returned his men's stolen possessions, and promised that his people would not molest them in future. Tinarou seemed delighted by this offer, telling his people to prepare 'ava; but as he offered this beverage to Christian, Mauatua warned him that treachery was afoot, and an ambush was imminent. According to 'Jenny', who had accompanied Alexander Smith to the island, some of the Tahitian men were also implicated in this plot; although when Mauatua, Fletcher Christian's partner, warned her lover, she did not betray them.[14] Christian told the sailors to arm themselves; and when he refused to drink the 'ava, Tinarou departed in high dudgeon. Christian, who had posted armed men on the ramparts of the fort, sent a boy to warn Coleman on the *Bounty* that an attack was in the offing. As a party of armed warriors gathered on the beach, Coleman fired a 4-pounder among them, the shot flying into a house and cutting away a rafter on which a gourd of water was suspended, terrifying the occupants who thought this was a god at work, and causing the warriors to flee.

Two days later, Ta'aroatohoa's elderly father Tahuhuatama accompanied by his younger son, Christian's bond friend Ta'aroamiva, and his daughter Waiaka arrived at the fort and presented Christian with gifts of provisions. After the young women from Tupua'i performed a dance, singing and beating time, the Tahitian women danced in reply. As the chiefs took their leave, Christian invited them to attend a *heiva* the next day. They agreed, and when they returned the following morning they found the Tahitian women dressed for the *hura* (ceremonial dance) and two of the Tahitian men wearing *parae* or chief *'arioi* costumes, who performed a *heiva* for the Tupua'i chiefs, impressing them with their elegant performance.

Although Christian began to talk of taking the masts out of the *Bounty* and dismantling the ship, Morrison, Stewart and Heywood were eager to return to Tahiti. At first the trio thought about sailing away in the cutter, but it was in poor condition and any attempt to fix it would have aroused Christian's suspicions. As it turned out, however, the other mutineers were also discontented, because although the Tupua'i men allowed them to sleep with women in their houses, the girls were not allowed to join the sailors at the fort. Some of the mutineers suggested that they should take the Tahitians who had accompanied them to Tupua'i as slaves, and cast lots for the Tahitian women, including Mauatua, Christian's lover. When Christian refused to allow this, they threatened to stop work unless he led an armed party to take some local women by force.[15] When Christian also turned down this proposal, there was a violent quarrel. Several of the mutineers demanded the key to the spirit room; and when Christian refused to hand it over, they smashed the lock. Finding his supporters unruly, Christian now called a meeting and asked them what they should do next. A motion was moved to sail the *Bounty* back to Tahiti, where women could be readily obtained and their party could separate, with those who wished being allowed to stay on the island. Although the motion was lost the first time it was put, the next day it passed with a show of hands, with sixteen men in favour, along with a resolution that those who stayed at Tahiti should have their fair share of the arms, ammunition and other things on board the *Bounty*. The sailors began to prepare the ship for the voyage, but when Christian sent some men to fetch the cow, they were attacked and stripped by Tinarou's warriors, and Smith's Tupua'i mistress left the fort without telling the British.

According to Alexander Smith (or John Adams, his true name), the Tupua'i people thought that the moat which the mutineers had dug around the fort was intended as a mass grave for the inhabitants of the island. The local priests may have spread this rumour, because as James Morrison noted:

> They could not bear to see such superiority as the Europeans in general usurp over those who differ from themselves, and became jealous of us with respect to their religious authority to which they saw that we not only refused to take notice of but even ridiculed, for this reason they used all the Means in their power to keep the Chiefs from making Friends, thinking perhaps that if we staid in the island, their Consequence would be lessen'd, which in all probability would have been the case.[16]

As Peter Heywood reported, Hitihiti had also quarrelled with the local people. On 13 September, Christian sent a party of twenty armed men to look for their livestock and punish the attackers, accompanied by the nine Tahitian men led by Hitihiti and four boys, one of whom carried the Union Jack. About a mile from the landing place they were ambushed by 700 Tupua'i warriors, armed with clubs and spears and wearing caps decorated with black feathers and red waistbands filled with stones, who attacked furiously but were soon repelled by musket-fire. In Polynesian warfare, when a chief was killed his men usually gave up the fight; and no doubt the Tahitians, who understood this, had deliberately targeted the Tupua'i leaders.

After the victory the mutineers gathered up the livestock, and Christian gave each of his men twenty-four rounds of ammunition and Hitihiti a musket, since he was an excellent shot. At the fort, they were met by Ta'aroatohoa, his father Tahuhuatama and his younger brother Ta'aroamiva (Christian's *taio*) and several others, who warned them that Tinarou's army was regrouping and that the chief was determined to reclaim the livestock. Alternating Tahitian men armed with clubs and sailors armed with muskets, Christian marched his men in silence into Tinarou's district. As they entered a thicket, however, they were ambushed. According to Morrison:

> Burkett, thinking that he heard something stir in the Bush, stepd to look, and receivd a wound in the left side with a Spear. The Taheitean who was next to Burkett instantly leveled the Man, and Seized his Spear; and before Burkett Could either Speak or fire his piece, they started up in a Swarm all round us, rushing on us with great fury & horrid yells, on which we instantly halted and

facing different ways, gave a smart fire, which we repeated several times with good effect.[17]

When the Tahitians counterattacked, several of them were wounded; but Christian was able to withdraw his men and shelter behind the raised banks of a taro garden, where they fired their muskets, driving back the Tupua'i warriors, who fought in groups of about twenty men, each with its own leader. Although one chief rallied his men, making menacing gestures, he was shot, as were several others who tried to follow him out of the thicket. Thomas Burkett (a sturdy, pockmarked, brown-haired man) was fainting from his wound, and his Tahitian *taio* escorted him to the boat. When Christian's men gave three cheers, the Tupua'i warriors fled, leaving the bodies of their dead comrades to be plundered by the Tahitians. Although one of the Tahitian boys asked if he could cut out the jawbone of a man he had shot, Christian indignantly refused. Back at the fort, the elderly chief Tahuhuatama greeted them with joy, and his son Ta'aroamiva reported that during the affray sixty of Tinarou's warriors had been killed, along with six women who had been handing them their weapons. The casualties included Tinarou's own brother, who had been shot by Christian himself. A great number of other warriors had been wounded; and Tinarou and his people were bitterly angry.

According to James Morrison, at least some of the 3000 inhabitants of Tupua'i were closely related to the inhabitants of the Society Islands.[18] The great-grandfather of Tamatoa, now the chief of the western district, had been a chief from the ruling family of Ra'iatea who was caught in a storm while he was out fishing, and driven to this island. At that time Tupua'i had been sparsely inhabited by people from Rurutu and Hiva (in the Marquesas), and when they recognised him as an *ari'i*, Tamatoa had settled on the island, naming several of the districts on the island 'Ra'iatea', 'Taha'a' and 'Huahine' after islands in the Society archipelago. When Morrison returned to Tahiti, Tu's mother Tetupaia told him that indeed, her ancestor Tamatoa had been blown away in a fishing canoe and lost at sea; and she was overjoyed to know what had become of him. During their visit to Tupua'i, the *Bounty* sailors also saw part of a Society Islands canoe on the *marae* known as Peetu; and Tapairu (the *taio* of Joseph Coleman and brother of Po'e'eno, the chief of Matavai Bay), recognised this craft as his own canoe that had been lost during a naval battle in Pa'ea. During that engagement, the warriors of Te Porionu'u (also known as Te 'Aharoa, the districts of Hitia'a, Matavai, Ha'apaino'o and Pare) had assembled at Pare and attacked the Pa'ea fleet, whose warriors had fought so fiercely that the Te Porionu'u men (including Tapairu) were forced to abandon their canoes, swimming ashore at Ta'apuna. Some of their canoes were wrecked on the reef while about eight craft were blown out to sea; and this canoe (which still held part of the decayed corpse of one of the Pa'ea warriors who had been killed and brought on board during the battle) was Tapairu's own vessel.

Despite these links, however, and the fondness of the Tupua'i people for red feathers, Morrison reported that there were no 'arioi on this island, and no infanticide, tattooing, voyaging, or any of the sexually graphic dancing that young 'arioi performed in the Society Islands, although the islanders did practise human sacrifice. They lived in long, oval houses with carved fronts and shutters, painted red, the interiors lined with reeds and divided into two sides, one side for the men and the other for the women. On the men's side, a tier of standing stones about 5 feet high held images of the ancestor gods, carved and decorated with human hair. Human sacrifices were offered on the marae, which had flat stone pavements and tiered platforms faced with standing stones. Their canoes were distinctive with sharp bows and sterns, painted red, the bow carved like an animal with a large mouth, and the stern rising in a neatly carved scroll; and none of these craft had sails.

Realising that he had no future in Tupua'i, Christian decided to return to Tahiti. Ta'aroamiva assured him that as his friend, he would certainly be killed if he stayed on the island; and when he and two companions begged to sail with him to Tahiti, they were overjoyed when Christian agreed to take them. On 17 September the Bounty's anchors were weighed, and as soon as the ship was clear of the reef the mutineers sailed away from the island, heading for Tahiti. Three days later they anchored briefly off Me'eti'a where the trade goods, arms, ammunition, wine and clothing were divided between those sixteen men who had decided to stay in Tahiti, and the eight who had pledged themselves to remain on board the Bounty with Fletcher Christian, saying, 'We shall never leave you, Mr. Christian, go where you will.'[19]

When the Bounty arrived back in Matavai Bay on 22 September 1789, the mutineers were disconcerted to discover that during their absence, another European ship had arrived at the island. On August 9, the Mercury had sailed within 2 miles of the north coast of Tupua'i in the dark, and seeing fires on the beach, had fired two cannons as a signal. The breakers were crashing so high on the reef, however, that they tacked away from the island. Fortunately for the mutineers, this was not a British naval vessel, but a privateer commanded by

Captain John Henry Cox. The *Mercury* (also known as *Gustavus III*) was a brand-new copper-bottomed 16-gun British brig with a crew of about thirty, sailing under the Swedish flag, despatched by the King of Sweden to attack Russian fur-trade settlements in the North Pacific.[20] On 15 August when Captain Cox and Lieutenant Mortimer, the commander of the marines, had landed in Matavai Bay, Po'e'eno showed them the famous oil painting of Captain Cook. On the back they found the following inscription:

> Lieut. Bligh, of his Britannick Majesty's ship Bounty, anchored in Matavia Bay the 25th of October 1788; but, owing to bad weather, was obliged to sail to Oparre on the 25th of December, where he remained until the 30th of March 1789; was then ready for sea, with one thousand and fifteen bread-fruit plants on board, besides many other fruits, and only waited an opportunity to get to sea; at which time this picture was given up. Sailed the 4th of April 1789.[21]

Although they went to view this portrait on several occasions, the *Mercury*'s officers never found out where it was kept, because Po'e'eno always sent two of his servants to fetch it, who brought it wrapped up in bark cloth. The islanders also showed them the place where one of the *Bounty*'s officers, one 'Torono' (whom Mortimer later identified as Huggan, the ship's surgeon) was buried; professing a great respect for his memory, and pointing to places on their bodies where he had healed dreadful ulcers. While they were gazing at his grave, an English pointer dog left by Bligh came up wagging its tail, greeting them with joy; and they found some gardens nearby, choked with weeds, where European plants were growing.

According to Mortimer, everywhere they went during this visit, they were followed by crowds of curious islanders who stroked their hands and bodies, admiring their clothes; although they also pilfered their possessions. On 15 August, Mortimer lost a small Tahitian vocabulary that he carried in his pocket; and that night one of the *Mercury*'s crew, John Brown, slashed one of his shipmates across the face with an old razor, and was thrown into irons. The following day, 'Itia, Tu's astute and capable wife, arrived on board the brig, and as they were about to pull off in the boat, the high chief himself came alongside in a double canoe. When Tu boarded the boat, he shook Captain Cox warmly by the hand and asked for the names of his officers; and when they invited him to board the *Mercury*, he inspected the ship with minute attention, expressing his surprise that so small a vessel could sail upright without an outrigger. Some nights later when he slept on board the ship, Tu saw a pair of scissors with a long chain around the neck of the second mate's wife and begged for them; and when she refused him, wept bitterly until he was given a similar pair. Apart from Jean Baret, the female attendant of Bougainville's naturalist Commerson, who travelled in disguise, this was the first European woman to visit the island; and no doubt her presence was one reason why the Tahitians were so fascinated by this vessel. Like Bligh, Lieutenant Mortimer spoke of 'Itia with admiration, saying that she was a clever, sensible woman and the only Tahitian female who was permitted to eat in the presence of men. She was also an excellent shot, hitting the ship's buoy with her first attempt, although Tu was too frightened to handle the musket.

On 20 August when the *Mercury*'s lieutenant of marines took a walk on shore, he bartered for a strange-looking club. Its owner told him that this weapon had been brought to Tahiti from a place called 'Tootate' (Aitutaki) by 'Titereano' (Christian), Captain Bligh's chief officer who had returned to Tahiti in the *Bounty* about two months after the ship had sailed from the island. According to this man, during his visit to Aitutaki, Captain Bligh had fought with the local warriors and one of his men had been killed with this club, while several of the islanders had been shot with muskets, and Bligh had now settled on that island. The man also assured Mortimer that Titereano and his companions had sailed from Tahiti in the *Bounty* only fifteen days before the *Mercury*'s arrival, taking some Tahitians with them to Aitutaki. Likewise, Po'e'eno had a beautifully polished spear in his possession with which he would not part, saying that it had been brought from Aitutaki in the *Bounty*, although it looked very similar to spears from Tonga (indeed, this spear must have been procured during the *Bounty*'s visit to Nomuka, just before the mutiny off Tofua in the Tongan archipelago). Christian had strictly forbidden his shipmates to talk about the mutiny and their subsequent visit to Tupua'i; and this misinformation successfully concealed these events from Captain Cox and his companions.

Several days later, when Tu set off in his double canoe for Pare, he took with him John Brown, the sailor who had been put in irons on board the *Mercury* after badly wounding a messmate with his knife; and who was eager to stay in Tahiti. Seating himself in the canoe and asking his island companions to pass down his hammock, Brown showed no signs of regret on leaving the ship; and as he departed, Tu asked Captain Cox to ask King George to send him a large ship with many guns and armed men, and a quantity of scarlet and blue jackets. The following morning Brown sent a letter to Cox, saying that he was happy in his new situation and asking for a Bible, some carpenter's tools and a quantity of large nails to build a boat; items which were sent to him along with a letter from the captain, advising him how to conduct himself in future. Evidently Brown was an ingenious man with many practical skills, although he became almost crazy when he was drunk with liquor.

On 1 September the *Mercury*'s anchors were raised, but finding that some articles, including a flag, had been stolen from the ship, Cox took Tetupaia, Tu's aristocratic mother, and her brother, an old priest named Tutaha (also known as Ha'amanimani) as hostages, declaring that unless these goods were returned, he would carry them away from the island. That afternoon Ari'ipaea went off in pursuit of the thief while Lieutenant Mortimer and two of the officers went ashore, where they saw an 'uncommonly indecent and lascivious' *heiva*. This performance reminded Mortimer of an occasion when he had accompanied two of the mates ashore one night to attend a similar entertainment. One of the mates, smitten by a pretty *'arioi* dancing girl, had showered her with beads and begged her to come with him out to the ship. Eventually she agreed, but when they arrived on the beach and she stripped off her theatrical costume, the dancer proved to be 'a smart, dapper lad'. Witnessing the mate's horrified expression, the Tahitians who had followed them to the beach, awaiting this denouement, laughed so hard that they almost collapsed, screaming with mirth. As Mortimer remarked, no doubt this trick later made a fine subject for one of their burlesque performances.

The next morning, 2 September 1789, the *Mercury* had sailed out of Matavai Bay, brushing past Dolphin Bank but fortunately avoiding any damage. When Ari'ipaea came out to the ship to say goodbye, he returned some of the stolen goods and insisted that he would hang the thieves when he caught them, although they suspected that he had been responsible for the thefts; and when Tetupaia farewelled them, she wept 'in such an affected manner, that it was almost impossible to refrain from laughing'.[22] The *Mercury*'s brief visit would convince Fletcher Christian that if he stayed in Tahiti, he would inevitably be captured by a British ship, taken back to England and put on trial.

# Murder and Mayhem

On 22 September 1789, just three weeks after the *Mercury*'s departure from Tahiti, the *Bounty* arrived back in Matavai Bay. Eight of her crew had decided to remain on board with Fletcher Christian: the dark-skinned midshipman Edward Young, his loyal friend born in the West Indies; William Brown, the assistant gardener; the gunner's mate John Mills; and five of the able-bodied sailors – John Williams, a Guernsey man who spoke French as well as English; Isaac Martin, the American; Alexander Smith (or John Adams), Matthew Quintal and William McCoy. The young chief Ta'aroamiva from Tupua'i (or Tetahiti, as he was later known) and his attendant Oha, who were both fond of Christian, also decided to join them, along with Christian's partner Isabella (or Mauatua), William McCoy's partner Mary (Te'o) with her little daughter from another liaison, and John Mills's lover Prudence (or Vahineatua), who were willing to accompany their lovers on board the *Bounty*.[1]

Sixteen of their shipmates had decided to remain in Tahiti, however, including Joseph Coleman, the powerful, sensible, grey-haired armourer who was now forty years old; Thomas McIntosh and Charles Norman, the carpenter's mates; and Michael Byrne, the fiddler, all of whom had been kept on board the *Bounty* against their will. More surprisingly, they were joined by George Stewart and Peter Heywood, Christian's fellow midshipmen, who later protested that they were innocent of mutiny, although the balance of evidence suggests that Stewart, Christian's confidant, had helped to instigate the uprising.[2] There was also the boatswain's mate James Morrison (who like Stewart, Martin and Christian had a star tattooed on his left breast, the insignia of the 'Knights of Otaheite'); the ship's corporal, Charles Churchill, who along with his two shipmates, John Millward (a dark, strong young man) and William Muspratt (a black-bearded, dark-skinned sailor), had tried to desert in Tahiti and been flogged; along with six others of the able-bodied seamen – Thompson, Sumner, Burkett, Heildbrandt, Skinner and Ellison.

The chests and hammocks of these men, along with a grindstone, bar iron, some flags, iron pots, a copper kettle, wine, and some carpenter's and armourer's tools were piled up on deck, and each man except Michael Byrne (who had a troublesome disposition) was given a musket, pistol, cutlass, bayonet, cartridge box, lead for ball and 17 pounds of powder. Lots were drawn for two spare muskets, which were won by Norman and Burkett, while Morrison took the musketoon. Although Christian refused to give them any saws, he handed over two spyglasses, ten swivels (although these were of no use), an old azimuth compass, some spare sails and the household gods from Tupua'i as a gift for Pomare II. He told his shipmates that he intended to stay at Tahiti for several days, loading the ship with fresh water, animals and crops before sailing to some uninhabited island where he planned to burn the ship and spend the rest of his days in complete isolation from other Europeans.

When the islanders came on board the *Bounty*, they asked Christian:

- Where is Parai?
- He is gone to England
- In what Ship?
- In Tute's Ship
- How came you to meet Tute and where is he?
- We met at Aitutaki where he is going to live, and has sent me for all those who will come and live with him. The Bull and Cows and as many Hogs as you will send him.
- What is become of the Breadfruit?
- He has sent it home to England with Bligh.[3]

Although Tu, who had returned home to southern Tahiti, did not make an appearance on this occasion, his younger brother Vaetua (Hayward's *taio*) soon came out to greet them. The surf was running high, and they worked all the next day to take goods ashore for those who were staying on the island, and loaded the animals and plants (which were readily given to Christian for delivery to Captain Bligh) on board the *Bounty*. As each man landed, those with *taio* or lovers from Matavai Bay were greeted by their families, who took them to their houses. Since Po'e'eno was James Morrison's *taio* (as well as Bligh's), and his wife was Millward's bond friend, they were escorted to Po'e'eno's house where they were treated like members of the family, although 'with more attention and respect'.[4]

*The death of Captain Cook by Johann Zoffany.*

Joseph Coleman and Matthew Thompson were escorted by Coleman's *taio* Tapairu (Po'e'eno's younger brother, who had travelled with them to Tupua'i) to his dwelling in Matavai Bay. Sumner, Burkett and Ellison were greeted by Sumner's bond friend; Richard Skinner (a fair, good-looking young man who was heavily tattooed) by his lover's father; while the ship's corporal Charles Churchill was welcomed by his *taio* from Matavai Bay.

When Fletcher Christian, Stewart and Heywood went ashore, Vaetua told them that a ship (the *Mercury*) had recently visited the island, leaving behind a man named John Brown who had gone with Tu on a visit to southern Tahiti. According to Vaetua, when Tu told the captain of the *Mercury* that Captain Cook was still alive and living in Aitutaki, and that Cook's 'son' Bligh had recently visited the island, the captain had assured him that Captain Cook was dead, showing him Zoffany's famous image of Cook's death at the hands of the Hawai'ian warriors. According to Vaetua, Tu was furious with Bligh for 'saying that [Captain Cook] was alive in England, that He was Capt. Cooks Son which they were informd to the Contrary of by Captain Cox, who told them that Captain Cook's son was then in England'.[5] After hearing this story, Stewart and his companions told Vaetua about the mutiny; and Vaetua remarked that they should have killed Bligh while they had the chance. Tu's younger brother, an *'arioi* warrior renowned for his addiction to *'ava*, now confessed that when Bligh had put his *taio* Hayward in irons and threatened to flog him, it was he who had cut the *Bounty*'s cable as an act of revenge, hoping that the ship would drift onto the reef so that he could rescue his bond friend. Vaetua added that if Bligh had ordered Hayward to be flogged, he had decided to kill him with a club, and to escape by diving overboard and swimming underwater back to shore. He declared that if ever Bligh returned to Tahiti, he would kill him.

When he was told about the *Mercury*'s visit, however, Fletcher Christian was appalled; and determined to leave Tahiti as soon as possible. Tu and his family now knew that he was a liar; and since the mutiny, he had often sworn that he would die rather than be captured and taken back to England: 'Though thousands and ten thousands attacked me, I'd DIE ere I would surrender. I'd rather meet A HOST OF DEVILS than once see the injured Captain Bligh's relations.'[6] That afternoon he had a long discussion with Peter Heywood and George Stewart, saying that a warship would certainly be sent in search of them, and advising them to give themselves up on its arrival. After asking Heywood to pass on some private details to his family which would explain his part in the mutiny, Christian rowed out to the *Bounty* where he scribbled a note absolving Heywood of any part in the uprising, asking one of the Tahitians to deliver it to him the next morning. According to Heywood, in this letter Christian wrote that after learning that the islanders intended to try and capture the *Bounty*, he had resolved to leave at once; and that because he knew that Heywood intended to return to England, he decided against warning him about his impending departure.[7]

To their astonishment, later that night the sailors on shore saw the *Bounty* sailing out of Matavai Bay, heading north. There was little wind, however, and it was not until noon the following day that the ship vanished over the horizon. Christian and his companions had cut the anchor cable, carrying away with them a number of islanders who had been dining below and thought that the ship was heading for Pare. These included eighteen Tahitian women (most of whom were taken against their will); three male commoners from Tahiti (Niau, a boy; Manari'i and Temua); one man from Ra'iatea (Tararo); and Christian's friends from Tupua'i. Although Christian had ordered the armourer Joseph Coleman to stay on board, valuing him for his ironworking and military skills, at the last minute Coleman dived overboard and swam ashore; and one of the women followed him soon afterwards. When the *Bounty* arrived off Mo'orea later that day and a canoe came alongside, Christian had allowed six of the older women to go ashore, leaving just twelve Tahitian women on board the *Bounty* as consorts for the fourteen men who remained on the vessel.[8]

As soon as the *Bounty* sailed out of sight, the sailors who had remained ashore began to disperse. Those with girlfriends and *taio* at Matavai Bay accompanied them to their houses; while George Stewart and his close friend Peter Heywood went with Heywood's *taio* Te Pau, the father of Stewart's partner 'Peggy' and the *ari'i* of the Fa'a'a district. Te Pau's house stood on the border with Matavai Bay, probably at One Tree Hill (although Peter later acquired his own Tahitian lover and an idyllic house nearby, set in gardens at the foot of a hill and approached by an avenue of shaddock trees).[9] The two carpenter's mates McIntosh and Norman, Heildbrandt, Muspratt and Byrne accompanied Ari'ipaea, Tu's other brother, to Pare. None of the *Bounty* sailors went to stay with Tu and 'Itia, who were now living on his mother's lands in southern Tahiti.

On 27 September 1789 the *Bounty*'s men at Matavai Bay marched with muskets on their shoulders to meet their comrades at Pare, carrying the Tupua'i gods decorated with red feathers, bark cloth from Tonga and Tupua'i, fine mats, weapons and iron goods as gifts for Pomare II, the young paramount chief of the island. When they reached Pare, they were joined by those of their shipmates who had been staying in that district with Ari'ipaea, and a priest welcomed them, making a long speech and presenting each of them with a plantain branch and a suckling pig or a chicken. Ari'ipaea (who was now Pomare II's regent) advised the *Bounty*'s men that the young *ari'i rahi* was so sacred that they must strip their heads and shoulders in his presence; but they refused, saying that even when they met the King of England, they were not required to remove their headgear. As a compromise, bark cloth was draped over their shoulders, and they marched towards Pomare II's dwelling, accompanied by their Tahitian *taio*.

Upon entering the sacred precinct, followed by a large crowd of men and women, their bond friends stripped themselves to the waist and removed the bark cloth from their *taio*'s shoulders. Beside the *fare ra'a* (sacred house), which stood on the opposite side of the river, they saw the young paramount chief 'flying' on the shoulders of his attendant, his face almost hidden by a headdress of black and red feathers. He welcomed the British, saluting them and addressing them by the names of their Tahitian *taio*; and Hitihiti stripped naked and carried their gifts across the river, especially the gods from Tupua'i, bedecked with their red feathers; telling a long story about these gods that evoked gasps of astonishment when he held up the images, displaying them to the crowd.

After this presentation, each man sent across his own gift of red feathers and bark cloth to the young *ari'i rahi*, an open-faced boy who gazed at them with avid interest; and afterwards they assembled in three divisions and fired off their muskets, delighting Pomare II, who assured them that from now on they should not worry about *tapu* restrictions, but could follow their own customs. Afterwards the British sailors were taken to Ari'ipaea's house where a lavish feast of baked pork, fish, breadfruit, taro, plantains and coconuts was served, and an area of land was pointed out for their use while they were visiting the district. That night they returned to Matavai Bay, and the next day a messenger arrived from Tu with a pig and a length of bark cloth for each of the *Bounty*'s men, who pointed out two other areas that had been set aside for their use – the whole of Point Venus where they could collect coconuts, and an area near Po'e'eno's house with a large grove of breadfruit trees. As Morrison observed, however, they did not need land to provide them with food, because their *taio* and their families kept them lavishly supplied with provisions.

Later that day, John Millward and Charles Churchill set off by canoe to Tahiti-iti (southern Tahiti), laden with gifts including a bottle of wine and several large *'ava* roots from Tupua'i for Tu, who was living there with 'Itia. According to Coleman, Churchill had been the first among them to try *'ava*, although it made him sick.[10] As Millward and Churchill sailed past Pa'ea, at their companions' request they ignored an invitation from Teto'ofa (the Admiral's son and heir) to visit him in this district. When they landed at Papara, Amo and Purea's son Teri'irere, the high chief of this district (and formerly a claimant to the status of paramount chief of the island), a fine-looking, affable man, gave them a warm welcome. Teri'irere was a highly sacred individual, renowned as a medium and priest, and often referred to by his people as an *atua* (god). When they arrived at Tu's house in southern Tahiti, he loaded them with gifts and told them to regard his land as their own, and Vehiatua III gave them rich presents and invited them to stay with him in Tai'arapu.

On 10 October when Millward and Churchill returned from southern Tahiti to Matavai Bay, they were accompanied by John Brown, the sailor from the *Mercury* who had been cast ashore. Captain Cox had given him an auger, some gimlets and a plane, but no axe or saw; although Cox had bartered many axes and saws during his visit to the island. He had also presented Tu with a musket, some pistols and a quantity of flints and ammunition, but gave Brown no firearms. According to Brown's own account, he had been a sergeant of marines in Portsmouth before joining the *Eurydice* and sailing to India, where he had worked for Colonel Bailey as a cook before entering the service of an Indian prince, converting to Islam and serving as an officer in the prince's army. When he had tired of this service, he and some friends seized a small East India Company vessel laden with a cargo, but were captured and put on trial. For want of evidence Brown was not convicted but sent back to England, where he joined HMS *Pomona* and then the *Mercury*, which carried him to Tahiti. After Brown's departure, Po'e'eno produced a letter from Captain Cox of His Swedish Majesty's Armed Brig *Gustavus III* (the *Mercury*'s Swedish name) declaring that although Brown was an ingenious and handy man when sober, he was very dangerous when drunk.

Morrison now made up his mind to build a small vessel to sail to Batavia and back to England; and when he shared this idea with Thomas McIntosh (one of the carpenter's mates) and John Millward, they agreed to build this craft together but to keep their plan a secret, telling their shipmates that they were building this vessel to sail around the islands. Upon leaving the *Bounty*, the sailor Matthew Thompson (a dark-skinned man who at forty was older than most of his shipmates) had taken Bligh's quadrant and some of Hayward's books, although he was illiterate; and Morrison, who already had a *Seaman's Daily Assistant*, managed to barter the quadrant for trade adzes and a gallon of wine. When Morrison also tried to acquire the navigational books, however, Thompson became suspicious, offering him cartridge paper instead. Hearing about their plan to build a vessel, the other carpenter's mate Charles Norman and Henry Heildbrandt (the Hanoverian cooper, who spoke English with a strong accent) agreed to join them, and shifted back to Matavai Bay where the islanders built houses for them around a parade ground where they raised a flagstaff, hoisting the British colours, holding divine service every Sunday, and observing a day of rest. As Morrison noted, the Tahitians were fascinated by these ceremonies, 'and they always behooved with much decency when present at our worship; tho they Could not understand one word; yet several were desirous to have it explained to them, and some of them wished to learn our prayers'.[11]

As soon as the compound at Matavai Bay was finished, Sumner, Burkett and Ellison, the ship's corporal Charles Churchill, Michael Byrne and John Brown, the sailor from the *Mercury*, arrived to join Morrison and his comrades. When they told Bligh's *taio* Po'e'eno about their plan to build a small ship, saying that they would use this craft to carry him and Tu to the neighbouring islands, Po'e'eno was delighted, giving them permission to cut down any tree they liked to construct the vessel. On 6 November, Brown and Ellison left Matavai Bay and set off for Tai'arapu, returning five days later. During their visit to Pa'ea, Brown had borrowed Ellison's cutlass and when he played tricks with it, teasing the local people, one of these men grabbed the cutlass, cutting Brown across the hand with a bamboo knife. In the scuffle that followed, Brown was stripped of his bark-cloth garments; but when he asked his shipmates at Matavai Bay to help him get them back, they refused, telling him to settle down peacefully in Matavai Bay, where Po'e'eno had given him a house and garden. As Morrison remarked ruefully, the Tahitians did not trouble Brown, 'suppos[ing] He was under Our protection, tho they knew he was a Stranger to us, and he often Used them very ill'.[12]

During Brown and Ellison's absence, their shipmates had already begun to build their ship, drawing up plans for a 30-foot schooner, cutting down trees and laying its keel on blocks. With the help of the carpenters, the sailors made moulds which Morrison and Churchill took around the different districts, looking for suitable timbers. The unskilled sailors did the rough work, although it took them two days to cut a plank 30 feet long, which the carpenter's assistants trimmed and fitted. After building a shed to shelter the schooner, they shaped the bow, sternposts and plank for the stern, learning by trial and error which timbers were suitable for different purposes, and drying the wood before fitting the pieces in place, so that they would not twist out of shape. Their *taio* willingly helped the sailors to haul the trees as they were felled, and split them, at which they were very skilled, roughing out the breadfruit planks and *purau* (hibiscus) timbers with stone adzes. This work was very laborious, however, because Morrison and his companions had no saws and only two iron adzes to finish these boards. As the frame of the schooner began to take shape under its shelter, they set Heildbrandt to work cutting hardwood pegs.

On Christmas Day 1789 the men at the compound killed a pig for a festive dinner and conducted divine service, which was attended by the chiefs who listened quietly to the story of Christ's birth. Soon afterwards a blind islander visited the site who felt the frame of their ship all over, declaring to his fellow islanders, 'Our Canoes are foolish things compared to this one.'[13]

On 1 February 1790 a great *heiva* was held at Matavai Bay to celebrate the end of the summer breadfruit harvest. When the people assembled near Po'e'eno's house, an old man produced Captain Cook's portrait, and as he unwrapped its bark-cloth covering, all of the men including Po'e'eno reverently stripped to the waist and the women uncovered their shoulders. Afterwards the priest made an *utu* or offering of a plantain branch and a young pig, which he tethered in front of Cook's portrait, giving a long speech which began with a chant:

> Hail, all hail Cook, Chief of Air Earth and Water
> We acknowledge you Chief from the Beach to the Mountains

Over Men, Trees and Cattle, over the Birds of the Air and the Fishes of
the Sea . . .[14]

After acknowledging Captain Cook as an *ari'i* of Matavai Bay, two young
chiefly women dressed in fine bark cloth accompanied by two male *'arioi* performed a series of dances which lasted for about four hours, accompanied by
drums and nose flutes. At the end of this performance the women slipped off
their bark-cloth costumes and retired, and their bark-cloth clothing and the fine
mats upon which they had danced were rolled up and laid as tribute in front
of Captain Cook's portrait. Several baskets of food including fish, plantains,
breadfruit, taro and coconuts were given to the *Bounty* sailors, and at Po'e'eno's
request they fired a musketoon loaded with slugs into a *vi* tree, bringing down
a shower of Tahitian apples to the delight of the spectators.

The next day Po'e'eno presided over another *heiva*, this time on the parade
ground, although Cook's portrait was not produced on this occasion. During
this ritual, Po'e'eno received the presentations of food and about a hundred
fathoms of bark cloth and matting, which he divided among the sailors. When the
islanders departed, the *Bounty*'s men found that the halyards from their flagstaff,
a pair of trousers and three pigs had been stolen. After chasing the thief as far
as Pare, they retrieved the halyards, although the trousers and the pigs had vanished. When the culprit was captured and brought to Matavai Bay, he was given
a flogging of 100 lashes; and Brown, whose pig had been stolen, cut off his ears.
Although Po'e'eno had advised them to shoot the offender, they released him
and he ran away, bleeding profusely and jeered at by his fellow islanders. When
another man who had stolen a knife was brought to the parade ground and given
'a smart flogging', the rash of thieving stopped. As Morrison remarked, by this
time the sailors were also beginning 'to get hold of their language so fast that we
could understand evry thing they said, and make a good shift to discourse with
them'.[15] No doubt because of his grasp of Tahitian, his close relationship with
many of the islanders and the length of time he spent on the island, Morrison's
account of life in Tahiti is illuminating (although it lacks the vivid detail of the
day-to-day logs and journals, especially those of William Bligh).

On 6 February when 'Itia arrived at the compound on her way to visit her
young son Pomare II, she and her younger sister Pateama'i, the wife of Vehiatua
III, presented each of the *Bounty* sailors with a length of bark cloth. These
women stayed with the British for several days, and during their visit the *'arioi*
gathered at the compound, using the village green as an arena for dancing, wrestling and throwing the javelin, and entertaining the sailors every evening. When

she saw the schooner in its shed, 'Itia was so impressed that she offered them a handsaw that Captain Cox had given to Tu, and sent one of her attendants to fetch it. It was an excellent tool, which Morrison thought must have cost at least five shillings in London. Before she left, this 'Great Woman' ordered the local people to keep the sailors well supplied with food; and they lived on excellent terms with the Matavai people.

One day, however, Matthew Thompson, the forty-year old, black-haired sailor who was living at Point Venus with the armourer Joseph Coleman, savagely raped a young woman. After giving Thompson a beating, her brother fled from the bay and, in a fury, Thompson vowed to take his revenge. Later that day a group of 'arioi from Lake Vaihiria (inland by Mt Tetufera, where the 'arioi went to stay and make a strong grey bark cloth with bark from the 'ora tree) arrived at Point Venus, a popular stopping place for pleasure tours around the island. When Thompson ordered them to leave the site, they did not understand him; and thinking that they were deliberately ignoring him, he took up his musket and fired, killing a man and a child whom he held in his arms, wounding a woman through the jaw and grazing a man on his back. Although the Bounty sailors were sure that these people would try to avenge the shootings, nothing happened. Peter Heywood gave a white shirt to the wife of the man who had been killed, and Churchill, who had aspirations to replace Christian as their leader, offered to command his shipmates in any battle that might follow the shootings. The group of Bounty sailors at Matavai Bay declined his offer, however, and Thompson sent Brown to Tai'arapu to ask Vehiatua III for a canoe. When the canoe arrived on 20 February, Churchill, Thompson and Brown left Matavai Bay, heading for southern Tahiti.

Despite the shootings, the people at Matavai Bay remained friendly with Morrison and his companions at the compound, since the 'arioi who had been killed belonged to another district. At the beginning of March, however, when Peter Heywood set off with his taio Te Pau (the ari'i of the Pa'ea district) on a visit to Papara, rumours soon arrived that he had been murdered at Lake Vaihiria. On 6 March when he returned safely to Matavai Bay, Heywood brought the barrel of Tom Ellison's pistol, which had been stolen from his house. He reported that one night at Pa'ea he had overheard the local warriors plotting to strip him, so he gave his knife and hat to the local ari'i Teto'ofa, and was allowed to carry on unmolested. At Papara he had been warmly welcomed by Teri'irere, the high chief of that district, and afterwards had travelled inland to visit Tu's mother Tetupaia. As he approached Lake Vaihiria, however, a man had seized him by the hair and was about to knock out his brains with a stone when another man grabbed his arm and stopped him. His assailant proved to be the brother of the man whom Thompson had murdered, who had mistaken him for Thompson; but luckily the other man remembered Heywood, who had visited the dead man's wife and given her some presents. Apologising profusely, his assailant invited Heywood to stay in his house, but instead the young midshipman visited Tetupaia and then carried on to Tai'arapu, where Vehiatua III loaded him with presents. At Tu's house, Heywood had also been showered with gifts, although Tu begged him not to shift from Matavai Bay, since Churchill, Thompson and Brown had now decided to settle in southern Tahiti with Vehiatua. He promised to stay at Matavai Bay; and after farewelling Tu, carried on up the east coast where he had been given a friendly welcome at every place that he stopped during his journey.

Now that a number of British sailors had settled on the island, each of the major chiefs was competing to secure their services. As the *Bounty*'s men dispersed across the landscape, they forged relationships and alliances that were more complex and shifting than those of any previous group of Europeans. On 8 March 1790 when a messenger arrived from Vehiatua III, inviting Morrison and Millward to shift to Tai'arapu and delivering a letter from Charles Churchill (who was now Vehiatua's *taio*), offering them riches if they came to southern Tahiti, Morrison's party, glad to be rid of Churchill, sent a polite message to Vehiatua declining his kind invitation, along with some gifts. The following day a messenger arrived from Pare, reporting that a fleet of canoes was approaching from Mo'orea with Mahau (now the high chief of that island), bringing a large quantity of bark cloth and pigs for Pomare II. The Pa'ea warriors had threatened to plunder the fleet, and Pomare II would be grateful for their assistance. Morrison and his shipmates set off armed with muskets, and when they arrived at Pare the visiting fleet from Mo'orea were allowed to land unmolested. In his gratitude, Pomare II ordered a feast, and assured them that they could take fish from his canoes whenever they wanted.

Several nights later, Matthew Thompson arrived back at Matavai Bay, begging for a musket to replace his gun, which had been stolen by one of Tu's men. He told them that he and Charles Churchill had quarrelled, and were now living in different places in southern Tahiti. Thompson had settled at Tautira with his *taio* Ti'itorea, formerly Vehiatua II's regent; while Churchill was living at Vaiaotea in the Teahupo'o district; and John Brown was living with Tu at Tautira. When Charles Norman loaned Thompson his spare musket, he went off threatening to shoot the thief as soon as he saw him. After his departure, their *taio* told them that while Coleman had been ill, Thompson had robbed the armourer; and that in fact it was Churchill who had stolen Thompson's musket while he was sleeping, although he had managed to convince Thompson that one of Tu's men was the culprit.

Now that the schooner's frame was complete, James Morrison and his comrades began to sheathe the vessel. Joseph Coleman had recovered from his illness, and when they asked him to make the ironwork he said that he was willing to do so, as long as they supplied him with coal and bellows. Coleman was popular among the Tahitians, helping them to mend their iron tools; and 'being remarkably clever both for invention and the execution of his works, he rendered no small assistance to the people of the island'.[16] The men at the compound began to make charcoal by burning wood; fashioning the bellows out of breadfruit wood, using wet canvas instead of leather and the handle of an iron saucepan for the nozzle; and building a frame for the forge which they filled with clay. Assisted by Heildbrandt, Coleman used this makeshift equipment to fashion eye bolts for the rudder. Soon afterwards, John Sumner, a fair-skinned young sailor with a scar on the left side of his face, got tired of working on the schooner and went to visit Tu in southern Tahiti.

When he returned ten days later with Charles Churchill, Churchill reported that Thompson had managed to retrieve his musket. He also told them that his *taio* Vehiatua III had died suddenly, and that as his bond friend, he had inherited his titles as the *ari'i rahi* of the southern districts. Although he urged his shipmates to accompany him to his new fiefdom in Tai'arapu, they declined, preferring to remain at Matavai Bay rather than trust themselves to Churchill's violent caprices. During their journey Teri'irere, the high chief of Papara, had made Sumner his *taio* and invited him to live with him at Papara. Since he and Teri'irere were now allies, Tu had no objections to this shift; and shortly afterwards, Teri'irere sent canoes to carry Sumner and his friend Thomas Burkett (now recovered from the wound he had received in Tupua'i) to his district.

On 1 April 1790, Michael Byrne and Thomas Ellison also stopped working on the schooner, having decided to return to live at Pare with Ari'ipaea and William Muspratt. The remaining sailors divided the tasks among themselves – Norman and Millward making the planks; McIntosh and Morrison attaching them to the frame; and Coleman and Heildbrandt forging the ironwork. It is notable that apart from Heywood and Stewart, who remained good friends and lived close to each other under Te Pau's protection on the border between Matavai Bay and Pare, and the core group of Morrison, Norman, Millward, McIntosh, Coleman and Heildbrandt who lived at the compound at Matavai Bay under Po'e'eno's protection, building the schooner, the rest of the *Bounty*'s men kept changing their allegiances.

After his visit to Matavai Bay, Charles Churchill decided to accompany Byrne, Ellison and Muspratt to Pare, but during their journey while he was stalking a group of ducks, he shot at some Tahitians who had disturbed his quarry, wounding one man in the back and a boy in the heel; and when their companions grabbed and disarmed Churchill, they broke his collarbone. The boy's injury became infected; and when he died, Muspratt and Churchill decided to leave the district and go to Tai'arapu, where Tu staged a lavish feast of welcome. Muspratt had invited John Brown (the sailor from the *Mercury* who was now living in Tai'arapu) to join them; but after the feast, while Tu's people were packing up the remaining food, Brown demanded some of this food for his dog. When the leader of these people refused, saying that they were waiting for other guests to arrive, Brown flew into a violent rage, throwing a punch at this man who blocked the blow so effectively that Brown's arm was broken. Although Brown dashed off to get his pistol to shoot him, when he returned he found that the man had vanished.

On 12 April, William Muspratt returned to Matavai Bay to report this fracas to his shipmates, who were still working on the schooner. According to Muspratt, after Churchill became the *ari'i rahi* of southern Tahiti, he and Thompson had quarrelled again. One day when Churchill ordered Thompson to fill some vessels with water, Thompson, offended, asked him if he knew to whom he was speaking. 'To a *seaman*,' said Churchill, 'but perhaps you forget that I am *master at arms*.' Furious at being patronised, Thompson retorted: 'I remember what you *were* when Bligh was our commander; but as to what you *are*, I think you now no better than myself, although the people here have *dubbed* you a chief. To be a servant to a villain is intolerable, for we are all villains alike.'[17] Hearing raised voices, some of Churchill's attendants had arrived and forced Thompson to leave.

Shortly after Muspratt's arrival, Tu sent a message to the *Bounty* sailors at Matavai Bay, saying that a party of Mo'orea people who were still loyal to Mahine's adopted son had risen up against Mahau, the 'rightful' high chief of Mo'orea; and asking for their assistance in quelling the uprising. Morrison and his companions sent back a message saying that while they were happy to clean and load Tu's muskets, Tu should send his own men with these weapons to Mo'orea. When the muskets arrived at Matavai Bay, along with a group of warriors led by Hitihiti, they cleaned and loaded the guns and the war party set off for Mo'orea, where Hitihiti shot the prophet of the rebel party dead and Tu's men won an easy victory. Mahine's adopted son was forced to flee to Pa'ea, and then to Papara where Teri'irere gave him some land; and he settled down with his mother and his aunt (Amo's sister and Mahine's widow), leaving Mahau in possession of Mo'orea.

On 15 April, letters from Burkett and Brown arrived at the compound in Matavai Bay, saying that both Charles Churchill and Matthew Thompson had been killed. According to Burkett, after his visit to Tu he had accompanied Churchill back to Tai'arapu. During Churchill's absence, however, a man named 'Ma'iriri' had told Thompson that in fact, it was Churchill who had stolen his musket. In a fury Thompson vowed to kill his shipmate, although when Burkett and Churchill arrived at Vaiaotea, he greeted them in a friendly manner, saying only that he had discovered the identity of the thief. The following morning when Burkett went to his canoe, he heard a shot; and when he ran up to the house Thompson barred his way, saying, 'I have done him.' Looking into the house, Burkett saw Churchill's body lying on the floor, shot from behind through the shoulder; and he took the corpse and buried it. When he asked Thompson for some of Churchill's books, Thompson refused to hand them over, so Burkett took his canoe and returned to Papara. Soon afterwards he heard that Vehiatua's people had killed Thompson in revenge for murdering their *ari'i*, and that his corpse had been taken to Vai'otaha *marae*.[18]

When John Brown arrived at the compound in Matavai Bay the following day, he told the *Bounty* sailors an almost identical story. Wanting to find out what had happened for himself, however, Morrison set off the next day to Tai'arapu, accompanied by Brown. When they arrived at Tautira, Tu greeted them warmly, although he begged Morrison not to stay in southern Tahiti. Reassuring him that he had no intention of leaving Po'e'eno or the compound at Matavai Bay, but that he wanted mats and ropes for the schooner, Morrison told Tu that he had come to hear the truth about the deaths of Churchill and Thompson; and Tu sent a messenger to summon a man named Patiri.

When he arrived, Patiri told Morrison that he had killed Thompson in revenge for Churchill's death. After gathering five or six of his friends, he had gone to Thompson's house, saluting him as 'Vehiatua' and saying that now that Churchill was dead, they wanted him to be their *ari'i*. Flattered, Thompson let them into the house where Patiri knocked the sailor down. While his companions put a plank across Thompson's chest, one sitting on each end, Patiri fetched a large stone and bashed his head in. After killing Thompson, they plundered his house, cut off his head and buried his body, taking his shattered skull to Vai'otaha *marae*, where it was offered as a sacrifice to 'Oro.[19] After telling Morrison this story, Patiri took him to Vai'otaha *marae* where he produced part of Thompson's skull, which Morrison recognised from a scar across the forehead. Convinced by this proof, Morrison assured Patiri that he would not be punished for killing Thompson, who was a murderer; and that 'I lookd on Him as an instrument in the Hand of Providence to punnish such Crimes'.[20]

During his three-day visit to Tautira, Tu told James Morrison that Vehiatua's nephew, a boy only four years old, had been appointed as Churchill's successor, although the boy's mother would act as his regent until he was formally installed as the *ari'i* of southern Tahiti. The people of southern Tahiti still staunchly refused to acknowledge his son Pomare II as their paramount chief, saying that 'he was a Bastard and not the son of Matte [Tu]'.[21] This referred to widespread gossip that Pomare II was in fact the son of 'Itia's attendant and lover, although she and Tu always said that the boy had been conceived by the god Tane, who came to her in the night. When Morrison set off for Matavai Bay, Tu presented him with a gift of a large pig, three bamboo containers of *monoi* or scented oil and a large quantity of bark cloth.

Arriving back at the compound on 24 April 1790, Morrison found that work on the schooner was progressing, and both sides of the ship had been planked and the beams secured. The next task was to collect breadfruit gum, boil it into pitch and mix it with pig's lard as a substitute for tar; and to gather enough oakum to caulk the vessel. While this work was under way, Mahau, the *ari'i rahi* of Mo'orea, paid them a visit, bringing two baked pigs and some bark cloth to thank them for their help in quelling the rebellion on his island. He was accompanied by a dog named Bacchus and a bitch named Venus that Bligh had left on Mo'orea; and to the chief's amazement, these dogs immediately recognised the sailors. Morrison and his comrades now invited a number of commoners to feast on Mahau's pigs, in return for collecting quantities of breadfruit gum, which they did by driving pegs made of *toa* wood into the trunks of breadfruit trees, and gathering the gum every morning.

By 1 June the deck of the schooner was finished. On 4 June the men at the compound in Matavai Bay fired a volley and drank a keg of cider (which they had made from Tahitian apples) to celebrate this milestone. Afterwards they set to work making casks for water and salted pork, and fashioning masts, booms, gaffs and a bowsprit for the schooner. When Byrne and Ellison visited them en route to Teti'aroa to join the *'arioi* celebrations on the islets, they helped them to fix the rudder, and to caulk and pitch the schooner. By 1 July they were ready to launch their little craft, slinging the masts by using a rope cradle. Po'e'eno insisted that the schooner must be blessed before his men would launch her, however, and on 5 July a priest arrived at the compound, where he was presented with a small pig and a plantain branch. Walking around the little craft, muttering short sentences in the priestly dialect, and tossing a plantain branch on the deck, the priest carried on chanting all night, finishing only at sunrise when Po'e'eno and Teu (Tu's father) arrived with about 600 men. After each of the chiefs had made a speech, the men either seized the schooner or grabbed long poles as levers. When the priest boarded the craft, plantain branches were tossed on board; and as he gave a signal, they began to sing in chorus, heaving the schooner, moving it off the blocks, and hauling it three-quarters of a mile to the beach, which took about half an hour. At the edge of the sea, the schooner was blessed and launched, named the *Resolution* after Captain Cook's famous ship and towed behind a canoe around Point Venus to a small bay east of the point, where they moored her safely. Over the next few days they shifted their houses to 'Cockroach Point', a small promontory that sheltered this bay, so that they could keep watch over their new vessel.[22]

During August, Morrison and his companions distilled salt to preserve pork, covered the schooner with mats of coconut leaves to prevent the timbers from warping and made more barrels to store their supplies of salted pork and water. When Tu sent them 400 fathoms of rope, they rigged the masts; and Morrison managed to repair his watch, ingeniously fixing its broken chain with a pair of compasses and a filed nail. They also made a log reel and line; a half minute glass using a glass phial cut in half; and a compass box out of a small gourd slung on gimbals in the binnacle, lit by an oil lamp and goat's fat candles. Thomas McIntosh (the fair-headed carpenter's mate) built a cooking enclosure out of planks, lined with squared stones and plastered with clay; but they had no sails for the schooner, having very little canvas, and the Tahitians were reluctant to provide them with fine mats for this purpose.

On 12 September 1790, Pomare II sent another message requesting their assistance. According to the messenger, the people of the Fa'a'a district under Teto'ofa (the 'Admiral's' son and heir) had risen up against the Pomare lineage, invading Pare and burning and destroying everything in their path. When the Pare warriors drove back the enemy warriors, they had fled leaving two of their dead comrades behind, whose corpses were taken to Pomare's *marae* (presumably Taraho'i). The Pa'ea people led by the great warrior Pohuetea had since joined the Fa'a'a army, however, and were preparing to make another descent on Pare. The messenger also reported that Ari'ipaea Vahine, Tu's elder sister and the highest-ranking woman in Tahiti, had returned to Pare after a long stay in Ra'iatea, accompanied by a large fleet of canoes that were ready for battle.

The next morning, Morrison and his comrades armed themselves and marched to Pare where Ari'ipaea Vahine welcomed them warmly, presenting them with a baked pig to thank them for their assistance. Because Byrne and Ellison were away at Teti'aroa and Muspratt was visiting Papara with his *taio* Ari'ipaea, there were only eight in their party on this occasion; although John Brown soon joined them, reporting that Pohuetea's warriors had also attacked Teri'irere at Papara. A priest dressed in red and black feathers was sent to the *marae*, emerging a few minutes later sneezing, his eyes staring and his body distorted into strange shapes, predicting a favourable outcome to the battle.[23]

After breakfast, the *Bounty* sailors set out for the Fa'a'a district, accompanied by a large war party from Matavai Bay, headed by Po'e'eno (the *ari'i* of the bay) and Vaetua (Tu's younger brother).[24] After marching for about half an hour, they found a *maro atua* (literally a 'god's girdle') of bark cloth draped across the path, tied between trees to which several pigs were tethered. This was a ritual barrier, placed to stop an enemy from advancing; and when the Matavai warriors seized it and untied the pigs, the Fa'a'a warriors, who had been hiding in the bushes, leaped up and ambushed them. As soon as they saw the British, however, they fled, mingling with the Matavai warriors in such a way that the sailors, unable to tell friends from enemies, could not shoot them with their muskets and pistols. As the Matavai warriors and their allies ravaged the Fa'a'a district, its inhabitants fled to the mountains. After this victory, the *Bounty* sailors asked Ari'ipaea Vahine for mats and ropes for their schooner; and told Po'e'eno and Vaetua that during the next skirmish, their warriors must wear identifying marks so that they did not accidentally shoot them, to which the chiefs agreed.

Although Ari'ipaea Vahine was the first-born in the chiefly line of Pare-'Arue with the right to govern those districts, she had lived in Ra'iatea for many years; and as a leading *'arioi*, she had no children. During her absences from Tahiti, she customarily handed over the *hau* or governance of the island to Tu and latterly to his son Pomare II, although whenever she returned to Tahiti she resumed her pre-eminent position. After collecting enough fine mats to make three sails for the schooner, she sent these to the British sailors with piles of provisions to thank them for their assistance in the recent skirmish. Pomare II also gave them a double canoe, and each of them a pig, a piece of bark cloth and a bamboo container of *monoi*. Back at 'Cockroach Point', James Morrison and his shipmates made the fine mats into sails, quilting and seaming the matting at regular intervals to strengthen it, using iron needles that Coleman had made; rigged the ship with ropes made of hibiscus bark; and prepared to leave the island. Before they were ready, however, the Pa'ea/Fa'a'a warriors sent them messages threatening to burn the schooner and challenging each of them to fight, claiming their bodies for their *marae*. After the enemy army mounted more raids on Pare and Papara, on 20 September the *Bounty* sailors were again called to assist Pomare II and his warriors.

Early the next morning, Morrison and his companions took their weapons and went by canoe to Pare, where Po'e'eno, Teu and Ari'ipaea Vahine greeted them. Almost every able-bodied man from Matavai Bay had gathered, led by Vaetua and Matahiapo, the principal warriors of their army, dressed in scraps of European clothing to distinguish them from the enemy forces. After breakfast, the *Bounty* sailors marched to Fa'a'a, surrounded by Matavai warriors; and when they saw them coming, the Fa'a'a warriors retreated to a high mountain pass where they had built a fortified village. It was a very hot day, and as they climbed up to the fort, Morrison and his companions refreshed themselves by drinking from coconuts. When Vaetua, Matahiapo and a group of Matavai warriors led them across a narrow ridge into the pass, the enemy warriors pelted them with a barrage of rocks, and the armourer Joseph Coleman was hit on the leg while his Tahitian *taio*, dressed in European clothing, struck between the mouth and nose, fell bleeding to the ground. His fall was greeted by triumphant cries from their enemies, who mistook him for one of the British sailors. About twenty of their Tahitian companions were also hit until the sailors, finally able to use their muskets, took aim and opened fire, shooting three of the leading enemy warriors and forcing their army to abandon the fort. As the Matavai warriors chased their enemies down the mountainside to Fa'a'a, burning houses and canoes and plundering their pigs and gardens, the Pare men destroyed the fortified village. The following morning the *Bounty* men realised that on this day, they had lived for exactly one year on the island.

Although the Fa'a'a army under Teto'ofa had been routed, the Pa'ea warriors under Pohuetea were still under arms; and several days later Pomare II asked his European friends to help him defeat them, forcing them to surrender the sacred relics that the high priest Tupaia had brought from the sacred *marae* of Taputapuatea on Ra'iatea to Papara in Tahiti many years earlier. These included Te Ra'i-puatata, the famous *maro 'ura* or red feather sash to which Tupaia had stitched the red bunting from the *Dolphin* for Teri'irere's installation; the portable *marae* known as Taputapuatea in which the image of 'Oro was kept; and its *fare atua* or god-house. These powerful objects held the *mana* of 'Oro, the god of fertility and war. According to Pomare II, when the Pare warriors headed by Tutaha (or Ha'amanimani) and the Atehuru army led by Pohuetea and Teto'ofa had attacked the Papara dynasty many years earlier at the great *marae* of Mahaiatea, preventing Teri'irere from being installed as the paramount chief of the island, Teto'ofa (the father of the current title-holder in Pa'ea) and Pohuetea had seized the red feather girdle and the image of 'Oro and taken these sacred relics to 'Utu-'ai-mahurau, their own *marae* in the Pa'ea district, on the west coast of the island. Since that time, although Tu and now Pomare II were the only *ari'i* who had the right to wear the red feather girdle, they had been forced to go to Pa'ea to perform the rituals dedicated to 'Oro.[25] Frustrated by this humiliating situation, Pomare II was determined to capture these sacred objects and take them to his own *marae* in Pare.

Weary after their long march, the *Bounty* sailors paddled back to 'Cockroach Point' where they loaded seven hundredweight of pork on board the schooner and raised the sails, heading back to Pare on 26 September 1790. Because Skinner's eyes were sore and infected, he remained at Matavai Bay. When they arrived at Pare, they met Hitihiti, the young Ra'iatean *arioi* who had sailed with Captain Cook, and who had just arrived from Papara, where Teri'irere's army assisted by Hitihiti, Sumner, Burkett, Muspratt and Brown had repulsed the Pa'ea and Fa'a'a forces with great slaughter. Their enemies still refused to surrender, however, and Teri'irere had sent Hitihiti to ask Pomare II to appoint a day on which the armies of Papara and Te Porionu'u would fight a pitched battle with their enemies at Pa'ea.[26] Arming Hitihiti with Tu's musket, Morrison and his companions boarded the schooner and joined a large fleet of forty canoes that had assembled under the command of the Te Porionu'u chiefs, each with fifty or sixty paddlers and flying a painted bark-cloth banner at its stern; accompanied by small tenders filled with provisions. As the drums beat and nose flutes played, the warriors capered on their fighting stages, wearing feather headdresses and gesticulating with their weapons; and the canoes lined up in the 'net of war' formation and paddled inside the reef to Pa'ea, followed on shore by a large army.

As they approached Pa'ea, the enemy warriors fled to the mountains, chased by the Pare and Papara warriors who ravaged their district, 'Burning the Houses, and destroying the Country by rooting up the Plantains & Tarro, and notching the bark round the Breadfruit trees to stop their Growth, and laying all in ashes before them'.[27] By noon when they arrived at Ta'apuna in Pohuetea's district, they found the Pare fleet hauled up on the beach, where the warriors had set up a shore camp. The British were told that their enemies had retreated to their mountain stronghold, a famous refuge with a stone wall,[28] and using their spyglasses, watched the warriors in their lair. Hitihiti was sent with two parties of men to set fire to the hillside, which was covered with reeds, and envoys were sent ahead to demand a surrender, while a white flag was hoisted on the schooner and another about two miles away on shore. While the hills were burning, the enemy warriors attacked Hitihiti and his men several times, but he always managed to shoot their leaders with his musket and they were forced to retreat back to the fort.

That night, Hitihiti's sentries in the camp cried out 'All's well' at thirty-minute intervals, while on board the schooner a sentry struck an iron hoop from an anchor stock with a hammer at the same time, showing that they were also on the alert. The following afternoon, they saw a party carrying a white flag coming down the mountainside; and at about sunset the great warrior Pohuetea and his wife arrived on the beach, accompanied by a priest who acted as their flag-bearer. A council was held with all the chiefs and leading men; and Pohuetea and his people agreed to make peace and hand over the sacred relics to the young *ari'i rahi*, acknowledging Pomare II as the paramount chief of the island. Teto'ofa still held some of the sacred relics, however, and Pohuetea and his wife boarded the schooner as voluntary hostages while a messenger was sent ordering him to surrender these within twenty-four hours, or his district would be devastated. When Burkett came out to the schooner, Morrison told him what had happened; and Burkett (who was the *taio* of Amo, Teri'irere's father) returned to Papara to inform Teri'irere.

Early on the morning of 31 September, the men on board the schooner were told that Teto'ofa had passed by during the night, going by canoe to Pare where he intended to hand over the *maro 'ura* in person to Pomare II, although he still hoped to keep the image of 'Oro for his own people. A double canoe was prepared, and John Millward was sent to bring Teto'ofa back to the schooner, which he did that evening. During the day, Ari'ipaea (Tu's brother) and his *taio*, William Muspratt, also visited the schooner, and Ari'ipaea presented each of the *Bounty* sailors with a pig and a length of bark cloth before carrying on to Pare. That night, Teto'ofa, the son and successor of the 'Admiral', a fine-looking man about twenty-two years old and 6 feet tall, arrived on board the *Resolution* with Pohuetea (the great warrior, whom Morrison described as about sixty-five years old and now very rotund). When Teto'ofa confessed that he was afraid they would be killed, Pohuetea comforted him, saying that he was a friend of Captain Cook's and that the British always honoured their friendships. The

*Bounty* sailors also reassured Teto'ofa, saying that the British never killed their prisoners, and that as long as he met their demands he would be freed and all his possessions returned to him. After hearing this, Teto'ofa sent his attendants to fetch the remaining sacred objects from 'Utu-'ai-mahurau *marae*, so that they could be handed over to Pomare II's priests and taken to Pare.

The next morning, 'Oro's sacred canoe, the *Rainbow*, arrived alongside the schooner, carrying the portable *marae* Taputapuatea (a box about 3 feet long, decorated with bunches of red and yellow feathers and surmounted by carved birds with their wings outstretched, in which the images of the gods were kept) and the *fare atua* (a moveable house, which stood on the same stand as the *marae* and held the *maro 'ura*), wrapped in the finest-coloured bark cloth, along with other sacred paraphernalia. Pomare II's fleet escorted the *Rainbow* to Pare where the Pa'ea priests handed over these relics to the priests from Matavai Bay and Pare – a momentous occasion in the history of the island.

When a breeze sprang up that afternoon, James Morrison and his comrades sailed the schooner to Fa'a'a with Po'e'eno, Teto'ofa and Pohuetea on board, anchoring off the coast where they were joined by Thomas Burkett and Amo. At 9 a.m. the next day they sailed to To'aroa Harbour where they accompanied the chiefs to Taraho'i *marae*, and the peace was formally ratified. The *Bounty* sailors suggested that Teto'ofa and Pohuetea should be left in possession of their districts, and in exchange Teto'ofa and Pohuetea swore undying loyalty to Pomare II, and each took one of the mutineers as their *taio*. During a great feast, they fired off volleys of musket-fire, and on 4 October 1790 the British returned to Matavai Bay, where Burkett and Amo, Teri'irere's father and Purea's ex-husband, came to visit them. Teto'ofa also came to see them, although soon afterwards he died of a fever and was succeeded by his sister's son, a boy about four years old who took over the title of Teto'ofa, with his mother acting as his regent.

# Pandora's Box

After returning to Matavai Bay, Morrison and his comrades resumed work on their new schooner, cutting and greasing new masts, boiling salt and re-rigging the vessel. On 9 October 1790 when William Muspratt arrived from the islets of Teti'aroa, the sailors decided to make a trial run to this *'arioi* resort. Against the advice of their friends, they set off in a fresh breeze which quickly turned into a gale. The *Resolution* handled these rough conditions well, although they could not land on the islets, returning to Fa'a'a three days later and running inside the reef to Ta'apuna in Pa'ea, where they landed to repair their tattered sails. At Pa'ea, the great warrior chief Pohuetea came on board with two roasted pigs and some breadfruit, and they also met Po'e'eno, the chief of Matavai Bay and Morrison's *taio*, who was touring around the island. He gave them one of his men as a pilot; and after mending the sails, they ran across to Mo'orea where they anchored in Vai'are Bay, a snug haven on the east side of the island. Ari'ipaea Vahine, who was visiting Mahau, the high chief of Mo'orea, arrived soon afterwards with a message from the *ari'i rahi*, inviting them to visit him at Papeto'ai Harbour where Captain Cook had anchored.

On 14 October they sailed to Papeto'ai, escorted by Tu's elder sister Ari'ipaea Vahine in her canoe. When Mahau and his wife Auo (Tu's younger sister) came on board, they were saluted with six musket shots. Morrison was eager to procure more mats; but by now the islanders, aware that the sailors were eager to sail away from Tahiti, were reluctant to give them mats, although they gladly provided them with pigs and other produce. The *Bounty*'s men went to see the cattle that Captain Cook had originally left on Tahiti, finding one bull, five cows and a calf in a western bay, all healthy and in fine condition, but very wild.

On 25 October, Morrison and his comrades sailed the schooner back to Vai'are with Mahau and his wife on board, intending to return to Matavai

Bay as soon as possible, although Mahau had pressed them to stay longer at Mo'orea. By the time they reached Vai'are, they had forty-eight pigs on board and many bales of bark cloth. When Joseph Coleman, who wanted some fine sand to clean the muskets, went ashore to fetch it, he was grabbed by a man who threatened to kill him, accusing him of raping his wife on board the schooner. This man demanded a large present, and although Coleman agreed to give it to him, when he returned on board his comrades realised that the armourer been duped, and decided to punish the offender. Early the next morning, Coleman, accompanied by Millward, McIntosh and Heildbrandt went ashore at Vai'are, armed with muskets, and as the people fled they shot two men, one in the thigh and body and the other in the arm. Their companions, who acknowledged that Coleman had been tricked, told them that the offender had escaped but took them to his house, which the British plundered, taking pigs, bark cloth, *monoi* or scented oil and a canoe sail. When they returned to the schooner, they sent a messenger to Mahau to tell him what had happened, and he sent the offender into exile. On 27 October they sailed back to Tahiti, entering the reef through the pass at Ta'apuna and sailing in the lagoon to Pare, where they landed the pigs that they had been given.

When they returned to Matavai Bay on this occasion, accompanied by Ari'ipaea, the beach at Point Venus was lined with crowds of people, who greeted them ecstatically '& seemd as much rejoiced as if they had found some of their lost relations'.[1] Joseph Coleman now returned to live with his *taio* at Point Venus, where he fell ill from a severe fever and almost died, although he recovered after a while. As Christmas Day approached again, Michael Byrne and his young friend Tom Ellison came back from Teti'aroa to celebrate the festive day at the compound before going to visit Mahau at Mo'orea. The rainy season was imminent, and Morrison and his companions hauled the schooner back under its shelter. Unsure of Morrison's navigational ability and realising that they could not reach Batavia without canvas sails, the men at the compound finally gave up the idea of leaving Tahiti, and decided to distribute the salted pork amongst those sailors who had worked on the vessel.

On 27 December a thief crept into Morrison's house and stole his writing equipment – quill, ink and paper – which he had been using to note down the events since the mutiny began, and was chased but got away. Fortunately, the next morning, one of Morrison's neighbours, who was climbing a coconut tree to gather nuts, spotted the box, which had been hidden in some bushes, and gave it back to him, to his relief and joy. Apparently the thief was an *'arioi* who had accompanied Ari'ipaea Vahine from Ra'iatea, and seeing the box open on the table, had impulsively decided to take it. He was captured soon afterwards and brought to 'Cockroach Point' where the *Bounty* sailors gave him a 'good smart Whipping' before releasing him.

During the month of January 1791, canoes began to arrive at Matavai Bay from Ra'iatea, whose crews eagerly asked after Captain Cook and Joseph Banks. When a group of chiefs arrived from Huahine, Morrison asked them about Ma'i, and his fate after Captain Cook's departure from that island. According to these chiefs, approximately four years after Cook left him behind on Huahine, Ma'i had died of *hotate* (a wasting fever), followed soon afterwards by Te Weherua and Koa, the two Māori youths, who were homesick and convinced that they would never return home to Te Wai Pounamu (the South Island). The Huahine chiefs also noted that Ma'i was a *manahune* or commoner. Prior to his voyage to England, he had been condemned to die for 'Blasphemy against one of the Chiefs',[2] but his brother had helped him to escape; and when the *Adventure* arrived, he sailed with Furneaux to avoid being offered as a human sacrifice.

Captain Cook had given Ma'i many treasures, but he was not respected by his fellow islanders, although they were in awe of his European weapons. Soon after Captain Cook left the island, Ma'i's horse had been gored in the belly by a billy goat and died; although the mare was still at Huahine, along with part of the house that Captain Cook's men had built for him. After his death, Ma'i's gardens had been destroyed, the poultry died and his possessions were distributed around the Society Islands. His *taio* Tenani'a, the brother of Teri'itaria, the *ari'i rahi* or high chief of Huahine, still had his muskets, although they no longer worked. According to one of Ma'i's attendants, whenever he went to battle, dressed in his helmet and breastplate and mounted on horseback, the enemy warriors had always fled and his party won the victory. Likewise at sea, sailing the canoe that he had acquired in Tahiti and firing his muskets and pistols, Ma'i had been invincible.

On 10 January 1791, 'Itia arrived from Tai'arapu with her younger sister Teano (or Vaiareti), Vehiatua III's widow and now Tu's junior wife, escorted by their attendants. After thanking Morrison and his comrades for their support in the recent war, 'Itia gave them gifts and announced that her son Pomare II was about to be invested with the *maro 'ura* Te Ra'i-puatata, formally succeeding his father Tu as the paramount chief of the island; and she had come to prepare for the ceremony. The priests had sent sacred plaits of coconut leaves to each household to indicate the dimensions of the stones that were required for the new *marae* that was built at Taraho'i for the investiture, with a human sacrifice buried under each of its cornerstones. The following day, the *'arioi* from Ra'iatea celebrated 'Itia's arrival with a boxing match, while the *'arioi* from Tahiti put on a display of wrestling and dancing with 'Itia presiding as mistress of ceremonies. A vast crowd had gathered, including Ari'ipaea Vahine, the black leg *'arioi* who had returned from Mo'orea to participate in her nephew's installation.

On 12 January, James Morrison went with 'Itia to visit Pomare II. Although 'Itia had to change her clothes before she could enter her son's sacred house, the young *ari'i rahi* excused Morrison from this ritual precaution. A pig was baked, although 'Itia could not eat in her son's presence. Until the investiture was performed and some of his *ra'a* or ancestral power was removed, he was too sacred to be touched, which is why he had been forced to stay away from the *Bounty*, the schooner and the Europeans' compound. On 14 January, Burkett arrived from Papara, and three days later Morrison accompanied him on a visit to Papara to meet Teri'irere, Purea's aristocratic son, describing him as a handsome, robust man, about 6 feet tall, now twenty-seven years old. Teri'irere welcomed Morrison warmly and adopted him as a *taio*, and they soon became intimate friends, sharing a feast every day during his visit to Papara.

While James Morrison was still staying with Teri'irere, Pomare II's flag arrived in Papara. Teri'irere received this emblem, a Union Jack that according to the Tahitians, Captain Cox had presented to the young chief (although in fact it had been stolen from the *Mercury*), slung across a staff on a bar and decorated with red feathers, breastplates and tassels; conducting the envoy along the edge of the sea to Mahaiatea *marae*. As they passed the houses, the inhabitants hid themselves and put out their fires, and no canoes were launched into the ocean. At the *marae*, Teri'irere's priests set up the sacred emblem, presenting offerings of a pig and a plantain tree to the envoys and making long speeches, followed by Teri'irere who declared his allegiance to Tu-nui-a'a-i-te-atua (Pomare II's title, formerly held by his father) as the *ari'i maro 'ura* (paramount chief of the red feather girdle) of Tahiti, inviting the envoys to a feast. When Morrison and Burkett fired their muskets to celebrate this occasion, the Tahitians understood this to be a declaration of loyalty, taking it for granted that the *Bounty*'s men would now support the flag against any challenge as it travelled around the island.

The priests chanted and prayed all night over the Union Jack; and early the next morning took it to the water's edge, and carried the sacred emblem south to Tai'arapu. On 23 January, Morrison farewelled Teri'irere, who presented him with two canoes and several pigs, along with bark cloth and other gifts in recognition of their friendship; and he and Burkett set off for Vaiari where they were welcomed by Ha'amanimani and Moana, the black leg *'arioi* whose attendants helped them haul their canoe 3 miles across the island at the Taravao isthmus. On 25 January when they reached the eastern coast, a messenger arrived from Tu inviting them to visit him at Afa'ahiti about 6 miles away, where a feast had been prepared.

When they arrived at Afa'ahiti, Tu told Morrison and Burkett that the Tai'arapu people had been very uncivil. Although they had allowed his son's flag to pass through their district for fear of the *Bounty* sailors, they had not accepted Pomare II as their *ari'i maro 'ura* or paramount chief. He urged them to punish these people for killing Thompson, saying that as soon as Morrison and his comrades appeared in arms in Tahiti-iti, its inhabitants would immediately surrender, leaving his son in a secure position. He assured them that Teri'irere would assist them, providing them with canoes and warriors for this purpose. They were eager to return home, however, and sailed to Hitia'a where they were given a feast, returning to Matavai Bay on 29 January where a huge crowd had gathered for Pomare II's installation. Mahau, the high chief of Mo'orea, had arrived with Norman, Ellison and Byrne; and all the principal chiefs of the island had landed at Matavai Bay, except those from Tai'arapu. On 1 February, John Millward and the carpenter's mate Thomas McIntosh set off for Papara to discuss the attack on Tai'arapu with Teri'irere; and ten days later 'Itia arrived with Tu's ammunition chest and a pair of pistols and a bayonet which she handed to Morrison for this expedition.


On 13 February 1791, as the end of the Season of Plenty approached, the cere-mony to invest Pomare II with the *maro 'ura* Te Ra'i-puatata was held at the new *marae* at Taraho'i in the Pare district, which had been built especially for this occasion. This new *marae* was called Taputapuatea, since the image of 'Oro and the *maro 'ura* were now held there; and at the same time, *marae* 'Uta-'ai-mahurau in the Pa'ea district lost this title. All of the chiefs from Mo'orea and Te Porionu'u attended this ritual, although none of those from Tai'arapu were present. The new *marae* had a stone pavement about 64 feet long and 42 feet wide, with some upright stones for the priests to lean on; and at one end there was an *ahu* (stone platform) 4 or 5 feet high, formed in two steps that were decorated with carved wooden figures representing *'arioi* dancers, birds and lizards.[3] Near the *marae* stood a large stage for offerings, about 40 feet long, supported by three rows of carved pillars about 8 feet high and decorated with a fringe of coconut leaves.

As the young *ari'i* was escorted to the *marae*, the high priest chanted a long prayer, took the *maro 'ura* out of its red bark-cloth wrapping and spread it out on the pavement. Morrison, who was present on this occasion, described this famous icon as a sash about 3 yards long, made of a fine network to which red and yellow feathers were fastened, with six tassels of red, black and yellow feathers at each end, each named after one of Pomare II's ancestors whose *mana* entered him when he wore the *maro 'ura*. This sash could be worn only once in a lifetime, during the investiture, and afterwards it was stored with the sacred eyeshade, which was also decorated with red feathers, in the *fare atua* or god-house. Interestingly, Morrison did not mention the red bunting from the *Dolphin*, a notable feature of this famous girdle, although William Bligh described it when he examined Te Ra'i-puatata not long afterwards. This is understandable, however, because Morrison's account was written from memory, much later in England. According to Pomare II, a number of red feathers given to him by Lieutenant Watts of the *Lady Penrhyn* had also been used to embellish the new section added to the *maro 'ura* on this occasion, once again drawing upon the mana of the British.[4]

As the *maro 'ura* was unrolled, the sacred drums thundered. After another long chant, the priest took the feathered girdle and put it around Pomare II's waist and the sacred eyeshade on his head, hailing him as the *ari'i maro 'ura* or paramount chief of the island. After a long speech by Mahau's orator acknowledging Pomare II as his *ari'i*, three human sacrifices from Mo'orea (including the corpse of one chief who had refused to let Pomare II's flag pass through his district) were laid on the *marae*, trussed up in plaited coconut leaves on poles, with their heads facing towards him. Making an oration over each of the sacrifices, Mahau's priest took an eye from each corpse with a piece of split bamboo and placing it on a leaf, held up the leaf to the young king, who sat above him with his mouth open, allowing the victim's spirit to enter his body. When his speech was over, the priest laid the plantain branches in front of Pomare II and his assistants buried the sacrificial corpses in the *marae*, while he placed the eyes and the plantain branches on the altar. Mahau was followed by the other leading chiefs, each of whom delivered one or two human sacrifices from their district to the *marae* and went through an identical ceremony.[5] Afterwards, huge numbers of pigs, turtles, fish and immense heaps of breadfruit, yams, taro, plantains and coconuts were presented to the young *ari'i rahi*, and several large canoes laden with hundreds of fathoms of bark cloth, red feathers, breastplates and other treasures were hauled up to the *marae*. When these presentations were over, the *maro 'ura* was unwound from Pomare II's waist, wrapped up in scarlet cloth and hidden away in the *fare atua*, and the spectators were regaled with feasts and celebrations that lasted for a fortnight.[6]

When Morrison asked his friends why the eyes had been offered to Pomare II, they explained that since the *ari'i maro 'ura* was the head of his people, the head was the most sacred part of the body, and as the eyes were the most sacred part of the head, eyes were the most appropriate offering on such an occasion. The *ari'i* opened his mouth to let the spirits of the sacrifice enter his *varua* or spiritual being, giving him additional strength. During the ceremony, several large pigs were also placed on the altar, and altogether thirty human sacrifices were offered on this occasion, some of whom had been dead for a month or more. According to Morrison, during the entire time that he had been on the island, these were the first human sacrifices that had been offered; and as soon as the timing of the ceremony was announced, many of the most likely victims (including those who had committed thefts or insulted a chief) had fled to the Europeans' houses, seeking sanctuary from Pomare's men.

Because none of the Tai'arapu chiefs had attended Pomare II's installation, Morrison, John Millward and Thomas McIntosh decided to help his warriors bring them to heel. Teri'irere (a *taio* of Tu's) proposed to give a great feast for the new paramount chief at which he would gather his warriors and canoes, along with the *Bounty* sailors and their schooner. When he gave the signal, the force would descend upon Tai'arapu, catching the chiefs of southern Tahiti unawares. Agreeing to this plan, Morrison and his comrades returned to Matavai Bay and began to prepare the schooner for the expedition.

On 13 March, Pomare II came to visit the compound, carried on his attendant's shoulders and wearing a black feather cloak, his head decorated with a large garland of red and black feathers. The principal chiefs of Matavai Bay followed him, carrying the Union Jack horizontally above their heads, to which several fathoms of painted bark cloth had been added. Because the ritual cycle that lifted the *ra'a* or sacred power from Pomare II was not yet over, the young *ari'i* had to stay on the sacred ground beside the beach. Although he could not go inland or visit the houses of the *Bounty* sailors, he gave each of them gifts including a plot of land, addressing them as *matua* (uncles or parents). Now that he had been installed with Te Ra'i-puatata (the red feather girdle that Tupaia had brought from Taputapuatea) along with the red feather girdle brought by his grandmother Tetupaia from Ra'iatea upon her marriage, while the image of 'Oro from Ra'iatea was held at his *marae*, Pomare II had at last succeeded his father Tu in being invested with the *mana* of all of these sacred objects.[7]

With Pomare II's installation, a series of events that had begun thirty years earlier was coming to a climax. From the conquest of Ra'iatea in about 1760, when the Porapora warriors had ravaged Taputapuatea *marae*, felling the sacred trees; to the high priest-navigator Tupaia's departure from Taputapuatea on his sacred canoe, taking Te Ra'i-puatata and the image of 'Oro to Papara; from the stitching of the *Dolphin*'s red banner to the *maro 'ura* for Teri'irere's investiture, and the subsequent conquest of Amo and Purea's army with the seizure of these sacred relics by the Atehuru warriors; to Tupaia's departure from the island on board the *Endeavour* with Captain Cook; from Tu's bond friendship with Cook and his investiture with Te Ra'i-puatata to Pomare II's bond friendship with Captain Cox; and Pomare II's installation with this famous red feather girdle with the help of the *Bounty* sailors and their muskets, Vaita's prophecy at Taputapuatea *marae* had been vindicated:

> The glorious children of Tetumu
> will come and see this forest at Taputapuatea.
> Their body is different, our body is different
> We are one species only from Tetumu.
> And this land will be taken by them
>
> The old rules will be destroyed
> And sacred birds of the land and the sea
> Will also arrive here, will come and lament
> Over that which this lopped tree has to teach
> They are coming up on a canoe without an outrigger.[8]

In their 'canoe without an outrigger,' the British (the 'glorious children of Tetumu') had helped Pomare II to win a series of victories, defeating his enemies and giving him unprecedented powers. From this time onwards, Pomare II's supporters referred to him as the *ari'i maro 'ura* (high chief of the red feather girdle), saying that while there might be a number of *ari'i rahi* (great chiefs) in the Society Islands at one time, there could only be one 'high chief of the red feather girdle' (although some other lineages had a different opinion).[9] In his gratitude, however, the young high chief gave the *Bounty* sailors land and excused them from the 'old rules', thus foreshadowing the demise of the *tapu* system in Tahiti.

As for the *Bounty*'s men, by this time they looked almost indistinguishable from the Tahitians. Tanned by the tropical sun, they were tattooed, and wore bark-cloth clothing. According to Coleman in a later interview:

Though deprived of every wretch's comfort, *hope*, yet they kept up their spirits, and supported themselves in a most amazing manner through the cheering assistance of the women, whose transcendant love and affection served in a great measure to alleviate their sufferings. These generous females endeavoured all in their power to dispel their fears, and defend them from the insults of their men.

The chiefs who had made them their Tyos were exceedingly good natured and honorable. They were not only willing to assist them, but seemed proud of giving their protection.[10]

Once Pomare II had been invested with Te Ra'i-puatata, however, it was as though their presence on the island was no longer needed. On 21 March 1791, Morrison and his comrades, McIntosh, Millward and Heildbrandt, boarded the schooner and sailed to Pare, leaving behind Stewart, Heywood, Coleman and Skinner at Matavai Bay. When they arrived at Pare, Charles Norman, the other carpenter's mate, joined them along with Ellison and Byrne, accompanying them to Papara. As they sailed along the white beaches of the Pa'ea district, the great warrior Pohuetea sent a messenger inviting them to visit him at Taitapu, where he was now living; but there was no safe anchorage, and they decided to carry on to Papara.

On 23 March they anchored opposite Mahaiatea *marae* – the great tiered stone temple where Pohuetea's warriors had seized Te Ra'i-puatata – and went ashore, where they met Burkett, Sumner, Brown and Muspratt. Almost as soon as they sat down for breakfast at Teri'irere's house, however, a messenger arrived from Hitihiti, telling them that two days after their departure from Matavai Bay, a strange ship had anchored, and armed boats had been sent to Pa'ea in pursuit of the schooner, determined to take them prisoner. The two midshipmen at Matavai Bay – Peter Heywood and George Stewart – had freely gone on board the vessel, where at first they were mistaken for Tahitians; but as soon as they identified themselves, the pair had been clapped in irons. When Skinner and Coleman went out to the ship, they were accorded the same harsh treatment. In token of their friendship, Hitihiti, who was guiding the boats, was giving their shipmates fair warning. Determined to avoid the armed boats, all of the Europeans at Papara except for Michael Byrne and John Brown now boarded the schooner, and headed south. Although Morrison later claimed that they had decided to surrender rather than being captured, hoping that this might lead to better treatment, it seems likely that they were trying to evade the British vessel.

Once again the matting sails could not handle the strong winds, however, and on 27 March, Morrison and his shipmates were forced to return to Papara. Upon their arrival, they were told that despite being nearly blind, Michael Byrne had walked through the night to Matavai Bay and boarded the ship; and that after plundering Burkett's house, John Brown from the *Mercury* had followed him on board, where he was quick to dissociate himself from the *Bounty* sailors. Thomas Hayward, Bligh's most loyal supporter on board the *Bounty* (although Bligh had clapped him in irons for sleeping on duty when some of his shipmates had deserted in Tahiti), was a lieutenant in charge of one of the armed boats, which had now returned to the ship; and Teri'irere had sent the rest of the sailors' goods to the mountains.

Most of their party now decided to follow Teri'irere inland, leaving Morrison, Norman and Ellison in charge of the schooner. When Morrison went ashore to fetch coconuts, and told his *taio* Teri'irere that he had decided to go out to the British ship and hand himself over, Tere'irere was furious. According to Morrison, he said that if he gave himself up, Lieutenant Hayward, who was bitterly angry with his former shipmates, would kill him. While Tere'irere was urging him to go inland, Morrison looked out to sea and saw his *taio*'s men boarding the schooner, and tossing Norman and Ellison overboard. As the *Bounty* sailors swam ashore, a thousand of Teri'irere's men swarmed over the *Resolution*, tipping her sideways and stripping her of her sails, rigging and fittings.

After swimming to the beach, Norman and Ellison reproached Teri'irere, asking why he had betrayed them. The high chief retorted that by planning to leave the island, they had deceived him. If they joined him in the mountains, however, he would keep them safe and all their possessions would be returned. When they still refused to go inland, Teri'irere exclaimed, 'Then I'll make you go!', ordering his men to seize them and carry them to the mountains; but when they begged to see their shipmates one last time, however, he relented, sending them to Mahine's nephew's house where they spent the next two days, and were kindly treated. In fact, Edward Edwards, the captain of the British frigate, the *Pandora*, had threatened Teri'irere, saying that if he did not give them up, he would destroy his district; and it seems that after some reflection, the chief had decided to hand them over to the Europeans.

While Morrison, Norman and Ellison were staying with Mahine's nephew, one of Po'e'eno's men promised Morrison that he would bring him a canoe so that he could return to Matavai Bay; and that night John Brown, the sailor from the *Mercury*, entered the house, armed with two hatchets and a knife, and carrying a bottle of gin. After offering them each a dram, he told them that Lieutenant

Hayward had landed him north of the Taravao isthmus and sent him on foot to Papara with gifts for Teri'irere, but instead of visiting the *ari'i*, he had been ambushed near Mahaiatea *marae* and almost killed, because the powder in his pistol was wet and would not fire. When the *Bounty* sailors told Brown that they had decided to go out to the ship, he said that it was an English man-of-war but gave them no further details. In fact Brown had told Captain Edwards everything he knew about them, and in return Edwards, who considered Brown 'very intelligent and useful' had entered him in the *Pandora* books, entitling him to rations and clothing and employing him as a spy.

Arming themselves with hatchets and a knife but leaving the pistol with Brown, the trio paddled to Pa'ea in a canoe, landed and walked 12 miles in the dark along the white sand of the beach to Pohuetea's house, arriving at about 4 a.m. Seeing a launch anchored off the beach, Morrison and his companions hailed it, but the men on board were all fast asleep. The canoes on the beach belonged to Ari'ipaea, who was guiding the launch, which proved to be commanded by Robert Corner, the second lieutenant of HMS *Pandora*. Corner was asleep in one of the canoes and, after rousing him, Morrison, Norman and Ellison surrendered, handing over their weapons and telling him where the schooner was anchored. Leaving them under guard in the launch, Corner set off by land for Papara, guided by Brown; and the following afternoon Thomas Hayward (now third lieutenant of the *Pandora*), accompanied by his *taio* Vaetua, arrived at Pa'ea in the pinnace with twenty armed men, where he ordered his former shipmates' hands to be tied, put a midshipman in charge of the launch and escorted them back to the ship, which was about 30 miles away. During this passage the midshipman gave each of the *Bounty*'s men half a pint of wine, told them what had happened to the *Bounty*'s launch, and that Bligh had been promoted.

Back in England, Bligh had been court-martialled and exonerated of any culpability for the loss of the *Bounty*; and with the assistance of Sir Joseph Banks (who had married and set up house in Soho Square) had won the coveted promotion to post-captain.[11] On the very day that the Admiralty ordered Bligh and those who had shared his ordeal on the launch (except for Purcell, the insubordinate carpenter) to be given their back pay, the Board of the Admiralty had signed the sailing orders for the *Pandora*, a 24-gun frigate with a crew of 140 men, to hunt down the mutineers.[12] When they selected Captain Edward Edwards to command this expedition, however, the Admiralty had been in a punitive mood. Edwards had suffered a near mutiny of his own on board the

*George Hamilton, surgeon of the* Pandora.

*Narcissus* during a voyage to America nine years earlier; and in the aftermath of that uprising, five of the conspirators had been hanged in New York, two received floggings of 250 and 500 lashes respectively, while their leader was hanged in chains.

On board the *Pandora*, Edwards had been joined by John Larkham as first lieutenant; Robert Corner, a humane, decent officer who had formerly served in the army, as second lieutenant; and Thomas Hayward, the 'loyalist' midshipman on the *Bounty* who had sobbed out his loyalty to Bligh, as third lieutenant. George Hamilton, a humorous, middle-aged Northumbrian who wrote a vivid, rollicking journal of the expedition, remarkable for its irreverence and gusto, sailed as the *Pandora*'s surgeon.[13] Their orders from the Admiralty instructed Captain Edwards to sail around Cape Horn to Tahiti, where he should try to get information about the mutineers from the local people. If any were still on the island, he was ordered to take one of the chiefs hostage, and send an armed party to capture the mutineers. Having taken them prisoner, he was 'to keep the Mutineers as closely confined as may preclude all possibility of their escaping, having, however, proper regard to the preservation of their Lives, that they may be brought home to undergo the Punishment due to their Demerits'.[14]

Because war with Spain seemed imminent, most experienced sailors had already either enlisted or been impressed into warships during the 'Spanish Re-armament'. As a result, many of the *Pandora*'s crew were landsmen, pressed for the voyage around the world; and Edwards had no marines. Almost as soon as the *Pandora* sailed from England on 7 November 1790, as Hamilton remarked glumly, '[T]he *Pandora* now seemed inclined to shed her baneful influence among us.'[15] There was an outbreak of fever, and thirty-five of the sailors were confined to their hammocks, including the surgeon's mate. At Tenerife they learned that war with Spain had been averted; and at Rio de Janeiro, after a tussle with the Brazilian authorities who tried to send a troop of soldiers on board, Edwards and his officers were given an affable welcome. Eager to avoid the bad weather that had plagued the *Bounty*'s voyage, Edwards hastened south, and the *Pandora* rounded Cape Horn in good weather, sighting Easter Island on 4 March; and sailing through the Tuamotu archipelago towards Me'eti'a.

On 23 March 1791 when the *Pandora* arrived at Matavai Bay, Captain Edwards showed no interest in trying to discover who had been involved in the mutiny, and who might be innocent of wrongdoing. In his journal, he referred to all of the *Bounty*'s former crew as 'pirates' and 'villains', treating them indiscriminately in the same harsh fashion (although to be fair, the Admiralty had ordered him to keep these men in close confinement, making no distinctions among them until they had been tried). The first man to come out to the ship was Joseph Coleman, who had been kept on board the *Bounty* against his will. Racing out in a canoe with Po'e'eno, the *ari'i* of Matavai Bay and William Bligh's *taio*, and his own *taio* Tapairu, Po'e'eno's brother, even before the *Pandora* had anchored, they capsized in the surf before Coleman could board the frigate. After giving Edwards a brief account of the mutiny, Christian's departure on the *Bounty* and the deaths of Churchill and Thompson, and telling him where the other sailors were staying on the island, the armourer was unceremoniously clapped in irons.

As soon as the *Pandora* anchored, Peter Heywood and George Stewart came out on a canoe, bringing out their sea chests which held their journals and papers, including a number of sketches and poems that Heywood had composed on the island. Edwards had them put under guard, watched by two seamen and a midshipman armed with pistols and bayonets.[16] When Heywood asked to see Thomas Hayward, hoping that his former friend would speak up for them, Hayward entered the Great Cabin, gazed at them contemptuously and 'pretended ignorance of our Affairs'.[17] Heywood protested, and when Hayward began to argue with him about what had happened, Edwards told his third lieutenant to leave. As Hayward left the Great Cabin, Peter Heywood insisted that he could vindicate himself, and that he was innocent of the crime of mutiny.

When Coleman's Tahitian friends told Captain Edwards that Richard Skinner was also at Matavai Bay, he sent Po'e'eno to fetch him, but Skinner had already decided to come out to the *Pandora*. When he arrived on board that afternoon, he was also clapped in irons. After discovering the whereabouts of the remaining *Bounty* men on the island from Po'e'eno and Tapairu, Edwards sent the launch commanded by his second lieutenant Robert Corner and the pinnace commanded by Lieutenant Hayward to the north-west coast (i.e. to Pare) in pursuit of the 'pirates', taking Hitihiti as a guide. As Hamilton remarked: '[A]lthough perfectly devoted to our interest, on being appointed one of the guides in the expedition against the mutineers, [Hitihiti] expressed great horror at the act he was going to commit, in betraying his friend, being Tyo to one of them.'[18] Soon afterwards a Tahitian envoy was sent on board the *Pandora*, carrying the portrait of Captain Cook which he ceremoniously placed in the Great Cabin. As soon as this man recognised the ship's purser, Mr Bentham, who had sailed with Cook, he made it plain that he and his people believed that Captain Cook was still alive in England.

On 26 March, Captain Edwards sent the pinnace to Tu with a bottle of rum as a gift (which Tu and his brothers humorously called 'ava taio, or 'drink of friendship'),[19] inviting him to dine with him on board the *Pandora*. The next day when Tu (whom Hamilton described as 'a tall handsome looking man, about six feet three inches high, good natured, and affable in his manners'[20]) arrived on board with his two wives, 'Itia (a 'robust looking, coarse woman, about thirty') and her younger sister Vaiareti ('a pretty young creature, about sixteen years of age'), 'Itia drank tea with the Europeans. They told Edwards that after returning to Papara in the schooner, 'the pirates' had landed and retreated to the mountains. After discussing tactics with Tu, Edwards decided that there was no need to take the high chief hostage. Although Tu seemed happy to help him, he made it plain that he had very little authority in Papara, where the high chief Teri'irere had recently declared his independence, having acquired a number of muskets with his capture of the *Bounty* sailors' schooner. Instead, Edwards sent Lieutenant Corner in the launch with twenty-six armed men, attended by the 'principal chiefs', with rich gifts and a message for Teri'irere, saying that if he did not hand over the mutineers, he and his men would ravage the Papara district. That night, Tu and his wives slept on board the *Pandora*, Hamilton remarking with surprise that 'they all three sleep together, and live in the most perfect harmony'.[21]

Early the next morning when Lieutenant Hayward went in the pinnace to join the party in the launch at Papara, he was accompanied by his *taio* Vaetua, Tu's younger brother. Later, finding that he needed the launch to water the ship, Edwards sent the yawl to fetch it back to Matavai Bay. At 9 p.m. on 29 March when the launch returned to the *Pandora* with Morrison, Norman and Ellison, who had given themselves up, Edwards ordered the captives to be imprisoned in leg irons under the halfdeck, where they joined Stewart, Heywood, Coleman, Skinner and Michael Byrne. Soon afterwards when Teri'irere's men delivered the schooner *Resolution*, which the ship's surgeon Hamilton described as 'decked, beautifully built, and the size of a Gravesend boat',[22] Captain Edwards ordered the little craft to be repaired as a tender for the *Pandora*, fitting it with canvas sails and other gear and renaming it the *Matavy*.

Now that most of the *Bounty*'s men were on board the *Pandora*, the ship's carpenters began to build a kind of roundhouse on the quarterdeck for the prisoners, and the armourer was put to work making handcuffs, clamping these on their wrists the following morning. On 5 April, Lieutenant Hayward, accompanied by Tu, Vaetua, Brown, several young Tahitians and twenty-five armed sailors, embarked in the yawl and the schooner *Matavy*, which was now manned by the *Pandora*'s men, and sailed back to Papara. Two days later, Lieutenant Corner with sixteen men, accompanied by Ari'ipaea and a party of warriors, landed at Point Venus and marched to the back of the mountains, where the remaining *Bounty* sailors had taken refuge. After crossing the Tuauru River sixteen times, using ropes and tackles to climb the steepest cliffs, they stopped for dinner. One of their companions ran to a local *marae* and came back with a roasted pig that had been offered as a sacrifice, giving this to them for their meal. Their Tahitian guides also plundered some *'ava* plantations, belonging to an enemy group. When they arrived at the home of a 'great chief', this man took them to visit his father's funerary platform, where Lieutenant Corner ordered his men to fire three volleys as a sign of respect. Unfortunately, one of the burning cartridges landed on the bark-cloth garments of the dead chief, which caught fire, to the consternation of their hosts. Soon afterwards, Morrison, Norman and Ellison surrendered to Lieutenant Corner, and were delivered to the *Pandora*.

When Lieutenant Hayward landed at Papara, guided by John Brown, 'a keen, penetrating, active fellow', they climbed into the mountains. The next night when the Tahitians attacked their camp, the guard shot at some men who were pelting him with stones, killing one whose companions rushed in and carried away his body. Later, their Tahitian companions attacked the *Bounty*'s men beside a river, and one islander felled one of their wives with a stone. Enraged, the *Bounty* sailor immediately shot him dead. On 7 March, finding some of these men asleep in a house in the woods, Brown crept up to the place where they lay, and 'distinguished them from the natives by feeling their toes; as people unaccustomed to wear shoes are easily discovered from the spread of their toes'.[23] When Hayward and his men attacked the next morning, the sailors surrendered at once. On 9 March when Lieutenant Hayward returned in the schooner, he brought to the *Pandora* Heildbrandt, McIntosh, Burkett, Millward, Sumner and Muspratt, who were also clapped in irons under the halfdeck.

The following day was a Sunday, and after mustering the ship's company, Captain Edwards read out the Articles of War, including 'Article XIX: If any Person in or belonging to the Fleet shall make or endeavour to make any mutinous Assembly upon any Pretence whatsoever, every Person offending herein, and being convicted thereof by the Sentence of the Court-martial, shall suffer Death.' Afterwards, three of the *Pandora*'s crew were punished with a dozen lashes each for 'theft and drunkenness'.[24] The roundhouse, a locked enclosure 11 feet long by 18 feet wide, was ready, and the fourteen prisoners were forced in through a bolted scuttle not quite 2 feet square, still pinioned in their irons. Their prison had two smaller scuttles, 9 inches square, for ventilation, with iron grates blocking the flow of the air. In this hell-hole, it was so hot that their sweat streamed into the scuppers, and lice, maggots and other vermin swarmed in their clothes and the hammocks on which they lay. According to Edwards, when the prisoners went to the heads to relieve themselves, they could not be prevented from conversing with the sailors,[25] so they were provided with tubs for their excrement and urine, which stank terribly. The *Bounty*'s men dubbed this foetid prison 'Pandora's Box', resorting to black humour to ease their suffering.

As the prisoners lay there naked, their wives (including 'Peggy' Stewart, 'Mary' McIntosh and the wife of Richard Skinner, each of whom had little daughters by their sailor lovers; along with 'Mary' Burkett and John Millward's partner, each of whom had sons)[26] came out to the *Pandora*'s stern, bringing these children to see their fathers. Six children altogether had already been born to the *Bounty* sailors, and some of their partners were pregnant again. According to the surgeon George Hamilton, the sentries allowed the women to hand up the infants to their fathers and give their menfolk food: 'To see the poor captives in irons, weeping over their tender offspring, was too moving a scene for any feeling heart. Their wives brought them ample supplies of every delicacy that the country afforded while we laid there, and behaved with the greatest fidelity and affection to them.'[27] When the sentries sent them away, however, these women sat in their canoes, slashing their heads until the sea was red with blood. As Morrison remarked: '[T]heir Mourning rites were sufficient to evince the truth of their Grief & melt the most obdurate Heart.'[28]

When these harrowing visits were finally forbidden, Te Pau, the ari'i of the Fa'a'a district, Peter Heywood's taio and the father of George Stewart's wife Peggy, plotted to cut the Pandora's cables in a gale, so that the frigate would be driven ashore and his people could rescue Heywood and Stewart. Ari'ipaea (a 'discerning, sensible and intelligent chief')[29] warned Edwards about this plot, however, and the following night he, Tu and Vaetua kept a close watch on the ship's cables, warning the sentries to be vigilant. Vaetua had remained loyal to his taio Thomas Hayward, who told him how the mutineers had treated him and William Bligh (Tu's taio), casting them adrift in a small boat in the middle of the Pacific. Now that he knew that Christian and the other mutineers had lied to him about their meeting with Captain Cook, Tu also decided to throw in his lot with Captain Edwards.

The day after Vaetua had given Edwards this warning, Tu and his two wives with their attendants paid the Pandora a ceremonial visit, preceded by 'arioi musicians. Each of Tu's wives was wrapped in about 60 or 70 yards of bark cloth, and had to be hoisted on board in slings like cattle, along with lavish gifts of pigs, coconuts, bananas and baked puddings. When they arrived in the Great Cabin, Edwards accepted their gifts by rolling the bark cloth around his waist, and when Ari'ipaea's wife Vahine Metua admired his laced coat, he gallantly draped it around her shoulders; although his return gifts were so miserly that the Tahitians called him piripiri, or stingy.[30] When Edwards presented Vahine Metua with red feathers, instead of saving these to present to 'Oro, this leading 'arioi had her servants sew them onto her fly flaps and other personal ornaments. As this visit progressed, the Bounty's men, who lay naked in their reeking roundhouse, must have heard their voices and realised that Tu and his family had betrayed them.

The following day, Tu invited Edwards and his officers to a great heiva at Point Venus. After landing in some style, preceded by 'arioi musicians, Edwards and his men entered the arena to watch the heiva. Two 'arioi men began the entertainment, posturing in 'filthy lascivious attitudes, with frightful distortions of their mouths'; followed by two women who were dressed for the hura, with fans of feathers fixed to their backsides. They looked elegant when they faced the British, but 'when in a bending attitude, they presented their rumps, to shew the wonderful agility of their loins', startling the Europeans with the sight. According to Hamilton:

> After half an hour's hard exercise, the dear creatures had remüe themselves into a perfect fureur, and the piece concluded by the ladies exposing that which is better felt than seen; and, in that state of nature, walked from the bottom of the theatre to the top where we were sitting on the grass, till they approached just by us, and we complimented them in bowing, with all the honours of war.[31]

During this festival Mahau, the *ari'i rahi* of Mo'orea who had arrived at Point Venus with his wife, adopted George Hamilton as his *taio*; and although the surgeon was no longer young, indicated that he expected him to sleep with his wife, Tu's sister Auo, and seemed insulted when he did not do so. When the offence was explained, Hamilton did his duty and all was forgiven; although afterwards Mahau expressed a concern that his wife, who was six months pregnant, would have a piebald baby when the child was delivered.

While Edwards and his officers were enjoying these entertainments, Larkham, the first lieutenant, inspecting the 'pirates' in their prison, found that McIntosh had freed one of his legs from its shackle. Summoning the armourer to tighten their leg irons and handcuffs, Larkham put his foot against each man's chest and pulled the cuffs as hard as he could against their wrists and feet to make sure that they could not escape, breaking the skin so that their limbs became terribly swollen. Fearing that they might persuade his sailors to help them, or that the prisoners would conspire with each other, Edwards had them guarded by two armed sailors and a midshipman, forbidding his crew to speak to the prisoners, and telling the *Bounty* sailors (who now spoke Tahitian as well as English) that if they spoke Tahitian to one another, they would be gagged. Over the days that followed, Tu and his people sent quantities of pigs, goats, chickens, coconuts, breadfruit and other provisions out to the ship, and when Captain Edwards announced that he was about to leave the island, Tu and 'Itia begged him to take them to England, although Ari'ipaea remonstrated with them, saying that this was impossible because war would soon break out on the island.

Before returning the portrait of Captain Cook, whom the Tahitians regarded with utmost reverence, to Tu, Captain Edwards wrote on the back: 'His Britannick Majesty's Ship Pandora Sailed from Matavai Bay Otaheite 9 May

1791.'[32] When the portrait was sent ashore to Tu, almost every canoe on the island flocked around the *Pandora*. Later that day, the frigate sailed past Mo'orea in a light, pleasant breeze, followed by the *Matavy*, the schooner that Edwards had taken from the *Bounty* sailors as a prize and commissioned as a tender, giving the command to his master's mate William Oliver. The prisoners' wives, lovers and *taio* followed the ships in their canoes, the women baring their upper bodies, cutting their heads with shells and weeping bitterly; and with 'tears trickling down his cheeks, [Tu] begged to be remembered to King George'.[33] All of the Europeans who had recently settled on the island were sailing away at once, leaving the islanders to deal with the fall-out from their friendships and betrayals.

And as they sailed away from Tahiti, the *Pandora*'s surgeon penned his verdict on the island. It was a Paradise, where food grew spontaneously, and love was innocent and free:

> This may well be called the Cytheria of the southern hemisphere, not only from the beauty and elegance of the women, but their being so deeply versed in, and so passionately fond of the Eleusinian mysteries;[34] and what poetic fiction has painted of Eden, or Arcadia, is here realised, where the earth without tillage produces both food and cloathing, the trees loaded with the richest fruit, the carpet of nature spread with the most odiferous flowers, and the fair ones ever willing to fill your arms with love.
>
> It affords a happy instance of contradicting an opinion propagated by philosophers of a less bountiful soil, who maintain that every virtuous or charitable act a man commits, is from selfish or interested views. Here human nature appears in more amiable colours, and the soul of man, free from the gripping hand of want, acts with a liberality and bounty that does honour to his God.[35]

Hamilton added: 'This I believe was the first time that an Englishman got up his anchor, at the remotest part of the globe, with a heavy heart, to go home to his own country.'[36] As one can see from this ecstatic account, after twenty-four years of intensive contact by ships of different European nations – British, French and Spanish – the myth of Tahiti as New Cythera, Aphrodite's birthplace and an Island of Love had triumphantly survived, unscathed by experience.

At the same time, Hamilton recognised that life in Tahiti was changing: 'Happy would it have been for those people had they never been visited by Europeans; for, to our shame be it spoken, disease and gunpowder is all the benefit they have ever received from us, in return for their hospitality and kindness. The ravages of the venereal disease is evident from the mutilated objects so frequent amongst them; [also] a disease of the consumptive kind has of late made great havoc amongst them; this they call the British disease, as they have only had it since their intercourse with the English.'[37] As the Greek poet Hesiod lamented when the goddess Pandora opened her jar:

> Numberless miseries were spread over all mankind
> The earth is crowded with anguish, also the sea,
> Some pestilence strikes men by day; some comes on as it will
> In night's quiet dark, its voice being silenced by Zeus's command.[38]

# 16

# Wreck of the *Pandora*

In Tahiti, Edwards had been informed that before sailing away on the *Bounty*, Fletcher Christian had declared that he would look for an unknown or uninhabited island with no harbour for visiting vessels, and run the ship ashore, although these hints were deliberately obscure. As Edwards later remarked to the Admiralty:

> This information was too vague to be follow'd in an immense Ocean strew'd with an almost innumerable number of known and unknown Islands.[1]

In his sailing orders, Edwards had been instructed that if he did not find the *Bounty* at Tahiti, he should look for the ship at Huahine and Ra'iatea before proceeding to Aitutaki and the neighbouring islands, and then on to Palmerston Island and Nomuka in the Tongan archipelago. If the *Bounty* was not in any of these places, he should return home via the Endeavour Straits. Although Edwards had captured a number of the *Bounty*'s men in Tahiti, Fletcher Christian and the *Bounty* were still at large. In the absence of any better information, he headed for Huahine where he sent the boats in to examine the harbours, and Hitihiti went ashore to ask for news of the mutineers.

When Hitihiti returned on board the *Pandora*, accompanied by several Huahine chiefs and one of Ma'i's former attendants, these men reported that they had not seen the *Bounty*, and that Ma'i had died of a venereal disease two years after his arrival at the island. Every time that Ma'i's fate was reported to the British, it seemed to be a different story. At first these chiefs seemed eager to accompany Hitihiti to Ra'iatea, but they suddenly changed their minds, returning ashore. From Huahine, the ship carried on to Ra'iatea, Taha'a and Porapora, where the high chief Tahatu (the successor of Puni, the old warrior chief, who had died since Bligh's visit to his island) came on board and said that he had recently visited Tupua'i, Maurua and Mopiha, and that there were no white men at these islands. According to Hamilton, Tahatu and his entourage of Porapora warriors had distinctive tattoos, with the glans of the phallus covered with blue patterns; and they were very proud of their military prowess, boasting of their conquests. When Hitihiti, who had been born in Porapora, went ashore to drink 'ava with his friends, he did not return on board the *Pandora*.

During the *Pandora*'s wild goose chase across the Pacific, the misinformation that Christian had left behind baffled his pursuers. During a conversation with Henry Heildbrandt, Christian had remarked that he might sail to the Duke of York's Island (Atafu) via Palmerston Atoll; and eventually the cooper passed this information on to Captain Edwards. When they reached Aitutaki, and Lieutenant Hayward recognised a man whom he had met during the *Bounty*'s visit to that island, he was assured that they had seen no sign of the mutineers. At Palmerston Island where Lieutenant Corner landed on the northernmost islet on 23 May 1791, finding spars and a yard embossed with the Admiralty's broad arrow and the inscription '*Bounty*'s Driver Yard', they searched the atoll. The boats were sent to scour the islets, and Corner and Hayward, both strong swimmers, donned cork jackets and swam ashore; while the midshipman Mr Sevill returned with strangely coloured canoes decorated with carvings of men, fish and animals.

During that day, however, the weather became thick and hazy, and in the evening the crew of one of the boats, worn out with their efforts, camped on an islet, and lit a fire. When a coconut that they had put on the embers exploded with a loud bang, as Hamilton later remarked with amusement, 'Expecting muskets to be fired at them from every bush, they all jumped up, seized their arms, and were some time before they could undeceive themselves, that they were really not attacked.'[2] The danger lay elsewhere, however, and the next day a storm blew up, bringing screaming winds and high waves. At the height of the tempest, the *Pandora*'s yawl under the command of Sevill and her five-man crew (which included the boatswain's son) disappeared. As the storm battered the ship, the *Bounty*'s men were tossed in their shackles, and their bruised limbs swelled to alarming proportions. When the tempest finally subsided, although Edwards and his men combed the seas around the atoll for the yawl, no trace of the missing boat or their shipmates could be found.

Eventually Captain Edwards gave up the search, and sailed to Atafu. Arriving at this island on 7 June, which had been uninhabited during Captain John Byron's visit in 1765, they found empty houses and wharves with canoes, convincing some of the sailors that the *Bounty*'s men had built these structures. Although a large wooden ship's buoy was found washed up on a beach, it soon became clear that the island was a seasonal fishing camp, used by the inhabitants of neighbouring islands. Finding no mutineers at Atafu, Edwards headed for the Samoan archipelago; and on 12 June sighted the atoll of Nukunonu, a new discovery, where canoes were sailing across the lagoon. Lieutenant Hayward was sent across in the yawl, but every time he beckoned to the inhabitants, they paddled away in the opposite direction. By the time that Hayward and Corner landed the next day, the people and the canoes had vanished, and the island (which had a number of ritual sites) was deserted, although it seemed to be their principal residence. Six days later at Savai'i, Edwards met a Tongan chief named Finau, the brother of the navigator who had guided William Bligh and Cook through the Tongan archipelago in 1777. He reported that his brother had since died, and that although he had seen Cook and his ships in the Tongan archipelago, the *Pandora* was the first European ship to visit this Samoan island.[3]

At 'Upolu on 21 June, some people boarded the ship who presented them with delicious spicy puddings. Such was their amazement that it appeared that Edwards and his men were the first Europeans they had seen. These visitors included a naked woman, exquisitely beautiful and 6 feet tall, whom Captain Edwards monopolised. As Hamilton noted sardonically:

> Many mouths were watering for her; but Capt. Edwards, with great humanity and prudence, had given previous orders, that no woman should be permitted to go below, as our health had not quite recovered the shock it received at Otaheite; and the lady was obliged to be contented with viewing the great cabin, where she was shewn the wonders of the Lord on the face of the mighty deep.[4]

When the women were sent ashore, the men began to barter with the sailors. While they were distracted, one man stole a jacket out of Hayward's cabin; and when the wind blew up, the *Pandora* sailed away from their canoes. When they finally noticed that their canoes were drifting at a distance, the Samoans 'jumped into the water like a flock of wild geese', although one clung on to the *Pandora*'s anchor chains, staying with the ship for several miles.

On 25 July while the *Matavy* was exploring the coast of Tutuila, another island in the Samoan group, a fleet of canoes surrounded the tender, whose crews refused to barter with the British. When the wind died, the crews of the canoes attacked the little schooner. Although the sailors fended them off with boarding pikes, one warrior managed to leap over the boarding net and tried to club down the master's mate, William Oliver, before being shot dead. When a sudden gale blew up, bringing torrential rain, the *Pandora* headed away from the coast, and at nightfall lost sight of the *Matavy*, leaving behind Oliver in command of the tender with a crew of seven men – the second of the *Pandora*'s boats to be lost during this futile hunt for the mutineers. Although Edwards fired the ship's cannons and lit false lights as signals during the night, no signals came in reply.

The following day the two vessels sailed around Tutuila, looking for each other. There were very few provisions on board the *Matavy*, almost no water and no charts, although they had two quadrants, a boarding net, six muskets, two seven-barrelled guns and three pairs of pistols. On 23 June when his men had drunk the last drop of water, Oliver decided to take the *Bounty*'s sailors' little schooner to Nomuka in the Tongan islands, 700 miles away, which Edwards had nominated as a rendezvous.[5] During the journey to Tonga they suffered terribly from thirst, and the midshipman Renouard became delirious, a state in which he remained for many weeks. On 25 June when they landed at Fonualei, another of the Tongan islands, they found no fresh water ashore. Almost dead with thirst they carried on, still looking for Nomuka, and on 29 June arrived at the Ono-i-lau Islands, one of which they mistook for the rendezvous. Fortunately, the people there were kindly and hospitable, giving them sweet potatoes, and drinking coconuts to quench their thirst; and the next night there was a providential downpour, which filled their water casks.

After cruising around the Ono-i-lau group for several weeks, Oliver and his men made a brief visit to Tuvana-i-ra, a small island to the south, to fetch more water. When the watering party took the boat and returned to the schooner, the local people attacked in their canoes, and were fired on. Oliver and his men spent two more weeks in the Ono-i-lau group, bartering for provisions before heading west towards the Endeavour Straits. Upon their arrival, they found themselves embayed within an encircling reef, being driven towards the rocks. Just as they were about to be wrecked, however, the wind changed at the last moment. After exploring an intricate maze of reefs and islets, Oliver sailed the *Matavy* over the reef into the Straits, where they met a small Dutch vessel whose crew gave them food and water. When they finally reached Surabaya in the East Indies, the Dutch governor, who had received Bligh's account of the mutineers and noticed that the *Matavy* was made out of tropical timbers, mistook them for the *Bounty* pirates and kept Oliver and his men under guard, although he treated them kindly. They were finally escorted to Semarang, still suspected of being mutineers, where Renouard was put in hospital – a bitter, ironic finale to the saga of this little ship, built with such devotion in Tahiti by Morrison and his shipmates.

Soon after the *Matavy* had sailed for the Tongan islands, the *Pandora* headed in the same direction, arriving at Nomuka on 29 June, the day that the schooner was attacked off Tuvana-i-ra. When the chief of Nomuka, Tupoulagi, came out to greet them, followed by Fatafehi, 'the Chief of all the Islands & who generally resides at Tongataboo'[6] (Captain Cook's ceremonial friend whose *'inasi* ritual he had attended, letting down his hair), these men denied any knowledge of the *Matavy*, Fletcher Christian and his fellow mutineers, or the *Bounty* – although they certainly knew all about the attack on Bligh after he had been set adrift in the *Bounty*'s launch. Having hired Tupoulagi's double canoe, Edwards sent Lieutenant Hayward ashore, where he found no trace of the *Matavy* or the mutineers. After the insults their chiefs had received, first from Captain Cook and then Captain Bligh, the Nomuka people were still angry with the British; and when Edwards landed and sent his servant back to the boat with a message, the islanders attacked, stripping the servant naked and leaving 'the great Irishman, with his shoe full in one hand, and a bayonet in the other, naked and foaming mad with revenge on the natives for the treatment he had received'.[7]

At Nomuka, where beautiful girls were brought on board and bartered for broad axes, 'the quarter-deck became the scene of the most indelicate familiarities'.[8] On shore, the islanders were hostile, one man clubbing Lieutenant Corner on the back of the neck and snatching his handkerchief; and Corner shot him dead. When they left Nomuka on 10 July, sailing to Tofua with Fatafehi and Tupoulagi as their passengers, two large sailing canoes followed in their wake. At Tofua, the local inhabitants prostrated themselves as they came alongside in their canoes, allowing Fatafehi to put his foot on their heads; although these people also denied any knowledge of the *Bounty* or the schooner.

That night the volcano flared and flamed inland. The following morning when Lieutenants Corner and Hayward accompanied by Fatafehi and Tupoulagi landed at Tofua, Hayward identified a number of the warriors who had attacked Captain Bligh, himself and their companions during their brief visit to that island, killing the quartermaster John Norton. When these men saw Hayward, they shrank away (although one of them later managed to steal a new uniform jacket from out of his cabin). Edwards did not punish these warriors for their attack on Bligh, fearing that the Tongans would avenge themselves on the crew of his lost tender if they had survived the voyage to the archipelago. During this visit to Tofua it poured with rain, drenching the prisoners in the roundhouse. When the *Bounty* sailors asked Larkham, the first lieutenant, to fix the leaks, he replied brusquely, 'I am Wet too and evry body on Deck and it will dry when the Weather clears up.'[9] During this passage the roundhouse had been washed out twice a week, soaking its occupants, and a number of the prisoners were ill. Although Edwards had ordered that they should receive no medical attention, Hamilton (whom Morrison described as 'a very humane Gentleman') and the second lieutenant Robert Corner arranged for cocoa to be boiled for them in a copper kettle, served with sugar to ease their misery.

Finding no signs of the *Bounty* or the schooner at Nomuka or Tofua, Edwards farewelled Fatafehi and Tupoulagi, and decided to return to the Samoan islands to continue the hunt for the mutineers. At Manu'a, where the local people came out in canoes, they were very reluctant to come on board; and when they landed at Tutuila, where the *Pandora* had lost sight of the *Matavy*, the sailors found a French uniform belonging to one of La Pérouse's men, who had been killed ashore. There were no signs of their shipmates or the *Bounty* mutineers, however. Upon returning to the Tongan archipelago, where Edwards discovered a magnificent landlocked harbour at Vava'u, they sailed between 'Eua and Tongatapu and then returned to Nomuka on 28 July, where he hoped that the tender might have arrived at the rendezvous during his absence.

At Nomuka, where a young high-born chief came out to the ship, the people prostrated themselves, but stole fearlessly from the Europeans. Their hostility continued unabated, and when the wooding and watering parties landed, the islanders attacked, seizing their oars, but were driven off by musket-fire. As soon as the young chief heard about this, he became agitated and tried to jump out of a window, although Captain Edwards prevented him from escaping. Edwards assured him that his men would shoot any thieves, firing a 6-pounder inland and an 18-pound cannon loaded with grape shot into the sea to underline this message. After three months of searching, however, he had found no sign of Fletcher Christian and his fellow mutineers, and the *Pandora*'s supplies were running low. On 2 August 1791, Edwards finally decided to give up the hunt and return to England with his prisoners. As he later reported to the Admiralty: 'Thinking it time to return to England, I did not think proper to wait any longer for the Tender, but left instructions for her Commander should she happen to arrive after my departure.'[10]

Setting a course towards the Torres Straits, the *Pandora* sailed past Wallis, Rotuma and Vanikoro islands, where they saw fires burning on the beach. Weary of searching, Captain Edwards did not send the ship's boats ashore to investigate, although it is possible that these fires had been lit by the survivors from the missing French expedition commanded by La Pérouse, who had been marooned on this island. After sighting the coast of New Guinea, they reached the Great Barrier Reef on 25 August 1791, sailing south until finally they sighted a gap in the reef (now known as 'Pandora Passage'), where Edwards sent Lieutenant Corner in the yawl to take soundings. At 5 p.m. on 27 August when Corner signalled that the passage was clear, Edwards ordered the yawl to return on board. As night fell, Corner fired muskets to keep in touch with the *Pandora* while Edwards had false fires lit on board. At 7 p.m. while the *Pandora* was sailing through the darkness, waiting for the yawl to reach the stern, the ship suddenly struck on a coral outcrop, smashing the rudder, and the current drove her onto the Great Barrier Reef. Perhaps the officer on watch was drunk, or asleep, for as Morrison later wrote meaningfully, 'I might say how the *Pandora* went on a reef, but it would be to no purpose.'[11]

While water poured into the ship's hull, the sailors manned the pumps and desperately tried to fother a thrummed sail over the splintered planks, stitching short lengths of yarn to the canvas and stretching it over the gaping hole; and Edwards released three of the prisoners whom Bligh had exonerated – McIntosh, Norman and Coleman – to help with the pumping. When two of the chain pumps broke down, the sea flooded into the hold until the water was 11 feet deep. Although the prisoners in the roundhouse begged for mercy, Edwards ignored them. Terrified and screaming, they managed to loosen their shackles; and when they told Lieutenant Corner what they had done, he told them to remain quiet, assuring them that they would not be left to drown.

As soon as Edwards realised that the prisoners had freed themselves, however, he ordered the armourer to replace their shackles and had the scuttle bolted, placing the master-of-arms and the corporal, each armed with a brace of pistols, on guard with orders to shoot anyone who tried to escape, or hang them from the yardarm. As the boats were loaded with provisions, the sailors threw overboard anything that would float. When the prisoners, hearing some of the sailors curse 'I'll be damnd if they shall go without us', frantically tried to attract their attention, clanking their irons, the master-of-arms exclaimed, 'Fire upon the Buggers!'[12] Morrison begged him not to shoot, saying that none of them would move. At that moment one of the boats broke adrift from the stern, distracting the master-of-arms and their other guards.

At sunrise the next morning, 28 August, the *Pandora* heeled over. The topmast crashed on the deck, killing one of the sailors, and another man was crushed by a careering cannon. When Edwards gave the order to abandon ship, the boats were lowered into the sea; and Joseph Hodges, the armourer's mate, was sent to open the scuttle and free Muspratt, Skinner and Byrne, who clambered up

*Wreck of the* Pandora.

on deck. While Hodges was still below, however, someone shut and bolted the scuttle, trapping him below with the captives. Although Morrison shouted out to the master-of-arms, begging him to open the scuttle, he yelled back, 'Never fear my boys we'll all go to Hell together!' As the *Pandora* gave a final lurch to port, the sailors cried, 'There She Goes!' Looking through the stern porthole, the prisoners could see Captain Edwards swimming for the pinnace, and the master-of-arms and the corporal toppling into the water. As water poured into the roundhouse, Hodges managed to free Morrison and Stewart; and hearing their frantic cries, William Moulter, the boatswain's mate, pulled back the bolt and threw away the scuttle before he also jumped into the water.

As they scrambled out of the roundhouse, George Stewart and John Sumner were hit and killed by a falling gangway, while Richard Skinner, who was still in handcuffs, fell into the sea and drowned. Heildbrandt, locked in his irons, went down with the ship. Grabbing each end of a floating gangway, Morrison and Millward saw Heywood, Burkett, Coleman and Lieutenant Corner on the roundhouse, which was floating on the ocean. As Heywood seized a plank and swam for one of the boats, Morrison pulled off his trousers, and tying a sash around his waist like a Tahitian *maro* (loincloth), took a plank and followed him, reaching the blue yawl where the master's mate, Mr Bowling, pulled them aboard. Upon reaching a white sandy islet, the ten surviving *Bounty* sailors found that thirty-one of the *Pandora*'s men had been lost in the shipwreck, including the master-of-arms and the corporal who had been guarding the roundhouse, although all of the officers and William Moulter, their saviour, had survived.[13]

The next day, Edwards and his men lay exhausted on the sandy islet, recovering from their terrible ordeal. When they had recovered a little, they examined the boats and the provisions that had been saved, a surprisingly small quantity considering the length of time that the ship had been stuck on the reef before it sank — one barrel of water, a quantity of biscuit, a parcel of tea, a saw and a hammer. Although it was scorching hot, and one of the *Pandora*'s sailors, maddened with thirst, drank salt water and became delirious, Edwards refused to allow the *Bounty*'s men any shelter, forcing them to stay at one end of the islet and forbidding them to speak to his crew. After their long imprisonment their skin was soft and white, and blistered and peeled in the sun. In a desperate effort to protect themselves, they buried themselves up to the necks in the sand, and slept in the lee of a sandy bulwark that night. The next morning when Edwards sent the mate to examine the wreck of the *Pandora*, Passmore returned with a length of the top-gallant mast, some copper wire from the lightning chain and the ship's cat, which he found desperately clinging to the head of the mast.[14]

Afterwards, the boats set off in a ragged procession, led by Captain Edwards and Lieutenant Hayward in the pinnace with nineteen officers and men and three prisoners on board (Morrison, Ellison and McIntosh), followed by Lieutenant Larkham and George Hamilton in the red yawl with twenty sailors and two prisoners (Burkett and Millward); Lieutenant Corner in the launch with twenty-seven sailors and three prisoners (Heywood, Coleman and Byrne); and Passmore, the mate, in the blue yawl with nineteen sailors and two prisoners (Norman and Muspratt). As Edwards edged his little flotilla northwards along the Great Barrier Reef, stopping on offshore islands to find food and fresh water while trying to avoid the local inhabitants, his men, terrified of being separated, lashed the boats together at night with tow-lines; while during the day, they huddled together.

Finally, on 2 September 1791, Edwards set off across the Endeavour Straits on the 1000-mile passage to Timor. During their crossing, the *Pandora*'s men followed Bligh's example, drenching their shirts in seawater to cool their bodies, although the salt water soaked into their parched skins, making their saliva intolerably salty. The canvas bags that held the water had leaked, and some of the men drank their own urine. According to Hamilton, the older sailors suffered more from thirst than their younger comrades, but as the voyage went on, they all became 'very cross and savage in their temper'.[15] Although the weather was kinder than it had been to Bligh and his men on the *Bounty*'s launch, on several occasions the swell ran so high that it snapped the tow-ropes that linked the boats at night. When one of the prisoners on board the pinnace (probably Morrison) began to hold a daily service, as Hamilton sardonically remarked, '[T]he Captain, suspecting the purity of his doctrines, and unwilling he should make a monopoly of the business, gave prayers himself.'[16]

Even after this disaster, Edwards was brutal towards the *Bounty*'s men, no doubt blaming them for the loss of the *Pandora*. According to Morrison, one day while he was leaning on his oars, talking to McIntosh, Edwards had him and Ellison pinioned in the bottom of the boat. When he protested, Edwards screamed, 'Silence, you Murdering Villain, are you not a Prisoner? You Piratical Dog what better treatment do you expect? By God if you speak another Word I'll heave the Log with you.'[17] For the rest of the passage, Morrison and Ellison were kept in shackles.

On 13 September 1791 when they sighted Timor, the shipwrecked sailors gave thanks for their deliverance. They stood in for the land, carried by fine breezes, and three days later when the boats anchored off Kupang, Governor Wanjon, who during his time as a deputy governor had been kind to William Bligh, invited them to his house and gave them a meal. During their visit to Kupang, Captain Edwards and Lieutenant Hayward stayed with the governor, spending every evening at concerts or playing cards, while the *Bounty*'s men, who had been put in the stocks at the fort, were forced to relieve themselves where they lay. At first they were stark naked, but their guards fetched them some leaves to weave into hats, which they sold to buy clothing. On 5 October when Lieutenant Larkham fetched them to go on board a Dutch ship, the *Rembang*, which was heading for Batavia, he pinioned their arms behind their backs, tightening their bonds by putting his foot against their backs and pulling so hard that he almost hauled their arms out of their sockets. When they sailed to Batavia on 6 October they were accompanied by another group of prisoners – eleven convicts (eight men, a woman and two children) who had escaped from Port Jackson in a six-oared cutter, making their way to Kupang in this tiny vessel.[18] During their passage to Batavia, while Captain Edwards allowed McIntosh, Coleman and Norman to walk around on deck, the other prisoners were kept in irons. When the *Rembang* was hit by a fierce storm, with violent flashes of lightning and claps of thunder, the Dutch sailors fled to their hammocks, and Larkham had the prisoners released to work the pumps. When Morrison protested that he was too weak to stand this labour, Larkham yelled, 'You damned Villain You have brought it on yourself, & I'll make you stand it, had it not been for you, we should not have been in this Trouble.'[19] According to the surgeon Hamilton: '[T]he ship was preserved from destruction by the manly exertion of our English tars, whose souls seemed to catch redoubled ardour from the tempest's rage . . . I [would not] wish to throw any stigma on the Dutch, who I believe would fight the devil, should he appear in any shape to them but that of thunder and lightning.'[20]

When they arrived at Semarang on 30 October, Edwards and his men were overjoyed to find their lost tender, the *Matavy*, at anchor. The Dutch authorities had imprisoned Oliver and his crew on suspicion of piracy, but Edwards quickly had them freed; and they followed him to Batavia in the schooner built by the *Bounty*'s men, arriving in early November at this 'golgotha of Europe', as Hamilton called Batavia with its fevers and stinking canals. When Captain Edwards wrote to the Admiralty, he reported the capture of some of the *Bounty*'s men in Tahiti, his failure to find the *Bounty* or Fletcher Christian, the loss of the *Pandora* and the journey to Timor, ending on an apologetic note:

> Although I have not had the good fortune to fully accomplish the object of my voyage, and that it has in other respects been strongly marked with great misfortune, I hope it will be thought that the first is not for want of perserver- ance, or the latter for want of the care and attention of myself and those under my command. Should their Lordships upon the whole think that the voyage will be profitable to our country it will be a great consolation to,
>
> Sir,
> Your most humble and obedient servant,
> Edward Edwards[21]

Overjoyed to have survived the shipwreck, one of the *Pandora*'s crew wrote a long poem in Batavia to commemorate their ordeal. Although Edwards was harsh with the *Bounty* sailors, he was lenient with his own men, who held him in high regard:

> Seamen All Attention Lend
>     to these few Lines that here are Pen'd,
>     the *Bounty*'s Loss I'll here Relate
>     And the Good Ship *Pandora*'s fate.

Say muse, What Dire affects are found
When evil Discord, doth Abound
And So it was in the Bounty
Which Rag'd at Last to Mutany

Our Master's mate did head a Gang
By name was Called Christian
The Simple Men he Did mislead,
And tempted them to do the Deed.

When this was Done, their hearts was vex'd
And Greatly Was their Souls Perplex'd
Christian knew not Where to find
A Refuge for his troubled Mind.

He Sail'd Away his Skill to try
To Save themselves from Infamy
And Still Remains in Climes Unknown,
Their Injured Country for to Shun . . .

After describing their futile hunt for the mutineers, the shipwreck of the
*Pandora*, their journey in the boats to Timor and their passage to Semarang,
the poem ended:

We Weigh'd Again and put to Sea
Our tender then in company
And for the main of Java Stood
And Anchor'd in Batavia Road,
Now to Conclude and End the Theme,
Bless'd be Captn. Edwards name
May All like him be just and true
The Darling of his Whole Ship's Crew.[22]

At Batavia, Lieutenant Larkham boarded a Dutch ship and sailed to Europe
with most of the *Pandora*'s crew, while Edwards sold the schooner built by
Morrison and his shipmates to cover some of his expenses. On 23 December
1791, Edwards embarked on another Dutch ship, the *Vreedenbergh*, with the
remaining prisoners (including Morrison), leaving them without provisions for

the first three days, and forcing them to lie on rough baulks of timber, soaked with urine from the pigsties on deck; and sailed for the Cape of Good Hope with the 'pirates', as he invariably called them. At the Cape, he took a passage for himself and the *Bounty*'s men on HMS *Gorgon*, which was returning to England from Port Jackson. While they were still in port, the *Gorgon*'s first lieutenant gave the prisoners a sail to lie on and provided them with shirts and trousers, allowing them to spend some time on deck each day and putting them on a full allowance of provisions for the first time since they had left Tahiti. On 2 April 1792, Captain Edwards's despatches arrived in London,[23] and two days later at the Cape of Good Hope, Edwards boarded the *Gorgon*. The next day the ship set sail for England, anchoring at Spithead on 19 June.

# The Mutineers' Babies

While the *Pandora* was being pounded to pieces on the Great Barrier Reef, two ships from another British expedition were crossing the Indian Ocean. The *Discovery* and *Chatham* were commanded by George Vancouver, who had twice sailed around the world with Captain Cook, and now had orders to complete Cook's search for the Northwest Passage. Vancouver had served as a midshipman on board the *Discovery* during Cook's third voyage, while William Bligh was the *Resolution*'s master, and they knew each other well. In some ways, it is surprising that Bligh was not asked to command this expedition, because during his voyage with Captain Cook, he had distinguished himself in the boats off the north-west coast of America, helping his commander to chart its intricate tracery of inlets, bays and islands. Instead, Vancouver had been ordered to take his ships in the wake of the *Bounty* and the *Pandora* to Matavai Bay, now well established as the favourite British port in the Pacific, where he might pick up news of the *Pandora*, the mutiny on the *Bounty* and Fletcher Christian and his companions, before heading to Hawai'i and the north-west coast of America. Joseph Banks had other plans for Bligh, and while he was waiting for a new command, he was put on half pay, having not fully recovered from his ordeal in the longboat. No doubt he met Vancouver before the ships set sail, and briefed him in preparation for the voyage.

Described by John Elliott, a *Resolution* shipmate, as a 'Quiet inoffensive young man',[1] George Vancouver had joined Captain Cook's second Pacific expedition as an able-bodied seaman at the age of fourteen (although he had been treated as a midshipman during the voyage). According to Elliott:

In the early part of the Voyage, Captn. Cook made all us young Gentlemen,
do the duty aloft, the same as the Sailors, learning to hand, and reef the sails,

*Captain George Vancouver.*

and steer the ship, exercise Small Arms & thereby making us good Sailors as well as Good Officers.[2]

During this expedition, William Wales, the astronomer, had instructed the 'young gentlemen' in navigation, mathematics and astronomy, while Cook taught them the arts of surveying and charting. When the *Resolution* headed to the far southern latitudes in search of Terra Australis and reached 71 degrees 10 minutes south, Vancouver distinguished himself by scrambling out on the bowsprit, waving his hat over his head, and shouting, 'Ne plus ultra!' ('This far and no further!').[3]

When the *Resolution* returned to England, Vancouver joined the *Discovery*, Captain Cook's consort ship for the third Pacific expedition, where he got to know Bligh. As we have seen, during their visit to Hawai'i, the young midshipman had been involved in a fracas with Palea, the male lover of the high chief, which led to the theft of the *Discovery*'s cutter and the death of his commander. Vancouver had learned to speak some Hawai'ian, and after Cook's death was sent to negotiate with the local people for his commander's remains. When a priest came out to the *Resolution* with a small box containing Captain Cook's 'scalp, all the long bones, thighs, legs, arms and the skull', according to Clerke, this man had been glad to talk with Vancouver, who 'best understood them'.[4]

Since his return to England, Vancouver had served in the West Indies, and like William Bligh, he became a skilled surveyor and hydrographer. Although during the third voyage, Cook had failed to find the fabled Northwest Passage, there were still influential men in England who thought that it might still be discovered in that frozen maze of inlets and islands. There was also the lure of the fur trade. In his journal, Captain Clerke had reported that seal and sea otter pelts, which could be bought cheaply on the north-west coast, could be sold for as much as 100 roubles each in China.[5] This observation was apparently based on a coup by William Bligh in Tahiti and Alaska, reported by his shipmate James Trevenen:

> To give some idea of the vast profit to be expected here in a trade for skins, I may mention the following circumstance. Mr. Bligh, the Master, while at Otaheite had given a shilling hatchet for thirty large green Spanish beads on which the natives there set little value, but which he thought might be useful in the course of the voyage; accordingly in this country [King William's Sound, Alaska] he purchased six sea otter skins with twelve of the beads. These skins might have sold in China at a low average of £15 each. Here we find a quick return of £90 for one shilling![6]

Lieutenant King had described this lucrative opportunity in the official account of Cook's last voyage, and afterwards British, Russian and European merchants flocked to the north-west coast of America.

On the same day that William Bligh was promoted to post-captain, George Vancouver replaced Henry Roberts, Bligh's former mate, as commander of this expedition. For reasons that remain obscure, Roberts was posted elsewhere and Vancouver took over his role. In addition to completing the exploration of the north-west coast, Vancouver was ordered to receive back the land and property at Nootka Sound that a Spanish captain had seized from British subjects. The Admiralty gave him three ships for this expedition: the *Discovery* (a small ship about the same size as the *Endeavour*, named after Captain Cook's consort vessel during his third, fatal voyage); a brig, the *Chatham*, commanded by Lieutenant

Broughton, who had served during the Nootka Sound crisis; and at the last moment, a storeship, which sailed independently. Once again, Sir Joseph Banks was involved in the arrangements for this voyage. When Lord Grenville, the Secretary of State, sought his advice, Banks commissioned two sets of detailed instructions for the survey of the north-west coast, one drafted by William Bligh (although in the event, Vancouver did not use them),[7] proposing that the *Discovery* should carry a botanist to study the 'natural history' of the north-west coast and the Pacific; and discover what had happened to the *Bounty*. When the Admiralty agreed, Banks appointed Archibald Menzies, a Scottish naval surgeon and botanist who had sailed with Colnett to the north-west coast, and afterwards worked with Banks, documenting his private collections.

George Vancouver was wary of Joseph Banks, however. As a young midshipman on Cook's second expedition, he and his shipmates had watched Banks persuade the Naval Board to add an extra deck to the *Resolution*, making it unseaworthy. In addition, there had been gossip in naval circles about the unlucky arrangements that Banks had made for Bligh's *Bounty* expedition. When Vancouver resisted some of Banks's directives, Banks was affronted, drafting detailed instructions about how Vancouver must treat Menzies during the voyage; and designing a large glass-topped garden frame for the *Discovery*'s quarterdeck – the captain's domain, where the ship was usually commanded at sea. During the voyage, this structure (which Banks filled with pots and tubs for Menzies's plants) proved to be an intolerable nuisance.[8] In addition, Banks arranged for Vancouver to return 'Towereroo' [Kualelo], a young Hawai'ian who had arrived in England with Colnett, back to his home island; and instructed Menzies to keep his own private journal on the voyage, urging the botanist to document any occasion on which Vancouver tried to obstruct him in carrying out his duties.

Although Vancouver had recruited some good men for this voyage, his crew also included a bevy of young aristocrats led by the Hon. Thomas Pitt, the sixteen-year-old son and heir of Lord Camelford (and a first cousin to the Prime Minister, William Pitt and his brother the Earl of Chatham, the First Lord of the Admiralty, all friends of Joseph Banks). While this young man had a reputation for impetuous bravery, he was also arrogant, with an unbridled temper. Pitt became the midshipmen's ringleader, resisting Vancouver's authority on a number of occasions. A number of the other midshipmen were also very well connected, including the Hon. Charles Stuart, son of the Marquis of Bute. Although Thomas Manby, a mate on board *Discovery*, had no influential relatives, he wrote an entertaining, vivid series of letters during the voyage, describing the strange customs and alluring women that he encountered; while Peter Puget, an enthusiastic twenty-one-year-old who became Vancouver's second lieutenant, kept an excellent journal of their adventures.

While the ships were being fitted out in the naval dockyards, however, Vancouver suffered an attack of malarial fever. When he had partially recovered, the Admiralty provided him with a collection of accounts of previous Pacific voyages, and allowed him to take his journals and charts from his expeditions with Captain Cook, including their visits to Tahiti. During this voyage, like Bligh before him, Vancouver largely retraced Cook's tracks across the Pacific. However, shortly after sailing from Tenerife, he suffered another bout of malaria and Menzies put him on a special diet which relieved the symptoms; although according to Sir James Watt, this illness affected his thyroid gland, causing him to gain weight and his skin to wrinkle, making him look prematurely aged.[9] This disorder may also have affected Vancouver's shipboard behaviour, which provides a chilling contrast with Bligh's style of command. Ironically, although William Bligh went down in history as a harsh and brutal commander, it was George Vancouver who truly deserved that reputation.[10]

En route to Tahiti, for instance, Vancouver ordered twenty-four men to be flogged, compared with just four on board the *Bounty* in the same passage.[11] During his voyage, Vancouver had almost half of his men flogged (45 per cent – more than twice the rate for voyages in the Pacific at this time), compared with 10 per cent on board the *Bounty*. To make matters worse, Vancouver's sentences were often excessive – two, three and four dozen lashes, although a dozen lashes was the legal limit – a mean of 21 lashes for each sailor on board the *Discovery*, compared with a mean of only 1.5 lashes on board the *Bounty*.[12] Determined to avoid Bligh's fate, Vancouver was also harsh with his midshipmen, 'mastheading' Stuart on many occasions; and when Thomas Pitt (later Lord Camelford) lay down on his greatcoat while on watch, Vancouver had him clapped in irons. During the voyage he had Pitt whipped three times in front of the other 'young gentlemen' in the Great Cabin, once for smashing the compass glass while sky-larking on the quarterdeck. After this degrading punishment, Stuart quarrelled with his captain, showing him a razor and saying that if ever he was ordered to be flogged, he would cut his own throat.[13] Compared with these humiliations, Bligh's treatment of Fletcher Christian was mild. There were rumours of mutiny but, unlike Bligh, Vancouver had a full complement of officers and marines on board the *Discovery*. These aristocratic young men loathed their commander, and after the voyage when they returned to England, Lord Camelford met Vancouver in the street and gave him a thrashing to avenge these abuses.

After sailing from the Cape of Good Hope, Vancouver took his ships to Dusky Sound in New Zealand, allowing his men to go ashore where they drank 'a cheerful glass to the memory of Captain Cook'. Despite Cook's meticulous exploration of the sound, the openings of two passages on his chart had been labelled 'No Body Knows What'; and after exploring these two small inlets, Vancouver completed the coastline with a triumphant inscription: 'Some Body Knows What!' When the two ships sailed out of the sound, heading for Tahiti, they were hit by a ferocious storm, and were separated.

On 28 December 1791 when the *Chatham* anchored in Matavai Bay, there was no sign of the *Discovery*. They had arrived in the midst of the Season of Plenty, when the Matahiti festival was imminent and the *'arioi* were flocking to the island. So many people clung to the sides of the *Chatham* that the brig heeled over; and when the islanders crowded on board, the men pilfered everything in sight, including the ship's flag (an enviable trophy), while the women had sex with the sailors. All that day it rained in torrents, with claps of thunder and brilliant flashes of lightning. That night the Tuauru River burst its banks and surged into Matavai Bay, sweeping numbers of large breadfruit trees into the harbour. According to Edward Bell, the young clerk on board the *Chatham*, upon seeing this the islanders 'shouted in a kind of extacy and many immediately Paddled for the place where we afterwards saw them from the ship, swimming & playing in the water'.[14]

The next morning, Pomare II sent a messenger out to the ship, carrying a plantain branch and bringing two big pigs and a gift of fruit. After making a speech of welcome, the herald told Lieutenant Broughton that Tu was at Mo'orea with the rest of his family, and asked him to send a ship's boat to fetch them. Later that afternoon, three young women wearing white linen shirts paddled out to the ship, each carrying a light-skinned baby. These women – 'Peggy' Stewart (who brought her little daughter Charlotte), 'Mary' McIntosh and 'Mary' Burkett – explained that they were the wives of *Bounty* sailors, and that these babies were their children. When Peggy Stewart asked Broughton whether George Stewart would be hanged when the *Pandora* returned to England, and he replied that this was likely, she burst into tears. She insisted that when Bligh had been taken prisoner, Stewart and Heywood were asleep and knew nothing about the uprising; and that Christian had left behind a letter on the island, clearing them of any involvement in the mutiny. Although none of them knew it, however, George Stewart was already dead, having been killed by a falling gangway four months earlier when the *Pandora* was wrecked on the Great Barrier Reef, off the coast of Australia.

During this conversation, Peggy told the officers about the *Bounty*'s departure from Tahiti under William Bligh, and how surprised the islanders had been when the ship returned under Fletcher Christian's command. After unsuccessfully trying to persuade the Tahitians that he had been to England, Christian had told them that the *Bounty* had met Cook's two ships, the *Resolution* and *Discovery*, at sea, and that Bligh and the others had joined Captain Cook, sending Christian with the *Bounty* to Tahiti for supplies. She also described the mutineers' visit to Tupua'i; their quarrel with local warriors; the *Bounty*'s return to Tahiti; and the quarrels among the *Bounty* sailors. Peggy told Broughton that Churchill was a very bad man who had killed one of his companions, and in turn had been killed by his shipmate's Tahitian *taio*. She added that the *Bounty*'s men had built a schooner and fought for Pomare II, winning a great victory for his lineage, and had subsequently been captured by Captain Edwards of the *Pandora*, who had sailed away, taking their little schooner with him.

According to Peggy, the *Bounty* men had been faithful to their Tahitian wives, treating them and their children with great kindness. During their time on the island, Stewart and Heywood had planted gardens with European plants – pineapples, chilli peppers, corn and lemon and orange trees – and adopted local customs, uncovering themselves in Pomare's presence. Although Edward Bell, the *Chatham*'s young clerk, had no sympathy for Fletcher Christian, exclaiming that his 'conduct proves him to be one of the most inhuman Villains that ever existed – pity it is that he was not taken, at his death I shou'd feel no regret', he felt sorry for Stewart and Heywood, adding, 'I shou'd be extremely happy to hear that the Midshipmen's lives were sav'd and that their innocence could be proved.'[15]

On 29 December, Pomare II sent a messenger to Lieutenant Broughton, saying that he would arrive at Matavai Bay the following day. The herald, who delivered a gift of two large live pigs, a barbecued hog and an immense quantity of breadfruit, was followed by Stewart's wife, who brought out gifts for Broughton and his companions, including delicious baked taro. That evening when the surf died down, Po'e'eno's brother Tapairu (who had befriended Charles Churchill, John Millward and William Muspratt during Bligh's visit with the *Bounty*, and encouraged them to desert the ship, later adopting the armourer Joseph Coleman as his *taio*) led Broughton to his house on the opposite side of the river, where they enjoyed a lavish feast. This dwelling, which was raised on a stone platform, was named 'The House for the Men from England' in memory of the relationship between Tapairu's family and William Bligh, and later with the *Bounty* sailors.[16]

After a night of pouring rain, with claps of thunder and lightning flashes, the next morning dawned bright and clear. At 8 a.m. a messenger arrived with the news that a ship had been sighted east of Port Venus. At first the men thought that it might be the *Bounty*, but to their delight it proved to be their consort ship, *Discovery*.[17] Soon after his arrival, when Vancouver was told that Pomare II had come to meet him, he and his officers went ashore. A herald greeted them, holding up a plantain branch, presenting Vancouver with a pig, and delivered a speech of welcome. Afterwards a canoe carried them across the river where they found the paramount chief, Pomare II, now about eleven years old, sitting on the shoulders of his attendant and wearing a cloak of English scarlet cloth ornamented with a ruff of feathers. Ha'amanimani (also known as Mauri), Pomare II's high priest from Ra'iatea and William Bligh's 'uncle', who had taught him Tahitian, took charge of this ceremony, dividing their gifts into four so that each of the British officers could present their own tribute to the boy.

When the ceremony was over, the young paramount chief relaxed and became friendly and animated. Remarking that his father Tu was at Mo'orea, and would be upset if he did not see them, he asked Vancouver to send a boat to bring Tu from that island. The botanist Menzies was impressed by the young paramount chief, describing him 'as firm & graceful, his behaviour affable & easy & his features pleasant & regular though sometimes clouded with a degree of austerity that enables him already to command immediate obedience to his will among these mild people'.[18] Although they discussed the visit by the *Bounty* under Fletcher Christian, the *Pandora*, and Edwards's capture of the *Bounty* sailors on the island, Pomare II had no news of Fletcher Christian and the *Bounty*; and Vancouver still knew nothing about the shipwreck of the *Pandora* on the Great Barrier Reef, and the loss of some of the *Bounty*'s men in that disaster.

Realising that the carpenters would have to build a new jolly-boat for the *Chatham*, and repair her great cutter that had been damaged in the storm, Vancouver now decided to spend the winter on the island, and informed the crews of his intentions. At first they were ecstatic, but when orders were posted prohibiting them from bartering their clothes or tools for sex, curiosities or other goods, or leaving the ships unless they were on shore duty, delight turned to angry frustration. Mindful of the mutiny on the *Bounty*, which Bligh had blamed on the allure of the Tahitian girls, Vancouver was determined to try and prevent his men from forming intimate liaisons on shore.

Early the next morning, 31 December 1791, Vancouver despatched Lieutenant Broughton, Menzies the botanist, and Collett the gunner (who had

sailed with Captain Cook in 1777, and now acted as their interpreter) in the
pinnace to fetch Tu from Mo'orea. After passing Papeto'ai Bay, which William
Bligh had charted, they arrived at Varari, where they met Tu, who arrived with
his family to greet them, accompanied by a large crowd. Although among the
British, Tu had the reputation of being timid, even cowardly, Broughton and
Menzies were impressed by his firm, erect stance and majestic demeanour. Bark
cloth was laid on the beach, and after the British walked across it, Tu embraced
them warmly, introducing them to his 'Queen' 'Itia, a mild, affable woman,
stout and very strong; and two other women (his junior wife Vaiareti, 'Itia's
sister; and his younger sister Auo), all intimates of William Bligh. Menzies was
fascinated by Tu's relationship with his two wives, remarking that although
Tu seemed to revere 'Itia, seeking her advice on all important matters and
treating her with respect and affection, most of his leisure time was spent with
her younger sister Vaiareti, a shy, plump, alluring woman who was clearly his
preferred bedmate.[19]

Tu and his wives were accompanied by Mahau, the high chief of Mo'orea,
who was the brother of 'Itia and Vaiareti, and the husband of Tu's sister Auo.
Tall and handsome at the time of the *Bounty*'s visits to the island, Mahau had
since been stricken by a severe illness, and was now so emaciated that he could
no longer stand, and had to be carried on a litter. When Tu recognised Collett,
the *Discovery*'s gunner who had previously visited Tahiti with Captain Cook,
he greeted him warmly and questioned him about Tute, 'whose fate he seemd to
bewail with real sorrow',[20] and 'Pane' (Joseph Banks), rejoicing that he was alive
and well in England. He did not ask after William Bligh, Fletcher Christian or
Edward Edwards, however, perhaps indicating a lack of concern for these men,
or unwillingness to refer to his relationships with them. Bligh and Christian had
both lied to him, and Edwards had threatened his *taio* Teri'irere and treated the
*Bounty* sailors with brutality, including Heywood and Coleman, who had been
popular with the islanders. Instead, Tu asked for the names of Vancouver's two
ships and their commanders, the places they had visited and intended to visit,
and whether Mr Webber was on board. He was eager to have a portrait of his son
Pomare II painted so that he could send it to King George, and was downcast
when he was told that this would be impossible.

After this conversation, Tu took the British aside and introduced them to
his father Teu, an upright, agile old man with silver hair and a long beard who
was sitting on a mat. Afterwards, they went to a house where a feast had been
prepared, and that night Tu's family took turns to care for Mahau, their sick
kinsman, massaging him with great 'care & tenderness'. The following morning,

1 January 1792, while the chiefs and their British companions were heading in the pinnace back to Matavai Bay, off the south-west point of Mo'orea, Tu's mother Tetupaia came out in a double canoe, bringing a gift of bark cloth, weeping, and calling out Captain Cook's name and lamenting his death, 'which sufficiently showed the sincerity of her affections & the tenderness of her feeling for the memory of a Man whose whole tenor of conduct was constantly actuated for the good of mankind in general & in the latter part of his life for those happy isles in particular'.[21] Like her son Tu, Tetupaia did not ask after William Bligh. They presented her with some trinkets, and felt sorry that they had no more gifts to offer this fine, good-hearted old lady.

Back in Matavai Bay, Vancouver's men celebrated New Year's Day with a lavish dinner and a double allowance of grog. Because both ships had been at sea on Christmas Day, the sailors had missed their extra ration of rum. After toasting their old sweethearts in England, the sailors embraced their island lovers. As Manby remarked: 'Mirth and good humour prevailed throughout and altho' we had not roast beef and plumb pudding, we were equally happy and delighted with roast pig and pretty girls.'[22] Vancouver added laconically: '[I]t is somewhat singular that the gunner of the *Discovery* was the only married man of the whole party.'[23] Later that day, Tu's younger brother Vaetua, a leading *'arioi* whom the sailors quickly nicknamed 'Watty', boarded the *Discovery*, presenting Vancouver with pigs, fruit and other provisions. Vaetua was accompanied by his wife Tai Aiva, a very beautiful woman with 'very fine Eyes and Teeth her long Black hair was Curl'd in the front with becoming taste, her face was well form'd and her skin remarkably smooth, all which added to a sweetness of Countenance and an Air of Majesty render'd her an object of general admiration'. The day was hot, and when this chiefly woman stripped off her shirt, 'and appeard down to her waist perfectly naked', the sailors were spellbound. Bell remarked appreciatively: 'I think I never saw a finer figure.'[24]

The following day, Vancouver ordered his men to set up the shore camp on Point Venus. Broughton and Menzies had spent the night at Pare with Tu and Mahau, and after visiting Taputapuatea *marae*, where the famous red feather girdle Te Ra'i-puatata was now held, they carried on to Matavai Bay. As they entered the harbour, Tu was saluted with four guns from each ship and cries of greeting from the crowd in the canoes, which 'gratified him extremely'. Alongside the *Discovery* he made a long speech, saluting Vancouver, and Vancouver replied, prompted by the high priest Ha'amanimani, who soon took over the oration. After Vancouver and Tu had exchanged names, in the tradition of bond friendship initiated by Captain Cook and William Bligh, the high chief boarded the ship, followed by Mahau in his litter. As Vancouver noted with concern, the high chief of Mo'orea 'appeared to be in the last stage of a deep and rapid decline; his person was reduced to a mere skeleton. The reasons that could induce a man in his deplorable condition to undertake such a visit, must, without doubt, be not less curious than extraordinary!'[25] It is likely that Mahau was suffering from a European disease (probably tuberculosis), and hoped to be healed on board the British vessel.

Soon afterwards, Po'e'eno, the chief of Matavai Bay, boarded the *Discovery* with Captain Cook's portrait, which he ceremoniously placed in the Great Cabin before adopting Menzies as his *taio*. When Vancouver and his officers examined the back of this famous portrait, they found that the last entry recorded the date of the *Pandora*'s departure – '8 May 1791'. Vancouver presented Tu with red cloth, printed linen and two axes; and while Tu was delighted, he begged his new bond friend to hide the two axes under his bureau, so that his brothers could not see them. He remembered Vancouver well from his previous visit to the island with Captain Cook, although to the commander's chagrin, he remarked that since that time, he had grown very old.

Soon afterwards, Tu's two brothers, Vaetua (Hayward's *taio*) and Ari'ipaea (Captain Clerke's *taio*) and their wives arrived alongside in canoes laden with gifts of pigs, bark cloth, chickens and vegetables. When Vancouver gave them lavish presents in return, they were speechless with delight. He invited the 'royal family' to dinner, and 'Itia and Auo, the wives of Tu and Mahau, joined their menfolk. During this meal, Vancouver questioned the chiefs about the mutiny on the *Bounty*, the stay of the *Bounty* sailors on the island and Captain Edwards's visit, events that they described in minute detail. Afterwards, Vancouver drafted a detailed report that he intended to hand over to the Admiralty if the *Pandora* did not reach England (although unfortunately its contents were not recorded in his journal, and the report has not survived). Tu and his brothers also told Vancouver that after the death of Charles Churchill, the *Bounty* mutineer who had succeeded Vehiatua III as the chief of southern Tahiti, a distant relative tried to claim the leadership of the district, but instead they had installed Pomare II's younger brother as his successor; and his uncle Ari'ipaea, a noted warrior, settled near the boundary between Tahiti-nui and Tahiti-iti to ensure that there were no uprisings.

Now that the shore camp had been set up, the men who were confined to the ships became incensed at the injustice of this arrangement. As Hewitt, a surgeon's mate, remarked acerbically, although Vancouver had been young when he visited Tahiti with Captain Cook, 'that not being now the case the Ladies were not so attractive'; while Edward Bell, the clerk of the *Chatham*, lamented:

> When we consider for a moment, how very anxious every person must be to get ashore – and what a relaxation it must be, after having been five weeks at Sea – and more especially when at such a place as Otaheite – one of the most charming Countries in the world, – Why should poor Sailors who have as little pleasure, and as much hard work as most people be debarr'd those recreations which they see every Officer on board enjoy?

All the same, Bell was forced to admit that Vancouver had good reason for this prohibition: '[His] motive was nevertheless good, for he was apprehensive of quarrels happening between the Sailors & the Natives.'[26]

When Po'e'eno, the chief of Matavai Bay, with many of his people, arrived at the shore camp, they dined in the marquee, carefully imitating everything that the British officers did, and trying all the dishes that were put before them. By this time, many of the local people could speak some English, as Bell reported:

> A man in the morning will accost you with "*how d'ye do Sir*," and the next hour at going away will bid you "*Good night*." One old Chief could count from one to a hundred, and another in imitation of the Boatswain cou'd "*turn the hands up out Boats*," but as most of those who had any of our words had learnt them of the Common Sailors, and as every one Knows what instructive tutors they are, they will not be surprised to hear that "*Damn your Eyes*" and such like expressions were most common among them.[27]

The weather still continued foul, and on 5 January, Ari'ipaea and his wife Tai Aiva came out to the *Discovery*. After warning Vancouver that a big storm was coming, they offered to stay on board to keep an eye on the vessels. *Te tau miti rahi*, the season of high seas, had arrived, which had earlier forced Bligh to shift the *Bounty* from Matavai Bay to Pare. The weather was dark and gloomy, with torrential rain, and as 'an amazing heavy swell tumbled into the bay'[28] islanders swam out to the ship with coconuts for their *taio*. The next morning, as predicted, a northwesterly gale howled into the bay, huge breakers crashing over the decks of the ships; and Vancouver had to lower an extra anchor. Ashore, Ha'amanimani went to Taputapuatea *marae* where he offered a pig, a dog and a chicken to ask 'Oro for fine weather, which the *atua* promised in four days' time. When flocks of birds began to circle over the land, however, other Tahitians assured Vancouver that the storm was almost over.

That afternoon, 'contrary to the Otaheitean oracle' at the *marae* but obedient to the circling birds, the sky cleared, with just a few light showers. When the waves died down, Tu and his wives paddled out to visit the ships, followed by Peggy Stewart and her baby daughter, bringing gifts for Vancouver and his officers. When Peggy asked Vancouver about the fate of Stewart and Heywood, however, and he assured her that they would probably be hanged upon their arrival back in England, she again burst into bitter tears.

Ari'ipaea had stayed all night on board the *Discovery*, waking at regular intervals to check on the weather and the cables. According to the botanist Menzies, this younger brother of Tu's was now the greatest warrior in the islands, having abandoned the fleets of unwieldy war canoes used by his predecessors in favour of lighter canoes that carried his men on lightning raids upon his enemies. Menzies admired Ari'ipaea, describing him as 'pleasing in his manner, firm and graceful in his gait, communicative in his conversations, pert in his enquiries, quick in his discernment, and sincere in his attachments'.[29] This chief, who had remained loyal to the memory of his *taio* Captain Clerke, always insisted upon being addressed as 'Tate' (Clerke's Tahitian name) in preference to any other title.

The next morning, 6 January, the weather was fine and clear, and Ari'ipaea and his wife, seeing that the ships were no longer in danger, decided to return ashore.[30] After dining with the officers in the marquee, he and Vaetua, his younger brother, presented them with coconuts and breadfruit and were given shirts, scissors and axes in return. Pomare II also made his first visit to the shore camp, riding on his attendant's shoulders. The paramount chief refused to enter any of the tents, however, because as his companions explained, if he did the tents would become *tapu* and no one else could go there. During this visit, Tu asked Vancouver to arrange a fireworks display before he and his party returned with Mahau to Mo'orea, and when they fixed upon the following evening for this *heiva Peretane* (British entertainment), Tu sent messengers around the island to invite the other chiefs to the festivity. Later that afternoon, a chief from southern Tahiti brought a Union Jack out to the *Chatham*, saying that it belonged to them, although clearly it came from a larger vessel (probably Captain Cook's *Resolution*).

Over the days that followed, the *Chatham*'s officers made an expedition inland, following the banks of the Tuauru River. During their journey, they were shown Fletcher Christian's garden, now overgrown with weeds, and some tobacco plants which according to their companions, Captain Cook had planted. Soon afterwards, Vancouver staged a 'British *heiva*', during which the ship's guns were fired, and the marines performed their drill. As a finale, there were fireworks, which terrified Tu, although his young wife Vaiareti fired off rockets, a Catherine wheel and some flowerpots with aplomb. When Mahau was taken back to Pare, carried on his litter, Tu presented Vancouver with three *parae* or 'black leg' *'arioi*'s costumes, the most prized gifts on the island, refusing to accept any gifts in return, and entertaining him with a *heiva* performed by an *'arioi* troupe, with dancing and chanting. During a visit to Po'e'eno's house in Matavai Bay, the chief showed Menzies some thriving orange trees that had been planted by William Bligh.

On 13 January, Bligh's 'uncle' Ha'amanimani, the high priest, invited the officers – Broughton, Puget, Menzies and some others, to visit Taputapuatea, the new *marae* near Taraho'i that had been erected for Pomare II's investiture while the *Bounty* sailors were living on the island. When they arrived at the sacred site, Ha'amanimani asked them to wait while he prayed before the 'Altar'. The *ahu* or stone platform was ornamented with carved *'unu* boards, and an elderly man placed a large bundle of white bark cloth and a bunch of red feathers upon it. During his chant, the high priest recited all of their names twice in succession, along with the names of the commanders of the ships that had previously visited the island (including James Cook, William Bligh and Edward Edwards), and the names of King George and 'Peretane' or Britain. Afterwards Ha'amanimani showed them around the *marae*, explaining each of its parts and their ritual roles; although as Menzies ruefully remarked: '[W]e could not help lamenting that [our] knowledge of the language was by no means sufficient to comprehend except in very few instances, otherwise we should have left this place much better informd.'[31]

At dusk that evening, when a messenger arrived to report that the 'royal family' were landing on the beach, they hurried out to meet them. Tu, who looked sombre and wretched, told them in a low voice that Mahau had just died, and that he had come to Pare to conduct the funeral at Taputapuatea. When Ari'ipaea and Vaetua joined them and Tu told his brothers the news, they burst into tears. Walking along the beach, they found Tu's two wives weeping beside the canoe in which Mahau's body was lying, wrapped in a length of English scarlet cloth. Searching for a bundle of shark's teeth, Vaiareti handed one to 'Itia and they began to lacerate their heads, weeping tears of blood for Mahau. Afterwards, the two women went into a nearby garden where they laid down a fine mat and sat there, weeping and slashing their scalps. According to Tu's companions, the entire district of Pare had been placed under a *tapu* for three days, with white flags hoisted on the paths leading to all of its boundaries to announce that no fires were to be lit, the people should stay in their houses and there would be no travel by canoe.

Early the next morning, Broughton and his companions saw a large crowd heading towards Taputapuatea *marae*; and shortly afterwards, a canoe with an awning paddled slowly in that direction, carrying Mahau's body. The mourning rituals were carried out in seclusion; and later that afternoon, the officers visited Tu's compound, two large houses beside the sea, one about 60 feet long, where young *'arioi* girls and a male performer danced for the gods. Mahau's death in the midst of the Season of Plenty had disrupted the ceremonial cycle, and these dances were an attempt to put things right. When a man with a large phallus performed a series of bizarre genital distortions, these were greeted with loud applause, although the British expressed their displeasure. He was followed by a group of young girls who danced for the Europeans, periodically opening their loincloths to expose their 'Native Charms'. After this performance, Broughton and his shipmates presented the girls with beads and carried on to a chief's house which stood outside the boundaries of the *tapu* district, where Vaetua gave them a lavish meal. When they offered him some *'ava Peretane* to salute their friends in England, he refused, joining in the toast with a bowl of *'ava* from Tahiti.

The next day, when Broughton's party returned to the shore camp, Vancouver began to load his ships, preparing to sail from the island. The following morning just as Pomare II arrived with his uncles and several other chiefs from Pare, a man who had stolen a hat from the *Discovery* was pursued by a boat and captured. He was taken to the shore camp, and in the presence of the chiefs, he and several other men who had stolen smaller items (including a painting knife) were tied to a tree, their heads were shaved and each was given two dozen lashes. The chiefs watched impassively, relieved that the punishment was not more severe. Bligh had given at least one Tahitian a savage flogging during his last visit, and some of the *Bounty*'s men had also reacted violently to thefts during their time on the island. After the flogging, Tu invited Vancouver and Broughton to visit Taputapuatea *marae*, asking them to bring their muskets, and fire volleys of gunshot over Mahau's body. They did so, presenting the new widow, Auo, with a length of scarlet cloth, while she gave them two large pigs.

Now that the sailors knew that the ships were about to leave Tahiti, discipline began to unravel. When Thomas Pitt defied the prohibition upon offering iron for sex, Vancouver was furious and, haunted by the spectre of the mutiny on the *Bounty*, ordered the boatswain to whip the midshipman in the Great Cabin, watched by the other 'young gentleman'. To make matters worse, when he sent a message to Ha'amanimani, who had been so helpful to the British, the high priest refused to send back the two axes he had borrowed to cut firewood, no doubt thinking that he had earned them several times over. In a fury, Vancouver raged at him, saying that if he did not return the axes, he would burn down his house and destroy all his possessions. With these threats and intimidations, Vancouver was putting at risk the alliance which had been forged between the Pomare lineage and Captain Cook, upheld by a series of British commanders – John Watts, William Bligh and Edward Edwards.

On 19 January 1792, Tu and his wives returned from Pare, sending large quantities of pigs, chickens, goats, vegetables and fruit out to the ships as gifts. Peggy Stewart came on board the *Chatham* with a *parae* (Chief Mourner's costume) for Mr Johnstone and a *taumi* or warrior's breastplate for Bell, in memory of her husband George Stewart; and when she refused to accept any presents in return, Bell dressed her in a white shirt. Seeing these magnificent gifts, a young girl who had adopted Bell as her *taio* burst into tears, upset that she could not match such chiefly generosity.

The following day, however, a bag containing a dozen white shirts belonging to Lieutenant Broughton (which had been left outside the marquee all night) was stolen. When Ari'ipaea arrived at the shore camp with a lavish gift of pigs, goats and other provisions, Vancouver complained about the theft and Ha'amanimani's refusal to return the axes. Ari'ipaea had brought a troupe of 'arioi with him, intending to farewell the British with a *heiva*; but when he invited Vancouver to watch the entertainment, the commander retorted that since his people had betrayed his trust, the less he had to do with them the better; adding that unless the stolen articles were returned, he would burn down every house in Matavai Bay.

Startled by Vancouver's anger, Ari'ipaea asked for a musket and ammunition so that he could shoot the thieves. When Vancouver loaned him a musket, refusing to give him any cartridges or powder, Ari'ipaea stormed off, returning with one of the axes at noon and reporting that Ha'amanimani had refused to give up the other until an adze which was being repaired in the shore camp was returned. Ha'amanimani and Ari'ipaea, Pomare II's high priest and his war leader, had been hospitable to William Bligh, and Vancouver's conduct seemed gauche and ungenerous. During these exchanges, despite his instructions from the Admiralty to avoid disputes with the local people, Vancouver had managed to alienate the two most powerful men on the island. Ha'amanimani and Ari'ipaea, the guardians of Pomare II, would never again place any confidence in the British.

When Vancouver boarded the *Discovery* the next morning, he found to his chagrin that the young Hawai'ian Kualelo, 'a boy of weak intellect, a sullen disposition, and excessively obstinate',[32] had absconded. During his visit to Tahiti, Kualelo had behaved just like Ma'i, lavishing gifts on those who flattered him, boasting and giving himself airs. After falling in love with Po'e'eno's daughter, he had showered her with treasures from England. When Vancouver met Tu with his wives and brothers at the shore camp, he flew into a rage, demanding the return of the young Hawai'ian along with Broughton's shirts and the axe from Ha'amanimani, and threatening to destroy all the houses in Matavai Bay. When he told Tu and his brothers that he had decided to cancel the fireworks display and withhold their farewell gifts unless Broughton's shirts and the young Hawai'ian were returned, they left the shore camp, seething with anger. The large work tent was lowered and brought out to the ship, leaving only the marquee, the guard tent and the cannons standing at Point Venus. After this confrontation the local people were so *matau* or afraid that they fled from the bay, abandoning the houses.

Early on 22 January, the day that Vancouver had fixed for his departure, Tu told his *taio* that the young Hawai'ian had been carried off to the mountains behind Pare. He assured him that he would bring him back, while Vaetua promised to retrieve the stolen garments. At the marquee, Lieutenant Puget awaited Tu's return with a guard of marines while the rest of the shore camp was packed up and sent on board. That afternoon Broughton crossed the river to visit his *taio*, but far from finding his stolen shirts, he discovered Vaetua making love with his wife. Disengaging himself, Vaetua confessed that he had been too afraid to visit the shore camp.

It was pouring with rain the next morning, and in the swell the *Chatham*'s stream cable parted on the coral. There was still no sign of Tu or Ari'ipaea, and Broughton and Menzies volunteered to go with Vaetua to Pare to look for them. Soon afterwards when 'Itia, Vaiareti and Auo came on board, offering to accompany the envoys, Vancouver replied that Tu's two wives and his sister would be kept on board until Broughton returned safely. The 'Royal Dames' found this hilarious, 'jocularly adding that if Pomarre [Tu] did not come for them, they would go to Britanee & get other husbands'.[33] Escorted by a guard of marines, Broughton, Menzies and Vaetua were rowed past One Tree Hill and landed on the beach, where they found Tu with Kualelo, who was dressed in Tahitian bark cloth.

As the young Hawai'ian was carried to the boat, he complained that after slipping overboard he had lost a rifle-barrelled musket given to him by Colonel Gordon at the Cape of Good Hope in the surf, along with a brace of pistols. When Broughton and Menzies urged Tu and Ari'ipaea to make a farewell visit to the ships, they set out together, followed by two fleets of canoes laden with pigs and vegetables intended for the *Discovery* and the *Chatham*. When they arrived at the ships, Kualelo was put in irons, and Tu and 'Itia slept on board the *Discovery* that night, while Ari'ipaea and his wife slept on board the *Chatham*.

The next day, 24 January, dawned fine and bright, with a light easterly breeze. At about 10 a.m. the sailors raised the anchors, and the ships were towed out of the harbour. When Peggy Stewart, whom Bell described as a rather plain, but very sweet-tempered, young woman and devoted to her small daughter, arrived alongside the *Chatham* with a canoe-load of pigs and fruit, she farewelled the crew (particularly Johnstone and Bell) with tears in her eyes, saying that she 'lov'd the English and wished we could come back and live at Otaheite'. Before leaving the ship, she went to visit Edward Bell in his cabin and asked him once more whether her husband George Stewart would be hanged. When he replied that he did not know, but that perhaps he would escape, she replied:

> If he is alive when you return tell him that you saw his Peggy and his little Charlotte, and they were both well and tell him to come to Otaheite, and live with them or they will be unhappy.[34]

As she climbed down into her canoe, Peggy Stewart burst into tears, and sat there holding on to her little daughter and waving goodbye as the ships vanished over the horizon.

On board the *Discovery*, Vancouver presented Tu and 'Itia with many gifts, including some ammunition. During this visit, Vancouver had become fond of Tu, describing him as having a good knowledge of himself, and 'an open, generous, and feeling heart'. Although Tu had often pleaded with Vancouver to support him in establishing his son's authority over the Society Islands, because the people of Ra'iatea and Taha'a did not recognise him, and even Ha'amanimani had limited influence over these islands, Vancouver had refused, but assured him that upon his return to England, he would ask King George to send a ship with some soldiers to Tahiti to conquer those islands if they were still resisting Pomare II's *mana*. When Ari'ipaea and Vaetua arrived from the *Chatham*, Vancouver, who was still angry with them, gave them no presents, although when they climbed into their canoes, he ordered them to be saluted with four guns. Tu was the last person to leave the *Discovery*, and as he boarded his canoe and began to paddle back to Pare, another four-gun salute was fired.


Like the *Bounty*'s men, Vancouver's crew adored their time in Tahiti. As Bell remarked, despite the diseases that were ravaging the local population, the women were delectable, with their lovely figures, beautiful teeth, sparkling black eyes and heads adorned with bright garlands of flowers. The sailors had been riveted by the sexually graphic dances that were now openly performed in their presence (whereas in Cook's time, such *'arioi* performances had been held in secret). According to Manby: 'The delightful scenes I met with transported me with pleasure, and allowing of [no] other comparison than the Garden of Eden.'[35] As for the Tahitians, apart from those like Peggy Stewart, who had close relationships with particular men, they had become increasingly disenchanted with the British. While they had revered Captain Cook, lamenting his untimely death, few spoke about William Bligh or Fletcher Christian, and none with any warmth. During his visit, Vancouver had quarrelled with Ari'ipaea, and insulted and threatened Ha'amanimani, Pomare II's guardian and the high priest of 'Oro on the island. As soon as his ships sailed away, a devastating epidemic broke out on the island, which killed many people. No doubt this was blamed on the anger of the gods. No one lamented Vancouver's departure; and when he returned to the island for the last time, Bligh would suffer the consequences.

## 18

## *Providence*

Just as Vancouver's ships set sail from England for Tahiti, the second breadfruit voyage was being planned. From the outset, it had been decided that William Bligh would lead this expedition. As Bligh wrote in excitement on 8 February 1791 to his young cousin, Francis Godolphin Bond, a naval lieutenant:

SECRET

Dear Frank,
There is a talk of my being sent out to Otaheite for the Breadfruit plant. – I shall in that case have perhaps two Lieutenants. – They may be appointed by the Admiralty. – Should you like such a long and very unpleasant Voyage, as well as dangerous, things may turn out so as I may be able to get you appointed, but it is very uncertain, and particularly in what rank . . .

There is no ship yet bought for the purpose, or am I officially spoke to on the busyness, yet I think it will take place, and that case I shall sail in May – don't determine rashly, or think you will displease me by refusing . . .[1]

Once again, Joseph Banks was largely responsible for this project. After the mutiny on the *Bounty*, he had learned his lesson; and both he and the Admiralty were determined not to stint on ships or men for the second breadfruit expedition. Accordingly, Banks took care to ask Bligh what he would need for the journey and, in reply, Bligh requested a three-deck ship with a crew of about ninety (including twenty marines and three lieutenants), along with a small tender with a crew of thirty, which would allow him to chart the Endeavour Straits north of Australia as a passage for the convict transports between Batavia and Port Jackson.[2]

By 23 February 1791, Bligh had located two suitable ships in Mr Perry's yard in Blackwell – a three-deck West Indiaman about twice the size of the *Bounty*; and a much smaller brig. A month later, the Admiralty had purchased these vessels, renaming them the *Providence* (no doubt a sign of Bligh's gratitude for his deliverance) and the *Assistant*, and sending them to Woolwich to be coppered. After his ordeal in the *Bounty*'s longboat, Bligh was also provided with two large launches in addition to the usual cutters and jolly-boats, and a crew of 100 for the *Providence*, including twenty marines from the Chatham division. At this time, however, war with Russia seemed imminent and experienced sailors were being pressed into the Navy's fighting vessels, so that Bligh had stiff competition in recruiting his crews, and it took him some time to man the vessels.

On this occasion, Banks allowed Bligh to choose his own officers. Bligh was eager to sail with Nathaniel Portlock, a calm, capable American who after the death of Captain Clerke had acted as his mate on board the *Resolution*. Since their time together during Cook's last Pacific expedition, Portlock had served in the Channel Fleet, and commanded the *King George*, a ship owned by the King George's Sound Company in which Joseph Banks had an interest, sailing to Alaska to collect furs to sell in China, and spending the winter months in Hawai'i. Portlock had written a fine account of this voyage (with a list of flora and fauna and ethnographic notes for Joseph Banks), which was later published – although surprisingly, his journal of the breadfruit voyage is sparse and prosaic. Portlock had been chosen as George Vancouver's consort captain, but withdrew from that voyage at the last moment. When Lieutenant Guthrie, an inexperienced young officer who enjoyed the patronage of Lord Samuel Hood (a member of the Board of the Admiralty) sought the command of the *Assistant*, Banks made sure that Portlock got the appointment instead.[3] Bligh's nephew Francis Bond, the son of his half-sister, a battle-hardened mariner who had been scarred in a gunpowder explosion, was appointed as the *Providence*'s first lieutenant,[4] while Guthrie became her second lieutenant.

For his second breadfruit voyage, William Bligh recruited some promising young officers. George Tobin, the modest and gifted 23-year-old third lieutenant on board the *Providence*, wrote an entertaining, lively journal of their adventures, illustrated by a series of watercolour sketches in an appealing, naive style. The son of a wealthy merchant in the West Indies, Tobin had served in the Navy since he was a boy, fighting in the Battle of the Saints in 1782 when he was only thirteen years old. Although his mother was a relative of the wife of Lord Nelson, who kept a benevolent eye on his career, Tobin (like Bligh) found himself without a ship after the Peace of Paris in 1783 and joined the merchant navy, travelling to

India and China. With this appointment to the *Providence*, he was returning to the Royal Navy. Matthew Flinders, the son of a Lincolnshire surgeon, enlisted in the Navy after reading *Robinson Crusoe* and joined the voyage as a midshipman with the encouragement of Thomas Pasley (Peter Heywood's uncle), his former captain on the *Bellepheron*. Flinders, who later became famous for his explorations of the Australian coastline, at seventeen years old was already a fine cartographer, although during the voyage he clashed with Bligh about the authorship of a particular chart – an ironic echo of Bligh's struggles after Cook's last voyage for recognition of his own hydrographic work. There was also John Gore, the son of Bligh's former commander on the *Resolution* (who after succeeding Cook and then Clerke, had failed to recommend his master for promotion), although this young man was recruited by Nathaniel Portlock.

For this voyage, Bligh adamantly refused to sail with any of his former officers from the *Bounty*. When William Peckover, the *Bounty*'s gunner, applied for a post in the *Providence*, Bligh turned him down flat (telling Banks that if Peckover approached him, he should say that Bligh had described him as a 'vicious and worthless fellow').[5] The only two former *Bounty*s who were allowed to join the *Providence* were Lawrence Lebogue, the sailmaker who had sailed with Bligh on board the *Britannia*, the *Bounty* and in the *Bounty*'s longboat, remaining staunchly loyal to his captain; and the sailor John Smith, who had also sailed on the *Bounty*'s launch, although his health suffered badly from that ordeal. Once again, Joseph Banks appointed two botanist-gardeners – James Wiles and Christopher Smith from Kew – to care for the breadfruit plants, paying for their wages and equipment; and helped Bligh to organise the internal layout of the ship to accommodate the breadfruit plants. Bank's instructions to the gardeners were meticulous, warning them of the dangers of salt spray, cold weather, lack of water, animals and insects; recommending a detailed regime for their preservation during the voyage; and urging them always to obey the orders of their commander.[6] Banks also arranged for an artist to sail with Bligh to the Society Islands; although according to Tobin, this man fell ill before the voyage and was unable to join them.

When Bligh's commission arrived on 16 April 1791, he and Portlock raced to get their ships ready.[7] Twelve carriage guns and fourteen swivels were brought on board the *Providence*; and as the ships were loaded with gear and provisions, Bligh ordered an assortment of 'Cotton long gowns for the Queen and Chief Women', lengths of printed cotton, shirts, and a collection of iron tools, nails, mirrors, beads and earrings for the Tahitians.[8] He also urged Sir Evan Nepean (the Undersecretary of State for the Home Department) to suggest to the Dutch

Ambassador that in recognition of his kindness to the men from the *Bounty*'s launch, Mr Wanjon, the deputy governor in Timor, should be promoted.[9]

At about this time in Britain, a number of influential Evangelical Christians who had read the official accounts of Cook's voyages became inspired with the idea of taking the Gospel to the heathen in the Society Islands. As Dr Thomas Haweis, chaplain to the Countess of Huntingdon, explained:

> The voyages of the great and adventurous Cook to the Southern Ocean, and his discoveries . . . could not but engage the most universal attention. Among others I read them with delight and wonder, and . . . I could not but feel a deep regret that so beautiful a part of the Creation, and the inhabitants of those innumerable Islands of the Southern Ocean should be regions of the shadow of Death, the Dens of every unclean Beast, and Habitation of Cruelty devouring literally one another.[10]

Enthralled by the idea of converting the 'heathen' inhabitants of the Pacific, Haweis spoke with Joseph Banks about taking missionaries to Tahiti on the second breadfruit voyage; and he must have been persuasive, because Banks agreed, providing that the government gave their permission. Haweis was also in touch with William Wilberforce, the anti-slavery campaigner, who helped to secure the government's support for this proposal, as long as Haweis trained the missionaries and paid for their passage and equipment.

In June 1791, Banks and 'other persons of consequence' visited William Bligh, and afterwards Bligh reported to Frank Bond that 'we shall have with us two Men who are to remain in Otaheite'.[11] Dr Haweis already had two missionaries in mind, young men named Waugh and Price from the Trevecca Wesleyan college in Wales; but they refused to sail on the *Providence* unless they were given a pension in the event of their untimely return to England. After this had been arranged, they demanded to be ordained. When the Bishop of London refused because neither of these men had studied at Oxford or Cambridge, they withdrew from the voyage. By this time Haweis had lost patience with them, remarking caustically, '[T]he event left me with no regrets.'[12]

Although by this time Banks was a baronet, the President of the Royal Society and a respectably married man, he looked askance at the Dissenters and their pious habits. During his youthful visit to Tahiti, he had revelled in the delights of the *'arioi* society; and when Ma'i arrived in London in 1774, Banks and his close friend Lord Sandwich had introduced the young Ra'iatean to high society, taking him on jaunts into the country, where they diverted themselves with concerts, feasts and ladies of pleasure, scandalising those who thought that they should be teaching Ma'i about Christianity, and how to read the Bible. As Sir Harry Trelawny had exclaimed to Revd Mr Broughton of the Society for Promoting Christian Knowledge: 'I hint to you what has I doubt not, appeared to you as it does to me a strange and diabolical neglect – the non-baptism & non instruction of the Indian Omiah – he is brought here where the full light of the glorious Gospel shines unclouded – and what has he learned? Why, to make refinements on sin in his own country.'[13] Horace Walpole, the British literary eminence, had remarked in a letter to Rev. William Cole in 1780: 'How I abominate Mr Banks and Dr Solander who routed the poor Otaheitians out of the center of the ocean, and carried our abominable passions among them!'[14]

Stung by these criticisms, one of Banks's circle had penned a satirical pamphlet, *A Letter from Omai, to the Right Honourable the Earl of [Sandwich], In which, amongst other things, is fairly and irrefragably stated, the Nature of Original Sin, together with a Proposal for Planting Christianity in the Islands of the Pacific Ocean.* In this tract, Ma'i was made to describe his encounter with a 'Methodist preacher, who told me that I had been damned to all eternity, had I not been so happy as to have heard the name of Christ, [and] talked about Adam and Eve, and original sin'. He also passionately defended Tahitian morality, arguing the lack of Christian charity in such blanket condemnations. Through Ma'i's fictitious voice, the evangelicals were mercilessly lampooned and accused of preaching 'the efficacy of faith without works, [and] doing much harm to the common people of England'.

No doubt this reflected Banks's own private opinions. Sceptical of evangelical zeal, he was 'little inclined to Conversions'.[15] In a letter to Count William Bentinck on the 'Manners of Otaheite', he had praised the Tahitians for their sexual tolerance, observing that there 'the want of Chastity does not preclude a woman from the esteem of those who have it . . . yet are there women there as inviolable in their attachments as here'.[16] Haweis used a variety of pragmatic arguments to win Banks over, promising to send him botanical specimens from any evangelical outposts that were established, and suggesting that a missionary settlement in Tahiti would provide the convict colony at New South Wales with a steady flow of pigs and other supplies.

Apart from the evangelical Christians, others took a close interest in the second breadfruit voyage. In early March 1791, Lord Chatham, the First Lord of the Admiralty, met with William Bligh to discuss the arrangements for the expedition.[17] After a meeting with the hydrographer Alexander Dalrymple (who had hoped to command the *Endeavour* instead of James Cook), Bligh drafted a meticulous chart of Pare Harbour from memory, lending Dalrymple a copy of his log kept on the *Resource* during his voyage from Timor to Batavia. At the same time, Sir Joseph Banks arranged for James Burney (the former first lieutenant of the *Discovery*) to edit Bligh's *Bounty* journal for publication, a narrative that Bligh was eager to dedicate to his patron.[18] When Bligh wrote to Burney, saying that he had left his log with Dalrymple, he reported that Captain Cox of the *Mercury* had visited Tahiti, where he learned that Christian had returned to the island with the *Bounty*, and had assured the Tahitians that Bligh had settled at Aitutaki. Bligh made several suggestions about the introduction to his journal, urging Burney to correct a number of errors (based on careless copying from his originals) in the charts that had been published in the official account of Captain Cook's last voyage.[19]

In 1791 when the Assembly of Jamaica voted Bligh a reward of £500 for his first breadfruit voyage on board the *Bounty*, even though it had failed,[20] Banks's letter of thanks to the Assembly on his behalf was published in the *Royal Gazette*:

> By the generous vote of the Assembly in favour of Capt. Bligh you have made a good man happy, and a poor man comparatively rich. He is highly grateful for, and sensible of, the honour which has been done him by so truly respectable a body as the Assembly of Jamaica. . . .
>
> I take some credit to myself for having successfully urged Government to forward the equipment of another bread-fruit ship, during the present turbulent times. Good fortune was my friend . . . and had it come later, the business of bread-fruit would inevitably have been postponed, and perhaps have been totally neglected. . . .
>
> It is difficult, in my opinion, to point out an undertaking . . . more likely to add comforts to existing people, and even to augment the number of those for whom the bounties of creation were intended, than that of transporting useful vegetables from one part of the earth to another where they do not exist.[21]

During his discussions with the Admiralty, Banks suggested that Bligh might visit Norfolk Island during his next voyage, and carry trees from there to Port Jackson; or alternatively pick up 'one or two New Zelanders accustomed to the Dressing of flax' and take them to Norfolk Island or Port Jackson to help the convicts weave their own clothing.[22] Although the Admiralty set aside these proposals, Banks assured Bligh that because he had 'the highest opinion both of

PLATE 12: *Breadfruit plant, by George Tobin.*

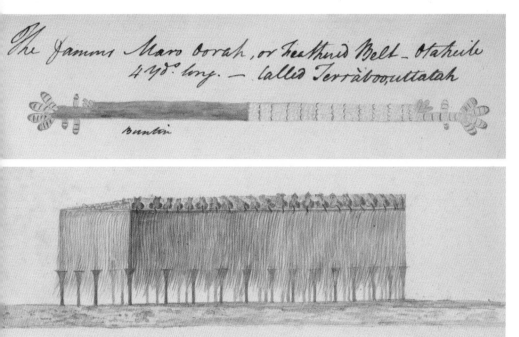

PLATE 13: *Te Raʻi-puatata, sketched by Bligh, above the great altar.*

PLATE 14: *Captain William Bligh, 1791, by John Russell.*

PLATE 15: *Elizabeth Bligh, by John Russell.*

PLATE 16: *Bligh's attempt to land at Tofua.*

PLATE 17: Providence *and* Assistant, *by George Tobin.*

PLATE 18: *Adventure Bay, by George Tobin.*

PLATE 19: Providence *and* Assistant *in Matavai Bay, by George Tobin.*

PLATE 20: *Pi'aroa cascade, Tahiti, by George Tobin.*

PLATE 21: *Fare tupapa'u, Tahiti, by George Tobin.*

PLATE 22: *Pomare II's sacred canoe, by George Tobin.*

PLATE 23: *Fishing by the Papeno'o River.*

PLATE 24: *The great marae of Taputapuatea, in Pare.*

PLATE 25: *Taraho'i marae, Pare.*

[his] Zeal and intelligence', he had ensured that his instructions for the voyage would be as flexible as possible.[23] By the end of July, however, the *Providence* and *Assistant* were still at anchor in Spithead, awaiting their final orders. Bligh pleaded with Banks to tell the Admiralty that if they waited any longer, the ships would be delayed by the monsoon season,[24] putting the expedition at risk, just as they had done with the *Bounty* voyage.

Bligh's orders arrived soon afterwards. On 2 August 1791, as the ships set sail on a calm sea with fair winds, he wrote Banks a heartfelt letter: 'Farewell My Dear Sir, be assured of every thing being done by me that is possible for a human Being to accomplish . . . Your letter expressing a regard to my family is a real treasure to me.'[25] The sailors were in high spirits, eagerly anticipating their sojourn in Tahiti. As his nephew Frank Bond confessed in his journal: 'The most friendly behaviour marks the conduct of each of my shipmates, and we are all alive with expectation of enjoying that blissful shore centred in the Pacific Ocean.'[26]

Two weeks into the voyage, Bligh organised his men into three watches, as he had done on board the *Bounty*, to ensure that they got plenty of rest. On 19 August 1791 when a gale blew up, he had fires lit below to dry the men's clothes. The ships made fine progress, the *Assistant* sometimes outsailing the *Providence*; but when they reached Tenerife on 30 August, Bligh suffered a relapse of malaria that he had contracted in the East Indies, suffering terrible headaches and 'all the Violent Batavia Symptoms' that left him crazed with pain. In Tenerife Harbour, where the air was so hot that the night breezes seemed to 'flow from a furnace', Bligh was forced to ask Lieutenant Portlock to take command of the *Providence*, sending his nephew Frank Bond to take over the *Assistant* [PLATE 17]. Although Bond was offended that his uncle had not asked him to take over his own ship, sending him to command the consort vessel instead, Portlock was the more experienced navigator, and Bligh was oblivious to the slight. As he wrote to Banks: 'Portlock behaves very attentive & is a very good natured worthy man, as is my first Lieutenant.'[27] Despite his illness, Bligh managed to procure two casks of the finest wine for Banks at Tenerife, which was transferred into English oak barrels.[28]

When the ships set off for St Jago, Bligh was still confined to his cabin. As Frank Bond remarked, during this passage the *Assistant* resembled a 'marine farm':

Today the sun shone out and our stock basked on the quarter deck: viz., a half-starved bitch with two playful pups, 2 months old; an old sow, with nine young ones skipping about; a sheep taught to feed from anyone's hands and as tame as a house lamb; 2 cats sleeping among the pigs; 2 blind ducks and 2 fowls with the coop. Thus did the parade of the *Assistant* afford a spectacle which might give pleasure to a philosopher.[29]

Although Portlock hoped to hire a house at St Jago where Bligh could recuperate, when they arrived at the island, a dangerous epidemic was raging; and after collecting a few oranges for Bligh, he set sail again. Before they departed, Bligh dictated a loving letter to his wife:

My Dear Betsy, I beg you will not be alarmed at not seeing my own writing. But as my [ailment] is of a nervouse kind, Mr. Harwood thought it improper from me to attempt writing. I anchored here to day to procure a little fruit, and shall leave it by midnight, as I find it an unhealthy time of year. I am now taking the bark and feel considerably stronger; so that [I] hope before we reach the Cape to be perfectly re-established in my health.

I am confident it is ordained for us once more to meet, you may therefore cherish your dear little girls in that happy hope . . . I remain, Yr. sincere & affecte husband Wm Bligh, I have written to Sir. J. Banks but no one else. You will therefore remember me kindly to your uncle and family.[30]

Alongside his signature, he scrawled in his own hand: 'God bless you my dear love and my little angles. God bless and preserve you.'

However, as Bligh confessed in his journal: 'I was constantly afflicted with a dreadfull Head Ach and burning heat in my Skin, with distracted brain on the least Noise; so that to preserve my Sences it was necessary a profound silence should be kept in the Ship, and I should be ungratefull not to acknowledge how wonderfully & kindly it was preserved.'[31] At the same time, Portlock wrote to Joseph Banks, passing on a reassuring message for Elizabeth Bligh about her husband's health; and she wrote back gratefully to Sir Joseph, thanking him for his kindness and concern.[32]

On this occasion, Bligh had no orders to sail around Cape Horn, and Portlock decided to head south along the west coast of Africa towards the Cape of Good Hope. On 3 October when they 'crossed the line', as was his habit, Bligh would not allow any of the crew to be ducked from the yardarm, although the 'gallows' (an iron cross with an iron collar attached, with a handspike as a crossbar) had been rigged, the novices among the crew sent below, and the hatchways covered with tarpaulins. Matthew Flinders gave a vivid description of the ceremony that followed – which in many ways evoked the *'arioi* skits in Tahiti:

> We heard a voice hailing the Ship, asking her Name and that of the Captain. Mr. Gutherie answered that it was the Providence commanded by Captn. Bligh, who will be very happy to see you and your retinue on board, most noble Neptune. Neptune answered that he would pay him and his children whom he had not seen before a visit.
>
> Two seamen who stiled themselves Constables, came down with their faces black'd, deputed by Neptune to bring up Mr. Nicols, tied a Handkerchief over his Eyes and led him up the after hatchway, walking on each side of him with Tridents or Broomsticks in their hands as marks of their Authority. We soon heard a swashing of Water of Deck and a great deal of talking and laughing, presently they came down for another and then for poor I, they blinded me, led me upon Deck, and made me sit down, and [told] me that Neptune was come on board, they hoped I would not let him go without something to drink.
>
> Oh the Gallows thinks I, how much do you want. The Captain says, why he must give you a Bottle, the same as the rest. Yes sir, says Neptune, a Bottle will do . . . O Yes, with all my Heart, accordingly they began to daub my face and scrap it with the smooth Edge of his Razor, tho' I did not find it remarkably so. Now says Neptune, we must give him a wash, lay hold here and give us a Hoist – its only three Times. Yes thinks I, that's often enough – in a moment my Seat went from under me, I fell back when the water sluice comes, They took the handkerchief off my Eyes, and I found my self in a large Tub full of water, and every body with Buckets in their Hands Heaving at me.
>
> On my left had stood our Gunners mate and two other Seamen disguised as Neptune, his Wife and the Barber, such horrid figures, plaistered, black'd, Swabs for Tails . . . After every Man had been brought up in Succession and passed under the Hands of the Tonsor [barber], a kind of Water War commenced, one Party against another, which ceasd gradually and was given up at the Captains expressing a Desire that it shoud, then everyone went below, put on dry Cloathes and the whole was concluded by the Captains giving each Man a Dram – thus this famous Ceremony ended.[33]

By early December when the ships arrived at the Cape of Good Hope, Bligh was feeling better; and he went ashore to call upon the lieutenant-governor, who greeted him courteously. During this meeting, however, Bligh managed to offend both Portlock and Bond by ignoring them and presenting a junior lieutenant to the governor instead; and during their time at the Cape, he was reluctant to give them shore leave. Soon afterwards, when an English ship flying distress flags approached the coast, the *Providence* fired her guns and sent out boats to tow the ship into the harbour. This proved to be a Dutch ship hired by John Hunter, the captain of the *Sirius*, the flagship of the First Fleet that had sailed to New South Wales, and during her return voyage had been wrecked on Norfolk Island. In fact, Hunter was the officer whose promotion to post-captain had galvanised Bligh into seeking a similar promotion before his voyage on the *Bounty*. After talking with him, Bligh wrote to Banks, advising him that the convict settlement at Port Jackson was short of food, but that if cattle were sent, manure could be added to the soil and the colony might become self-supporting.[34] There was no news of the *Pandora* at the Cape or at Rio de Janeiro, however, where the *Daedalus* (Vancouver's storeship) had visited, and he speculated that Captain Edwards might have returned to England via Cape Horn.

Bligh was still suffering from an intermittent fever and headaches that made him irritable; and on one occasion when Frank Bond sent the boats ashore without tackles to lift the stores, he wrote his nephew a testy letter, rebuking him for this blunder. Despite these tensions, his men had a wonderful time at the Cape, where Tobin described a carriage pulled by four tame zebras; although as he confessed ruefully, when he tried to flirt with the daughter of a Dutch burgher in English, 'the language of Botany Bay would have been equally successful'.[35]

By 23 December 1791 when the *Providence* and *Assistant* sailed from the Cape of Good Hope, Bligh had almost recovered. After giving Lieutenant Portlock a copy of his orders, he sent him back to the *Assistant*, resumed command of the *Providence* and summoned Frank Bond to return on board as his first lieutenant, to Bond's dismay. As the ships headed out to sea, Hunter and his *Sirius* crew saluted them with three hearty cheers. On Christmas Day, Bligh ordered the men to be given the ingredients to make themselves a sea pie each, a modest celebration.

Now that Bligh was back in command, he resumed the kind of needling that had infuriated his immediate subordinates on board the *Bounty*. On the *Providence*, the main scapegoat was his first lieutenant and nephew Frank Bond, who complained bitterly of Bligh's 'dictatorial insistence on trifles, everlasting fault-finding, and strong and passionate condemnation of little errors of judgement', exclaiming, 'I shall think the Grand Turk complacency itself after this!'[36] His shipmates took these clashes less seriously – for instance, George Tobin, who remarked: 'A few passing squalls had taken us, within board as well as without, but by clearing up in time, without any serious mischief.'[37] Passing the island of St Paul in a thick fog, the ships headed east for Adventure Bay off the south coast of Tasmania, where Bligh had first anchored with Captain Cook in 1777, and afterwards on board the *Bounty* in 1788.

On 9 February 1792 when the ships anchored in Adventure Bay [PLATE 18], the shore party cooked fresh fish, birds and shellfish on the campfire; and a volunteer named Bennet tried to desert from the *Assistant*. Exploring the bay, they found an old saw pit made by the *Bounty*'s men, and a piece of red baize lying on the ground, looking as fresh as if it had just been dropped. At Gully Head, some of the officers met a group of Tasmanians, who asked for a hat but soon fled, leaving behind four spears. During this visit, Bligh planted oak trees, fruit trees, strawberries, pomegranates and a rosemary bush beside the lake at the end of the beach; named a hill on Bruny Island 'Nelson's Hill' after David Nelson, the *Bounty* botanist who had been the first European to climb it; and below an inscription carved on a tree during Cook's visit, recorded the arrival of the *Providence* and the *Assistant* with the words: 'Near this tree captain William Bligh planted seven fruit trees 1792: – Messrs S. and W., botanists'. As the ships sailed out of the bay, they were hit by a savage gale that blew away the *Assistant*'s foreyard, and were forced to return for repairs. It was not until 24 February 1792 that Bligh finally set off on the next leg of his journey, heading for the southern end of New Zealand.

In the frigid, rolling wastes of the deep Southern Ocean, Bligh excelled himself in his care of the men. Sauerkraut, dried cabbage and portable soup were served as anti-scorbutics, and every morning the sailors were given warm gruel for breakfast. Spruce beer alternated with grog, and the ship was kept meticulously clean and warm, with fires burning in both cockpits (which made it intolerably smoky below). His men admired Bligh's seamanship, for as Tobin remarked, he had 'the quickest sailor's eye, guided by a thorough knowledge of every branch of the profession necessary on such a voyage. It is easy of belief that on first joining a man of such experience, my own youth and inferiority were rather busy visitors. [Nevertheless], I had courage to believe that my captain was not dissatisfied with me.'[38] As always, Bligh was at his best as a mentor. It was when his superiority was challenged or his high standards were not met – especially by his immediate subordinates – that he became quick to insist upon his authority. According to Frank Bond, during this passage the men nicknamed Bligh 'the Don', likening him to a Spanish grandee in his arrogance and pride (although probably this nickname was more often used in the wardroom than among the sailors).

As the ships headed north towards the tropics, Bligh's terrible headaches returned to plague him. Nevertheless, there are poetic moments in his journal – for instance, on 16 March 1792, as they sailed through colonies of phosphorescent seaworms like 'thousands of small lamps lighted on the water'; or a meteor blazed across the sky, 'like a plate of burning brandy held in the wind'. En route to Tahiti, the ships sailed within 500 miles of Pitcairn's Island, where unknown to Bligh, Fletcher Christian's band of 'pirates' had settled.

Although Bligh knew nothing about Fletcher Christian's fate at this time, after the mutineers' final departure from Tahiti, there had been dramatic developments on board the *Bounty*. These are best recorded in accounts by 'Jenny', one of the Tahitian women whom they kidnapped; and by Alexander Smith in 1825, during a meeting with Captain Beechey on Pitcairn's Island.[39]

According to these narratives, on 23 September 1789 after Fletcher Christian had cut the *Bounty*'s anchor cable, he sailed away from Tahiti with eight of his *Bounty* shipmates on board, accompanied by two men from Tupua'i, one man from Ra'iatea and fourteen Tahitians (three men and eleven women). In his journey, he was guided by Bligh's surveys and charts, including his personal copy of the official account of Cook's last voyage, which Bligh had profusely annotated in pencil.[40]

After leaving Tahiti, Christian had headed for the southern Cook Islands, where they visited an island called 'Purutea'. When a canoe from this island approached the *Bounty*, and one of its men admired the pearl-shell buttons on Christian's uniform jacket, Christian allowed him to put it on. As the man stood on the gunwale, preening himself, however, one of the mutineers shot him, to Christian's fury, and he toppled into the ocean.[41] It has been suggested that this island was Rarotonga, because according to the missionary John Williams, who visited that island in 1823, the people told him about the visit of a ship that he identified as the *Bounty*, where one man had gone on board. According to Williams, when this man returned:

> He told his astonished countrymen that it was a floating island; that there were two rivers flowing on it; that two large *taro* plantations, with sugar-cane, bread-fruit, and other trees, were growing there, that the keel scraped the bottom of the ocean, for he dived as deep as man could go, and could not see its termination.
>
> I account for these singular statements, by supposing that the pumps were

at work while the man was on board, which he mistook for rivers, or streams, and that the two plantations, bread-fruit trees, etc. were the large boxes which were fitted up throughout this vessel for these exotics. From this vessel was obtained a pointed piece of iron, about two feet six inches in length, which the natives immediately dedicated to the gods.[42]

Most of the breadfruit plants had been thrown overboard from the *Bounty*, although the mutineers had kept a few for their own use, and brought a variety of other island plants on board, including the seeds of sweet potatoes and yams.[43] Another oral account recorded in 1823 identified the captain of this ship as Makere (McCoy?), and described the taro plants, young banana and breadfruit trees on board, saying that their first oranges were stolen from this vessel.[44] Although these hints may be suggestive, however, they do not prove that this ship was the *Bounty*, or that the island they visited was Rarotonga.

Christian and his shipmates also visited Tongatapu in the Tongan archipelago, where the local inhabitants spoke about Captain Cook's visit to that island, reporting that the horned cattle that he had left ashore were still living;[45] and 'Vivini', an atoll in the southern Lau Islands (perhaps Ono-i-lau, or Vatoa), where they collected birds, eggs and coconuts, searching for a fertile uninhabited island where they could settle. Finally, after thumbing through Bligh's set of Hawkesworth's *Voyages* (1773), Christian found Carteret's description of Pitcairn's Island, which he had discovered during the *Swallow*'s Pacific crossing in 1767. After the *Swallow* and the *Dolphin* had been separated by a storm, Carteret sighted Pitcairn's Island, making an error of three degrees in its longitude, while Hawkesworth made a further error of five degrees in its latitude in his published account of the voyage.[46] According to Carteret, this tiny, remote, high island had both forest and fresh water, although it took Christian two months of beating into the trade winds to locate his promised land.

It was midsummer when they arrived off Pitcairn (or Hiti-au-rereva, as the Tahitians called it),[47] but the weather was so wild and boisterous that Christian was forced to wait for three long days before going ashore. On 15 January 1790 when the Tahitians told him that a landing might be possible, he went ashore with an armed party – Brown, Williams, McCoy and three of their Tahitian companions. When they returned to the ship two days later, Fletcher Christian wore 'a joyful expression such as we had not seen on him for a long time past'. As Carteret had reported, the island was fertile, temperate and uninhabited, with no safe landing place – a perfect haven. After shifting the *Bounty* to Bounty Bay, Fletcher and his men stripped everything useful out of the ship, floating these items ashore on a raft tied to the rocks and carrying them up the 'Hill of Difficulty' to a small grassy flat below the island's main *marae*. Although Pitcairn was uninhabited at the time of their arrival, it had formerly been occupied, as they could see from the ancient *marae*, where four stone gods still stood upright as sentinels over the island; the pictographs carved into the cliffs; the stone house platforms; and numerous stone adzes, gouges and other tools that were strewn upon the ground.

After making temporary shelters with *ti* leaves and saplings, the mutineers and their island companions began to build permanent houses on the plateau where the village of Adamstown now stands, mostly two-storeyed cottages with upstairs loft bedrooms, around a fenced common, using timbers from the *Bounty*. Although they cleared the ground for gardens, a row of trees was left to screen the village from any passing ships. They had brought pigs, chickens and goats with them from Tahiti, as well as yam and sweet potato seeds, although bark-cloth trees, taro, coconut trees, breadfruit, plantain, bananas and sugar cane were already growing ashore.

When the houses were ready, Fletcher Christian, Adams and most of the mutineers agreed that the *Bounty* should be wrecked on the rocks. Fearful that the masts might betray them, however, that night Matthew Quintal went out and set fire to the carpenter's storeroom.[48] As the ship burned to the water line, 'all were in tears at seeing her in flames'.[49] After the burning of the *Bounty*, the mutineers lived peacefully together for a time, Fletcher Christian settling down with his stately high-born wife Isabella (or Mauatua), who was pregnant. When their first son was born on a Thursday in October 1790, they named him 'Thursday October Christian' to commemorate his birthday; and over the next three years, Mauatua bore him two more children. William McCoy lived with his wife Mary (or Te'o) and her little daughter Sully by a previous partner, a baby who according to island tradition had been floated ashore in a barrel;[50] while John Mills lived with his partner Prudence (or Vahineatua), who gave him a daughter.

Most of the other liaisons were volatile and shifting, however. Although Jenny (or Te'ehuteatuaonoa) accompanied Alexander Smith on board the *Bounty*, during their search for a new home she had an affair with Isaac Martin and lived with him on Pitcairn's Island; while Smith took up with Puarai, one of the Tahitian women whom they had kidnapped. The other sailors – the midshipman Edward Young; William Brown the assistant gardener; the gunner's mate John Mills; and the able-bodied sailors Quintal and Williams – also took partners from among the kidnapped women. The midshipman Ned Young claimed the beautiful young girl Susannah (or Teraura), while John Williams took the fleet-footed Fa'ahotu, and Matthew Quintal lived with Sarah (or Tevarua), abusing her brutally during their liaison.[51]

As shipmates who had both joined the *Bounty* from their old ship, the *Triumph*, Matthew Quintal and William McCoy were often together.[52] They regarded the Tahitian men as their servants, forcing them to do much of the hard work in their gardens. Although it is said that Christian, Young and Adams treated the islanders kindly, none of the British regarded these men as their equals. While the young high-born Ra'iatean, Tararo, had his own wife, To'ofaiti, the Tupua'i chief Ta'aroamiva (or Tetahiti, as he was known on Pitcairn) and his servant Oha had to share one woman (Tinafanaea); and the three Tahitian commoners had only one woman (Mareva) between them.

About three years after their arrival on Pitcairn, these tensions came to a climax. After John Williams's wife Fa'ahotu died, either from yaws or by falling off a cliff (according to different reports), he demanded a woman to replace her. When he threatened to leave the island with one of the *Bounty*'s boats, his shipmates forced the island men to draw lots, and To'ofaiti was forcibly taken from Tararo and handed over to Williams. Distraught at losing his wife, the young Ra'iatean plotted with the two islanders from Tupua'i to kill the white men and retrieve To'ofaiti, although she evidently preferred John Williams. One day she sang to herself, 'Why does black man sharpen axe? To kill white man', in the presence of Christian's wife Mauatua. When Mauatua warned her husband, Christian threatened the ringleaders with his musket and fired at them (although he had only loaded it with powder), so they fled into the bush. Three days later, however, Tararo, seeing To'ofaiti fishing on the reef, persuaded her to join him. By a combination of threats and promises, the Europeans now persuaded Manari'i, one of the Tahitian commoners, to shoot Oha, the Tupua'i servant, and afterwards with the help of the faithless To'ofaiti, he also shot Tararo, her former partner.

After this spate of murders, an uneasy peace prevailed for several months, but McCoy and Quintal continued to mistreat the surviving male islanders, beating them and rubbing salt in their wounds as an extra punishment. Although Bligh knew nothing about the fate of the mutineers on Pitcairn, he would have been gratified by the bloody cataclysm that occurred about eighteen months after he sailed past the island. One day when Manari'i took one of McCoy's pigs and his *taio* took yams from Quintal's garden, these two men were flogged. Infuriated by the punishment, they talked with the other male islanders and agreed to wipe out the British. In late September 1793, while the sailors were working in different parts of the island, the Tupua'i chief Tetahiti, who had borrowed a musket ostensibly to shoot wild pigs, shot and killed John Williams, who was building a fence in his garden. Afterwards, accompanied by the three Tahitians, he found his own *taio* Fletcher Christian clearing a garden and shot him in the back, smashing in his head with an axe and leaving his body on the ground. As Christian groaned in his death agony, McCoy heard him, although Mills thought that it was Mauatua, calling her husband to dinner.

After killing Christian, the Tahitians shot and wounded the American sailor, Isaac Martin. When he ran to Brown's house, they shot him a second time and killed him, smashing in his head with a hammer. William Brown was also club-bed down, and although one of the Tahitians pretended to shoot him, trying to save his life, he staggered to his feet and Manari'i saw him, shooting him in the back.[53] Next Tetahiti managed to separate McCoy and Mills, luring McCoy into an ambush by saying that the Tahitians were stealing things from his house. As he ran towards his dwelling, they shot at him but missed, and he hurried to warn Mills, who was so certain that his *taio* would protect him that when McCoy and Quintal fled into the mountains, Mills stayed behind and was shot in his turn. By this time, the Tahitian women had warned Edward Young (a favourite among them, with his dark skin and West Indian blood), and Alexander Smith (known on Pitcairn by his true name, John Adams), who fled into the mountains. When Adams returned to collect food from his gardens, Tetahiti shot him in the right shoulder and neck, and when he parried a blow from the butt of a musket, the little fingers on his left hand were smashed. Although Tetahiti tried to shoot him again, poking the musket in his side, the gun misfired, and Adams fled to Christian's house, where the women threw themselves across his body, protec-ting him from their male compatriots.

After these killings, the 'blacks', as Adams always called them, began to quarrel over the women. Within a week, one of the Tahitian men, Manari'i, shot another, Teimua, who was playing his nose flute to allure the seductive Teraura. As Teimua lay wounded, Manari'i shot him again and killed him. After trying to shoot Tetahiti, Christian's *taio*, Manari'i ran into the mountains and joined McCoy and Quintal, offering to work for them. At the urging of their shipmates, however, they shot him, and as a reward, were allowed to return to the village. Angry at the deaths of their European husbands, the women now plotted with Edward Young to kill the two surviving island men. As the Tupua'i chief Tetahiti slept beside William Brown's widow, Edward Young's beguiling wife Teraura cut off his head with an axe; and soon afterwards Young shot Niau, the last of the male Tahitians.

Although these deaths were followed by a period of peace, the surviving mutineers still abused the Tahitian women. The following year, the women tried to escape from the island on a boat, which sank just off the coast. Afterwards, they made several unsuccessful attacks on the white men, trying to kill them all. In 1798, William McCoy, who had worked in a Scottish distillery, managed to make a potent spirit from the roots of the *ti* plant, which led to drunken abuse and many fiery quarrels. In 1799 when Matthew Quintal's wife died, he tried to take Young's wife, and declared that he would murder both Young and Adams, who got together and killed him with an axe. Shortly afterwards, McCoy, mad with drink, drowned himself at sea; and in 1800 Edward Young died of an asthma attack, leaving John Adams (formerly Alexander Smith) as the sole surviving *Bounty* mutineer on Pitcairn Island, with ten Tahitian women.

Although Pitcairn lay quite close to the track of the *Providence* and *Assistant*, its location was inaccurately recorded in the shipboard charts, and Bligh remained oblivious to the existence of the 'pirate' settlement on this tiny island. Heading for Tahiti, he discovered Te Matangi, a low, uninhabited atoll in the Tuamotu archipelago which he named 'Lagoon Island'. He was also unaware of the fate of the *Pandora*, Edwards's visit to Tahiti and his capture of some of the *Bounty*'s men. On 1 April 1792, anticipating trouble upon their arrival in Tahiti – perhaps a clash with the 'pirates' – Bligh ordered Frank Bond to keep the officers' cabins and the between-decks clear, so that in the case of an attack, the ship could run out its guns.[54] As they sailed towards Me'eti'a on 7 April, he instructed the surgeons to examine the crews for signs of venereal disease, and had an inventory of their garments made to prevent them from bartering their clothes for sex with the Tahitian women.

The next day was a Sunday, and after hoisting the British flag and conducting divine service on their ships, Bligh and Portlock each read out a list of rules to guide the conduct of their crews when they landed on the island. In these orders, Bligh strictly forbade his men to mention Captain Cook's death or the loss of the *Bounty*; to inform the Tahitians that they had come for breadfruit; or to allow their firearms to be stolen. They were ordered to treat the islanders kindly and avoid any violence. Any sailor infected with venereal disease (four of whom had been identified on board the *Providence*) was forbidden to have sex with the local women.[55] No canoes would be permitted to come alongside at night, and the officer on watch was strictly forbidden to speak with their crews; while all barter would be handled by a person specifically appointed for that purpose.

That afternoon they arrived off the tiny high island of Me'eti'a, described by Tobin as 'one of the most beautiful spots that can be conceived',[56] where four canoes came out whose crews bartered breadfruit and coconuts for nails. When the *ari'i* or high chief, dressed in a shirt and giddy with *'ava*, came on board the *Providence*, he told Bligh that about three months earlier, two English ships (which Bligh correctly concluded must be Vancouver's vessels, which had sighted Me'eti'a on 26 December 1791) had sailed past his island en route to Tahiti. When the *Providence* set sail again, this man and his companions jumped overboard, clutching their European goods, and swam ashore.

# This Modern Cyprus

At daylight on 9 April 1792, when the blue mountains of Tahiti appeared on the horizon, the sailors were overjoyed to have arrived at this 'modern Cyprus [Cythera]', as Matthew Flinders called it. It had rained heavily all night, and as the ships sailed towards Point Venus, waterfalls tumbled down the mountains. Crowds of people stood on the beaches, and canoes paddled inside the reef where others were collecting shellfish or fishing, although they did not seem surprised by the sight of the European vessels [PLATE 19]. Vancouver had sailed from Matavai Bay only ten weeks earlier, having managed to offend most of the leading chiefs on the island; and at noon when the *Providence* and *Assistant* anchored in Matavai Bay, and a cask of spruce beer was served to the sailors, to their amazement, a whaleboat raced out, crewed by seven European sailors, all wearing Tahitian bark-cloth costumes.

When Mr Norris, a ship's surgeon, boarded the *Providence*, he told Bligh a terrible tale. Their vessel, the *Matilda*, a transport commanded by Captain Matthew Weatherhead, had carried 230 convicts to New South Wales, but after heading for South America on a whaling voyage, they crashed onto the reef of Vanavana in the Actaeon group.[1] After taking to the boats, Weatherhead and his men had sailed 700 miles to Me'eti'a, where the *ari'i* treated them kindly. Off the coast of Tahiti, however, the boats were scattered by a storm; and on 6 March 1792, just six weeks after Vancouver's departure, two of the boats had landed at Matavai Bay (one carrying Norris, Connor [an Irish sailor] and their companions; the other commanded by Captain Weatherhead). Although the chiefs at Matavai Bay gave them shelter at first, they soon stripped them of their guns, money and papers. The third boat (which carried a Scotsman, James Butcher, among others)[2] landed in Papara, Teri'irere's district; while the fourth boat came ashore at Pare (carrying Marshall, the first mate; Campbell, the second mate;

and a Swedish sailor Andrew Lind, a man in his late twenties from Stockholm).[3] At Pare, Pomare II's district, the sailors were also stripped of their possessions, although otherwise they were treated kindly. While the British had been furious about losing their possessions, this was in keeping with local custom, by which the chief of a district had the right to claim any flotsam and jetsam, including drifting canoes, their crews and cargo.

According to Norris, the *Matilda*'s men soon discovered that the Matavai people, led by Po'e'eno and Tapairu (his brother, who had lured away several of the *Bounty*'s crew during Bligh's last visit to the island, acquiring a number of muskets), were desperate to assert their independence from Pomare II, the paramount chief at Pare. After confiscating five muskets and a quantity of Spanish dollars from Captain Weatherhead and his men, the Matavai chiefs had commandeered the two whaleboats that landed in their district, ordering the sailors to row them to Pare. When they arrived there, on their instructions Norris, in the name of the King of England, demanded the return of the guns taken from the whaleboat that had landed in that district. The Pomare family, led by Ari'ipaea and Vaetua, handed over the weapons; but when they realised that they had been tricked, and that the Matavai chiefs now had their muskets, they were bitterly angry. No doubt they threatened to take revenge upon the *Matilda*'s men in Pare, because soon afterwards, the second mate, Campbell, and two sailors, equipped only with a quadrant, a compass and mat sails, set off in their whaleboat from the island, heading for Port Jackson.

Almost as soon as they had departed, however, on 26 March 1792 a schooner from Bristol, the *Jenny* commanded by Captain Sutter, arrived in Matavai Bay, where Captain Weatherhead of the *Matilda* boarded the vessel. The *Jenny* was on her way to the north-west coast of America to trade for furs, and when she sailed from the bay five days later, Captain Weatherhead, two sailors and ten boys from the *Matilda* went with her. Weatherhead had left behind a letter, which was delivered to William Bligh upon his arrival.[4] In this letter, he complained that after spending a few days under the protection of the Matavai chiefs, all of his guns and a box containing 407 Spanish dollars, seventeen guineas, about four pounds of English silver and some clothing had been stolen, and he and his men had been stripped of their clothes and left to fend for themselves. According to Norris, after the *Jenny* sailed from the island, Ari'ipaea and Vaetua had attacked Matavai Bay, trying to retrieve the lost muskets, and on this occasion the surgeon and his shipmate Connor fought in support of Po'e'eno and his brother Tapairu, Norris almost shooting Ari'ipaea. During the battle, the Matavai chiefs were driven into the mountains and their district was ravaged, although they managed to keep five of the *Matilda*'s muskets in their possession. Although Connor, the Irishman, now had a wife on shore, Norris was desperate to leave the island.

During his visit to the *Providence*, Norris must have told William Bligh about Edwards's visit in the *Pandora*, when he captured and took away a number of the *Bounty*'s men as prisoners; and Vancouver's more recent visit, during which he had offended Ari'ipaea and Ha'amanimani, Bligh's adoptive 'brother' and 'uncle'. No doubt these insults influenced the chiefs' decision to plunder the *Matilda* castaways, since they were also British, but vulnerable. Ari'ipaea must have been very worried, however, when he learned that Norris had gone on board the *Providence*, since the ship's surgeon was an ally of their Matavai enemies and Bligh's former friends, Moana, Po'e'eno and Tapairu. Soon after Norris's arrival, several canoes hastened alongside bringing Bligh's 'old acquaintances' from Pare, including Ari'ipaea and Vaetua (Tu's younger brothers, both notable warriors), 'Itia (Tu's wife) with her favourite attendant Maititi, and Ha'amanimani (or Tutaha), the old high priest from Ra'iatea, Bligh's 'uncle', who held up a plantain branch in welcome.

Upon greeting William Bligh, these chiefs no doubt had mixed emotions. As the men of the *Bounty*, the *Pandora* and the *Matilda* had told them, during his visit on the *Bounty*, Bligh had lied to them, saying that Captain Cook was still alive in England and that he was Cook's 'son'. Indeed, Vaetua had sworn to kill Bligh if he dared to return to the island, for ill-treating his bond friend, Thomas Hayward. Since that time, however, Tu had allied himself with Captain Edwards of the *Pandora*, taking him as his *taio*; and Edwards had told them about the mutiny, and that Fletcher Christian had also lied to them, and cast Bligh adrift from the *Bounty*. They were also very angry with George Vancouver, who had insulted them; and no doubt by comparison, Bligh seemed a paragon who had treated them kindly on most occasions, even under severe provocation. Although Bligh's *mana* had been greatly damaged by his deceit, the Pare chiefs were desperate to ensure that, as Tu's bond friend, he would continue to be their ally, and not support his old friends from Matavai Bay in their efforts to assert their independence from Pare.

When they came on board the *Providence*, Ari'ipaea and 'Itia greeted Bligh warmly, presenting him with a plantain branch. 'Itia wrapped a length of bark cloth around him, and 'the ship was covered with hogs, bread-fruit, cocoanuts, plantains and apples'.[5] After telling Bligh about the visits by the *Pandora* and Captain Vancouver's two vessels, 'Itia remarked that his *taio* Tu was at Mo'orea, and would be eager to see him. Because Norris was on board, however, this meeting was uneasy; and the chiefs soon returned to Pare, leaving 'Itia and

Maititi on board with a large number of women; or as the midshipman George Tobin remarked whimsically — 'the most desirable part of their freight, which after the trying self-denial of a long voyage, shut out from the dearest solace life affords, could not but be truly acceptable'.[6]

Early the next morning, canoes flocked around the two ships, bringing out pigs, breadfruit and other fruit which their occupants bartered eagerly for iron and other European goods, offering a medium-sized pig for an iron adze while the women tried to obtain scissors, sheets and shirts. 'Itia had spent the night on board the *Providence*, and when Tobin gave her gifts, she offered to become his *taio*. At dinner with Bligh and Norris in the Great Cabin, she ate with a knife and fork, tossing down bumpers of Tenerife wine. During the meal, 'Itia told Bligh about Fletcher Christian's last visit to the island and his hasty departure, when he had cut the *Bounty*'s cable and left behind an anchor. She also told him about the *Pandora*'s visit, noting that the islanders, after retrieving the *Bounty*'s anchor, had presented it to Captain Edwards. She gave him a list of the *Bounty* sailors who had been carried away in the *Pandora*, telling him which of these men had children on the island (Stewart, McIntosh and Skinner, each of whom had a daughter; and Burkett and Millward, each of whom had a son). Bligh was elated to hear that Edwards had captured a number of the 'pirates', exclaiming that night in his journal: 'It may readily be believed that I found great satisfaction and pleasure to hear of these Wretches all being taken by Captain Edwards, except two who were killed by the Indians.'[7]

In addition, 'Itia described Vancouver's five-week visit to Tahiti, saying that after his ships sailed away, a terrible epidemic had swept across the island, killing so many people 'that they speak of the Ships with a degree of horror and declare that [the disease] was caught on board'.[8] During his visit, Vancouver had insulted Ha'amanimani, 'Oro's high priest from Ra'iatea, and it seems that the epidemic was understood as a punishment by the war god. Although Bligh was held responsible for his compatriot's conduct, and its consequences, the Pomare lineage needed him as their ally; and 'Itia pleaded with him to remain loyal to his *taio* Tu, and assist them in their struggle with the Matavai people.

Later that day when the Pare chiefs returned to the ship, their canoes laden with gifts, 'Itia presented Tobin with a large pig, clothed him in a *tiputa* (like a poncho made of bark cloth), wrapped a very long length of bark cloth around his waist and kissed him. After they had pressed noses and exchanged names, he gave her gifts in return. At the same time, the other chiefs took their own *taio* — Ari'ipaea (who according to Portlock was 'an Excellent figure of a man, remarkably strong and commanding')[9] taking Lieutenant Bond as his friend, while the old priest Ha'amanimani adopted Lieutenant Pearce, and Vaetua took the *Providence*'s surgeon Edward Harwood as his *taio*. Matthew Flinders gave a vivid account of this custom, which as it now applied to Europeans, had been transformed into a kind of barter:

> I thought the Custom they have of each selecting a Tayo or Friend rather singular . . . if you consented he went to his Canoe and brought two Pieces of Cloth, the one a square piece generally with a Hole cut in the Middle to put the Head in, he put over your Shoulders, the other a long white piece and much finer than the other he draped round you perhaps ten or twelve Yards long according to the Quality of your Tayo & this he accompanies with a Hog perhaps two and a Quantity of Bread fruit and Cocoa-nutts – the next Day you will have him again but with his Present not quite so large the first Day he will receive nothing from you but the second or third if you press him he will receive your Present in return which will mostly consist of a Shirt, a Hatchet, looking Glass and a few other Trifles all which he will be much delighted with.
>
> Afterwards you will find him not so scrupulous; his Presents will come about once in three or four Days and he will take the Liberty to ask for what he wants which will often be every thing he sees and if he knows you have given anything to any body else he will not fail to reproach you for it, for they look upon a Man as perjured if he has two Tayos, you must take Care your Presents are not too large at first, for if they much exceed his or he thinks he has got [the] greatest part of your Trade, you may trust not to seeing him again.[10]

On 11 April the weather was fine, and Bligh left the ship early to visit Pomare II at Pare. The young paramount chief, who was 'flying' on his attendant's shoulders, had grown into 'a fine Youth', and Bligh presented him with lavish gifts, although their meeting was relatively informal. Using a switch to beat back the crowd, Pomare II greeted Bligh warmly, holding his hand as he urged him to shift the ships back to the anchorage in Pare. This was a remarkable change from Bligh's previous visit on the *Bounty*, when he had been allowed to talk with Pomare II only at a distance, across a river. When Bligh met Terano, the widow of Te Pau, the high chief of Fa'a'a whom he had befriended during his previous visit, she hung around his neck, thanking the *atua* (god) who had saved him from the loss of the *Bounty*, and saying that since his last visit, her husband died from the cancer in the roof of his mouth that had plagued him, and been succeeded by his younger brother. She added that Mou'aroa (Teu's elder brother, also known as Teri'i-hinoi-atua), with whom Bligh had often talked, had also died shortly after Captain Vancouver's departure and was now lying on a funerary bier at Pare; and that Hitihiti had sailed with Captain Edwards to Ra'iatea. In the heat of the day, Bligh's headache returned. Almost blinded by the pain, he was forced to farewell these people and return to Matavai Bay.

As he was rowed back to the *Providence*, Bligh saw a large group of Pare warriors gathering on the low ground at Matavai Bay, led by Ari'ipaea and Vaetua, both of whom wore *taumi* or breastplates, confronting the Matavai army, commanded by his bond friend Po'e'eno and his younger brother Tapairu (who had helped some of his men to desert from the *Bounty*). In all, about 1300 warriors were assembled on the beach. When they began to sling stones at each other, Ha'amanimani hurried out to the *Providence*, urging Bligh to assist the family of his *taio*, Tu, who were trying to retrieve 'King George's muskets'. Although he refused to land the marines or fire at the Matavai warriors, Bligh promised that he would not allow them to pass Tahara'a (One Tree Hill), and sent Norris ashore to order Po'e'eno and Tapairu to hand over the *Matilda*'s muskets. With this action, he had chosen to take sides with Tu and the Pomare family.

When Norris returned to the ship, he reported that upon his arrival, he had been led through the crowd of warriors, all armed with long spears and slings, who were very anxious to know what Bligh was planning. He spoke to the Matavai chiefs, who promised that they would surrender the guns in a day or two, but refused to do so immediately (hardly surprising, under the circumstances). As soon as Norris embarked on the boat and was rowed back to the *Providence*, the armies engaged, the warriors hurling spears and rocks and occasionally firing muskets at each other, until one of the Matavai men was shot through the head with a musket ball. When he fell, the Matavai warriors retreated into the hills, standing behind trees at intervals to fire their muskets, pursued by the Pare army who began to burn their houses and canoes. That evening when Tu's family visited the ship, they reported that Tapairu's men had retreated about 8 miles east to the hills behind Pare, foully cursing their enemies in English. As Bligh remarked in dismay, they used such 'vile and blackguard expressions [that] I declare I would rather forfeit any thing than to have been in the list of Ships that have touched here since April 1789'.[11]

Early the next morning, the carpenters began to caulk the side of the *Providence* and the sailors repaired the rigging. A messenger came to inform Bligh that the Matavai people had been driven into the mountains, and that the fighting would stop as soon as Tu arrived from Mo'orea. On shore, canoes were landing people from Pare who plundered the bay, seizing everything portable and loading it into their canoes, including the sides of houses. When Ari'ipaea came out to the ships, he urged Bligh to stay on board the *Providence* until Tu arrived from Mo'orea, when a peacemaking ritual would be held.

Soon afterwards, a man who had stolen some clothing from the *Assistant* was brought on board the *Providence* and thrown in irons; although when Ari'ipaea assured Bligh that this man was insane, he had him released. Later that evening, the same man was found clinging to the *Assistant*'s cable; and when Portlock took a boat to chase him, he swam and dived so quickly, even after being hit in the head with a boathook, that if Maititi had not dived overboard and grabbed him, he would have escaped. He was delivered to the *Providence*, and put back in irons. That night Lieutenant Portlock set up a swivel and two brass blunderbusses on the deck of the *Assistant*, although as Lieutenant Bond remarked drily, there was very little danger from the local warriors: 'The Natives were observed daily to make attacks on the enemy, as one Parish might assault another in England, but little danger attended those expeditions, and the death of one or two men made a bloody campaign.'[12]

By 13 April 1792, Matavai Bay was almost deserted. Although the Season of Scarcity was approaching, canoes from Pare kept arriving alongside the ships, laden with pigs, breadfruit, plantains, taro, coconuts and *vi* or Tahitian apples, no doubt plundered from their Matavai enemies. In the hot, sultry conditions, Bligh's headache was atrocious. He ordered the *Providence* to be shifted closer to Point Venus, so that the ship's guns could cover the shore camp; and when 'Itia came on board and asked for a boat to fetch Tu from Mo'orea, he spoke to her brusquely, saying that if she wanted to retain his friendship, she should go herself. Alarmed by his tone, 'Itia took a double sailing canoe and set off at once to Mo'orea, promising that if the weather was fine, she would return with Tu in two days' time. When Bligh told Ari'ipaea that he was not willing to wait for Tu's arrival before setting up the shore camp, Ari'ipaea escorted him ashore and they fixed on a site close to the Tuauru River, where the chief promised to clear the ground and erect a large shed for the breadfruit plants, and two small houses for the officers and the men on duty.

Later that day, Bligh sent George Tobin and Ari'ipaea in the cutter to Pare to collect the *Matilda*'s first mate Marshall, who was still living in that district. When Tobin landed at Pare, carrying gifts from Bligh, Pomare II greeted him courteously, riding on his attendant's shoulders. Tobin described the paramount chief as 'a youth about twelve years of age; his countenance free and open, yet with much curiosity painted in it'.[13] Telling the midshipman to hand his gifts to his attendants, Pomare II gazed eagerly at some buttons on the petty officer's sleeve, which were cut off and given to him. Upon their return to Matavai Bay, where a number of sailing canoes were arriving from Mo'orea, Tobin remarked upon the tall, narrow sails. Ari'ipaea explained that these canoes often capsized in contrary winds, and that during a recent trip to Teti'aroa, his own double canoe had tipped over, and he and his wife and attendants had spent several hours in the sea before being rescued by another canoe. When one of these craft swamped, the crew would jump into the sea and, moving the hull back and forwards, forced the water out over each end. After this conversation with Tobin, Ari'ipaea went off to the *Assistant* where he presented Lieutenant Portlock with a gift of a pig, two dozen coconuts and dressed breadfruit, saying that he intended to sleep at Point Venus that night so that early the next morning, he could begin work on the shore camp. By nightfall, however, Ari'ipaea had returned to the *Providence*, where he drank a great deal of *'ava no Peretane* (British *kava* or grog) at supper and became very animated, making exuberant promises to his new *taio* Lieutenant Bond.

At dawn the next morning when Portlock and Bligh went to Point Venus, they found Ari'ipaea and his people already hard at work, clearing the site. At Ari'ipaea's urging, Bligh sent Norris back to Po'e'eno and Tapairu to demand the return of Captain Weatherhead's money and the muskets from the *Matilda*. When Ha'amanimani arrived at the shore camp, Portlock invited him to dinner on board the *Assistant*, describing the old high priest as one of 'the most intelligent men of the Island' who could speak some words of English very plainly, and was 'always delighted to be taught more'.[14] By nightfall, a fence had been built around the shore camp, and a house about 90 feet long and 18 feet wide for the plants was already two-thirds completed.

Early the next morning, a Sunday, Norris returned to the *Providence* and reported that Po'e'eno had fled to Ha'apaino'o on the east coast, where the local chief had given him refuge. Although Po'e'eno greeted him kindly, promising to return the money as soon as he could retrieve it from the islets of Teti'aroa, where it had been taken for safekeeping, he had adamantly refused to hand over the muskets to Norris unless the Pare people also surrendered their guns; saying defiantly that if he was attacked, he would retreat to a narrow pass in the mountains and fight to the death. During his meeting with Norris, Po'e'eno seemed very sad, begging that Bligh, his former friend and ally, not be angry with him. He told Norris that it was the commoners who had plundered the *Matilda*'s boats and stripped the sailors, and that he and Tapairu had been unable to stop them. After describing Matavai Bay as 'Bligh's own country' (a reference to the fact that Bligh had been installed as an *ari'i* of Matavai Bay during his *Bounty* visit), Po'e'eno lamented that the Pare warriors had destroyed their houses, barked the trees and ruined their gardens. When Norris met Tapairu, who had been wounded in the recent battle, the chief asked the surgeon to cure him; and ruefully confessed that he and Po'e'eno had only forty balled cartridges left between them.

Although Bligh felt some sympathy for his *taio* Po'e'eno and his family, the conflict between them and Tu's family had forced him to take sides, and he decided to throw in his hand with the Pomare lineage. Fortunately, as he remarked, despite the ravages by the Pare warriors, there were still plenty of breadfruit plants left in the district. He had already demonstrated the best techniques for transplanting breadfruit to Banks's gardeners, and recruited several Tahitians who had previously worked with David Nelson during his *Bounty* visit. One of these men, Paupo, took James Wiles as his *taio*, working with him devotedly during their time on the island. After mustering the crew and performing divine service, Bligh put the men on a short allowance of liquor, since there was plenty of coconut milk, so that their grog could be shared with the remaining crew of the *Matilda*. When Lieutenant Bond went ashore, Ari'ipaea treated his *taio* to a feast of dog, a chiefly food on the island. The dog was smothered, its hide singed and scraped to remove the hair, and the carcass was cut up and cleaned. Layers of small stones alternating with wood were laid in a shallow hole, and a fire was lit to heat the stones. When the stones were hot, the wood was removed, and some of the stones were spread in the bottom of the hole and covered with green leaves upon which the dog was laid, wrapped in leaves. The oven was sealed with earth and left for about four hours, after which the meat was taken out, perfectly cooked and delicious. As Bond remarked, these dogs were regarded as chiefly food, 'bred for eating, living only on breadfruit, cocoanuts, yams and other vegetables'.[15] Visiting the shore camp later that afternoon, Bligh and Portlock found that Ari'ipaea's people had made good progress with the two houses for the marines, while the shade house for the plants and a small house for the officers were completed, although the officers' house had been built too close to the Tuauru River, and Bligh asked Ari'ipaea to have it shifted.

On 16 April, Bligh sent a party to occupy the shore camp at Point Venus. Apart from the two gardeners, Wiles and Smith, and the breadfruit plants under their shade house, this 'post' was a military establishment, manned by Lieutenant Pearce and twenty of his marines from Chatham; together with Lieutenant Guthrie, the second lieutenant of the *Providence*, two midshipmen, a master's mate and Norris, the *Matilda*'s surgeon, who was acting as an interpreter and mediator with the Tahitians. After the difficulties he experienced with Fletcher Christian, who had commanded the shore camp during his *Bounty* visit, Bligh was taking no chances on this occasion. Matavai Bay was quiet, with no more skirmishing, although while a cargo of garden pots was being loaded into the boats, the man who had tried to rob the *Assistant* jumped off the deck of the *Providence*, still in irons, and had to be rescued from drowning.

Later that day, Bligh's other bond friend, Tu, arrived from Mo'orea in a double canoe with 'Itia and her younger sister Vaiareti, accompanied by his father Teu in another canoe. Tobin described Tu as a tall, muscular, lightly tattooed man about forty-five years old; and Teu as 'a venerable old man apparently about seventy; very grey and infirm, and whose skin was much affected from drinking of *kava*'.[16] Delighted to be reunited with his bond friend, Bligh ordered a ten-gun salute to be fired, although it made Tu tremble with fear. In Tu's canoe, the portrait of Captain Cook was prominently displayed; and when he came on board the *Providence*, his *taio* presented Bligh with a large pig, breadfruit, plantains and coconuts, while Vaiareti wrapped him in lengths of bark cloth. In return, Bligh presented Tu with a suit of crimson cloth decorated with gold lace on the cape and sleeves, and each of his two wives with printed calico nightgowns. Despite these exchanges, however, their encounter was unceremonious. As Bligh lamented in his journal that night: 'It is rather a difficulty to get them to speak their own language without mixing a jargon of English, and they are so generally altered, that I believe no European in future will ever know what their ancient Customs of Receiving Strangers were.'[17]

Notwithstanding the informality of their meeting, Tu and Teu seemed genuinely delighted to see Bligh again. They exclaimed how glad they were that he was still alive, and said that when they heard the mutineers had marooned him in a little boat without food or drink and set him adrift, they were sure that he must have died. They asked Bligh whether he had seen King George, and what the King had said to him; congratulating him on his fine new vessel. When Bligh reproached Tu for having treated Fletcher Christian so kindly, Tu explained that when the *Bounty* had returned to the island for the first time, he believed Christian when he said that Bligh had gone to England. It was only when the *Bounty* returned from Tupua'i that he learned about the mutiny; and he had been so angry with Christian that the young man had stayed on shore only a few hours, departing the island in such a hurry that he left an anchor behind. After hearing this account, Bligh forgave his *taio* – 'Thus he freed himself from any suspicion on my side, & with his usual good nature and cheerfulness regained my esteem and regard.'[18] According to Portlock: 'It was a very happy meeting of old friends and their joy was so great that it was now visible in all countenances ... This King is one of the most friendly and best disposed men in the world, he still looks remarkably well and is much belovd by his subjects.'¹⁹

When Captain Cook's portrait was brought into the Great Cabin, Bligh inspected the back of the painting, noting that his own record of the *Bounty*'s visit was now followed by the dates of the visits by the *Pandora* and Vancouver's ships, although there was no record of the *Bounty*'s visit under Fletcher Christian, or the capture of the *Bounty* sailors by the *Pandora*. Later, he lamented that Captain Edwards had not left behind a detailed report of what had happened during his visit. On deck, when Tu noticed the man in irons he laughed, saying that this man was *nevaneva* or crazy; and asked Bligh to release him. As soon as he was freed, the man jumped up joyously, leaped overboard and swam ashore. During this meeting, Bligh was surprised to learn that since his last visit to the island, Tu had taken Vaiareti, 'Itia's younger sister (who had previously been married to Vehiatua III), as his second wife, although he noted that she was much prettier than 'Itia. Since her deceased husband had no surviving brothers (or according to island custom, she would have married one of them), Tu had married Vaiareti instead, and she and her elder sister 'Itia seemed on the best of terms.

That afternoon when Tobin went to get something from the cabin of Lieutenant Guthrie (who was ashore at the post), he was startled to find Vaiareti and Ari'ipaea making love – 'nor should I have entered the six foot cabin of my friend Guthrie – at least without knocking – had I in the slightest degree suspected it had been converted into a rendezvous for gallantry'.²⁰ As Bligh had previously reported, chiefly brothers sometimes slept with each other's wives, the women regarding this as an honour. Afterwards when 'Itia visited her *taio* Tobin, however, presenting him with a pig, some breadfruit and lengths of bark cloth that she wrapped around him, she tried to protect her younger sister by begging him to keep his discovery a secret from Tu, who might be jealous of this amorous encounter.

At supper that evening, 'Itia and Vaiareti ate with the menfolk, breaking the usual restriction upon the sexes dining together; and Tu was 'crammed like a turkey' by his 'feeder' while Tobin poured wine down his throat. During the meal, Tu and Teu railed against Po'e'eno and his Matavai people, asking Bligh to attack and destroy them, along with the people at Papara and Vaitepiha Bay who had also acquired a number of muskets. They explained that when Teri'irere's men at Papara had sacked the *Resolution*, the little schooner built by the *Bounty*'s men, they seized their muskets; and they also confiscated some guns from the *Matilda*'s boat when it landed in their district. Although Bligh refused to wage war on his *taio*'s enemies, saying that it would interfere with his task of collecting the breadfruit, he promised Tu that he would try to recover the money and the muskets from the *Matilda*.

Early the next morning when Bligh and Portlock landed at the shore camp, Pomare II paid them a visit, riding on his attendant's shoulders, proudly wearing a scarlet jacket that Pearce, the lieutenant of marines, had given him. Pomare was now unabashed about asking for gifts, identifying the objects in English and offering presents in return; and during this visit he stayed in the shade of a bread-fruit tree when it rained, rather than coming inside the shelter. Although Bligh invited the young paramount chief to visit him on board the *Providence*, the *ari'i maro 'ura* was still so sacred that he could not visit the ships, and did not accept the invitation. On this occasion Pomare II was accompanied by his attendant, an albino man with light grey, squinting eyes, flaxen hair and eyebrows and white skin that blistered in the sun, whom Bligh remembered from his *Bounty* visit.

Although Pomare II could not join Bligh on board the *Providence*, Tu, his wives, Ari'ipaea and Ha'amanimani dined with him; after a hearty meal they boarded the cutter, which rowed them to Pare. Thanking Bligh for this courtesy and for his ten-gun salute of welcome, Tu remarked with satisfaction that 'it will show all his enemies that we are good Friends'.[21] After the Pare chiefs had departed, Matavai Bay seemed desolate and empty. Almost all of the houses had been burned or demolished in the wake of the recent fighting, and the place was deserted. As Bligh reflected, this was perhaps just as well, because his headaches were now so bad that he felt sickened with pain. During that day, the gardeners found a place up the Tuauru River valley to gather breadfruit, and potted thirty-two plants; although when Bligh realised that they had forgotten to put shells or gravel in the bottom of the pots for drainage, he made them plant them all again.

On 18 April 1792 the weather was hot and sultry, and Bligh's headache was so severe that he stayed on board the *Providence*. Portlock visited the post, where he found the sailors digging a defensive ditch; and Pomare II paid him a visit. Portlock was impressed by the young paramount chief, describing him as about thirteen years old, active and lively, with 'a countenance that commands respect already from the Inhabitants'.[22] That morning Peggy Stewart (George Stewart's high-born wife Teria, the daughter of Te Pau) took her daughter out to the *Providence*, a very pretty, brown-skinned child about one year old. According to Frank Bond, Peggy bitterly mourned the loss of her husband, weeping incessantly for months, sleeping little and staying away from her friends and family.[23] Bligh, who was very bitter against Stewart, offered Peggy no comfort about his fate.

During their absence, Bligh missed Tu and his family, who were still at Pare, discussing the war against the Matavai chiefs. By this time, he had realised why they were so anxious to retrieve the *Matilda*'s muskets. According to his calculations, the Pare chiefs now had eight muskets and five pistols; the Vaitepiha people had five muskets and five pistols; those at Hitia'a had just one musket; the Atehuru warriors had five pistols; while the Matavai chiefs had five muskets from the *Matilda*. Teri'irere's people at Papara, however, outgunned all the other districts with an armoury of eight muskets, six pistols and a swivel gun, acquired when they had plundered the schooner built by the *Bounty* sailors and the *Matilda*'s boat.

The following evening when Tu, his wives and three attendants returned from Pare, Bligh was delighted to see them. At supper he asked Tu and 'Itia why they were both addressed as 'Pomare' (although Tu was also called 'Teina' at this time), and they explained that after their eldest daughter died from an illness which made her cough at night, they had adopted the name of the malady that killed her. As Bligh had previously noted, the chiefs on Tahiti frequently changed their names. Tu had also taken the name 'Mate' ('death'), while Ari'ipaea adopted the name 'Apopo' ('tomorrow'); and as a result, those common words became *tapu* or sacred, and had to be replaced in everyday speech with new equivalents – *pohe* instead of *mate* for illness or death; and *ananahi* (which had meant 'yesterday') instead of *apopo* ('tomorrow'). This must have been very confusing. That night, Tu and his wives and attendants took over Bligh's cabin, sleeping side by side on a mat on the floor; and during this visit to Matavai Bay, they dined with Bligh every day, and slept in his cabin every evening.

The next day when Pomare II visited the post again, riding on the shoulders of his attendant, Bligh tried to find out when the young paramount chief would be allowed to walk on the ground. He was told that this would not happen until he was fully grown, although at home in Pare, Pomare II was allowed to run around like an ordinary boy. He was so *ra'a* or sacred that a series of *amo'a* rituals was required to release him from the presence of the gods, culminating in a feast known as the *fa'atoira'a* at which a human sacrifice would be offered.[24] Although very few canoes visited the ships at this time, they were plentifully supplied with provisions; and as Bligh remarked buoyantly, 'Every thing goes on as well as I could possibly wish.'[25]

By Sunday 22 April, the gardeners had already filled 730 pots with plants; and Bligh told them to collect their plants later in the day to stop them wilting; and to gather plants from each of the different varieties of breadfruit on the island. According to Matthew Flinders: 'The Natives enumerate more than 20 varieties of this tree differing in the Time of bringing their <u>Fruit</u> to perfection, which also differs considerably in each – The Tree when in perfection is the Size of a midling Oak, affording a beautiful, extensive and almost impenetrable Shade.'[26] On board the *Providence* the sailors mustered in divisions; and Bligh inspected them, and after conducting divine service gave them shore leave, six at a time. That morning, Tobin set off with his friends the surgeons (Harwood from the *Providence*, Franklin from the *Assistant*, and Norris from the *Matilda*) on a trip to search for the source of the Tuauru River. At its mouth, the river valley was about half a mile wide, with rich, fertile soil, although all of the houses in this neighbourhood had been burned or demolished during the recent fighting. Many of the trees had been ring-barked, and some had been plastered with a poultice of clay covered with leaves to try and heal the wounds. As they climbed higher up the river, Tobin and his companions were joined by a party of thirty Matavai people who greeted them warmly, lamenting that because of the war, they were unable to visit Bligh and his people.

About 3 miles up the valley, crossing the river on their companions' shoulders, Tobin's party came to a cluster of inhabited houses beside the *marae* that Bligh had visited during his *Bounty* visit. At this *marae*, four sacrificial platforms holding twelve rotting pigs stood beside a stone pavement about 12 feet square, which held twenty stone uprights, each ornamented with a woven bonnet. An old priest spoke about Captain Cook with admiration, lamenting when he heard that he had died. By this time, Bligh had realised the folly of trying to lie to the Tahitians, and lifted his prohibition on telling the islanders about the fate of Captain Cook. A little higher up the valley, they came across three fine shaddock trees from Tonga, planted by David Nelson during his 1777 visit on board the *Resolution*, although their Tahitian companions did not like the fruit (which they called '*uru no Peretane* or English breadfruit). There were no breadfruit or coconut trees in this area, where waterfalls cascaded around them.

By the time they reached Pi-'a-roa, a spectacular cataract that tumbled over a sheer cliff of basalt pillars about a hundred feet high into a wide pool [PLATE 20], most of their Tahitian companions had left them. The young men sat on a rock in midstream, refreshing themselves with drinking coconuts; and when he returned to the ship, Tobin sketched this picturesque scene. The day was passing, and they were forced to turn back before reaching the source of the river. As they climbed down the valley, carrying shaddocks for Captain Bligh, they found groups of people making small dams in the river with stones, using bushes to beat the fish into a gap where a woven basket or a landing net had been placed to catch them. Their Matavai companions refused to accompany them to the post, however, saying that it was too dangerous, and that they were terrified of the warriors from Pare.

Early the next morning before dawn, the officer on watch on the *Assistant* woke Portlock and reported that two large canoes were sailing towards the ships, although in fact they headed for the eastern side of Point Venus. A few people were beginning to straggle back to Matavai Bay; and when Bligh went ashore, he found the local people making *mahi* or fermented breadfruit. After collecting the near-ripe fruit and scraping off the rind with split bamboo, they laid these in a hole lined with green ginger leaves, where they were left to soften. When the fruit were ready several days later, the *mahi* was tightly packed, wrapped in leaves, covered with a heavy pile of stones and earth, and left to ferment for about three weeks. Finally, the *mahi* was removed from the hole, wrapped in clean breadfruit leaves and baked. This baked breadfruit was often bartered to the British, who enjoyed its light, doughy texture and slightly sweet taste, preferring it to ship's biscuits.

While Bligh was ashore on this occasion, Pomare II paid him a visit, ordering a woman and four male *'arioi* to perform a *heiva* to entertain him. Afterwards, when one of the marines was reported for having mislaid a full cartridge and one of his shirts, which he had bartered with one of the visiting *'arioi*, he was sent on board the *Providence* and punished with eighteen lashes. Returning to the ship for dinner, Bligh found that Tu and his two wives, his father Teu and his brother Vaetua had arrived with another party of *'arioi* from Mo'orea, the first strangers to visit the *Providence*. Po'e'eno had sued for peace, and the *'arioi* had arrived to assist with the ceremony. These people were led by Mahau, a fine, strapping, handsome man, 6 feet 3 inches tall, who carried the name of the former high chief of Mo'orea, who had died during Vancouver's visit. This was probably the result of a *taio* relationship, because the original Mahau had been succeeded by his son Tetuanui, a boy about four years old. When Tu showed Mahau around the *Providence*, he asked Bligh for presents to give him, describing him as a friend of Vaiareti's. As Bligh remarked with annoyance: 'Tu is a perfect fool to this Woman. She rules him as she pleases, while Iddeeah ['Itia] quietly submits, and is contented with a moderate share of influence.'

At this time, Tu and 'Itia had four living children – Pomare II, his younger brother Teri'itapunui, a sister Tahamaitua, and a small son Oroho, born since Bligh's *Bounty* visit. Soon afterwards, Tu's elder sister, Ari'ipaea Vahine, from Ra'iatea, boarded the *Providence* with Ari'ipaea and his wife Vahine Metua, a leading *'arioi* who was in a state of *ra'a* (sacred restriction). One of her close relatives had died, and she wore a lock of her relative's hair in her ear and was so sacred that she had to be fed at dinner. After their meal, Ari'ipaea offered his wife to his *taio* Lieutenant Guthrie, who in response to this courtesy, made love with her. The *'arioi* had brought *'ava* with them, and their attendants chewed the fresh root, spitting the juice into a wooden tray and straining it with bunches of grass. After drinking a large quantity of this chiefly beverage, one of the *'arioi* 'came reeling into the ward-room, displaying the symptoms of epilepsy or St. Vitus's dance'.[27] When 'Itia, who had drunk about a pint of *'ava*, offered a cup to Lieutenant Tobin, and Mahau did the same to Lieutenant Guthrie, whom he had adopted as his *taio*, the young officers decided to try it. At first they felt a pleasurable giddy sensation, and then fell into a delicious, refreshing sleep that lasted for about three hours, followed by a slight headache.

That night at sunset, the marines performed their drill at the post, watched by a curious crowd of visitors. Later, on board the ships, led by Ari'ipaea Vahine, a marvellous dancer, a group of about twenty girls performed the *heiva*, clapping, chanting and announcing 'the scandal of the day, where our names as well as those of our island friends, were frequently introduced' (no doubt including ribald comments on Vahine Metua's session with Lieutenant Guthrie).[28] According to Frank Bond:

> In their *Haivas* [*heiva*] they represent with good humour the follies of their visitors, as well as their domestic scenes; for mimickry is acquired by them with great facility, and much genius. Their dances are graceful and lascivious – those of the men by wonderful contorsions of the body & limbs, and most extravagant gestures of the countenance. The drum & flute their chief musick; the latter highly pathetic and Plaintive.[29]

By 24 April 1792, all of Tu's family were living in Matavai Bay. His father Teu had built a house on Point Venus, while Ari'ipaea erected a shelter on the beach, and Tu and his son Pomare II both had houses on the east side of the point. When Tobin and Harwood, the surgeon of the *Providence*, went for a stroll that morning to Taipipi (or 'Cockroach Point', as the *Bounty* sailors had dubbed it) on the east side of Point Venus, just inside Motu Au where Morrison and his friends had anchored their home-made schooner, they discovered that a small house had been built for Pomare II, with his double canoe hauled up outside on the beach. Because this place was *ra'a* or sacred, the young chief could stand and sit down, but as soon as he saw the British officers approaching, he became very agitated. His attendants cried out '*Atua! Atua!*' ('The god! the god!'), and the British stayed back, although Tobin sat at a safe distance to sketch 'Oro's sacred double canoe, noting a roasted pig and an offering of breadfruit, plantains and sugar cane on one of its prows, while a large bundle containing the *to 'o* or image of 'Oro, about 5 feet long and wrapped in red European cloth, lay on the other. The canoe was decorated with bunches of feathers, and a platform about 3 feet high stood near the prows, surrounded by a railing which supported a long box shaped like a coffin. This box, which held the god when the weather was bad, was shaded by a canopy of wickerwork and reeds. Two drums covered with European cloth stood on the beach, and Pomare II's small house was like a museum, packed with prized objects presented by the commanders of visiting ships, including a St George's Ensign that Captain Cook had presented to his father.

At about this time, one of the young sailors from the shore camp was married to his Tahitian lover. At her family *marae*, a runner of bark cloth about 17 yards long was laid upon the ground, leading to the stone pavement. As he and his *taio* walked along the bark cloth, the bride sat at a distance. Her father went to the *ahu* (stone platform), said some prayers and gathered leaves, laying them on the pavement while her mother took a shark's-tooth instrument and slashed her daughter's head, allowing the blood to flow onto the leaves. Afterwards, her father picked up two of these leaves, and raising them as high as his forehead, 'presented them in this fashion to his European son', binding their lineages together.[30]

Early the next morning, Tu told Captain Bligh that his *taio* Po'e'eno had asked to make peace, offering to return Captain Weatherhead's money. To ratify the truce, his son had arrived in Matavai Bay with Ha'amanimani, the high priest from Ra'iatea, who would perform a ritual in Bligh's presence. Bligh admired this old man, his 'uncle' whom he described as 'a great Orator, and highly respected for his abilities . . . the Prime Minister of Tynah [Tu], their Oracle and Historian of this country, and possesses a great fund of humour';[31] noting that the high priest had now acquired a vocabulary of more than a thousand English words. Many of the Pare people were now arriving in Matavai Bay, and occupying houses and gardens, assured of their safety by the presence of the British ships. As Portlock remarked, although some of the other chiefs in the island had wanted to join Po'e'eno and Tapairu in their rebellion against the Pomare dynasty, Bligh's arrival and his steadfast support of Tu and his family deterred them; and the Pare people now regarded Matavai Bay as conquered territory.

That afternoon, Tobin and Franklin, the surgeon of the *Assistant*, were carried by canoe to Pare. As they were paddled along the coast, the sea was as smooth as glass, brilliantly coloured fish darting below them in the lagoon. When they landed, they were joined by Franklin's *taio* Taro, a senior *'arioi* who ordered a pig to be baked for their dinner. While they were waiting, they walked to the west side of Taone Bay to a large thatched house belonging to Tu, occupied by an old Ra'iatean man who gave them a warm welcome. This house was very large, 68 yards long by 15 yards wide, and built on nine pillars 16 feet high which supported its ridgepole, with seventy-two lower pillars holding up the eaves. The old man sent his attendants to fetch coconuts, and Tobin watched curiously as the servants swarmed up the palms, gripping with a rope tied between their feet and throwing down nuts with a deft flick of the wrist so that they spiralled, landing on their points, and did not shatter.

Afterwards, they carried on to the house of Torano ('Solander', no doubt a *taio* of Dr Solander, Banks's scientific companion on board the *Endeavour*), one of Tu's female relatives, who served them with more refreshments. On their way back to Taro's house for dinner, Tobin saw a boy fishing with a rod and a line with a small noose on the end, snaring fish as they passed through gaps in the coral; and several *marae* or burying places; and he sketched a *fare tupapa'u* or funerary platform with a stage 6 feet high, carrying the body of an *ari'i*'s child wrapped in red and white bark cloth. The corpse was shaded by a canopy of reeds covered with black and white cloth and decorated with tassels of cock's feathers, and white bark-cloth curtains at the back and sides. Underneath the stage, which was surrounded by a reed fence, a large sleeping mat lay with a quantity of white bark cloth where the dead person's spirit could sleep; while a small *marae* stood nearby with a square pavement decorated with the carved stone bust of a man [PLATE 21].

At Taro's house, the roasted pig was taken out of the earth oven, wrapped in large leaves, and served on a tablecloth in the British style, laid with bamboo forks. After dinner, Tobin and Franklin walked about 2 miles back to the post, passing Tahara'a or One Tree Hill, the boundary between the Pare-'Arue and Ha'apape districts where they met a party of *'arioi* girls heading for the ships, who danced and sang for them before resuming their journey. Back at the post, they were told that Po'e'eno had returned to the bay; and that Mr Whyte, one of the surgeon's mates, had been robbed of a handkerchief during an excursion in the hills. That evening, Captain Bligh invited Tobin to join Tu and his two wives at supper, and the young man watched as Tu caressed his young wife Vaiareti, who lay seductively on a fine mat on the cabin floor. The men were delighted to be in Tahiti, and relished their time on the island.

# 20

# Belle of the Isle

At dawn on 26 April 1792, Tu and the high priest Ha'amanimani took Bligh and Lieutenant Portlock to Taipipi, the bay on the east side of Point Venus, for the peacemaking ceremony between Tu and Po'e'eno. When they arrived, Bligh found Taputapuatea, the shrine of 'Oro, standing on Pomare II's sacred canoe [PLATE 22]. Later, he described this 'ark' as comprised of a series of wooden arches or 'legs' which supported two troughs or *ro'i* (beds). One of these troughs, sheltered by a small roof, was called the *fare atua* (god-house), while the other, decorated with four carvings, was called the *marae*. Sitting in the canoe, Ha'amanimani began to pray for King George, Captain Bligh and Lieutenant Portlock, holding up a plume of red feathers fixed to the end of a bamboo stick and asking 'Oro to protect them from their enemies. As he chanted, a priest and a marine kept time by beating their drums. At the finale of the ceremony, the high priest stripped naked and held up the bundle of the god, which was wrapped in red cloth. Afterwards, Po'e'eno promised Tu that he would return the guns and the money from the *Matilda*. Although the two chiefs pressed noses as a sign of reconciliation, Portlock was sceptical, remarking, '[F]or my part, I think that they cordially hate each other, and that Poeno does not mean to observe the conditions of the peace.'[1]

Although Tu had promised to take Bligh to Pare the next day, during that afternoon he and his companions (including 'Itia) drank so much *'ava* that they could not stir from the *Providence*. During Bligh's two previous visits, Te Ra'i-puatata, the famous red feather girdle, had been kept at Atehuru, but Tu told him that this sacred relic was now held on his own *marae* at Pare. When he asked how this had happened, Tu told Bligh that after Christian's flight from the island, some of his *Bounty* crew had fought with Tu and his army, helping them to defeat the Atehuru warriors who had been forced to surrender the *maro 'ura* and Taputapuatea (the ark containing the image of 'Oro) to the Pare people; and that these sacred objects had been carried to Pare for Pomare II's installation. On this occasion, Tu introduced Bligh to another visitor, a friend of his named Mapu who had brought a human sacrifice from Mo'orea to thank 'Oro for the defeat of Po'e'eno and Tapairu. That afternoon when Bligh went ashore to inspect the breadfruit plants, he was delighted to find that one thousand pots had now been planted. As he passed a house in which Po'e'eno and his family were seated, they called out but Bligh ignored them, determined to have nothing to do with his former friends from Matavai Bay until the money and muskets from the *Matilda* had been handed over. That night, Ari'ipaea and 'Itia stayed at the post, where Ari'ipaea tried to persuade the sergeant of marines to barter five cartridges in exchange for 'curiosities'.

At dawn on 28 April, Tu and Ari'ipaea accompanied Captain Bligh, Lieutenant Bond and Mr Harwood in the cutter to Pare, where Ha'amanimani was waiting at the new *marae*, Taputapuatea, which stood beside Taraho'i *marae*, a little inland. This sacred site had a two-tiered *ahu* or stone platform about 30 feet long and 4 feet high, standing in front of a pavement with a number of stone uprights against which the priests leaned their backs. These uprights were decorated with seventeen carved wood ornaments (or *'unu* boards), some in the shape of a man and others resembling birds. Upon their arrival, the old high priest began to chant, accompanied by two *tahu'a* (priests) and two *marae* attendants, with the image of 'Oro wrapped in red cloth lying before him, and a small fish to one side. To the right of the god lay the human sacrifice from Mo'orea, trussed in the plaited branch of a coconut palm and tied to a pole; with two sacred drums, one large and one smaller, standing nearby. Beside the *marae*, Bligh could see a great *fata* or sacrificial platform about 40 feet long, decorated with a skirt of coconut leaves and laden with twenty-nine dead pigs and a medium-sized turtle. One *fare atua* (god-house) stood by the *marae* on nine strong pillars, while two others stood nearby on their canoes. On this occasion, an array of gods had been summoned to the *marae*; and Pomare II was present, sitting on his attendant's shoulders, chatting to Bligh and playing tricks throughout the ceremony.

After his opening chant, Ha'amanimani unwrapped the image of 'Oro, a bound cylinder covered with red and yellow feathers, and four others with a sennit binding that held the lesser gods. Next he unwrapped the *maro 'ura*, Te Ra'i-puatata, laying it on the pavement of the *marae*. Bligh noted that this famous girdle (which he later sketched, along with the *fata* or sacrificial platform) [PLATE 13] was about 12 feet long, with one half made of yellow feathers striped with red feathers and stitched to bark cloth; and the other half made of red English bunting without feathers and the ends split into feathered divisions. As he unwrapped these sacred relics, the priest chanted a long prayer, telling 'Oro that a man had been sacrificed and his eye had been offered to the god. Pigs and a large turtle had also been offered, and in exchange he and his people wanted prosperity, and victory over their enemies. As the drums throbbed loudly, Ha'amanimani presented 'Oro with a tuft of feathers on the end of a bamboo cane, and the corpse of the human sacrifice was buried in a shallow grave beside the *marae*. A pig's carcass was scorched over a sacred fire (which was kindled with two pieces of wood) to remove the bristles, and the entrails were removed and burned, except for the liver, which was cooked on the sacred fire. After the scorched pig was smeared with its own blood, the animal and its liver were placed on the *fata* or sacrificial platform as an offering from Tu, and a prayer was chanted for King George, Captain Bligh and all of his people. After this finale, the image of 'Oro and the red feather girdle were wrapped up again, and the ceremony ended.

Only about 150 people had attended the ritual, and when it was over, Ha'amanimani began to joke and caper, making 'obscene' gestures. Bligh inspected the *marae*, noticing that two other human sacrifices had recently been buried there, which according to Tu had been offered to 'Oro at the beginning of the recent war. While another, slightly smaller, turtle was being cooked for them, fresh leaves were laid beneath a shady tree, and Tu invited Bligh and his companions to sit down for an *erauaua* ceremony, acknowledging his friends and allies. Having collecting twelve leaves, Ha'amanimani recited the name of each of Pomare II's allies, handing each leaf in succession to the young paramount chief.

When Tu asked Bligh, Lieutenant Bond and the surgeon Mr Harwood to repeat the name of each person, and they did so, the spectators rocked with laughter, finding their mangled pronunciation hilarious. As their own names were called, they stepped forward in turn. After the ritual, the turtle (a chiefly food) was served with vegetables and other delicacies, and the chiefs spoke about Christian and his friends, saying that they had been glad when Captain Edwards carried the *Bounty*'s men away, although Coleman always wept whenever he spoke about the mutiny, and they considered him innocent of any wrong-doing. They told Bligh about the deaths of Churchill and Thompson, saying that after persuading the Tai'arapu chiefs to steal Thompson's musket and pistol, Churchill had blamed the theft on the chiefs; and when he learned the truth, Thompson had shot his shipmate. Afterwards, enraged by the death of their *taio*, Churchill's friends beat out Thompson's brains, and his skull now lay on this *marae*. In his journal that night, Bligh rejoiced: 'Thus these two Villains affected their own destruction!' (although later, he scratched out 'Villains', writing instead 'unfortunate Wretches').

The next day, a Sunday, the crews were mustered and their captains performed divine service. A cask of spruce beer was broached and the crew were given shore leave. At dawn, Tobin with his friends, the surgeons Harwood and Franklin, left on another excursion, this time to Ha'apaino'o at the mouth of the Papeno'o Valley. When they landed at Matavai Bay, their canoe tipped over in the surf, tossing them into the ocean. Although Harwood could not swim, he grabbed the outrigger and held on tight until they were rescued. After drying their clothes at the shore camp, they set off for the east coast, where waves crashed on the beach. About 4 miles from the camp, they came to the foot of a high cliff, the west boundary of the Ha'apaino'o district. According to their guides, in Captain Wallis's time the sea level had been higher, and waves had crashed against the base of this precipice.

When they entered the Ha'apaino'o district, Tobin and his companions were met by Tapairu and his family, who seemed very apprehensive. Tapairu, a vigorous, dignified man who was missing most of his front teeth, had been wounded in the knee during the recent fighting. After some conversation, Tobin fired his pistol at a mark, hitting it in the centre and impressing the chief's family, who applauded. Afterwards, they were served fruit and coconut milk. Not wanting to offend Tapairu, Tobin did not mention the *Matilda*'s muskets, although later he learned that Tapairu kept these prized objects under his sleeping mat each night, and was determined not to surrender them.

About 2 miles further down the east coast, Tobin's party came to the mouth of the Papeno'o River, which was about 300 feet wide with a bed of large dark pebbles. Their guides carried them across on their backs, and at the opposite bank they were greeted by Vaetua, Tu's younger brother and Harwood's *taio*, who had a house in this district. Welcoming them warmly, Vaetua ordered a leg of pork to be baked in an earth oven; and while it was cooking, they strolled to a sacred spot surrounded by a large railing fence, with a stone *marae* nearby and a sacrificial platform laden with offerings, including a shell trumpet. Although Vaetua explained the significance of this place, they could not understand him, except that the *marae* was dedicated to an *atua*. When they returned to his house, his wife Tai Aiva, a beautiful young woman whom the sailors had already dubbed 'the Belle of the Isle', welcomed them and served their dinner. During their walk, Vaetua drank some *'ava*, and after the meal he lay on his wife's lap for a massage and went to sleep for several hours. Tobin and his friends were also given a massage and had a nap, and when they awoke, Vaetua and Tai Aiva escorted them back to the Papeno'o River. As they crossed, the 'Belle of the Isle' stripped off her bark-cloth garments, and 'unconscious of her hitherto hidden charms, for the translucency of the stream but ill-served to envelop them',[2] waded through the water. On their way to Tapairu's house, Tobin sketched the local people fishing for mullet, some using a rod and line [PLATE 23].

Over the next few days, Matavai Bay was very quiet. Few canoes came out to the ship or visited the post, although every evening, people gathered to watch the marines performing their drill. On board the *Assistant*, Vaiareti presented Lieutenant Portlock with a large pig and some coconuts, and the next day Tu and 'Itia gave him a pig, bark cloth, breadfruit and some coconuts, adopting the consort captain as their *taio*. Women and children were drifting back to Matavai Bay, and on 2 May 1792, Mary McIntosh, the wife of the *Bounty* carpenter's mate Thomas McIntosh, brought her little daughter Elizabeth, a fine child about eighteen months old, to see Captain Bligh. She told Bligh that she had accompanied McIntosh to Tupua'i, where Christian had intended to settle and had built a fort defended by the ship's guns. When Tinarou and Ta'aroatohoa, the two principal chiefs of the island, had objected, however, war broke out, and many of the Tupua'i warriors were killed. In the aftermath, when Christian and his shipmates decided to return to Tahiti, Tu had treated Christian so coolly that within a matter of hours, he set sail again, saying that he would look for an island to settle where he would haul the *Bounty* ashore and demolish her.

According to Mary McIntosh, although her husband, Coleman, Heildbrandt, Norman and Ellison always wept when they spoke about Bligh, 'Stewart and Haywood [Heywood] were perfectly satisfied with their situation as any two Villains could be' (although Bligh later crossed out that last, bitter phrase). She knew exactly what had happened during the mutiny, even repeating the names of those men who had surprised Bligh in his cabin, and helped to tie up his hands.

While Bligh was talking with Mary McIntosh, Tobin and Franklin set off to explore the mountains inland towards Orohena, escorted by three guides. The soil on the foothills seemed poor, although higher up in the hills it was more fertile. After climbing for about 4 miles, they entered a forest and came to a ridge which separated the Tuauru River from a smaller stream to the east (the Vaiava). It was a very hot day, and when two of their guides farewelled them, they were glad to see a path heading down the east side of the ridge, through shady forests of wild plantain trees. Above them, they could see a village of about a dozen houses at the base of Orohena Mountain, which according to their remaining guide was a place where the *'arioi* 'resorted at particular periods to indulge uninterruptedly in unbounded licentiousness'.³ It was now noon, and although this man assured them that a path led directly to this village, they were tired; and decided to return to the post. Before they did so, Tobin sketched the scene in the bay, the *Providence* and *Assistant* sitting like 'specks on the blue surface of the sea', and the islets of Teti'aroa in the distance, encircled by a reef.

As they headed down, their guide offered to carry Tobin's pistols, their jackets and a piece of pork that they had brought for their dinner. When they entered the forest, however, he disappeared into the trees, taking their possessions and leaving them to find their own way back to the post. They got lost several times, and by the time they arrived back at the shore camp, the moon was high in the sky. Their shipmates laughed at their discomfiture, although a good supper and brandy soon restored their good humour. Bligh was annoyed when he heard about this episode, exclaiming in his journal: 'These Gentlemen, tired even of wearing their own Jackets, pulled them off with the only Arms they had being in the Pockets, and gave the whole to a worthless fellow to carry, who [led] them into an intricate and blind Path, where without any ceremony he abruptly took his leave.'⁴ Since this man was a servant of 'Itia's, Bligh decided not to pursue the matter, but blamed Tobin and Franklin for their foolhardiness on this occasion.

The following day, Tu's mother Tetupaia arrived from Teti'aroa with her daughter Auo, Mahau's widow. Tetupaia, now about sixty years old and more corpulent than ever, was hoisted up the side of the *Providence* in a bosun's chair; and when she entered the Great Cabin, she threw herself on the floor, weeping loudly to express her joy at seeing her 'son' Bligh again. When her daughter and their companions joined her, they wept for about an hour until Bligh cheered them up with gifts including sheets and nightgowns. Tetupaia, who assured Bligh that she and her family had not befriended Fletcher Christian, warmly congratulated him upon his miraculous escape in the launch. Her daughter Auo, who had been cured of yaws by the *Bounty*'s surgeon, Ledward, enquired after the doctor, and asked whether the surgeon on the *Providence* could treat an ulcer on her right shin. She explained that since Bligh's last visit, her husband Mahau had died and been succeeded by a nephew of Tetupaia's, the current title-holder. During this first visit to the *Providence*, neither Tetupaia nor Auo would eat on board the vessel.

When Tu, 'Itia, Vaiareti and Ha'amanimani joined Bligh for dinner, they reported that although Vaetua had tried to retrieve the *Matilda*'s muskets from Tapairu, Po'e'eno had again fled from Matavai Bay. When Ha'amanimani tried to persuade Bligh to invite Po'e'eno on board the ship and take him hostage, Bligh refused, perhaps feeling some sympathy for his former *taio*, but saying that this would put his men at risk, and he was not yet ready to leave the island. During this visit, 'Itia presented Tobin with a length of plaited human hair (used by *'arioi* dancing girls as a headdress), the first gift that she had given him for some time; and when she reproached him for failing to give her a return gift, Tobin hinted that he was waiting for a war mat and other 'curiosities'. Afterwards, he noted that many local artefacts, especially stone adzes, were now falling out of use, the people preferring to use iron tools and weapons. Although 'Itia laughed at Tobin for his collecting, he noted in his journal that there were also collectors of European artefacts among the Tahitians, with their own 'cabinets of curiosities'. Ha'amanimani, for instance, treasured a volume of *Statutes at Large* that he had acquired from a visiting ship; while as we have seen, Pomare II kept a large collection of European objects in his dwelling.

On 5 May 1792, Tu escorted William Bligh to an *'arioi* performance. Although these were formerly known as *heiva*, they were now called *upaupa*, since Teri'irere, the high chief of Papara and a senior *'arioi*, had taken 'Heiva' as one of his names. Three *'arioi* played their nose flutes, accompanied by two drummers – a performance that delighted the Tahitian audience, although Bligh found the music monotonous and boring. Later that day, 'Itia sent her *taio* Tobin a large pig and some breadfruit in return for a gift that he had given her. Unfortunately, however, his small cabin lay on the side of the ship that had been set aside for barter, and he was plagued by constant grunting and squealing as the pigs were hauled up the side one by one, just outside his porthole.

Taro, Franklin's *taio*, also visited Tobin's cabin, where he powdered his hair. Although Taro was a senior *'arioi*, Tobin confessed that 'with scarcely any knowledge of the language, I am precluded speaking confidently of any of their mysterious ceremonies'.[5] When Tobin tried to convince this man that the *'arioi* practice of destroying their children just after birth was wicked, Taro retorted that it was good, and an ancestral custom; and he said the same about human sacrifice. As Tobin mused, apart from the children of the *Bounty*'s men, who had had settled relationships with their Tahitian women, he had seen no offspring of white sailors on the island; concluding that like the children of active *'arioi*, they must have been destroyed.

Early the next morning, a Sunday, Ari'ipaea arrived on board the *Providence* to return the pistols that had been stolen from Tobin in the mountains. Explaining that Vaetua had captured the thief at Ha'apaino'o, en route to Teahupo, the windward peninsula, he loudly condemned this man as a *ta'ata 'ino* or bad fellow. According to Tobin, Vahine Metua, Ari'ipaea's wife, was jealous of his affair with Vaiareti, although she spoke affectionately about her husband. The ship's company was mustered as usual, and after divine service Bligh went ashore, where he met a dwarf named Toma, a boy eight years old and only 31 inches tall, who had four of his upper front teeth missing.

On 7 May when a messenger arrived from Tapairu, saying that he had managed to retrieve Captain Weatherhead's money from Teti'aroa, Bligh sent Norris with some armed men to collect it. The following morning, Toipoi, the widow of Pohuetea Ti'i, the young high chief from Hitia'a who had visited Bligh during his *Bounty* voyage, came to see him. Bligh vividly remembered this young chief, the only man apart from Pomare II and Tu who had been so sacred that he was fed by hand; and he was saddened to hear that after visiting the *Discovery*, Vancouver's ship, Pohuetea Ti'i and many others had died from a fever, vomiting and flux (probably dysentery). He gave the widow many gifts, but could not convince her that Vancouver's ship was not responsible for the epidemic. During this visit, an enterprising thief stole Tobin's sheets through the porthole, although Maititi, 'Itia's attendant and a 'clever, active fellow', managed to retrieve the linen.

While Bligh was talking with Toipoi, Tu was suddenly called away to Pare. 'Itia remained on board the *Providence*, and at noon she pointed out a canoe passing the ships, carrying a human sacrifice that had been sent to Tu by Wana, the chief of Ha'apaino'o, in apology for having sheltered Tapairu after his defeat in Matavai Bay. Bligh, who was feeling unwell, did not try to attend this ceremony, remarking, 'These Sacrifices are truly Shocking and Savage, and I am sorry to say I find they are made not only on solemn occasions, but on the most trifling differences between great & inferior Chiefs.'[6]

That night in his journal, Bligh made an effort to unravel the intricacies of Tahitian politics. During his previous visits, he noted, although the Tai'arapu people of southern Tahiti had always insisted that Vehiatua was their high chief (or *ari'i rahi*) while Tu was only the high chief of the western districts, Tu's family was adamant that there was just one *ari'i rahi* on the island. The Vehiatua line had now died out, however; and in 1790, Tu's second son Teri'itapunui, at the age of three, had taken over the Vehiatua title. In order to complete this network of alliances, Pomare II, the paramount chief of Tahiti, was now betrothed to Ta'aroahine, a fine young girl only twelve months old and the daughter of Tu's sister Auo and Mahau (the former high chief of Mo'orea), indicating that in dynastic marriages in Tahiti, first cousins were allowed to marry.

On 9 May, Mr Norris, the *Matilda*'s surgeon, and Mr Marshall her first mate, returned from Ha'apaino'o with less than half of Captain Weatherhead's money – 172 Spanish dollars and three half-crown pieces; and a silver watch belonging to the first mate. When they met Tapairu high in the Papeno'o Valley, accompanied by about a hundred of his people, the Matavai chief had told them that the rest of the money was held by another chief, who refused to return it. After trying and failing to turn the dollars into fish-hooks, his people had played with the coins, skipping them on the sea and losing most of the money in the lagoon.[7] Adamantly refusing to give up the five muskets from the *Matilda*, Tapairu declared that he would rather retreat to the mountains and fight to the death; and contemptuously dismissed his brother Po'e'eno, who had made peace with Tu, as a coward.

Several days later, one of the marines was given twelve lashes for sleeping with a woman while he had a venereal infection; and Bligh was visited by Moana, the old chief of Matavai Bay and the father of Po'e'eno and Tapairu, who had befriended him during the *Bounty* visit, but left him alone after three of the *Bounty* sailors had deserted.

On Saturday 12 May, Ari'ipaea, his nephew Pomare II, and Ha'amanimani came to say goodbye to Bligh, explaining that they were going to visit Papara where Teri'irere was on his deathbed. When Tu asked Bligh for gifts to take to Papara, Bligh gave them an assortment of European goods. Ari'ipaea, who hoped that the Papara people would be lulled by this appearance of friendship, was planning to seize the muskets and pistols that Teri'irere's people had taken from the *Bounty* sailors, along with a boat from the *Matilda*. After their departure, Matavai Bay was almost deserted, although Tu stayed on, dining with Bligh on board the *Providence* every day. When Bligh showed him the engravings from Captain Cook's last voyage, he was only interested in the sea horses from Kamchatka, but asked if he could show Vaiareti some curious Chinese objects that Bligh had collected.

Although 'nothing could be more cheerful and amiable than their demeanour', the officers and crews were relieved when Ari'ipaea, Ha'amanimani and their attendants set off for Pare, and they had the ships to themselves again. William Bligh was disconsolate and lonely, however. During his previous visit to Matavai Bay, the 'Paradise of the World', he had been honoured as a high chief, showered with gifts, placed at the heart of the seasonal rituals and entertained by the *'arioi* with feasts, wrestling, skits, dancing, music and athletics contests. Now as he walked along the coast, Bligh was irked to see Peter Heywood's house with its avenue of shaddock trees (a vivid reminder of the mutiny); and distressed by the devastation of Matavai Bay in the wake of the recent wars. He was also troubled by the way the chiefs had adopted alcohol, filthy swear words and dirty, ragged European garments – signs of corruption, as he saw it, in the wake of contact with Europeans.

Although Tu remained his true friend, Moana and Po'e'eno, who had once treated him so kindly, were now in exile. Pomare II, the young paramount chief, had become closer to his uncle, Ari'ipaea, and his great-uncle the high priest Ha'amanimani, than to his father Tu, Bligh's *taio*, causing Bligh's own influence to wane. In addition, Bligh's lies during his last visit, when he had claimed to be Captain Cook's son, and that Cook was still alive in England, had diminished his *mana*; along with the discourteous behaviour of his compatriot, George Vancouver, who had insulted Ha'amanimani and Tu's brothers, and left a virulent epidemic in his wake. During this visit, too, Bligh was plagued with unbearable headaches, a sign of 'Oro's displeasure; and he stayed on board the *Providence* instead of living ashore with his friends, while Matavai Bay had become a war zone. With little to comfort him in Tahiti, Bligh's thoughts turned increasingly to England, and the honours that would be showered upon him when he delivered the cargo of breadfruit and other plants to the West Indies, and to Kew Gardens. He also wondered what had happened to the *Pandora*, and the mutineers – those 'wretches' and 'villains entrapped through their own seduction'. After the shock and humiliation of losing the *Bounty*, it would be glorious to return home in triumph, with his honour restored and his reputation vindicated.

The 13th of May 1792 was a Sunday, '*Po nui o te Atua*' – 'The great day of the god', as the Tahitians called it. Knowing that this was a day of rest for the British, most of the islanders stayed away from Matavai Bay, while Bligh kept himself busy by inspecting the breadfruit plants, supervising the carpenters who were repairing the launch, and making astronomical observations. Only Tu and Vaiareti kept him company, 'so that we have no bustle or anything passing curious or interesting'.[8] The sailors hauled the seine, catching fine loads of fish, and Tu's people supplied the ships with provisions. On 18 May, however, a group of Ari'ipaea's followers tried to rob the watering party, pelting them with dirt and stones; and when one of these men was captured and taken on board the *Providence*, Bligh had him put in irons. After midnight that evening, another man opened the port of Lieutenant Bond's cabin and stole his sheet while he was sleeping. Although the sentries fired their muskets and the boats chased the thief, he managed to elude them.

At dinner the next day, Bligh told Tu that he intended to punish the man captured by the watering party. When Tu agreed, the man was given thirty-six lashes on his bare backside, although he did not cry out or moan. On shore, another of Ari'ipaea's men fought with a sailor and gave him a black eye; and when both men were brought on board and he heard their accounts, Bligh allowed the sailor to give the man a beating. After he had been punched several times, the Tahitian jumped overboard and swam ashore. That afternoon, 'Itia returned from Papara with gifts of bark cloth, and a load of pigs was delivered by canoe from Pare.

On Sunday 20 May, having filled their pockets with trinkets to barter for curiosities, Tobin and the surgeon, Harwood, went to Pare to visit Taputapuatea *marae*. People flocked around, teasing them by offering a stone, or a feather, for their trade goods. After bartering for four little blue parakeets in a cage, Tobin promised to pick them up when he returned, although soon afterwards the man ran after him, lamenting that two of the birds had escaped. About an hour later when a boy offered him two more of these birds and Tobin paid for them, he realised from the amused reaction of the crowd that he had been tricked, and these were the same birds that had 'escaped' from the cage. En route to Pare, they visited the *fare tupapa'u* or funerary platform of Tu's uncle, the venerable old chief Mou'aroa. The corpse had been embalmed in a sitting position with loins and forehead covered with bands of white bark cloth, leaving its heavy tattoos exposed. Mou'aroa, who was survived by his widow, Mari'ia, had been a 'black leg' or senior *'arioi*, and his legs and thighs were tattooed a solid black, with curving lines on his arms from the shoulder to the wrist; and under his left breast, the broad oblong of the *'arioi* society.

When Tobin and Harwood approached Point 'Utuhaihai, they came across some *ti'i*, one of which was carved into the trunk of a coconut tree 20 feet high, with female figures at the base and male figures on top, their sexual organs prominently displayed. Tobin sketched Taputapuatea, the inland *marae* built for Pomare II's investiture; and that night he described its sacrificial platforms and the two-tiered *ahu* upon which the gods alighted during the ceremonies, facing the stone pavement [PLATE 24]. According to Tobin, the *'unu* boards on the platform were carved with the images of *heiva* dancers, birds or lizards. Beside the *marae*, a human skull and the skull of a pig hung on carved figures, and a *fare atua* or god-house stood nearby. One of their guides showed them the skull of Thompson, the mutineer who had killed Churchill and in his turn had been killed by Churchill's friends, saying that it was kept on this *marae*. Tobin also sketched and described Taraho'i, the *marae* on the nearby point belonging

Ti'i, *by George Tobin.*

to Tu. This stood only about 100 yards from his son's *marae* Taputapuatea, and had a four-tiered *ahu* adorned with carved *'unu* boards. On the seaward side the *marae* was sheltered by a low wall, with several human skeletons lying inside it. [PLATE 25] As they returned to Matavai Bay, Tobin and Harwood watched two men fighting, kicking, pulling each other's hair and biting as several women stood by, weeping and lamenting with loud shrieks, although no reason was given for this dispute.

The following day, many of the Pare people returned to Matavai Bay, including Mari'ia, Mou'aroa's widow; although Ari'ipaea, Ha'amanimani and Pomare II were still absent. Teri'irere, the high chief of Papara, had recovered from his illness, and Ari'ipaea had failed in his attempt to capture the *Matilda*'s muskets from his Papara district. Although ceremonies had been held – perhaps the autumn harvest festival – Bligh had not been invited; and afterwards Pomare II, his high priest Ha'amanimani and his uncle and protector Ari'ipaea set off with the *'arioi* on a circuit of the island, leaving Tu alone with his British *taio*. By this time, both Tu and Bligh were being marginalised by Pomare II and his allies. That afternoon the man who had been flogged on board the *Providence* arrived at the watering place, where he mocked his punishment in a burlesque display.

The Season of Scarcity had now begun, and very few supplies were brought out to the ships, forcing Bligh to send a boat to Pare for provisions. Meanwhile, he forbade the sailors to trade for any more 'curiosities', hoping that this would force the islanders to bring food to Matavai Bay. The next night when Tu arrived late from Pare, he sent his attendants ahead with torches along the pathway across One Tree Hill; and as Bligh remarked: '[P]erhaps a prettier sight was never seen [than the torches flickering] on the smooth water about the Shore, for the lights were brilliant and numerous.'[9] This was a rare occurrence, however, because most Tahitians preferred to stay at home after dark, apart from those male *'arioi* who came to steal from the ships or the post, under the cover of darkness and with the blessing of Hiro, the god of thieves. Tu told Bligh that he had no control over these men, although he urged Bligh to follow the local custom, and kill any thief who fell into his hands.

On 25 May 1792, Tu and his wives invited William Bligh to a *heiva*. As Bligh noted, his presence at these events usually galvanised the *'arioi*, inspiring burlesque skits that delighted the crowds; and the people enjoyed the gifts that he distributed. A fine mat was laid on the ground, and two male *'arioi* helped to dress a pretty little girl of about eleven and a woman in lengths of red, black and pleated white bark cloth, while the female dancers donned black-feathered bodices. As one of these men gave a loud call, the women sat on the mat, leaning upon their elbows. Chanting a prologue, the other male *'arioi* entered the ring holding two plaited plantain leaves, one within the other, a tribute to a visiting chief, striking his chest with his right hand and posturing dramatically. He took one of the leaves (plaited in the shape of a shoe) and placed it on Bligh's left foot, and retired as the girl and the woman began to dance to the drums, gesturing gracefully and twisting their mouths awry. When the men joined them, quickly moving their hands and knees, there was loud applause; and after this dance, the women twirled around, unwinding the lengths of bark cloth from their bodies, and laid them before Captain Bligh. Afterwards, the male *'arioi* asked a sailor from the post to dance with them, imitating his movements so perfectly that the crowd rocked with laughter. Bligh was dispirited and grumpy, however, and did not enjoy the *heiva*, complaining that there was 'not anything new in the performance'.[10] Nevertheless, he ordered his men to fire off a dozen sky rockets, thrilling the spectators.

The next day, plants of a very fine variety of breadfruit were brought to Bligh from Tai'arapu. By this time, his collection of breadfruit and other local plants was flourishing, 'in charming order, spreading their leaves delightfully'. He had brought a cargo of exotic plants, including orange and lime trees, pineapples, guavas, pomegranates, figs and eight young fir trees from England and the Cape of Good Hope,[11] and ordered these to be taken ashore to be planted, especially at Pare, hoping that the old man who had cared for Captain Cook's shaddock trees would look after them. The next day was a Sunday, and after mustering his crew and performing divine service, Bligh went on board the *Assistant*, where he found everything shipshape. He was full of praise for Lieutenant Portlock, who shared his determination to keep the vessels in meticulous order.

At dinner that day, Tu, who had drunk '*ava* before coming on board, consumed a quantity of rum and suffered convulsions so severe that it took six men to hold him down. Although Vaiareti took little notice of his fit, 'Itia looked after Tu tenderly, giving him a massage that put him to sleep until the next morning, when he woke up feeling fit and cheerful. In his journal that night, Bligh mused about marriage in Tahiti, noting that a male *teuteu* or servant could never marry a high-born wife; and that a chief had to win the permission of a woman's parents before they could marry. Once their consent was obtained, a ceremony was performed on the *marae*, although only for the first wife; and afterwards the couple could separate whenever they chose. A man could have many wives, although those with children had more rights than the others. While a husband could punish a wife who committed adultery, high-born women could take as many lovers as they wanted.

That Sunday, Tobin and Guthrie returned to Ha'apaino'o to look at a war canoe that Tu had praised in their presence. En route they were shown the site of the recent battle, where the trunks of the trees had been scarred by flying stones. Soon afterwards they came to the house of Vaetua, Tu's younger brother, whom Tobin described as a handsome man about 27 years old, famed as a warrior for having killed Mahine (the high chief of Mo'orea) some years earlier – although as Tobin sardonically remarked, Mahine had in fact been captured by two of Vaetua's men, who held him down while the young chief beat in his head with a stone. His beautiful wife Tai Aiva, the 'Belle of the Isle', was eating a breakfast of fish in a small shed nearby. As the young lieutenant remarked ruefully: 'Ruffled or unruffled, she was still the same cold, repellent fair one. Had Tai Aiva been more yielding, the wardrobe of many an English chief would have been expended, and this kindly isle far the richer in various sorts of foreign drapery.'[12] Vaetua was jealous of his lovely young wife, however; and since she was of a lower rank than her husband, she did not dare to offend him.

After this encounter Tobin and Lieutenant Guthrie crossed the Papeno'o River, carried on the shoulders of their guides; and after landing and walking about a quarter of a mile, arrived at the shed where the war canoe was being built. Its prow was decorated with the figure of a man and the stern and sides with carvings of turtles and lizards, while a wooden god-house stood near the stern to hold the image of 'Oro. In a shed, a carved sternpost 20 feet high was stored with a high wickerwork helmet decorated with cock's feathers, worn by the priests in battle. According to their companions, when the canoe was finished it would be carried to the river on poles on men's shoulders. By this time, only this war canoe and another at Pare remained on the island. When they returned to Vaetua's house, Tapairu paid them a visit, although he and Vaetua were at war. Nevertheless, he shared their meal of baked pig, breadfruit and plantains, with coconut milk and salt water to go with the meat, remarking ruefully that most of the things in the house had been plundered from his own dwelling; and when they set off to return to Matavai Bay, he loaded their attendants with gifts of fruit.

On 28 May, a messenger arrived to tell Tu and 'Itia that their daughter Tahamaitua had died at Papara. After being taken to the *heiva* in that district, the girl had caught a chill and died. Tu seemed unmoved; and when 'Itia shed only a few tears, Bligh reproached her for caring so little for her dead child. The next day, Bligh went to Tu's house in the country, which stood on a beautiful site in the hills, hoping to check on some orange and lemon trees, pineapples and fir trees that his men had planted. When he returned to the coast, he found 'Itia mourning her dead daughter who was laid out under a shed, wrapped in scarlet English cloth and bark cloth, hands folded on her chest. There were very few people in attendance, and the servants were preparing the *fare tupapa'u*, a bier about 6 feet high, fenced around with reeds and decorated with coloured bark cloth, leaves and flowers.

Upon seeing Bligh, 'Itia slashed her head, weeping, although she soon became cheerful again. When Bligh asked her attendants how corpses were embalmed on the island, he was told that after four or five days on the funerary bier, an 'undertaker' came at night to flay the skin with a wooden scraper, leaving the body perfectly white. The flesh was oiled, the bowels and intestines were removed, and the interior cavity was washed with water steeped with herbs and dried. The eyes were also washed, and the lids carefully closed. They assured him, however, that the body of Tu's daughter would not be treated in this way, since she was only a child.

The next day when Ari'ipaea returned to the *Providence*, Bligh upset him by asking how many muskets he had seized at Papara, shaming the great warrior (who had not captured any). During this meeting, when a messenger arrived from a chief in one of the rival eastern districts, carrying a bough as an invitation for a visit, Bligh compounded his offence by fastening a red feather to the bough as a sign of acceptance. Soon afterwards when it began to pour with rain, Vaiareti, Tu's young wife who had been having an affair with Ari'ipaea, appeared from a cabin, stark naked, and romped around in the downpour before returning to the cabin. As Tobin remarked: 'She was a wicked jade, and we should all have been much more pleased had it been Taiaiva [the Belle of the Isle].'[13]

Although Tobin was censorious about Vaiareti's 'wanton' display, thinking that she was betraying his *taio* 'Itia, her older sister, in Tahiti it was an honour for a chief to sleep with his brother's wife. Back in Britain, however, puritanical attitudes (associated with evangelical Christianity) were gaining ground, condemning sexuality as a sign of original sin and attacking the hedonistic paganism of 'gentlemen' such as Joseph Banks and the Earl of Sandwich. As Tobin mused, perhaps the sexual tolerance of Tahiti was preferable to the strait-laced piety of British society, in which young women who strayed from the 'straight and narrow' were cruelly ostracised:

> The instructed daughters of chastity in our colder regions, no doubt, in their own strength, look with pity and contempt on the infirmity of these poor islands. True, from their infancy they are taught that this alone will pave their way to heaven. This jewel inviolate, every discordant passion may riot without impeachment or control. The children of these southern isles know no such doctrine, nor are they the less happy for it. If frail, yet do they largely teem with charity and benevolence.
>
> Yet do our own fair fall, and deep indeed, for such is the prejudice of an unfeeling world . . . that the once fond mother who watched sedulously their infant years, and sisters who shared the warm confidence of their bosoms must know them no more. This is a heart-rending truth. Better then, perhaps do the thoughtless South Sea Islanders act in looking with a benevolent eye on what mankind has from the 'beginning' and will to the 'end' err in.[14]

# 21

# Paradise Lost

The day after Vaiareti's naked frolic, Bligh was stricken again with his nervous headache. As he lamented in his journal: 'When these dreadfull fitts lay hold of me I am almost distracted. My mind being constantly on the stretch will I fear never suffer me to be free of these complaints until I return into a Cold Climate.'[1] Without doubt, the Tahitians took these attacks to be inspired by the anger of 'Oro, casting a shadow over Tu's *taio*, although they were coming to have some faith in Western remedies. While Bligh eased his headache by bathing at dawn in the chilly waters of the Tuauru River, a number of islanders came out to the *Providence* asking the ship's surgeon to cure them of ulcers and sores.

Soon afterwards, Tu asked the surgeon, Harwood, to treat his youngest child, Oroho, who was very ill and under the care of an old man (since no women were allowed to approach these sacred children). The boy's stomach was distended, and an ulcer had erupted in his groin. When Bligh rebuked 'Itia, saying that she should take better care of her children, she angrily retorted that this was Vaiareti's responsibility. Although Bligh was amazed that Tu did not seem fond of his children, he mused that this was probably because his eldest son had taken over Tu's rank and many of his privileges as soon as he had been born, and he and his children were forced to live apart from each other. Only 'Itia (who had breastfed her babies) and their male nursemaid were allowed to approach these sacred children, so that Tu could not 'view with pleasure the progress of the infants', being forced to address them from a distance of at least 15 yards until after the *amo'a* ceremonies were performed, when they could spend some time together. Bligh noted, however, that this situation was atypical in Tahiti, where most parents treated their children with tenderness and affection. As he confessed in a sadly revealing comment, 'few more engaging and pretty Children are to be met with, could we divest ourselves of the dislike to the Colour'.[2]

On 4 July 1792, King George III's birthday, the ships were decorated with flags, and the officers donned their best uniforms. At noon, the marines lined up and fired three volleys; and an hour later, the cannons on each ship fired twenty-one guns, and every person on board was served a tot of rum. As Tobin commented when he tossed down his dram, 'the gay, the jovial Vaetua' remarked that the 'ava of Britain was better than that of Tahiti, because although it took away the use of his limbs, it freed his tongue, and after drinking it, he always felt very bold; while Ari'ipaea was loud in the praise of 'Kini Iore' (King George).[3] At noon, all of the chiefs came on board the *Providence* to dine with Bligh. He had asked George Tobin to make two silver paper balloons for the celebration, and that night the gleaming spheres flew up into the sky and a dozen rockets were fired, to the ecstasy of about 600 spectators.

Despite this joyous celebration, Bligh was increasingly critical of the Tahitians. As the provisions ran short, he remarked that these 'lazy Wretches' were so indolent that they hardly cultivated any yams or sweet potatoes, and went hungry as soon as the breadfruit season ended.[4] The next day, he sent Tobin to accompany Tu to fetch supplies from Fa'a'a. When Tobin arrived at Tu's house in Matavai Bay, he found the chief eating his breakfast (about 3 pounds of baked fish), and caressing 'the false Vaiareti'. As soon as the boat was sailing down the west coast, however, Tu began to joke and clown, imitating the way in which the British steered their boats. At their first landing he ordered a pig to be baked for dinner, and gathered plantains from the nearby trees. Although Tu could not find any ripe breadfruit, the trees were loaded with young fruit, and Tobin noted that after preserving their *mahi* (fermented breadfruit), the islanders only had about a month (in June) when they lacked this invaluable crop, of which about thirty different varieties grew on the island.

While their meal was cooking, Tu and Tobin strolled several miles down the west coast, the young lieutenant noting that it was densely inhabited with large groves of breadfruit, *vi* and Tahitian chestnut trees. Passing the funerary bier of one of the mutineers' children, they met Moana, who provided them with refreshments. Afterwards some men carried them back to their landing place, and the pig was brought from the earth oven and served for their dinner. After bathing in a nearby stream, Tu ate alone (as was his custom) under a shady breadfruit tree. About 3 miles further west, they paddled past a small island close to the coastline through a narrow passage, where flocks of wild ducks perched in the trees.

As they sailed inside the reef back to Pare, Tu remarked that although he was not courageous, this was not necessary for a high chief. When he asked Tobin whether King George ever fought in battle, and Tobin told him that he did not, Tu was delighted, exclaiming, '*Maita'i!*' ('Good!'). In his family, Ari'ipaea and Vaetua were the warriors, and Tu felt no shame about his timidity, having been 'taught that a king should not appear in battle'.[5] As Tobin mused, even in pre-revolutionary France, Frenchmen did not worship their King as much as Tahitians revered their *ari'i*, for in Tahiti, in the presence of the 'royal' children who had inherited their titles, their parents had to strip to the waist and bow.

By this time, however, the Pomare family had become tired of William Bligh, and his ailments and grumpy behaviour. Although Ari'ipaea was now back in Pare, he rarely visited the ship, and Vaetua also stayed away, drinking '*ava*; while Pomare II and Ha'amanimani absented themselves, accompanying the '*arioi* on their circuit of the island. Only Tu and his wives remained loyal, and every day at noon Bligh sent the boat to Pare to fetch them to share his dinner. On the rare occasions when Ari'ipaea and Vaetua joined them, the three brothers and their wives got very drunk, Tu forgetting his vow of abstinence, until finally Bligh ordered that his *taio* should be given no more alcohol. They were irritated by Bligh's questions about local customs, no doubt because he was judgemental, and increasingly mistrusted his intentions. As he remarked sadly: 'It is difficult to get information respecting their manners or Country; they seem suspicious of every enquiry.' Although Tu was living close to the post, there were often prowlers around the camp, trying to steal from the British; and on 11 June, a man was shot and wounded by the sentry, dying several days later. That same evening, Lieutenant Pearce, the commander of the marines, reported his sergeant to Bligh for insolence, and asked to have him court-martialled.

By this time, many of the sailors had been infected with venereal diseases; and breadfruit, yams, sweet potatoes and firewood were scarce. In order to keep them supplied, Tu marked a tree in Matavai Bay that they could cut down and sent provisions to the ships, including about a thousand coconuts every day. As the breadfruit plants were collected, potted up and placed in the greenhouse at the shore camp, the sailors hauled the seine, repaired the ships and painted the boats.

During one of his walks around Point Venus, Bligh had noticed a small stone shrine where some plaited coconut leaves had been laid, placed on a palm stump which served as a sacrificial platform for offerings of a coconut grater, some coconut and *mahi*. He was told that Tu had set up this *marae*, named Ruahatu after the sea god, to ensure the success of a new fish weir that his people had built near Point Venus. Increasingly, he was learning about the relationship between the islanders and their ancestor gods. To his disappointment, however, Matavai Bay was still very quiet, and only about twenty people visited the ship each day, compared with the hundreds who had gathered every evening during the *Bounty*'s visit. Like the Pomare family, Bligh had grown bored and disaffected: 'Very few Natives about us, they regard us with very great indifference, so that we see no strange People of any consequence, or does any thing pass interesting or worth notice.'[6]

On 17 June when a party from Tai'arapu visited Matavai Bay for some wrestling matches, there was a brief flurry of excitement, although the visitors seemed uneasy each time that one of Tu's men was defeated. The following day Ha'amanimani returned from his tour of the island, although Pomare II and Teu were still absent; and two of the sailors were flogged on board the *Providence* for theft and insolence — a rare punishment during this voyage. Soon afterwards when Bligh came across another human sacrifice, trussed up on a pole and away from any houses, he was told that this victim had been sent to Tu as an apology from the Huahine chiefs, who had assisted Po'e'eno and Tapairu in the recent fighting. On 20 June while he was surveying Matavai Bay, Bligh was stricken by another fever. That night he wrote in his journal: 'Besides a constant Head Ach, I have a sinking at the pit of my stomach, then a dreadfull heat flies up into my Face, which seems to fly out the top of my head, as if shot through me — a lowness and flurry of my spirits takes place.'[7] Although the Tahitians gave him coconut milk and *vi* to ease his symptoms, it seemed clear that Bligh had angered the gods. When Lieutenant Portlock took over his duties, Bligh remarked gratefully: '[His] allertness and attention to his duty, and every thing I direct him to do, makes me at all times think of him with regard and esteem.'[8]

The 21st of June 1792 was the day of the winter solstice, when the gods were farewelled from the island, heralding the beginning of the Season of Scarcity. Although on this occasion the ceremonies were conducted away from Matavai Bay and Pare, explaining Pomare II's continued absence, a fleet of fifteen canoes arrived from Teti'aroa, bringing loads of dried tuna (which the British did not like). That night a thief, aided by the trickster god Hiro, stole a bag of dirty clothing belonging to Lieutenant Guthrie at the shore camp, although three sentries were awake and on guard. The next morning, Bligh, still plagued with headaches, consoled himself by visiting the breadfruit plants: 'It gives me peculiar satisfaction to see my Plants thriving. I have now once more with unwearied Zeal and attention procured that great and valuable object, and hope God will grant my endeavours may be crowned with success.'[9]

Several days later, Tu and Tobin went in an armed boat to Fa'a'a to retrieve Guthrie's stolen clothing, and Bligh sent Lieutenant Portlock to collect the *Matilda*'s whaleboat from Atehuru. Landing in a cove opposite the small offshore island in Fa'a'a, Tu pointed out a small stream that marked the boundary between this district and Teahupo'o. When they walked to the house of the man who had been accused of the theft, a plantain branch was placed at Tu's feet and the women protested the man's innocence, saying that he had fled for fear of being captured. Although Tobin threatened that Captain Bligh would burn down all of their houses unless the stolen linen was returned, Tu said little, annoying the young lieutenant. They were served a meal of two baked pigs, which Tu ate alone, as usual, and returned to Matavai Bay.

During his expedition to Atehuru (which as Bligh now learned, was divided into two districts – Pa'ea, ruled by Pohuetea, who had been succeeded by a minor chief; and Patere, governed by Teto'ofa, the grandson of the 'Admiral'), Portlock had succeeded in retrieving the *Matilda*'s whaleboat. The whaleboat was kept in Teto'ofa's territory, and his widow, supported by an intelligent young priest, insisted on handing it over to the British, despite some opposition from the local people. The widow, a 'stout, good-looking woman', told Portlock that although the chiefs of Matavai and Pare had forbidden them to visit the ships, now that he had arrived, she and her new husband with her brother would accompany him and dine with Captain Bligh. When she boarded the *Providence*, Tu, 'Itia and Vaiareti were wary at first, but Bligh gave her valuable gifts and treated her kindly; and after dinner (which included cheese, which the chiefs jokingly called *tupapa'u*, or part of a dead body) Tu took her and her companions ashore and welcomed them to Pare. As Bligh remarked, however, Teto'ofa's widow did not eat on board the ship. In fact, the only women who ever ate with him were 'Itia and Vaiareti; and on shore, even these high-born women ate apart from their menfolk.

After this meeting with the Atehuru chiefs, Bligh attempted to describe the political geography of the island. At this time, he wrote, there were four main divisions in Tahiti – Te Porionu'u, Atehuru, Teva-i-uta, and Teva-i-tai (or Tai'arapu). Te Porionu'u, which was ruled by Pomare II and covered the north-east part of the island, was divided into six 'counties' or districts – Matavai, Pare, Ha'apaino'o, Ti'arei, Mahaena and Hitia'a. Atehuru, the division to the west, ruled by Pohuetea and Teto'ofa and their successors, was divided into three districts – Tetaha [Fa'a'a], Pa'ea and Patere. Teva-i-uta to the south-west, which had four districts – Papara, Atimaono, Vai'uriri and Vaiari – was ruled by Teri'irere, who 'has had equal and like Power to Otoo [Tu]. He had the Eye of the human sacrifice presented to him – wore the Maro, and every person uncovered to him.'[10] After his defeat by Tu's uncle many years earlier, during the peacemaking rituals Teri'irere had become Tu's *taio*, marrying his sister Teri'inavaharoa. Finally Teva-i-tai or Tai'arapu, the division at the southern end of the island, traditionally ruled by the Vehiatua clan, was divided into twelve districts, the title being held by Pomare II's younger brother Teri'itapunui (Tu's second son) since the extinction of the original chiefly line. Although during this visit Bligh was disheartened and often ill, and did not make as many detailed enquiries as he had done during his visit on the *Bounty*, his command of Tahitian kept improving, and he was gaining more intricate insights into the political networks on the island.

By the time of Bligh's visit on the *Providence*, everyone acknowledged Pomare II as the *ari'i maro 'ura* or paramount chief of the island, with the sole right to wear the red feather girdle and 'eat' the spirits of human sacrifices; although his family remained vigilant against his enemies. While Ari'ipaea ensured that the people of southern Tahiti remained loyal to their high chief, Pomare II's younger brother, Vaetua kept a watch on the eastern districts; and Ha'amanimani, the high priest from Ra'iatea and Pomare II's great-uncle, ensured that the gods were on the young chief's side, governing the worship of 'Oro on the island.

As for Tu, he was now living in Mo'orea with Mahau's heir and successor, in a marginal position. The *taio* relationship that he had forged with Captain Cook, and his bond friendships with successive British commanders including Captain Bligh (and the gifts he received from them), had proved to be his most enduring claims to *mana*. Although Tu and his wife 'Itia still had political ambitions, these were increasingly contested by his younger brothers Ari'ipaea and Vaetua, his old uncle Ha'amanimani (Pomare II's high priest and advisor), and their eldest son Pomare II – none of whom shared his loyalty to the British.

After the visit by Teto'ofa's widow and her companions, very few canoes visited the ships. As Bligh remarked plaintively: 'The Natives appear to care but little about us.' Although fleets of canoes carrying parties of *'arioi* passed to and from Teti'aroa, they did not visit Matavai Bay; and now that the Season of Scarcity had begun, very few provisions were delivered to the ships. On 2 July when a few inferior chiefs from the eastern districts of Te Porionu'u visited the *Providence*, they recited the names of each of the ships that had visited the island and their commanders, calling Bligh's ships the 'healthy' vessels, unlike the ships of Captain Vancouver that had brought disease and death to Tahiti; and describing the *Jenny* as a 'miserable vessel', and her commander as a 'great Rascal'.[11]

Ever since the theft of Guthrie's linen, Tu had been incensed with his brother, calling him 'ungrateful' for failing to retrieve the stolen garments. Deciding to do something about this situation, Tu set off on 4 July, and after a night of wild storms and lightning, returned with some of the stolen clothing, saying that the thief had fled with the other items. Several of the *Matilda*'s men were still living in southern Tahiti, where part of a yard and a plank from their ship had been washed ashore. Bligh also learned that Teri'irere, the high chief of Papara, had a number of his own books in his possession, plundered from the schooner built by his men, the *Resolution*. One of these volumes, Dampier's *Voyages*, was delivered to him with a provocative message from Teri'irere saying that if he wanted the rest, he could exchange them for cartridge paper. Apparently, Teri'irere had been tearing out the pages of Bligh's books to make cartridges for his plundered muskets.

Although Bligh sent a message to Teri'irere, inviting him to visit the ships, he received no reply. In any case, he had decided that the time had come to leave the island: the breadfruit plants were flourishing, the ships were in good order, and the carpenters had almost repaired the *Matilda*'s whaleboat. When he announced his decision to his *taio*, Tu told his family; and on 8 July, they all boarded the *Providence* with their parents, Teu and Tetupaia. These old people were now very infirm, and Tu's mother Tetupaia, who could barely walk, had to be hoisted up the side of the ship in a bosun's chair. Tetupaia wept bitterly when she met Bligh, and warmly greeted her sons. As Bligh noted: 'They are happy in their Children, who show them every mark of affection and respect, and their filial attention is such a blessing to the Old Pair as delights me on every occasion.'[12] Tu wore his bark-cloth robes on this occasion, while 'Itia had donned a crimson coat with gold buttonholes (a gift from Bligh). Vaiareti was dressed in a similar coat in blue, and Ari'ipaea was resplendent in a captain's uniform coat that Captain Edwards had given him. They all assured Bligh that when he left the island, the people would lament, weeping and slashing their heads with shark's teeth.

Of them all, Tu was the most disturbed to hear that Bligh's ships would soon be leaving the island. He begged Bligh to give him a passage to England to see his *taio* King George, reminding him of all the things that he had done to help the British, including the assistance that he had given to Captain Edwards in capturing the *Bounty* sailors. When Bligh replied that he could not take him to Britain, Tu was very distressed, asking him to take 'Itia's attendant Maititi instead, a 'Fine Active Person about 22 Years of Age' who would learn a great deal in England, and be of great assistance to him when he returned home. As Bligh remarked: 'I could not help thinking it was the least thing I could do for him, and that whether the Man returned or not it would be no great burthen to our Country.'[13] When Bligh gave his consent, Tu urged his friend to ask King George to send a ship to bring him to England, because this great chief would never have sent him so many gifts unless he wanted to see him.

On 11 July, Pomare II arrived in Matavai Bay, having cut short his tour around the island to farewell William Bligh. He was accompanied by about 500 'arioi, and when he came alongside the ships in his double canoe, Bligh saluted the young paramount chief with seven guns, which 'fed his Pride not a little'. When Pomare II landed, the 'arioi staged an entertainment with wrestling matches and other diversions, and that night Bligh ordered a fireworks display for the strangers. Upon meeting each other, the young chief and his mother 'Itia showed few signs of affection, although she uncovered herself to the waist. As Bligh teased her again about her indifference to her children, 'Itia picked up her son and held him on her hip, the first time that she had done such a thing in his presence. The following morning, the human sacrifice was placed in a double canoe that Hotu, the chief of Huahine, had also sent as a sign of atonement. The canoe was hung with coarse white 'arioi bark cloth and decorated with nine long rods called manutea or marae, each with a short crosspiece lashed on and decorated with red feathers, and slowly headed for Taputapuatea marae, the drums beating to keep the paddlers in time.

When Bligh set off in the pinnace for this ceremony, accompanied by Tu, Teu, 'Itia and Vaiareti, they quickly overtook the sacred canoe. At Pare they were greeted by Pomare II, riding on the shoulders of his attendant; and Ha'amanimani escorted them to Taputapuatea marae where the high priest chanted, summoning up the gods. His prayer ended with a great shout as the priests and the people called upon 'Oro; and a man entered the marae, carrying the bundle which contained the god upon his shoulders. At the same time, the double canoe was hauled up beside the marae and Pomare II and Ha'amanimani sat down on either side of it. While Ha'amanimani chanted, the drums beat in a strange rhythm, and three bunches of red feathers and the manutea rods were presented to the young paramount chief. The human sacrifice was laid in front of him, head facing, and as the drums beat loudly, the outer wrapping was taken off and the head was exposed. An old priest took a piece of bamboo and taking out the two eyes, placed them on leaves, laying one on the marae and holding up the other to Pomare II's mouth, so that the spirit of the dead man could enter his varua or spirit.

Afterwards, the young paramount chief was carried to a small shrine named Tepa, where he dismounted from his attendant's shoulders. When the image of 'Oro was laid on the ground, the red feather girdle, Te Ra'i-puatata, was unwrapped and laid on the stone pavement. As the priests chanted, Ha'amanimani wrapped the girdle around the young chief's waist and the crowd cried out 'Maeva Ari'i' ('Hail to the high chief!') three times, the marines firing a volley at each shout of acclamation. Bligh noticed that since his last sight of this famous feather girdle, its body had been decorated with red hair from Richard Skinner, the *Bounty*'s red-headed barber. In Tahiti, the head was the most *tapu* (sacred) part of the body, and because hair was a direct link with the gods, a barber was a sacred person. Red hair was more sacred still, since red was the colour of the gods. Along with the red bunting from the *Dolphin*, this red hair joined the power of the British gods to the *mana* of 'Oro. At the end of the ritual, the human sacrifice, which had been offered to Pomare II rather than to 'Oro, was buried beside Taraho'i *marae* at the entrance of the bay. Only human sacrifices offered to the god could be buried on this *marae*.

This ritual marked the climax of Bligh's third and last visit to Tahiti. This time he was determined not to linger on the island; and when he returned to Matavai Bay, he ordered the breadfruit plants to be loaded on board the *Providence*, which had been fumigated with boiling water to kill the teeming cockroaches, and the water casks to be refilled. Although Tu and 'Itia seemed saddened by his imminent departure, presenting him with pigs, coconuts and plantains, Vaiareti, who disliked Bligh, was rejoicing. As he prepared to sail from Tahiti, Bligh was dejected, remarking that while 'some others express sorrow; it is very remarkable to me the indifference with which the general run of People treat us. Very few People come about us, and the Natives have formed few attachments with any of my People. Hitherto I have been accustomed to see them show great concern at parting, and load their Friends with presents of every thing they thought would be desireable to them, but now they offer nothing remarkable.'[14]

Tobin saw it differently, however, remarking that 'every hour served to convince me of the unfeigned sorrow of these gentle people at our approaching separation'.[15] When the young lieutenant presented 'Itia with farewell gifts, she indicated that she wanted a fowling piece instead; and after asking Bligh's permission, Tobin gave it to his *taio*, along with a small portrait of himself marked on the back with the dates of his visit to the island. For his part, Tobin covetously eyed the portrait of Captain Cook that Tu had brought on board the *Providence*, although no space remained on the back of the portrait for other ships to mark the dates of their arrivals and departures. As he remarked ruefully: 'Much did I covet the polygraphic secret, to steal the portrait of this immortal navigator, which was said by those who knew him to be a most striking resemblance. Nothing I suppose could tempt this amiable chief to part with it.'[16]

Although most of the former *Matilda*s were eager to leave Tahiti in the ships, four of them had decided to remain on the island – a Jewish convict, Samuel Tollen, who had stowed away on the vessel when she sailed from New South Wales; Andrew Lind, the young Swedish sailor from Stockholm; the Irish sailor simply known as 'Connor'; and the Scotsman, James Butcher. After exhorting these men to support Tu and his family, rather than their enemies, Bligh wrote them a letter, saying that unless they acted as allies to the Pomare family, they would be treated as deserters by the next British ship that visited the island. This missive was entrusted to Ha'amanimani, who brought it to Tobin and several others to check upon its contents – a sign that after Bligh's earlier lies, the chiefs did not trust him. Other islanders, eager to sail to Peretane, tried to persuade their *taio* to hide them on board the ships in chests or barrels.

On 15 July 1792 the weather was rough and windy, with loud claps of thunder and vivid lightning flashes – signs of 'Oro's power. Bligh was forced to delay the loading of the plants; although after completing his astronomical observations, he ordered the observatory tent to be struck and taken back on board. Despite the high seas, a large double canoe with an awning arrived from Ra'iatea, bringing a party of fifteen *'arioi* to farewell the ships. The next morning was calm, and the rest of the plants were brought out to the *Providence* and loaded into the Great Cabin and on the quarterdeck, where a greenhouse had been built. Bligh gave gifts to the leading *'arioi* from Ra'iatea and a lavish present to Teu, who wept as he received it. Later that afternoon, Lieutenant Pearce drew up the marines and marched them to the boats, which had been hauled up on Point Venus. As they rowed away, the marines gave three cheers, and the islanders replied in kind; although according to Lieutenant Bond, these salutations were signs of joy that the British were leaving: 'The Natives seemed much delighted at the Evacuation and many shouts were heard, which shewed how sensible these pacific Beings were of a state of Liberty and Freedom.'[17] Later that day, Bligh sent Tobin ashore to supervise the watering party, which was filling a few last barrels. Matavai Bay was deserted and the shore camp looked so desolate that Tobin was glad to row away from 'this cheerless spot'.[18]

Although Pomare II spent most of the day paddling around the ships in his double canoe, he did not come on board; and when Bligh said goodbye, the young paramount chief wept and held on tightly to his hand until Bligh promised to see him again the next morning. When he set off for Pare, the young chief was saluted with three cheers, and his crew replied 'with great ardour'. The *Matilda*'s whaleboat was lashed to the deck of the *Providence*, and Tu, 'Itia, Vaiareti and Ari'ipaea came to spend the night on board with Bligh and Maititi, 'Itia's attendant who was about to set sail for Peretane. That evening, Bligh sent a letter to Lieutenant Portlock, saying that if they were separated at sea before reaching the Tongan islands, he would cruise around Tofua and Kao for twenty-four hours, waiting for the *Assistant*; and if they were separated after leaving the Tongan islands, he would wait for him off the coast of the New Hebrides. Since the westerly monsoon was approaching, they would not have time to explore the Endeavour Straits, but would have to sail directly to Timor.

At daylight the next morning, 100 canoes flocked around the ships, the biggest fleet that they had seen since arriving at the island. To the delight of Tu and his family, the wind died and the ships were becalmed, delaying their departure. Bligh presented many of the commoners with gifts; and as the vessels were warped out of the harbour, the crews of the canoes tore their hair and slashed their heads with shark's teeth. As Bond remarked with satisfaction, after just three months in Tahiti, they had a full cargo of plants:

> 780 large, & 3012 small Pots: 35 Tubs and 28 Boxes of Bread fruit. Of Avees [*vi* or Tahitian apple, *Spondius dulcis*], 8 large & 17 small Pots. Mattee [*Ficus tinctoria*], 5 large and one small Pot. A-ee-yah, 4 large and 31 small Pots, and 2 Tubs. Oreeah (fine Plantain [*Musa paradisiaca*]) 10 large Pots. Frahee (Mountain Plantain) two large Pots. Peeha [*Tacca leontopletaloides*], 7 large Pots. Ratta [*Inocarpus edulis*], 18 large and 7 small Pots. Ettow [*Cordia subcordata*], 2 large and 4 small Pots. Curiosity Plants, 2 large 8 small Pots & 2 Tubs.[19]

Bligh was happy with this flourishing nursery, knowing that Sir Joseph Banks and King George would be delighted that he had collected so many new species for the greenhouses at Kew Gardens. That night, Tu, 'Itia and Vaiareti slept peacefully in his cabin, and according to Tobin: 'We had the whole court on board; yet such was their good faith, this cruise did not at all alarm them.'[20]

The next day, 18 July, dawned bright and clear, but now the winds had become contrary, blowing from the north-west. No doubt Tu and his family had commanded the priests who controlled the winds to delay the ships as long as possible. Early that morning, Bligh headed from Matavai Bay to Pare, where he went ashore to take his leave of Tetupaia and Teu, his 'parents'. The old lady wept bitterly as she said goodbye; and when he returned to the *Providence*, Pomare II came alongside in his double canoe, staying there until noon, when Bligh presented him with a rich farewell gift of shirts, printed linen, axes, knives, hatchets, toys, scissors, saws, nails and beads. When Pomare II farewelled him, they shook hands – the first time that they had touched, and a striking gesture, given the paramount chief's tapu, or state of sacred restriction – and made Bligh promise to return again to the island. As the sea breeze blew up, canoes flocked around the ships, and Tu, 'Itia and Ari'ipaea insisted upon being the last to go ashore; although Vaiareti, who had quarrelled with Tu, had already landed at Pare. Out at sea, the wind was so strong that Bligh was forced to let the chiefs spend one last night in his cabin.

At dawn on 19 July 1792, the weather was calm; and Bligh loaded Tu and his family with gifts, including a musket and 500 rounds of powder and shot that Tu had urgently requested, and farewelled them. As the chiefs said goodbye to Maititi, Tu reminded his attendant to visit King George and ask him to send another ship to Tahiti to carry Tu to England. As a final act, Bligh handed over the portrait of Captain Cook, inscribed with the dates of the arrival and departure of his ships on the back, and the number of plants on board the *Providence*. As the *Matilda*'s whaleboat under Tobin set off for the shore, however, only 'Itia and the officers' washerwoman, whom they called 'Venus', were crying.

As Frank Bond remarked: 'I saw nothing of the weeping spoken of by Mr. Mortimer and others, [although] a silent sorrow hung on the brow of several persons.' According to Bond, 'Itia was popular in the wardroom, 'possessing a good heart, the most pleasing manners, and a kind of obliging disposition'; while his own *taio* Ari'ipaea was courageous and impressive, 'his manner good, his carriage princely'.[21] Captain Bligh had urged Tobin not to linger ashore, which 'made my farewell interview with these happy islanders but short, yet was it so distressing, I was glad to hurry from the scene'. The old lady Torano, who had formerly welcomed him to Pare, pressed Tobin's hand, weeping and saying, 'God bless you on the deep.'[22]

As William Bligh mused that night: 'We had marks both of regret & indifference in leaving this hospitable place. This is the second time I have experienced their friendship and regard, and I have done every thing in my power to reward them. I can venture to say that they are sensible of it.'[23] Apart from the attentions of Tu and 'Itia, however, during this visit to the island Bligh had been treated with reserve. As Morrison, one of his *Bounty* crew, later remarked, the chiefs did not really like Bligh, although during his visits they flattered him for political reasons. George Vancouver, who followed him to the island, had insulted both the high priest Ha'amanimani and Tu's brothers, and since they were both British, Bligh was held responsible for his behaviour, and the epidemic that had followed Vancouver's visit. Vaetua hated Bligh for putting his *taio* Hayward in irons on board the *Bounty*, and since his return to the island, he had offended other members of Tu's family – criticising the Tahitians for 'laziness'; reproaching 'Itia for not caring for her children; and mocking Ari'ipaea for failing to retrieve the *Matilda*'s muskets from Papara. Vaiareti, Tu's young wife, detested him (perhaps he had chided her for her naked frolics on board the *Providence*). Only Tu remained steadfastly loyal, upholding the bonds that he had forged with Captain Cook and Captain Bligh; although he was bitterly disappointed when Bligh refused to take him to England.

During his *Bounty* visit to Tahiti, Bligh had delighted in local customs, describing the island as the 'Paradise of the World', and demonstrating real insight in his descriptions of Tahitian society. After the mutiny, however, he was quick to blame the island's seductive women for leading his men astray, like the Sirens in the *Odyssey* or Eve before the Fall. In his search for self-justification, Bligh showed no mercy towards the mutineers – those 'pirates', 'wretches' and 'villains' – and their island partners. It is also probable that before he sailed from England, his attitudes towards the Tahitians had been coloured by the contacts with Dr Haweis and the other evangelical Christians, who saw the islanders as living under the dark shadow of Satan, and hoped to bring them into the light of God. The officers on board Bligh's ships knew about the proposal to bring missionaries to the island, and as they sailed away from Tahiti, George Tobin pronounced his verdict on this pious scheme:

> What the exact creed of the Tahitians is, it is not in my power to explain. Yet it [is] a good one, if faith and good works travel in amity with each other. In the latter, these islanders are "eminent beyond compare." They encourage a lesson of morality and good will among one another that puts civilised religion to blush.
>
> Let us then – still I may be in error – in the name of Providence have done with missions of the kind. Take a retrospect of their sanguinary exterminating consequences in many a large portion of the world, and humanity will tremble. The Tahitian needs no conversion; he divides what he has with the stranger, as with his neighbour. He administers to, he anticipates their wants. Can he be taught more, and still retain these amiable and generous qualities?[24]

No doubt Joseph Banks would have heartily agreed.

For the evangelical Christians and increasingly for William Bligh, however, it seemed a blasphemy to think of Tahiti as a Paradise on earth. According to a work that described the first mission on the island: 'There were some people who loved God in England who were grieved to think of the poor natives of Tahiti. "Ah!" thought they, "You may sit under the spreading trees, eating the golden bread-fruit, or drinking the sweet milk of the cocoa-nut: but how can you be happy when you know not of the Paradise above, nor of the Saviour who can wash out your many crimes in his blood? For soon death will snatch you from your sunny isle, and bring you before the judgement-seat."'[25]

And in response to a report that, unlike European swine, the Polynesian pigs in Tahiti did not roll in the mud, the *Evangelical Magazine* argued that the islanders themselves were wallowing in sensuality and sin. Instead of a terrestrial Paradise, the evangelical Christians were recasting Tahiti as Paradise after the Fall, when having eaten the forbidden fruit, Eve realised that she and Adam were naked, bringing sin into the world:

> Delightful scenes! Ye southern isles!
> Where yet a fruitful Eden smiles,
> And plenty flows around!
> Your shores no beasts of prey infest
> Nor pois'nous creatures e'er molest;
> As if un-curst the ground!
>
> Strange! That your *Swine* should not desire
> To roll, like ours, in filthy mire,
> But choose a cleanlier rest!
> But yet – unhappy still the place!
> Immers'd in sin, a sensual race,
> Man wallows there – a beast!
>
> All-hail! The gen'rous plan of love
> (The spark descended from above
> That wak'd the sacred fire.)
> Tis yours, ye messengers of grace,
> Who flew to help a ruin'd race
> To raise them *from the Mire!*[26]

# 22

## The Awful Day of Trial

As early as 2 April 1792, just before the *Providence* arrived in Tahiti, the British newspapers reported that some of the *Bounty*'s men had been captured and were being brought back home to be tried in England. Three weeks later the *Historical Chronicle* claimed that 'two of Christian's crew', one of whom was Peter Heywood, had swum out to the *Pandora* at Matavai Bay and surrendered to Captain Edwards, although they were so tanned and heavily tattooed that at first the crew mistook them for Tahitians.[1] While Fletcher Christian's relatives were terrified about what the court martial might reveal, Peter Heywood's family, convinced of his innocence and thrilled that he was alive, set about doing everything possible to save him. His sister Nessy fired off letters in all directions – to Hallett, one of the young *Bounty* midshipmen, who assured her that while Peter had been held in great esteem, he had sided 'with the criminal party; but it was a time of great Confusion among us', but added, 'notwithstanding the Friendship I had for your Brother, I shall be strictly bound by Oath to adhere to Truth'; to her father's cousin James Modiford Heywood of Marristow House, Devon, who had married the sister of Admiral Lord Howe, protesting her brother's 'extreme Youth and perfect Innocence, which nobody who knew him will for a Moment doubt'; and to Commodore Thomas Pasley, her uncle by marriage and captain of the *Vengeance*, a stern-faced, corpulent man who was fond of his niece and personally acquainted with William Bligh.[2]

Nessy also wrote a letter to her brother, describing his family's horror and distress that he had been dubbed a 'Mutineer' but saying that she would stake her life on his innocence; assuring him: 'We are at present making all possible Interest with every Friend & Connection we have to ensure you a sufficient Support & Protection at your approaching Trial.' In her letter she told Peter that during his absence their father, much troubled by his business affairs, had died, although he had known nothing about Peter's misfortunes and blessed his son on his deathbed.[3]

On 11 June 1792 the *Weekly Entertainer* published a detailed account of the voyage and shipwreck of the *Pandora*. A week later when the first bedraggled contingent of the *Pandora*'s crew, headed by Lieutenant Larkham, arrived in England from the Netherlands (where the Dutch East Indiaman *Zwan* had taken them), they were transferred to Commodore Pasley's own ship, the *Vengeance*, at Sheerness. Soon afterwards, her uncle sent Nessy a frightening letter. From what these men had said, the tale that Peter had swum out to the *Pandora* was untrue; and 'your Brother appears by all Account to be the greatest Culprit of all, Christian alone excepted. Every exertion you may rest assured I shall use to save his Life – but on Trial I have no hope of his not being condemned.' After reading this letter, their kinsman J.M. Heywood became gloomy about Peter's prospects of acquittal, saying that although he was a good-hearted boy, this would not help him 'when he is convicted of a Crime, which, viewed in a political Light, is of the blackest Dye'. Four days later, however, when Nessy's mother received a long letter from Peter, written in Batavia in December and smuggled to another ship by one of the *Pandora*'s men, the family's spirits soared.[4] In this letter, Peter ('your ill-fated Son') gave his mother a detailed account of the mutiny and his time on board the *Pandora*, assuring her 'before the Face of God of my innocence'. As Nessy exclaimed joyously in a letter to her uncle, Commodore Pasley, '[W]hen we consider his extreme Youth; only sixteen at the Time of the Mutiny, & now but nineteen; his Fortitude, Patience and manly Resignation under the pressure of Sufferings and Misfortunes . . . what Man on Earth can doubt of the Innocence which cou'd dictate such a Letter?'

According to Heywood's account, he had been asleep in his hammock when the ship was taken. Waking just after daybreak, he saw a man [Thompson] sitting on the arms chest, holding a naked cutlass. When he asked what he was doing, Thompson told him that Christian and some of his shipmates had captured the *Bounty* and taken Captain Bligh as a prisoner, intending to carry him to Britain to be tried for 'his long tyrannical, & oppressive Behaviour to his people'. Thunderstruck, Heywood woke Stewart, his messmate, and after telling him the news, climbed up the foreladder to see Bligh standing on the quarterdeck with his hands tied behind his back, guarded by Fletcher Christian, who was armed with a drawn bayonet and a pistol. When Heywood questioned his shipmates, some said that Bligh would be taken ashore to Tofua in the launch, while others said that he would be carried in irons to Tahiti. Since Tofua was a long way off and the inhabitants were fierce, he had been afraid to board

*Nessy Heywood, Peter Heywood.*

the launch, supposing that its crew would be killed by the Tongans, drown, or die of starvation or thirst.

In his letter, Heywood explained that as he stood there in amazement, 'a silent spectator', Christian ordered Hayward and Hallett into the launch; and when he heard them begging to stay on board the *Bounty*, this had confirmed his fears that a journey on the boat was likely to prove fatal. Bligh was sent down into the launch, and soon afterwards when Heywood's messmate and friend George Stewart came on deck, and asked him what he intended to do, and he answered that he had decided to stay on board the *Bounty*, Stewart told him to go below at once and fetch his things, and accompany him on the launch. As soon as they returned to their berths, however, Churchill gave Thompson orders to keep them below; and they were prevented from joining Captain Bligh on the launch.

Heywood assured his mother that when the *Bounty* returned to Tahiti after its brief visit to Tupua'i, he had hoped to escape, but the mutineers kept a close watch, threatening to shoot anyone who tried to run from the ship. Back in Tupua'i, he and Stewart joined the group which decided to return to Tahiti. During his time on that island, 'we were used by our Friends the Natives with a Friendship, & Generosity, & Humanity almost unparalleled, being such as never was equalled by the People of any civilized Nations. To the Disgrace of all

Christians.' Although he had fought in several skirmishes with their enemies, 'I was always protected by a never failing Providence'. When the *Pandora* arrived off Matavai Bay, he had been about to set off to the mountains, and sent one of his attendants to tell Coleman about the ship's arrival. Taking a single canoe, the armourer set off but capsized before reaching the frigate. Seeing this, Stewart and Heywood decided to wait until the ship was at anchor, and then paddled out in a double canoe and boarded the ship; although at first the sailors, seeing them dressed in bark cloth and heavily tattooed, mistook them for Tahitians. When he asked to see his former messmate, Hayward, 'like all Worldlings when raised a little in Life he received us very coolly, & pretended Ignorance of our Affairs; yet formerly he & I were bound in brotherly Friendship . . . We were ordered in Irons and looked upon – infernal Words! – as piratical Villains.'

After describing his sufferings on board the *Pandora*, Heywood ended his letter with loving assurances to his mother that, despite these adversities, he was well, and calm in spirit:

> I endeavour to qualify my Affliction with these three Considerations – first, my Innocence, not deserving them – second, that they cannot last long – & third, that the Change may be for the better. The first improves my Hopes – the second my Patience – & the third my Courage, & makes me thankful to God for them.
>
> I am young in Years, but old in what the World calls Adversity, & it has had such an Effect upon me, as to make me consider it as the most beneficial Incident that could have occurred.
>
> It has made me acquainted with three Things which are little known – first, the Villainy & Censoriousness of Mankind – second, the Futility of all Human Hopes, – & third, the Enjoyment of being content in whatever Station it pleases Providence to place me in. – in short it has made me more of a Philosopher than many years of a Life spent in Ease & pleasure cou'd have done.

Not realising that Bligh's father-in-law Dr Betham had died during his absence, Heywood also sent his patron and old friend an account of his calamities, asking him to intercede with his son-in-law and begging for 'pity for my Youth, Inexperience, & Misfortunes'. Elated by Peter's account of what had happened, Nessy wrote him an ecstatic letter, assuring him of her faith in him:

> My dearest & most beloved Brother. Thanks to Almighty Providence which has so miraculously preserved you, – your fond, anxious, & till now, miserable

Nessy is at last permitted to address the Object of her tenderest Affection in England! – Oh! my admirable, my heroic Boy – what have we felt on your Account! Surely my beloved Boy, you could not for a Moment imagine we ever supposed you guilty of the Crime of Mutiny.[5]

She also sent a letter to Thomas Hayward, the other midshipman and now lieutenant of the *Pandora*, seeking his support; although his father wrote back instead, saying that his son could not discuss the matter until after the court martial, but telling her when Peter might return to England.

On 21 June 1792, the *Gorgon* finally arrived in Portsmouth with Captain Edwards, who handed over the ten surviving *Bounty* prisoners to the Admiralty. After losing his ship on the Great Barrier Reef, along with thirty-one of his men and four of the 'pirates', as he habitually called them, Edwards knew that he would face a court martial, although like Bligh and his own master's mate Oliver, he had made the perilous boat crossing to Timor. There was something about the *Bounty* that seemed to provoke the loss of ships, followed by heroic small-boat voyages.

Soon after their arrival, the prisoners were transferred to the *Hector* and locked in the ship's gunroom. A week later, Captain Montagu shifted the *Hector* to Gosport, awaiting the court martial. Fortunately for the prisoners, Montagu was a close friend of Commodore Pasley's, and he was kind to Heywood and his shipmates; while J.M. Heywood's daughter Emma Bertie (who lived with her husband Captain Albemarle Bertie on board his ship the *Edgar*, now moored next to the *Hector*) provided them with every comfort, although they were shackled in leg irons.[6] While Nessy was desperate to visit him, Peter told his sister that this was impossible, but asked his mother to send a little money so that he could buy himself clothing and other items. Less diplomatically, he also wrote to Captain Bligh's wife Betsy, asking her to return some clothes that he had left with her to be laundered before setting sail on the *Bounty*. This was also an anxious time for Bligh's family, who had heard nothing from him since the *Providence* and *Assistant* sailed from the Cape of Good Hope six months earlier. When Betsy's sister Henrietta wrote to her from America, she rejoiced that after recovering his health, Bligh had been rewarded for his 'unparralled sufferings', but commiserated with her sister's distress that they had once again been separated.[7] In her next letter, Henrietta expressed an ardent wish that:

Your most sanguine hopes may be realised, that you may pass the remainder of
your lives in affluence & happiness is my earnest prayer! Surely your worthy
Husband's sufferings will be rewarded by a future exemption from toil & care,
& the improvement and growth of your pretty little flock will be at once a
source of comfort & amusement through hope to you both.[8]

At this time, there was a discussion in the Admiralty about whether or not
the prisoners should be tried immediately. Like Bligh's wife Betsy, they had
heard nothing from him since the *Providence* and *Assistant* had left the Cape of
Good Hope. Under the circumstances, they would have to wait until Lieutenant
Hayward returned to England, to give his evidence. While Peter Heywood
waited to hear about the court martial, his mother, his seven brothers and sisters
and various family friends showered him with fond messages, expressing their
belief in him and promising him every assistance. Nessy in particular was an
ardent and effective advocate, persuading many of her correspondents to see her
brother as Bligh's victim, not a villain. According to Bligh, at about this time
the Heywoods also circulated a rumour that during his absence on the second
breadfruit voyage, there had been another mutiny, and he had been sent as a
prisoner to the East Indies.[9]

In preparation for Heywood's trial, Commodore Pasley hired a legal advisor,
John Delafons, a man with a fine reputation as a counsel for courts martial who
had published a treatise on the subject. On his advice, Peter sent a petition to
the Commissioners of the Admiralty, asking for a speedy hearing. This proved
to be impossible, however, because Edwards's court martial had to be held first,
and both trials had to wait until twelve senior captains could be assembled in
Portsmouth, and Lord Hood, who would act as President in both courts martial,
returned from sea patrol.

In the meantime, his father's cousin J.M. Heywood pursued his own inquiries,
interviewing a number of the *Bounty* sailors. Afterwards, he assured Peter that his
findings gave him 'the strongest Hopes that you will clear your Character when
you are put upon your Trial'. Commodore Pasley also spoke with Fryer, Cole,
Peckover and Purcell, each of whom spoke highly of his nephew, corroborating
his account of the mutiny. Fryer's memories of the uprising had evidently altered,
because in a letter written to his wife from Batavia, he had remarked that 'the
captain & me were surprised by Misters Christian, Stewart, Young & Haywood
& the Master at Arms'.[10] In a letter to Nessy, Pasley exclaimed: 'I have likewise
seen that <u>Fellow</u> Captain Edwards, whose inhuman rigor of Confinement I
shall never forget.' Like Bligh, Edwards was being portrayed as a naval tyrant

(although according to the ship's log, only seven men out of 160, or 4 per cent, on board the *Pandora* were flogged during this voyage, and never with more than a dozen lashes – the best record of any British ship to sail in the Pacific during this period – even better than Bligh's).[11] Worried that Nessy was being over-optimistic about the outcome of the trial, Pasley warned his niece that martial law was very severe, and that 'the Man who stands neuter is equally guilty with him who lifts his Arm against his Captain in such cases. – his extreme Youth, & his delivering himself up are the strong Points of his Defence'. At the same time, Captain Bertie sent his first lieutenant to visit Heywood and advise him on how to conduct himself during the trial.

While Peter was comforted by these attentions, when he heard that his twelve-year-old brother Henry had followed him to sea, he was horrified, exclaiming, 'God help him! – he like me knew not the Troubles he was soon to encounter. I wish he was safe at Home again.' Upon learning the date that his father had died, 6 February 1790, he sent Nessy a long poem that he had composed in Tahiti on the day of his father's death, and later committed to memory – a vivid, visionary epic that opens with a lyrical evocation of his life on the island:

> Within those Limits, where the Southern Course
> Of beaming Sol by Capricorn is bound,
> Those fertile Islands lie whose ancient source
> Cannot be trac'd, nor Origin be found.
>
> The free-born Natives of whose happy soil,
> Favor'd of Heav'n, in Peace, & Plenty, live
> Crown'd with her copious Blessings, without Toil,
> With Joy receive – but with still greater give.
>
> Sure Friendship's there, & Gratitude, & Love,
> Such as ne'er reigns in European Blood
> In these degen'rate Days; tho' from Above
> We precepts have, & know what's right and good.
>
> What we pretend to – yet scarce e'er perform,
> They duly practise, & untaught, observe;
> Those Tenets, unto which, we rare conform;
> The Name we bear, they with more Truth deserve.

Halfway through the poem, as the hero is sitting on a green hill, mourning his lost home, the sky grows dark, and a loud, hollow voice booms out from the clouds, telling him not to bewail his fate, but to trust in God:

> – So depend
> On God in all Conditions, & submit
> Thyself & thy Concerns, till Life shall end,
> To his Disposal as he may think fit . . .
>
> He felt, till now unknown, a Force within,
> Resisting Passion, & subverting Sin. –
> Lo! – thus one sight of visionary Truth
> Check'd the impetuous Foibles of the Youth.[12]

As this poem suggests, during their confinement in 'Pandora's Box', Heywood and his other shipmates, led by James Morrison, the boatswain's mate, had found consolation in religion; and while he and his shipmates waited for their court martial, Heywood's letters were filled with pious resignation. At the same time, however, he prepared his defence; worked on a vocabulary of the Tahitian language that ran to 100 folio pages; and made a few sketches, including two of the wreck of the *Pandora* and one of himself, for his devoted sisters. When Nessy expressed her surprise that he was not taller, Peter responded tartly:

> Let me ask you this. Suppose the last two years of *your* growth had been retarded by close Confinement nearly deprived of all kinds of necessary Aliment – shut up from the all-chearing Light of the sun for the space of five months – & never suffered to breathe the fresh Air – without any kind of Exercise to stretch & supple my Limbs – how tall shou'd you have been my dear sister?

During this period, Morrison, a sharp, intelligent man, also prepared his defence and drafted a brief two-part Memorandum of their voyage up to the mutiny which included specific accusations against Bligh and described their voyage from Tahiti to England with Captain Edwards and the sufferings that they had endured, which was eventually sent to Sir Joseph Banks. Morrison and Heywood worked together on these projects, sharing their knowledge and memories and annotating each other's manuscripts – a welcome distraction as they awaited their trial.

On 15 August 1792, Lord Hood arrived back in Portsmouth, hurrying to

London to report on his cruise and receive instructions for the courts martial of Edwards and the *Bounty* prisoners. These were ominous times in Europe. On 10 August the Tuileries Palace in Paris was stormed and the Swiss Guard massacred; and over the days that followed, Louis XVI was arrested and imprisoned with his family. Lord Hood knew that naval law must be upheld, despite the torrent of appeals from Heywood's family, and growing doubts about the conduct of Captains Bligh and Edwards. At the same time, for the sake of morale in the Navy, justice must be seen to be done without undue brutality. Despite Commodore Pasley's warning that 'Sea Officers have a great aversion to Council', Peter's family hired a lawyer, Mr Const; while a great friend of Pasley's, Mr Graham, a former secretary of successive admirals who acted as judge advocate (or supervising officer) at many courts martial, also offered his services. Later, Graham would work for the Admiralty as a spy, and was known to pay his informants.[13] As John Bond wrote to his brother Frank, there were suspicions that witnesses had been paid to testify in Heywood's favour: 'Heywood's friends have bribed through thick and thin to save him.'[14] In the event, the two lawyers worked closely together. Muspratt also hired a lawyer, Barney, who kept a detailed set of minutes of the trial.

On 21 August, Lord Hood returned to Portsmouth; and on 5 September, Lieutenant Hayward arrived for Edwards's court martial for the loss of the *Pandora*. Upon hearing this news, and no doubt smarting over his memories of how his shipmate had treated him on board that vessel, Peter Heywood wrote to his mother, describing the *Pandora*'s arrival in Tahiti, and how he and George Stewart had taken a double canoe and paddled out to greet her captain. He explained that he had taken the tattoos that caused the *Pandora* sailors to mistake him for a Tahitian because, on the island, a man without tattoos was an outcast; assuring her: 'I was a universal Favorite amongst those Indians, & perfectly conversant in their Language . . . I was the great favorite of any Englishman on Shore & treated with respect by every Person on the Island in whose Mouths *my* Name ever was, as an Object of their Love and Esteem.'

Five days later, Edwards's trial was held, and after a cursory inquiry, he was honourably acquitted. On 11 September, Peter wrote again to his mother to say that his own court martial was imminent:

> The awful Day of Trial now draws nigh
> When I shall see another day — or — die!

*Samuel Hood, First Viscount Hood by Lemuel Francis Abbott.*

Urging her to prepare herself for either outcome, 'with the Fortitude & Resignation of a true Christian', he asked her to tell his sisters 'to <u>set</u> <u>taut</u> <u>the</u> <u>Topping-lifts</u> of their Hearts'.

On 12 September 1792, a wet squally day, the court martial of the *Bounty*'s men began on board the *Duke* in Portsmouth Harbour. The Rt Hon. Lord Hood, Vice-Admiral of the Blue, was assisted by eleven post-captains, including Captain Bertie, whose wife had done so much to assist Peter Heywood before his trial; Sir Andrew Snape Hamond, a 'particular friend' of Captain Pasley's; and Sir Roger Curtis, who was already familiar with various circumstances of the mutiny, having been one of the judges at William Bligh's court martial for the loss of the *Bounty*. In his absence, Bligh's report about the mutiny from Timor was read out to the court. This was a brief document, accusing Fletcher Christian of leading the mutiny without mentioning any of the prisoners as participants in the uprising, although it did list those men who had remained on board the *Bounty*. In addition, excerpts from Bligh's *Narrative of the Mutiny on board His Majesty's Ship* Bounty, published two years earlier, were read. In that account, Bligh identified Christian as 'the captain of the gang', and his messmates Heywood, Stewart and Young as ringleaders, while Burkett was named as among those who had taken their captain prisoner. On the other hand, Bligh noted that the armourer Joseph Coleman, the carpenter's mates Thomas McIntosh and Charles Norman, and Michael Byrne, the half-blind fiddler, had all been detained on board the *Bounty* against their wills. Although Stewart had died in the wreck of the *Pandora* and Young accompanied Christian to Pitcairn, both Heywood and Burkett were standing trial, along with the four men whom Bligh had declared innocent, and three of their shipmates – Morrison, Millward and Muspratt.

During the court martial Morrison, the thirty-year-old boatswain's mate, conducted his own defence, as did the other prisoners except for William Muspratt and Peter Heywood. With two lawyers to assist him, Heywood placed a letter before the Court asking to be tried on his own; but after retiring, the Court declined his submission. Ominously, Lord Hood argued that 'the *Bounty*'s Mutineers being charged with and . . . guilty of the same atrocious Crime', should all be tried together; and this view prevailed. The trial began with evidence from John Fryer, the master, and William Cole, the boatswain, both of whom had joined Bligh in the launch and been honourably acquitted when Bligh was tried for the loss of the *Bounty*. Fryer, who had often clashed with Bligh during the *Bounty*'s voyage, was intent upon clearing his own name, because Bligh had accused the master of not helping him to retake the ship, despite a direct request, although Fryer had a brace of pistols in his cabin.

In his evidence, John Fryer testified that on the morning of the mutiny, he was woken by the noise of shouting. Quintal and Sumner burst into his cabin, saying that he was their prisoner, and that if he did not hold his tongue he was a dead man. Although he had a brace of pistols and a sword in his cabin, he had no ammunition (although Bligh later disputed this), and in any case these weapons were quickly confiscated by Charles Churchill. On deck, when Bligh asked the master to knock Christian down, Quintal and Sumner were standing behind him, armed with muskets and bayonets. When he asked Christian what he was doing, Christian shouted:

"Hold your tongue, Sir. I have been in Hell for Weeks past – Captain Bligh has brought all this on himself." I told him that Mr. Bligh and his not agreeing was no reason for his taking the ship. "Hold your tongue Sir," he said. I said, "Mr. Christian you and I have been on friendly terms during the Voyage, therefore give me leave to speak; let Mr Bligh go down to his Cabin and I make no doubt but that we shall all be friends again in a very short time." He then repeated, "Hold your tongue, Sir, it is too late."[15]

Fryer told the court that after this exchange, he had decided to stay on board the *Bounty* to try and recapture the ship. When he spoke to the gunner about it, however, Heildbrandt overheard them and reported the conversation to Fletcher Christian; and he and Peckover were sent into the launch.

Of his shipmates who were standing trial, Fryer said that both Burkett and Millward had been armed during the mutiny; but Coleman, McIntosh, Norman and Byrne were innocent. During the uprising, he added, he had questioned the boatswain's mate James Morrison, who assured him that he knew nothing about the mutiny, although he was helping to lower the boats. When the launch rowed away from the *Bounty*, he had seen Tom Ellison loose the topgallant sails. In the launch, he had often told Bligh that during the mutiny, he did not see George Stewart or Peter Heywood ('the youngsters') on deck.

After being sworn in, William Cole, the boatswain, testified that on the morning of the mutiny he woke to hear Matthew Quintal telling Purcell, the carpenter, that the ship had been taken and Bligh was a prisoner. Climbing up the fore stairway, he saw Heywood leaning over his hammock; while on deck, Bligh was standing with his hands tied behind his back. When Cole returned below, he woke up Morrison, Millward and McIntosh, three of the prisoners, who assured him that they knew nothing about the uprising. Millward, however, remarked morosely that after 'the foolish Piece of Business before' (his desertion at Tahiti with Charles Churchill), the mutineers would certainly force him to join them; and soon afterwards, when Churchill arrived and ordered Millward to take a musket, he did so. When he saw Heywood, Coleman, Norman, McIntosh and Morrison helping to lower the launch, he supposed that they were trying to assist Captain Bligh. Soon afterwards, when Heywood went below, he heard Churchill call out, 'Keep them below', and assumed that Churchill was referring to the midshipmen Heywood and Stewart. According to the boatswain, Heywood had intended to come into the launch. Of the other prisoners, he saw Burkett, Muspratt, Ellison and Millward under arms; but Coleman, Norman and McIntosh were all detained on board the *Bounty* against their will.

The next morning when Morrison cross-examined Cole, the boatswain recalled that he had ordered his mate to help lower the boats. When Morrison asked him whether he remembered Captain Bligh protesting that the launch was overloaded, and that no more people should come on board, and that Morrison had said afterwards that he would take his chance with the ship, Cole agreed that he recalled this conversation. He also stated that Morrison had willingly followed his orders that day, and that he did not regard him as one of the mutineers.

When William Peckover, the gunner and Pacific veteran whom Bligh had refused to take on board the *Providence*, gave his evidence, he declared that during the mutiny, he had not seen Muspratt under arms. After he was sent into the launch, Thomas Burkett, one of the prisoners, fetched him some clothes. He did not see Heywood or Morrison that day; and of the prisoners, he could only say that Burkett had been armed, although he brought Peckover some clothes from his cabin. He did not see Millward carrying a musket. According to Peckover, Coleman, Norman, McIntosh and Byrne were all innocent of mutiny, and Captain Bligh had often said so during their journey in the launch.

In his testimony, William Purcell, the carpenter, reported that, like Cole, he had seen Peter Heywood and George Stewart standing by their hammocks just after the mutiny, guarded by Thompson. Later, on deck, he saw Heywood standing on the booms with his hand touching a cutlass. When he exclaimed, 'In the Name of God, Peter, what do you do with that!', Heywood immediately let the weapon drop. When the lawyers questioned him about this damning statement, Purcell said, 'I looked upon him as a person confused', and insisted that Heywood had taken no part in the conspiracy to capture the *Bounty*.[16]

The following day when the two midshipmen, Thomas Hayward and John Hallett, gave their evidence, they condemned a number of their shipmates. According to Hayward, during the mutiny he saw Ellison, one of the prisoners, arm himself with a bayonet; and both Muspratt and Millward were armed. Ellison had volunteered to guard his captain; and Millward jeered at Bligh and his companions while they were floating alongside in the launch. During that morning, Hayward had seen Peter Heywood, his messmate George Stewart and James Morrison all unarmed, standing on the *Bounty*'s booms. Later when he went below to fetch some of his possessions, noticing Heywood beside his hammock, he told him to go into the launch; but Heywood ignored him, although he was not under guard. Hayward claimed that while the launch was being lowered, James Morrison, the boatswain's mate, had looked 'rejoiced'. When Morrison cross-questioned him, asking Lieutenant Hayward whether he remembered him saying that they might retake the ship, and telling the midshipman that he would back him up, Hayward answered, 'I have a faint Remembrance of a Circumstance of that Nature.'[17] Hayward also testified that upon the *Pandora*'s arrival in Tahiti, both Heywood and Stewart had come on board as soon as the frigate anchored, and seemed happy to see Captain Edwards.

It was John Hallett, however – 'that little Wretch', as Nessy Heywood indignantly called him – who gave the most damning evidence against his shipmates. According to Morrison's account of the mutiny, this midshipman (who was only fifteen at the time of the mutiny, a year younger than Peter Heywood) had been asleep on watch when Bligh was captured, an offence punishable by death under the Articles of War; and in his letter to his wife Betsy about the mutiny, Bligh had described Hallett as a 'worthless impudent scoundrel'.[18] In his evidence, Hallett claimed that during the mutiny, he saw Ellison, Burkett and Morrison under arms – the only man to claim that Morrison had carried a weapon. He also saw Peter Heywood on deck, who was not under guard at that time, looking attentively at Captain Bligh; and when Bligh said something to him, Heywood had laughed and turned away – a suggestion that the young midshipman had mocked his commander. Of James Morrison, Hallett testified that he saw him talking to Millward, and afterwards, armed with a musket. When the launch was lowered and lay astern, Morrison had called out to his shipmates in a jeering tone, 'If my friends enquire after me, tell them I am somewhere in the South Seas.' Hallett added that he did not see Muspratt during the mutiny; that Coleman, Norman and McIntosh were kept on board against their wills; and that Byrne appeared sorrowful. In cross-questioning, when Morrison asked him to declare before God that it was Morrison whom he saw under arms, and who had jeered at his shipmates, and not any other person, Hallett replied, 'I have declared it.'[19]

When John Smith (Bligh's servant whom Fletcher Christian had ordered to serve a dram of rum to the armed men) testified, he said that after the mutiny, seeing Captain Bligh standing on the deck in his nightshirt, he went below and brought up his clothes, putting on Bligh's trousers and draping his jacket over his shoulders. When Christian ordered him to serve the armed men some rum, Peter Heywood would not drink it, and he did not notice him talking to anybody (including William Bligh), although Millward, Burkett and Ellison all had a dram. Morrison was not armed, and he did not see Muspratt.

When Captain Edwards and Lieutenant Larkham of the *Pandora* were called, they stated that upon their arrival at Matavai Bay, the armourer Coleman came on board first, followed by Stewart and Peter Heywood. According to Edwards, when Lieutenant Hayward treated Stewart and Heywood with contempt, Heywood had indignantly exclaimed that he 'should be able to vindicate his

Conduct'.[20] On the advice of his lawyers, Heywood now asked for permission to reserve his defence and his questions until the evidence had all been given, and the Court adjourned to give him this opportunity.

During the adjournment, the newspapers were filled with news of the violence in France. The mobs in Paris were killing thousands of aristocrats, transfixing them with pikes or daggers, sticking their heads on pikes, throwing the corpses in large mass graves or burning them in bonfires. Just across the Channel in Britain, the dangers of mob rule were being graphically enacted. When the court martial resumed on 17 September 1792, Mr Const read out Peter Heywood's statement of defence, explaining that after the rigours of his confinement, he could not do himself justice in an oral statement (although in fact, Const had written this statement for Heywood, replacing a version that Heywood himself had drafted). In this statement, Heywood gave a very similar account, although more detailed, to the one that he had sent his mother from Batavia. He agreed that he had helped to lower the launch, and handed things down into it; and that while he was doing this, he must have put his hand on a cutlass, although it was only for a moment and no one save Purcell had noticed it. Pleading his 'extreme youth and inexperience', Heywood admitted that he had been afraid to go in the launch, given the dangers of starvation, drowning or being killed by the natives. When his messmates Hallett and Hayward were ordered into the boat, they had both seemed alarmed; and although Hayward was an experienced sailor, he wept at the prospect. Heywood added that when the master John Fryer decided to stay on board to try and retake the ship, this had seemed to justify his decision.

In his defence, Heywood denied speaking to Bligh or laughing at him during the uprising, pointing out that in his *Narrative*, Bligh himself had said that while he was held under guard, no one was allowed to come near him. He also pointed out inconsistencies in Hayward's evidence; noting that it was Stewart, not Hayward, who had ordered him to go in the launch, and that Thompson, who was acting as their guard, had prevented them from doing so. In his testimony and afterwards, Heywood was eager to clear his friend and messmate George Stewart of any complicity in the mutiny. His own defence rested on the claim that both he and Stewart were asleep at the time of the uprising; and that afterwards, when they returned to their quarters in the cockpit, although Stewart urged him to gather his possessions and join Bligh in the launch, Thompson had prevented them from joining their comrades. While the Court did not know it, however, this part of his evidence was inconsistent with Heywood's own letter to his mother from Batavia, in which he confessed that Bligh was already in the launch when he made up his mind not to go with him. Since Bligh had not been sent into the launch until the last moment, Heywood must still have been on deck at that time, and not below with Stewart.

On the other hand, in his own manuscript account of the mutiny, Bligh wrote: 'As for the officers . . . they endeavoured to come to my assistance, but were not allowed to put their heads above the hatchway',[21] a statement that supported Heywood's story, although it was excised before the *Narrative* was published. Heywood also noted that Captain Edwards had kept him and the other prisoners in irons when the *Pandora* was sinking; and swore 'in the name of the tremendous Judge of Heaven and Earth (before whose vindictive Majesty I may be destined soon to appear)' that he was innocent of plotting, abetting or assisting in mutiny.

Under cross-questioning from Peter Heywood, John Fryer stated that when he entered the launch, the gunwales were only 8 inches above the water. He regarded Heywood as one of the captain's party, and that on board the *Bounty*, he was 'Beloved by every body, to the best of my Recollection'.[22] Cole, the boat-swain, testified that he did not hear Captain Bligh say anything to Heywood, nor had Heywood laughed during the mutiny; and that in his opinion, the young man had been on the captain's side. When Churchill called out to Thompson to 'keep them below', he believed that this referred to Heywood, who had gone below to fetch his belongings. Cole also confirmed the story about the master's plan to retake the ship. He noted that during the mutiny, Hallett and Hayward seemed agitated and very alarmed (suggesting that their evidence might be unreliable).

The gunner Peckover added that on board the *Bounty*, Heywood was 'the most amiable, deserving of every one's Esteem';[23] while the carpenter William Purcell testified that he had not heard any conversation between Bligh and Heywood during the mutiny, nor did Heywood laugh or look merry. On the contrary, he heard Churchill tell Thompson to 'keep them below'. Purcell added that at the time of the mutiny, Hallett and Hayward were both very confused, and testified that Peter Heywood's conduct was 'in every respect becoming the Character of a Gentleman, and such as merited the Esteem of every body'.[24] Captain Edwards, upon questioning, reluctantly agreed that Heywood had freely come on board the *Pandora* and helped him to locate the other mutineers, answering his questions and helping him to go through his journals. No doubt Edwards was still smarting about Heywood's testimony that, contrary to his orders, when the *Pandora* was sinking he had kept his prisoners in irons.

James Morrison, the next to defend himself, also stoutly declared his inno-cence. This slender, sallow-faced boatswain, with his long black hair and tattoos, impressed the court martial, having 'stood his own counsel, questioned all the evidences, and in a manner so arranged and pertinent that the spectators waited with impatience for his turn to call on them, and listened with attention and delight during the discussion'.[25] According to Morrison, when he helped to lower the boats, he had been following William Cole's orders; and when Fryer asked him to support him in retaking the ship, he said that although he feared it was too late, he would try. Immediately after this exchange, however, Fryer had been taken below, and was soon sent into the launch. By the time that Fryer boarded the launch, it was very low in the water, and Bligh declared that no one else could come on board. When he heard this, Morrison said to Cole that he intended to stay on the ship, and Cole shook his hand, saying, 'God bless you, my boy, I will do you Justice if ever I reach England.'[26] Morrison added that when Hayward spoke to him, signalling his intention to knock down Charles Churchill, he had offered his help. He had loaded pork, gourds of water and two cutlasses into the boat for Captain Bligh; although when Churchill handed down two more, he sneered at Bligh, '*There*, Captain Bligh! you *don't* stand in Need of *fire-arms* as you are Going among your *friends*'[27] – making it plain that he knew that Bligh was likely to be attacked in Tonga. Like Peter Heywood, Morrison absolutely denied any complicity with the mutineers.

Norman and McIntosh both had letters from Captain Bligh, declaring that they had been kept on board the *Bounty*; and since their innocence was clear, they said very little. As for Tom Ellison, the short, stocky young sailor with his name and the date of his arrival in Tahiti tattooed on his arm, a protégé of Duncan Campbell's, he pleaded that at the time of the mutiny, he had been only sixteen years old. When he saw Mr Christian, looking like 'a Madman, his long hair luse, his shirt Collair open', bringing Captain Bligh on deck as a prisoner, he was 'amaz'd and Terrifyde'.[28] Seeing the two midshipmen, Hayward and Hallett, weeping when they were sent into the launch, he had been too afraid to follow them; and in any case, Bligh had 'begged for god sake that no more would come In, for she would be over loaded and sink with them'.

Thomas Burkett, twenty-two years old, tall, fair, heavily tattooed and pock-marked, gave the most vivid account of the uprising. He claimed that when the mutiny began, Fletcher Christian, 'with Fury in his looks', had forced him to take a musket. Afterwards when Christian went below to Bligh's cabin, he heard a door being kicked in, and glass smashing. Churchill called out for cord to bind Bligh's hands, and when no one responded, roared, 'You Infernal buggers, hand down a seizing or I'll come and play hell with you all.' When Christian brought Bligh on deck without his trousers, Burkett, noticing Bligh's shirt caught up in his bonds, exposing his genitals, pulled down the garment and told John Smith to fetch his clothes, saying, 'It is a shame to see him naked.'[29]

John Millward, the able-bodied sailor with a tattoo of a Tahitian breastplate on his belly, confirmed Morrison's claim that Fryer had asked them to help retake the ship, and said that he had agreed to assist them. When Quintal forced him to take a musket, he had accepted the weapon, hoping that he could use it to assist Morrison and Fryer. William Muspratt, another of the sailors, who was thirty years old, also admitted that he had picked up a musket, but declared that he had done so in order to help Fryer retake the ship. At this point, Muspratt asked the Court to pass sentence, acquitting Byrne and Norman so that he could call them as witnesses, but the Court refused its permission.

When the court martial reassembled the following day, Lord Hood read out the verdicts. He announced that the charges of mutiny against Peter Heywood, James Morrison, Thomas Ellison, Thomas Burkett, John Millward and William Muspratt had been proved, and that each of them should 'suffer Death by being hanged by the Neck' on board one of His Majesty's ships. He added, however, that given a number of circumstances, the Court 'most humbly and earnestly' recommended Peter Heywood and James Morrison for a royal pardon. The charges of mutiny had not been proved against Charles Norman, Joseph Coleman, Thomas McIntosh and Michael Byrne, each of whom was acquitted. As soon as the sentences were pronounced, Muspratt handed over a note penned by his lawyer, protesting that he had not been permitted to call those declared innocent as witnesses, although in the criminal courts, an early verdict of not guilty for some parties in a group action would allow others to call upon them to testify.

Horrified by this verdict, Heywood wrote his mother a despairing letter: 'I must now communicate to You the melancholy Issue . . . All Hope of Worldly Joy is fled far from me! On Tuesday Morning the 18 inst. the dreadful Sentence of Death was announced upon me!'[30]

Meanwhile, on the Isle of Man, the Heywood family were in agonies, awaiting the news. Nessy and Peter had been exchanging poems, and on 10 September 1792 when she feared that the court martial was imminent, Nessy wrote a poem called 'Anxiety':

> Doubting, dreading, fretful Guest
> Quit, ah! Quit this tortur'd Breast!

Why with thou my peace invade
And each brighter prospect shade?

Pain me not with endless Fear,
But let Hope my Bosom chear;
While she softly whispers me,
"Lycidas again is free . . ."

Hence – nor darken Joy's soft Bloom,
With thy pale, & sickly Gloom:
Nought have I to do with thee –
Hence – begone –Anxiety.

On the morning of 17 September when a little boy, the son of one of the Heywood's friends, ran into their house, he blurted out that the trial was over, and that all the prisoners had been condemned, although Peter was recommended for mercy. The boy had heard the news from a fisherman who read the story in a Liverpool newspaper, but had forgotten to bring the paper with him. Heywood's family was distraught – and to make matters worse, over the next seven days the winds were contrary, and no ship could enter or leave Douglas Harbour. Finally, Peter's brother James took a ship to Liverpool where he was able to confirm the report.

Although their friends on the island assured them that a recommendation of mercy from a court martial was almost the same as an acquittal in a criminal court, the Heywood family was terrified that Peter would be hanged. Mrs Bertie hastened to write to Mrs Heywood, assuring her that in the court martial, the _Bounty_'s officers had given her son 'the highest Character imaginable', and that his life was safe; while Heywood's lawyer Mr Graham told her that although 'from a Combination of Circumstances, Ill-nature, & mistaken Friendship, the Sentence is terrible', according to the King's Attorney-General, Peter was 'as safe as if he had not been condemned!'. Despite similar assurances, Peter was shattered, and once again he turned to religion, declaring to a family friend: 'I bow my devoted Head, with that Fortitude, Chearfulness, resignation, which is the duty of every Member of the Church, of our blessed Saviour and Redeemer Christ Jesus!'

After the sentences had been pronounced, the chaplain from the _Bedford_, Reverend William Howell, the minister of St John's Chapel, Porteas, who had often visited the _Bounty_ sailors during their confinement, prayed with the condemned prisoners, trying to calm their fears. He also spent time with Heywood and Morrison, encouraging them to work on their manuscripts about Tahiti, the mutiny and their voyage as prisoners to England, which they intended to publish together. Heywood worked on his vocabulary; and after completing his shorter Memorandum, sent it as a letter to Reverend Howell and headed '*Hector* 10 October 1792',[31] Morrison began a much longer manuscript (which eventually numbered 384 folio pages) describing his memories of their journey to Tahiti, which recounted many episodes unfavourable to Bligh, and a detailed account of life on the island, which he was preparing for publication (with Howell's assistance), along with Heywood's vocabulary.[32] As he listened to their tales about Bligh's behaviour towards his crew, the chaplain became increasingly indignant, convinced that Christian had been driven to mutiny by his commander; and that the *Bounty*'s crew had also been unjustly treated.

On 11 October, when still no decision had been reached about Peter's fate, Nessy Heywood wrote a poignant letter to Lord Chatham (who had close ties to William Wilberforce, the best friend of his brother Lord Pitt, and a close friend of Edward Christian's), assuring him that her brother was 'dearer & more precious to me than any Object on Earth', and enclosing ten pages of explanatory comments that Heywood (or perhaps his lawyer Const) had written about the various points of evidence against him at the court martial. Two weeks later, Peter Heywood and James Morrison were pardoned; and William Muspratt, whose legal gamble had paid off, was given a stay of execution (and later also pardoned).[33] After weighing all the evidence, the authorities had decided that those men who had taken the least active part in the mutiny should be set free. Although none of them had actively tried to help their captain or retake the ship, this was equally true of the master Fryer and the two midshipmen, Hayward and Hallett, who had been forced into the *Bounty*'s launch by the mutineers against their will, but were nevertheless acquitted at Bligh's court martial. Captain Montague of the *Hector* was ordered to release Heywood and Morrison.

According to the *Morning Chronicle*, after reading out the order in front of the prisoners and the ship's company, 'Captain Montague, in the most elegant and officer-like manner, pointed out to the prisoners the evil of their past conduct; and, in language that drew tears from all who heard him, recommended to them to make atonement by their future good behaviour.'[34] Shortly after the pardons, Reverend Howell wrote to his friend and former shipmate Molesworth Phillips (a friend of Banks's), the lieutenant of marines who had served with Bligh during Cook's third voyage, confiding:

It is very natural for Sir Joseph Banks not to think so unfavorably of Bligh as you or I may – there was a time when no one could have an higher opinion of an officer than I had of him – so many circumstances, however, have arisen up against him attended with such striking marks of veracity that I have been compelled to change that idea of him into one of a very contrary nature.[35]

Howell also spoke about Morrison's short two-part Memorandum, offering to send the manuscript to Banks so that he could read it. In this account, Morrison claimed among other things that Bligh had cheated his men of their provisions, and accused him of fraudulent conduct, saying that 'the Bills drawn at the Cape of Good Hope will prove, that Wm. Muspratt and Thos. Hayward, both belonging to the *Bounty* have signed as respectable merchants of that place', so that Bligh could claim for purchases that never happened. The boatswain's mate added that the mutiny had succeeded because these men 'had been base enough to sign false Survey-Books and papers, to the prejudice of his Majesty & Government, & perhaps now, stung with remorse, their Courage fled; the Love of their Country was gone before'.[36]

While Morrison's accusations were aimed at Bligh, they also cast doubt upon Banks's judgement as Bligh's patron and mentor. After reading his short account, it seems likely that Banks used his influence to prevent the publication of the longer manuscript that Morrison was writing, and later helped to secure him a place as a gunner in the Navy, in return for his silence.[37]

On the evening of 28 November 1792, Nessy Heywood was reunited with her brother in London. At 10 a.m. the next morning she wrote to her mother: 'I have seen him – clasped him to my Bosom – & my Felicity is beyond Expression. I can write no more but to tell you that the three happiest Beings at this Moment on Earth are your most dutiful Children.' The letter was signed by Nessy, Peter and their brother James. At 9 a.m. that same morning, a gun was fired on board HMS *Brunswick* and a yellow flag raised to assemble the boats from all the ships in the fleet, manned and armed to witness the executions. At 10 a.m. when Burkett, Ellison and Millward were led out of the *Brunswick*'s gunroom, the sailors thanked Captain Curtis for the humane way in which they had been treated during their confinement after the court martial. While Peter was celebrating with his brother and sister in London, Millward stood and addressed his fellow sailors:

Brother Seamen, you see before you three lusty young fellows about to suffer a shameful death for the dreadful crime of mutiny and desertion. Take warning by our example never to desert your officers, and should they behave ill to you, remember it is not their cause, it is the cause of your country you are bound to support.[38]

Nooses were tied around the prisoners' necks, with ropes leading aloft, and James Morrison blessed each of his shipmates. At 11.26 a.m. when a gun was fired, the sailors assigned to each rope hauled hard away, leaving the corpses dangling from the yardarms.

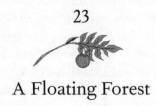

# A Floating Forest

When William Bligh set sail from Tahiti on 19 June 1792, he knew nothing about the wreck of the *Pandora*, or that some of the *Bounty* mutineers had been taken to England. Now that his dream of an island Utopia in the South Seas was over, he fixed his gaze upon the glory and rewards that awaited him in the West Indies and London when his cargo of breadfruit was safely delivered. As the *Providence* and the *Assistant* sailed past the coast of Tahiti, Maititi ('Itia's high-born attendant) gazed wistfully at his homeland; and as the ships headed for Huahine, Paupo, the *taio* of Mr Wiles, the gardener, who had stowed away between-decks on the *Providence*, emerged from his hiding place. Although Bligh was unaware of his past history, Paupo had attached himself to Fletcher Christian after the mutiny on the *Bounty*, accompanying him to Tupua'i where he had fought in the battle against Tinarou's warriors, shooting several men and killing another with a club. Christian had given him a naval coat, of which he was so proud that the sailors called him 'Jacket'; and since Christian's departure from Tahiti, Paupo had served in Po'e'eno's army, shooting three of Tu's men with the musket that he had learned to use in Tupua'i.[1] Bligh was reluctant to take any islanders with him to England, but Smith and Wiles, the two botanist-gardeners employed by Joseph Banks, managed to persuade him that Paupo's knowledge of Tahitian plants would be invaluable during the voyage.

Intent upon making a fast passage to the East Indies, Bligh was unwilling to stop at any of the Society Islands, sailing past them at a distance. Eager to discover more about the *Bounty* and the *Pandora*, however, he decided to call at Aitutaki (which he had visited in the *Bounty* in 1789), because the Tahitians had assured him that during his visits to Tahiti, Fletcher Christian had said that Captain Cook and Bligh himself had settled on that island. On 23 July the cone-shaped peak of Aitutaki appeared on the horizon, and early the next morning canoes were launched from the beaches. When three of these craft came alongside the *Assistant*, a priest holding a plaited coconut branch and a piece of white cloth in each hand chanted an incantation, handing a branch up to Lieutenant Portlock. As Portlock sent down gifts, the men boarded the *Assistant* where they greeted the strangers by pressing noses; although three women, each about thirty years old, stout and poorly clad, stayed on board their canoes. These people had brought plantains, coconuts and some baked breadfruit; and eagerly bartered pieces of glazed bark cloth painted in small red, black and white squares; little mats woven in differently coloured fibres; four paddles, carved 'like Cornish work' and stained with black patterns; five spears (including one tipped with a stingray barb); four pearl-shell gorgets and a necklace made of palm nuts, for large adzes and nails. Their hair was lightened with lime, their faces daubed with red ochre, and their legs, arms and torsos were tattooed although their backsides were not marked.

Soon afterwards, a canoe carrying about a dozen men approached the *Providence*, which had stayed further out to sea, where they conversed with Maititi and Paupo. Although their languages were different, the islanders could understand each other; and the Aitutaki men assured the Tahitians that although no white men had landed on their island, three ships had sailed past (which Bligh guessed must have been the *Bounty*, the *Pandora* and the little schooner that Edwards had confiscated from the *Bounty* sailors). They pronounced the names 'Peretane' (Britain) and 'Tahiti' very distinctly; and identified the chiefs of their island as Kamakaia and Tongaware. When these men invited Maititi and Paupo ashore, however, the Tahitians just laughed. The visitors avidly bartered spears, pearl-shell breastplates hung on collars of plaited human hair, turtle-shell fish-hooks with copra lines and a stone adze with a circular edge, for nails and iron tools; and when one of them saw Bligh looking at a piece of bark cloth, he handed it to him, saying courteously, 'Take it – you are wellcome, but it is wet with the Sea.'[2]

Realising that the *Providence* was drifting westwards, these men jumped into their canoes and paddled ashore, leaving two of their companions behind. Unwilling to take any more passengers, Bligh forced them to jump into the sea; and although they swam towards the shore, one of them became so exhausted that if Lieutenant Portlock had not taken him into the *Assistant*, he would have drowned. Stopping the canoes, Portlock made them take him back to shore. As Tobin remarked: '[T]he conduct of the islanders on this occasion gave us but an unfavourable opinion of their humanity, nor could our kind and gentle Tahitians help expressing their indignation in the most feeling manner against those in the canoes for deserting their countrymen.'[3]

*Aitutaki by George Tobin.*

During this brief visit to Aitutaki, Bligh saw fifteen dugout canoes, some long and single with outriggers and four of them double, the largest carrying fifteen people; and about 400 inhabitants. The canoes were made of breadfruit wood, very white and decorated with a line of red peas with black eyes along the hull; while the larger ones, which carried about twenty people, had a kind of 'gallows' 8 feet high at the stern, decorated with man-o'-war bird feathers. None of these canoes had sails, although occasionally their crews slung a small piece of cloth between two spears to catch the wind; and in the lagoon, they punted with long poles. Most of the houses at Aitutaki seemed to be open-sided sheds, but among the coconut trees Bligh could see some large shelters, high and pointed like haystacks, similar to those in Hawai'i. On the beach, the women danced the *heiva*, making enticing gestures towards the strangers. As Tobin remarked, the *Providence* and *Assistant*, loaded as they were with plants, must have looked like 'floating gardens'. From the masthead, as he gazed down at the breadfruit and other plants on the quarterdeck, and the rigging decked with plantains, coconuts and other fruit and vegetables, this 'bird's eye' view presented the *Providence* in a garb of green, attended by the *Assistant* in 'the same gay livery'.[4]

After sailing from Aitutaki on 25 July, the ships headed west, passing the coast of Niue (which Captain Cook had dubbed 'Savage Island') and the northern Tongan islands. Although Cook had named the Tongan archipelago the 'Friendly Isles', Bligh, who had bitter memories of Tongan warriors after the attack on the launch at Tofua, gave these islands a wide berth. On 5 August, approaching the

Fijian archipelago, they came to the island of Mothe (now Sunday Island), and very early the next morning a small outrigger canoe with a curved prow paddled out to the *Providence* with two men on board, who bartered a few coconuts for adzes and nails. After sunrise when another canoe with a crew of four came alongside, two of these men boarded the *Providence*, offering spears and clubs as well as coconuts in exchange for iron tools and nails. The hair of one of these men was greased and plaited in long tails, while the others had their hair cut short and whitened with lime. Although they had no tattoos (except for one who had a few markings on his heel), another of these men had his ear pierced and stretched almost to his shoulder, while several had two joints amputated from the little finger, a sign of mourning. Their canoes were 18 feet long, sharp at both ends and hewn from logs of dark red wood. At a distance, the sailors saw a very large sailing canoe with a cabin; and when they spoke to their visitors about Tongatapu, they seemed familiar with that island. As Tobin concluded: 'That there is an intercourse between [Fiji and Tonga] can hardly be doubted.'⁵

As the ships sailed through the islands of the Fijian archipelago, Bligh, fearful of desertions, added a warrant officer to each watch to keep a close eye on the men, as well as a lookout for shoals, reefs and coastlines. On 8 August when they passed the island of Ngau, which looked so enticing that he called it 'Paradise Island', he was glad of these precautions. Inside the reef the sea was as flat as a mirror, and on shore 'nothing could exceed the beauty of the Country, it was cultivated far up into the Mountains in a regular and pretty manner. Fine Plantain Walks and Shades of Cocoa Nutt and other Trees were rendered more picturesque by the dwellings that were among them.'⁶ One large village stood on the top of a hill, reached by a well-beaten path and shaded by a 'charming Grove of Trees'. Its houses were thatched on the sides as well as on the roof, with just one doorway. As Bligh watched through his spyglass, two flags were hoisted ashore on tall coconut trees as a signal, warning the inhabitants of danger.

Although three canoes raced out from the shore, trying to overtake the ships, they were unable to catch the *Providence* and her consort. Their crews wore pearl-shell breastplates, and some had white bark-cloth turbans. One man gestured at a piece of red cloth, perhaps trying to indicate a previous encounter with Europeans. As Lieutenant Portlock wrote: 'There can remain but little doubt of these islands being the Feejee Islands that the Friendly Islanders speak so much about. Tasman, it appears (in 1643) fell in with the eastern or small cluster of this group, but certainly Captain Bligh is the discoverer of the Western or large group.'⁷ Indeed, Bligh had previously sailed past some of the Fijian islands in the *Bounty*'s launch. Although he was sorely tempted to visit this lovely place, he decided to ensure the safety of the plants by making a rapid passage to the East Indies. As he later wrote to Joseph Banks: 'I must bear the mortification of having no intercourse with the Natives – I never gave up any thing so reluctantly.'[8] After sighting Kandavu, the ships headed for the northern New Hebrides (which Bligh had also passed in the *Bounty*'s launch).

At this time Bligh and Bond continued to argue, and as the young man wrote in his journal:

> Several affairs have lately occurred to prevent the cordiality wh should have existed between my commander and myself, and his remarks tended to deprive me of self-confidence. I was, e.g., reproached and threatened because my men in the Fore Tops yard were beaten by Tobin's and Guthrie's, the carpenter was abused for acting on my orders and ordered to take the skippers out, the boatswain was similarly treated. The usual etiquette in our respective positions was quite set aside.[9]

On 28 August when the *Providence* and *Assistant* approached the waters of the Torres Straits, a large waterspout spiralled down from a small black cloud, spinning and zig-zagging ahead of the *Providence*. The next day, a white studding-sail boom floated past which they thought might belong to one of the ships of La Pérouse, which were still missing in these waters.

On 31 August, Bligh sent Lieutenant Portlock ahead in the *Assistant*, who climbed to the masthead of his little ship to try and detect a channel through this 'labyrinth of rocks and shoals'.[10] Sailing through a passage that Bligh named 'Bligh's Entrance', they reached the Murray Islands; and on 6 September, four large canoes raced out towards the whaleboat and cutter, which were ahead of the *Providence*, their crews wearing chest and back protectors in case the locals proved hostile. Although Lieutenant Tobin hoisted a signal in the cutter asking for help, the ships did not see it; and as a canoe about 50 feet long intercepted the cutter, their leader sat on the roof of a little hut amidships while another man held up a green coconut. At a signal from their leader, its crew of nine naked men began to arm themselves with bows and arrows; and just as they were about to shoot, Tobin ordered his men to fire a volley with their muskets. A number of the warriors fell wounded; and seeing their leader still sitting on his perch, the coxswain shot him dead. When this canoe dropped back, three others came to join it, heading towards the cutter. Paupo, who was keeping watch from the masthead of the *Providence*, saw the smoke from the muskets and informed the officers, who sent the pinnace, crewed by armed men, racing to their rescue.

Over the days that followed, there were several peaceful encounters with other canoes, whose crews quietly bartered their bows and arrows for iron. On 8 September the men in the boats, led by Mr Nichols, briefly visited a village on Dalrymple Island, where the inhabitants welcomed them, waving green branches and clapping their hands; and were given gifts of iron. These people indicated that they were familiar with firearms by whistling and making a noise like a ball whizzing through the air.

On 11 September as they sailed past Dungeness and Warrior islands, the two ships were ambushed. Nine canoes approached the *Providence* while others surrounded the *Assistant*, shooting arrows and wounding three of her crew. When Portlock raised the signal calling for help, Bligh ordered his men to fire two quarterdeck guns loaded with round shot and grape into the attacking flotilla, and 'they fled, and the Natives jumped from their Cannoes into the Sea and Swam to the Windward like Porpoises'.[11] As they swam, these men stroked with alternate hands – the first description of the swimming style now known as the 'Australian crawl'.

During this passage, the weather was dry and scorching hot, and the water on the ships was running low. In obedience to his orders, Bligh gave priority to the plants, and the men were soon so thirsty that, in desperation, they licked drops of water from the watering can; and once, filled it with seawater instead, which was then accidentally sprinkled on some of the plants. In a rage, Bligh threatened to flog the offenders, but the sailors refused to identify them.[12] On 21 September they finally reached the open sea, and several days later one of the men who had been shot with an arrow died of his wounds.

When the expedition anchored at Kupang on 2 October 1792, the Dutch authorities greeted the ships with a salute of fifteen guns, and Bligh was given the 'melancholy intelligence of the shipwreck of the *Pandora* at the eastern entrance of the straits through which we had so providentially searched our way'.[13] Before going ashore, he wrote a letter to Sir Joseph Banks, listing the islands he had visited and reporting triumphantly that upon sailing from Tahiti, he had 1281 pots and tubs on board filled with 2634 plants; although during their passage to the East Indies, the contents of 200 of these pots had perished. At the end of this letter, he added, 'I trust that after all I have done I shall once see you to prove I have accomplished every thing that could be expected and to give you joy of the Plants being safe landed at Jamaica. My Eyes are so inflamed it distresses me to write . . . Pray remember me to my poor little Family.'[14]

During this visit, the East Indies once again proved to be an unhealthy destination. Many of Bligh's men were stricken with malaria and dysentery; and his feverish headaches returned, so that 'my Brains feel like being in a state of boiling'. Mr Wanjon, the Dutch officer who had been so kind to Bligh after his ordeal in the *Bounty*'s launch, and had been promoted to governor as a result of Bligh's intervention, showered him and his officers with hospitality, inviting them to dinner at his cool, shady house on the banks of the Pantassey River. He also showed Bligh a copy of his original deposition to the Dutch authorities upon the mutiny of the *Bounty*, although unfortunately Edwards's account of the loss of the *Pandora* and the fate of the *Bounty* sailors whom they had captured had been mislaid. Over the next few days, the two botanist-gardeners, Wiles and Smith, collected ninety-two pots of local plants (including mangoes, betel nut and a seed-bearing breadfruit) to replace the breadfruit plants that had died in the Torres Straits.

Although Maititi and Paupo were delighted to have arrived in a European settlement, they found the Malays repellent because of their black teeth.[15] From Kupang, Bligh sent an adoring letter to his wife:

> My Dear Dear Love and My Dear Children,
> This is the last Voyage I will ever make if it pleases God to restore me safe to you. I hope I shall live to see you & my Dear Little Girls. Success I hope will crown my Endeavours & that we shall at last be truly happy.
> Next June, my Dear Betsy, I hope you will have me home to protect you myself – I love you dearer than ever a Woman was loved – You are, nor have not been a moment out of mind – Every joy and blessing attend you my Life, and bless my Dear Harriet, My Dear Mary, My Dear Betsy, My Dear Fanny and my Dear Ann. I send you all many Kisses on this paper & ever pray to God to bless you. I will not say farewell to you now my Dear Betsy because I am homeward bound – I shall lose no time every happyness attend you my Dearest Life and ever remember me your best of Friends & most affectionate Husband.
> My Eyes are now ready to start out of my head & I am tortured with the heat. God bless you my Dear Betsy.[16]

After the collapse of his vision of a 'Paradise of the World' in Tahiti, where he had been so greatly honoured, Bligh's solace in life, his wife and six daughters (for some reason, he forgot to mention Fanny's twin sister Jane), had become even more precious.

After only eight days at Kupang, Bligh hastened to St Helena, arriving there on 17 December 1792, although 272 more breadfruit plants perished during the passage. One of the marines also died, an older man 'whose constitution was much impaired by intemperance'. When this man was given a sea burial, Paupo was horrified, protesting that it would be too cold in the water, and the sharks would eat him. Now that his nervous headaches had returned, Bligh was irascible and peremptory, harassing his officers, particularly Frank Bond, his nephew and first lieutenant. Intent on rescuing his reputation by celebrating the success of this expedition, several days out from St Helena he ordered his men to hand in their journals. Although at this time, journals from voyages of discovery were routinely required to be handed in to the Admiralty, his officers were surprised and angry. Bond, who had written a detailed account of their voyage, was outraged, writing a fiery letter to his brother accusing William Bligh of tyranny, vanity and overweening arrogance, and giving a keen insight into the kind of conduct that so often left Bligh's subordinates seething with impotent rage:

Yes Tom, our relation had the credit of being a tyrant in his last expedition, where his misfortunes and good fortune have elevated him to a situation he is incapable of supporting with decent modesty. The very high opinion he has of himself makes him hold every one of our profession with contempt, perhaps envy: nay, the Navy is but [a] sphere for fops and lubbers to swarm in, without one gem to vie in brilliancy with himself. I don't mean to depretiate his extensive knowledge as a seaman and nautical astronomer, but condemn that want of modesty, in self-estimation.

To be less prolix I will inform you that he has treated me (nay, all on board) with the insolence and arrogance of a Jacobs; and not withstanding his passion is partly to be attributed to a nervous fever, with which he has been attacked most of the voyage, the chief part of his conduct must have arisen from the fury of an ungovernable temper. Soon after leaving England I wished to receive instruction from this imperious master, until I found he publickly exposed any deficiency on my part in the Nautical Art, &c.

His maxims are of that nature that at once pronounce him an enemy to the lovers of Natural Philosophy, for to make use of his own words, "No person can do the duty of a 1st Lieut. who does more than write the day's work of his publick Journal!" This is so inimical to the sentiments I always hope to retain, that I find the utmost difficulty in keeping on tolerable terms with him.

Every dogma of power and consequence has been taken from the Lieutenants, to establish, as he thinks, his own reputation – what imbecility for a post Captn! One of the last and most benificent commands was, that the Carpenter's Crew should not drive a nail for me without I would first ask his permission – but my heart is filled with the proper materials always to disdain this humiliation.

Among many circumstances of envy and jealousy, he used to deride my keeping a private journal, and would often ironically say he supposed I meant to publish. My messmates have remarked he never spoke of my possessing one virtue – tho' by the bye he has never dared to say I have none. Every officer who has nautical information, a knowledge of natural history, a taste for drawing, or anything to constitute him proper for circumnavigating, becomes odious; for great as he is in his own good opinion, he must have entertained fears some of his ship's company meant to submit a spurious Narrative to the judgment and perusal of the publick.

Tired heartily with my present situation, I will conclude it by inserting the most recent and illegal order. Every Officer is expected to deliver in their private Logs ere we anchor at St. Helena. As our expedition has not been on discoveries, should suppose this an arbitrary command, altho the words King's request; Good of the Country, Order of the Admiralty &c &c &c., are frequently in his mouth – but unparelled [sic] pride is the principal ingredient of his composition.

The future will determine whether promotion will be the reward of this voyage: I still flatter myself it will, notwithstanding what I have said . . . My time is so effectually taken up by Duty that to keep peace I neglect all kind of study, yet the company of a set of well-informed Messmates make my moments pass very agreeably, so that I am by no means in purgatory.[17]

If Fletcher Christian had written a letter to one of his brothers off the coast of Tofua, it would have had an identical tone of incandescent fury.

When he landed at St Helena, Bligh presented Governor Brooke with a number of plants including a dozen breadfruit plants; and the seeds of mountain rice. The local officials sent him a letter expressing their gratitude, saying that the sight of the ships 'had raised in them an inexpressible degree of wonder and delight to contemplate a floating garden transported in luxuriance from one extremity of the world to the other'.[18] Delighted to have delivered his first cargo of plants, Bligh wrote another letter to Sir Joseph Banks, giving an inventory of these plants and adding: 'I most sincerely pray you may live to hear they flourish, and to know Thousands are fed with their Fruit – Posterity will ever remember you for being the means of transmitting to them such an inestimable Jewel.'[19] In closing, he remarked plaintively that since his departure from England, he had received no letters from his family or friends.

Bligh's men enjoyed their time at St Helena, with its mild, refreshing climate and hospitable people. The local women were fair-skinned and attractive, and many of the sailors were smitten. As Tobin remarked: 'I verily believe that no one was ever five days at this island without getting a wound from the eyes of some fair damsel or other.'[20] Maititi and Paupo were fascinated by the buildings and the fortifications; and when the governor gave them each a suit of red clothing (the sacred colour in the islands) and ordered his troops to demonstrate their drill, with the military band playing and the soldiers firing cannons, they were ecstatic. When he invited them to a play, however, the two islanders remarked that 'it was very bad and that their own country Heivas were much preferable'.[21] The Malay inhabitants often questioned these men about their homeland; and one day while Tobin was walking with Maititi, they met a couple of old British soldiers who stood and gaped at the islander. After a while, one asked the other, 'And what do you suppose will be done with him on his arrival in England?' 'Why you fool,' said his friend, 'what should I suppose? Why he will be put in the Tower to be sure for a rare sight.' Although Tobin was unhappy to hear these men 'disposing of our friend with the wild beasts of the creation',[22] Maititi, an aristocrat in his home island, was mortified. After this incident, he drank too much at dinner and became inebriated, a state he considered uncouth (although Paupo, a commoner, often got drunk), later apologising for this lapse with intense embarrassment.

During their visit to St Helena, one of the young gentlemen from the *Providence* caught yellow fever, and died. Smallpox was raging on the island, and when Bligh arranged for Maititi and Paupo to be inoculated, a kindly gentleman named Mr Raymond placed his house, horses and carriage at their disposal. While they were recuperating, they found it almost impossible to drink the milk prescribed as a remedy, finding its taste revolting; and although Maititi was a good patient, Paupo was often short-tempered, quarrelling with their black nurse. One day when she tried to persuade him to eat, he exclaimed, 'I do not want to eat, my belly is full'; and when she persisted, took her finger and poking it in his ear, shouted, 'Perhaps you might find room in my head!' Although they survived the inoculations, neither of them was ever well again. Raymond, an eccentric, humorous man, often entertained the ships' officers, and during these convivial evenings the young men sang and composed poetry about their adventures, including the following immortal lines:

> Two Whales were seen upon the sea,
> Wagging their tails in extacy.[23]

When Maititi recovered, Raymond taught him how to ride; and upon returning to the *Providence*, Tu's envoy sent him a gift of bark cloth, begged from his
shipmates.

As soon as his ships were refitted, Bligh sailed for the West Indies, losing
another of his men en route from dysentery. On 22 January 1793 they sighted
Barbados, and the next morning the island of St Vincent appeared on the horizon.
Bligh had last visited these islands in 1787, as a merchant captain for Duncan
Campbell, his wife's uncle. As soon as the ships were anchored, Bligh sent a
message to the governor, asking for the plants destined for this island to be taken
ashore as soon as possible; and early the next morning a line of black men arrived
at the ships and picked up the pots, carrying 544 potted breadfruit plants balanced
on their heads 2 miles to the Botanic Garden, returning to the *Providence* with 465
pots containing a selection of West Indies plants for the King's gardens at Kew.

That afternoon, a deputation of local dignitaries invited Bligh and his officers
to a formal dinner, where Bligh was presented with an official citation and silver
plate to the value of 100 guineas in recognition of the safe delivery of the breadfruit plants. Afterwards, he wrote to Sir Joseph Banks, enclosing a copy of the
citation and adding warmly: 'The greatest pleasure I have is thinking you will
be very happy to hear of my success.'[24] Ironically, however, the black slaves in
the West Indies did not like breadfruit at first, preferring their traditional diet of
plantain and yams, although later it became a staple food on the island. Instead it
was the sugar cane which Bligh brought from Tahiti, which proved to be larger
and juicier than Creole cane, that was a hit, quickly replacing the local variety
in the West Indies plantations.[25] During this visit to St Vincent, Bligh lost two
more of his men, one of whom fell overboard and drowned, while the other, one
of the sailors from the *Matilda*, ran ashore.

On 30 January 1793, Bligh's ships set sail for Jamaica. When they anchored in
Port Royal Harbour on 5 February, the black slaves marvelled at the *Providence*,
which they called 'de ship da hab de bush', paddling around the frigate in their
canoes in amazement.[26] After reporting to Commodore Ford, putting himself
under his command, Bligh sent a letter to the governor-general, asking that the
breadfruit and other plants for Jamaica should be disembarked as quickly as
possible. At a meeting ashore, it was decided that these plants should be divided
among the various counties, although some would be cared for in two local
nurseries. Bligh recommended James Wiles, one of Banks's botanist-gardeners

*Bligh's breadfruit plants arrive in the West Indies, by Thomas Gosse.*

(who was offered a salary of £200 a year plus board, lodgings and laundry) to look after the plants, along with Paupo or 'Jacket' (whom Wiles described as 'an exceeding good natured harmless creature')[27] who had learned very little English. The gardener's assistant, Maititi, Tu's envoy, had no particular interest in plants; and in any case he was heading for England to see King George and to study shipbuilding.[28]

Soon afterwards when the *Duke of Cumberland* arrived in Jamaica, her captain brought news that France had declared war on England; and Bligh was ordered to stay in the West Indies until reinforcements arrived. He took out his frustration on Frank Bond, sending him a flurry of peremptory orders in writing, noting that the stern hawser had not been properly laid, and ordering him to take care of this task himself whenever the master was absent;[29] and castigating him for putting drunk sailors on duty: 'You will see what a situation you have brought us in by your improper conduct in sending Drunkards and persons not fitt to be relied on any point of duty.'[30] It must have been with no small satisfaction that Bond showed Bligh a letter from his brother Tom, telling him about the court martial of the *Bounty*'s men. It ended: 'I am very sorry the Minutes of the Tryal are not in print, nor can I get them to send to Capt Bligh for his inspection. Heywood's friends, have bribed through thick and thin to save him, and from publick report, have not been backward in defaming our uncle's character. Government in my judgment, should have waited until Captn. Bligh's arrival in England, before those Mutineers were brought to trial . . . Your affectionate brother, T. Bond.'[31]

Although the commodore had hoisted his broad pennant on the *Providence*, taking over the vessel as his flagship, Bligh must have been consoled when in March the Assembly voted him £1,000 and Lieutenant Portlock £500 for safely delivering their cargo of breadfruit plants to the West Indies.[32] He also made a handsome profit when a local privateer sailed into port with prizes worth £2,500, and Bligh contrived to be the first naval commander to receive him. Since the privateer had no official letter of marque, Bligh was entitled to claim these prizes.[33] It was not until 10 June that he finally received his orders to sail for England. Although the *Assistant* was on convoy duty, Bligh decided to load his cargo of plants for Kew at once and sail to meet Lieutenant Portlock. On 17 June the *Providence* joined the *Assistant* and sailed with the convoy to England, arriving off the Irish coast in thick fog on 27 July 1793.

When the two ships entered the Downs on 2 August, they were cheered by the crews of the ships at anchor. Two days later, Bligh wrote to Sir Joseph Banks, announcing the safe delivery of his plants and saying how delighted he was to hear that he and his family were all well. He added: 'My Little Flock are anxious to see me & I must go to the Admiralty otherwise I should wait on you to day.'[34] Soon afterwards when Sir Joseph visited the ship, he expressed his pleasure at the thriving condition of the plants. Although Banks must have met Maititi on this occasion, Tu's envoy had fallen ill, and on 3 September he died from a lung infection.[35] As Bligh wrote sadly in his journal: 'Friday, September 6th, our Otaheitan friend was buried at Deptford New Church Yard in the parish of St. Paul's. I shall ever remember him with esteem.'[36] Tu's representative had perished before he could meet the King of England, and pass on Tu's urgent requests for a passage to England, a ship, soldiers and guns. Back in Jamaica, Paupo, who was still suffering from his smallpox inoculation, refused to talk to anyone or to take any European medicines; and on 27 October, he also died.[37]


Although Banks was delighted with Bligh's conduct of the second breadfruit voyage, trouble was brewing at the Admiralty. To Bligh's dismay, Lord Chatham, the First Lord of the Admiralty who had appointed him to command the second breadfruit expedition, did not come to the Downs to congratulate him and his men on the success of the voyage. When the Duke of Clarence boarded the

*Providence* and asked whether Lord Chatham had presented Bligh to the King, Bligh had to confess that he had not seen the First Lord since his arrival in England. According to Bligh, the Duke exclaimed, 'Here is an officer that has acquitted himself in the highest manner, and the First Lord of the Admiralty would not see him.' Indignant at this snub, the Duke invited Bligh to dine at Richmond and asked to see his charts; and soon afterwards, Admiral Affleck presented Bligh to Queen Charlotte at St James's Palace.[38]

Buoyed by these signs of royal favour, the crew was in a high good humour when on 7 August, the *Providence* was paid off at Deptford. As the *Kentish Register* reported:

> It was a scene highly gratifying to observe the cordial unanimity which prevailed amongst the Officers; the decency of conduct and the healthy and respectable appearance of the seamen, after so long and perilous a voyage, not one of whom but evinced that good order and discipline had been invariably observed.
>
> The high estimation in which Captain Bligh was deservedly held by the whole crew, was conspicuous to all present. He was cheered on quitting the ship to attend the Commissioner; and at the dock-gates, the men drew up and repeated the passing acclamation.[39]

Uplifted by this demonstration of goodwill from his men, Bligh sent Sir Joseph Banks a turtle and two Tahitian bows with a quiver and seventeen arrows, adding jovially, 'I imagine the Ladies may wish to try them in the country';[40] while Nathaniel Portlock also sent Banks some curiosities. Soon afterwards, Sir Joseph wrote to Lord Chatham, pointing out that the breadfruit expedition had been an overwhelming success, and that 'the Judicious and Able Conduct of Capt. Bligh exceeded my most Sanguine expectations'.[41] He also urged the First Lord to promote Nathaniel Portlock, the last of Captain Cook's midshipmen who was still a lieutenant, to master and commander.

Despite Banks's efforts on his behalf, however, the First Lord resolutely ignored William Bligh. Although he made repeated efforts to gain an audience, Lord Chatham (to whom Nessy Heywood had appealed after Peter Heywood's conviction) always seemed to be busy. On 28 September when Lieutenant Portlock was given an audience while Bligh was left cooling his heels, he was upset and humiliated, writing to Sir Joseph to complain about the way in which he had been treated.[42] It must have awakened painful memories of how the Admiralty had snubbed him after Captain Cook's last voyage; and once again he found himself on half pay, this time for a lengthy period. Matthew Flinders, one of Bligh's midshipmen, had already been warned by Thomas Pasley (his former commander, and the uncle of Peter Heywood) that Bligh would find himself *persona non grata* in London: 'Your Capt. will meet a very hard reception – he has Dam'd himself.'[43] This proved to be an accurate prediction. While he was sailing to the West Indies with his cargo of plants, damaging stories about how Bligh had treated the *Bounty*'s crew had been circulating in England, and Lord Chatham had found them persuasive.

During Bligh's court martial for the loss of the *Bounty* and the court martial of her surviving crew, although no testimony was given about Bligh's style of command, serious questions had been raised in private. Reverend William Howell, for instance, the naval chaplain who had frequently visited the prisoners, had written to Molesworth Phillips, a friend of Sir Joseph Banks, in November 1792, passing on information that the *Bounty*'s men had given him about Bligh's command; and the next month sent him Morrison's short account of the *Bounty*'s voyage to Tahiti, which contained a number of allegations about Bligh's conduct as a commander and a purser. Howell also shared his concerns with influential members of the London Missionary Society; and later passed on Heywood's vocabulary and Morrison's longer account of his adventures and life on the island (supplemented with material taken from Hawkesworth's publication of Cook's first voyage), which they had intended for joint publication, to Reverend Thomas Haweis, who was again planning to send a group of missionaries to Tahiti, allowing him to copy these invaluable materials for the use of the missionaries on the *Duff*, which carried the first evangelical party to the island.[44]

In addition, after Peter Heywood was sentenced and before he was pardoned, his sister Nessy had written a flurry of impassioned letters in his defence to a range of people in high places. Nessy's letter to Lord Chatham had included an enclosure from Heywood himself, rebutting each of the main points of evidence raised against him at the trial. Impressed by Nessy's belief in her brother, Lord Chatham must have spoken to the King, because Heywood and Morrison were pardoned two days later. After their release, it is likely that Reverend Howell encouraged Heywood to share his story with Fletcher Christian's family, who were suffering agonies of humiliation over Christian's part in the mutiny. In November 1792, Heywood wrote from London to Edward Christian, who held a chair in Common Law at Cambridge, offering to 'prove that your brother was not that vile wretch void of all gratitude, which the world had the unkindness to think him: but, on the contrary, a most worthy character; ruined only by having the misfortune . . . of being a young man of strict honour, adorned with every virtue, and beloved by all (except one, whose ill report is his greatest praise) who had the pleasure of his acquaintance'.[45]

At about the same time, John Fryer had gone to see Joseph Christian, another of the clan, to give him his version of what had happened on board the *Bounty*. After meeting Heywood and hearing about Fryer's account, Edward Christian became convinced that Bligh had seriously maligned his brother. When three of the *Bounty*'s officers and two of the sailors who had been acquitted at the court martial were interviewed, these men confirmed Heywood's version of events on board the *Bounty*. As one of the sailors exclaimed of Fletcher Christian: 'Oh! he was a gentleman, and a brave man, and every officer and sailor on board the ship, would have gone through fire and water to have served him.' Soon afterwards, Edward published Heywood's letter (without giving his name) and these remarks in the *Cumberland Packet*, ending with the ominous comment: 'The mystery of this melancholy transaction will soon be unravelled, and then the shame and infamy of it will be distributed in just proportions.'[46]

The Heywood and Christian families were influential and well connected, and no doubt there were meetings and conversations with people in power about the mutiny on the *Bounty*, which have left no documentary traces. Once aroused, Edward Christian proved to be a formidable opponent. Over the months that followed, while William Bligh was still in the West Indies, Christian pursued his enquiries, gathering together a group of 'respectable gentlemen' (almost all of whom were in fact, close friends of the Christian and Heywood families) to help him establish the 'truth' of what had happened on the *Bounty*, who collected further testimony from the men who had sailed with William Bligh. During this period, Edward Christian wrote several letters to Sir Joseph Banks, raising questions about Bligh's conduct, and the veracity of his published account of the voyage. At first, it seems that Banks, intent on preserving his own reputation and considering Christian's interventions self-serving, set these letters aside; and even after Bligh's return to England, Banks remained loyal to his protégé, continuing to defend him and urge that he and Portlock should be rewarded for the success of the second breadfruit voyage.

Finally, however, as the pressure mounted, Banks sent Christian's letters and a copy of Morrison's 'Memorandum and Particulars' to Bligh, asking him for his comments. After requesting a copy of the official transcript of the court martial from the Admiralty, on 30 October 1793 Bligh drafted a reply to Banks, dismissing these documents by saying that Christian's letters made no particular charges. Remarking loftily that the 'low abuse contained in the Notes upon my Narrative are beneath my notice', he added that Morrison's accounts were made up of 'vile falsehoods' and 'malicious insinuations'; assuring Banks that nothing in these documents contradicted the account that he had given of the voyage and the mutiny on the *Bounty*.[47] Fortunately, the bills drawn at the Cape of Good Hope had been sent to his wife's uncle, Duncan Campbell, and Bligh was able to use these to demonstrate the probity of his transactions.

From that moment on the *Bounty*'s launch when he had declared himself blameless for the mutiny on board his ship, Bligh's conviction of his own innocence and his fury with Fletcher Christian and the other 'villains' had never wavered. The notes that he made in response to Christian's accusations, which still survive, reflect a burning, self-righteous rage. He argued that although Christian argued that his 'Brother has been driven to desperation – [and] would have been a Glory to his Friends had he not sailed with Captain Bligh', in fact Christian had sailed with him over three years previous to the *Bounty* voyage, during which he was 'promoted to Acting Lieutenant, [and] occupied the same place of confidence & Trust to the moment of his Horrid act of ingratitude'.[48] All of those who had spoken to Edward Christian had been in disgrace during the voyage – for instance, John Fryer had been imprisoned in the East Indies, Purcell the carpenter had been tried by a court martial, while William Peckover the gunner had 'received some proof of his disapprobation'; and because of this, their accounts of the voyage could not be trusted. Indeed, he was convinced that their testimony to Christian's 'group of gentlemen' had been tampered with.

In his response to Joseph Banks, Bligh also vigorously rebutted a number of statements made to the court martial, dismissing Fryer as 'a dastardly Scoundrel' who had asked Christian if he could stay on the ship, and had assured him in the launch that Heywood was 'at the head of the Mutiny' with Christian.[49] He vehemently denied each of the charges in Morrison's short account. With respect to the episode of the 'stolen' cheeses before the *Bounty* sailed, Bligh said that when the cask had been opened and the cheeses counted, they had in fact been at sea; and that two of the cheeses had disappeared while he was at dinner. For this reason, it was impossible that these cheeses could have been sent to his house, as Morrison had asserted. With respect to the 'theft' of the coconuts off the coast of Tofua, Bligh said that when he noticed that the pile of coconuts had shrunk, and demanded that the officers of the watch should replace them, they had refused, saying that the coconuts had been taken by stealth. He exclaimed to Banks: 'Here was a publick theft; a contumacy, & direct disobedience of orders!' He also claimed that 'Captain Bligh never had a symptom of the Scurvy in any

Ship he commanded' – surely a case of self-deception, because even under Captain Cook's rigorous regime, there had been symptoms of scurvy after long passages at sea.[50] Contrary to Edward Christian, he stated that '[Fletcher] Christian had a particular female – Coleman remembering her, & Lebogue saw her this time we were at Otaheite. She went with Christian always untill his last Departure.'[51]

Although Banks remained loyal to Bligh, he felt compromised by Christian's campaign, later confessing to Lord Chatham (in a letter marked 'Private'): 'I Felt my character in some degree involved in the Charge brought against Capt. Bligh as being the Person who recommended him to the Admiralty.'[52] In the Admiralty, too, many had resented Banks's high-handed meddling in naval matters, and when the *Bounty* expedition collapsed in so spectacular a fashion, it must have provoked glee in a number of quarters.

Quite unfairly, Bligh's officers on board the *Providence* also shared in his ignominy. Instead of being rewarded for the success of the second breadfruit voyage, they (like Bligh) were kept on half pay and passed over for promotion, tainted by the gossip about their captain's role in the mutiny on the *Bounty*. On 9 December 1793, when the Society for the Encouragement of Arts, Manufactures and Commerce awarded Bligh the gold medal for the first person to take bread-fruit plants to the West Indies,[53] his men received no reward for their efforts. Although Tobin and Harwood, the surgeon of the *Providence*, assured Frank Bond that 'the Don' (Bligh's shipboard nickname) was making repeated efforts to get him promoted,[54] Lord Chatham resolutely ignored him;[55] and in January 1794 when one of his family friends wrote to Bond, thanking him for despatching a Tahitian canoe, he added: 'I still expect you will get your well-earned promo-tion before you go again to sea; and I cannot help thinking that the officers of the *Providence* have been very hardly dealt by. I believe it is the first instance of any such voyage, even when unsuccessful, not being followed by promotion – how much more do Capt. Bligh and his officers deserve it who accomplished every object upon which they were sent.'[56] In March, when Portlock was finally given the command of a ship heading for Botany Bay (which he refused when he realised that he was expected to be subordinate to Captain Hunter), Bligh had to confess to his nephew that not only was Lord Chatham refusing to see him, he was also ignoring his letters.[57]

Worse was still to come. On 1 May 1794, Edward Christian published a devastating broadside. Although the Admiralty had refused to release the official minutes of the court martial, Christian persuaded Muspratt's lawyer, who was sympathetic to the *Bounty* sailors, to publish his own transcript of the trial (although only the testimony for the prosecution was included). This account of the court martial included an *Appendix* written by Edward Christian, which began with a clever disclaimer – that the author had no intention of trying to justify the crime of mutiny. Irrespective of the causes, this was an offence so heinous that it 'should be punished with inexorable rigour'. Nevertheless, Christian added, 'every friend to truth and strict justice must feel his attention awakened to the true causes and circumstances, which have hitherto been concealed or misrepresented, of one of the most remarkable events in the annals of the Navy'.[58]

In the *Appendix*, Christian painted a vivid picture of the sufferings of the families of the accused. At first, they had not questioned Bligh's accounts because 'they came from those whose sufferings had unquestionably been extreme, and preservation almost miraculous. Their lips were closed, they mourned in silence, and shuddering at the most distant allusion to this melancholy subject, they were of all persons the least likely to discover the real truth of the transaction.'[59] After the stunning shock of his conversation with Peter Heywood, however, he had gathered together a group of gentlemen to witness his interviews with various parties involved in the mutiny, whom he listed by name – the master John Fryer; the gunner William Peckover; the carpenter William Purcell; Thomas Hayward the midshipman; the boatswain's mate James Morrison; the cook John Smith; Joseph Coleman the armourer; Lawrence Lebogue the sailmaker; Thomas McIntosh the carpenter's mate; and Michael Byrne the fiddler, who gave him very different accounts of the *Bounty* voyage from those that had emerged at the court martial.

In fact, however, Christian's informal tribunal was far from dispassionate. His 'group of gentlemen' included William Wordsworth's uncle Rev. Cookson; Rev. Dr Frewen, Wordsworth's tutor at St John's College, Cambridge, where Edward Christian had also studied; Rev. Mr Antrobus from Cockermouth, the Christians' home town, and chaplain to the Bishop of London; Captain John Wordsworth, a relative of William Wordsworth; Rev. Dr Fisher, a friend of Fletcher Christian's first cousin; James Losh, a lawyer and friend of Wordsworth, and the family of Peter Heywood's mother; Samuel Romilly, another lawyer and friend of Edward Christian, like William Wilberforce (who himself was the intimate friend of the Prime Minister William Pitt, the brother of Lord Chatham).[60] There was a tightly overlapping network of ties between these men, Fletcher Christian's old schoolmate William Wordsworth and Christian's family; and many of them were fervent abolitionists (and unlikely to be sympathetic to Bligh, who had worked for his wife's uncle Duncan Campbell, a prominent slave-owner), or like Wordsworth himself, sympathised with the French Revolution.[61]

In his *Appendix*, Christian published testimony about Bligh's conduct on the *Bounty* that had not been presented to the court martial, an inquiry restricted to the question: 'Who took part in the mutiny?' According to the men interviewed by Christian and his panel, during the voyage Captain Bligh had often abused his officers, calling them 'scoundrels, damned rascals, hounds, hell-hounds, beasts, and infamous wretches'.[62] Fletcher Christian had been his favourite target; and during these tirades, Bligh had sometimes shaken his fist in Christian's face. After the disappearance of the coconuts, when Bligh summoned his acting lieutenant, for example, he yelled, 'Damn your blood, you have stolen my coconuts.' When Christian replied, 'I was dry. I thought it of no consequence, I took one only, and I am sure no one touched another', Bligh shook his fist at him, saying, 'You lie, you scoundrel, you have stolen one half.' Afterwards (although the men insisted that he was 'no milk sop'), Christian was in tears, exclaiming, 'I would rather die ten thousand deaths, than to bear this treatment; I always do my duty as an officer and as a man ought to do, yet I receive this scandalous usage.'[63] Later, when he decided to take the ship, Christian had resolved that no one was to be killed; and as the launch rowed away, he declared that 'he would readily sacrifice his own life, if the persons in the launch were all safe in the ship again'. According to the *Appendix*, when Fletcher Christian took a high-born *taio* in Tahiti, Bligh jeeringly said to the chiefs that Christian was only a *teuteu*, or servant.[64] The gist of Edward Christian's argument in the *Appendix* was that William Bligh himself was responsible for the mutiny on the *Bounty*, having subjected Fletcher Christian and his fellow officers to insults and humiliations that no true gentleman could endure.

Unwisely, however (since this was quickly contradicted by his informants), Christian claimed that his brother 'never had a female favourite at Otaheite, nor any attachment or particular connexion among the women'.[65] Despite their sufferings in the launch, he noted, each of the men who left the *Bounty* with Bligh warmly praised Fletcher Christian, saying, for instance, 'He was a gentleman, and a brave man; and every officer and seaman on board the ship would have gone through fire and water to have served him'; or 'He was a gentleman every inch of him, and I would still wade up to the arm-pits in blood to serve him'.[66] The *Appendix* concluded with a dire warning to the naval authorities: 'The crime in this instance may afford an awful lesson to the Navy, and to mankind, that there is a degree of pressure, beyond which the best formed and principled mind must either break or recoil.' Despite his earlier disclaimer, Edward Christian's pamphlet was in fact a sustained defence of his brother; and in its last lines, he asked the reader to join him in his sorrow 'that a young man is condemned to perpetual infamy, who, if he had served on board any other ship, or had perhaps been absent from the Bounty a single day, or one ill-fated hour, might still have been an honour to his country, and a glory and a comfort to his friends'.[67]

In the *Appendix*, it is likely that Edward Christian (who, after all, was a Professor of Common Law) was trying to goad Bligh into suing him for slander. Instead of confronting him in court, however, Bligh sought to undermine the credibility of the *Appendix* by persuading various of the *Bounty* sailors to withdraw the statements that they had made. Writing to his nephew Frank Bond, for instance, who was now on the same ship as Michael Byrne, he asked him to put a list of questions to the fiddler, and get him to disavow the statements that he had made to Edward Christian. When Bond wrote back and reported that Byrne had adamantly refused, Bligh exploded: 'As to the blind scoundrel, I can only beg of you to make the best of him, and get him flogged nobly whenever he deserves it, for he is certainly a very great villain.'[68] When Byrne finally gave his answers to Bligh's questions, moreover, they were unhelpful to his cause, and Bligh could not use them. The same questions were also put to John Smith, Joseph Coleman and Lawrence Lebogue, no doubt using a similar combination of threats and promises.

In drafting his reply, *An Answer to certain Assertions contained in the Appendix to a Pamphlet entitled, Minutes of the Proceedings of the Courtmartial* (1794), Bligh made a blunder. Instead of vigorously defending his own conduct on board the *Bounty*, and demonstrating that each of Christian's main informants had been placed under discipline during the voyage (as he had done in his notes to Sir Joseph Banks), Bligh published a miscellaneous collection of documents that only indirectly addressed the question: 'Who was responsible for the mutiny on the *Bounty*?' These documents, edited for publication by a family friend of his wife's, the poet George Keate, included his orders for the conduct of his men at Tahiti, and the punishment of the three men who had deserted on the island, with their abject apology; the transcript of the trial of Fryer and other officers at Batavia, during which they had cleared Bligh of any blame for the mutiny (although this testimony had been given under duress); Bligh's description of the men who remained on board the *Bounty*; a letter from Peter Heywood to his wife Elizabeth, protesting his innocence of any involvement in the uprising, and his statement to the court martial that 'indeed, from [Bligh's] attention to, and very kind treatment of me, personally, I should have been a monster of depravity to have betrayed him', juxtaposed with Heywood's letter to Edward

Christian, warmly defending Fletcher Christian. There was also a letter from Hallett describing the accusations against Bligh as 'malevolent', but offering little by way of rebuttal; a strongly worded letter to *The Times* from Edward Harwood, the surgeon on the *Providence*, decrying the *Appendix* as an 'imbecile and highly illiberal attack' while praising Bligh's 'affability to his officers, and humane attention to his men' during his latest expedition (although Harwood, of course, was not on board the *Bounty*); and one from Edward Lamb, who had sailed with Bligh and Christian on the *Britannia*, stating that during those early voyages, Bligh had been very partial to Fletcher Christian.

Although in the *Appendix*, it had been claimed that in Tahiti, Christian had no attachment among the women, Lamb tartly remarked that if that was the case: 'He must have been much altered since he was with you in the *Britannia*; he was then one of the most foolish young men I ever knew in regard to the sex.'[69] There were also the affidavits from Coleman, Smith and Lebogue, intended as the centrepiece of Bligh's *Answer*, flatly denying most of the assertions attributed to them in the *Appendix*; but these failed to give any vigorous defence of Bligh's command. Although collectively, these documents cast doubt upon the truth of some statements in the *Appendix*, they did not offer a compelling alternative account of Bligh's conduct on the *Bounty*.

Nevertheless, Bligh's defence of his reputation won him sympathy in some quarters. In August 1794, for example, their family friend George Keate published a poem commemorating the return of the *Providence*, which hailed Bligh as a hero:

> O, Welcome home with thy triumphant sail!
> Achiev'd the noble task to thee assign'd;
> With ardour such as thine it scarce could fail;
>
> To such a cause the Heav'n's protection lend!
> Thou felt their influence in a trying hour;
> When all around menac'd a fatal end,
> From the black stratagems of lawless power.[70]

In its review of the *Answer*, the *Critical Review* remarked that Bligh had 'fully vindicated his character against the censures advanced by Mr. Christian, and the manner of defence he has chosen, is not its least recommendation';[71] while the *British Critic* declared that 'without entering into any personal vindication of himself, or indulging those feelings unavoidable to the predicament in which he is placed, [Bligh] has produced authentic documents and testimonies from others, which contain the fullest and most satisfactory refutation of all that was insinuated against his character. We cannot help thinking, that the friends of Christian will act the wisest part, in throwing as much as possible into oblivion, the transaction in which that young man played so conspicuous, and so criminal a part.'[72]

Far from heeding the *Critic*'s advice, however, in 1795 Edward Christian published his *Short Reply to Captain Bligh's Answer*, which demolished the affidavits of Smith, Coleman and Lebogue by pointing out that John Smith was Bligh's servant who lived in his house; that Joseph Coleman, who was 'old and dull', was now a pensioner in Chelsea Hospital (implying that this had been a reward for withdrawing his statement); and that Lawrence Lebogue's affidavit, which flatly denied statements that he had made to Edward Christian in front of a number of witnesses, was the 'grossest and foulest perjury'. Christian's withering contempt for Lebogue was telling. He added that Hallett's letter had been sent to Bligh before he had seen the *Appendix*, and was published after his death; and that after the publication of the *Appendix*, he himself and his friends had interviewed Peckover and Purcell, who stated 'that every part within [their] knowledge was correctly stated'.[73]

As a polemicist, it appears, William Bligh was no match for Edward Christian. After reading the *Short Reply*, he soberly wrote to his nephew Frank Bond: 'I have not yet published my *Voyage* and shall wait till better times.'[74] This included his charts from the voyage, now held in the National Library in Canberra, Australia.[75] Misfortune piled upon misfortune, though, because during 1795 his wife lost another baby, and almost died.[76] In the end, as history has demonstrated, Christian won the battle of the pamphlets. His vivid portrait of William Bligh as an abusive and tyrannical commander, which captured the popular imagination, has endured for more than 200 years.

# Epilogue

# Death of 'the Don'

If one reads all of the documents relating to the mutiny on the *Bounty*, it is clear that Edward Christian's vindication of his brother and his fellow mutineers was over-stated. Although Fletcher Christian was capable and popular, his shipmates all agreed that he was susceptible to women, and no doubt his decision to take over the ship was influenced by his desire to return to Tahiti. And while Peter Heywood always insisted that George Stewart was a loyal officer who remained true to his captain, several of the *Bounty*'s men indicated that Stewart had sympathised with the mutiny. Indeed, according to John Fryer and James Morrison, Stewart had helped to inspire the uprising by suggesting to Christian that the 'men are ripe for anything'. If Heywood's defence of Stewart fails (and it does seem far-fetched), then his account of his own conduct during the mutiny also falters. Since Stewart was his friend and mentor, it seems more likely that the younger midshipman followed Stewart's example, and simply let the mutiny unfold.

At the same time, William Bligh was seriously flawed as a commander. Vain and ungenerous, he had a volatile temper and a biting tongue. Unlike his mentor, Captain Cook, he lacked charisma or an imposing physical presence; and unlike Charles Clerke, he had no sense of humour. Obtuse to the point of cruelty, he had little empathy, except for his family and a few young protégés; and no gift for the arts of political management. Often spoken of as a 'passionate' man, William Bligh had a violent, impetuous temper that exploded when he was thwarted. Given his bitter experiences after Cook's last Pacific expedition, he had too much to prove. Determined to silence his critics by making a perfect voyage in the *Bounty*, and then in the *Providence*, he was enraged by any lapses that threatened his record; and knew how to humiliate those responsible for such infractions. As an insecure man, prone to elaborate feats of self-justification,

Bligh had a gift, almost amounting to genius, for insulting and infuriating his immediate subordinates. N.A.M. Rodger's crisp verdict on the mutiny on the *Bounty* – 'Bligh was an outstanding seaman with an ungovernable temper and no idea about how to get the best out of his officers', and Fletcher Christian was 'an unstable young man who could not stand being shouted at' – gets close to the heart of the matter.[1]

Compared with Captain Edwards, however, Bligh could be warm and engaging (especially with those who posed no threat to his reputation). In his domestic life, he was ardent and faithful, in stark contrast to many of his former shipmates (Molesworth Phillips, for example, the *Resolution*'s lieutenant of marines, who was an infamous brute to his wife and a bully to his children; while James Burney, Phillips's brother-in-law, had a series of affairs, including an incestuous one with his half-sister).[2] In this respect, he was more like Captain Cook than most of their comrades. Compared with George Vancouver (and almost every other British commander in the Pacific), too, Bligh was a paragon of restraint in his methods of discipline (flogging only 10 per cent of the *Bounty*'s crew and 8 per cent on board the *Providence*, compared with 25 per cent on board Cook's *Resolution*, and 45 per cent on board Vancouver's *Discovery*, for instance).[3] On the basis of these figures, his reputation for brutality – initiated by Edward Christian (although Christian did not accuse him of physical violence), and later elaborated into a popular myth of Bligh as an archetypal 'flogging captain' – was a triumph of rhetoric over reality. William Bligh was a fine practical sailor and hydrographer, and a gifted ethnographer, who had gained some real insights into life in Tahiti. If he tormented his men, they knew how to pay him back with insolence and passive resistance. The responsibility for the breakdown in relationships on board the *Bounty* cannot be sheeted home to Bligh alone, but must be shared by his officers, especially George Stewart and Fletcher Christian.

Under most circumstances, too, the tensions on board the *Bounty* would not have led to a collapse of command. Unfortunately, the planning of the expedition by Joseph Banks and the Admiralty had been fatally flawed, placing Bligh and his officers under intolerable pressures. If the government had been more generous, or Banks had selected a larger ship for the breadfruit expedition, with a Great Cabin for her captain and room for her officers and crew, the atmosphere on board might have been different. If the Admiralty had sent his orders to Bligh in time for him to sail around the Horn, his stay in Tahiti would have been brief, just a matter of weeks; and shipboard discipline is unlikely to have unravelled. Had there been other commissioned officers on board, Fletcher Christian would not have been appointed an acting lieutenant, without a proper commission and dependent on the whim of a quick-tempered, verbally abusive commander. If there had been a contingent of marines on board, fearful of being shot, the young officer is unlikely to have indulged himself with fantasies of mutiny and desertion. Like Frank Bond on the *Providence*, Christian would have been forced to swallow Bligh's insults, and do his duty; and the mutiny would not have happened.

To make matters worse, by the time that the *Bounty*'s men were brought back to England, the French Revolution was unfolding; and the government and the Admiralty could not afford to admit their own part in the responsibility for the mutiny (along with that of Sir Joseph Banks, a close friend of King George III). Instead, the *Bounty* sailors were put on trial; and after the court martial, three of them were hanged from the yardarm. When public sympathy for the *Bounty* officers, especially Peter Heywood and Fletcher Christian, was aroused by their relatives, William Bligh became the scapegoat. At the same time, Bligh's intemperate tirades were the sparks that ignited the mutiny, driving his subordinates to distraction. His bad luck and his bad language proved to be an inflammable combination.

These were turbulent times. When France declared war on Britain in 1793, there were roughly 16,000 sailors in the Navy; but by 1795, this figure had grown to 85,000 men, many of whom had been impressed, some criminal or unfit; while others were literate and politically aware. After poor harvests and bitter winters, food prices had doubled; and after riots and disturbances, habeas corpus had been suspended. On board the ships, conditions were miserable, and although pay in the Army was increased in 1795, sailors' wages had remained the same for more than a century. Men in the Royal Navy were now paid three or four times less than their counterparts in the merchant navy; and they often received their wages two, five, eight or even fifteen years after they were due. Shipboard conditions were also worse than in the merchant service; the time at sea was longer, and the discipline more harsh. Tom Paine's *The Rights of Man*, published in 1791–92, was circulating widely in Britain, encouraging the men to think about their rights and grievances.

Under these conditions, seasoned officers were desperately needed; and in 1795 when Evan Nepean, who had worked with Duncan Campbell on the transport of convicts to New South Wales, became Secretary of the Navy with William Marsden, a member of the Royal Society and a good friend of Sir Joseph Banks, as his assistant, Bligh's prospects of advancement brightened. On 30

April 1795, he was finally appointed to command the *Calcutta*, a former East Indiaman converted into an armed 24-gun transport, and offered the position of first lieutenant to Frank Bond. Blind to his nephew's bitter resentment of his conduct on board the *Providence*, Bligh was surprised and hurt when Bond turned down the appointment. The *Calcutta* was part of a small North Sea fleet based at Leith in Scotland under the command of Admiral Duncan, one of the strictest disciplinarians in the Navy. Their task was to blockade the Dutch coast, where the French were assembling a fleet to invade Britain; and when Bligh safely escorted the Hudson Bay's fleet into Leith Harbour, Duncan praised him in an official despatch.

In October while the *Calcutta* was in port, a mutiny broke out on board the *Defiance*, whose captain had watered down the men's grog and stopped their shore leave. The mutineers included a number of political prisoners, some from Ireland and others who sympathised with the French Revolution, who demanded that less water should be used in their rum, their shore leave be reinstated, and their captain and a brutal, alcoholic lieutenant be replaced. After the officers had seized eight of these men and clapped them in irons, the captain called for outside assistance. When Bligh and the commander of the *Asia* went on board the *Defiance*, they told the crew that their comrades could not be freed; but later that night, to Bligh's fury, their captain acceded to these demands. The Admiral called a meeting, and according to Bligh:

> Many plans were mentioned, & the best way discussed, how to subdue this mutiny, & I did not hesitate to declare that a party of Troops embarked on board of another Ship & laid alongside, was the most effectual manner that I knew of, because they would be protected, which by any other means they would not, if resistance was made.[4]

No doubt because of his own experience with the *Bounty* mutineers, the other captains were inclined to listen to Bligh; but soon afterwards, the Admiral changed his mind, deciding not to place the troops in the safety of another ship and drift it alongside the *Defiance*, but to send them across on boats, without any protection. Bligh was put in charge of the operation, and when he and the commander of the troops went ahead, arriving alongside the *Defiance*, the mutineers yelled, 'Clear away the Guns – sink them!' Urged on by their officers, the soldiers clambered up the side and took over the vessel before the mutineers could run out the guns, forcing them to drop the cannonballs into the attacking boats by hand. They were arrested, and those men who had remained loyal to their captain were transferred to other ships, including the *Calcutta*.[5] After a court martial, eight of the ringleaders were sentenced to hang from the yardarm, while four were each sentenced to 300 lashes.[6]

By this time, Bligh's wife Elizabeth had six small children, including their epileptic daughter Ann, born in 1791. Betsy had lost twin sons soon after birth in 1795, damaging her health, and in December of that year she wrote to Sir Joseph Banks, asking for a shore posting for her husband, perhaps as a captain at Greenwich Hospital (the sinecure that the Admiralty had offered to both Captain Cook and Captain Gore).[7] When Banks pleaded for Bligh at the Admiralty, saying that he had suffered greatly for little reward, and that his health had been ruined by his ordeal in the *Bounty*'s launch, leaving him crippled with rheumatism during the cold, dark North Sea patrols,[8] the First Lord of the Admiralty replied that the vacancy at Greenwich had already been filled. In January 1796, however, Bligh was promoted to a larger ship, the 64-gun warship *Director*. By this time he was forty-two years old, and had served twenty-six years in the Navy. He was pleased with this appointment, which as Sir Joseph observed, helped to heal 'the wound his spirit has received by the illiberal & unjust treatment his Character has met from the Relatives of the Mutineers on the *Bounty*'.[9]

In March 1787, men on sixteen ships of the line in the Channel Fleet in Spithead signed a petition asking for a pay rise, regular wages, better food, care for sick sailors, shore leave and the removal of unpopular officers. When the fleet commander ignored their requests, the crews on board two ships at Spithead mutinied. Discipline among the sailors, who were led by some of the most respected men among them, was tight. Although the Admiralty belatedly agreed to a rise and a King's pardon for the mutineers, the crews refused to man their ships unless these promises were ratified by Parliament. After delays in meeting this demand, the mutiny spread to Plymouth. It was only when the fleet commander, Lord Howe, and his wife invited the leaders to dinner and removed a number of officers named by the sailors that the mutiny ended. After triumphant celebrations at Plymouth, the Channel Fleet returned to sea.

By this time, however, the unrest had spread to the Nore off Sheerness, where Admiral Duncan had sent the *Director* for a refit. On 12 May 1796 while Bligh was on court-martial duty on board another ship, a mutiny broke out in the fleet, co-ordinated by men on board the *Sandwich*, which was grossly overcrowded. When Bligh returned to the *Director*, his crew (who had not been paid since January) presented him with a list of demands, including the removal of three of his officers, although they made no complaints against their captain. He suspended the officers, but when a leader from the *Sandwich* came on board to urge the crew to seize the ship's arsenal, Bligh abused him roundly, angering some of the men. A week later a majority of the *Director*'s sailors voted to remove Bligh from his command, sending him and several of his midshipmen ashore – his second mutiny, although by that time a number of other captains in the fleet had already been toppled.[10] Each of the ships in the mutiny appointed a management committee, forming a 'Floating Republic', a self-governing naval democracy. While the mutiny at the Nore was under way, in a gesture of confidence, the Admiralty despatched Bligh to Duncan's fleet at Yarmouth to talk with the men and assess their morale. He reported that there was considerable unrest in the fleet, with some crews refusing to go to sea until they were paid and their other demands were met, and that an attack on the Nore mutineers by 'loyal' ships from Yarmouth would not be feasible.

At the Nore, the government was better prepared. From the outset, they decided to take a tough line, treating the mutineers as rebels inspired by the French Revolution. After sending army regiments to blockade the ships, they removed the buoys that marked the safe channels out of the harbour. Meanwhile, on board the *Director*, the loyalists among the crew twice tried to retake the ship. Trapped in port and intimidated by the government's resolute actions, the leaders of the mutineers eventually offered to surrender as long as the men's back wages were paid. The authorities were obdurate, however, and when the mutineers, including those on board the *Director*, finally submitted, ten of the ringleaders from each ship were handed over, and twenty-nine of these men were hanged while many others received savage floggings. Later, when more mutineers were demanded for punishment, Bligh (who was now back in command) protected his crew, saying that after the ten leaders had been sent ashore, the rest of the men had been given the King's pardon. He wrote first to Admiral Keith, and then to the port admiral, stressing the promises that had been made and refusing to provide any information against his men,[11] in striking contrast with his long-standing, vindictive hostility towards the *Bounty* mutineers.

After the mutiny on the Nore, the ships, including the *Director*, rejoined Admiral Duncan's fleet.[12] When the news arrived at Yarmouth that the Dutch fleet had left Texel and were at sea, Duncan decided to chase them. After heading down the coast, the Dutch commander-in-chief, Admiral de Winter, changed his mind and sailed back to port, hugging the shore. Upon sighting the Dutch fleet, however, Duncan divided his ships into two groups, ordering them to attack the Dutch ships at close quarters. Bligh in the *Director* joined the northerly squadron, led by Admiral Onslow, who attacked the Dutch vice-admiral's ship, while Admiral Duncan in his flagship *Venerable* assailed de Winter's vessel. After heavy firing, the Dutch line broke and its ships began to strike. Noticing that the Dutch flagship was no longer under attack, Bligh headed towards the *Vrijheid*, which had been badly battered. As his men shot away its masts one by one and disabled its guns, de Winter's flag fell; and when Bligh went to get orders from Admiral Duncan, he was told to take possession of the Dutch flagship.

During this engagement, John Williamson, the third lieutenant of the *Resolution* who had abandoned Captain Cook in Kealakekua Bay (and now the commander of the *Agincourt*), failed to take his ship into action; he was later court-martialled for cowardice and disobedience of orders. When Bligh was called to testify, he said little, but what he did say was on Williamson's side. According to Bligh, he had not noticed the *Agincourt* during the battle, but thought that all of the ships in the rear division were fighting; and he did not see Williamson's ship standing to windward of the fleet. For whatever reason, Bligh refused to condemn his former comrade. The testimony of others was damning, however, and Williamson was found 'in part' to have disobeyed a signal, and declared incapable of ever serving again in the Navy.

Horatio Nelson, the great commander, considered this verdict deplorable, protesting, 'I should have every man believe, I shall not only take my chance of being shot by the Enemy, but if I do not take that chance, I am certain of being shot by my friends.'[13] During the battle of Camperdown, Bligh had fought bravely; and when they returned to the Nore, Admiral Duncan wrote to him: 'I have mentioned to the Admiralty that if your ship is paid off I hope they will immediately give you another as I have always observed her conducted like a Man of War.'[14] In December 1797 when the victory at Camperdown among others was celebrated by a royal procession to St Paul's Cathedral, the procession, which included the King and Queen and many members of the royal family, the House of Lords, the House of Commons and the judiciary in order from lowest to highest, was led by wagons carrying the flags captured from the French, Spanish and Dutch navies, attended by flag officers and captains. Bligh marched in the group led by Admiral Duncan, who carried the flag of Admiral de Winter, which Bligh's men had seized.[15]

Through 1798, Bligh was back on blockade duty on board the *Director*, although in September 1799 he was sent to convoy a fleet of East Indiamen from St Helena to England. During this cruise, two of his lieutenants were confined for refusing to take his orders; and when he arrived at St Helena, he found that the fleet had sailed without him. After collecting a cargo of plants for Kew Gardens, he sailed back home, en route producing the first chart of the Atlantic that recorded the effects of the currents.[16] During that year an account of the voyage of the *Duff*, the ship that had carried the first party of London Missionary Society missionaries to Tahiti, was published, and Bligh must have read it eagerly, curious to know what had happened on the island since his departure. According to the *Voyage*, when the *Duff* anchored in Matavai Bay on 5 March 1797, his 'uncle' the old high priest Ha'amanimani came on board, followed by Haggerstein and Lind, the Swedes from the *Matilda*, who told the missionaries that just before their arrival, there had been a terrible storm and an earthquake on the island, the first that the people had ever experienced. Twenty months earlier, according to Captain Wilson, Pomare's men had defeated Teri'irere and the Papara army in a great battle, and Pomare II was now the acknowledged paramount chief of the island.[17]

According to Wilson's account, when the missionaries landed, the chief of Matavai Bay produced the famous portrait of Captain Cook, and led them to the 'Fare no Peretane', the house that had been built for William Bligh during his *Providence* visit. Later, when Tu and 'Itia came to meet them, Ha'amanimani recited the names of each of the European captains who had visited the island, including 'Parai'; and in reply, the interpreter assured Tu that 'King George loved him, and the earees [*ari'i* or high chiefs] of Pretane; and that out of regard for him and his people, they had sent this ship with some of the best men in England, purposely to do them good'.[18] The district of Matavai had been ceremoniously presented to the missionaries, as it was to Bligh before them; but when Tu and 'Itia asked to have the occasion celebrated with sky rockets, violin music, dancing and bagpipers, the missionaries had to confess that they could not oblige.

When the *Director* was decommissioned in July 1800, Bligh once again served a period on half pay, and was given the task of surveying Dublin Harbour.[19] In March the following year, the new First Lord of the Admiralty, Sir John Jervis, the Earl of St Vincent, who had presided over Bligh's court martial for the loss of the *Bounty*, appointed him to command the *Glatton*, a 54-gun former East Indiaman in the Baltic fleet. Bligh, who had hoped that he would be given an independent command, was dashed to discover that he would be sailing under Admiral Sir Hyde Parker, a man in his late sixties who had just married a girl of twenty-four. As he wrote to Banks:

I do not like my ship, as she has nothing to recommend her as a Man of War, but her great shot. Captain Stephens who I releive, and all the Fleet, he tells me, were astonished to hear I was to command her, but we will do our part very well I have no doubt & I trust will not keep her long.[20]

At this time, Russia and four other Baltic states, including Denmark, had placed an embargo on British ships sailing in the Baltic, which the government was eager to contest, but Parker was reluctant to go to sea. As soon as Horatio Nelson, his impetuous but heroic vice-admiral, complained to the Admiralty about his dilatory conduct, however, Parker sprang into action. The *Glatton* was ready for sea, and Bligh was appointed as Nelson's second, joining his squadron.[21]

By the time that Admiral Parker's fleet arrived off the Danish coast on 19 March 1801, the Danish defences had been strengthened. Although Nelson was eager to attack, Parker wished to resolve the conflict by diplomacy. Finally, on 26 March, he agreed to allow Nelson to take his squadron along a narrow channel off the south coast of Copenhagen, where the defences were relatively weak, and attack the Danish fleet and their shore batteries. Nelson proposed that each of his ships should sail northward in succession, with the wind astern, and then drop anchor and bombard the enemy. As each ship anchored, the next would sail past it and take its station just north of the anchored vessel, protected by their bombardment, in a leapfrog manoeuvre. Although his captains, including Bligh, were dubious about this plan, considering it very dangerous, Nelson won them over, organising his own men to sound the channel and mark it with temporary buoys. After boarding the *Amazon*, a frigate commanded by Edward Riou (who had sailed with Captain Cook as a midshipman on board the *Discovery*, and later detained John Fryer at the Cape of Good Hope after the mutiny on the *Bounty*) to examine the Danish defences, Nelson held a conference with his captains, giving each of them detailed orders. Although one of the ships ran aground even before the fighting began, disrupting the plan, the other captains pressed ahead. Having fired on several of the Dutch vessels, Bligh's ship the *Glatton* anchored immediately behind Nelson and they bombarded the Dutch flagship, which returned fire, shooting down the *Glatton*'s topmast, disabling a number of her carronades and killing and wounding many of the sailors. While this action was under way, two more of the British vessels, led astray by their pilots, ran aground.

When the shore batteries opened fire, Edward Riou, who was badly out-gunned, went in to bombard them. After two hours of heavy firing, the flagship surrendered, but other Dutch ships continued to fight. Just as the Dutch vessels began to strike to the British, Admiral Parker, who had kept his squadron at a distance instead of joining the battle, and could barely see through the billowing gunsmoke, flew the signal to 'discontinue the action', directed to each ship individually. Although some of the captains were forced to obey, Horatio Nelson had no intention of quitting the battle. Clapping his telescope to his blind eye, he exclaimed to his flag-captain, 'You know Foley, I have only one eye – and I really have a right to be blind sometimes', and, fuming at Parker's timidity, ignored the signal.[22]

Riou, on the other hand, who had no such excuse, felt obliged to obey Parker's order. When he left off the attack, however, and the smoke cleared, the shore batteries fired at his ship, and a cannonball cut him in half. Like Nelson, Bligh ignored Parker's signal, and the ships behind him in the line followed suit. After another hour of heavy fighting, Nelson sent a message ashore to the Crown Prince, saying that unless the Danes surrendered, he would burn all of the floating batteries that he had captured. In another, more conciliatory message, he assured the Crown Prince that if the flag of truce was accepted, it was his hope that Denmark and Britain would become friends and allies. Shortly after receiving this note, the Danes stopped firing, and Nelson invited William Bligh on board his flagship, where he thanked him for his support, which had helped to win the battle.[23] Proud of his role in this great victory, Bligh made a sketch of the disposition of the Danish ships during the battle, and listed the number of men killed and wounded in each of the British vessels (including seventeen killed and thirty-four wounded on board the *Glatton*, which had been badly damaged).[24]

Strangely enough, John Fryer, Bligh's old adversary on board the *Bounty*, was the sailing master on board Admiral Parker's flagship; while Fryer's young brother-in-law Robert Tinkler, who had sailed with them on the *Bounty*'s launch, was a lieutenant in the *Isis*, which fought with Nelson during this engagement. Furious with Nelson for ignoring his signal, Admiral Parker nevertheless claimed the fruits of the victory. He made all of the promotions himself, and to Nelson's indignation, burned a number of the prize ships that his squadron had captured. Some Danish prisoners were taken on board the *Glatton*; and when they were released, one of them, a lieutenant, complained that the ship's captain had taken his sword. When the Danes asked Bligh for an explanation, after saying that another of the prisoners had sold him the sword for a pound, he brusquely refused to surrender the weapon, defying naval tradition and tarnishing his own reputation.[25]

Despite this, in reward for his role in the victory, Admiral Parker promoted Bligh into the *Monarch*, a 74-gun ship of the line; and at Bligh's urging, Nelson wrote him a testimonial for the Admiralty:

Captain Bligh (of the *Glatton* who had commanded the *Director* at Camperdown) has desired my testimony to his conduct, which although perfectly unnecessary, I cannot refuse; his behaviour on this occasion can reap no additional credit from my testimony. He was my second, and the moment the Action ceased, I sent for him . . . to thank him for his support.[26]

Notwithstanding his courage in battle, however, the *Monarch*'s men heartily disliked their new commander. During the journey home, one of his midshipmen wrote: 'Captain Bligh was an excellent navigator, and I believe in every respect a good seaman, but his manners and disposition were not pleasant, and his appointment to the *Monarch* gave very general disgust to the officers.'[27] When Bligh weighed anchor, for example, he abused the ship's officers as 'dolts' and 'blockheads' and decided to pilot the ship out of the harbour himself. As the midshipman, Millard, remarked: 'This was as unnecessary as it was unusual. These men had been accustomed to the Baltic trade the greater part of their lives, and were certainly as well able to conduct the ship from the Naze of Norward to Lowestoffe Point as Captain Bligh.'[28] When they arrived back in Britain, instead of doing as he had promised and landing the wounded men and officers at Yarmouth, where there was a naval hospital and many of them had families, Bligh hastily shifted them to another ship, and sailed off in the *Monarch* to the Nore. As Millard remarked acidly, 'So much for the humanity and politeness of Captain Bligh.'

Feeling that his faith in Bligh had been vindicated, in 1801 Sir Joseph Banks, the President of the Royal Society, nominated him for election as a Fellow 'in consideration of his distinguished services to navigation' and, this time, Bligh was successful. When his eldest daughter married and bore him a grandson, Bligh was delighted, although the boy died several years later. In May of that year, he was promoted to the command of the *Irresistible*, another 74-gun ship of the line, a position he kept until May of the following year, when the Peace of Amiens was signed.[29] One of the men who served with him on this ship, Lieutenant John Putland, later married his daughter Mary. Once again, Bligh served a period on half pay, spending much of his time with his wife and family. In March 1803 when he asked the Admiralty for work, he was given a Dover Revenue cutter and a tender that he named the *Betsy*; and the task of surveying Dungeness Roads and the Flushing coast. In early 1804, he was appointed acting Director of the Hydrographic Department – where he wrote his searing remarks on the margins of their copy of the official account of Cook's last voyage.

Finally, in May 1804, Bligh was offered the command of the *Warrior*, a 74-gun ship of the line under Lord Cornwallis. The *Warrior* had only half of her normal complement, however, very few of whom were experienced seamen; and his first lieutenant was ill, while his second lieutenant John Frazier, who had reported fit for duty, had been lamed by an accident on a merchant vessel. Towards the end of a patrol when Frazier asked for a medical survey, hoping to be discharged from the Navy, the surgeon put him on the sick list. Convinced that the lieutenant was malingering, Bligh ordered the surgeon to take him off the list; but when he told Frazier to stand watch, the lieutenant refused, saying that he was not well enough. After repeated refusals, Bligh had him arrested for disobedience and court-martialled. At the trial, however, when other officers gave evidence that Frazier had injured his ankle again and could hardly walk, and the surgeon testified that Frazier had been on the sick list, and was only taken off it on Bligh's orders, the Court dismissed the charges against him.

Incensed by the way he had been treated, and well aware of Bligh's history, Frazier now took his revenge, demanding that Bligh should be court-martialled for insulting him on deck and 'tyrannical and oppressive and unofficerlike behaviour, contrary to the rules and discipline of the Navy'.[30] Although Bligh appealed directly to Lord Cornwallis, who assured him that 'your conduct since you have been under my orders has always been perfectly to my satisfaction', the court martial went ahead in February 1805.

The testimony in the *Warrior* court martial is illuminating about Bligh's style of command, which had evidently changed little since his days on the *Bounty* and the *Providence* – although after Edward Christian's attacks on his reputation, and the damage these had caused, he was probably even more irascible. In addition, Christian's suggestion that he was a tyrannical commander, responsible for driving his men on the *Bounty* to mutiny, made him vulnerable to similar accusations. In his evidence for the prosecution, Henry Cock, a master's mate, testified that one day while Lieutenant Frazier had been talking with the ship's corporal about an incident in the wardroom, Bligh came out of his cabin and asked him why he spoke so loudly. When Frazier replied, 'I beg your pardon, Sir, I am not, I am answerable for the occurrences in my watch', Bligh exploded, saying, 'What, Sir, you damn'd rascal, you damn'd scoundrel, never was a man troubled with such a set of blackguards as I am. Take care, Sir, I am looking out for you.' Under cross-examination, Cock explained that Frazier habitually spoke in a loud voice; and that he would have forgotten about the incident if the lieutenant had not asked him to make a note of it. He added that he himself had often declared to his *Warrior* shipmates about Bligh that he had never sailed with a better captain than Bligh in his life.

According to Lieutenant Boyack, who supported Frazier in his court martial, he had heard Bligh say that 'he would rule the officers of the *Warrior* with an iron rod'; and he called Mr Jewell, the boatswain, 'a rascal and a scoundrel', shaking his fist at his head. As for himself, Boyack added: 'One day when hoisting a boat in, Captain Bligh called out "God damn me (or God damn you) Sir," and shook his fist at me, saying, "Why don't you hoist the boat in?"' On cross-examination by Bligh, who asked, 'Is it usual for me when any duty is carrying on to make use of a great deal of action, with my hands, without having any particular meaning in it?', Boyack replied, 'He has a great deal of action with his hands, as if he was going to knock a person down.' The surgeon, Robert Cinnamon, declared that when he told Bligh that Frazier could not do his duty, Bligh used 'violent language'; although in his view Frazier's leg was badly swollen, and he was not fit to stand watch. The surgeon's mate added that he had once seen Bligh grab the boatswain, telling him to execute various orders; and that his manner was generally 'rather abusive and irritating'.

Lieutenant William Pascoe affirmed that he had heard Bligh call the master 'a Jesuit and an old rogue', and say, 'let me have none of your rigadoon steps here'; and to the gunner that 'he was a damn'd long pelt of a bitch'; but that Bligh had never behaved in a 'tyrannical, unofficer-like or oppressive manner' to any of his officers. When the boatswain Jewell took the stand, he testified that Captain Bligh had said that if he had him in a dark corner he would do his business for him; and that he had frequently called him 'you scoundrel and you villain', but that he put no particular interpretation on his words. Captain Bligh was very hot and hasty, and he believed that he no sooner uttered these words than his passion ended.

The testimony for the defence was led by the *Warrior*'s first lieutenant, George Johnston, who had previously served with him as first lieutenant of the *Director* (although according to Bligh, he had since 'become the Greatest Drunkard').[31] Johnston affirmed that Bligh had been considerate towards Frazier, allowing him to sit on the quarterdeck, and excusing him from keeping watch and allowing him to sleep in on at least one occasion. He denied that Bligh had called Frazier a rascal or a scoundrel, or shaken his fist in his face. According to Johnston, Frazier had told him that if Bligh had not court-martialled him, he would not have pressed these charges. He admitted that Bligh often swore at the quartermasters or men who were idle, or officers who were derelict in their duties, but considered this justifiable anger, not to be taken as personal insults. In his view, Frazier had been capable of keeping watch, but had refused for fear that he would not be discharged from the Navy. According to Peter Mills, a midshipman, Frazier had said to him: 'I am told Captain Bligh intends to try me, but, if he does, I'll try him, and I'm damn'd if I don't do him.' He added that Jewell, the boatswain, was often drunk and incapable of doing his duty.

When Bligh asked him to describe his conduct towards his officers, Mills said that he tried to teach them good seamanship and navigation, regularly invited them to dinner and was just in dealing with any complaints; 'and if you happened to be in a passion with them, which you sometimes were, from the officers not carrying on the duty to your liking, you have spoken harshly to them, when you have asked them in the same voice to dine with you'. William Ranswell, master's mate, added that although Captain Bligh's expressions were sometimes hasty, they were commonly used in the Navy 'for the good of the service, to make the men smart'.

In his own defence, Bligh claimed that Frazier's accusations were driven by malice; and that any commander might be subject to 'ebullition of mind' when his officers neglected their duty. One can readily imagine that after his ordeals in the *Bounty*'s launch and on the *Providence*, and his time in the Pacific, when many of the sailors had suffered from scurvy (which made their limbs ulcerated and swollen), he would have been impatient with a lieutenant who refused to do his duty because his leg was painful. Bligh added:

> I candidly and without reserve avow that I am not a tame & indifferent observer of the manner in which Officers placed under my orders conducted themselves in the performance of their several duties. A signal or any communication from a commanding officer have ever been to me an indication for exertion & alacrity; . . . and peradventure I may occasionally have appeared to some of those officers as unnecessarily anxious for its execution by exhibiting any action or gesture peculiar to myself.
>
> Mr President & the members of this Court, who know & have experienced the arduous task of responsibility, and that of the magnitude of one of His Majesty's seventy-four gun ships, will, I am persuaded, acquit me of any apparent impetuosity & would plead in extenuation for my imputed charges, attributing the warmth of temper to my zeal for that service in which I have been employed without an imaginary blemish on my character for upwards of 35 years.[32]

After all the evidence had been heard, the Court concluded that the charges were in part proved, and Bligh was reprimanded and told to 'be more correct in his language'.

This rebuke was mild, and probably would not have been given but for wider concerns about the conduct of naval officers, and a wish to avoid future uprisings in the Navy. On the whole, like Fletcher Christian, the men on board the *Warrior* saw Bligh as a 'passionate' man. Although he cursed them heartily, he quickly forgot his rage, and was likely to do them a kindness or invite them to dinner immediately after. While his tongue could be lacerating (one can almost admire the eloquence of Bligh's invective), bad language was commonplace in the eighteenth-century Navy. As the *Warrior* court-martial testimony suggests, most sailors preferred to be cursed than to be flogged, and William Bligh was not a flogging captain. When Bligh castigated someone to whom he had formerly been kind, however, upbraiding them in front of the crew for not doing their duty, his habit of cursing and wild gesticulation often led to trouble. This was particularly the case with men who cherished their dignity as officers – Fletcher Christian, Frank Bond and John Frazier, for instance – who felt affronted and humiliated by his tirades. Others – Nathaniel Portlock, George Tobin and George Johnston, for example – were more tolerant of Bligh's outbursts, weighing these against his seamanship, courage and high standards.

Sir Joseph Banks was among this latter group, although he had never felt the sharp edge of Bligh's tongue. He was always kind to Elizabeth Bligh, and resolutely loyal to her husband. After the *Warrior* court martial, when Bligh wrote Banks a furious note, castigating four of his officers as 'the worst of serpents', Frazier as 'low and disgraceful', and the surgeon Cinnamon as 'the most designing wicked man ever came into a ship, and most highly perjured', and asked him to have them removed, Banks wrote him a sympathetic letter, promising his assistance.[33] When the two lieutenants were transferred from the *Warrior*, Bligh thanked him warmly for this 'proof of your great friendship and esteem, which to me is everything', adding plaintively: 'I have thought from the natural feelings of my mind that my moral character was as high as any man's.'[34] Banks's last beneficent gesture to William Bligh, however, almost proved fatal to his protégé.

Banks was still a key advisor to the government on the penal colony at New South Wales, which had become riddled with corruption. The New South Wales Corps, sent to guard the convicts, had taken control of the colony, receiving large land grants, using convict labour paid for by the government, and controlling the import and sale of food, liquor and clothing. As the governor, Philip Gidley King, reported: 'There is no society where the clashing of duty and interest between the Governor and the governed are more violent than in New South Wales, and more particularly so if the Governor does his duty.'[35] When King, worn out by these stresses, asked to be recalled, Sir Joseph was asked to suggest likely candidates. He immediately thought of William Bligh, and on 15 March 1805 wrote him a flattering letter, asking him to consider the position:

> In conversation [with Lord Camden], I was this day asked if I knew a man proper to be sent out in his stead – one who has integrity unimpeached, a mind capable of providing its own resources in difficulties without leaning on others for advice, firm in discipline, civil in deportment and not subject to whimper and whine when severity of discipline is wanted to meet [emergencies].
>
> I immediately answered: As this man must be chosen from among the post captains, I know of no one but Captain Bligh who will suit, but whether it will meet his views is another question.[36]

The government wanted the penal colony restored to order; and William Bligh, with his reputation as a stern, unflinching disciplinarian, seemed ideal for the task. In this letter, Banks assured him that if he took the post, the governor's salary would be doubled to £2,000; he would have 'the whole of Government power and stores' at his disposal; his daughters would have better marriage prospects in the colony than in England; and that his seniority and pension rights would not be harmed.

Although he was attracted by this offer, Bligh hesitated, knowing that his wife Betsy, to whom he was devoted, was unlikely to go with him. As he explained to Banks, Betsy now had a morbid fear of the sea: 'What a serious thing it is, you will allow, to take leave for ever of a wife who has united her lot with mine for 30 years . . . her undertaking the voyage I fear would be her death, owing to her extreme horror of the sea, the sound of a gun or thunder.' He was also worried that since the government intended to separate the governorship from the Navy, this might end his chances of becoming an admiral. After Banks settled many of his doubts, on 25 April 1805 Bligh finally accepted the appointment.[37] At the same time, Lieutenant Putland from the *Invincible*, now his son-in-law, was promoted to master and commander and appointed as his aide (so that his loyal, beloved daughter Mary could travel with him to Sydney); and in September, Bligh was appointed as the nominal captain of the *Porpoise* and commander-in-chief of His

Majesty's ships in the New South Wales station on full pay. In preparation for this posting, Bligh applied for a chronometer, intending to carry out surveys in Australia, and was granted the use of an Arnold instrument previously used by Vancouver during his survey of the north-west coast of America.[38]

On the voyage out, Bligh wrote at length to his wife, 'whom he is always thinking and talking of', as Mary reported to her sisters. He purchased jewellery for her and his daughters; 'Mama of course to be the handsomest,' Mary added.[39] During the passage to the Cape of Good Hope, however, Bligh engaged in a running battle with Captain Short, the commander of the convoy. As commander-in-chief, he assumed that he had the supreme command of the ships, while Short violently disagreed with this. When Bligh took control of the transport on which he was sailing and altered her course without prior warning, Short ordered Lieutenant Putland to fire two shots, one across her bows and one astern, and to load another shot to fire at the ship that was carrying Putland's wife and father-in-law. As Mary wrote to her mother:

> [Putland] can scarcely speak from agitation upon the subject of the Shots which were fired at us . . . Captn. S. had the brutality, to make him fire them; and told him, to prepare a third, for if we did not bear down immediately, he was to fire right into us. I think such an inhuman thing, as making a man fire at his Father and Wife, was never done before.[40]

At the Cape of Good Hope, Francis Beaufort, the commander of another British ship who observed the disputes between Bligh and Short, gave his verdict on their clashes:

> They were both wrong, both had acted intemperately and foolishly, both had laid themselves open to censure, and both were equally resolved to stick to what they had already done and not to retract a single expression. I immediately pronounced for Capt. Bligh – and whatever I thought of their mutual conduct, I perceived that one was a man of talents and the other an ass.[41]

During the voyage, Short also quarrelled with his officers; and upon their arrival in Sydney, Bligh convened an inquiry into these disputes, which found against Short, who was sent home for court martial. Back in London, Short was honourably acquitted, however, and the Court stated that in their opinion, Bligh had instigated the charges against him and that Short had been unjustly treated.

Furious on her husband's behalf, Bligh's wife Elizabeth interceded with Banks, hotly defending his conduct; and sent a letter to the Admiralty, asking that 'in their great justice and goodness [they should] consider the extreme hardship it is for an Officer of Rank & Character who is far distant executing an arduous duty, to be thus traduced & defamed, with out being defended or heard'; along with affidavits which indicated that on a number of matters, Short had lied to the tribunal.[42] In a loving letter, she sent her husband a detailed account of the machinations against him in England, warning him that he had many enemies, and imploring him to be cautious and keep his temper, because 'the malice and cruelty of the people who were engaged in this business exceeds everything I ever thought men capable of'.[43] Expressing her trust in Samuel Marsden, the New South Wales chaplain who had given her warm support, she warned Bligh against various individuals, including his predecessor Governor King, who had tried to reassure her in an 'artfull bombast letter' but was nevertheless intriguing to return to Sydney in his place. When their daughter Elizabeth wrote to her sister Mary on the same subject, she added: '[T]hank God we have got quite the better of the wicked set who would have injured him, & they have fallen into the pit they dug for him.'[44] On Betsy's urging, Banks contacted the Admiralty, and later wrote to Bligh that 'all I hear in Lord Castlereagh's office is in your favour; your talents, your perseverance, and your spirited conduct are spoken of in terms of praise'.[45]

Betsy's warnings came too late to save Bligh as Governor of New South Wales, however. Soon after arriving in Sydney, his 'Oeconomy' overcame him. Before Governor King left office, he awarded Bligh three land grants – one of 240 acres near Sydney to be called 'Camperdown'; another of 105 acres near Parramatta to be known as 'Mount Betham', his wife's maiden name; and a third grant of 1000 acres near Rouse Hill, named 'Copenhagen' after his other great sea battle – estates which he began to farm using government stores and convict labour. In exchange, as soon as he took office, Bligh granted King's wife an area of 790 acres, which she incautiously named 'Thanks' – suggesting that neither he nor the Kings saw much wrong with these transactions. He also indulged his daughter, allowing her to lay out elaborate gardens in Government House grounds. Although Joseph Banks had urged Bligh to accept the governorship on the grounds that he would have 'the Government power and stores at his command', these actions undermined his authority just as he set about trying to curb the corruption of the New South Wales Corps.

In the colony, rum was the sole currency, and the officers had a monopoly on its trade and supply. After sizing up the situation, Bligh advised Banks that stern measures were needed. The use of spirits as a currency must be abolished; the Corps should be recalled, perhaps to India; and the civil and criminal courts should be regulated by rules like those in Britain. These were astute recommendations, but Bligh's own conduct lacked discretion. When Judge Advocate Richard Atkins told him that a decision to suspend an assistant surgeon was contrary to law, Bligh retorted: 'The law, sir! Damn the law: my will is the law, and woe unto the man that dares to disobey it!' According to his own account, Atkins found the governor's demeanour during this confrontation intolerable, confessing that it 'is yet impressed on my mind'.[46]

Bligh also clashed with John Macarthur, a former member of the Corps, an arrogant, unprincipled man who was one of the richest settlers in the colony. During his time in the Corps, Macarthur had been court-martialled in England for duelling with his commanding officer. Afterwards, he had resigned his commission and in 1804 received a land grant of 5000 acres to set up a merino wool industry in New South Wales. Although Banks opposed this scheme, saying that an English company should be given the task instead, Macarthur managed to gain access to the royal flocks of merino sheep, which Banks himself had established. As Governor King wrote about Macarthur:

> His employment during the eleven years he has been here has been that of making a large fortune, helping his brother officers to make small ones (mostly at the publick expense) and sowing discord and strife . . . Many and many instances of his diabolical spirit had shown itself before Govr. Phillip left this colony, and since, altho' in many instances he has been the master worker of the puppetts he has set in motion.[47]

Bligh was well aware of Bank's views. According to John Macarthur, when he came to Government House and tried to talk with him about the wool industry in Australia, Bligh exploded:

> What have I to do with your sheep, sir; what have I to do with your cattle? Are you to have such flocks of sheep and such herds of cattle as no man ever heard of before? – No, Sir! I have heard of your concerns, sir; you have got 5000 acres of land in the finest situation in the country; but by God, you shan't keep it!

When Macarthur stood his ground, saying that he would complain to his influential friends in England, the governor exclaimed furiously, 'Damn the Privy Council! And damn the Secretary of State too! What have they to do with me?'[48]

Having made an enemy of the most powerful man in the colony while insulting some of the most powerful men in England, Bligh now insisted that all land grants (apart from his own) must be formally approved in London, and cancelled a number of leases of the land around Government House and the church in Sydney, ordering that the houses which had been built on them should be demolished. This angered many of the military and a number of free settlers (including John Macarthur, who held one of these leases) – although the farmers appreciated his efforts to break the power of Macarthur and the Corps. He replaced many officials with his own appointments, and according to the soldiers, failed to treat the Corps with 'proper' respect, calling them 'wretches', 'villains' and 'tremendous buggers'.[49] When Provost Marshal William Gore, his loyal ally, was prosecuted for the illegal sale of a house, Bligh declared that as governor, his authority was equal to the laws of England, and soon afterwards Gore was acquitted. Almost immediately, those whom he had affronted began to recall the mutiny on the *Bounty*; the Corps' surgeon John Harris, for instance (who had been dismissed), writing indignantly:

> It is completely the reign of Robertspere [Robespierre], or that of Terror . . . I have heard much about Bounty Bligh before I saw him, but no person could conceive that he could be such a fellow – Caligula himself never reigned with more despotic sway than he does.[50]

Exploiting the gossip about the mutiny on the *Bounty*, Macarthur remarked ominously that the governor 'will perhaps get another voyage in his launch again';[51] and by October 1807 a poem about Bligh was circulating in Sydney:

> Oh tempora! Oh Mores! Is there
> No *Christian* in New South Wales to put
> A stop to the Tyranny of the Governor.[52]

Once again, Bligh was the subject of a campaign of vilification, fuelled by his own lack of political judgement and discretion, this time led by John Macarthur, which aimed to whip up anger against him and destroy his reputation. In Sydney, thoughts of insurrection were already in the air.

When the crisis came in December 1807, it was orchestrated by Macarthur. Judge Advocate Atkins ordered Macarthur to pay a bond that he had forfeited when a convict escaped from one of his ships. He refused, and when Atkins issued a warrant summoning him to appear in court, Macarthur ignored it, and was arrested and committed for trial. On the night before the trial, a mess dinner was held for the New South Wales Corps, attended by Macarthur's son and nephew. Afterwards, their commanding officer, Major George Johnston, had an accident in his carriage, bruising his face and hurting his arm. In the court, which consisted of the judge advocate and six Corps officers, Macarthur declared: 'It is to the Officers of the New South Wales Corps that the administration of Justice is committed; and who that is just has anything to fear?' After this incitement, the Corps officers refused to serve as a jury under Atkins, aborting the trial. When Bligh wrote to Johnston, asking him to come to Government House to discuss the matter, Johnston replied that he was unable to do this, since he was confined to his sickbed.

Incensed by these events, Bligh had Macarthur thrown into jail. When he sent a letter to Johnston, declaring that the actions of his officers were treasonable (a capital offence), the major panicked. Hurrying into town, he went to the Corps barracks, where the officers and a handful of settlers were conferring. As one of the soldiers later recalled, Lieutenant Laycock exclaimed, 'By God, we are all going to be hanged!' When another of the officers asked, 'Why so?' and Laycock answered, 'Old Bligh has summoned us to appear before him,' Adjutant Minchin retorted, 'Mr. Laycock if you are afraid I am not and we will find a way to cool him.' 'How is that?' 'By arresting him before he arrests us.'[53]

When these men assured Johnston that unless he put the governor under arrest, there would be an uprising, he assumed the title of lieutenant-governor and signed a warrant for Macarthur's release. Towards sunset on 26 January 1808, 400 soldiers of the New South Wales Corps, led by Major Johnston, his arm in a sling and his face bruised, and accompanied by John Macarthur, marched to Government House with bayonets fixed, flags flying and the band playing 'The British Grenadiers', followed by a large crowd. As they approached the governor's residence Macarthur cried out, 'My Boys, this Memorable day will be the most Glorious day the New South Wales Corps ever experienced!'[54]

At the gates of Government House, Bligh's daughter Mary, whose husband Lieutenant Putland had died just four days earlier, tried to bar their way, confronting the soldiers with their naked bayonets, brandishing her parasol and crying out, 'You traitors, you rebels, you have just walked over my husband's grave & now come to murder my father.'[55] Bligh had hidden inside the house, and when the soldiers found him two hours later, his uniform was dishevelled, and covered with dust, cobwebs and feathers. Afterwards, although some claimed that he had been found under a bed, Bligh insisted that he had been concealing some papers; and the eyewitness accounts were confused and contradictory. His papers were confiscated, and he was arrested and confined to quarters. Outside, as bonfires blazed, Bligh's effigy was burned, and Macarthur was chaired on the shoulders of his jubilant supporters. Afterwards, Macarthur wrote to his wife: 'I am happy to say I have succeeded beyond what I expected. The Tyrant is now no doubt gnashing his Teeth with vexation at his overthrow. May he often have cause to do the like.'[56]

With Bligh confined in Government House, Johnston and Macarthur set about overturning his reforms. Almost all of his appointees were dismissed from office; and after a farcical trial, Macarthur was acquitted of the charges against him and appointed a magistrate and secretary to the colony. A flurry of land grants and appointments were given to officers of the Corps and their friends and supporters; and those who sympathised with Bligh were brought before Johnston's court and given harsh sentences, while the rum trade resumed unabated.[57] In March 1809 when Bligh agreed to return to England, having promised on 'his honour as an officer and a gentleman' that if he was released, he would not interfere with the government, he was freed. As soon as he boarded the *Porpoise*, however, a naval vessel that he nominally commanded, he reneged on his promise, saying that it had been made under duress; and took control of the *Porpoise*, sailing to Hobart, where he hoped to find assistance, although this was not forthcoming. From the ship, he sent Betsy a long, formal account of the rebellion, hoping that she could use it in England to clear his name.[58] In January 1810, when a new governor, Lachlan Macquarie, arrived in New South Wales, Bligh sailed to Sydney to greet him. Although at first Macquarie was sympathetic, he soon lost patience with his predecessor, writing to his brother:

> Bligh is certainly a most disagreeable Person to have any dealings, or Publick business to transact with; having no regard whatever to his promise or engagements however sacred, and his natural temper is uncommonly harsh, and tyrannical in the extreme. He is certainly generally detested by high, low, rich and poor, but more specially by the higher Classes of People.[59]

Despite his disaffection with Bligh, Macquarie took firm action to restore order to the colony. Macarthur and Johnston were arrested, and sent to England for trial. All appointments and land grants made since Bligh's arrest were revoked; Judge Advocate Atkins was sent home; the decisions of Johnston's court were declared null and void; and the New South Wales Corps was recalled to England, in keeping with Bligh's earlier recommendations. After giving

*The capture of Governor Bligh.*

Mary's hand in marriage to her new husband, Lieutenant-Colonel O'Connell, Bligh returned to England, writing plaintively to Betsy from Rio de Janeiro:

> Thus My Dear Love, when I thought nothing could have induced our dear Child to have quitted me, have I left her behind me in the finest climate in the World, which to have taken her from into the tempestuous Voyage I have performed I now believe would have caused her death . . . If I had forced her away & I had lost her on the Voyage I could never have survived it – she remains as a Pattern of Virtue and admired by everyone.[60]

In October 1810 when his ship anchored, Bligh hurried to London to see his wife and other daughters, who had lobbied indefatigably on his behalf.[61] As he reported disconsolately to Frank Bond (with whom he was now reconciled), however, Betsy's health had suffered badly from these latest trials: 'Mrs. Bligh is not well, her Nerves being very much broke.'[62] When he met with Sir Joseph Banks, after discussing the situation in New South Wales, Banks told him some extraordinary news – the Pacific hideout of Fletcher Christian and the *Bounty* mutineers had recently been discovered. According to Admiralty sources, when an American sealer, the *Topaz* commanded by Mayhew Folger, had anchored off

Pitcairn's Island in 1808, three young men came out in a double canoe, bringing a pig and some fruit as a gift. Speaking in English, they told Folger that they had been born on the island, and that their father had sailed with William Bligh. When Folger went ashore, he met their 'father', an Englishman who identified himself as Alexander Smith (John Adams), one of the *Bounty* mutineers.

According to Smith, after sending Captain Bligh into the ship's boat, Fletcher Christian had taken command of the *Bounty*, sailing to Tahiti where most of the men had stayed ashore. Soon afterwards, Christian, Smith himself and seven others, each with their Tahitian 'wives' and accompanied by six island men or 'servants', had sailed to Pitcairn's Island, where they stripped everything useful out of the *Bounty*, and ran her on the rocks. Several months later, in a fit of insanity, Christian had thrown himself off a cliff (although in fact, this was William McCoy). About six years (or four years) after their arrival, according to Smith in various statements (in fact, three years, in 1793), the Tahitian men had rebelled and killed all of the Englishmen except himself, although he was shot in the neck with a pistol ball. That same night, the widows of the sailors killed all of the island men, leaving Smith alone on the island with nine women and several small children.

When Folger asked Smith whether he had heard about the great battles between the English and French navies, the old man exclaimed, 'How could I? Unless the birds of the air had been my heralds.' When he was told about the great victories of Earl St Vincent, Lord Duncan and Lord Nelson, Smith threw his hat into the air, gave three cheers and shouted with joy, 'Old England forever!' During the visit he presented Folger with the Kendall chronometer from the *Bounty* (which was later taken from the captain by the governor of Juan Fernandez) and an azimuth compass, which Folger forwarded to the Lords of the Admiralty. According to Folger, there were now about thirty-five people living on the island, who regarded Smith as their father. They all spoke English, and lived 'in a Religious and moral way'.[63] Given his memories of Alexander Smith, Bligh would have been bemused to find him the pious patriarch of a tranquil island community. No doubt he was gratified to learn that all of the other 'pirates', including Fletcher Christian, had perished.

When Major George Johnston was put on trial in London in May 1811 for leading the Rum Rebellion, Bligh was exonerated (although in the process, his conduct as Governor of New South Wales was subjected to merciless scrutiny). Johnston was declared guilty of mutiny and cashiered, while for the next eight years, Macarthur found himself unable to return to New South Wales for fear of facing civil charges. Although mutiny was a capital offence, the court martial held that under the extraordinary circumstances prevailing towards the end of Bligh's tenure as governor, Johnston could not be held wholly responsible for the uprising. Once again, Bligh's violent temper, which led one of the Corps soldiers who gave evidence against him to describe him (yet again) as 'a passionate man', cost him dearly.[64]

Nevertheless, his seniority in the Navy led to further, automatic promotions (although he remained on half pay, and never went to sea again); and four weeks after Johnston was sentenced, Bligh was gazetted a Rear-Admiral of the Blue. In July, when Bligh wrote to Frank Bond about Johnston's court martial, reporting that he was editing the minutes for publication, he remarked with satisfaction: 'They entered into all the irrelevant matter they could, but they could not fix one spot on my Character which I am happy to say was proved most perfect notwithstanding their attempts to slander it.'[65]

Later that year, however, one of the Romantic poets, Mary Russell Mitford, published a narrative poem, *Christina, the Maid of the South Seas*, based on the reports of Folger's visit to Pitcairn's Island. In the course of writing this work, Mitford was advised by Samuel Taylor Coleridge (whose Ancient Mariner, like Fletcher Christian, had exclaimed 'I am in hell. I am in hell!'), and James Burney, who had sailed with Bligh on Cook's third expedition. In *Christina*, after anchoring off an Arcadian island in the South Seas, Captain Folger ('Seymor') is greeted by three fine young men in a double canoe. When he goes ashore, he is astonished to meet an old man who had sailed with William Bligh, and was involved in the mutiny of the *Bounty*:

> For well he knew – who knows it not?
> Misguided Christian's ruthless plot.
> And he had read, with horror pale,
> The suffering Bligh's heart-thrilling tale,
> When from his gallant vessel driv'n,
> Of every earthly comfort riv'n;
> Remote from kind and friendly land,
> The rebels chas'd his faithful band.

While Seymor is talking with Alexander Smith ('Fitzallan'), one of his young sailors ('Henry') comes upon Christina, the daughter of Fletcher Christian, weeping at the tomb of her Tahitian mother. Moved by the sight of this beautiful

*Landing at Bounty Bay, Pitcairn Island.*

*John Adams, surviving* Bounty *mutineer.*

young girl, he falls in love with her, instigating a bitter rivalry with her island suitor. While Henry is dallying with Christina, Seymor tells Fitzallan that Bligh is still alive, shocking the old man:

> With Bligh I sailed — Whence comes so chill
> At that once hated name the thrill
> He lives! He lives! My heart be still.

Startled into candour, Fitzallan tells Seymor the story of the mutiny — how during their visit to Tahiti, Fletcher Christian had fallen in love with the chieftain's daughter, Iddea ('Itia, Tu's wife in Tahiti), who became pregnant with their child. Terrified that the *'arioi* would destroy his baby, Christian begged Bligh to take Iddea on board the *Bounty*, but his captain refused, earning Christian's undying hatred:

> Say, would not Bligh? O, name him not!
> From nature's scroll that foul line blot;
> He has refus'd a husband's prayer,
> Refus'd! and fears not my despair!

In revenge Christian decided to take over the ship; and after seizing Bligh and sending him and many of his shipmates into the ship's launch, returned to his lover in Tahiti. In the wake of the mutiny, Christian became morose and withdrawn. Soon after arriving in Tahiti, he and Iddea with some of the *Bounty*'s men had sailed to Pitcairn, a deserted island, where they settled. When their baby died, stricken with remorse, Christian committed suicide by jumping off a cliff.

No doubt William Bligh and his wife read this poem, which was published in London. In the advertisement, Mitford nervously anticipated their reactions, as well as those of the mutineers' families:

> In detailing an event, still remembered with anguish by those who shared the sufferings of Captain Bligh, as well as by the friends and relations of the unfortunate persons, who occasioned those sufferings, it was difficult so as to write, as to avoid on the one hand the charge of palliating a most fatal conspiracy, and, on the other, an imputation far more dreaded by the Author! — of irritating the feelings of a highly respectable family, and tearing open the scarcely healed wounds of kindred affection.[66]

Indeed, Bligh and his wife must have been appalled by Mitford's depiction of him as a heartless tyrant, her tale of Christian's curse upon their children, and her sympathetic portrayal of the mutineers.

In November 1811, Bligh sent Frank Bond a copy of the minutes of Johnston's court martial, which he had edited, remarking: 'You will find that all the Witnesses on his side were the Villains connected in the Usurpation, and besides their perjuries and prevarications they were allowed to go into every scheme they could, to show something against me.' He added unhappily: 'I am sorry to inform you that Mrs. Bligh has been for some Months Dangerously Ill, and now altho an Invalid, yet the seat of the disease not being removed, I fear she will never be reinstated in her health again. She has been five Weeks at Brighton, and only gathered a little strength, and continues an Invalid not being able to digest any Solid Food, or exposed to the Air but for a quarter of an hour While the Sun Shines.'[67]

Worn out by all her trials, on 15 April 1812 Betsy Bligh died after a long illness. She and William Bligh had eight children together, six girls and the twin boys who died shortly after their birth; and she had made him happy. A fulsome obituary in the *Gentleman's Magazine* described her as 'a woman of superior abilities and attainments, and a rare example of every virtue and amiable quality – an inestimable treasure'. According to this account, Elizabeth Bligh was intelligent, high-spirited, well-educated, and widely read, with a large library; and a devoted collector of prints and shells.[68] On her tombstone, Bligh had the following text inscribed:

> Her spirit soar'd to Heav'n, the blest domain,
> Where virtue only can its mead obtain.
> All the great duties she perform'd thro' life,
> Those of a child, a parent and a wife.[69]

After Betsy's death, William Bligh was awarded a pension for his services as Governor of New South Wales, and another naval promotion, becoming a Vice-Admiral of the Blue in June 1814. He left the family house at Lambeth, moving with his unmarried daughters to a manor house at Farningham in Kent. Dr Gatty, who often visited the manor as a boy, later described Bligh's love of small children, saying that the admiral used to take him on his knee and let him play with a bullet that he always wore on a blue ribbon around his neck – the same bullet that he had used as a weight when doling out the rations on board the *Bounty*'s launch during her odyssey across the western Pacific.[70] In marked contrast with his disputatious conduct as a commander, Bligh's family life was contented and good-humoured. On one occasion, his unmarried twin daughters Frances and Jane, noticing that a man had advertised for a wife, invited him to a service at Farningham Church, telling him to identify himself by loudly blowing his nose in the aisle. When he did so, they laughed so hard that they almost disgraced themselves; and when the hapless suitor followed them home, Bligh sent him packing.

In 1815, further reports of the colony on Pitcairn Island arrived in London, after a brief visit by Captain Sir Thomas Staines in the *Briton* and Captain Pipon in the *Tagus* in September 1814. In a sympathetic account, Staines praised Alexander Smith's 'exemplary conduct & fatherly care of the whole of the little Colony, [which] could not but command admiration. The pious manner in which all those born on the Island have been reared, the correct sense of Religion which has been instilled into their young minds by this old man, has given him the preeminence over the whole of them, to whom they look up as the Father of the whole & one family.'[71] According to Staines and Pipon, Smith (John Adams) declared that he had been asleep in his hammock when the mutiny broke out, and that 'he always lamented the transaction'. The descendants of the mutineers had fine gardens and plantations, and plenty of pigs, goats and chickens; and in Smith's house, which was furnished with a table, chairs and benches, with windows and shutters, Staines saw some muskets in poor condition, and a number of Bligh's books from the *Bounty* (including his personal copy of the official *Voyage* from Cook's third expedition). When these volumes were taken out to the *Briton*, the officers examined them with great interest. According to Lieutenant Shillibeer:

> In the title page of each volume the name of Captain Bligh was written, and I suppose in his own writing Christian had written his name immediately under it without running his pen through, or defacing in the least, that of Captain Bligh. On the margins of several of the leaves are written in pencil, numerous remarks on the work, but as I consider them the private observations of Captain Bligh, and written unsuspecting the much lamented event which subsequently took place, they shall by me be held sacred.[72]

Just as Bligh, impelled by outrage, had scrawled comments in the copy of the *Voyage* in the Hydrographic Office, it seems that he had also annotated his own personal copy of these volumes (especially the last) before or during the *Bounty* voyage. While Shillibeer's discretion is understandable, since Bligh was still alive during his visit to Pitcairn's island, it is very frustrating. It would be fascinating to be able to compare Bligh's comments written in his own personal set of the *Voyage*, held on board the *Bounty*, with his later marginalia in the Hydrographic Office copy.[73]

In his account of this visit, Captain Pipon described Pitcairn Island as an evangelical Utopia, inhabited by 'extremely fine young Men, very athletic, with the finest forms, & countenances indicating much benevolence & goodness. The young women are still more to be admired, wonderfully strong, most pleasing countenances, & a degree of modesty & bashfulness that would do honour to the most virtuous nation . . . There is no debauchery here, no immoral conduct, & Adams [Smith] informed me, there is not one instance of any young Woman having proved unchaste: the men appear equally Moral & well behaved.' Fletcher Christian's son, Thursday October Christian, the first baby to be born on the island, was a 'tall fine young Man about 6 feet high . . . with a great share of good humour & a disposition & willingness to oblige, we were very glad to trace in his benevolent countenance, all the features of an honest English face'.[74] These young people all spoke English and Tahitian, although they could not read or write, and held prayers every morning and evening, reciting grace before each meal. When Alexander Smith expressed a wish to return to England, they clustered around him, weeping and calling him father, and imploring him to stay with them; and he consented.[75] Pipon concluded: 'It would have been a heart-breaking circumstance, to have torn him from those he most dearly loved, as well as cruel to a degree to have left a young Colony to perish without such a protector.'[76] For William Bligh, these glowing reports of the colony established by the 'pirates' must have been galling. The attacks upon his reputation by Edward Christian and John Macarthur had captured the popular imagination, while Fletcher Christian and Alexander Smith were becoming Romantic heroes, featuring in a melodrama in Drury Lane in 1816, and immortalised by British poets.[77]

After retreating into the consolations of family life, on 7 December 1817 William Bligh collapsed and died from cancer, at the age of sixty-four. He was buried next to Elizabeth in Lambeth graveyard in London, mourned by his children and grandchildren. The inscription on his tombstone reads:

Sacred
To the Memory of

William Bligh Esq., F.R.S.
Vice-Admiral
of the Blue
The celebrated navigator
who first transplanted the Bread fruit tree
from Otaheite to the West Indies
Bravely fought the battles of his country
and died beloved, respected and lamented
on the 7th day of December 1817
Aged 64.

After hearing the news of the death of 'the Don', George Tobin, former midshipman on the *Providence*, wrote to his shipmate, Bligh's nephew Frank Bond:

So poor Bligh, for with all his infirmities, you and I cannot but think of him, has followed Portlock. He has had a busy and turbulent journey of it – no one more so, and since the unfortunate Mutiny in the *Bounty*, has been rather in the Shade. Yet perhaps was he not altogether understood.

– I am sure, my dear Friend that in the *Providence* there was no settled <u>system</u> of Tyranny exercised by him likely to produce dissatisfaction. It was in those violent <u>Tornados</u> of temper when he lost himself, yet, when all in his opinion, <u>went right</u>, when could a man be more placid and interesting?

For myself I feel that I am indebted to him. It was the first ship in which I ever served as an Officer – I joined full of apprehension, – I soon thought he was not dissatisfied with me – it gave me encouragement and on the whole we journeyed smoothly on. Once or twice indeed I felt the <u>Unbridled</u> licence of <u>his power of Speech</u> yet never without soon receiving some thing like an emollient plaister to heal the wound.

Let our old Captain's frailties be forgotten and view him as a man of Science and excellent practical Seaman. He had suffered much, and ever in difficulty, by labour and perseverance extricated himself. But his great quality was Foresight. In this, I think, Bond, you will accord with me. I have seen many men in his profession with more resources, but never one with so much precaution – I mean as a Navigator.[78]

This was a fitting epitaph for William Bligh, sailor and South Sea explorer. On the other side of the world from Lambeth, in Matavai Bay in Tahiti – Captain Cook's favourite Pacific port – there stands another memorial to

William Bligh. In 2005, a volcanic stone upright was erected on the black sands of Point Venus, surrounded by pebbles set in concrete and adorned with bronze images of the *Bounty*, Fletcher Christian and Captain Bligh. Once in a while, the descendants of the mutineers (from Pitcairn, Norfolk Island, Australia, New Zealand and elsewhere) visit Tahiti, and gather around the obelisk to honour their ancestors. Of all the early European navigators who visited this lovely island, only Bligh and his *Bounty* sailors have their own *marae*.

# Selected Bibliography

(See other sources cited in the notes.)

Alexander, Caroline, 2003, *The Bounty: The True Story of the Mutiny on the* Bounty (New York, Penguin).

Bach, John, ed., 1987, *The Bligh Notebook: 'Rough Account – Lieutenant Wm. Bligh's Voyage in the* Bounty*'s Launch from the Ship to Tofua and from Thence to Timor'*, *28 April to 14 June 1789, with a draft list of the* Bounty *mutineers*, facsimile ed., 2 volumes (Sydney, Allen & Unwin in association with the National Library of Australia).

Banks, R.E.R. et al., 1994, *Sir Joseph Banks: A Global Perspective* (London, Kew Publishing).

Beaglehole, J.C., ed., 1955, *The Journals of Captain James Cook on His Voyages of Discovery, Vol. I: The Voyage of the* Endeavour *1768–1771* (Cambridge, at the University Press, for the Hakluyt Society).

——, ed., 1962, *The* Endeavour *Journal of Joseph Banks 1768–1771, Vols I and II* (Sydney, Angus & Robertson).

——, 1967, *Captain Cook and Captain Bligh* (Wellington, Whitcombe & Tombs Ltd).

——, ed., 1967, *The Journals of Captain Cook, Vol. 3: The Voyage of the* Resolution *and* Discovery *1776–1780*, Parts I and II (Cambridge, at the University Press, for the Hakluyt Society).

——, ed., 1969, *The Journals of Captain Cook, Vol. 2: The Voyage of the* Resolution *and* Adventure *1772–1775* (Cambridge, at the University Press, for the Hakluyt Society).

Beechey, Captain F.W., 1831, *Narrative of a Voyage to the Pacific and Beering's Strait, to co-operate with the Polar Expeditions: Performed in His Majesty's Ship* Blossom, *under the Command of Captain F.W. Beechey, R.N, F.R.S., &c., in the years 1825, 26, 27, 28*, I, II (London, Henry Colburn and Richard Bentley).

Bladen, F.M., ed., 1898, *Historical Records of New South Wales, King and Bligh* (Sydney, William Applegate Gullick, Government Printer).

Bligh, William, 1790, *A Narrative of the Mutiny on Board His Majesty's ship the* Bounty *and the subsequent voyage of part of the crew, in the ship's boat* (London, G. Nicol).

——, 1792, *A voyage to the South Sea, undertaken by command of His Majesty, for the purpose of conveying the breadfruit-tree to the West Indies in His Majesty's Ship the* Bounty (London, G. Nicol).

——, 1794, *An Answer to certain Assertions contained in the Appendix to a Pamphlet entitled, Minutes of the Proceedings of the Courtmartial held at Portsmouth August 12th, 1792, on Ten Persons charged with Mutiny on Board His Majesty's Ship the* Bounty (London, G. Nicol).

—— (and Fryer, John) in Owen Rutter, ed., 1934, *The Voyage of the* Bounty*'s Launch as related in William Bligh's Despatch to the Admiralty and the Journal of John Fryer* (London, Golden Cockerel Press).

—— in Owen Rutter, ed., 1937a, *The Log of the* Bounty*: Being Lieutenant William Bligh's Log of the Proceedings of His Majesty's Armed Vessel* Bounty *in a Voyage to the South Seas, to Take the Breadfruit from the Society Islands to the West Indies,* 2 volumes (London, Golden Cockerel Press, and in facsimile by Pageminster Press, Guildford, Surrey, 1981).

—— in Owen Rutter, ed., 1937b, *Bligh's Voyage in the* Resource *from Coupang to Batavia, Together with the Log of His Subsequent Passage to England in the Dutch Packet* Vlydt *and His Remarks on Morrison's Journal. All Printed for the First Time from the Manuscripts in the Mitchell Library of New South Wales* (London, Golden Cockerel Press).

—— in Stephen Walters, ed., 1981, *The Mutiny on Board HMS* Bounty. *The Log in Facsimile,* I (Guildford, Surrey, Pageminster Press).

—— in John Bach, ed., 1987, *The Bligh Notebook: Rough Account: Lieutenant Wm. Bligh's Voyage in the Bounty's Launch from the Ship to Tofua and from Thence to Timor,* facsimile ed., 2 volumes (North Sydney, Allen & Unwin in association with the National Library of Australia).

—— in Paul Brunton, ed., 1989, *Awake, Bold Bligh! William Bligh's letters describing the mutiny on HMS* Bounty (Sydney, Allen & Unwin).

Boswell, James, 1791/1992, *The Life of Samuel Johnson* (New York, Alfred A. Knopf).

Bougainville, Louis-Antoine in John Dunmore, trans. and ed., 2002, *The Pacific Journal of Louis-Antoine de Bougainville* (Cambridge, at the University Press, for the Hakluyt Society).

Brunton, Paul, ed., 1989, *Awake, Bold Bligh! William Bligh's letters describing the mutiny on HMS* Bounty (Sydney, Allen & Unwin).

Christian, Edward, 1794, [*Appendix*], *Minutes of the Proceedings of the Court-Martial held at Portsmouth August 12, 1792 on Ten Persons charged with Mutiny on Board His Majesty's Ship the* Bounty*: With an Appendix containing a full Account of the real Causes and Circumstances of that unhappy Transaction, the most material of which have hitherto been withheld from the Public* (London, J. Deighton).

——, 1795, *A Short Reply to Captain William Bligh's Answer* (London, J. Deighton).

Christian, Glynn, 1982 / 2005, *Fragile Paradise: The Discovery of Fletcher Christian,* Bounty *Mutineer* (London, H. Hamilton / The Long Riders' Guild Press).

Cook, James and King, James, 1784, *A Voyage to the Pacific Ocean. Undertaken, by the Command of his Majesty, for making Discoveries in the Northern Hemisphere. Performed under the direction of Captains Cook, Clerke, and Gore, In his Majesty's Ships the* Resolution *and* Discovery. *In the Years 1776, 1777, 1778, 1779, and 1780. In Three Volumes,* Vols I and II written by Captain James Cook, F.R.S., Vol. III by Captain James King, L.L.D. and F.R.S. (London).

David, A.C.F, Lieutenant Commander, 1982, 'The Surveyors of the *Bounty:* A preliminary study of the hydrographic surveys of William Bligh, Thomas Hayward and Peter Heywood and the charts published from them', typescript, Royal Navy Hydrographic Department, Ministry of Defence, Taunton, Somerset.

——, 1997, *The Charts & Coastal Views of Captain Cook's Voyages, Volume Three: The Voyage of the* Resolution *and* Discovery *1776–1780* (London, The Hakluyt Society, in Association with the Australian Academy of the Humanities).

Dening, Greg, 1992, *Mr Bligh's Bad Language: Passion, Power and Theatre on the* Bounty (Cambridge, Cambridge University Press).

Denman, Arthur, 1903, 'Captain Bligh and the Mutiny of the *Bounty*', *Notes and Queries* 9th s. XII: 501.

Du Rietz, Rolf E., 1981, *Fresh Light on John Fryer of the* Bounty (Uppsala, Sweden, Dahlia Books, Banksia 2).

——, 1986, *Peter Heywood's Tahitian Vocabulary and the Narrative by James Morrison: Some Notes on their Origin and History* (Uppsala, Sweden, Dahlia Books, Banksia 3).

——, 2003 / 2009, *The Bias of Bligh: An Investigation into the Credibility of William Bligh's Version of the* Bounty *Mutiny* (Uppsala, Sweden, Dahlia Books, Banksia 7).

Ellis, William, 1859, *Polynesian Researches during a Residence of Nearly Eight Years in the Society and Sandwich Islands, Vols I–IV* (London, Bohn).

Forster, George, 1787, *Cook der Entdecker*, published in facsimile with a translation, 2007, *Cook the Discoverer* (Sydney, Hordern House, for the National Maritime Museum).

Fryer, John, ed. Stephen Walter, 1979, *The Voyage of the* Bounty*'s Launch. John Fryer's Narrative* (Guildford, Surrey, Genesis Publications).

Gesner, Peter, ed., 1998, *A Voyage Round the World in His Majesty's Frigate* Pandora (Sydney, Hordern House, for the Australian National Maritime Museum).

Gould, Rupert, 1928, 'Bligh's Notes on Cook's Last Voyage', *Mariner's Mirror* 14: 371–85.

Greatheed, Samuel, 1820, National Library of Australia, NK9566, 'Authentic history of the mutineers of the *Bounty*', in *Sailors' Magazine and Naval Miscellany*, I: 402–6, 449–56.

Haweis, Thomas, ed., 1799, *A Missionary Voyage to the Southern Pacific Ocean, Performed in the Years 1796, 1797, 1798, in the Ship* Duff, *commanded by Captain James Wilson* (London, T. Chapman).

Henry, Teuira, 1928 / 1971, *Ancient Tahiti* (Honolulu, Bishop Museum / New York, Kraus Reprint Co.).

Holmes, Christine, ed., 1982, *Captain Cook's Final Voyage: The Journal of Midshipman George Gilbert* (Partridge Green, Sussex, Caliban Books).

'Jenny' [Te'ehuteatuaonoa], 1819, 'Account of the mutineers of the Ship *Bounty* and their Descendants at Pitcairn's Island', *Sydney Gazette* July 17: 817.

——, 1829, 'Pitcairn's Island: The *Bounty*'s crew', *United Service Journal and Naval and Military Magazine* II: 589–93.

Kennedy, Gavin, 1978, *Bligh* (London, Duckworth).

——, 1989, *Captain Bligh: The Man and his Mutinies* (London, Gerald Duckworth & Co.).

Knight, C., 1936, 'HM Armed Vessel *Bounty*', *Mariner's Mirror* 22: 183–99.

Lamb, W. Kaye, ed., 1984, *A Voyage of Discovery to the North Pacific Ocean and Round the World 1791–1795, Vols I, II and III* (London, The Hakluyt Society).

Lansdown, Richard, ed., 2006, *Strangers in the South Seas: The Idea of the Pacific in Western Thought* (Honolulu, University of Hawai'i).

Lee, Ida, 1920, *Captain Bligh's Second Voyage to the South Sea* (London, Longmans, Green & Co.).

Lloyd, Christopher and Anderson, R.C., eds, 1959, *A Memoir of James Trevenen* (London, Navy Records Society).

Mackaness, George, 1936, *The Life of Vice-Admiral William Bligh* (New York and Toronto, Farrar & Rinehart, Inc.).

——, ed., 1938, reissued 1981, *A Book of the* Bounty*: William Bligh and Others* (London, Dent / New York, Everyman's Library).

——, ed., 1949, *Some Correspondence of Captain William Bligh, R.N., with John and Francis Godolphin Bond, 1766–1811* (Sydney, D.S. Ford, Printers).

——, 1951, *The Life of Vice-Admiral William Bligh R.N., F.R.S*, I & II (New York, Farrar & Rinehart).

——, ed., 1953, *Fresh Light on Bligh: being Some Unpublished Correspondence of Captain William Bligh R.N. and Lieutenant Francis Godolphin Bond, R.N.* (Sydney, privately printed by the author).

——, ed., 1960, 'Extracts from a Log-Book of HMS *Providence*, kept by Lieut. Francis Godolphin Bond, RN, on Bligh's Second Breadfruit Voyage, 1791–3', *Journal of the Royal Australian Historical Society* 46/1: 24–57.

Manby, Thomas, ed. Dale La Tendresse, 1988, *Journal of the Voyages of the HMS* Discovery *and* Chatham (Fairfield, Washington, Ye Galleon Press).

Marra, John, 1775, *Journal of the* Resolution*'s Voyage in 1771–1775* (Amsterdam, Bibliotheca Australiana #15).

Maude, H.E., 1958, 'In Search of a Home: From the Mutiny to Pitcairn Island (1789–1790)', *Journal of the Polynesian Society* 67/2: 104–31.

——, 1964, 'The History of Pitcairn Island', in Alan Ross and A.W. Moverley, eds, *The Pitcairnese Language* (New York, Oxford University Press).

Menzies, Archibald, 2007, *Journal of Archibald Menzies, Surgeon and Botanist on Board* Discovery (Marlborough, England, Adam Matthew Digital).

Moerenhout, J.A., 1837, in Arthur R. Borden, Jr, trans. and ed., 1983, *Travels to The Islands of the Pacific Ocean* (Lanham, New York, University Press of America).

Morrison, James in Owen Rutter, ed., 1935, *The Journal of James Morrison* (London, Golden Cockerel Press).

Oliver, Douglas, 1974, *Ancient Tahitian Society, Vols I–III* (Honolulu, University of Hawai'i Press).

——, ed., 1988, *Return to Tahiti: Bligh's Second Breadfruit Voyage* (Melbourne, Melbourne University Press at the Miegunyah Press).

Orsmond, J.M., The Papers of Rev. J.M. Orsmond, Vol. 4, 'The 'Arioi War in Tahiti', National Library of Australia Mfm G7706, Mitchell Library A2608, Meredith Filihia transcript.

Pope, Dudley, 1972, *The Great Gamble* (New York, Simon & Schuster).

Powell, Dulcie, 1977, 'The Voyage of the Plant Nursery, H.M.S. *Providence*', *Economic Botany* 31/4: 387–431.

Ritchie, John, ed., 1988, *A Charge of Mutiny* (Canberra, National Library of Australia).

Rodger, N.A.M., 2005, *The Command of the Ocean: A Naval History of Britain, 1649–1815* (London, Penguin Books and the National Maritime Museum).

Ross, Alan and Moverley, A.W., eds, 1964, *The Pitcairnese Language* (New York, Oxford University Press).

Rutter, Owen, 1931, *The Court-martial of the* Bounty *Mutineers* (Edinburgh, William Hodge & Company, Ltd).

——, 1934, *The Voyage of the* Bounty*'s Launch as related in William Bligh's Despatch to the Admiralty and the Journal of John Fryer* (London, Golden Cockerel Press).

——, ed., 1935, *The Journal of James Morrison* (London, Golden Cockerel Press).

——, 1936, *Turbulent Journey: A Life of William Bligh, Vice-Admiral of the Blue* (London, Ivor Nicholson & Watson).

——, ed., 1937a, *The Log of the* Bounty*: Being Lieutenant William Bligh's Log of the Proceedings of His Majesty's Armed Vessel* Bounty *in a Voyage to the South Seas, to Take the Breadfruit from the Society Islands to the West Indies,* 2 volumes (London, Golden Cockerel Press).

——, ed., 1937b, *Bligh's Voyage in the* Resource *from Coupang to Batavia, Together with the Log of His Subsequent Passage to England in the Dutch Packet* Vlydt *and His Remarks on Morrison's Journal. All Printed for the First Time from the Manuscripts in the Mitchell Library of New South Wales* (London, Golden Cockerel Press).

——, 1939, *John Fryer of the* Bounty. *Notes on His Career Written by his Daughter Mary Ann (Gamble)* (London, Golden Cockerel Press).

Salmond, Anne, 2003, *The Trial of the Cannibal Dog: Captain Cook in the South Seas* (Auckland, Penguin NZ / London, Penguin UK).

——, 2009, *Aphrodite's Island: The European Discovery of Tahiti* (Auckland, Penguin NZ / Berkeley, University of California Press).

Schreiber, Roy E., 1991, *The Fortunate Adversities of William Bligh* (New York, Peter Lang).

——, ed., 2007, *Captain Bligh's Second Chance: An Eyewitness Account of his Return to the South Seas* (London, Chatham Publishing).

Sheridan, Richard B., 1989, 'Captain Bligh, the Breadfruit and the Botanic Gardens of Jamaica', *Journal of Caribbean History* 23/1: 28–50.

Smith, D. Bonner, 1936, 'Some Remarks about the Mutiny on the *Bounty*', *Mariner's Mirror* 22/2: 200–37.

Thomas, Nicholas, Guest, Harriet and Dettelbach, Michael, eds, 1996, *Observations Made During a Voyage Round the World* (Honolulu, University of Hawai'i Press).

Thomson, Basil, ed., 1915, *Voyage of H.M.S.* Pandora *despatched to arrest the mutineers of the* Bounty *in the South Seas, 1790–91* (London, Francis Edwards).

Turnbull, John, 1810, *A Voyage Round the World in the Years 1800, 1801, 1802, 1803, and 1804* (Philadelphia, Benjamin & Thomas Kite).

# Notes

## INTRODUCTION: THE PARADISE OF THE WORLD

1   For a commentary on various portraits of Bligh (but not including this one), see Callendar, Geoffrey, 1936, 'The Portraiture of Bligh', in *Mariner's Mirror* 22: 172–78.

2   Commerson in Dunmore, ed. and trans., 2002b, 94.

3   Banks in Beaglehole, ed., 1962, I: 252.

4   Boswell, 1992, May 1773, 477.

5   For discussions of this satirical 'literature', see Roderick, Colin, 1972, 'Sir Joseph Banks, Queen Oberea and the Satirists', in Walter Veit, ed., *Captain James Cook: Image and Impact. South Seas Discoveries and the World of Letters* (Melbourne, Hawthorn Press), 67–89; Bewell, Alan, 1996, '"On the Banks of the South Sea": botany and sexual controversy in the late eighteenth century', in David Philip Miller and Peter Hanns Reill, eds, *Visions of Empire: Voyages, Botany, and Representations of Nature* (Cambridge, Cambridge University Press), 173–93.

    These poems and satires include, in order of publication: Oberea (pseud.), attributed to Major John Scott-Waring, 1773, *An Epistle from Oberea, Queen of Otaheite, to Joseph Banks, Esq.* (London, J. Almon); Mr. Banks (pseud.), 1773, *An Epistle from Mr. Banks, Voyager, Monster-hunter and Amoroso, to Oberea, Queen of Otaheite* (London, John Swan and Thomas Axtell); Blosset, Harriet (pseud.), 1774, *The Court of Apollo. An Heroic Epistle from the injured Harriet, Mistress to Mr Banks, to Oberea Queen of Otaheite* (London, Westminster Magazine); Oberea (pseud.), attributed to John Scott-Waring, 1774, *An Epistle from Oberea, Queen of Otaheite, to Joseph Banks, Esq.* (London); Oberea (pseud.), attributed to John Scott-Waring, 1774, *A Second Letter from Oberea Queen of Otaheite to Joseph Banks* (London, T.J. Carnegay); Omiah (pseud.), 1775, *An Historical Epistle from Omiah to the Queen of Otaheite* (London, T. Evans); Omiah (pseud.), 1776, *Omiah's Farewell, Inscribed to the Ladies of London* (London, G. Kearsley); Oberea (pseud.), Gerald Fitzgerald, 1779, *The Injured Islanders, or the Influence of Art upon the Happiness of Nature. A Poetical Epistle from Oberea of Otaheite to Captain Wallis* (Dublin, T.T. Faulkner); Anonymous, 1779, *Mimosa or the Sensitive Plant* (London, printed for W. Sandwich near the Admiralty); Omai (pseud.), 1780, *A Letter from Omai to the Right Honourable the Earl of ********, Translated from the Ulaietean Tongue, In which, amongst other things, is fairly and irrefragably stated, the Nature of Original Sin* (London, J. Bell).

6   Forster, Johann in Michael Hoare, ed., 1982, *The Resolution Journal of Johann Reinhold Forster 1772–1775, Vols I–IV* (London, the Hakluyt Society), II: 336.

7   Cook in Beaglehole, ed., 1969, II: 428.

8   For an excellent discussion of the 'Islands of the Blest', see Lovejoy, A.O. and Boas, G., 1980, *Primitivism and Related Ideas in Antiquity* (New York, Octagon Books), 290–367. For island Utopias, see Cheek, Pamela, 2003, *Sexual Antipodes: Enlightenment, Globalisation and the Placing of Sex* (Stanford, California, Stanford University Press); Fausett, David, 1993, *Writing the New World: Imaginary Voyages and Utopias of the Great Southern Land* (Syracuse, New York, Syracuse University Press); Société des Etudes Océaniennes, 2004, *Utopies Insulaires* (Papeete, Bulletin de la Société des Etudes Océaniennes); and Lansdown, Richard, ed., 2006, Introduction, and 'The Noble Savage', in *Strangers in the South Seas: The Idea of the Pacific in Western Thought* (Honolulu, University of Hawai'i Press), 1–27, 64–72.

9   Bligh in Rutter, ed., 1936, I: 381.

10   *General Evening Post*, 16 March 1790. For a discussion of the imaginary power of the tale of Circe and Odysseus, see Segal, Charles, 1968, 'Circean Temptations: Homer, Vergil and Ovid', *Transactions and Proceedings of the American Philological Association* 99: 419–42.

11   McKusick, James, 1992, 'The Politics of Language in Byron's *The Island*', *ELH* 59: 839–56.

12    In this endeavour, I am indebted to Marshall Sahlins, Natalie Zemon Davis and Inga Clendinnen among
      others for leading the way; and above all to Greg Dening for his fine pioneering exploration of the
      Tahitian and British 'worlds' involved in the mutiny on the *Bounty*. This book also draws upon my own
      study of Tahiti just before and during the early contact period: Salmond, Anne, 2009, *Aphrodite's Island:
      The European Discovery of Tahiti* (Auckland, Penguin NZ; Berkeley, University of California Press);
      Teuira Henry's *Ancient Tahiti*, published in 1971 by the Bishop Museum (Honolulu, Bishop Museum);
      and Douglas Oliver's classical 1974 three-volume work *Ancient Tahitian Society* (Honolulu, University
      of Hawai'i Press). Glynn Christian's book about his forebear, *Fragile Paradise: The Discovery of Fletcher
      Christian, Bounty Mutineer* (The Long Riders Guild Press), was published in 2005, while Caroline
      Alexander's impressive researches into the British side of the *Bounty* expedition are vividly deployed
      in her book *The* Bounty: *The True Story of the Mutiny on the* Bounty (New York, Penguin), published
      in 2003. For the rest of the huge literature on William Bligh and his Pacific voyages, see the notes that
      follow.

## CHAPTER 1: THE DEATH OF CAPTAIN COOK

1    As Ledyard, an American marine on board the *Resolution*, remarked at this time: '[It] appeared very
     manifest that Cook's conduct was wholly influenced by motives of interest, to which he was evidently
     sacrificing not only the ships, but the healths and happiness of the brave men, who were weaving the
     laurel that was hereafter to adorn his brow': Ledyard, John, in James Zug, ed., 2005, *The Last Voyages of
     Captain Cook: The Collected Writings of John Ledyard* (Washington, DC, National Geographic Society),
     69. The 'mutinous' conduct of the sailors is discussed in Cook in J.C. Beaglehole, ed., 1967, *The Journal
     of Captain James Cook on his Voyages of Discovery: The Voyage of the* Resolution *and* Discovery, Part 1
     (Cambridge, published for the Hakluyt Society at the University Press), 478 fn., 479; King in Beaglehole,
     ed., 1967, I: 503; and Watts in Beaglehole, ed., 1967, I: 479–80 fn.
2    [Rickman, John], 1781 (1967 facsimile), *Journal of Captain Cook's Last Voyage to the Pacific Ocean*
     (Amsterdam, N. Israel, Bibliotheca Australiana #16), 295.
3    Bligh's description of Kealakekua Bay is given in King in Beaglehole, ed., 1967, I: 502. For a meticulous
     description of the surveying methods used in Cook's third voyage, see David, A.C.F., 1997, *The Charts
     & Coastal Views of Captain Cook's Voyages, Volume Three: The Voyage of the* Resolution *and* Discovery
     *1776–1780* (London, the Hakluyt Society, in Association with the Australian Academy of the Humanities),
     xxvi–lxii, especially xxxiii: 'To sketch in the coastline and to sound out the harbour, Robertson [i.e. John
     Robertson, author of *Elements of Navigation*] suggested that a boat should be taken inshore to examine the
     coastline and . . . make sketches thereof, estimating the lengths and breadths of the several inlets, either
     by the rowing, or sailing of the boat, taking as many bearings, soundings and other notes, as may be
     thought necessary.' For a detailed account of Bligh's surveying and charting work during the voyage, see
     David, A.C.F, Lieutenant Commander, 1982, 'The Surveyors of the *Bounty:* A preliminary study of the
     hydrographic surveys of William Bligh, Thomas Hayward and Peter Heywood and the charts published
     from them', typescript, Royal Navy Hydrographic Department, Ministry of Defence, Taunton, Somerset.
4    [Rickman], 1781, 296.
5    The manuscript accounts of Cook's two visits to Kealakekua Bay and the events surrounding his death
     include the following documents: British Museum: James Burney's *Discovery* Journal, Add Ms 8955;
     George Gilbert's *Discovery* Journal, Add Ms 38530; David Samwell's *Discovery* Journal, Egerton 2591.
     Public Record Office: Anonymous log, Adm 51/4530/71; William Bayly's *Discovery* Log and Journal,
     Adm 55/20; William Charlton's *Resolution* Journal, Adm 51/4557/191–193; Charles Clerke's Log and
     Observations, Adm 51/4561/217, 220–221; Charles Clerke's *Discovery* Log, Adm 55/23; Thomas Edgar's
     *Discovery* Log, Adm 55/24; William Harvey's *Discovery* Log, Adm 55/110; George Gilbert's *Resolution*
     Journal, Adm 51/4559/214; John Gore's *Resolution* Log, Adm 55/120; James King's *Resolution* Log,
     Adm 55/116, 122; William Lanyon's *Resolution* Journal, Adm 51/4558/196–198; John Henry Martin's
     *Discovery* Journal, Adm 51/4531/47; John Rickman's *Discovery* Log, Adm 51/4529/46; Edward Riou's
     *Discovery* Journal, Adm 51/4529/41–44; William Shuttleworth's *Resolution* Journal, Adm 51/4561/211;
     John Watts's *Resolution* Log, Adm 51/4559/212. Dixson Library, State Library of New South Wales: J.
     Dimsdell, Account of the Death and Remains of Capt. Cook – at Owhyhee recd from Joshua Lee Dimsdell
     Quarter Master of the Gunjara Capt. James Barber, 1801, Ms Q/154; William Griffin's Narrative, Ms
     98, Ms Q/155; Henry Roberts' *Resolution* Log, Ms Q/151–152. Mitchell Library, State Library of New
     South Wales: James Burney's *Discovery* Journal; Anonymous, 1781, Copy of Letter to Mrs Strachan
     of Spithead, 23 January 1781 (Safe 1/67). National Library of Australia: Alexander Home's *Discovery*
     notes and typescript (Ms 690); Anonymous, Account of the Death of Cook, 9–22 February 1779, by
     an Eyewitness. Alexander Turnbull Library, Wellington: William Bayly's *Discovery* Journal; James
     Trevenen's *Resolution* notes; William Brown, Letter to Mr. George Lane, 12 February 1827.
        For published accounts of these events, see Cook, James and King, James, 1784, *A Voyage to the Pacific
     Ocean. Undertaken, by the Command of his Majesty, for making Discoveries in the Northern Hemisphere.
     Performed under the direction of Captains Cook, Clerke, and Gore, In his Majesty's Ships the Resolution and
     Discovery. In the Years 1776, 1777, 1778, 1779, and 1780. In Three Volumes.* Vols I and II written by Captain
     James Cook, F.R.S., Vol. III by Captain James King, L.L.D. and F.R.S. (London); 1784, 'An Account

of the Death of the late Captain Cook, and some Memoirs of his Life, by Captain King, with a Tribute to his Memory, by a noble Lord high in the Profession', *The Universal Magazine* 33–40; Beaglehole, J.C., ed., 1967, *The Journals of Captain James Cook on His Voyages of Discovery, Volume III, parts i and ii* (Cambridge, at the University Press, for the Hakluyt Society); Ellis, William, 1782, *An Authentic Narrative of a Voyage performed by Captain Cook and Captain Clerke in His Majesty's Ships Resolution and Discovery, during the Years 1776, 1777, 1778, 1779, and 1780*, Vols. *I and II* (London, G. Robinson); Gilbert, George in Christine Holmes, ed., 1982, *Captain Cook's Final Voyage: The Journal of Midshipman George Gilbert* (Partridge Green, Sussex, Caliban Books); Gould, Rupert T., ed., 1928, Some Unpublished Accounts of Cook's Death, *Mariner's Mirror* 14/4: 300–19; Home, George, 1838, *Memoirs of an Aristocrat* (London, Whittaker & Co); Ledyard, John, 1783, *A Journal of Captain Cook's last Voyage to the Pacific Ocean, and in quest of a North-West Passage, between Asia & America. Faithfully narrated from the original MS. Of Mr. John Ledyard* (Hartford), and Ledyard, John, in James Zug, ed., 2005, *The Last Voyages of Captain Cook: The Collected Writings of John Ledyard* (Washington, DC, National Geographic Society); Marra, John, 1775, *Journal of the* Resolution's *Voyage in 1771–1775* (Amsterdam, Bibliotheca Australiana #15); Rickman, John, 1781 (1967 facsimile), *Journal of Captain Cook's Last Voyage to the Pacific Ocean* (Amsterdam, N. Israel, Bibliotheca Australiana #16); Samwell, David in Martin Fitzpatrick, Nicholas Thomas and Jennifer Newell, 2007, eds, *The Death of Captain Cook, and other Writings by David Samwell* (Cardiff, University of Wales Press); Trevenen, James in Christopher Lloyd and R.C. Anderson, eds, 1959, *A Memoir of James Trevenen* (London, Navy Records Society); Zimmerman, Henry in F.W. Howay, ed., 1929, *Zimmerman's Captain Cook* (Toronto, The Ryerson Press).

6   Ledyard in Zug, ed., 2005, 69.

7   The note about the Hawai'ians swimming 'like shoals of fish' is an unusually poetic description from Cook, in Beaglehole, ed., 1967, I: 491. His journal, however, ends shortly after he went ashore.

8   Ellis, 1782, 85.

9   Gilbert in Holmes, ed., 1982, 101.

10   Cordy, Ross, 2000, *Exalted Sits the Chief: The Ancient History of Hawai'i Island* (Honolulu, Mutual Publishing), 225–239 gives an excellent critical account of the various stories about Lono-i-ka-Makahiki. Cordy dates Lono-i-ka-Makahiki's rule to AD 1640–1660.

11   Samwell in Beaglehole, ed., 1967, II: 1159.

12   Ledyard in Zug, ed., 2005, 74.

13   For an account of the sacred high chief Kalani'opu'u, his ancestors and his battles, see Kamakau, Samuel 1992, *Ruling Chiefs of Hawaii* (Honolulu, The Kamehameha Schools Press), 34–104. See also Charles Ahlo and Jerry Walker, eds, 2000, *Kamehameha's Children Today* (Honolulu, J. Walker), 21–42; and Kuykendall, R.S., 1938, *The Hawaiian Kingdom* (Honolulu, University of Hawai'i Press), 30–34.

14   Ledyard in Zug, ed., 2005, 75.

15   Samwell in Beaglehole, ed., 1967, II: 1168.

16   For the status of the high priest of Lono, a man named Omea, see Samwell in Beaglehole, ed., 1967, II: 1184.

17   Samwell in Beaglehole, ed., 1967, II: 1170.

18   Ledyard in Zug, ed., 2005, 77.

19   Samwell in Beaglehole, ed., 1967, II: 1170–71.

20   The breach of *kapu* by the sailors is described by Ledyard, who notes: 'In a few days the white rods were taken down by some of the Inhabitants, and a free egress and regress took place: the inhabitants had access to our tents, viewed our conduct in private and unguarded hours, had every opportunity to form an opinion of our manners and abilities, and contrast them with their own, nay, were even instructed in the nature and use of our firearms' (Ledyard, in Zug ed., 2005, 73).

21   Ledyard joined them that evening, and described the rituals (Ledyard, in Zug, ed., 2005, 84–85).

22   Cook and King, 1784, Book V: 26.

23   Ledyard in Zug, ed., 2005, 85.

24   Ledyard reported the fact that the trees around Kealakekua Bay had all been cleared for a distance of 4 to 5 miles (ibid., 81). He also described the Hawai'ians' reaction when the sailors demolished the palisade from the *heiau* and the semi-circle of gods; and their conduct when the master's mate struck some of their number while trying to haul the *Resolution*'s rudder (ibid., 91–92).

     As an American at a time when the American colonies were at war with Britain, Ledyard felt no compunction about reporting incidents unfavourable to the British and Captain Cook, although he held his commander in very high esteem. (See Davie, Donald, 1970, 'John Ledyard: The American Traveler and His Sentimental Journeys', *Eighteenth Century Studies* 4/1: 57–70.)

25   Ledyard in Zug, ed., 2005, 92.

26   The comment about Cook's pride in his discovery of the Hawai'ian islands is from the Anonymous account in the Mitchell Library, 14.

27   Cook and King, 1784, Book V: 32.

28   King in Beaglehole, ed., 1967, I: 527.

29   Ledyard in Zug, ed., 2005, 95.

30   Anonymous, Mitchell Library, 14.

31   The theft of the armourer's tongs and the pursuit of the thief in the *Discovery*'s cutter and its aftermath

are recorded in the eyewitness accounts by Charles Clerke, Thomas Edgar, and Heinrich Zimmerman (who was with Edgar and Vancouver in the cutter); and Cook and King's pursuit of the thief by King in his journal (King in Beaglehole, ed., 1967, I: 529–30).

32    King in Beaglehole, ed., 1967, I: 530.

33    Ibid., 530.

34    Anonymous, Mitchell Library; and Ledyard, 1783, 143.

35    Cook's certainty that the Hawai'ians would not resist if they were fired on is described in Burney's Journal in the Mitchell Library, 253–54; and Samwell in Beaglehole, ed., 1967, II: 1194.

36    According to Samuel Kamakau, Kamehameha's fighting instructor, a chief named Kehuhaupi'o, seeing Captain Cook heading towards Ka'awaloa in the pinnace, set out from Ke'ei with another chief called Kalimu. Seeing a man sitting in the canoe with a feather cape, the strangers shot Kalimu and killed him. When Kehuhaupi'o arrived on the beach at Ka'awaloa, he saw the high chief Kalani'opu'u preparing to go on board the ship with the strangers and warned him of the danger (Kamakau, 1992, 102).

37    King in Beaglehole, ed., 1967, I: 535.

38    Ledyard in Zug, ed., 2005, 100.

39    For Watts's account of Captain Cook's death, see Watts, Adm 51/4559/212: 95–96.

40    Samwell names the man who struck Captain Cook with the dagger as Nu'a [Noo-ah], on the basis of the testimony of the priest Keli'ikea; describing him as follows: 'He was of high rank, and a near relation of the king: he was stout and tall, with a fierce look and demeanour, and one who united in his figure the two qualities of strength and agility, in a greater degree, than ever I remembered to have seen before in any other man. His age might be about thirty, and by the white scurf on his skin, and his sore eyes, he appeared to be a hard drinker of Kava. He was a constant companion of the king' (Samwell in Thomas et al., eds, 2007, 78). It is likely that this man was Nu'uanupa'ahu, a chief from Ka'u who later rebelled against Kalani'opu'u and was killed by him. (See Cordy, 2000, 295.)

41    For the killing of Captain Cook, see Samwell (in Beaglehole, ed., 1967, II: 1198), who interviewed many of the eyewitnesses soon after they returned to the ships. The only eyewitness accounts of the events on shore at Ka'awaloa, however, are those by Molesworth Phillips (as told to Charles Clerke); Henry Roberts (who commanded the *Resolution*'s pinnace); and William Lanyon (who commanded the *Resolution*'s small cutter), William Charlton and James Trevenen (who also were on board the cutter with two other midshipmen), each of whom arrived after Cook had already been killed. Until the rest of the ships' boats arrived at the shore camp, the only eyewitness accounts of what happened there are by William Bayly, James King, and in the marginalia by William Bligh in a copy of King's account of Cook's death (reproduced in Gould, 1928). John Watts, a midshipman who also visited Tahiti on the *Lady Penrhyn*, was evidently with the ships' boats, and gave an interesting account of what happened that day (John Watts's *Resolution* Log, Adm 51/4559/212).

      Any reconstruction of the events surrounding Cook's death is made more problematic by the fact that almost all of the shipboard accounts for several weeks before and just after Cook's death seem to have been written well after the event. These versions are thus based on memory and sometimes guesswork about particular sequences of events, while others were written years later. The written accounts of the death of Cook are also almost all partisan – trying to avoid or fix blame – because very few of the journal-keepers felt free of guilt about what had happened. In this reconstruction, I have relied as much as possible on those eyewitness accounts that were recorded soon after the event.

42    Samwell in Beaglehole, ed., 1967, II: 1200.

43    Gilbert in Holmes, ed., 1982, 107–8.

44    This was John Martin, who had replaced William Harvey as Bligh's mate when Harvey was disrated and sent to the *Discovery* (Anonymous, Mitchell Library).

45    Trevenen in Lloyd et al., eds, 1959, 35–36.

46    Samwell in Beaglehole, ed., 1967, II: 1204.

47    The refusal of most of the launch's crew to testify against Williamson is also described in Anonymous, Mitchell Library; along with Clerke's speech to his men on board the *Discovery*.

48    For more recent commentaries on Cook's death, see Marshall, 1985, *Islands of History* (Chicago, University of Chicago), 104–35; Bergendoff, Steen, Ulla Hasager and Peter Henriques, 1988, 'Mythopraxis and History: on the Interpretation of the Makahiki', *Journal of the Polynesian Society* 97: 391–408; Sahlins, Marshall, 1989, 'Captain Cook at Hawaii', *Journal of the Polynesian Society* 98/4: 371–423; Obeyesekere, Gananath, 1992, *The Apotheosis of Captain Cook: European Myth-making in the Pacific* (New Jersey, Princeton University Press); Sahlins, Marshall, 1995, *How "Natives" Think: About Captain Cook, For Example* (Chicago, University of Chicago Press); Ashley, Scott, 2007, 'How Navigators Think: The Death of Captain Cook Revisited', *Past and Present* 194/1: 107–37; and Williams, Glyndwr, 2008, *The Death of Captain Cook: A Hero Made and Unmade* (Cambridge, Mass., Harvard University Press).

      The debate between Marshall Sahlins and Gananath Obeyesekere has inspired many comments and reviews; see Borofsky, Robert, 1997, 'Cook, Lono, Obeyesekere and Sahlins', *Current Anthropology* 38/2: 255–82 for many citations. Although Sahlins argues that Cook was taken for the ancestor god Lono, worshipped because he arrived at the right time in the Makahiki cycle, and killed because he returned at the wrong ritual moment, my reading of the journal accounts suggests that this interpretation is too simple. There were at least three individuals in Kealakekua Bay during Cook's visit who were addressed as 'Lono' – Captain Cook, Kalani'opu'u and Omia, the high priest of Lono; and it is clear that this ancestor god had more than one human avatar. Equally, it is obvious that the Hawai'ians had many reasons for being offended with Cook and his men; and that the attack on Palea, the killing of Kalimu in the bay and the attempt to take Kalani'opu'u hostage all helped to provoke the attack on Cook and his death at the hands of Hawai'ian warriors. Obeyesekere argues that Sahlins, overcome with European imperial hubris, claimed that the Hawai'ians greeted Captain Cook as a god when they only hailed him as a high chief. This, however, is based on ignorance of Hawai'ian (and Polynesian) tradition, where high chiefs were seen as the living embodiments of their ancestors, and thus often addressed as *akua*, or ancestor gods. (For a longer and more detailed discussion, see Salmond, Anne, 1993, 'Whose God, or not?', *Social Analysis* 34: 50–55; and 2003, *The Trial of the Cannibal Dog: Captain Cook in the South Seas* (London, Penguin UK), 386–431.)

49    Watts, John, Journal, Adm 51/4559, 96.
50    Unfortunately, Bligh's first-hand account must have been lost with the *Bounty*. His annotations on the three-volume official account of Cook's third voyage (London, 1784), and particularly the third volume written by James King, are on a copy of the work once held in the Hydrographic Office, and now in the Naval Historical Library. They are reproduced with a commentary in Gould, Rupert, 1928, *Mariner's Mirror* 14: 371–85. Lieutenant Commander A.C.F. David suggests that these annotations must have been made in 1804, when Bligh was in charge of the Hydrographic Office, thus 'ensuring that his comments would have wide publicity in official circles' (David, A.C.F, 1981, *Mariner's Mirror* 67: 102). In that case, however, it is likely that the comments would have been written in ink, rather than pencil (which allowed for second thoughts, at least one of which led to an erasure). David also gives a detailed account of the annotations on the charts in this publication in David, A.C.F, Lieutenant Commander, 1982, 'The Surveyors of the *Bounty*: A preliminary study of the hydrographic surveys of William Bligh, Thomas Hayward and Peter Heywood and the charts published from them', typescript, Royal Navy Hydrographic Department, Ministry of Defence, Taunton, Somerset.
51    In his 1984 article, O.H.K. Spate agrees with Bligh that King's account of the later part of the voyage was often snide and self-serving (Spate, O.H.K., 1984, 'Splicing the Log at Kealakekua Bay: James King's sleight of hand', *The Journal of Pacific History* 19/2: 117–20). After reading King's excuses in Adm 55/116, 1–3, in which he effectively blamed the state of the ship's logs on Captains Cook and Clerke (both of whom had conveniently died by that time), I can only agree. According to King, 'the principal cause of the logs being very different from what I could have wished; was the situation it was left in on the death of Capt. Cook. As we had jointly undertaken to make astronomical observations and what was recommended in Mr. Bailey's instructions as far as circumstances & our respective employments permitted, we in some measure separated our labour, the computations for the most part were to be done by me, and he gave me to understand that he should comply with the instructions requiring logs & charts, and as I relyed principally upon his representation of my conduct, for any promotion, and advantage that might arise from the Voyage, I was regardless of what related to those parts of the log out of the common form . . . On the death of Capt Cook, his papers being taken into the custody of the next commander, I was left only with the books in which the astronomical observations are entered, with no logs or charts but what I had of my own, & intended for the Admiralty . . .'
52    David, 1981, 380.
53    Ibid., 382.
54    Ibid., 381.
55    Ibid., 381–82.
56    Cook and King, 1784, Book V: 57.
57    Quoted in Gould, 1928, 383.
58    James Trevenen to his brother Matthew at Trinity College Cambridge, *Memoirs of James Trevenen, by C.V. Penrose*, National Maritime Museum Greenwich, App., 108.
59    Quoted in Burney, Fanny, 1843, *Diary and Letters of Madame D'Arblay, edited by her niece, Vols I, II and III* (London), 113.
60    Quoted in Gould, 1928, 384. It is, however, true that during this period Bligh was active in the boats, and took an increasing number of lunar distances (which helped to fix their longitude, and required lengthy, complicated calculations) for his commander.
61    Bligh's passing certificate as Lieutenant is in PRO Adm 6/50 (Appointment Book). The promotions of Harvey and Lanyon were acting appointments, made because after the deaths of Cook, and then Clerke, new watch-keepers were required. (Many thanks to N.A.M. Rodger for explaining this situation, pers. comm. 2010.) A young officer who performed well in an acting role, however, could hope to have the commission confirmed when the ship returned to England; and in fact this happened in the case of Bligh's two mates. If Bligh had hoped to win a commission at sea, there were precedents, especially during a long and dangerous voyage of exploration, when officers died and had to be replaced far from England. As Rodger notes, 'it was quite possible to rise directly from a warrant to a commission . . . Justinian Nutt sailed with Anson on the *Centurion*'s famous voyage round the world in 1740 as a lieutenant's servant . . . By the end of the voyage he had risen first to master, then to acting third lieutenant. Masters, being the best-educated warrant officers, were in a particularly good position to reach commissioned rank' (Rodger, N.A.M., *The Wooden World: An Anatomy of the Georgian Navy* (Annapolis, Maryland, Naval Institute

Press), 267–68). During Vancouver's voyage around the world, too, Thomas Manby and Spelman Swaine were each promoted from master's mate to mate of the *Chatham*, and then back to the *Discovery* as third lieutenants. (Many thanks to Nigel Rigby for alerting me to the examples from Vancouver's expedition.)

62   According to Trevenen, on his deathbed Captain Clerke destroyed the damning depositions about Williamson's conduct (Trevenen in Lloyd et al., eds, 1959, 82).

63   For a detailed discussion of the fate of Cook's journal, log and papers, see Williams, Glyndwr, 2008, *The Death of Captain Cook: A Hero Made and Unmade* (Cambridge, Mass., Harvard University Press), 49–60.

64   Molesworth Phillips, National Library of Australia, Ms 333.

65   Home's claim that Williamson formed a 'Mason's lodge' is made in Home, 1838, 305. In their journal accounts, many of his shipmates were scathing about Williamson's conduct; and after the voyage Edward Thompson, a naval captain to whom King gave an unguarded account of Cook's death, fumed that the official account of the voyage made no mention of Williamson's desertion of Cook: 'He lost his life, by not being supported by Lieut. Williamson, who shoved off the boats, yet no word is mentioned of it' (Thompson, Edward, Diary entry, 27 November 1784, Add Ms 46, 120). There is perhaps poetic justice in the fact that after the battle of Camperdown, in which Bligh also fought, Williamson was court-martialled for 'disaffection, cowardice, disobedience to signals and not having done his duty in rendering all assistance possible'; convicted of the two last charges; and sentenced to be 'placed at the bottom of the list of Post-Captains, and be rendered incapable of ever serving on board of any of His Majesty's Ships' (Gould, 1928, 380).

66   This is Article XII. See also Article XI: 'Every person in the fleet, who shall not duly observe the orders of the admiral, flag officer, commander, or his superior officer, for assailing, joining battle . . ., and being convicted thereof by the sentence of a court-martial, shall suffer death, or such other punishment, as from the nature and degree of the court-martial shall deem him to deserve.'

67   The charge that Cook helped to provoke his own death by an outburst of anger was given wide circulation in England; and in his Narrative, David Samwell felt it necessary to defend Cook against the accusation that he had acted rashly, and with 'a precipitate self-confidence' (Samwell in Thomas et al., eds, 2007, 72). The testimony by William Brown, a gunner's mate on the *Resolution*, in the Alexander Turnbull Library, which was written so that a certain George Lane could assess Cook's culpability or otherwise for the confrontation at Kealakekua, also strongly defends Captain Cook, insisting that he was 'a very Cool, Deliberate and very Determined Man – on every occasion', and ending by saying: 'If any misconduct has been attached to Captn. Cook it is beyond my knowledge. I only speak from what I thought of him, as being always much collected – and a very brave man.'

68   The other two officers who conspicuously failed to win promotion were Rickman, first lieutenant of the *Discovery*, and her master Thomas Edgar. Rickman's action in shooting a Hawai'ian out in the bay was said to have inflamed the warriors, leading to Cook's death (see Ashley, Scott, 2007, 'How Navigators Think: The Death of Captain Cook Revisited', *Past and Present* 194/1: 107–37 for an argument that Rickman was made a scapegoat, and insights into Williamson's Whig connections); and he had also published an anonymous account of the voyage. Edgar, who had passed his lieutenant's exam some years earlier and, like Bligh, made a major contribution to the hydrographic surveys, was also passed over when he made a personal application for a commission as lieutenant after the voyage. Interestingly, his account of Cook's death is also missing.

69   Beaglehole, J.C., 1967, *Captain Cook and Captain Bligh* (Wellington, Whitcombe & Tombs Ltd).

## CHAPTER 2: THE *RESOLUTION*'S MASTER

1   According to the Rev. R. Polwhele in his 1831 *Biographical Sketches in Cornwall*, I–III (Truro, Polyblank), I: 19, 'Bligh (as he himself informed me,) was a native of St. Tudy.' See also 'Copy of a Memorandum respecting the genealogy of the Bligh family given to Richard Bligh my brother by my mother Elizabeth Bligh at Sydney New South Wales in the year 1862', ML A2049.

Biographies of Bligh include Mackaness, George, 1936, *The Life of Vice-Admiral William Bligh* (New York and Toronto, Farrar & Rinehart, Inc.); Rutter, Owen, 1936, *Turbulent Journey: A Life of William Bligh, Vice-Admiral of the Blue* (London, Ivor Nicholson & Watson Ltd); Kennedy, Gavin, 1978, *Bligh* (London, Duckworth), 1989, *Captain Bligh: The Man and his Mutinies* (London, Gerald Duckworth & Co.); and Schreiber, Roy E., 1991, *The Fortunate Adversities of William Bligh* (New York, Peter Lang).

2   For a disentangling of these genealogical details, see Mackaness, George, ed., 1953, *Fresh Light on Bligh: being Some Unpublished Correspondence of Captain William Bligh R.N. and Lieutenant Francis Godolphin Bond, R.N.* (Sydney, privately printed by the author), 5–6.

3   Log of the *Monmouth*, Adm 51/3916; muster roll PRO Adm 36/6103–4.

4   Tregellas, Walter, 1884, *Cornish Worthies: Sketches of Some Eminent Cornish Men and Families*, I & II (London, Elliot Stock), 145–46.

5   When Bligh's mother, Jane Pearce, married Francis Bligh on 3 November 1753, it was a second marriage for them both.

6   Log of the *Hunter*, Adm 51/451; muster roll PRO Adm 36/7868–9.

7   Log of the *Crescent*, Adm 51/204; muster roll PRO Adm 36/7573–4. After the mutiny on the *Bounty*, Bligh complained that he had been unable to save a box containing 'his surveys, drawings and

remarks for fifteen years past, which were numerous' (Bligh, 1792, 157), suggesting that some of these surveys may have been made at least two years before he joined the *Resolution*, probably on board the *Ranger*.

8    Log of the *Ranger*, Adm 51/768; muster roll PRO Adm 36/7665–6.

9    For Bligh's letter of discharge from the *Ranger*, see Adm 1/2672.

10   Falconer, William, 1780, *Dictionary of the Marine* (London, Thomas Cadell), 191: 'Master of a ship of war, an officer appointed by the commissioners of the navy to assist in fitting, and to take charge of the navigating and conducting a ship from port to port, under the direction of the captain, or other his superior officer. The management and disposition of the sails, the working of the ship into her station in the order of battle, and the directions of her movements . . . in the other circumstances of danger, are also more particularly under his inspection. He is to be careful that the rigging, sails, and stores, be duly preserved: to see that the log and log-book be regularly and correctly kept: accurately to observe the appearances of corals, rocks, and shoals, with their depths of water and bearings, noting them in his journal. He is to keep the hawser clear when the ship is at anchor, and to provide himself with proper instruments, maps, and books of navigation. It is likewise his duty to examine the provisions . . . He is moreover charged with the stowage, or disposition of these materials in the ship's hold. . . . And to enable him the better to perform these services, he is allowed several assistants, who are properly termed mates . . .' Although Robert Molyneux, Captain Cook's master on board the *Endeavour*, was only 22 years old at the beginning of the voyage, for instance, he had previously sailed with Captain Wallis on the *Dolphin* to the Pacific; while Joseph Gilbert, Cook's master on the *Resolution* during the second voyage, had previously carried out surveys in Newfoundland with Captain Hugh Palliser (see David, 1997, lxxi).

11   Forster, George, 1787, *Cook der Entdecker*, published in facsimile with a translation, 2007, *Cook the Discoverer* (Sydney, Hordern House, for the National Maritime Museum), 207.

12   Bligh's discharge from the *Ranger* is recorded in Adm 1/2672. See Pulvertaft, David, 2000, Lieutenants' Passing Certificates: William Bligh and Peter Heywood, *Mariner's Mirror* 86: 197–98, which gives the details of Bligh's previous naval service, although Pulvertaft misreads *Ranger* as *Bangor*.

13   Daniel Solander to Joseph Banks, 14 August 1775, in Neil Chambers, ed., 2008, *The Indian and Pacific Correspondence of Sir Joseph Banks, 1768–1820* (London, Pickering & Chatto), I: 188.

14   Cook to Capt. John Walker, 19 August 1774, in Beaglehole, ed., 1969, II: 960.

15   Samwell in ibid., II: 1271–72.

16   For an excellent account of how Cook was persuaded to lead the third Pacific expedition, see David, 1997, xvii.

17   'Cooke was jealous of [Gore] . . . Gore had a sort of separate command in the vessel, . . . which gave him superintendence over all the transactions with the Indians. He made use of this sometimes to disobey Cooke; & therefore they hate each other.' Charles Blagden, recounting a conversation with Solander; quoted in Carter, Harold, 1988, *Sir Joseph Banks 1743–1820* (London, British Museum of Natural History), 86.

18   A close friend of Banks's, who committed his child to Banks's care if he failed to return to England: Williams, Glyndwr in Banks, R.E.R. et al., eds, 1994, *Sir Joseph Banks: A Global Perspective* (London, Kew Publishing), 177.

19   See Beaglehole, ed., 1967, II: 1503 for the order to Clerke on 5 June 1776; and 1506 for Clerke's request to the Admiralty, and Cook's response.

20   Charles Clerke to Joseph Banks, 28 June 1776, in Beaglehole, ed., 1967, II: 1508.

21   John Gore to Joseph Banks, 27 November 1776, in ibid., II: 1522.

22   William Bligh to John Bond, Cape of Good Hope, 23 October 1776, in Mackaness, George, ed., 1949, *Some Correspondence of Captain William Bligh, R.N., with John and Francis Godolphin Bond, 1766–1811* (Sydney, D.S. Ford Printers), 13.

23   Bligh in ibid., 14.

24   Clerke to Joseph Banks, 1 August 1776, in Beaglehole, ed., 1967, II: 1514.

25   Clerke to Joseph Banks, November 19–23, Cape of Good Hope, Papers of Sir Joseph Banks, 11.03 (http://www2.sl.nsw.gov.au/banks/).

26   Cook to Joseph Banks, 26 November 1776, in Chambers, ed., 2008, I: 221.

27   Forster, 1787, trans., 206.

28   Cook and King, 1784, Book I: 5. See also Forster, 1787, trans., 247–49, for an account of how Captain Cook trained his young officers.

29   Cook in Beaglehole, ed., 1969, I: 29.

30   Burney, James, BM Add Ms 8955, 25 December 1776.

31   For an excellent account of how a running survey was conducted at this time, see David, 1997, xxxiii–iv.

32   Bligh's charts of Christmas Harbour, Port Palliser and the north-east coast of Desolation Island are given in David, 1997, 13, 14, 15, 23, 28, 30.

33   Forster, 1787, trans., 230.

34   Gore, Adm 55/120, 31 December 1776.

35   This chart is given in David, 1997, 32–33; in style it looks similar to the chart of the north-east coast of Desolation Island. For the engraved version in the official *Voyage*, see Cook and King, 1784, Vol. I: pl. 5, 91. For comments on Bligh's coastal views, see David, 1997, lxiii.

36   Marra, 1775, 96.

37   Cook in Beaglehole, ed., 1969, II: 653.
38   Bayly, William, Adm 55/20, 48.
39   Cook in Beaglehole, ed., 1969, I: 69.
40   See especially Burney, quoted in ibid., I: 64 fn.
41   Ma'i's outburst to Captain Cook in Queen Charlotte Sound was reported by Cook himself in ibid., I: 68.
42   Burney, BM Add Ms 8955, 24 February 1777.
43   Lieutenant James King's comments about the 'disobedient' and 'mutinous' behaviour of the crew after
     their visit to Queen Charlotte Sound are quoted in Beaglehole, ed., 1967, I: 77 fn.
44   Salmond, 2003, 433–37.
45   See an account of Polynesian bones discovered in an archaeological dig in Chile, and dated to about
     AD 1400 in Storey, Alice; Ramirez, José Miguel; Quiroz, Daniel; Burley, David V.; Addison, David J.;
     Walter, Richard; Anderson, Atholl J.; Hunt, Terry L.; Athens, Stephen; Huynen, Leon and Matioso-
     Smith, Elizabeth, 2007, 'Radiocarbon and DNA evidence for a pre-Columbian introduction of Polynesian
     chickens', *Proceedings of the National Academy of Sciences*, online at www.pnas.orga/cgi/content/
     full/0703393104/DCI. The South American *kumara* or sweet potato was in Polynesia by about AD 1000.
46   On the Hydrographic Office copy of the official account of Cook's last voyage, Bligh wrote opposite the
     plans of 'Watteeo' [Atiu]; 'Mangeea' [Mangaia] and 'Toobouia' [Tupua'i], 'The above are coppies of my
     original drawings W. Bligh' (David, 1982, 20).
47   Driessen, Hank, 1982, 'Outriggerless canoes and glorious beings: pre-contact prophecies in the Society
     Islands', *Journal of Pacific History* XVII: 8–9; Tahitian text in Henry, 1928, 5. For variant versions of this
     story, see ibid., 4–6; 910.
48   Burney, BM Add Ms 8955, 16 April 1777.
49   Cook in Beaglehole, ed., 1967, I: 98.
50   For a detailed description of this surveying method, see David, 1997, xxxiii. In the Hydrographic Office
     copy of the official account of the Voyage, Bligh wrote against the survey of 'Owyhee', 'Capt. Cook left
     the survey to me and I completed [it]' (quoted in David, 1982, 20).
51   Ledyard in Zug, ed., 2005, 17.
52   Beaglehole, ed., 1967, II: 1361–62.
53   Cook in ibid., I: 119.
54   Ibid.
55   Bayly, Adm 55/20, 72.
56   Gilbert in Holmes, ed., 1982, 33–34.
57   Anderson in Beaglehole, ed., 1967, II: 874.
58   Bligh, quoted in Gould, 1928, 376.
59   Williamson in Beaglehole, ed., 1967, II: 1342–43; see also Cook in ibid., I: 136–37; King in ibid., II: 1362.
60   Bayly, Adm 55/20, 73.
61   Williamson in Beaglehole, ed., 1967, I: 151 fn.
62   Cook in ibid., I: 144.
63   See these charts and Bligh's comments about them in David, 1997, 67, 75.
64   Cook in Beaglehole, ed., 1967, I: 183.

## CHAPTER 3: ISLAND OF THE BLEST

 1   Horace Walpole to Rev. William Cole, 15 June 1780, in W.S. Lewis, ed., 1937, *Horace Walpole's
     Correspondence with the Rev. William Cole* (London, Oxford University Press), II: 225. For a detailed
     discussion of voyages to Tahiti before the *Resolution*'s arrival in 1777, see Salmond, Anne, 2009, *Aphrodite's
     Island: The European Discovery of Tahiti* (Auckland, Penguin NZ).
 2   Cook in Beaglehole, ed., 1967, I: 186.
 3   King in ibid., II: 1370.
 4   Samwell in ibid., II: 1054.
 5   Bayly, quoted in ibid., I: 187 fn.
 6   Cook in ibid., I: 187.
 7   Orsmond, 'The 'Arioi War in Tahiti', Filihia transcript.
 8   Ledyard in Zug, ed., 2005, 30.
 9   Samwell in Beaglehole, ed., 1967, II: 1059.
10   *Resolution*'s Log, Adm 55/114, 81.
11   Cook in Beaglehole, ed., 1967, I: 186.
12   Samwell in ibid., II; 978.
13   Cook in ibid., I: 201.
14   Griffin, 17 September, DL Ms 98, Ms Q/155; [Rickman], 1781, 140.
15   Griffin, ibid.
16   [Rickman], 1781, 140.
17   Home typescript, NLA.
18   James Burney, 1809, *Chronological History of North-Eastern Voyages of Discovery* (London), 233–34.
19   Samwell in Beaglehole, ed., 1967, II: 1055.

## CHAPTER 4: THE OLD BOY TIPS A *HEIVA*

1 On an engraved chart of the bay in the Admiralty Library, attributed to Henry Roberts, Bligh later noted in ink: 'The Harbour . . . is a copy of my Survey' (David, 1997, xlii, 86).
2 Samwell in Beaglehole, ed., 1967, II: 1067.
3 Gilbert, in Holmes, ed., 1982, 67.
4 Home typescript, NLA.
5 Ibid.
6 Trevenen in Lloyd et al., eds, 1959, 27–28.
7 Ibid., 21.
8 Gilbert in Holmes, ed., 1982, 46–47.
9 Williamson, quoted in Beaglehole, ed., 1967, I: 231 fn.
10 Orders from Cook to Bligh, Edgar and Portlock, in ibid., II: 1527–28.
11 Samwell in ibid., II: 1070.
12 Bayly in ibid., I: 238 fn.
13 Cook in ibid., I: 240–41.
14 [Rickman], 1781, 171.
15 Home typescript, NLA.
16 Ibid.
17 Williamson in Beaglehole, ed., 1967, I: 251 fn.
18 Ellis, 1782, I: 159–61.
19 Edgar, in Beaglehole, ed., 1967, I: 247 fn.
20 [Rickman], 1781, 138.
21 Home typescript, NLA.
22 [Rickman], 1781, 276. During their search for the Northwest Passage, Bligh had only one mishap, irritating Cook when he neglected to mark the spot where the kedge anchor, which had dropped when a rotten cable snapped, was hooked by the hawser and then sank again (Cook in Beaglehole, ed., 1967, I: 362 fn.).
23 For this chart, see David, 1997, 120–27. For the coastal views, see David, ibid., 140–41; and BM Add Mss 15513 & 15514. For a detailed examination of Bligh's survey work on the *Resolution* voyage, see David, 1982, 1–23.
24 Charles Clerke to Joseph Banks, *Resolution* at sea 10 August 1779, Papers of Sir Joseph Banks, 11.04.
25 Trevenen in Lloyd et al., eds, 1959, 35.

## CHAPTER 5: *BOUNTY*

1 Lord Sandwich to Joseph Banks, 10 January 1780, Papers of Sir Joseph Banks, 09.02.
2 Burney, Fanny, ed., 1842, *Diary and Letters of Madame D'Arblay* (Henry Colburn), I: 317–18.
3 King in Beaglehole, ed., 1967, I: 717.
4 Gore to Admiralty Secretary, 7 October 1780, Adm 1/1839.
5 Board of Longitude minute, 4 November 1780, 3 March 1781, quoted in Beaglehole, ed., 1967, II: 1561–63.
6 For a superb discussion of the surveys and charts from Cook's last voyage, see David, 1997.
7 For records of the promotions authorised by Lord Sandwich during this period, which show the close interest he took in the careers of all of those men who had sailed around the world with Byron, Wallis and Cook, see National Maritime Museum, SAN 1–6. For Bligh's application, see SAN 5, entry 64: 'Wm. Bligh, master of the Resolution sloop – himself – promotion – Round the World'. Unlike a number of the other entries, however, it doesn't note that he had passed his lieutenant's exam, or list a senior officer as his nominee, or record a decision; or include the notation 'GM' ['Good man'], Sandwich's private commendation. (Many thanks to Nicholas Rodger for this last detail.) For Edgar's application, see the same entry: 'Thos Edgar, late master of the Discovery – himself – to be a Lieut – passed in 1769'. In this same entry, King and Lord Orford recommended Vancouver, Trevenen, Mackie and Mouat from *Discovery*, while Gore recommended Hergest, Ward, Riou, Taylor and Watts from *Resolution*, noting in each case that they had 'Passed their Exam', but again, without Sandwich recording a decision.
8 John King to Joseph Banks, n.d., Holograph Letters and Documents relating to Captain Cook, Alexander Turnbull Library, Wellington.
9 Elizabeth Bligh to John Bond, Eaton Street, Pimlico, 18 July 1781, ML Ms 1016.
10 Log of the *Belle Poule*, PRO Adm 51/101; Bligh's log, Adm 52/2171.
11 Log of the *Berwick*, PRO Adm 51/101.
12 Lord Selkirk to Banks, 7 September 1787, Papers of Sir Joseph Banks, 45.11.
13 For Sandwich's attitude to promoting masters to lieutenants, see Schreiber, 1991, 24.
14 Bligh to John Bond, *Berwick*, 18 November 1781, in Mackaness, ed., 1949, 17–18.
15 Log of *Princess Amelia*, PRO Adm 51/737.
16 Elizabeth Bligh to John Bond, Douglas, Isle of Man, 28 July 1782, ML Ms 1016.
17 Log of *Cambridge*, PRO Adm 51/153, 158 and Adm 52/2194.
18 Elizabeth Bligh to John Bond, Douglas, Isle of Man, 7 November 1782, ML Ms 1016.

19   Quoted in Vickery, Amanda, 1998, *The Gentleman's Daughter: Women's Lives in Georgian England* (New Haven, Yale University Press), 41.

20   Bligh to John Bond, *Berwick*, 18 November 1781, in Mackaness, ed., 1949, 17–18.

21   Bligh to John Bond, 25 May 1783, in ibid., 20.

22   Bligh to Duncan Campbell, Douglas, Isle of Man, 18 July 1783, William Bligh Letters, 1782–1805, ML Safe 1/40.

23   John Campbell to Duncan Campbell, 21 November 1783, ibid.

24   For letters from Bligh to Duncan Campbell during this period, see ML Safe 1/40, CY Reel 178, 270–278.

25   Elizabeth Bligh to John Bond, London, 8 September 1784, ML Ms 1016.

26   Christian, Fletcher, quoted in Christian, Edward, 1794, *Appendix*, 77.

27   Edward Lamb to William Bligh, 28 October 1794, quoted in Mackaness, 1936, 45–46.

28   For an excellent account of the publication of the official record of Cook's last voyage, see David, 1997, xciv–ci.

29   Bligh, quoted in Gould, 1928, 371.

30   Bligh in ibid., 377–78.

31   William Bligh to James Burney, 26 July 1791, quoted in David, 1997, liv. See Beaglehole's detailed comments on this cartographic error in Beaglehole, ed., 1967, I: fn. 444.

32   Bligh, quoted in David, 1997, lxxi–ii.

33   Darwin, Erasmus, trans., 1783, Carl von Linné, *A System of Vegetables, According to their classes, orders, genera, species* (London, Lee & Sotheby).

34   For an excellent account of Banks's role in this regard, see Williams, Glyndwr in Banks et al., eds, 1994, 177–91.

35   Banks in Beaglehole, ed., 1962, I: 341.

36   Daniel Solander to John Ellis, 4 May 1776, in Edward Duyker and Per Tingbrand, eds, 1995, *Daniel Solander: Collected Correspondence 1753–82* (Melbourne, Melbourne University Press), 363–64.

37   Sheridan, Richard B., 1989, 'Captain Bligh, the Breadfruit and the Botanic Gardens of Jamaica', *Journal of Caribbean History* 23/1: 30. See also Mackay, David, 1985, *In the Wake of Cook: Exploration, Science & Empire, 1780–1801* (Wellington, Victoria University Press) for an excellent account of the transport of the breadfruit to the West Indies.

38   For a record of Joseph Banks's testimony about the virtues of Botany Bay as a site for a penal colony before the Bunbury Commission at the Houses of Parliament on 10 April 1779, see Neil Chambers, ed., 2008, *The Indian and Pacific Correspondence of Sir Joseph Banks 1768–1820* (London, Pickering & Chatto), I: 251–52.

39   Smith, D. Bonner, 1936, 'Some Remarks about the Mutiny on the *Bounty*', *Mariner's Mirror* 22/2: 210. For the description of the hulks, see Grose, Francis, 1785, *A Classical Dictionary of the Vulgar Tongue* (London), 11–12: 'The floating Academy, the lighters on board of which those persons are confined, who by a late regulation are sentenced to hard labour, instead of transportation. Campbell's Academy, the same, from a gentleman of that name, who had the contract for finding and victualling the hulks or lighters.'

40   For correspondence relating to the publication of the official version of Captain Cook's third voyage, see the Papers of Sir Joseph Banks, 09. For this quotation, see Joseph Banks, Copy of a Statement of the manner in which the publication of Cook's third voyage was managed, 16 July 1795, 09.15; and also Memorandum for the division of the Profits arising from the Sale of Captn. Cooks late voyage agreed in the Presence of Ld. Sandwich, Ld Howe, Sr Jos. Banks & Mr. Stephens, 28 July 1785, 09.14.

41   Burney, Fanny, in Marquis of Lansdowne, ed., 1934, *The Queeney Letters, Being Letters addressed to Hester Marie Thrale* (New York, Farrar and Rinehart), 111.

42   Bligh to Duncan Campbell, 23 April 1786, ML Safe 1/40, CY Reel 178, 271; published in Mackaness, 1936, 60.

43   For details of the birth dates and places of the children of Elizabeth and William Bligh, see http://81.21.76.62/devon-genealogy.org.uk.

44   For Banks's instructions for the convict transport, see Sir Joseph Banks, Instructions for the Vessell from Botany Bay, February 1787, Papers of Sir Joseph Banks, 45.03.

45   Originally an under-gardener at Kew, David Nelson brought 200 packets of seeds back to England for Joseph Banks after his voyage with Cook, which were shared between Kew Gardens and the Gottingen Botanical Gardens (Leventhall, David, 2002, 'Cook's *Bounty* Men', *Cook's Log* 25/1: 1911–12).

46   Although it has often been claimed (by Dening, for example) that the *Bethia* was owned by Duncan Campbell, Navy Records Office papers indicate that this is incorrect (Knight, C., 1936, 'HM Armed Vessel *Bounty*', *Mariner's Mirror* 22: 185–86; Watkin, R.C., 1970, 'Mutiny on the *Bounty*', *Isle of Man Natural History and Antiquarian Society* 7: 378). See also McKay, John, 1989, *Anatomy of the Ship: The Armed Transport* Bounty (London, Conway Maritime Press) for an authoritative account of the purchase, refit and structure of the *Bounty*.

47   Bligh to Banks, 6 August 1787, Papers of Sir Joseph Banks, 46.02.

48   Charles Clerke to Joseph Banks, quoted in Beaglehole, ed., 1969, II: xxx.

49   Elliott in Holmes, Christine, ed., 1984, *Captain Cook's Second Voyage: The Journals of Lieutenants Elliott and Pickersgill* (London, Caliban Books), 7–8.

50    For the impassioned exchanges between Banks and Sandwich about the alterations to the *Resolution*, see their letters in Neil Chambers, ed., 2008, *The Indian and Pacific Correspondence of Sir Joseph Banks, 1768–1820* (London, Pickering & Chatto), I: 112–14.

51    Dening, 1992, 24.

52    Banks to Admiralty, 12 August 1815, University of London Library, cited in Williams, Glyndwr, in Banks et al., eds, 1994, 184.

53    Banks, A note on the establishment for the *Bounty*, Papers of Sir Joseph Banks, 45.06.

54    Duncan Campbell to Dugald Campbell, 30 August 1787, in Mackaness, ed., 1953, 50.

55    Christian, Edward, 1794, *Appendix*, 76; quoted in Christian, Glynn, 2005, *Fragile Paradise: The Discovery of Fletcher Christian*, Bounty *Mutineer* (The Long Riders' Guild Press), 33. In this book, Christian gives an engaging, rich account of Fletcher Christian's life and career.

56    Fletcher Christian, quoted by Christian, Edward, 1794, *Appendix*, 77.

57    Christian, 2005, 87.

58    Fletcher Christian joined the *Eurydice* as a midshipman on 25 April 1783; and was promoted to Acting Lieutenant on 24 May 1784 (Christian, 2005, 43, 51).

59    Maude, H.E., 1964, 'The History of Pitcairn Island', in Alan Ross and A.W. Moverley, eds, *The Pitcairnese Language* (New York, Oxford University Press), 50.

60    Dr Betham to William Bligh, Douglas, Isle of Man, 21 September 1787, quoted in Mackaness, 1936, I: 56–57. For more on Peter Heywood's life and career, see Smyth, W.H., 1831, 'A Sketch of the Career of the later Capt. Peter Heywood, RN', *United Service Journal and Naval and Military Magazine* I: 468–81.

61    Captain Cook was not altogether pleased with William Peckover, however, noting that the *Discovery*'s gunner had slept with Tongan women, knowing that he was infected with venereal disease (Cook in Beaglehole, ed., 1967, I: 266).

62    Thomas Ledward in Denman, Arthur, 1903, 'Captain Bligh and the Mutiny of the *Bounty*', *Notes and Queries* 9th s. XII: 501.

63    Statement by Mrs Gamble, Fryer's daughter, in Rutter, ed., 1939, 25–27, in which she gives her memories of her father's career. See also Du Rietz, Rolf, 1981, *Fresh Light on John Fryer of the* Bounty (Uppsala, Sweden, Dahlia Books, Banksia 2) for an excellent account of Fryer's naval service, his time on board the *Bounty* and the *Resource*, and his actions during and after the court martial.

64    For details of Morrison's previous naval career on the *Suffolk*; the *Termagant* under Arthur Kempe, who had sailed on Cook's second voyage, and then Charles Stirling; and the *Hind*, see Grant, James Shaw, 1997, *Morrison of the* Bounty: *A Scotsman: Famous but Unknown* (Stornaway, Acair Ltd).

65    Smith, D. Bonner, 1936, 212 made this point after a meticulous study of the *Bounty*'s muster roll.

66    Knight, 1936, 191.

67    Sir George Yonge to Sir Joseph Banks, 7 September 1787, Sir Joseph Banks to Sir George Yonge, 9 September 1787, Papers of Sir Joseph Banks, 45.08.

68    Lord Selkirk to Banks, 7 September 1787, Papers of Sir Joseph Banks, 45.10.

69    Forster, 1787, trans., 199–200. The *Dolphin* commanded by Captains Byron and then Wallis had a crew of about 150; the *Boudeuse* commanded by Bougainville had a crew of 220; while the *Endeavour* commanded by James Cook had a crew of 94; compared with Bligh's crew of 45.

70    William Bligh to Banks, 9 October 1787, Papers of Sir Joseph Banks, 46.06; Edgell, J.A., Rear-Admiral, in Rutter, Owen, ed., 1936, *The Log of the* Bounty: *Being Lieutenant William Bligh's Log of the Proceedings of His Majesty's Armed Vessel* Bounty *in a Voyage to the South Seas, to Take the Breadfruit from the Society Islands to the West Indies* (London, Golden Cockerel Press), I: 11.

71    Bligh to Banks, 5 November 1787, Papers of Sir Joseph Banks, 46.08.

72    According to Harold Carter, from 1779 Banks would leave London in mid to late August each year, and head to Revesby Avenue with his wife and sister, where he stayed during September and October (Carter, Harold, in Banks et al., eds, 1994, 6). In 1787, however, he may have stayed later in London to take care of the arrangements for the *Bounty* voyage.

73    Bligh to Duncan Campbell, 6 November 1787, ML Safe 1/40, CY Reel 178, 279.

74    Bligh to Banks 5 December 1787, 6 December 1787, Papers of Sir Joseph Banks, 46.13, 14. See also Bligh to Duncan Campbell, 6 December 1787, 'I hear there is a promotion taken place if you can do any thing for me I shall be greatly obliged to you', ML Safe 1/40, CY Reel 178, 289.

75    Bligh to Banks, 10 December 1787, Papers of Sir Joseph Banks, 46.16.

76    Bligh to Duncan Campbell, 10 December 1787, William Bligh Letters, 1782–1805, ML Safe 1/40, CY Reel 178, 291.

77    Dr Richard Betham to William Bligh, 21 September 1787, quoted in Mackaness, George, ed., 1938, *A Book of the* Bounty: *William Bligh and Others* (London, Dent), 295.

78    Bligh to Duncan Campbell, 22 December 1787, ML Safe 1/40, CY Reel 178, 297.

79    Christian, Charles, quoted in Christian, Glynn, 1982, *Fragile Paradise, The Discovery of Fletcher Christian*, Bounty *Mutineer* (London, H. Hamilton), 87.

80    Bligh to Duncan Campbell, 22 December 1787, ML Safe 1/40, CY Reel 178, 296.

81    Elizabeth Bligh to Frank Bond, No. 4 Broad Street, St George's, East London, 24 June 1788, ML Ms 1016.

## CHAPTER 6: THE FINEST SEA BOAT

1    Bligh in Rutter, ed., 1936, I: 45.

Bligh's various accounts of the voyage of the *Bounty*, the mutiny, the voyage of the *Bounty*'s launch to Timor and Batavia, and his return passage from Batavia to London are as follows, in the order of production: 1. Bligh's pocket notebook from the voyage in the launch containing his running log and description of the mutineers (National Library of Australia, Ms 5393), published as Bligh, William, transcription and facsimile, ed. John Bach, 1987, *The Bligh notebook: 'Rough account – Lieutenant Wm Bligh's voyage in the* Bounty*'s launch from the ship to Tofua & from thence to Timor', 28 April to 14 June 1789. With a draft list of the Bounty mutineers*, I & II (Sydney, Allen & Unwin in association with the National Library of Australia); see also Description of the Pirates remaining on board His Majesty's Armed Vessel *Bounty*, Mitchell Library, Safe 1/43; 2. William Bligh, private holograph journal of the voyage up to the departure from Timor, although the volumes on Tahiti, and on the passage from Timor to Batavia, and Batavia to England are missing (Log of the proceedings of His Majesty's Ship *Bounty* in a Voyage to the South Seas 1 Dec 1787–22 October 1788, Mitchell Library, Safe 1/46; Log of the proceedings of His Majesty's Ship *Bounty* Lieut William Bligh Commander 5 April 1789–13 March 1790, ML Safe 1/47; Index to the Log Book of HMS *Bounty*, ML Safe 1/46a); 3. William Bligh, Account of the mutiny delivered on 1 July 1789 to the governor at Kupang (missing); 4. William Bligh, Coupang, 18 August 1789, Letter to Philip Stephens, the Admiralty (PRO Adm 55/151, National Archives, Kew, AJCP reel 1601), printed in Rutter, Owen, 1931, *The Courtmartial of the* Bounty *Mutineers* (Edinburgh, William Hodge), 20–22, 26–28; 5. William Bligh, Coupang, 19 August 1789, Letter to Elizabeth Bligh (Mitchell Library, ZS1/45, 17–24, published in transcript and facsimile in Paul Brunton, ed., 1989, *Awake Bold Bligh! William Bligh's letters describing the mutiny on HMS* Bounty (Sydney, Allen & Unwin), 22–25; 6. William Bligh, Report delivered to the governor at Semarang on 23 September 1789 (missing); 7. William Bligh, Report translated into Dutch and delivered to the governor-general at Batavia on 1 October 1789 (missing); 8. William Bligh, Batavia, 13 October 1789 to Duncan Campbell (Mitchell Library, ZS1/40, 59–72, published in Brunton, ed., 1989, 25–30); 9. William Bligh, Batavia, 13 October 1789 to Joseph Banks (Mitchell Library, ZA78-4, 104–7, and ZS1/36, Safe 1/36; published in Brunton, ed., 1989, 30–38); 10. William Bligh, Account of the voyage in the launch, 29 April 1789–2 January 1790, probably written in Batavia, prefaced by an undated copy of a letter to Sir Joseph Banks, informing him of the mutiny (Mitchell Library, Safe 1/37); 11. A copy of William Bligh's journal (or perhaps simply a list of the mutineers) sent to Lord Cornwallis, Governor-General of India, on 14 October 1789 (missing); 12. William Bligh, Testimony to the court of inquiry at Batavia, 13 and 15 October 1789 (original documents in Dutch with English translations); Attestation William Bligh Plaintiff, 13, 15 October 1789, NLA, Ms 5956); Attestation William Bligh Plaintiff, 13, 15 October 1789, Mitchell Library, Safe 1/43; 13. William Bligh, Despatch to Philip Stephens at the Admiralty from Batavia on 15 October 1789 (PRO Adm 1/1506, published in Bligh, William, ed. Owen Rutter, 1934, *The Voyage of the Bounty's Launch as related in William Bligh's Despatch to the Admiralty and the Journal of John Fryer* (London, Golden Cockerel Press), 29–51, with various transcripts; 14. William Bligh, Cape Town, to the Admiralty, 16 December 1789, a despatch that arrived in London on 14 March 1790 (in National Archives, Kew – Captain's Letters Adm 1); 15. William Bligh, Cape Town, 16 December 1789 to Joseph Banks (Papers of Sir Joseph Banks, 46.28); 16. William Bligh, official transcript of his log in 3 volumes, delivered to the Admiralty in March 1790 (William Bligh, Log of the *Bounty*, PRO Adm 55/151, published by Owen Rutter, ed., 1937a, *The Log of the* Bounty*: Being Lieutenant William Bligh's Log of the Proceedings of His Majesty's Armed Vessel* Bounty *in a Voyage to the South Seas, to Take the Breadfruit from the Society Islands to the West Indies*, 2 volumes (London, Golden Cockerel Press), and in facsimile by Pageminster Press (Guildford, Surrey, 1981); see also Muster rolls 1787–90, *Bounty* (Ship) 16 August 1787–19 November 1790, Commander William Bligh, London, PRO Muster Books 1768–98, Adm 36/10744; 17. William Bligh, London, 14 May 1790 to Joseph Banks, enclosing a (missing) account of the mutiny written by John Fryer in Batavia, 26 November 1789, Papers of Sir Joseph Banks, 46.29; 18. A transcript made in London from Bligh's log from Kupang in Timor to Batavia in the *Resource*, 21 August–15 October 1789; his stay in Batavia; in the *Vlydt* from Batavia to the Cape of Good Hope, 17 October–17 December 1789; his stay at the Cape from the Cape of Good Hope to England, 3 January–13 March 1790; published by Owen Rutter, ed., 1937b, *Bligh's Voyage in the* Resource *from Coupang to Batavia, Together with the Log of His Subsequent Passage to England in the Dutch Packet* Vlydt *and His Remarks on Morrison's Journal. All Printed for the First Time from the Manuscripts in the Mitchell Library of New South Wales* (London, Golden Cockerel Press); 19. Minutes of the Proceedings of a Court-Martial on Lieutenant William Bligh and certain members of his crew, to investigate the cause of the loss of HMS *Bounty*; Minutes of the Proceedings of a Court-Martial on Mr. William Purcell, Carpenter of HMS *Bounty* on charges formulated by Captain William Bligh, PRO Adm 1/5328, part 2; 20. Bligh, William, 1790, *A Narrative of the Mutiny on board His Majesty's Ship* Bounty*; and the subsequent Voyage of Part of the Crew, in the Ship's Boat, from Tofoa, one of the Friendly Islands, to Timor, a Dutch Settlement in the East Indies* (London, George Nicol); 21. Bligh, William, 1792, *A voyage to the South Sea, undertaken by command of His Majesty, for the purpose of conveying the breadfruit-tree to the West Indies in His Majesty's Ship the* Bounty (London, G. Nicol); 22. Bligh, William, 1794, *An Answer to certain Assertions contained in the Appendix to a Pamphlet entitled,*

*Minutes of the Proceedings of the Courtmartial held at Portsmouth August 12th, 1792, on Ten Persons charged with Mutiny on Board His Majesty's Ship the Bounty* (London, G. Nicol); 23. Bligh, William, 16 December 1793, Remarks on the Court-martial of the *Bounty* mutineers, on Morrison's Journal, or Mr [Edward] Christian's Letters, Mitchell Library, Safe 1/43, CY Reel 179.

The voyage of the *Bounty* to Tahiti is also recorded in the following manuscripts: National Archives, Kew: William Bligh, Captain's Letters, Adm 1; National Library of Australia: Bligh, William, Letters 1776–1811, Ms 62; Instructions to David Nelson, appointed to proceed with Lieutenant Bligh on the ship *Bounty*, Ms 166. Mitchell Library, Sydney: Bligh, William: Remarks on Court Martial, Safe 1/43; Remarks on Mr. Christian's Letters Dec. 16, 17, 1792, Safe 1/43; Remarks, Safe 1/43; Remarks on Morrison's Journal, 1793, Safe 1/43; William Bligh Charts, 1788–1805, DL Z BLIGH; Bligh, William – Family Correspondence, Safe 1/45; William Bligh, Letters 1782–1805, Safe 1/40; and Bligh's correspondence with Sir Joseph Banks in the Papers of Sir Joseph Banks. The Mitchell Library also holds an array of Bligh memorabilia – his telescope, signet ring and sword; and documents from the following: Duncan Campbell papers, 1766–1802; Ledward, Thomas, *Resource*'s Sickbook, 27 July 1789–20 August 1789, Safe 1/45; Affidavit of Joseph Coleman, 31 July 1794, MSQ 163; Anon. crew member of *Pandora*, Verses on the Loss of HMS *Bounty* and *Pandora*, Safe 1/44; Morrison, James, Journal on HMS *Bounty* and at Tahiti, 1792, Safe 1/42; and Memorandum and Particulars respecting the *Bounty* and her Crew, Safe 1/33; John Fryer, Narrative, letter to his wife and documents, 4 April 1789–16 July 1804, Safe 1/38; Heywood, Mary, letterbook, Ms 5719; Elizabeth Bligh, papers, Safe 1/45; Elizabeth Bligh, letters, Ms 1016; John Adams, Autograph Ms Narrative of the Mutiny of the *Bounty*, given to Captain Beechey of HMS *Blossom* off Pitcairn's Island, 5 December 1825; and Peter Heywood and George Stewart, Extracts by Captain Edward Edwards in The Royal Naval Museum and Admiralty Library, Portsmouth, Mitchell Library microfilm reel FM4 2098, A.L. Faber microfilm, Freelance Microfilm Library, film 43, Adm ref No. 180. Manx National Heritage Library: The defence of Peter Heywood at a Courtmartial held on him & others, on board HM Ship the *Duke* at Portsmouth September 12th, 13th, 14th, 15th, 16th, 17th, & 18th, 1792, Ms 09519/2/1; Transcribed poetry and correspondence, predominantly by or relating to Nessy Heywood and her brother Peter Heywood, Ms 01016; Letter and papers of Hester (Nessie) and Peter Heywood, Ms 09519; Facsimile of marriage entry of Captain William Bligh and Miss Elizabeth Betham from Onchan parish register, 10 February 1781. Newberry Library: Correspondence of Miss Nessy Heywood, E5. H5078. Alexander Turnbull Library, Wellington: Sir Joseph Banks, Autograph Instruction to the Gardener of the *Bounty* expedition, QMS 0123; Inward Correspondence to Sir Joseph Banks, William Bligh, Ms papers 0155-21.

Because of the mutiny, most of the other logs and journals were lost, although according to Captain Edward Edwards, after capturing the 'pirates' in Tahiti, a number of their journals were found in their sea chests, although these do not appear (except perhaps notes by James Morrison and brief summaries by Edwards of the journals of Heywood and Stewart) to have survived the wreck of the *Pandora*. In his account, Edwards drew particularly from Morrison's account, see Edwards, Edward in Basil Thomas, ed., 1915, *Voyage of H.M.S.* Pandora (London, Francis Edwards), 34; although he also incorporated some details from the journals of Heywood and Stewart.

There is, however, a huge published literature about the mutiny on the *Bounty*, including the following selected sources (in chronological order): Anon., 1792, *An Account of the Mutinous Seizure of the* Bounty, *with the Succeeding Hardships of the Crew, to which are Added Secret Anecdotes of the Otaheitean Females* (London, Robert Turner); Christian, Edward, 1794, *Minutes of the Proceedings of the Court-Martial held at Portsmouth August 12, 1792 on Ten Persons charged with Mutiny on Board His Majesty's Ship the* Bounty: *With an Appendix containing a full Account of the real Causes and Circumstances of that unhappy Transaction, the most material of which have hitherto been withheld from the Public* (London, J. Deighton); Christian, Edward, 1795, *A Short Reply to Capt. William Bligh's* Answer (London, J. Deighton); Smyth, W.H., 1813, 'A Sketch of the Career of the Late Peter Heywood, R.N.', *United Service Journal and Naval and Military Magazine* I: 468–87; Te'ehuteatuaonoa ['Jenny'], 1819, 'Account of the mutineers of the Ship *Bounty* and their Descendants at Pitcairn's Island', *Sydney Gazette*, July 17: 817; Greatheed, Samuel, 1820, National Library of Australia, NK9566, 'Authentic history of the mutineers of the *Bounty*', I: 402–6, 449–56, in *Sailors' Magazine and Naval Miscellany*; Te'ehuteatuaonoa ['Jenny'], 1829, 'Pitcairn's Island: The *Bounty*'s crew', *United Service Journal and Naval and Military Magazine* II: 589–93; Smyth, W.H., 1829, Letter to the Editor, *United Service Journal and Naval and Military Magazine* II: 366–67; Smyth, W.H., 1831, 'The *Bounty* Again!', *United Service Journal and Naval and Military Magazine* III: 305–15; Gould, Rupert, 1928, 'Bligh's Notes on Cook's Last Voyage', *Mariner's Mirror* 14: 371–85; Rutter, Owen, 1931, *The Courtmartial of the* Bounty *Mutineers* (Edinburgh, William Hodge); Chauvel, Charles, 1933, *In the wake of the* Bounty: *to Tahiti and Pitcairn Island* (Sydney, Endeavour Press); Morrison, James in Owen Rutter, ed., 1935, *The Journal of James Morrison* (London, Golden Cockerel Press); Rutter, Owen, 1936, 'Bligh's Log', *Mariner's Mirror* 22: 179–182; Knight, C., 1936, 'HM Armed Vessel *Bounty*', *Mariner's Mirror* 22: 183–99; Smith, D. Bonner, 1936, 'Some Remarks about the Mutiny of the *Bounty*', *Mariner's Mirror* 22/2: 200–37; Smith, D. Bonner, 1937, 'More Light on Bligh and the *Bounty*', *Mariner's Mirror* 23: 210–18; Mackaness, George, ed., 1938, *A Book of the* Bounty: *William Bligh and Others* (London, Dent); Rutter, Owen, 1939, *John Fryer of the* Bounty. *Notes on His Career Written by his Daughter Mary Ann (Gamble)* (London, Golden Cockerel Press); Montgomerie, H.S., 1941, 'The Morrison Myth', *Mariner's Mirror* 27: 69–76;

Mackaness, George, ed., 1949, *Some Correspondence of Captain William Bligh R.N., with John and Francis Godolphin Bond, 1776–1811* (Sydney, D.S. Ford, Printers); Fryer, John and Bligh, William in Stephen Walters, ed., Australiana Society, 1952, *Narrative of the mutiny on board HMS* Bounty . . . *Minutes of the court martial* . . . *Bligh's Answer to certain assertions* . . . *Edward Christian's short reply to Captain William Bligh's answer. 1790, 1792, 1794, 1795. Facsimiles* (Melbourne, Georgian House); Mackaness, George, ed., 1953, *Fresh Light on Bligh: being Some Unpublished Correspondence* (Sydney, privately printed by the author); Maude, H.E., 1958, 'In Search of a Home: From the Mutiny to Pitcairn Island (1789–1790)', *Journal of the Polynesian Society* 67/2: 104–31; Danielsson, Bengt, 1963, *What Happened on the* Bounty (London, George Allen & Unwin Ltd); Du Rietz, Rolf, 1963, Three Letters from James Burney to Sir Joseph Banks: A Contribution to the History of William Bligh's 'A Voyage to the South Seas' *Ethnos* (Ethnological Museum of Sweden) XXVII: 115–125; Du Rietz, Rolf, 1965, *The Causes of the* Bounty *Mutiny: some comments on a book by Madge Darby* (Uppsala, Sweden, Dahlia Books, Studia Bountyana 1); Darby, Madge, 1966, *The Causes of the* Bounty *Mutiny: a short reply to Mr. Rolf Du Rietz's comments* (Uppsala, Sweden, Dahlia Books, Studia Bountyana 2); Beaglehole, J.C., 1967, *Captain Cook and Captain Bligh* (Wellington, Whitcombe & Tombs Ltd); David, A.C.F, 1977, 'The surveys of William Bligh', *Mariner's Mirror* 63: 69–70; David, A.C.F., 1977b, 'Broughton's Schooner and the *Bounty* Mutineers', *Mariner's Mirror* 63: 207–13; Fryer, John, ed. Stephen Walter, 1979, *The Voyage of the* Bounty*'s Launch. John Fryer's Narrative* (Guildford, Surrey, Genesis Publications); Du Rietz, Rolf E., 1979, *Thoughts on the present state of Bligh scholarship* (Uppsala, Sweden, Dahlia Books, Banksia 1); Du Rietz, Rolf E., 1979b, 1981, *Fresh Light on John Fryer of the* Bounty (Uppsala, Sweden, Dahlia Books, Banksia 2); David, A.C.F., 1981, Bligh's Notes on Cook's Last Voyage, *Mariner's Mirror* 67: 102; Mackaness, George ed., 1981, *A Book of the* Bounty: *William Bligh and Others* (New York, Everyman's Library); Christian, Glynn, 1982, *Fragile Paradise: The Discovery of Fletcher Christian, Mutineer* (London, H. Hamilton); David, A.C.F, Lieutenant Commander, 1982, 'The Surveyors of the *Bounty*: A preliminary study of the hydrographic surveys of William Bligh, Thomas Hayward and Peter Heywood and the charts published from them', typescript, Royal Navy Hydrographic Department, Ministry of Defence, Taunton, Somerset; Danielsson, Marie-Thérèse and Bengt, 1985, 'Bligh's Cave: 196 years on', *Pacific Islands Monthly*, June, 25–26; Du Rietz, Rolf, 1986, *Peter Heywood's Tahitian Vocabulary and the Narrative by James Morrison: Some Notes on their Origin and History* (Uppsala, Sweden, Dahlia Books, Banksia 3); Kennedy, Gavin, 1989, *Captain Bligh: The Man and his Mutinies* (London, Gerald Duckworth & Co.); and the fine catalogue for the exhibition 'Mutiny on the *Bounty*' at the National Maritime Museum, to mark the 200th anniversary of the mutiny, 1989, *Mutiny on the* Bounty (London, Manorial Research).

More recently, see Dening, Greg, 1992, *Mr Bligh's Bad Language: Passion, Power and Theatre on the* Bounty (Cambridge, Cambridge University Press); Alexander, Caroline, 2003, *The* Bounty: *the True Story of the Mutiny on the* Bounty (New York, Viking); Du Rietz, Rolf E., 2003, 2009, *The Bias of Bligh: An Investigation into the Credibility of William Bligh's version of the* Bounty *Mutiny* (Uppsala, Sweden, Dahlia Books, Banksia 7); Rigby, Nigel, Van der Merwe, Pieter and Williams, Glyndwr, 2005, 'The Trials of Captain Bligh', in *Pioneers of the Pacific: Voyages of Exploration 1787–1810* (Crawley, West Australia, University of West Australia Press), 58–80; Lincoln, Margarette, 2007, 'Mutinous Behavior on Voyages to the South Seas and Its Impact on Eighteenth-Century Civil Society', *Eighteenth Century Life* 31/1: 62–80.

2   Bligh to Duncan Campbell, 9 January 1788, ML Safe 1/40, CY Reel 178, 300.
3   For a detailed account of how Captain Cook looked after the health of his men, see Forster, 1787, trans., 233–37.
4   Bligh in Rutter, ed., 1937a, I: 59 (23 January 1788).
5   Ibid., I: 76.
6   Bligh to Banks, 17 February 1788, Papers of Sir Joseph Banks, 42.21.
7   Bligh to Duncan Campbell, 20 February 1780, ML Safe 1/40, CY Reel 178, 314–15; quoted in Mackaness, 1936, 72.
8   Bligh to Duncan Campbell, 9 January 1788, ML Safe 1/40, CY Reel 178, 301, quoted in ibid., 69.
9   Morrison in Rutter, ed., 1935, 18–19.
10   Morrison refers to these as 'pumpions', an old English term for pumpkins.
11   Morrison, Memorandum and Particulars respecting the *Bounty* and her crew, ML Safe 1/33, 9.
12   Ibid., 13, 15–16.
13   Fryer in Rutter, ed., 1934, 63. For Bligh's reply to Morrison's accusations, see Bligh, ed. Rutter, 1937b.
14   King, quoted in Beaglehole, ed., 1967, I: 77 fn.
15   As Rolf Du Rietz has argued, masters were indispensable and only rarely promoted to lieutenant (of the same ship) during a voyage, and Fryer had not passed his lieutenant's exam, but was working his way through the ranks as a master – see Du Rietz, 1981, *Fresh Light on John Fryer of the* Bounty (Uppsala, Sweden, Dahlia Books, Banksia 2), 9–18.
16   Bligh, 1792, 26–27.
17   Forster, 1787, trans., 209–11.
18   Bligh in Rutter, ed., 1937a, I: 178.
19   This story was later told to W.H. Smyth by Peter Heywood himself (see Smyth, W.H., 1831, 'The *Bounty* again!', *United Service Journal and Naval and Military Magazine* III: 305).
20   Bligh in Rutter, ed., 1937a, I: 159.

21  Ibid., I: 220.
22  Ibid., I: 219.
23  Heywood, Peter, Anonymous letter from a midshipman (aged sixteen) on board his Majesty's ship *Bounty*, *Cumberland Pacquet*, quoted in Alexander, 2003, 95.
24  Bligh to Duncan Campbell, 25 May 1788, in ML Safe 1/40, CY Reel 178, 308.
25  Alexander Smith (or John Adams, his true name), as told to Captain Beechey, who visited Pitcairn Island in 1825. See Beechey, Captain F.W., 1831, *Narrative of a Voyage to the Pacific and Beering's Strait, to co-operate with the Polar Expeditions: Performed in His Majesty's Ship Blossom, under the Command of Captain F.W. Beechey, R.N, F.R.S., &c., in the years 1825, 26, 27, 28*, I, II (London, Henry Colburn and Richard Bentley), I: 70.
26  Ledward, in Denman, 1903, 501.
27  Bligh in Rutter, ed., 1937a, I: 298.
28  Tobin, George to Francis Bond, quoted in Brunton, ed., 1989, 16.
29  Bligh in Rutter, ed., 1937a, I: 306.
30  Ibid., I: 343.
31  Morrison in Rutter, ed., 1935, 27.
32  Bligh in Rutter, ed., 1937a, I: 219.
33  Ibid., I: 367.
34  Article II: 'All flag officers, and all persons in or belonging to His Majesty's ships, being guilty of profane oaths, cursings, execrations, drunkenness, uncleanness, or other scandalous actions . . . shall incur such punishment as a court martial shall think fit to impose, and as the nature and degree of their offence shall deserve.'
35  See Kennedy, 1989, 43.
36  Bligh, 1794, 4.
37  The surviving records from the *Lady Penrhyn*'s voyage have been published in Paul G. Fidlon and R.J. Ryan, eds, 1979, *The Journal of Arthur Bowes Smyth: Surgeon, Lady Penrhyn 1787–1789* (Sydney, Australian Documents Library), which appears to be a later, revised version of his original journal (see ibid., 1979, xvi–xviii), and Lieutenant Watts's Narrative of the Return of the *Lady Penrhyn* Transport, in Phillip, Arthur, 1789, *The Voyage of Governor Phillip to Botany Bay with an Account of the Establishment of the Colonies of Port Jackson & Norfolk Island* (London, John Stockdale), 150–64. See also Gillen, Mollie, 1989, *The Founders of Australia: A Biographical Dictionary of the First Fleet* (Sydney, Library of Australian History); Bateson, Charles, 1969, *The Convict Ships 1787–1868* (Glasgow, Brown, Son & Ferguson Ltd); and Keneally, Thomas, 2006, *A Commonwealth of Thieves: The Improbable Birth of Australia* (New York, Doubleday) for accounts of the *Lady Penrhyn*.
38  Phillip, 1789, 153.
39  Bowes Smyth in Fidlon and Ryan, eds, 1979, 102.
40  See James Morrison's account of these events in Morrison in Rutter, ed., 1935, 172–73. As Du Rietz (Du Rietz, Rolf, 1986, *Peter Heywood's Tahitian Vocabulary and the Narratives by James Morrison: Some Notes on their Origin and History* (Uppsala, Sweden, Dahlia books, Banksia 3) has suggested, this is a retrospective account, written without the aid of a log, journal or notes from the voyage, immediately after the trial of the *Bounty* mutineers in Portsmouth. There are few dates in the account, which is much less detailed than a daily journal or an account based on a log would have been. Like the journals written by Heywood and Stewart, it seems likely (and a very great loss) that Morrison's original journal (if any) vanished during the wreck of the *Pandora*.
41  Morrison in Rutter, ed., 1935, 229.
42  Bowes Smyth in Fidlon and Ryan, eds, 1979, 105.
43  Ibid., 161.
44  Ibid., 106.

## CHAPTER 7: CAPTAIN COOK'S 'SON'

1  Bligh in Rutter, ed., 1937a, I: 371.
2  Morrison in Rutter, ed., 1935, 31.
3  Note that although during Cook's voyages the convention had been for those writing a journal to shift into civil time (midnight to midnight) while the ship was at anchor, during the earlier part of Bligh's visit to Tahiti, he stayed with naval time in his journal (noon to noon, with the date coinciding with civil time on the second noon). In this reconstruction, I have shifted to civil time while the *Bounty* was in Tahiti.
4  Bligh in Rutter, ed., 1937a, I: 372.
5  Bligh in Oliver, Douglas, ed., 1988, *Return to Tahiti: Bligh's Second Breadfruit Voyage* (Melbourne, Melbourne University Press at the Miegunyah Press), 97.
6  Bligh in Rutter, ed., 1937a, I: 373.
7  Bligh in Oliver, ed., 1988, 89; although, according to Ellis, William, 1859, *Polynesian Researches during a Residence of Nearly Eight Years in the Society and Sandwich Islands* (London, Bohn), II: 70, Pomare took this name after an expedition to the mountains during which he caught a cold and coughed at night. Because Europeans first knew this chief as 'Tu', however, while his eldest son and successor is usually

referred to as Pomare II, these names are used throughout this work, to avoid confusion. As the reader can imagine, the Tahitian custom of frequently changing names poses a formidable challenge to those trying to decipher the oral traditions, genealogies, and European records of visits to the island.

8   Bligh in Rutter, ed., 1937a, I: 374.
9   Ibid., 375.
10  As James Morrison later explained: 'If any Man is Caught in the act of Theft and is immediately put to Death, the Person who kill'd him is brought to No account for it. But if the Thief escapes & the Property is afterwards found on him the Person whose property it is, may plunder him of His Goods and Chattels which the Thief always submits to' (Morrison in Rutter, ed., 1935, 192; see also Ellis, 1859, III: 125–27).
11  Ellis, 1859, I: 203.
12  Ibid., III: 113–14; see also Oliver, Douglas, 1974, *Ancient Tahitian Society*, I–III (Honolulu, University of Hawai'i Press), II: 1044–45.
13  According to Oliver, Pomare II had been born in about 1783; their daughter Teri'i-na-vaho-roa in about 1784, their son Teri'itapunui in about 1786; and their daughter Tahamaitua in about 1787 (Oliver, 1974, III: 1253–54).
14  Bligh in Rutter, ed., 1937a, I: 380.
15  Mou'aroa was the title of the leading *'arioi* from Te Porionu'u, whose great *'arioi* house was known as Nanu'u. Orsmond gives Mou'aroa's chant in his manuscript 'The 'Arioi War in Tahiti' (Filihia transcript, 9).


## CHAPTER 8: BLIGH / PARAI

1   Bligh in Rutter, ed., 1937a, I: 381.
2   Henry, 1928, 332, quoting King Pomare II.
3   As mentioned earlier, James Morrison noted that the breadfruit trees cropped earlier in the southern districts, where the rainfall was much higher (Morrison in Rutter, ed., 1935, 142). William Ellis noted that the early missionaries learned the names of 50 different varieties of breadfruit, each with different characteristics (Ellis, 1859, I: 43).
4   Tyerman, Rev. Daniel and Bennet, George, 1831, *Journal of Voyages and Travels by the Rev. Daniel Tyerman and George Bennet deputed from the London Missionary Society to visit their various Stations in the South Sea Islands, China, India, &c. between the years 1821 and 1829, compiled from the original documents by James Montgomery, Vols I and II* (London, Frederick Westley and A.H. Davis), I: 327–28, and Ellis, 1859, I: 203–4. See also Moerenhout for a detailed and vivid description of similar festivities (known as *taupiti* or *orou*) when *'arioi* assembled from different islands: Moerenhout, J.A., 1837, in Arthur R. Borden, Jr, trans. and ed., 1983, *Travels to The Islands of the Pacific Ocean* (Lanham, New York, University Press of America), 352–56; Oliver, 1974, II: 915–19; and Henry, 1928, 237–41.
5   When an *ari'i* landed for some important occasion, his paddlers would leap out of the canoe and carry it ashore on their shoulders. The missionary Orsmond was once honoured in this way in Ra'iatea: 'Once, at Ra'iatea, on my arrival, the king, the chiefs, and great numbers of the people, ran into the water, laid hold of my little boat, and carried it, including myself and all my cargo, upon their shoulders, about a furlong inland, into the royal yard, with masts, sails and rigging all displayed.' Quoted in Tyerman and Bennet, 1831, I: 175.
6   Bligh in Rutter, ed., 1937a, I: 383.
7   Ibid., I: 384.
8   Maude in Ross and Moverley, eds, 1964, 50.
9   Bligh in Rutter, ed., 1937a, I: 388.
10  Ibid., 390.
11  See Ellis, 1859, I: 49 for another account of this cooking method.
12  For a more extended discussion of the complexities of rank in Tahitian society, see Oliver, 1974, II: 749–98. Vancouver later elaborated Bligh's account of the *ari'i* by quoting Pomare II and his family, who said that in 1792, Pomare II was no longer addressed as *ari'i rahi* but as *ari'i maro 'ura*, saying that 'there be many *Arees de Hoi* [*ari'i rahi*], but there can be only one *Aree Maro Eoora* [*ari'i maro 'ura*]'. See Vancouver, George in W. Kaye Lamb, ed., 1984, *A Voyage of Discovery to the North Pacific Ocean and Round the World 1791–1795, Vols. I, II and III* (London, The Hakluyt Society), I: 433.
13  Bligh in Rutter, ed., 1937a, I: 395.
14  Ibid., I: 397.
15  See also Morrison in Rutter, ed., 1935, 231–32; and Oliver, 1974, I: 498–99, who reports that the corpse of a dead chief was rubbed with oil, while some *ari'i* were also embalmed. Bligh gave a detailed description of this practice in 1792 (Bligh in Oliver, ed., 1988, 187). A specialist scraped the body bare of its skin and rubbed it with oil, which made it supple; and then completely disembowelled the corpse through the anus with two fingers, since the bowels were the seat of thought and emotions; the body fluid was drained into a pit, and the body cavity was filled with bark cloth soaked in scented oil. The limbs were kept pliable by moving them frequently, the skin was toughened, and falling hair glued back on.
16  Morrison in Rutter, ed., 1935, 232–33.

17    See Handy, E.S., 1930, *History and Culture in the Society Islands* (Honolulu, Bernice P. Bishop Museum Bulletin 79), 30 for a discussion of this practice.

18    Morrison explains that the embalmed bodies or skulls of high chiefs were treated as embodiments of the *mana* of the dead person, and in times of war they were hidden away, just like Cook's portrait had been (Morrison in Rutter, ed., 1935, 233).

19    Orsmond, 'The 'Arioi War in Tahiti', Filihia transcript, 9.

20    Morrison in Rutter, ed., 1935, 86.

21    An early missionary, Davies, described a ceremony held to consecrate a new god house, and when the gods were brought by the priests, a coconut branch was brought and a number of the leaves were plaited into small bunches called *tapau* which were then placed in various ritual positions (Davies Journal 1808, Douglas Oliver Missionary Card Index, 278–79, The University of Auckland Library).

22    Bligh in Rutter, ed., 1937a, I: 403.

23    See Ellis, 1859, I: 235 for an account of the *heiva* (later called *upaupa*).

24    Bligh in Rutter, ed., 1937a, I: 403.

25    Ibid., 406.

26    For a more detailed analysis, see Smith, D. Bonner, 1936, 216–17.

27    Bligh in Rutter, ed., 1937a, I: 413.

28    Ibid., 414.

29    Dening, 1992, 384.

30    Cook in Beaglehole, ed., 1955, 154 fn., 156–57.

31    Turnbull, John, 1810, *A Voyage Round the World in the Years 1800, 1801, 1802, 1803, and 1804* (Philadelphia, Benjamin and Thomas Kite), 273–74.

32    Bligh in Rutter, ed., 1937a, I: 414.

33    Ibid., I: 416.

34    Ibid., I: 418.

35    Ibid., I: 419.

36    Ibid., II, 33.

37    Orsmond, 'The 'Arioi War in Tahiti', Filihia transcript, 7.

38    See Orsmond, 'The 'Arioi War in Tahiti', Filihia transcript, which gives the name of the head *'arioi* as *avae parae*.

39    'Presentations of this kind were not uncommon among the islanders, as a compliment, or matter of courtesy, to a visitor, and were regulated by the rank and means of the donors, or the dignity of the guests. Houses, plantations, districts and even whole islands, were sometimes presented; still, those who thus received them never thought of appropriating them to their own use' (Ellis, 1859, II: 8–9).

40    Morrison in Rutter, ed., 1935, 29.

41    See Ellis for an account of how taro and yams were cultivated – the 33 varieties of taro grown in low marshy places; and the yam cultivated with much care in terraced gardens, covered with rich earth and a mulch of rotted leaves (Ellis, 1859, I: 43–45).

42    See also Morrison's excellent description of this kind of fishing in Morrison in Rutter, ed., 1935, 155–56.

43    Bligh in Rutter, ed., 1937a, I: 428.


## CHAPTER 9: MR BLIGH'S BAD LUCK

1    Bligh in Rutter, ed., 1937a, II: 5.

2    Ibid., II: 6.

3    Ibid., II: 7.

4    For these fishing methods see Morrison in Rutter, ed., 1935, 157–58.

5    See Morrison in ibid., 154–55. For a comprehensive account of fishing methods, see Ellis, 1859, I: 138–50.

6    Bligh identified Tapairu as the chief who had enticed away his men during his visit on the *Providence* (Bond, F., Journal fragments, published by Mackaness, George, 1960, 'Extracts From a Log-Book of HMS *Providence*, kept by Lieut. Francis Godolphin Bond, RN, on Bligh's Second Breadfruit Voyage, 1791–3', *RAHS Journal* 46/1: 37–38).

7    Bligh in Rutter, ed., 1937a, II: 12.

8    Ibid.

9    Ibid.

10    Bligh in Mitchell Library, Safe 1/46a.

11    Morrison in Rutter, ed., 1935, 33.

12    [Coleman et al., as told to a reporter], 1794, Narrative of the Mutiny on board the *Bounty*, *Walker's Hibernian Magazine, or, Compendium of entertaining knowledge*, October 1794, 322. This story, which includes many fascinating nuggets, is also very unreliable, leaving out the excursion to Tupua'i altogether. Apart from Morrison's retrospective journal, the evidence given at the court martial and the very brief snippets from Heywood's and Stewart's journals kept by Captain Edwards, however, it is the only account of the time spent on Tahiti between the mutiny and the arrival of the *Pandora*.

13    Bligh in Oliver, ed., 1988, 71.

14 Dening, Greg, 1992, *Mr Bligh's Bad Language: Passion, Power and Theatre on the* Bounty (Cambridge, Cambridge University Press)

15 Bligh in Rutter, ed., 1937a, II: 13.

16 According to Bligh, this man 'had the appearance of a Woman, his Yard & Testicles being so drawn in under him, having the Art from custom of keeping them in this position; those who are connected with him have their beastly pleasures gratified between his thighs, but are no farther Sodomites as they all positively deny the Crime. On examining his privacies I found them both very small and the Testicle remarkably so, being no larger than a boys of 5 or 6 Years Old, and very soft as if in a State of decay or a total incapacity of being larger, so that in either case he appeared to me effectually a Eunuch as if his stones were away' (Bligh in Rutter, ed., 1936, II: 17). See also Morrison's account of the *mahu* in Morrison in Rutter, ed., 1935, 238).

17 Bligh in Rutter, ed., 1937a, II: 17.

18 Ibid., II: 18.

19 Ibid., II: 17.

20 Ibid., II: 18.

21 Ibid., II: 23.

22 Morrison in Rutter, ed., 1935, 226; see also Ellis, 1859, I: 221–22 for an account of *fa'atitoraumoa* (lit. making cocks fight).

23 Bligh in Rutter, ed., 1937a, II: 23–24; 26.

## CHAPTER 10: THESE HAPPY ISLANDERS

1 Bligh in Rutter, ed., 1937a, II: 25.

2 Ibid., II: 29.

3 Ibid., II: 28.

4 See also Morrison in Rutter, ed., 1935, 156–57 and Ellis, 1859, I: 147–49 for vivid descriptions of this fishing method.

5 Bligh, 1794, 5.

6 Morrison, in Rutter, ed., 1935, 34, 77.

7 Moerenhout, in Borden, ed., 1983, I: 286–87.

8 Bligh in Rutter, ed., 1937a, II: 32.

9 Ibid., II: 34.

10 Turnbull, 1810, 213.

11 Ellis, 1859, I: 160–63.

12 As the missionary Williams remarked: 'At least every two months there are westerly gales for a few days, and in February there are what the natives call *to'erau maeha'a*, or the westerly twins, when the wind blows from the west several days, then veers round the compass, and, in the course of twenty-four hours, comes from that point again. I have frequently seen it continue for eight and ten days; and on one occasion, for more than a fortnight'. See Williams, John, 1838, *A Narrative of Missionary Enterprises in the South Sea Islands* (London, J. Snow), 509.

13 Henry, 1928, 185–86.

14 'The men now began their performance which of all things that was ever beheld I imagine was the most uncommon and detestable. They suddenly took off what cloathing they had about their Hips and appeared quite Naked. One of the Men was prepared for his part, for the whole business now became the power and capability of distorting the Penis and Testicles, making at the same time wanton and lascivious motions. The Person who was ready to begin had his Penis swelled and distorted out into an erection by having a severe twine ligature close up to the Os Publis applied so tight that the Penis was apparently almost cut through. The Second brought his Stones to the head of his Penis and with a small cloth bandage he wrapt them round and round, up to-wards the Belly, stretching them at the same time very violently untill they were near a foot in length which the bandage kept them erect at, the two stones and head of the Penis being like three small Balls at the extremity. The Third person was more horrible than the other two, for with both hands seizing the extremity of the Scrotum he pulled it out with such force, that the penis went in totally out of sight and the Scrotum became Shockingly distended. In this Manner they danced about the Ring for a few minutes when I desired them to desist and the Heivah ended, it however afforded much laughter among the Spectators' (Bligh in Rutter, ed., 1936, II: 35).

15 The missionary John Orsmond's fragmentary Tahitian dictionary includes many entries relating to the use of bindings in ritual practices, such as the *'aha matatini* – the multicoloured sennit binding on a god-image; the *'aha mata ioio* – the sacred binding on an adze, dedicating it to Tane, the *'aha pahu* – the sacred binding on a sharkskin drum, dedicating it to Romatane, and the *'aha papa* – a flat sennit used to make an *ari'i*'s war helmet or the grip on a weapon; the *'aha tatai* (lit. the lacing that bound together a canoe or the rafters of a house), a pact to perform a journey or a particular ritual, and the *'aha moe* – a ritual to ensure a safe voyage, or a pact to carry out a particular sacred task; the *'aha huri fenua* (lit. sennit that overturns the land), a ritual to bring victory in war, and the *'aha ta'ata* – the sennit used to bind a human sacrifice head to foot, or his penis, killing off his lineage; the *'aha tia* – offering of the 'first fish', the first enemy killed in battle, the *'aha mareva* – fleet of canoes on a voyage, and the *'aha ra'a* – fleet of

canoes drawn up for battle or the 'net of war'; and the *'aha tianoo* – a sorcerer's chant to 'entangle' and destroy the spirit of his victim (Orsmond, Rev. John, n.d., Papers, Vol. 5, Part of Tahitian Dictionary, 1850, Mitchell Library, A2609 (Mfm Reel CY 3946).

16   See also Ellis, 1859, I: 49 for a description of this cooking method.

17   Henry, 1928, 75–76.

18   Bligh in Rutter, ed., 1937a, II: 38.

19   As Morrison explained, when a child was born it was taken to the *marae*, where the father and priests offered a young pig or a chicken to the god. The priest cut off the navel string and buried it in the *marae*, and a temporary hut was built near the *marae* for the mother, where she and the child stayed until the rest of the navel string fell off. During this period the mother had to be fed, along with anyone else who touched the child, until an *amo'a* ceremony was performed with offerings of plantain branches, pigs and chickens to raise some of the *ra'a* or ancestral power from the child, allowing the mother to feed herself. A second *amo'a* was performed to allow the father and uncles to enter the house without changing their clothes; a third allowed the mother and aunts to touch the child without changing their clothes; a fourth allowed the child to enter a house where his father and uncles were eating; a fifth allowed the child to enter a house where his mother and aunts were eating; a sixth might be performed when he took a *taio*. A high-ranking child was so sacred that he or she might be twelve years old before all these restrictions were raised (Morrison, in Rutter, ed., 1935, 186–87).

20   Driessen, 1991, 'From Ta'aroa to 'Oro: An Exploration of Themes in the Traditional Culture and History of the Leeward Society Islands', PhD thesis, Australian National University, 101–2.

21   Oliver, 1974, III: 1280.

22   By the time Bligh arrived back in Tahiti in the *Providence* in 1792, it is said that Ha'amanimani had a vocabulary of 1000 English words (Bligh in Oliver, ed., 1988, 114).

23   Bligh in Rutter, ed., 1937a, II: 48.

24   Ibid.

25   Ibid., II: 50.

26   Forster, Johann, in Nicholas Thomas, Harriet Guest and Michael Dettelbach, eds, 1996, *Observations Made During a Voyage Round the World* (Honolulu, University of Hawai'i Press), 148–49.

27   Morrison in Rutter, ed., 1935, 171. By 1797, just nine years later, Captain Wilson estimated that the population was only 16,000, suggesting an exponential decline in numbers (Ellis, 1859, I: 101).

28   Henry, 1928, 178.

29   See Ellis, 1859, II: 47–48. As Ellis also describes, in early 1816 Pomare II sent most of his family gods to the missionaries, and these were deposited in the Missionary Museum at Austin Friars in Britain (Ellis, 1859, II: 23–174). According to Ellis, in early 1798 after the image of 'Oro had once again been seized by the Paea warriors and taken back to 'Utu-'ai-mahurau *marae*, the *Porpoise* arrived from Australia with gifts for Pomare II from the governor of New South Wales, reaffirming British support for the Pomare dynasty. In 1802, London Missionary Society missionaries found Pomare II at 'Utu-'ai-mahurau marae, being saluted by the people along with the image of 'Oro, to whom the people exposed themselves 'in the most shameful manner' (Ibid., II: 45). When Pomare II demanded that the Paea people surrender the image of the god to him, they refused; and his attendants seized the god and carried him off to Tautira. Soon afterwards, the Paea warriors attacked Pare and Tai'arapu, and retook the image of 'Oro. In November 1802 Teu died, soon afterwards followed by Teari'inavahoroa, Pomare II's younger brother who was now the *ari'i* of southern Tahiti, his death being blamed upon Metia, a famous sorcerer and priest of 'Oro.

   In 1803 Pomare II again demanded the image of 'Oro, and although his enemies agreed to give it up, they delayed. As European diseases continued to ravage the island, some thought that these maladies were being sent by the god of the missionaries, while others thought they were sent by their own gods. When Tu, or Pomare I, died during September of that year, his death was blamed on his violent seizure of the god 'Oro.

   In January 1806 Pomare II returned with 'Oro from Mo'orea, bringing the god in his sacred canoe along with Ohiro, Tane, Temaharo, Ruahatu and Huaima'o (the last two being shark gods), and began to learn to read and write. 'Oro was taken to Tautira. In July 1806 his wife died after having a stillborn child, leaving him a widower and childless. In mid 1807 his warriors attacked the districts of Tai'arapu and Paea, killing many people who were offered as sacrifices to 'Oro at Tautira. During 1807 Pomare II was very ill, and his life was thought to be in danger. In October 1808 war broke out again when the enemy districts threatened to attack Matavai and Pare; and influenced by Metia, 'Oro's priest and prophet, Pomare II ordered an attack and was defeated, the enemy warriors devastating the Matavai and Pare districts. Pomare II went into exile in Mo'orea, and when 'Itia's daughter died he began 'to doubt the truth of that system of idol-worship to which he had formerly been devoted'.

   Pomare II now ordered a sacred turtle to be baked in his own kitchen rather than taken as an offering to 'Oro, and when no dire consequences followed, he unsuccessfully tried to persuade Tamatoa, his father-in-law and *ari'i rahi* of Ra'iatea, to convert to Christianity. In 1813 a church was built in Mo'orea, and Patii, the priest at Papeto'ai, publicly burnt the images of the gods from that *marae*. In January 1814 'Itia, who like Pomare I had remained faithful to 'Oro, died. Afterwards fighting broke out between the adherents of Jehovah and those of 'Oro; and after a victory by the Christians (led by Mahine, the *ari'i rahi* of Mo'orea) at Paea, peace was made. 'Utu-'ai-mahurau *marae* with all its gods, altars and sacred paraphernalia was destroyed, followed by Taraho'i, the main *marae* of 'Oro in southern Tahiti, where they stripped the gods and set up the image of 'Oro in Pomare II's kitchen, hanging food baskets upon it.

Many of the priests and high chiefs now converted to Christianity, including Tamatoa of Ra'iatea, and the *'arioi* society ceased to operate. In 1816, as mentioned above, Pomare II sent his family gods to the missionaries, who despatched them to the missionary museum in Britain. See also Davies, John in C.W. Newbury ed., 1961 (Cambridge, at the University Press for the Hakluyt Society) for a detailed account of these events.

30  Bligh in Rutter, ed., 1937a, II: 52.
31  See Morrison's detailed description of the *'ihi ari'i* ceremony in ibid., 216–17.
32  Smith, Howard M., 1975, 'The Introduction of Venereal Disease into Tahiti: A Re-examination', *Journal of Pacific History* 10/1, 38–45.
33  Bligh in Rutter ed., 1937a, II: 59.
34  Ibid., II: 61.
35  Morrison in Rutter, ed., 1935, 217–18. Here, Morrison also describes how the Tahitians collected black feathers from man-o'-war birds.
36  Bligh in Rutter ed., 1937a, II: 65.
37  Bligh to Elizabeth Bligh, Mitchell Library, Safe 1/45, 487.
38  Bligh in Rutter, ed., 1937a, I: 395.

# CHAPTER 11: HUZZA FOR OTAHEITI!

1  Morrison in Rutter, ed., 1935, 36.
2  Bligh in Rutter ed., 1937a, II: 78.
3  Ibid.
4  Ibid., II: 83.
5  In a later account of Ma'i, Ellis notes that the *ari'i rahi* of Huahine had married Ma'i to his daughter and gave him the name *Paari* (wise or knowledgeable). During Ellis's visit to the island in 1824 the site of Ma'i's house was still known as 'Peretane' or Britain; and the helmet given to Ma'i by King George along with several cutlasses were still preserved, along with a jack-in-the-box and a large quarto Bible (Ellis, 1859, II: 365–71).
6  Bligh in Oliver, ed., 1988 321.
7  Fryer in Rutter, ed., 1934, 53.
8  Bligh in Rutter ed., 1937a, II: 116.
9  Morrison in Rutter, ed., 1935, 37.
10  Bligh in Rutter, ed., 1934, 47.
11  Morrison in Rutter, ed., 1935, 38.
12  Fryer in Rutter, ed., 1934, 55.
13  Morrison in Rutter, ed., 1935, 39.
14  Bligh in Rutter ed., 1937a, II: 118.
15  Morrison in Rutter, ed., 1935, 40.
16  Fryer in Rutter, ed., 1934, 56.
17  Morrison in Rutter, ed., 1935, 41.
18  Ibid.
19  Forster, 1787, trans., 208.
20  Christian, Edward, 1794, *Appendix*, 64.
21  Fryer in Rutter, ed., 1934, 56.
22  Morrison in Rutter, ed., 1935, 44. Although Rolf Du Rietz has argued that in making this remark, Stewart was warning Christian that if he left the ship, it would be almost impossible to control the crew, I am not convinced by this interpretation: see Du Rietz, Rolf, 1965, *The Causes of the* Bounty *Mutiny: Some comments on a book by Madge Darby* (Uppsala, Sweden, Dahlia Books, Studia Bountyana 1), 13–14. Morrison's account of Stewart's role in the mutiny was independently supported by John Adams, when Captain Beechey spoke to him on Pitcairn in 1825: 'A young officer, who afterwards perished in the *Pandora*, to whom Christian communicated his intention, recommended him, rather than risk his life on so hazardous an expedition, to endeavour to take possession of the ship, which he thought would not be very difficult, as so many of the ship's company were not very well disposed towards the commander (in Beechey, 1831, 72; see also Adams, Mitchell Library, A1804). Although Peter Heywood later denied that Stewart made any such suggestion to Christian, he was very anxious to remove any suspicion of complicity in mutiny from his friend; since it was key to his own defence that Stewart had urged him to be loyal to his captain, and that they had both attempted to join Bligh in the longboat, but were prevented by the mutineers.
23  See Coleman et al., *Walker's Hibernian Magazine*, 1794, 324, which also gives Christian, Churchill, Mills and Burkett as the men who burst into Bligh's cabin.
24  Gamble, Mary Anne Fryer, in Rutter, Owen, 1939, *John Fryer of the* Bounty. *Notes on His Career Written by his Daughter Mary Ann (Gamble)* (London, Golden Cockerel Press), 12.

25   Morrison in Rutter, ed., 1935, 41.
26   Fryer, statement to the court martial, 1794, *Minutes of the Proceedings of the Court-Martial held at Portsmouth August 12, 1792, on Ten Persons charged with Mutiny on Board His Majesty's Ship the* Bounty (J. Deighton, London), 7.
27   Adams, ML A1804.
28   Morrison in Rutter, ed., 1935, 42.
29   Bligh in Rutter ed., 1937a, II: 121.
30   Fryer in Rutter, ed., 1934, 60.
31   See Coleman et al., *Walker's Hibernian Magazine*, 1794, 324, who claimed that Isaac Martin climbed into the launch.
32   Ibid., 325.
33   According to Fryer, however, when Bligh whispered to him to knock Christian down, Christian threatened him with his bayonet, saying, 'Sir if you advance one inch further I will run you thro,' and sent him back down below (Fryer in Rutter, ed., 1934, 58).
34   Fryer, John, statement to the court martial, 1794, 7; Cole, ibid., 15.
35   Edgell in Rutter, ed., 1936, states that after being taken to Pitcairn Island, the Kendall chronometer (K2) was held in the Royal United Service Institution in Whitehall. It has now been carefully restored, and is held in the National Maritime Museum at Kew.
36   Bligh, Log of HMS *Bounty*, Mitchell Library, Safe 1/42, 61.
37   Cole, statement to the court martial, 1794, 16.
38   Although it had been claimed that Stewart clapped his hands and said that the mutiny was the happiest day in his life, Michael Byrne, the fiddler, thought that it was Heywood who said this – but Byrne was half blind, and alongside in the cutter during the mutiny (Bligh, questions for Frank Bond to put to Michael Byrne, transcribed in Du Rietz, Rolf, 2009, 55).
39   Morrison in Rutter, ed., 1935, 43.
40   Although some of the mutineers later denied that they had cried out 'Huzza for Otaheite', John Adams (alias Alexander Smith) freely admitted it (see Beechey, 1831, I: 76–80).
41   Bligh in Rutter ed., 1937a, II: 123.
42   Ibid., II: 122.
43   From this point in the voyage of the *Bounty*'s launch, the sequence of events is taken from Bligh's notebook (Bligh in Bach, ed., 1987), which was kept in nautical time (i.e. noon to noon), but the dates are translated into civil time (i.e. midnight to midnight) for consistency with the rest of the narrative.
44   Fryer in Rutter, ed., 1934, 64.
45   According to Setaleki Iloa as told to Commander (Retd) Wm. H. McGrath, US Navy, 1989 (Setaleki Iloa, Nuku'alofa, Tongatapu), this included William Bligh, who slept with Lesieli, the daughter of Taufa Tofua, the leading chief on the island. According to this account by a direct descendant from the liaison, Bligh promised to stay with this high-born young woman, and when he fled from the island, she cried out, 'Sir Lie!' When their baby was born, she named her daughter Selai after Bligh's deception. Many thanks to Ruth Kerr, Managing Editor, Waitakere City History, for sending me a copy of this publication. This does seem unlikely, however, given Bligh's devotion to his wife Betsy, and the fact that none of his men ever mentioned it afterwards.
46   Bligh gives their names as Eegyeefow, Maccaacabou and Vageetee. See Bligh in Mackaness, ed., 1981 (London, Dent; New York, Everyman's Library), 314.
47   Bligh in Rutter, ed., 1937a, II: 131.
48   Fryer in Rutter, ed., 1934, 68.
49   Bligh in Rutter, ed., 1937a, II: 131.

## CHAPTER 12: I HAVE BEEN RUN DOWN BY MY OWN DOGS

 1   Noted in Alexander, 2003, 425. See also Fisher, Emma, 1978, 'William Bligh's Pocket Notebook', *Mariner's Mirror*, 64: 2.
 2   Fryer in Rutter, ed., 1934, 78.
 3   Bligh in Rutter ed., 1937a, II: 132.
 4   Ibid.
 5   David, A.C.F., 1977, 'The surveys of William Bligh', *Mariners' Mirror* 63: 69–70.
 6   Bligh in Rutter ed., 1937a, II: 171.
 7   Bligh in Bach, ed., 1987, 95.
 8   Ibid., 107.
 9   Fryer, in Rutter, ed., 1934, 68.
10   Ibid., 69.
11   Bligh in Bach, ed., 1987, 115.
12   Bligh in Rutter ed., 1937a, II: 189.
13   Bligh in Bach, ed., 1987, 119.
14   Fryer in Rutter, ed., 1934, 70.
15   Bligh in Rutter ed., 1937a, II: 192. Fryer's explanation for Purcell's anger is found in Rutter, ed., 1934, 70.

16   Fryer in Rutter, ed., 1934, 71.
17   Bligh in Rutter, ed., 1937a, II.
18   Matthew Flinders, HO, OD 799b, 601.
19   David, 1982, 23.
20   Bligh in Rutter, ed., 1937a, II: 205.
21   Bligh to Banks, Batavia, 13 October 13 1789 in Bligh, ed. Brunton, 1989, 36.
22   Bligh in Rutter ed., 1937a, II: 219.
23   Bligh in Rutter, ed., 1934, 12.
24   Fryer in ibid., 74.
25   Fryer in ibid., 76.
26   Bligh in Rutter, ed., 1937a, II: 229.
27   Rutter, 1931, 45.
28   Bligh to Elizabeth Bligh, Coupang, Mitchell Library, ZML Safe 1/45, 487–91.
29   For Bligh's account of this voyage, see William Bligh, ed. Owen Rutter, 1937b, *Bligh's Voyage in the Resource* (London, Golden Cockerel Press).
30   For Bligh's account of this confrontation with his men, see Bligh in Rutter, ed., 1937b, 64–68. See also the excellent commentary by Du Rietz on these matters in Du Rietz, Rolf, 1981, *Fresh Light on John Fryer of the* Bounty (Uppsala, Sweden, Dahlia Books, Banksia 2), 22–24; and 2009, 47–51.
31   Bligh in Rutter, ed., 1937b, 69.
32   Transcribed by Bligh in ibid., 82–83.
33   Bligh in ibid., 94.
34   Denman, 1903, 501.
35   Bligh to Joseph Banks, Batavia, 13 October 1789, Sir Joseph Banks Papers, 46.27, 138–39.
36   Bligh to Banks, Batavia, 13 October 1789, Mitchell Library, Safe 1/40, CY Reel 178, 327.
37   Bligh to Joseph Banks, Batavia, 13 October 1789, Sir Joseph Banks Papers, 46.27, 138–39.
38   Ibid., 144, 132.
39   For this list, see the notebook containing the log of the launch journey, NLA MS 5393.
40   Bligh to Joseph Banks, Batavia, 13 October 1789, Sir Joseph Banks Papers, 46.27, 137.
41   Bligh in Rutter, ed., 1937b, 113.
42   This encounter, and the near sinking of the *Guardian*, is described in Pope, Dudley, 1972, *The Great Gamble* (New York, Simon & Schuster), 230–33.
43   Du Rietz, Rolf, 1981, 31. As Du Rietz points out, Riou later declared Fryer to be a 'good honest plain modest man', asserting that without his help, the *Guardian* would never have stayed afloat.
44   Price, Richard, 1790, *A Discourse on the Love of our Country, delivered on November 4, 1789* (London, T. Cadell), 50.
45   Wordsworth, William, 1850, *The Prelude, or Growth of a Poet's Mind* (London, Edward Moxon), 299.
46   Burke, Edmund, 1790, *Reflections on the Revolution in France* (London, J. Dodsley), 127–28.
47   See Lincoln, Margarette, 2007, 'Mutinous Behavior on Voyages to the South Seas and Its Impact on Eighteenth-Century Civil Society', *Eighteenth-Century Life* 31/4: 62–80, who compares the mutiny on the *Bounty* to the two mutinies at about the same time against John Meares on his voyage from China to Nootka. Like Bligh, Meares portrayed himself as an exemplary commander whose men mutinied in order to escape to the 'voluptuous abodes' in the Pacific Islands (Hawai'i in this case). As in this account, Lincoln (on p. 66) concludes that the mutiny on the *Bounty* was 'only an extreme example of difficulties of command in the Pacific'.
48   *Daily Advertiser*, Issue 136, European Intelligence, 1–10 April 1790.
49   In Britain, see *English Chronicle or Universal Evening Post*, 13–16 March 1790; *General Evening Post*, 16–18 March 1790; *London Chronicle*, 16 March 1790; *The World*, 16 March 1790. In the West Indies, see the *Daily Advertiser* in Kingston, Issues 124, 131, 136, 137, 183 & 293, 1790; in India, see the *Calcutta Gazette, or Oriental Advertiser*, Vol. 4, Issue 350, Vol. 5, Issue 237; and the *Madras Courier*, Vol. 7, Issue 283, which reported that Captain Cox had touched at Tahiti, where he was told that the *Bounty* had returned there, and that 'Christian and his crew are turned pirates'.
50   *London Chronicle*, 5–8 June 1790, 538.
51   Quoted in Dening, 1992, 287–88.
52   William Bligh to Admiralty, Adm 1/1507. Bligh to Joseph Banks, Batavia, 13 October 1789, in Mackaness, ed., 1938, 313.
53   James Mario Matra to Joseph Banks, 7 May 1790, British Library, Add Ms 33979, 29–30.
54   Quoted in Burney, Fanny, ed. Austin Dobson, 1905, *Diary and Letters of Madame D'Arblay, edited by her niece, Vols I, II and III* (London), 378.
55   Keate, George, Verses to Capt. Bligh, on Reading his Narrative of the Mutiny on the *Bounty*, and his Passage in an open Boat across the Pacific Ocean, *Literary Magazine and British Review* 7, July 1791: 65; and in John Almon, ed., 1793, *An Asylum for Fugitive Pieces, in Prose and Verse* (London), IV: 107–9.
56   Quoted in Christian, Glynn, 2005, 258.
57   Charles Christian to Dr Betham, Manx National Heritage Library, Ms 09381.
58   These letters can be found in Heywood, Mary, letterbook, Mitchell Library, Sydney, Mss 5719; and also in 'Correspondence of Miss Nessy Heywood', Newberry Library, Chicago, E5. H5078.

59  J.M. Heywood to Miss Nessy Heywood, London, 14 April 1790, Mitchell Library, Mss 5719.
60  Denman, 1903, 502.
61  *Calcutta Gazette, or, Oriental Advertiser*, Vol. 14, 1790–1791, Issue 350.
62  See Du Rietz, 1981, 22–25, for an excellent discussion of this matter.
63  For records of the courts martial of Purcell and Bligh, Adm 1/5328. For Bligh's letter to Banks announcing his honourable acquittal, and begging him to arrange to have him made a post-captain, see William Bligh to Sir Joseph Banks, 24 October 1790, Papers of Sir Joseph Banks, 46.31.

## CHAPTER 13: AN ISLAND FORT

1   Morrison in Rutter, ed., 1935, 71.
2   Coleman et al., *Walker's Hibernian Magazine*, 1794, 327.
3   Morrison in Rutter, ed., 1935, 52.
4   Coleman et al., *Walker's Hibernian Magazine*, 1794, 415.
5   For discussions of the Tahitian women who became partners to the *Bounty* mutineers, see Langdon, Robert, 2000, '"Dusky Damsels": Pitcairn Island's Neglected Matriarchs of the *Bounty* Saga', *Journal of Pacific History* 35/1, 29–47; Te'ehuteatuaonoa ['Jenny'], 1819, Account of the mutineers of the Ship *Bounty* and their Descendants at Pitcairn's Island, *Sydney Gazette*, 17 July 1819: 817; Te'ehuteatuaonoa ['Jenny'], 1829, 'Pitcairn's Island: The *Bounty*'s crew', *United Service Journal and Naval and Military Magazine* II: 589–93; Maude in Ross and Moverley, eds, 1964.
6   Heywood, Peter, extract by Edward Edwards in the Royal Naval Museum and Admiralty Library, Portsmouth, Mitchell Library microfilm reel FM4 2098, Item 1.
7   Morrison in Rutter, ed., 1935, 55.
8   'Jenny' (or Te'ehuteatuaonoa), 1829, 589.
9   Ibid.
10  Fort George was visited by Moerenhout (Moerenhout, J.A., 1837, *Voyages aux Iles du Grand Ocean*, I, II (Paris, Arthus Bertrand), I: 149; and by Seale in 1902, Narrative of Trip to South Sea Islands, with Notes on Voyages, Islands and People 1901–2, Ms, Bernice P. Bishop Museum Library, Honolulu, who sketched it at that time.
11  Fort George was sketched by Seale in 1902, an image reproduced by Maude, H.E., 1958, 'In Search of a Home: From the Mutiny to Pitcairn Island (1789–1790)', *Journal of the Polynesian Society* 67/2: 112.
12  Extract from Peter Heywood's journal, in Admiral E. Edwards commanding HMS *Pandora*, concerning the Mutiny of the *Bounty* and the voyage of the *Pandora* 1789–91, A.L. Faber microfilm, 43, from the Admiralty Library, Adm ref No. 180.
13  Most of the narrative about what happened at Tupua'i is taken from Morrison's journal; but from the fragment of Peter Heywood's (unpaginated) journal recorded by Captain Edwards, it is clear that Morrison underplayed the brutality with which the mutineers treated the local people. The narrative is therefore supplemented with additional details from Heywood, and Te'ehuteatuaonoa's accounts of their visit to the island. Presumably the original journals of Stewart and Heywood were both lost in the wreck of the *Pandora*.
14  'Jenny', 1829, 589.
15  Heywood journal extract.
16  Morrison in Rutter, ed., 1935, 71.
17  Ibid., 62.
18  For a brief and skimpy ethnographic account of Tupua'i, see Aitken, Robert T., 1930, *Ethnology of Tubuai*, *Bernice P. Bishop Museum Bulletin 70* (Honolulu, Bishop Museum).
19  Christian, Edward, 1794, *Appendix*, 73.
20  For more about the background to the voyage of the *Mercury*, see Du Rietz, Rolf E., ed., 2002, *A Secret Anglo-Swedish naval expedition to the Pacific in 1789* (Uppsala, Sweden, Dahlia Books), which reproduces several articles in French by Commandant Cottez and explains that Captain Cox, eager to participate in the sea-otter trade but lacking a licence from the East India Company, persuaded the King of Sweden to give him a commission in the Swedish navy for a voyage to raid the Russian fur-trading posts in the Bering Sea – a commission that would allow him to live as a trader in China.

  For accounts of this voyage: Mortimer, Lieutenant George, 1791, *Observations and Remarks made during a Voyage to the Islands of Teneriffe, Amsterdam, Maria's islands; Otaheite, Sandwich islands; Owhyhee, the Fox Islands on the North West Coast of America, Tinian, and from thence to Canton* (London, printed by T. Cadell for the author). See also Cottez, J., 1951, 'Recherches historiques sur une expédition militaire Suédoise en Océanie à la fin du XVIIIme siècle', *Bulletin de la Societé des Etudes Océaniennes* 94: 173–82; 1952, 'Histoire d'une expédition militaire Suédoise dans le Pacifique à la fin du XVIIIme siècle (1789–90)', *Bulletin de la Societé des Etudes Océaniennes* 100: 425–53; 1955, 'Une expédition militaire Suédoise dans le Pacifique au XVIIIme siècle: John Henry Cox Esquire', *Bulletin de la Societé des Etudes Océaniennes* 110: 374–81.
21  Ibid., 25.
22  Ibid., 48.

## CHAPTER 14: MURDER AND MAYHEM

1 For the names of the men from Tahiti, Ra'iatea and Tupua'i see Te'ehuteatuaonoa ['Jenny'], 1819: 817; see also Maude in Ross and Moverley, eds, 1964, 52 for a list of names as given by a number of sources.

2 Morrison described watching Christian and Stewart going several times into the fore cockpit to visit the boatswain and the carpenter in their cabins on the night before the mutiny; and Coleman et al. insisted that Heywood, Young and Stewart had all agreed to desert the ship while they were still in Tahiti. Morrison in Rutter, ed., 1935, 45; Coleman et al., *Walker's Hibernian Magazine*, 1794, 323). It does appear that Heywood was asleep at the time of the mutiny, however, and knew nothing about it until it was over.

3 Bligh in Oliver, ed., 1988, 55.

4 Morrison in Rutter, ed., 1935, 76.

5 Ibid., 77.

6 Coleman et al., 1794, 417.

7 Ibid., 506.

8 These women included Maimiti / Mauatua / Isabella, Christian's partner; Tinafanaea, the partner of the two Tupua'ians, Tetahiti and Ohu; Mareva / Moetua, consort of the three Tahitians, Manarii, Teimua and Niau (a boy); Fa'ahutu, the partner of John Williams; Opuarei, John Adams's partner; Te'o / Mary, William McCoy's partner, with her little daughter; Teatuahitea or Sarah, William Brown's partner; Tihuteatuaonoa [Te'ehuteatuaonoa] / Tohimata / Jenny, Isaac Martin's partner; Teraura / Susannah, the partner of Edward Young; Tevarua or Sarah, Matthew Quintal's partner; Toofaiti or Nancy, Tararo's partner; and Vahineatua or Prudence, the partner of John Mills. See Te'ehuteatuaonoa ['Jenny'], 1819: 817; Maude in Ross and Moverley, eds, 1964, 52. See also 'The Women of the *Bounty*', based on research by Pat Bentley, graduate student at the University of Hawai'i, on www.lareau.org/Bounty which includes biographical details for a number of these women.

9 Heywood became a fluent speaker of Tahitian, later preparing a detailed vocabulary of the language: see Du Rietz, Rolf E., 1986, *Peter Heywood's Tahitian Vocabulary and the narratives by James Morrison: Some notes on their origin and history* (Uppsala, Sweden, Dahlia Books, Banksia 3).

10 Coleman et al., 1794, 417.

11 Morrison in Rutter, ed., 1935, 84.

12 Ibid., 81.

13 Ibid., 84.

14 Ibid., 86.

15 Ibid., 87.

16 Coleman et. al., 1794, 416.

17 Ibid., 419.

18 For Coleman's account of these events, see ibid., 419–20, 502–3.

19 Extract from Peter Heywood's journal, in Admiral E. Edwards commanding HMS *Pandora*, concerning the Mutiny of the *Bounty* and the voyage of the *Pandora* 1789–91, A.L. Faber microfilm, 43, from the Admiralty Library, Adm ref No. 180.

20 Morrison in Rutter, ed., 1935, 95.

21 Ibid., 96.

22 See Ellis for a later account of launching a ship (Ellis, 1859, II: 240–41).

23 Morrison in Rutter, ed., 1935, 181–82.

24 Turnbull, 1810, describes Paitia as the brother of Pomare I and the sister of Auo (244). Since Ari'ipaea is separately identified by Morrison, this must be another name for Vaetua, Tu's younger brother.

25 See Morrison's account of Tahiti's political history since the attack on Mahaiatea in Morrison in Rutter, ed., 1935, 171–72.

26 According to Morrison, at the time of his stay on the island, Tahiti-nui or northern Tahiti was divided into Te Porionu'u or Te 'Aharoa, an alliance of districts which included Pare, Matavai, Ha'apaino'o, Unuhea, Ti'arei and Hitia'a; Teva-i-uta, an alliance of districts which included Vaiari, Vai'uriri and Papara, who were allied with Te Porionu'u; Atehuru (Paea) and Tetaha (Fa'a'a); while Tahiti-iti included six districts – Afahiti, Tautira, Tepare, Vai'otaha, Mataoae and Vairao (ibid., 166.)

27 Morrison in Rutter, ed., 1935, 104.

28 Ellis, 1859, I: 313.

## CHAPTER 15: PANDORA'S BOX

1 Morrison in Rutter, ed., 1935, 111.

2 Ibid., 112.

3 Tobin in Oliver, ed., 1988, 126, who visited the *marae* in 1792. See also Bligh's description in ibid., 125; and his sketch of the *marae* and its platform for offerings (plates 15 and 16 in ibid., facing p. 138).

4 Pomare II letter, quoted in Ellis, 1859, II: 174.

5 See Bligh for a detailed account of an almost identical ceremony at this *marae* in 1792, which is probably more accurate since it was written shortly afterwards. By that time the *maro 'ura* had been decorated with some auburn hair from Skinner, the barber on board the *Bounty* (Bligh in Oliver, ed., 1988, 230–32).

6  It is not clear from Morrison's description whether he was present at this ritual, or at parts of it, or not at all. Morrison does not seem to have been an honorary *'arioi* or *ari'i*, and he may have been excluded from this sacred ceremony. In any case, his description seems to be incomplete. According to Ellis, the installation of a new *ari'i rahi* began when a new section was added to the *maro 'ura*, when human sacrifices were offered. When the parties processed to the *marae*, the image of 'Oro was stripped of its bark-cloth coverings and carried to the forecourt, where the *Paharahi o Ruea* or great bed of 'Oro, a large bench cut out of a solid piece of wood, was placed upon the *marae* as a seat for the paramount chief. After some rituals (which Ellis does not describe, although Morrison does), the procession – which was led by the high priest Tairi-moa who carried the image of 'Oro, followed by the *ari'i rahi* himself, then four chiefs carrying the bed of 'Oro, and the priests bringing the great sacred drum and conch-shell trumpets from the *marae*, each of whom wore braided coconut leaf twists or *tapa 'au* on their arms – marched towards the beach, where a fleet of canoes was waiting. 'Oro was carried on board the sacred canoe, which was decorated with *tapa 'au* (which were also worn by each of its crew), while the *ari'i rahi* sat on 'Oro's bed, which was placed at the water's edge. The chiefs stood around him and the priests stood around the god, until on a signal the *ari'i rahi* entered the sea and bathed himself. The head priest entered the water carrying a branch from a *miro* tree taken from the *marae* and struck the *ari'i rahi* on the back, offering up a prayer to Ta'aroa (the feathered creator god), thus clearing the paramount chief of all *hara* or wrongdoing.

   Afterwards, the high priest and the *ari'i rahi* entered the sacred canoe together, where in the presence of 'Oro the paramount chief was girded with the *maro 'ura* as the assembled multitude saluted him with jubilant cries of '*Maeva ari'i! Maeva ari'i!*' ('Hail to the high chief!'). The rowers of the sacred canoe began to paddle towards the reef, the priests beating the sacred drum and sounding their trumpets, followed by the spectators in their canoes, still shouting '*Maeva ari'i!*' At the reef, the two sacred sharks Tuu ma'o and Tahui approached the sacred canoe to salute the *ari'i rahi*. When they returned to the beach, the paramount chief was again placed on the sacred stool, reclining his head on the sacred pillow of Tafeu. The procession formed again and marched back to Taputapuatea, the priest Tairi-moa once again carrying the image of 'Oro. The *ari'i rahi*, still seated on the sacred stool, was carried behind him, followed by the priests with their trumpets and drum. At the *marae* the paramount chief upon his stool was placed on a raised stone platform on the *marae*, surrounded by the *unu* or carved wood ornaments honouring departed chiefs. The gods 'Oro and Hiro were placed beside him, and he was saluted by his people. According to other sources, at this time naked *'arioi* touched him with their genitals, covering him with urine and excrement to raise the *ra 'a* (ancestral power) of the occasion (Moerenhout in Borden, ed., 1983, 302); but Ellis simply says 'a veil must be drawn over the vices with which the ceremonies were concluded.' (Ellis, 1859, III, 108–14).

7  These ritual objects were later described by William Bligh during his second breadfruit voyage to Tahiti on the *Providence*: 'The Red Bundle their Etuah (which they called Oro) was nothing more than a number of Yellow and Red feathers, and four rolls about 18 Inches long platted over with Cocoa Nut fibres, to which they gave the Name of some inferior Deities . . . The Marro Oorah, or feathered Belt, which is put on the Erreerahigh when the Sacrifice is first made and the Eye presented, is about 12 feet long, and about 14 inches wide, one half is made of Yellow Feathers stitched on Cloth, and the other half is some Red English Buntin without any feathers. The Ends are wrought, with feathers, in divisions, which give a change to the form of it, and are the parts which hang as ornaments when worn by the King. The Yellow Feathers are diversified by narrow stripes of red feathers, it is however not remarkably ellegant or neatly made' (Bligh in Oliver, ed., 1988, 125). Bligh also sketched and named Te Ra'i-puatata; see ibid., 139, plate 16. Note that by that time the *maro 'ura* had been decorated with some auburn hair from Skinner, the *Bounty*'s barber (Bligh in Oliver, ed., 1988, 230–32).

8  Driessen, Hank, 1982, 'Outriggerless canoes and glorious beings: pre-contact prophecies in the Society Islands', *Journal of Pacific History* XVII, 8–9; Tahitian text in Henry, 1928, 5. For variant versions of this story, see Driessen, ibid., 4–6; 910.

9  Vancouver in Lamb, ed., 1984, I: 433.

10  Coleman et al., *Walker's Hibernian Magazine*, 1794, 16.

11  Bligh was appointed Commander of the *Falcon* on 3 November and Captain of the *Medea* on 15 December 1790, which latter promotion put him on the post-captain's list – see Smith, D. Bonner, 1936, 224. For his letter of grateful thanks to Joseph Banks, see William Bligh to Sir Joseph Banks, Papers of Sir Joseph Banks, 46.32.

12  The *Pandora* was a sixth-rate, 24-gun, Porcupine-class frigate, designed by Sir John William and built in Deptford in 1779 by Adam and Barnard, with a crew of 129 men – Gesner, Peter, ed., 1998, *A Voyage Round the World in His Majesty's Frigate* Pandora (Hordern House for the Australian National Maritime Museum), 17.

13  In 1777 Hamilton was appointed to a storeship, HMS *Tortoise*, as first surgeon's mate, and by 1783 was serving as the surgeon on a third-rate warship HMS *Agamemnon*. In 1786 he served as surgeon on the 14-gun cutter the *Brazen* before going onto half pay for four years. His appointment to the *Pandora* signalled his return to active duty. For more information on his career, see Gesner, ed., 1998, 23–26.

14  Personal papers of Admiral E. Edwards, commanding HMS *Pandora*, concerning the Mutiny of the *Bounty* and the voyage of the *Pandora* 1789–91, A.L. Faber microfilm, 43, from the Admiralty Library, Adm ref No. 180.

The voyage of the *Pandora* is recorded in the following original documents: National Archives, Kew: Captain Edward Edwards, Adm 1/1763: Report to the Admiralty, Teneriff, 25 November 1790; A List of Pirates late belonging to His Majesty's Armed Vessel *Bounty*, taken by His Majesty's Ship *Pandora*; State of the Company of His Majesty's Ship *Pandora* Capt. Edw. Edwards: and the manner disposed of on board Dutch East India Company Ships for their Passage to Europe; List of Islands and places discovered by His Majesty's Ship *Pandora*; Report to the Admiralty, Batavia, 29 May 1791; Letter to the Admiralty, Cape of Good Hope, 19 March 1792; Letters to the Admiralty from 8 Craven St., The Strand, London; *Pandora*'s Orders, Adm 2/20: 478; Muster roll of the *Pandora*, Captain Edward Edwards, Adm 35/1360; Monthly books, August 1790–September 1792, Adm 36/1136; Captain's Letters, Captain Edward Edwards, *Pandora*, Adm 52/2440/3. Naval Historical Library, London: Log of the *Pandora*, Ms 180. Mitchell Library, Sydney: Anon., 1790, Narrative of the Loss of HM Frigate *Pandora*, Safe 1/30; Edwards, Edward, 1789, Admiral Edwards Commanding HMS *Pandora*, concerning the Mutiny of the *Bounty* and the Voyage of the *Pandora* 1789–91, London: Admiralty Library, ML microfilm reel FM4 2098; Edwards, Edward, 1790, Letters to the Admiralty, AJCP 'Captains' Letters' 3270, no. 1763. National Library of Australia: Personal papers of Admiral E. Edwards, commanding HMS *Pandora*, concerning the Mutiny of the *Bounty* and the voyage of the *Pandora* 1789–91, A.L. Faber microfilm, 43, from the Admiralty Library, Adm ref No. 180.

Captain Edwards's report to the Admiralty from Batavia was published (a little inaccurately) by Basil Thomson, ed., 1915, *Voyage of H.M.S.* Pandora *despatched to arrest the mutineers of the* Bounty *in the South Seas, 1790–91* (London, Francis Edwards); while George Hamilton's account of the Voyage, published in 1793 as *A Voyage round the World in His Majesty's Frigate* Pandora (London, Berwick), was republished under the same title as a facsimile in 1998 (Sydney, Hordern House for the Australian National Maritime Museum). See also Du Rietz, Rolf, 1963, 'The Voyage of HMS *Pandora*', *Ethnos* 2–4: 216–18.

15  Hamilton in Gesner, ed., 1998, 5.
16  Captain Edwards of the *Pandora* made extracts of the journals of Heywood and Stewart, preserved in his personal papers in the National Library of Australia. See Du Rietz, Rolf, 1986, *Peter Heywood's Tahitian Vocabulary and the narratives by James Morrison: Some notes on their origin and history* (Uppsala, Sweden, Dahlia Books, Banksia 3), for a detailed discussion of these documents and their fate.
17  Peter Heywood, Correspondence of Miss Nessy Heywood, Newberry Library, Chicago, E5, H5708.
18  Hamilton in Gesner, ed., 1998, 41.
19  Bligh in Oliver, ed., 1988, 100.
20  Hamilton in Gesner, ed., 1998, 16.
21  Ibid., 26–27. See H.E. Maude's 1966 note about the discovery of the Edwards papers, including the journal of the *Pandora*, after they had been languishing for many years, wrapped up in brown paper, in a cupboard in the Admiralty Library, in *Journal of Pacific History* I: 184–85.
22  Hamilton, in Gesner, ed., 1998, 60.
23  Ibid., 31.
24  Rodger, N.A.M., 1982, *Articles of War: The Statutes which Governed our Fighting Navies, 1661, 1749 and 1886* (Kenneth Mason, Homewell, Havant, Hampshire).
25  Edwards, Edward, Memo made at Otaheite, Personal papers of Admiral E. Edwards, National Library of Australia, commanding HMS *Pandora*, concerning the Mutiny of the *Bounty* and the voyage of the *Pandora* 1789–91, A.L. Faber microfilm, 43, from the Admiralty Library, Adm ref No. 180.
26  Bligh in Oliver, ed., 1988, 55.
27  Hamilton in Gesner, ed., 1998, 34.
28  Morrison in Rutter, ed., 1935, 123.
29  Hamilton in Gesner, ed., 1998, 33.
30  Ibid., 39.
31  Ibid., 36–37.
32  Bligh in Oliver, ed., 1988, 75.
33  Hamilton in Gesner, ed., 1998, 58–59.
34  These fertility rituals dedicated to Demeter (the goddess of grain) and her daughter Persephone (the goddess of the annual renewal of life) were among the most sacred celebrations in ancient Greece. The participants took a vow of secrecy not to reveal what happened, but these rituals are thought to have featured ritual sex between the high priest and high priestess, and the offering of pigs.
35  Hamilton in Gesner, ed., 1998, 37–38.
36  Ibid., 59.
37  Ibid., 54.
38  Hesiod, translated in Powell, Barry, 2004, *Classical Myth* (New Jersey, Pearson / Prentice Hall), 118. Note that Pandora, the first woman, had an earthenware jar, not a box, which she had been forbidden to open; but driven by curiosity, she lifted the lid, releasing the diseases and miseries that afflict humankind.


## CHAPTER 16: WRECK OF THE *PANDORA*

1   Edward Edwards to the Admiralty, Batavia, 25 November 1791, Adm 1/1763.
2   Hamilton in Gesner, ed., 1998, 69.

3 In fact the island had been previously visited by Bougainville, La Pérouse and Freycinet (Hamilton in Thomson, ed., 1915, 49 fn.).
4 Hamilton in Gesner, ed., 1998, 79–80.
5 For more information on the voyage of the *Matavy*, see David Thomas Renouard – Narrative of the *Pandora*'s tender, 1791; transcript by Alfred Purshouse Driver, 7 Sept. 1864, from the original narrative by David Thomas Renouard, 1791, Mitchell Library, Sydney, D377; published in Maude, H.E., 1964, 'The Voyage of the *Pandora*'s Tender', *Mariner's Mirror* 50: 217–35; and earlier in Anon. [Smyth, William Henry], 1842, 'The Last of the *Pandora*s', *Colburn's United Service Magazine and Naval and Military Journal* III: 1–14. For a discussion of the ultimate fate of the tender, see David, A.C.F., 1977, 'Broughton's Schooner and the *Bounty* mutineers', *Mariner's Mirror* 63: 207–13.
6 Edwards report to the Admiralty, Batavia, 25 November 1791, 16.
7 Hamilton in Gesner, ed., 1998, 84.
8 Ibid., 87.
9 Morrison in Rutter, ed., 1935, 124.
10 Edwards report to the Admiralty, Batavia, 25 November 1791, 21.
11 Morrison, Memorandum and Particulars respecting the *Bounty* and her crew, ML Safe 1/33, 51.
12 Ibid., 55.
13 Although the *Pandora*'s muster roll gives the names of 24 men (not 31), including 5 landsmen, 10 ordinary sailors and 9 able-bodied sailors, who died in the shipwreck (Adm 36/7511), this appears to be an incomplete listing. In his biography of Heywood, Marshall notes that 'Moulter was subsequently made a warrant-officer through Captain Heywood's influence' (Marshall, John, 1825, *Memoirs of the services of all the flag-officers, superannuated rear-admirals, retired-captains, post-captains, and commanders, whose names appeared on the Admiralty list of sea officers at the commencement of the year 1823, or who have since been promoted; illustrated by a series of historical and explanatory notes* (London, Longman, Rees, Orme, Brown and Grey), 770 fn. (Many thanks to Rolf Du Rietz for pointing this out to me.)
14 The wreck of the *Pandora* still lies where she sank off the Great Barrier Reef. For information about the archaeological investigations of the wreck, see the website of the Queensland Museum, http://www.qm.qld.gov.au/features/pandora/pandora.asp.
15 Hamilton in Gesner, ed., 1998, 129.
16 Ibid., 129.
17 Morrison in Rutter, ed., 1935, 131.
18 For an account of their voyage, see Howay, F.W., 1944, 'Some Lengthy Open-boat Voyages in the Pacific Ocean', *American Neptune* 4: 53–57.
19 Morrison, Memorandum and Particulars respecting the *Bounty* and her crew, ML Safe 1/33, 65.
20 Hamilton in Gesner, ed., 1998, 149–50.
21 Edwards in Thomson, ed., 1915, 82.
22 Anon. crew member of *Pandora*, Verses on the Loss of HMS *Bounty* and *Pandora*, ML Safe 1/44, 444–447.
23 *Monthly Chronicle*, 2 April 1792, Issue 21: 317.

## CHAPTER 17: THE MUTINEERS' BABIES

1 Elliott, John in Christine Holmes, ed., 1984, *Captain Cook's Second Voyage: John Elliott & Richard Pickersgill* (London, Caliban Books), xxxi.
2 Ibid., 30.
3 Lamb, W. Kaye, 1984, *A Voyage of Discovery to the North Pacific Ocean and Round the World 1791–1795* (London, The Hakluyt Society), I: 5.
4 Clerke in Beaglehole, ed., 1967, I: 554.
5 For an authoritative account, see Williams, Glyndwr, 2002, *Voyages of Delusion: The Search for the Northwest Passage in the Age of Reason* (London, HarperCollins).
6 Trevenen in Lloyd et al., eds, 1959, 21–22.
7 General Instructions for Surveying, February 1791, Papers of Sir Joseph Banks, 60.05.
8 *Discovery*'s Garden Hutch as fitted on the Quarterdeck, ibid., 60.12.
9 Watt, Sir James, 1987, 'The Voyage of Captain George Vancouver 1791–5: The Interplay of Physical and Psychological Pressures', *Canadian Bulletin of Medical History* 4: 33–51.
10 The voyage of the *Discovery* and *Chatham* is recorded in the following logs and journals: National Archives, Kew: CO/187, Captain Vancouver's despatches; Adm 1/2628, Captain's Letters, George Vancouver; Adm 35/535, Log of the *Discovery*; Adm 51/2251, Lt R.W. Broughton, *Chatham*; Adm 51/4146/11, J. Hanson, Captain's Log; Adm 51/4532, Spelman Swaine, *Chatham*; Adm 51/4533/52, J. Mudge, *Discovery*; Adm 51/4533/52, John Aisley Browne, *Discovery*; Adm 51/4533/54, J. Stewart, *Discovery*; Adm 51/4533/55, John Stewart, *Discovery*; Adm 51/4534/50, J.W. Scott, *Discovery*; Adm 51/4534/51, Robert Pigot, *Discovery*; Adm 51/4534/56–57, George Charles McKenzie, *Discovery*; Adm 51/4534/58–59, Edward Roberts, *Discovery*; Adm 51/4534/60–61, T. Dobson, *Discovery*; Adm 51/4534/73, Anon.; Adm 52/2262, Joseph Whidbey, *Discovery*; Adm 53/334, *Chatham*'s Log Book, John Sherriff; Adm 55/335, J. Johnstone, *Chatham*; Adm 53/402, Zachary Mudge, Ship's Log, *Discovery*; Adm 53/402, Joseph Whidbey, *Discovery*; Adm 53/403, Thomas Manby, *Discovery*; Adm 55/6–7, Nathaniel

Portlock, *Chatham*; Adm 55/13, Anon., *Chatham*; Adm 55/14, Lt J.W. Scott, *Chatham*; Adm 55/15, Lt T. Heddington, *Chatham*; Adm 55/25, John Sykes, *Discovery*; Adm 55/26, Harry Humphreys, *Discovery*; Adm 55/27, Lt P. Puget, *Discovery*; Adm 55/28, Lt J. Stewart, *Discovery*; Adm 55/29, V. Ballard, *Discovery*; Adm 55/30, Lt R. Pigot, *Discovery*; Adm 55/31, H.M. Orchard, *Discovery*; Adm 55/32–33, Lt J. Baker, *Discovery*. British Library: Add Ms 32641, Archibald Menzies, Journal; Add Ms 17550, Lt P. Puget, Rough Log of the *Chatham*; Add Ms 17543, Lt P. Puget, Journal of the *Chatham*; Add Ms 17545–46, Lt P. Puget, Journal of the *Chatham*. National Library of Australia: Archibald Menzies, Journal, Ms 155. Alexander Turnbull Library, Wellington: Journal of Edward Bell, Voyage of HMS *Chatham* to the Pacific Ocean, Ms Papers 6373-46.

　　For preparations for the voyage and the involvement of Sir Joseph Banks, see Mitchell Library, State Library of New South Wales, Sir Joseph Banks Papers, [in date order] Series 60.12, 61.01, 61.02, 61.03, 60.01, 60.02, 60.03, 61.04, 61.05, 60.04, 60.05, 61.06, 61.07, 61.08, 61.09, 60.06, 61.10, 61.11, 61.12, 61.13, 60.07, 61.14, 61.15, 60.08, 60.09, 60.10, 60.11. National Library of Australia, Ms Papers of Sir Joseph Banks, 09.31.

　　For Vancouver's account of the voyage, see Vancouver, George, 1984, ed. W. Kaye Lamb, *A Voyage of Discovery to the North Pacific Ocean and Round the World 1791–1795*, I–IV (London, Hakluyt Society). For Menzies's account, see Menzies, Archibald, 2007, *Journal of Archibald Menzies, Surgeon and Botanist on Board* Discovery (Marlborough, England, Adam Matthew Digital). For Manby's account, see Manby, Thomas, ed. Dale La Tendresse, 1988, *Journal of the Voyages of the HMS* Discovery *and* Chatham. See also Fisher, Robin and Hugh Johnston, eds, 1993, *From Maps to Metaphors* (Vancouver, UBC Press); Rigby, Nigel, Pieter van der Merwe and Glyn Williams, 2005, *Pioneers of the Pacific: Voyages of Exploration, 1787–1810* (Fairbanks, University of Alaska Press); Bown, Stephen R., 2008, *Madness, Betrayal and the Lash: The Epic Voyage of George Vancouver* (Vancouver, Douglas & McIntyre Ltd).

11　Recorded by Zachariah Mudge in his logbook, Adm 53/402

12　For these metrics, see Darby, Madge, 2000, 'Bligh's Disciple: Matthew Flinders's Journals of HMS *Providence* (1791–3)', *Mariner's Mirror* 86/4: 402 and Dening, 1992, 62–63, 384.

13　These punishments are recorded in a letter by Joseph Banks after he had interviewed Lord Camelford about the voyage (National Library of Australia, Correspondence and papers of Sir Joseph Banks, 01, Item 31).

14　Bell, 71.

15　Ibid., 77.

16　Sherriff, 30.

17　Ibid., 38.

18　Menzies, 2007, 113.

19　See Vancouver in Lamb, ed., 1984, 429; Menzies, 2007, 161.

20　Menzies, ibid., 115.

21　Ibid., 118.

22　Manby in La Tendresse, ed., 1988, 103.

23　Vancouver in Lamb, ed., 1984, 397.

24　Bell, 82.

25　Vancouver in Lamb, ed., 1984, 398.

26　Bell, 86.

27　Ibid., 127.

28　Johnstone, 113.

29　Menzies, 2007, 126–27; see also Frank Bond's description of his *taio* in Bond in Mackaness, ed., 1960, 45.

30　From a close study of the journals and logs of Vancouver's visit to Tahiti, it is clear that in almost every case the entries were made after the fact, and different writers often attribute particular events to different days. This is also true of Vancouver's journal, although it seems the most reliable in its record of the sequence of events. In this account, the chronology as given by Vancouver is followed.

31　Menzies, 2007, 137.

32　Vancouver in Lamb, ed., 1984, 419.

33　Menzies, 2007, 157.

34　Bell, 112.

35　Manby in La Tendresse, ed., 1988, 111–12.

## CHAPTER 18: *PROVIDENCE*

1　Bligh to Francis Godolphin Bond, 8 February 1791, in Mackaness, ed., 1953. Frank Bond was the son of Catherine Bond, Bligh's stepsister and the daughter of Bligh's mother by her first marriage (see also Mackaness, ed., 1949, 3; for Bond's naval career, see Mackaness, ed., 1953, 7–11).

2　Captain Bligh's Hints for an Outfit, c. March 1791, Papers of Sir Joseph Banks, 49.05.

3　Bligh to Banks, c. January 1791, Papers of Sir Joseph Banks, 50.03.

4　For details of Frank Bond's naval career and his family relationship with William Bligh, see Darby, Madge, 1999, 'Lieutenant Francis Godolphin Bond and the Bligh Family', *Mariner's Mirror* 85: 203–5.

5　Bligh to Banks, 17 July 1791, Papers of Sir Joseph Banks, 50.05.

6   Joseph Banks to James Wiles and Christopher Smith, 'Gardiners on the *Providence*', Papers of Sir Joseph Banks, 52.

7   See also Admiralty Instructions for the *Providence*, Adm 2/121; Bligh's requisition for stores and despatches, Adm 1/1507.

8   Bligh to Evan Nepean, 24 April 1791, State Library of NSW, CY 4402.

9   Ibid.

10   Thomas Haweis, autobiography, quoted in Lansdown, ed., 2006, 113. Indeed, Haweis was not the only evangelical Christian to be inspired by the idea of a mission to Tahiti. William Carey, the pastor of a village church at Moulton and one of the founders of the Baptist Missionary Society in 1792, had already declared his intention of going as a missionary to Tahiti: '*Mr. Carey:* It is highly important that something should be done for the heathen. *Mr. Potts:* But how can it be done, and who will do it? *Mr Carey:* Why, I engage to go wherever Providence shall open a door. *Mr. Potts:* But where would you go? Have you thought of that, friend Carey? *Mr. Carey:* Yes, I certainly have. Were I to follow my inclination, and had the means at command, the islands of the South Seas would be the scene of my labours, and I would commence at Otaheite'. See Cox, Rev. F.A., 1842, *History of the Baptist Missionary Society, from 1792 to 1842* (London, T. Ward & Co.).

11   Bligh to Bond, c. June 1791 in Mackaness, ed., 1953, 19.

12   Ellis, William, 1844, *The History of the London Missionary Society* (London, John Snow), I: 6–7.

13   Quoted in McCormick, E.H., 1977, *Omai: Pacific Envoy* (Auckland, Auckland University Press), 164.

14   Horace Walpole to Cole, 15 June 1780, in W.S. Lewis, ed., 1937, *Horace Walpole's Correspondence with The Rev. William Cole* (London, Oxford University Press), II: 225.

15   Banks, quoted in Gascoigne, John, 1994, *Joseph Banks and the English Enlightenment: Useful Knowledge and Polite Culture* (Cambridge, Cambridge University Press), 42.

16   See Gascoigne's excellent discussion of Banks's religious sympathies, in ibid., 41–55.

17   William Pitt the Younger, Lord Chatham, to Sir Joseph Banks, 9 March 1791, Paper of Sir Joseph Banks, 49.04.

18   See Du Rietz, Rolf, 1962, 'Three Letters from James Burney to Sir Joseph Banks: A Contribution to the History of William Bligh's *A Voyage to the South Sea*', *Ethnos* 27: 115–25.

19   Bligh to James Burney, 26 July 1791, Mitchell Library, Ms Q 163, CY Reel 223, 958–964.

20   As reported in *Craftsman or Say's Weekly Journal*, Issue 16771, 14 January 1792.

21   Clipping from the *Royal Gazette*, 25 July 1791, Papers of Sir Joseph Banks, 50.09 (also West Indies, *Gentleman's Magazine*, August 1791, 61/2: 766).

22   Banks, Memorandum concerning the purchase of plants and the route of the voyage, 1791, Papers of Sir Joseph Banks, 49.11.

23   Bligh to Banks, 21 July 1791, Papers of Sir Joseph Banks, 50.08.

24   Bligh to Banks, 7 July 1791, ibid., 50.10.

25   Bligh to Banks, 2 August 1791, ibid., 50.11. Bligh's second breadfruit voyage is recorded in the following logs and journals: National Archives, Kew: Adm 35/1361, *Providence* muster books; Adm 36/11154, *Providence* muster book; Adm 36/11169, *Assistant* muster books; Adm 55/6–7, Nathaniel Portlock, *Assistant*; Adm 55/94–95, Lieutenant Tobin; Adm 55/96, Lieut. Bond; Adm 55/97–98, Matthew Flinders; Adm 55/152–53, William Bligh. National Maritime Museum, Greenwich: Ms 60/017, FLI/8a, Matthew Flinders. Mitchell Library, State Library of New South Wales: Papers relating to William Bligh, including *Providence* orders and logbook, Safe 1/48, A564/1–2; Orders for the Conduct of Affairs on HMS *Providence*, Safe 1/22b; Sketches of HMS *Providence*, George Tobin, PXA 563; Drawings by William Bligh, Commander of HMS *Providence*, PXA 565. National Library of Australia: Journal Kept on board HMS *Providence* by William Bligh, MS 4235; Sketches by George Tobin, Rex Nan Kivell collection, NK 4065, NK 6581.

     For published accounts of the voyage, see Lee, Ida, 1920, *Captain Bligh's Second Voyage to the South Sea* (London, Longmans, Green & Co.); Oliver, Douglas, 1988, *Return to Tahiti: Bligh's Second Breadfruit Voyage* (Honolulu, University of Hawai'i Press); Tobin, George, in Roy Schreiber, ed., 2007, *Captain Bligh's Second Chance: An Eyewitness Account of his Return to the South Seas* (London, Chatham Publishing).

26   Francis Godolphin Bond, 2 August 1791, in Mackaness, ed., 1960, 27.

27   Bligh to Banks, Tenerife, 30 August 1791, Papers of Sir Joseph Banks, 50.13.

28   Bligh to Banks, ibid.

29   Bond in Mackaness, ed., 1960, 31.

30   Bligh to Elizabeth Bligh, 13 September 1791, St Jago, ML Safe1/45, 498–99; quoted in Mackaness, ed., 1938, 319.

31   Bligh in Rutter, 1936, 133.

32   Portlock to Banks, 1 September 1791; Elizabeth Bligh to Sir Joseph Banks, 2 November 1791, Papers of Sir Joseph Banks 51.01, 51.02.

33   Matthew Flinders, Portion of a journal relating to a Voyage in the *Providence* with Captain Bligh, National Maritime Museum, Ms 60/017, FLI/8a. See also George Tobin's description in Schreiber, Roy, ed., 2007, *Captain Bligh's Second Chance: An Eyewitness Account of his Return to the South Seas* (London, Chatham Publishing), 27–28. See also Williams, Anne, 1989, 'Sowse over Head: Crossing the Line on

the *Providence'*, *Pacific Island Focus* (Laie, Hawai'i, Institute for Polynesian Studies, Brigham Young University, Hawai'i), 23–44 for a discussion of Tobin's account of this ceremony.

34   Bligh to Banks, 17 December 1791, Papers of Sir Joseph Banks, 50.17.
35   Tobin in Schreiber, ed., 2007, 45–46.
36   Bond in Mackaness, ed., 1960, 35. For an instance of the kind of micro-management that so infuriated Bond during the voyage, see William Bond to Lieut. Frank Bond, 19 June 1793, Orders for the conduct of affairs on HMS *Providence*, ML Safe 1/22b.
37   Tobin in Schreiber, ed., 2007, 54.
38   Ibid., 55.
39   The account of these events is based primarily on the following documents: Te'ehuteatuaonoa ['Jenny'], 1819, Account of the mutineers of the Ship *Bounty* and their Descendants at Pitcairn's Island, *Sydney Gazette*, 17 July: 817; Captain Beechey's published account of his visit in the *Blossom* in December 1825 (Beechey, 1831, I: 66–136); the manuscript account Beechey collected from John Adams on that occasion (ML A1804); and 'Jenny' or Te'ehuteatuaonoa's account, as told to Captain Dillon, 1829, *United Service Journal and Naval and Military Magazine* II: 590. In addition, Glynn Christian's *Fragile Paradise* adds further details from local island traditions. Further information was given by Alexander Smith to Captain Folger of the American ship *Topaz*, who briefly visited Pitcairn in February 1808, the first to do so since Christian and his companions arrived on the island; and Captain Pipon and Captain Sir Thomas Staines during their visit on HMS *Briton* and HMS *Tagus* on 17 September 1814 (Papers of Sir Joseph Banks, Series 71, State Library of New South Wales) – although Smith gave them many misleading details.
40   Shillibeer, Lieut. J. R.N., 1817, *A Narrative of the Briton's Voyage to Pitcairn's Island* (London, Law and Whittaker), 96–97.
41   Ibid., II: 590.
42   Williams, John, 1838, *A Narrative of Missionary Enterprises in the South Sea Islands* (London, J. Snow), 201–2; see Maude, H.E., 1958, 'In Search of a Home: From the Mutiny to Pitcairn Island (1789–1790)', *Journal of the Polynesian Society* 67/2: 121–24 for a discussion.
43   'Jenny', 1829, 591.
44   Gill, Wyatt, 1911, 'Extracts from Dr. Wyatt Gill's papers, No. 123: The coming of Goodenough's ship to Rarotonga in 1820', *Journal of the Polynesian Society* 20: 191–95. See also Maude, 1958, 104–31, who argues strongly that this visit was to Rarotonga.
45   'Jenny', 1829, 590.
46   Lansdown, ed., 2006, 7.
47   Henry, Teuira, 1928, 69. In Mangareva, Pitcairn was known as Matakiterangi, settled by the chief Taratahi (Maude, 1964, 45).
48   John Adams in Beechey, 1831, 81.
49   'Jenny', 1829, 591.
50   Christian, 2005, 243.
51   For the names of the men from Tahiti, Ra'iatea and Tupua'i see 'Jenny', 1819, 817; see also Maude, 1964, 52, who gives a list of names as recorded in a number of sources.
52   Maude, 1964, 51.
53   John Adams in Beechey, 1831, 85.
54   Bligh to Frank Bond, 1 April 1793, ML Mic CY 1480.
55   Bligh, 19 June 1793, Orders given at Otaheite, ML Mic CY 1480; Flinders, Adm 55/97–98, 8 April 1792.
56   Tobin in Schreiber, ed., 2007, 70.

## CHAPTER 19: THIS MODERN CYPRUS

1   Tobin gives the latitude of this island as 22 degrees south and 139 degrees 30 minutes west, which is closest to this atoll.
2   Wilson, James, ed. Thomas Haweis, 1799, *A Missionary Voyage to the Southern Pacific Ocean, Performed in the Years 1796, 1797, 1798, in the Ship* Duff, *commanded by Captain James Wilson* (London, T. Chapman), 183.
3   Ibid., 58.
4   Although in his introduction to the voyage of the *Duff*, Samuel Greatheed of the London Missionary Society claimed that the *Matavy*, the tender built by the *Bounty* mutineers, was later used in the sea otter trade and made the quickest voyage ever known from England to the Sandwich Islands, he appears to have confused the tender with another small ship named the *Prince William Henry*, which according to Greatheed visited Tahiti on 26 March 1792, staying only three days; and making a voyage from Britain to the Sandwich Islands so rapid that it took only four months. Mr Lamport, the first mate of the *Prince William Henry*, recorded further details of this voyage (ML A1963, Haweis papers, 271–72), which confirms this itinerary – so was the *Jenny* actually the *Prince William Henry*, since these vessels are said to have landed in Tahiti on the same day? For a discussion of this conundrum, see David, A.C.F, 1977, 'Broughton's Schooner and the *Bounty* Mutineers', *Mariner's Mirror* 63: 210–11.
5   Bond in Mackaness, ed., 1960, 38.
6   Tobin in Schreiber, ed., 2007, 72.

7   Bligh in Oliver, ed., 1988, 55.
8   Ibid., 56.
9   Portlock, Adm 55/6–7, 14 April 1792.
10  Flinders, Adm 55/97–98, 8 June 1792.
11  Bligh in Oliver, ed., 1988, 62.
12  Bond, Adm 55/96, 12 April 1792.
13  Tobin in Schreiber, ed., 2007, 74. Tobin's journal (which he cleverly disguised as letters) was evidently written after the event, and the chronology is often scrambled – generally it is a day out. The journal fragments from Frank Bond and Matthew Flinders also lack proper chronology. For the sequence of events, Bligh's own journal is largely relied on, which he kept in civil time during his stay in Tahiti (i.e. from midnight to midnight); supplemented by the shipboard logs written by Portlock, Bond and Flinders, all of which are kept in naval time (i.e. from noon to noon, with the date of the second noon corresponding to civil time).
14  Portlock, Adm 55/7, 14 April 1792.
15  Bond in Mackaness, ed., 1960, 40.
16  Tobin in Schreiber, ed., 2007, 78.
17  Bligh in Oliver, ed., 1988, 75.
18  Ibid., 75.
19  Portlock, Adm 55/7, 17 April 1792.
20  Tobin in Schreiber, ed., 2007, 79.
21  Bligh in Oliver, ed., 1988, 80.
22  Portlock, Adm 55/7, 17 April 1792.
23  Bond in Mackaness, ed., 1960, 44.
24  Henry, 1928, 188.
25  Bligh in Oliver, ed., 1988, 94.
26  Flinders, Adm 55/97–98, 16 July 1792.
27  Tobin in Schreiber, ed., 2007, 81.
28  Ibid., 82.
29  Bond, Adm 55/96, Account of Otaheite.
30  Bond in Mackaness, ed., 1960, 40.
31  Bligh in Oliver, ed., 1988, 114.

## CHAPTER 20: BELLE OF THE ISLE
1   Portlock, Adm 55/7, 27 April 1792.
2   Tobin in Schreiber, ed., 2007, 93.
3   Ibid., 94.
4   Bligh in Oliver, ed., 1988, 141.
5   Tobin in Schreiber, ed., 2007, 98.
6   Bligh in Oliver, ed., 1988, 150.
7   Smith, William, 1813, *Journal of a Voyage in the Missionary Ship* Duff, *to the Pacific Ocean in the Years 1796, 7, 8, 9, 1800, 1, 2 &c* (New York, Collins and Co.), 18.
8   Bligh in Oliver, ed., 1988, 162.
9   Ibid., 180.
10  Ibid., 174.
11  Sheridan, 1989, 41.
12  Tobin in Schreiber, ed., 2007, 107–8.
13  Ibid., 109.
14  Ibid., 76–77.

## CHAPTER 21: PARADISE LOST
1   Bligh in Oliver, ed., 1988, 190.
2   Ibid., 192.
3   Tobin in Schreiber, ed., 2007, 110.
4   Bligh in Oliver, ed., 1988, 195.
5   Tobin in Schreiber, ed., 2007, 112.
6   Bligh in Oliver, ed., 1988, 202.
7   Ibid., 210.
8   Ibid.
9   Ibid., 212.
10  Ibid., 215.
11  Ibid., 220. See also Cass, Alan D., 1996, 'The Schooner *Jenny*', *Mariner's Mirror* 83: 325–35.
12  Bligh in Oliver, ed., 1988, 226.

13    Ibid., 227.
14    Ibid., 233.
15    Tobin in Schreiber, ed., 2007, 117.
16    Ibid.
17    Bond, Adm 55/96, 15 July 1792.
18    Tobin in Schreiber, ed., 2007, 119.
19    Bond, Adm 55/96, 16 July 1792. The botanical names of these plants are given in Powell, 1977, 414–16.
20    Tobin in Schreiber, ed., 2007, 119.
21    Bond in Mackaness, ed., 1960, 45.
22    Tobin in Schreiber, ed., 2007, 120.
23    Bligh in Oliver, ed., 1988, 239.
24    Tobin in Schreiber, ed., 2007, 131.
25    Anonymous, 1844, *The Night of Toil: or a Familiar Account of the Labours of the First Missionaries in the South Sea Islands* (London, J. Hatchard and Son), 3.
26    'On reading that Hogs at Otaheite have not the custom of wallowing in the mire', *Evangelical Magazine*, April 1801, 176.

## CHAPTER 22: THE AWFUL DAY OF TRIAL

1    East India Intelligence, *Gentleman's Magazine*, April 1792, 62/4: 372; Historical Chronicle, *Universal Magazine of Knowledge and Pleasure*, May 1792, 90: 393.
2    Commodore (later Admiral Sir) Thomas Pasley was married to a daughter of Thomas Heywood of the Nunnery, Isle of Man, and was thus Heywood's uncle (Smith, D. Bonner, 1936, 228). The Heywood family correspondence, including a number of poems, survives in a number of places: Mitchell Library: Heywood, Mary, letterbook, Mss 5719. Manx National Heritage Library: Transcribed poetry and correspondence, predominantly by or relating to Nessy Heywood and her brother Peter Heywood, Ms 01016; Letter and papers of Hester (Nessie) and Peter Heywood, Ms 09519. Newberry Library: Correspondence of Miss Nessy Heywood, E5. H5078. For more on Peter Heywood, see Smyth, W.H., 1813, 'A Sketch of the Career of the Late Peter Heywood, R.N.', *United Service Journal and Naval and Military Magazine* I: 468–87; and Smyth, W.H., 1831, 'The *Bounty* Again', *United Service Journal and Naval and Military Magazine* III: 305–15.
3    The Heywood correspondence and poems quoted here are from Heywood, Mary, letterbook, ML Mss 5719, which is not paginated. For this reason, no detailed references can be given.
4    Peter Heywood to his mother, 20 November 1791, Batavia, ML M 3075.
5    Nessy Heywood to Peter Heywood, Isle of Man, 29 June 1792, ML Mic CY 2809.
6    Captain (afterwards Admiral Sir) Albemarle Bertie was married to a daughter of James Modiford Heywood of Marristow House, Devon (Smith, D. Bonner, 1936, 228).
7    Henrietta Polden to Elizabeth Bligh, Albany, 12 July 1792, ML Ms Q163, CY Reel 223, 967–70.
8    Henrietta Polden to Elizabeth Bligh, New York, 8 January 1793, ibid., 973.
9    Bligh, Adm 2/3091, R93, quoted in Schreiber, 1991, 71.
10    Fryer, John, in 'Narrative, letter to his wife and documents, 4 April 1789–16 July 1804', ML Safe 1/38.
11    Smyth, W.H., 1843, 'The *Pandora* Again', *Colburn's United Service Magazine and Naval and Military Journal*, 411–20.
12    Peter Heywood, in Heywood, Mary, letterbook, n.d., unpaginated.
13    For fascinating insights into Graham's career and an excellent account of the trial, see Alexander, 2003, 205–7. For a more detailed account of the court-martial, consult her excellent account.
14    T. Bond to F. Bond, ML Mss 6422.
15    Evidence of John Fryer, in Rutter, 1931, 73.
16    Evidence of William Purcell, in ibid., 104, 107.
17    Hayward in ibid., 122.
18    Bligh to Elizabeth Bligh, Coupang, Timor, 19 August 1789, Mitchell Library, ZML Safe 1/45.
19    Hallett in Rutter, 1931, 126–27.
20    Edwards in ibid., 132.
21    Bligh, Logbook of HMS *Bounty*, ML Safe 1/42, 60.
22    Fryer in Rutter, 1931, 149.
23    Cole in ibid., 152.
24    Purcell in ibid., 154.
25    *Gentleman's Magazine*, December 1792, 1097–98.
26    Morrison in Rutter, 1931, 164.
27    Morrison in ibid., 165.
28    Ellison in ibid., 175–76.
29    Burkett in ibid., 185.
30    Peter Heywood to his mother, *Hector*, 20 September 1792, Batavia, ML M 3075.
31    Du Rietz, 1986, 17.

32 See ibid. for a detailed and careful discussion of the history of these manuscripts, and the most likely time of their composition.
33 For a discussion of the legal debate over Muspratt's fate, see Smith, D. Bonner, 1936, 232–37.
34 Morning Chronicle, *European Magazine, and London Review*, 29 October 1792, 22: 395.
35 Rev. William Howell to Capt. Molesworth Phillips, 25 November 1792, Papers of Sir Joseph Banks, 48.01.
36 Morrison, James, 'Memorandum and Particulars respecting the *Bounty* and her Crew', ML Safe 1/33, 39.
37 Du Rietz, 1986, 18–23.
38 Christian, Edward, 1794, *Appendix*, 58.

## CHAPTER 23: A FLOATING FOREST

1 Wiles, James, *Postscript to the Royal Gazette*, 26 October 1793, 19; Papers of Sir Joseph Banks 89.02, 13.
2 Bligh in Oliver, ed., 1988, 267.
3 Tobin in Schreiber, ed., 2007, 138.
4 Ibid.
5 Ibid., 142.
6 Bligh in Oliver, ed., 1988, 249.
7 Portlock, Adm 55/6–7, 10 August 1792.
8 Bligh to Banks, 16 December 1792, Papers of Sir Joseph Banks, 50.21.
9 Bond in Mackaness, ed., 1960, 56–57.
10 Tobin in Schreiber, ed., 2007, 150.
11 Bligh in Oliver, ed., 1988, 255.
12 Scott, quoted in Powell, 1977, 412.
13 Tobin in Schreiber, ed., 2007, 159.
14 Bligh to Banks, 2 October 1792, Papers of Sir Joseph Banks, 50.19.
15 Wiles, James, quoted in Powell, 1977, 395.
16 William Bligh to Elizabeth Bligh, Coupang, 2 October 1792, Mitchell Library, Bligh Family Correspondence, Safe 1/45, CY Reel 178, 502–4.
17 T. Bond to F. Bond, n.d., quoted in Du Rietz, 1965, 1: 28–29. Matthew Flinders was also very upset by this order, and also wrote an angry letter to his brother, NMM, BND/1.
18 Bligh in Oliver, ed., 1988, 256.
19 Bligh to Banks, St Helena, 16 December 1792, Papers of Sir Joseph Banks, 50.21.
20 Tobin in Schreiber, ed., 2007, 164.
21 Wiles, James, *Postscript to the Royal Gazette*, 26 October 1793, 19; Papers of Sir Joseph Banks 89.02.
22 Tobin in Schreiber, ed., 2007, 166.
23 Ibid., 170.
24 Bligh to Banks, 27 January 1793, Papers of Sir Joseph Banks, 50.23.
25 Sheridan, 1989, 28. See also Powell, 1977. In these articles, Powell and Sheridan give excellent accounts of the introduction of the breadfruit to the West Indies.
26 Tobin in Schreiber ed., 2007, 167.
27 Wiles, James in *Postscript to the Royal Gazette*, 27 October 1793, Papers of Sir Joseph Banks 89.02.
28 *Royal Gazette*, Jamaica, 9 February 1793, 15: 10.
29 Bligh, Orders at Jamaica, ML Mic CY 1480.
30 Bligh to Bond, n.d., in Mackaness, ed., 1953, 27.
31 T. Bond to F. Bond, ML Ms 6422.
32 Newscutting from Jamaica, March 1793, Papers of Sir Joseph Banks, 50.26.
33 Schreiber, 1991, 86.
34 Bligh to Banks, 4 August 1793, Papers of Sir Joseph Banks, 50.29.
35 Historical Chronicle, *The Universal Magazine*, 4 September 1793, 93: 234.
36 Bligh in Lee, 1920, 219.
37 Wiles, James, *Postscript to the Royal Gazette*, 26 October 1793, 19; Papers of Sir Joseph Banks 89.02.
38 Bligh to Banks, 30 October 1793, Papers of Sir Joseph Banks, 50.32; and *Lloyd's Evening Post*, 14 August 1793, Issue 5640.
39 *Kentish Register*, 6 September 1793; *Public Advertiser*, 10 September 1793, Issue 18485.
40 Bligh to Banks, 16 August 1793, Papers of Sir Joseph Banks, 50.31.
41 Banks to Lord Chatham, 1 September 1793, Papers of Sir Joseph Banks, 54.01.
42 Bligh to Banks, 30 October 1793, Papers of Sir Joseph Banks, 50.32.
43 T. Pasley to Matthew Flinders, 8 August 1793, quoted in Darby, Madge, 2000, 'Bligh's Disciple: Matthew Flinders's Journals of HMS *Providence* (1791–3)', *Mariner's Mirror* 86/4: 401–11.
44 De Lacy, Gavin, 1997, 'Plagiarism on the *Bounty*', *Mariner's Mirror* 83: 84–90.
45 Peter Heywood, quoted in *Cumberland Packet*, Newspaper cutting, November 1792, Papers of Sir Joseph Banks, 46.35.
46 Ibid.
47 Bligh to Banks, 30 October 1793, Papers of Sir Joseph Banks, 50.32.

48  William Bligh, 16 December 1793, Remarks on Christian's letters, and Remarks on Morrison's Journal, ML Safe 1/43, CY Reel 179, 400.
49  Ibid., 407.
50  Ibid., 426.
51  Ibid., 417.
52  Banks to William Pitt the Younger, Lord Chatham, 5 January 1795, Papers of Sir Joseph Banks, 48.02.
53  *Arts and Entertainment World*, 9 December 1793, Issue 2168.
54  According to Tobin, the person who delivered the letter to the First Lord had been urged to 'observe his Lordship's phiz while perusing it', and reported that Chatham had read it with a smile on his face, and afterwards put it in his pouch. Despite these kindly interventions, however, it was several years before Bond was promoted to post-captain (in Mackaness, ed., 1953, 73–74).
55  Bligh to Bond, 15 January 1794, in Mackaness, ed., 1953, 51.
56  James Guthrie to Bond, 3 January 1794, in Mackaness, ed., 1953, 72.
57  Bligh to Bond, 29 March 1794, in Mackaness, ed., 1953, 52.
58  Christian, Edward, 1794, *Appendix*, 61.
59  Ibid., 61–62.
60  Alexander, 2003, 325–7.
61  Kennedy, 1989, 222–23.
62  Christian, Edward, 1794, *Appendix*, 63.
63  Ibid., 64–65.
64  Ibid., 71.
65  Ibid., 75.
66  Ibid., 76.
67  Ibid., 79.
68  Bligh to Bond, 26 July 1794, 14 August 1794, in Mackaness, ed., 1953, 57–58, 62.
69  Bligh, 1794, 30; see also Joseph Coleman Affidavit, Dixson Library, Sydney, CU Reel 223, Ms 163, 27–28.
70  Keate, George, Esq., 1794, To Captain Bligh, On his Return to England in June 1793, after having in so successful a manner having executed the Commission entrusted to his Care, of transporting the BREAD FRUIT TREE from OTAHEITE to the islands of JAMAICA and ST. VINCENT, in *European Magazine, and London Review*, August 1794, 26: 140.
71  *Critical Review, or Annals of Literature*, March 1795, 13: 359.
72  *British Critic*, December 1794, 4: 686.
73  The quotations from Christian's response to Bligh's *Answer* are taken from Christian, Edward, 1795, *A Short Reply to Captain William Bligh's Answer* (London, J. Deighton).
74  Bligh to Bond, 12 May 1795, in Mackaness, ed., 1953, 66. As Bligh also wrote to George Tobin's father at about the same time: 'I cannot possibly say when my voyage will be printed. – This some time past my drawings have been done, but I do not know if I shall be able to get the Admiralty to assist me. At present books of voyages sell so slow that they do not defray the expence of publishing' (Mackaness, ed., 1953, 81).
75  See David, 1982, 23h, for a listing. Some of these have been published in Lee, 1920.
76  William Bligh to Sir Joseph Banks, n.d., Papers of Sir Joseph Banks, 50.37.

## EPILOGUE: DEATH OF 'THE DON'

1  Rodger, N.A.M., *The Command of the Ocean: A Naval History of Britain, 1649–1815* (London, Penguin Books and the National Maritime Museum), 404.
2  McCormick, E.H., n.d., The Burneys of Queen Square, Alexander Turnbull Library, Ms-papers-5292-237, 358.
3  Dening, 1992, 114.
4  Bligh to Sir Joseph Banks, ML Mss 218.
5  Log of the *Calcutta*, Adm 51/1102. For Bligh's role in quelling the mutiny on the *Defiance*, see William Bligh to Sir Joseph Banks, 19 October 1795, Papers of Sir Joseph Banks, 58.01.
6  Kennedy, Gavin, 1979, 'Bligh and the *Defiance* Mutiny', *Mariner's Mirror* 65: 65–69.
7  Kennedy, 1989, 236.
8  Sir Joseph Banks to Lord Spenser, 10–11 December 1795, Papers of Sir Joseph Banks, 58.02.
9  Ibid.
10  Logs of *Director*, Adm 51/1156, 1195, 1229, 1285, 1398.
11  Bligh's reports of the mutiny on the Nore are in Adm 1/1516, /1524. For a detailed account of these mutinies, see Grint, Keith, 2000, 'The Floating Republics: Political Leadership in the Spithead and Nore Mutinies', *The Arts of Leadership* (Oxford, Oxford University Press); for Bligh's role, see Mackaness, 1951, II: 32–47; Kennedy, 1989, 236–47.
12  For a letter from the *Director* at Yarmouth, see Bligh to Duncan Campbell, 14 October 1796, ML Safe 1/40, CY Reel 178, 330–33.
13  Quoted in Kennedy, 1989, 255.

14  Admiral Duncan to William Bligh, ML Mss C218, 59.
15  *Universal Magazine of Knowledge and Pleasure*, December 1797, 101: 445–46.
16  See David, 1982, 8, 11, for an evaluation of this chart.
17  Wilson, James, ed. Haweis, 1799, 58–59.
18  Ibid., 73.
19  See David, 1982, 3, 8, and Daly, G., 'Captain William Bligh in Dublin, 1800–1801', *Dublin Historical Record* 44/1:20–33, for comments on Bligh's survey of Dublin Bay.
20  Quoted in Schreiber, 1991, 113.
21  Log of the *Glatton*, 51/1333.
22  Rodger, 2004, 470.
23  For an excellent account of Bligh's role in the battle of Copenhagen, see Kennedy, 1989, 259–71.
24  William Bligh, sketch of the Battle of Copenhagen, ML Safe 1/39, 16, and 19–21.
25  Pope, 1972, 177–78.
26  Mackaness, 1936, 64.
27  Millard, ML Mss Ab 60/15. See also Log of the *Monarch*, PRO Adm 51/1333.
28  Pope, 1972, 177–78.
29  Log of the *Irresistible*, PRO Adm 52/1407.
30  Log of the *Warrior*, PRO Adm 51/1407. For the records of the *Warrior* court martial, Adm 1/5349; Adm 1/5367 and Adm 1/5368. Lord Cornwallis letter to Bligh, Adm 1/5368.
31  William Bligh to Frank Bond, 10 July 1805, ML Ab 60/11.
32  For Bligh's defence against Frazier's charges, see William Bligh, 26 February 1805, Papers of Sir Joseph Banks, 58.27.
33  William Bligh to Sir Joseph Banks, 28 February 1805, Papers of Sir Joseph Banks 58.28.
34  Sir Joseph Banks to William Bligh, Torbay, 7 March 1805, Alexander Turnbull Library, Mic 196A. For a fine account of the *Warrior* court martial, which quotes much of the testimony in full, see Mackaness, 1951, 69–94.
35  King to Undersecretary Cooke, 18 June 1808, in F.M. Bladen, ed., 1898, *Historical Records of New South Wales, King and Bligh* (Sydney, William Applegate Gullick, Government Printer), 6: 656.
36  Sir Joseph Banks to William Bligh, quoted in ibid., 6: xxxv–xxxvi.
37  William Bligh to Sir Joseph Banks, 21 March 1805–14 July 1805, Papers of Sir Joseph Banks, 58.29–34.
38  David, 1982, 16a.
39  Mary Putland to her sisters, n.d., and 1 April 1806, ML Safe 1/45, CY Reel 178, 554–63.
40  Mary Putland to Elizabeth Bligh, ML Safe 1/45, CY Reel 178, 557.
41  Quoted in Kennedy, 1978, 345.
42  Elizabeth Bligh to Sir Joseph Banks, 25 January 1808, Papers of Sir Joseph Banks, Series 42; Elizabeth Bligh to the Lords Commissioners of the Navy, 1 February 1808 with enclosures (letter from Rear-Admiral Isaac Coffin, 13 December 1807; affidavit asserting that contrary to statements by Captain Short to the court martial, his wife was already dying when she arrived in New South Wales, having given birth on board the *Porpoise*; that no child of hers had died on the return voyage to England; that Governor Bligh had no orders from the Government to give a land grant to Captain Short). There was also a statement from Lieutenant Tetley, 5 February 1808, denying that Bligh had instigated him to lay charges against Capt. Short, ML Safe 1/43, CY Reel 179, 32–33; and a letter from Robert Campbell, Sydney, 18 February 1808, strongly defending Bligh against any charges, saying that these were due to the wrath of the Corps officers, who 'had acquired immense fortunes by their infamous activities' (ML Safe 1/43, 39–40).
43  Elizabeth Bligh to William Bligh, Durham Place, 15 February 1808, ML Safe 1/49, CY Reel 178, 586–91.
44  Betsy Bligh to Mary Putland, n.d., in ibid., 595–98.
45  Quoted in Mackaness, 1936, 106.
46  Richard Atkins, evidence, in Ritchie, John, ed., 1988, *A Charge of Mutiny* (Canberra, National Library of Australia), which includes a facsimile edition of Bartrum, Mr ed., 1811, *Proceedings of a General Court-Martial, held at Chelsea Hospital, Which Commenced on Tuesday May 7, 1811, and continued by Adjournment to Wednesday, 5 June, following, for the Trial of Lieut.-Col. Geo. Johnston, Major of the 102nd Regiment, late the New South Wales Corps on a Charge of Mutiny, Exhibited against him by the Crown, for Deposing on the 26th of January, 1808, William Bligh, Esq, F.R.S. Taken in short hand by Mr. Bartrum of Clement's Inn, Who attended on behalf of Governor Bligh, by permission of the Court* (London), 161. For an excellent account of Bligh's governorship and the Rum Rebellion, see Atkinson, Alan, 'Sydney's Rebellion', Chapter 13, *The Europeans in Australia* (Sydney, Oxford University Press).
47  King to Undersecretary King, 8 November 1801, National Archives, Kew, CO 201/20: 177–80.
48  William Bligh as quoted by John Macarthur, in Ritchie, ed., 1988, 178–79.
49  Evidence of Sergeant-Major Whittle, and Sergeant Mason, in ibid., 368, 375.
50  John Harris to Anna Josepha King, 25 October 1807, ML Mss A1980, 237–48.
51  Ritchie, ed., 1988, 136.
52  John Harris to Philip Gidley King, 25 October 1807, ML Mss 681/2, 401–8.
53  Statement of John Colonan, WO 32/75.
54  George Johnston to Bligh, 26 January 1808, *Historical Records of New South Wales*, Bladen, ed., 1898, 6: 417.

55    Quoted in Mackaness, 1936, 189.

56    Macarthur, John in Sibella Macarthur Onslow, ed., 1914, *Some Early Records of the Macarthurs of Camden* (Sydney), 153.

57    For letters about the Rum Rebellion, see William Bligh correspondence, ML Safe 1/45, CY Reel 178, 684–816, Safe 1/46, CY Reel 179, 37–381.

58    William Bligh to Elizabeth Bligh, His Majesty's Ship *Porpoise* in the Derwent, 16 June 1809, ML Safe 1/46, CY Reel 179, 205–60.

59    Macquarie, quoted in 1930, *Journal of the Royal Australian Historical Society* 16/1: 27.

60    William Bligh to Elizabeth Bligh, 11 August 1810, *Hindostan*, ML Safe 1/45, CY Reel 179, 739–46.

61    A series of letters over 1808–9 about the rebellion from Elizabeth Bligh to Sir Joseph Banks, with drafts of his replies, are to be found in the Papers of Sir Joseph Banks, Series 42. See also Bligh, William, ed. John Currey, 2003, *Account of the Rebellion of the New South Wales Corps, communicated to Lord Castlereagh and Joseph Banks* (Malvern, Banks Society Publications); and Bligh's account of the Rum Rebellion in *Historical Records of New South Wales*, Bladen, ed., 1898, 6.

62    William Bligh to Frank Bond, 16 December 1810, ML Ab 60/11.

63    Folger, Mayhew, Extracts from the Log Book of Captain Folger of the American ship *Topaz* of Boston; copy of a letter from Mr. Folger, forwarded to Mr. Croker by Rear Adml Rodham, 1 March 1813, Papers of Sir Joseph Banks, 71.01–3; see also Review of *Delano's Voyages and Travels* in *Northern American Miscellaneous Journal* 1815, 5: 244.

64    Sergeant John Harris, in Ritchie, ed., 1988, 327.

65    William Bligh to Frank Bond, 22 July 1811, ML Ab 60/11.

66    All quotes from Mitford, Mary Russell, 1811, *Christina, the Maid of the South Seas* (London, A.J. Valpey).

67    William Bligh to Frank Bond, 14 November 1811, ML Ab 60/11.

68    Additions to Former Obituaries, *Gentleman's Magazine*, May 1812, 486–87.

69    Quoted in Rutter, 1936, 262.

70    Tregellas, Walter, 1884, *Cornish Worthies: Sketches of Some Eminent Cornish Men and Families*, I & II (London, Elliot Stock), 145.

71    Staines, Sir Thomas to Vice-Admiral Dixon, Valparaiso, 1814, Papers of Sir Joseph Banks, 71.08.

72    Shillibeer, Lieut. J. R.N., 1817, *A Narrative of the Briton's Voyage to Pitcairn's Island* (London, Law and Whittaker), 96–97.

73    See David, 1982, 20a for a discussion of this matter.

74    Captain Pipon's Narrative of the State Mutineers of H.M. settled on Pitcairns Island in the South Sea; in Sept. 1814, Papers of Sir Joseph Banks, 71.05; see also *Quarterly Review*, July 1815, 13/26: 352–83; and 'The Descendants of the *Bounty*'s Crew', *United Service Journal*, 1834, pt 1: 191–99.

75    Keith, Brief memorandum relative to HM Ship *Bounty* & the mutineers of her Crew, Papers of Sir Joseph Banks, 71.09, 11 July 1815; see also 'Further account of the Descendants of the Mutineers of the *Bounty*', *Weekly Entertainer, or Agreeable and Instructive Repository*, December 1815, 55: 989–93 for a fuller account.

76    Captain Pipon's Narrative, Papers of Sir Joseph Banks, 71.05.

77    For an account of the melodrama *Pitcairn's Island*, see Alexander, 2003, 440. It seems that a number of the Romantic poets took their opinions about Bligh and the mutiny on the *Bounty* from Christian's family, through mutual friends, including William Wordsworth. Robert Southey, for instance, talked with James Losh, who had been present when Edward Christian interviewed the mutineers captured in Tahiti; and afterwards spoke of Bligh's 'unendurable tyranny', saying that 'if every man had his due Bligh would have had the halter instead of the poor fellows whom we brought from Taheiti'. See Southey, Robert, in Kenneth Curry, ed., *New Letters of Robert Southey*, I and II (New York, Columbia University Press), I: 19. Samuel Taylor Coleridge, who assisted Mary Russell Mitford with *Christina*, thought of writing a narrative poem about Fletcher Christian; while in 1823 Lord Byron (the grandson of Captain Byron, who had preceded Captain Cook into the Pacific) published a long epic, *The Island, or Christian and His Comrades*. Although this epic poem upheld naval discipline and did not vilify Bligh, it made a tragic hero out of Fletcher Christian (see McKusick, James C., 1992, 'The Politics of Language in Byron's *The Island*', *English Literary History* 59: 839–56; Addison, Catherine, 1995, '"Elysian and Effeminate": Byron's *The Island* as a Revisionary Text', *Studies in English Literature, 1500–1900* 35/4: 687–706).

78    George Tobin to Frank Bond, 15 December 1817, ML Ab 60/8.

# Index

Page numbers in *italics* refer to illustrations.

Abbott, Lemuel Francis 406
aborigines 55, 223–4, 341, *225*
Actaeon Group 349
Adam and Eve 396
Adams, John *467*
  *see also* Alexander Smith
Adamstown 344
*Adventure* 55–60
Adventure Bay 55, 129–30, 341
Affleck, Admiral 432
*Agincourt* 448
*ahu* (altars, stone pyramids) 283, 325, 365, 368, 377–8
Aitutaki 204, 244, 256, 259, 260, 299, 300, 336, 419–21, *421*
Alaska 314, 332
alcohol
  consumed by sailors *see* grog
  consumed by Tahitians 157, 326, 356, 376, 380, 384, 385, 428
*Alecto* 116
*Amazon* 450
ambushes and plans for ambushes 63, 182, 252, 274, 289, 346, 424
Amo (chief) 80, 263, 277, 278, 286
*amo'a* rituals 361
amputation of fingers in grief 266, 422
ancestors 60, 74, 142, 153, 157–8, 188, 284
anchor problems 63, 145–6, 171, 205–6, 243, 261, 485n
Anderson, William (surgeon) 65, 83, 94, 109, 192
animals
  brought in by Europeans 65, 78, 88, 134, 136, 140, 145, 146, 182, 249, 255, 279, 338
  taken out by mutineers 244, 245
Antarctic Circle 49, 96
Antrobus, Rev. Mr 437
*Appendix* (Edward Christian) 436–441
Aphrodite (goddess) 17
Arcadia 18, 297, 466
*ari'i* (chiefs) 156, 172

Ari'ipaea (Tu's brother, Teari'ifa'atau) 148
  and Bligh 140, 144–62, 174–200
  and *Bounty*'s men 262–3, 269, 274, 295
  and Cook 76–7, 78
  and *Providence* visit 351–95
  and *Mercury* visit 257
  and Vancouver's visit 322–30
  attack on Matavai Bay 350–1, 354–5
  jealous of Tu 154, 174
  taio of Clerke 140, 148, 322
Ari'ipaea-vahine 77, 274–5, 279, 282, 363–4
*'arioi* 74–5, 95, *177*
  amusements 89–90, 95, 149, 162–3, 185, 266, 375
  black-leg (*avae parae*) 75, 89, *177*
  burlesque performances 149, 169, 257, 364, 379
  dancing 90, *89*, 149, *150*, 188, 364, 379
  dress 149, 167, 188, 196, *199*
  *fa'amu'a* (feeding) ceremony 151
  *fanaunau* (loss of privileges) 166
  *heiva* performances 159–60, 188, 257, 295–6, 364, 379
  lifestyle 95, 202–3
  music 90, 148, 188, 266, 364, 373
  not permitted to have children 74, 143, 153, 166, 203, 373
  *parae* (costumes) 198–200, *199*, 251, 325, 327
  *parae heiva* 167, 181
  warriors *177*
arrowroot pudding 155, 189
artefacts and curiosities 72, 90–1, 207, 365, 373, 375, 379, 432
Articles of War 43–4, 123, 130, 131, 183, 294, 410
*Asia* 445
Assembly of Jamaica 336
*Assistant* 332–3, 337–8
astronomy 313
Atkins, Judge Advocate Richard 460–3
attacks and battles in Society Islands
  attack on Fa'a'a 275–6
  attack on Matavai Bay 350–1, 354–5, 357

  attack on Mo'orea 79, 82–3, 85
  attack on Pa'ea fleet at Pare 253–4
  attack on Papara 276, 449
  attack on Pare 273–4
  attack on Rai'atea 61
  battle at Pa'ea 276–7
attacks on or by Europeans
  at Pitcairn's Island 345–7
  at Tupua'i 242, 245–6, 250–4
  in Hawai'i 34–44
  in Murray Islands 423–4
  in New Zealand 57–9
  in Niue 204
  in Samoa 301
  in Society Islands 87–8, 159, 293–4
  in Tonga 66, 217–18, 303, 304
Atafu 300–1
Atiu 60–1
Auo (Tu's sister, Mahau's wife) 77, 78, 135, 162, 197, 279, 296, 320, 322, 328, 372, 374
  death of Mahau 326
Austral Islands 68, 93, 241–2, 245–54, *247*
Australia 55, 129, 210, 222–4, 333, 458, 459–63
autumn harvest festival 196, 378
*'ava, kava*
  *'ava* 71, 140, 141, 149, 157, 168, 250, 263, 364, 380
  *'ava Peretane* (alcohol) 157, 326, 356, 384
  *'ava* roots as peace offering 246, 249, 250
  *'ava taio* (rum) 292
  *kava* 25, 76, 157, 165, 356, 358, 482n
Avanui Bay, Porapora 94

Bacchus (Bligh's dog) 272
bagpipes 78, 449
Bailey, Colonel 263
Baltic States' embargo on British ships 450–2
Banks, Sir Joseph 18, 49–50, 51, 75, 90, 91, *106*
  and Bligh 109, 112–13, 117, 119, 123, 240, 336–7, 417, 427, 432–6, 446, 456–60

and breadfruit expeditions 108–9,
331–2, 336
and Vancouver's expedition 315
in England after *Endeavour* voyage
107–8
in Tahiti 18, 107, 334–5
Barbados 429
Baret, Jean 255
bark cloth 267
as gifts *142*, 188, 190
clothing 78, 190, 196
incorporation of European patterns
136
intensifying *mana* 135
manufacture and dyeing 165
plants 168, 191
ritual presentation 151, 155
*tiputa* (poncho) 352, 353
wrapping/unwrapping Cook's
portrait 135, 265
wrapping/unwrapping the gods
79, 135, 284, 368–9, 391
wrapping/unwrapping people 23,
24, 25, 135, 142–3, 159, 161, 167,
196–7, 352
Barney (lawyer for Muspratt) 405,
416, 436
barter
for artefacts, curiosities 207, 256,
319, 368, 377, 420
for iron items 136, 326, 333, 348,
352, 420, 422, 424
for red feathers 72, 136, 143
for sex 140, 303, 319, 326, 347
for weapons 31, 256
inventory of items on *Bounty*
116–17
rules and prohibitions 131–2, 168,
319, 326–7, 347, 363
Batavia (Jakarta) 231–2, 240, 308–11,
331
Bayly, William 28, 40, 42, 66, 67,
72, 90
Beaglehole, J.C. 44
Beaufort, Commander Francis 458
*Bedford* 415
Beechey, Captain (*Blossom*) 342
beer 122, 341, 349, 370
Bell, Edward 317, 318, 321, 323, 327,
329, 330
*Belle Poule* 101
*Bellepheron* 333
Bennet (volunteer) 341
Bentham (purser on *Pandora*) 292
Bentinck, William 335
Bertie, Captain Albermarle (*Edgar*)
401
Bertie, Emma 401
*Berwick* 101–2
Betham, Dr Richard 46, 105, 115, 400
*Bethia* 110–11
*Betsy* 452
birds 198, 199–200, 324
Bligh (née Betham), Elizabeth (Betsy)
children 102, 446, 452, 469
described in *Gentleman's Magazine*
469
epitaph 469
first meeting with Bligh 46
illness and death 446, 464, 469
relationship with W. Bligh 13–14,
50–1, 104, 121, 228, 229, 338,
425, 443, 458–9, 469
wedding day 101

Bligh, Anne 446
Bligh, Elizabeth 109, 371, 459
Bligh, Fanny 425
Bligh, Frances 469–70
Bligh, Harriet 102, 103, 104, 229, 425
Bligh, Henrietta 401–2
Bligh, Jane 425, 469–70
Bligh, Mary 104, 229, 425, 452, 457–8,
462, 464
Bligh, William ('Parai') 17, 19–21,
75, 142
account of Cook's death 41–4
accusing men of theft 208–9, 124,
435
admiration of Cook 129
ambitions 47, 50–1
and Banks 109, 112–13, 117, 119,
123, 240, 336–7, 417, 427, 432–6,
446, 456–60
and Bond *see* Bond, Frank
and Christian 105, 204–5, 206–7,
209–15, 435, 438, 456
and Cook
Bligh 'Cook's son' in Tahiti 20,
139, 159, 174, 260, 376
Cook as mentor 47–8, 54, 68,
94–5, 124–5, 158, 442–3
in Hawai'i with Cook 22–44
in Tahiti with Cook 69–97
*passim*
master of *Resolution* under
Cook 22–44, 47–96
and Fryer *see* Fryer, John
and Horatio Nelson 450–2
and John Gore 100
and John Macarthur 460–3
anti-scourbotic regime 117, 122–3,
128, 129, 131, 341
breadfruit collection and delivery
*see* breadfruit expeditions
character paradoxes summarised
13–14, 442–3, 472
charts and surveys 30, 56, *139*
Christian's use of 342
Hydrographic Office 41, 67–8,
106, 452
misattributed 44, 67–8, 100,
105–7
on *Bounty* 130, *139*
on *Bounty's* launch 221, 224–5
royalties 109
under Cook 19, *30*, 31, 54–5,
*56*, 62, 67–8, 96, 100, 105–7,
221, 225
compared to Cook, Edwards and
Vancouver 443
court martial re *Bounty* 240, 289,
433
court martial re *Warrior* 453–6
court martial threats made to men
130, 183, 186, 196, 210
death from cancer 471
devoted to wife and family 13–14,
121, 228, 229, 338, 425, 443, 469
domestic life contrasted with public
image 13–14, 443, 469
early life 45–6
early Naval career 45–7
epitaph 471–2
financial abuses 123–4, 232, 240,
417, 459
flawed as commander 442–3
'flogging captain' myth debunked
443

floggings *see* floggings
Governor of New South Wales
457, 459–63, *464*
arrested 462–3
captured *464*
effigy burned in New South
Wales 463
humiliating his men 20, 130–1,
196, 206–9, 426–7, 438, 442–3,
456
illness 156, 231, 232, 337–8, 340,
342, 354, 355, 360, 376, 383, 386,
425, 446
in Tahiti on *Bounty* and *Providence*
acquisition of Cook's *mana* 84
acquisition of Cook's *taio*
friendships 20, 77, 81,
141–2, 174–5
affection for people of Tahiti
201
ambivalence of chiefs on
*Providence* visit 351
ambushed 182
*ari'i* of Matavai Bay 167–8,
356–7
*ari'i* in Pare 189–90
disillusioned on *Providence* visit
375–6, 379–8, 386, 419
enjoyment of Tahitian life 20,
153–4, 183, 201
harsh treatment of men 176–9
*mana* damaged by deceit 351,
376, 392
marginalised on *Providence* visit
378–9, 385, 386, 388, 391,
394–5
offending Tu's family 381, 395
refraining from taking hostages
93, 145–6, 176, 372–3
support of Pomare lineage 351,
354, 357
*taio* of Po'e'eno 141, 165, 168,
169, 172, 179, 182
*taio* of Tu *see* Tu
taught about Tahitian ways 193
treated like *'arioi* 74, 95
treated with veneration 158–60
treatment of Tahitian thieves
176, 178, 195
in Tonga
attacked 66, 217–18
taking hostages 207–8
injured 53
insecure 442
joining merchant navy 332–3
journey to West Indies with
breadfruit plants 419–31
known as 'the Don' 341
lack of political awareness 442–3,
459–63
marriage to Elizabeth (Betsy)
Betham 101
member of Royal Society 452
memorial in Tahiti 472
mocked 131, 215
mutiny on *Bounty* and following
events 211–16
attacked on Tofua 216–18
back in England 237–40
defending reputation 439–41
exonerated for loss and
promoted 289
in East Indies on homeward
journey 226–34

journey to East Indies on launch 219–26
loss of books, maps, drawings 238
mutineers condemned by Bligh 228–9, 233–4, 239, 395, 435
on *Resource and Vlydt* 230–1, 234–5
on Restoration Island 223–4
on Sunday Island 224
on Turtle Island 225
*persona non grata* in London 433
personal report of mutiny 232–4
religious consolation 216, 220, 222, 223, 227–8, 227–8
self-exoneration 232, 435
snubbed by Lord Chatham 335, 416, 431–3, 436
treated as hero 237–8, 440
mutiny on *Director* 447
on half pay 103, 240, 312, 432, 449, 452, 466
passed over for promotion 44, 100–1, 117–21, 436
'passionate' man 105, 116, 340, 442, 456, 466
perceptions of self 455, 466
physical description 17, 125, 139
positions held after *Resolution* voyage 101–5
praised, honoured 116, 238, 431–2, 445, 448, 459
promoted 46, 102, 240, 445, 446, 451–2, 466, 469
commander of *Calcutta* 445–6
commander of *Director* 446–8
commander of *Glatton* 449–52
commander of *Irresistable* 452
commander of *Monarch* 451–2
commander of *Warrior* 453–6
Rear-Admiral of the Blue 466
Vice-Admiral of the Blue 469
reaction to *Voyage* account inaccuracies 105–7, 129, 470
skills and abilities
as charter and surveyor 224–5
as ethnographer 14, 95, 153, 156, 169, 443
as mentor 104, 113, 341
as seaman 14, 341, 443, 452, 456, 472
tolerated for his strengths 456
vanity 426, 442
verbal abuse and tyranny 14, 20, 125, 130, 164, 176, 178–9, 204, 206, 208–9, 340, 426, 438, 444, 452, 453–6, 461, 463
vilified 426–7, 436–41, 453, 461
*Voyage* annotations 44, 48, 55, 64, 101, 106–7, 470
Bligh, General Edward 45
Bligh, Francis 45, 46
Bligh, Sir Richard Rodney 45
*Bligh's Bad Language*, Mr (Dening) 178
'Bligh's Cap' 19, 54
'Bligh's Entrance' 423
'Bligh's Islands' 221
'Bloody Bay' 245
Boenechea, Don Domingo 71
Bond, Catherine 46
Bond, Frank 332

and Bligh 13, 337, 340, 341, 444, 445, 456, 472
Bligh and Bond reconciled 464
complaining bitterly about Bligh 426–7
in Tahiti with *Providence* 356, 364, 368–9, 376, 392, 393, 394
Bond, Frank Godolphin 331
Bond, John 45, 48, 53, 101, 102, 104, 405
Bond, Tom 430–1
Booby key 225
Borabora *see* Porapora
Boswell, James 18
botanical specimens 315, 335, 429
Botany Bay 109, 110, 114, 117–18, 133, 340, 436, 488n
*Bounty* 20
accusations of incompetence, disloyalty, negligence 151, 196
accusations of theft aboard 124, 208–9
attempted shipwreck by Vaetua 186, 187
Bligh as purser 123–4, 128, 168, 178, 213, 230, 240, 433
Bligh's lack of authority 179, 196
Bligh's lack of privacy 112–13, 125, 179
crew, numbers 112, 118
damaged 122, 173
deck plans *111*
delayed departure, implications 171, 179, 443
described as 'floating island' 342–3
desertion attempt 175–83
destroyed at Pitcairn's Island 344, 465
deterioration of relationships 129, 168, 196, 204–5, 443–4
discipline difficulties 125, 164, 443–4
figurehead 112, 160
formerly *Bethia* 110–11
grounded 171
health and hygiene regime 122–3, 127–8
journey to Society Islands 122–32
mutineers after mutiny *see* mutineers
mutiny 209–15
performance in storms 126–7, 128
preparations in England for voyage 110–21
provisions 117, 122, 123, 209
refit 110–13
repaired and reprovisioned 129
small size of ship 112–13, 118–19, 120, 123, 125, 178–9
taken over by Fletcher Christian 209–15, 241–2
at Pitcairn's Island 342, 343–8
at Tahiti 244–5, 258
at Tupua'i 242–4, 245–54
voyage to Tahiti from England 122–31
Bounty Bay 343–4, *467*
'Bounty Isles' 130
Bougainville, Louis-Antoine de 17, 118, 255, 489n
boxing matches 24, 27, 28, *28*, 29, 95, 181, 282

Boyack, Lieutenant (*Warrior*) 454
breadfruit 20
baked 174
flowering signalling Season of Plenty 150–1, 193
harvest celebrations 265–7
*mahi* (fermented) 363, 384
varieties 150–1, 193, 362, 384, 494n
breadfruit expeditions
Banks's role 108–13, 336
*Bounty* expedition
collection on Tahiti 141, 153, 154, 161, 171
dumped from *Bounty* after Mutiny 242, 244, 342–3
journey to Tahiti to obtain 122–37
plants on board 173, 179, 200–1
preparation for voyage 108–21
*Providence* expedition 331–96, 419–31, *430*
collection on Tahiti 357, 360, 361–2, 368, 380, 386, 389, 391
delivery at Jamaica 429–30
delivery at St Helena 427
delivery at St Vincent 429
inventory of plants 393, 424
journey to West Indies 419–27
perished plants 425, 426
praise and rewards 431, 432, 436
preparation for voyage 331–7
Britain ('Peretane') 88, 133, 139, 157, 172, 185, 325, 392, 420, 449
*Britannia* 104, 105, 113, 173, 218, 241, 333, 440
*British Queen* 123
*Briton* 470
Brooke, Governor 427
Brown, John 255, 256, 263–5, 270, 288–9, 293–4
Brown, William (gardener's assistant) and Cook 484n
death at Pitcairn's Island 346
during mutiny 212
in Tahiti with Bligh 141, 149, 153, 163
with Christian after mutiny 248, 258, 344
Broughton, Lieutenant 314, 317–29
*Brunswick* 417
Bruny Island 55, 129–30, 341
Burke, Edmund 236
Burkett, Thomas (able seaman) 163
and 'Mary' (Te'o) 245, 294, 317
and mutiny 211–12
at Tahiti after mutiny 259–60, 264, 269, 271, 276–8, 282–3, 287–8
attacked at Tupua'i 252–3
court martial evidence 413–14
hung 414, 417, 444
on *Pandora* 294–5, 306–7
return to England 308–11
shipwrecked 306–8
burlesque skits/plays 149, 169, 257, 364, 379
Burney, Fanny 98, 109, 238
Burney, James 35, 50, 54, 57, 59, 60, 61, 72, 83, 94, 100, 238, 336, 443, 466
Butcher, James (on *Matilda*) 349, 392

Byrne, Michael (able seaman) 116, 123, 163
  acquitted of mutiny 414
  and mutiny 213, 215, 407, 408, 409, 410, 437, 439
  at Tupua'i after mutiny 249
  at Tahiti after mutiny 258–9, 262, 264, 269–70, 272–3, 274, 280, 283, 287–8
  fiddler 123
  return home 305–6, 307
Byron, Captain John 300

Calcutta 445–6
Cambridge 102
Campbell (second mate on Matilda) 349, 350
Campbell, Duncan 46, 101–9, 113, 119, 120, 122, 123, 128, 229, 413, 429, 435, 437, 444
Campbell, Vice-Admiral John 101, 105
Campbell, Dr Neil 46
Camperdown 448
cannibalism 58, 59, 67, 225, 234
cannons 38, 40, 72, 112, 137, 200, 254, 384, 428
canoes
  at Aitutaki 300, 421, 421
  at Tupua'i 254
  belonging to Pomare II 365
  burnt or destroyed in raids 57, 87, 146, 275
  carrying human sacrifice 390
  in Fiji 422
  in Hawai'i 26
  in Tonga 207
  Matavai fleet 81–2, 82
  Rainbow (sacred canoe) 278
  va'a motu (large outrigger canoes) 187–8
Cape of Good Hope 53, 127–9, 143, 152, 234, 311, 338–40, 450, 458
Cape Horn 120, 126–7, 128, 291, 443
Carteret, Philip 343
cartography see maps
carvings 184, 254, 278, 283, 300, 367, 368, 377–8, 381, 420
cats 63, 88, 161, 163, 172, 200, 205, 245, 249, 307, 338
chants and songs
  'arioi 158–9, 189–90, 325
  priests 25, 167, 169, 265–7, 273, 284, 325, 368
  warriors 26, 37
  women 163, 364
Charlotte, Queen 77, 90, 432
charts and surveys, Bligh see Bligh
Chatham 314–15
Chatham, Lord 335, 416, 431–3, 436
Chelsea Physic Garden 108
chiefly system 153
childbirth 153, 192
children
  games 181
  infanticide 74, 143, 153, 166, 192, 203, 373
  of sailors 294–5, 317–18, 352, 373
  tama aitu (sacred children) 147–8, 197, 363–4, 383, 385
Chile 486n
China 133, 136, 314, 332
'cholera morbus' 150, 156
Christian, Charles 113, 238–9

Christian, Edward 105, 113, 114, 236
  Bligh's response to attack 439–41
  publication of account
    undermining Bligh 433–41, 442, 453, 471
Christian, Fletcher (master's mate, 'Titereano') 20, 105, 113–14
  and Bligh
    humiliated and verbally abused 204–5, 206–7, 209, 435, 438, 456
    indulged and promoted 105, 125, 435
    voyage to Tahiti 122–31
  and Mauatua ('Isabella') 245, 250, 251, 258, 344, 345, 346
  at Pitcairn's Island 343–8
  at Tupua'i after mutiny 242–4, 245–54
  children 344
  family reactions in England to mutiny 238–9, 433–41
  financial debt to Bligh 128
  in Cook Islands with mutineers 342–3
  in Tahiti
    after mutiny 244–5, 258–61, 318, 352, 358, 371
    fond of Tahitian women 176–7, 442
    in charge of shore camp 149
  in Tonga with mutineers 343
  killed at Pitcairn's Island 346
  mutiny events on Bounty 206–15, 408
  plan to desert from Bounty 176–7, 210
  popular 244–5, 433–4, 438, 442
  'romantic hero' 471
  skills and abilities 113–14, 120–1, 130
  stealing on Tupua'i 250, 259, 262
Christian, Joseph 433–4
Christian, Thursday October 344, 471
Christianity 497–8n
  and Tahitian beliefs 154
  at Pitcairn's Island 471
  Bligh's consolation after mutiny 216, 220, 222, 223, 227–8
  divine service 123, 167, 191, 223, 264, 265, 347, 357, 362, 370, 374, 380
  evangelical, in Britain 334–5, 382, 395, 396
  Heywood's faith 404, 415 16
  missionaries 74–5, 334–5, 395, 433, 449, 494n
  Morrison's faith 308, 404
  Tahitians interested in European gods 154, 264
Christina, the Maid of the South Seas (Mitford) 466, 468
Christmas 122, 171, 173, 265, 280, 321, 340
'Christmas Harbour' 54, 485n
Churchill, Charles (master at arms)
  at Tahiti after mutiny 244–5, 248, 260, 263–5, 267–72
  and Thompson 268–9, 270
  ari'i of Southern Tahiti 269, 322
  killed by Thompson 271, 318, 369–70, 377

  leadership aspirations 267
  shooting at Tahitians 270
  taio of Vehiatua III 268, 269
  desertion attempt 175–6, 182–3, 186–7, 258–9, 318
  during mutiny 210–12, 214–15, 399, 407, 408, 412, 413
Cinnamon, Robert (Warrior) 454, 456
Clarence, Duke of 431–2
classical allusions 17–21
Clerke, Captain Charles ('Tate') 49
  and Banks 49–50, 53
  commander of Discovery 22–44, 50–68
  illness, death 43, 51, 83–4, 91, 96–7
  in Hawai'i 26–44
  in Society Islands 69–97
  plot to kill Clerke 93
  relationship with Cook 51
Clerke, John 50
clothing and dress
  as gifts 94, 153, 358, 394
  bark cloth 78, 190, 196
  breastplates 190, 204, 281, 282, 284, 327, 354, 420, 422
  European clothing worn by islanders 163, 275, 389
  helmets, headdresses 26, 262, 276, 373, 381
  masks 167
  parae ('Chief Mourner' costumes) 189–200, 199, 251, 325, 327
  stolen 57, 266, 301, 303, 326, 327–8, 350, 355, 372, 386–7, 389
  worn by Ma'i 48, 281
Cock, Henry 453–4
cock-fighting 183
'Cockroach Point' (Taipipi) 273, 274, 276, 281, 364, 367
Cole, William (boatswain) 116, 163
  and mutiny 212–15, 402, 407, 408–9, 412–13
  berated by Bligh for neglect of duty 181–2
  with Bligh after mutiny 220, 230, 241
Coleman, Joseph (armourer) 116, 138
  acquitted of mutiny 414
  and mutiny 211–15, 241, 242, 369, 371, 407, 408, 409, 410, 437, 439, 440, 441
  at Tahiti after mutiny 258–93 passim, 318, 320, 400
  escaping from Bounty 261
  illness 280
  popular for ironwork skills 261, 269
  surrender 291
  tricked 280
  at Tupua'i after mutiny 244–54
  on Pandora 293, 305–8
  testimony at court martial 408–9
Coleridge, Samuel Taylor 466
Collet (gunner) 319–20
Colnett, James 315
Commerson, Philibert 17
Connor (sailor on Matilda) 349, 350–1, 392
Const (lawyer) 405, 411, 416
consumption see tuberculosis
convicts
  labour 457, 459

settlements 109–10, 133, 308, 336, 340, 349, 456–7
ship transport 46, 110, 133, 234, 331, 349
Cook, James ('Kuki', 'Tute') 67, *83, 99*
  attack on Mo'orea 87–8, 134
  death 38–44, 96, 98–9, *99, 260,* 314, 484n
  death concealed from Tahitians 132, 134, 139, 161, 244, 351, 362
  hero in England 98–9
  in Hawai'i 22–44
  in New Zealand 57–60
  in Society Islands 69–96
  in Tonga 62–8, 343
  journey to Tahiti from England 53–68
  'lapse of dignity' 67
  last voyage 22–96
  *mana* 125, 131–2
  navigational skills praised 53–4
  portrait 17, 20, *83*, 84, 134–5, 141, 292, 449
    desired by Tobin 391
    inscribed by Bligh 201, 255, 359, 394
    inscribed by Edwards 296–7, 322, 359
    inscribed by Vancouver 359
    no more room for inscriptions 391
    venerated 158–9, 160, 265–6
  punishment over-harsh 65, 90, 178
  refusal to engage in island warfare 79
  refusal to punish or avenge 58–9, 66, 67, 124
  reputation 42–3, 44, 84, 98
  search for Terra Australis 313
  *taio* of Kalani'opu'u 25–6
  *taio* of Tu 73–88, 94
  violent outbursts 67, 86–8, 90, 91, 125
Cook Inlet 96
Cook Islands 60–1, 204, 244, 256, 259, 260, 299, 300, 336, 342, 419–21, *421*
Cookson, Rev. 437
Corner, Captain (*Crescent*) 46
Corner, Robert 289, 290, 292–3, 300–7
Cornwallis, Lord 453
cosmos 74, 167, 188, 191
courts martial
  Bligh 240, 289, 433, 453–6
  *Bounty* mutineers 406–18
  Edwards 405
  Johnstone 465–6, 468–9
  Short 458
cows 78, 88, 156–7, 246–6, 251, 259
Cox, Captain John Henry (*Mercury*) 254, 255–7, 260, 263–4, 282, 286, 336
creation story of Tahiti 74
*Crescent* 46
Cythera 17, 297, 349

*Daedalus* 340
daggers 26, 31, 37–8
Dalrymple, Alexander 336
Dalrymple Island 424
dancing
  *'arioi 89,* 90, *89,* 149, *150,* 188, 364, 379

erotic 78–9, 159–60, 257, 364
  *hura* 295–6
  in Tonga 63
dark and light *see* Te Po; Te Ao
Darwin, Erasmus 107–8
David, A.C.F. 221
Davis, Natalie Zemon 21
death
  burials 28, 165–6, 192, 426
  chiefs 157–8, 325–6
  embalming 157–8, 381–2
  funerary biers/burial platforms 157, 166, 192, *366, 377,* 381, 384
  mourning rituals 157–8, 194–5, 206, 326, 381, 422
  *ra'a* (sacred restriction) 364
  sailors' funerals 28, 165–6, 354, 381–2
  slashing of head in grief 92, 165, 194, 195, 208, 249, 295, 325, 381, 389, 393
  *tapu* 325–6
  use of coffins by Tahitians 192, 195
Delafons, John 402
*Defiance* 445–6
Dening, Greg 21, 178
Denman, Arthur 240
Denmark 450–2
desertion and potential desertion 76, 152, 418
  under Bligh 91–6, 116, 175–83, 186–7, 210, 233, 318, 341, 354, 392, 418, 422, 429, 444
  under Cook 46, 83–4, 136, 178, 179, 233, 242
  under Fletcher Christian 244
Desolation Island 19, 54, 55, 100
*Director* 446–8
*Discovery* 17
  mast snapped on way to Tahiti 68
  on Cook's last voyage 22–96
  under Vancouver 312–30
*Discovery* (named after Cook's consort vessel) 314, 315
disease *see* sickness and disease; venereal disease
dogs
  as gifts 172
  as pets 270, 272
  bartered 206
  cooked 357
  dumped at Tahiti 200
  from England 60, 255, 272
  hair used for decoration 89
  killed in rampages 87
  sacrificed 323–4
  trial of 'cannibal dog' 59, 234
Dogger Bank battle 101, 102
*Dolphin* 69, 80, 143, 243, 275, 284, 343, 391, 489n
Dolphin Bank 164, 170, 245, 257
drums 63, 80, 90, 148, 188, 266, 284, 364, 368, 373, 503n
Dublin Harbour 449
*Duff* 433, 449
*Duke of Cumberland* 430
Duke of York's Island (Atafu) 300–1
Duncan, Admiral 445, 447
Dungeness Island 424
Dusky Sound 317
dysentery 374, 425, 429

earthquake 449

East Indies 226–34, *227,* 308–11, 424–5
Easter Island 60, 245, 291
eclipses 67, 68
*Edgar* 401
Edgar, Thomas 55, 100
  in Austral Islands 68
  in Cook Islands 60
  in Hawai'i 29, 33–4
  in Society Islands 71, 95, 96
  in Tonga 63, 65
Edwards, Captain Edward (*Pandora*)
  court martial 405
  in Tahiti 291–9
  praised in verse 309–10
  portrayed as tyrant 402–3
  return to England from East Indies 308–11, 401
  search for mutineers 289, 291–304
  shipwrecked 305–8
  testimony at mutineers' court martial 410–11
Ellis, William (surgeon) 95, 101
Ellis, William (missionary) 146, 147, 187
Ellison, Thomas (able seaman) 114
  and mutiny 211, 371
  at Tahiti after mutiny 259, 260, 264–5, 269–70, 272–3, 274, 280, 283, 287–9
  court martial evidence 408, 409, 410, 413, 414
  hung 414, 417, 444
  surrender and return to England 289, 293, 307, 308
  with Christian after mutiny 229, 241, 248–9
Elphinstone, William (master's mate) 116, 205, 206, 208, 230, 240
  death in Batavia 240
Elysium/Elysian fields 19, 81, 297
embalming 157–8, 381–2
*Endeavour* 18, 42, 69, 80, 107, 108, 286, 314
Endeavour Straits 208, 299, 302, 307–8, 331, 393
entertainment *see* boxing; dancing; music; skits; wrestling
equatorial crossings 53, 123, 338–9
*erauaua* ceremony 369
'Eua 304
European mythic projections 17–21, 297–8
*Eurydice* 114, 263
*Evangelical Magazine* 396
Eve 395, 396
exchanges of names 25–6, 85, 141–2, 189–90, 246, 322, 352–3
  *see also taio*

Fa'ahotu 344–5
*fa'toira'a* feast 361
face and body painting 89, 420
*Falcon* 240
*fare atua* (god-houses) *170, 275, 278, 284, 367, 368, 377*
Fare Harbour, Huahine 88
*Fare no Peretane* built for Bligh 449
*fare noa* (profane, unrestricted houses) 197
*fare ra'a* (sacred house) 262
*fare tupapa'u* (funerary platform) *366, 377*
Farero 'i *marae* 157

*fata* (sacrificial platforms) 368–9
Fatafehi (Tu'i Tonga) 62–7, 303–4
feasts 263, 318, 361
fertility rituals 24, 159–60
Fiji archipelago 221, 442–3
Finau 62–6, 205, 207, 216, 217, 301
fine mats 165, 181, 246, 266, 274–5
fireworks displays 63–4, 65, 74, 90, 91, 324, 325, 384, 390
Fisher, Rev. Dr 437
fishing 174, 185–6, 363, 366, 371, 385
Flinders, Matthew 224–5, 333, 339, 349, 353, 362, 432
floggings 178, 316, 403
 Bligh's men 126, 128, 152, 164, 178, 183, 186, 194, 204, 363, 375, 386, 446
 by Christian at Tupua'i 243
 Cook's men 59–60, 90, 91, 94, 178
 Edwards' men 294, 403
 Hawai'ians 33
 Tahitians 90, 194, 195, 266, 281, 326, 377
 Tongans 63, 65, 205
 Vancouver's men 316, 326
Folger, Matthew 464–5, 466
Fonualei 302
food
 as gifts 133, 322, 327
 Bligh and men starving after mutiny 216, 219–26
 chiefly food 369
 lavish feasts 263, 318
 served British-style 366
 shortages for slaves in West Indies 109, 110
 Tahitian diet 174
 *see also specific foods*
Ford, Commodore 429
Forster, George 47, 53–4, 55, 118, 126
Forster, Johann Reinhold 18–19, 195
Fort George 249–54
France 69, 132
 Revolution 21, 235–6, 405, 411, 437, 445, 447
 war on Britain 430, 444–5
Franklin (surgeon on *Assistant*) 362, 365–6, 370, 371–2, 373
Frazier, John (*Warrior*) 453
French West Indies 110
Fresne, Marion du 47
Frewen, Rev. 437
friendship 369
 *see also taio*
Fryer, John (master) *115*, 116
 and Bligh 124, 125, 129–31, 168, 181–2, 204, 212, 207, 208
 at Bligh's court martial 240
 during mutiny 208–15, 407–8
 evidence at mutineers' court martial 407–8
 with Bligh after mutiny 216–35
fur trade 255, 314, 332, 350, 501n

games 19, 181, 183
gardens *see also* plantations; trees
 destroyed 85, 90, 146, 275, 276, 281, 357
 planted by Bligh 130, 144, 152, 153, 325, 341, 380
 planted by Christian 324
 planted by Cook 78, 88, 144, 325

planted by Stewart and Heywood 318
planted on Pitcairn's Island 470
 Tahitian 168, 191
Garden of Eden 20, 297, 330, 396
gastroenteritis 150, 156
Gatty, Dr 469
genital distortion (male) 188, 326
genital exposure 74, 78–9, 159, 163, 188, 296, 326, 497n
George III, King ('Kini Iore') 77, 82, 108, 147, 367, 384–5, 389, 390, 394, 449
Gibraltar 102
Gibson, Samuel 69, 139
gift-exchanging rituals 26–7
Gilbert, George 39, 65, 85, 87–8, 95
*Glatton* 449–52
'Glorious children of Tetumu' 60–1, 286
gods
 abandoned 195
 behaviour of people during sacred rituals 180
 *fare-atua* (god-houses) *170, 275, 278, 284, 367, 368, 377*
 farewell to the gods for Season of Scarcity 386
 generative power 188
 god-images in Hawai'i 24–5, 26, 29, 32
 god-images in Tahiti 79, 188, 365
 peace-making ritual 367–8
 'Oro 73, 74, 78–9, 184, 195
 Season of Plenty rituals 159–60
 *to'o* images 188, 365
 Tupua'i household gods stolen by Christian 250, 259, 262
 wrapping/unwrapping the gods in rituals 79, 80, 135, 284, 368–9, 391
Gore, John 38, 39, 50, 51, 60, 69, 75, 90, 97, 100
Gore, John (son) 333
Gore, Provost Marshall William 461
*Gorgon* 311, 401
Gosse, Thomas 430
Graham (lawyer) 405, 415
Grass Cove killings 57–9, 67
Great Barrier Reef 222, 305–7, 312, 317, 319, 401, 505n
Great Women (of Tahiti) 135, 143, 193, 267
Greek and Roman mythic parallels *see* European mythic projections
grog 22, 131, 173, 209, 249, 341, 445
 *see also* rum
*Guardian* 234
guns and ammunition
 as gifts 201, 263, 329
 desired by Tahitians 84, 148, 152, 256
 salutes 84, 279, 321, 329–30, 358, 360, 390, 424
Guthrie, Lieutenant 332, 339, 357, 359, 364, 380–1, 386–7, 389, 423

Ha'amanimani (priest) 193, 356
 and Bligh's *Bounty* visit 14, 152, 192–3, 351
 and Bligh's *Providence* visit 351–95 *passim*
 and *Duff* missionary visit 449
 and Vancouver's visit 319, 321–2,

323–4, 327–30, 351, 352, 376, 394–5
 at Taputapuatea *marae* 325, 368–9, 390
 attack on Papara dynasty 276
 English vocabulary 365
 installation of Pomare II 283
 taken hostage 257, 276
Ha'amanino Bay 91, 93
Ha'apai Islands 63
Haggerstein (*Matilda*) 449
hair used decoratively 204, 250, 254, 373, 391, 502n, 503n
Hall, Thomas (ship's cook) 163, 231
Hallet, John (midshipman) 114, 176
 acquitted of mutiny 416
 and Bligh after mutiny 223, 229, 230, 241
 and mutiny 211–13, 399, 439, 441
 back in England 397
 court martial evidence 409–13
 evidence at court martial 409–10
Hamilton, George 290, *290*, 291–301 *passim*
Harris, John 461
Harrison, John 91
Harvey, William 43, 50, 90, 100, 483n
Harwood, Edward (surgeon on *Providence*) 338, 353, 362, 364, 368–70, 377–8, 383, 436, 439–40
Hastings, Warren 238
Hawai'i 22–44, 60, 96
Haweis, Dr Thomas 334–5, 395, 433, 507n
Hayward, Thomas (midshipman) 114
 and Bligh 175–6, 183, 209, 215, 30, 288, 290
 and mutineers at Tahiti 288–95
 back in England 401
 during mutiny 211–13, 341
 evidence at court martial 409–10
 *taio* of Vaetua 154, 175, 183, 186, 261, 289, 293, 295, 321
*Hector* 401, 416
*heiau* (stone temple) 22, 24, 26–7, 28, 29, 32, 40, 42, 217, 481n
Heildbrandt, Henry (cooper) 163
 and Bligh 371
 and Christian after mutiny 249
 and mutiny 212, 408
 at Tahiti after mutiny 259, 262, 264, 265, 269, 270, 280, 287
 drowned in shipwreck 306
 on *Pandora* 294, 300, 306
*heiva* ('*arioi* performances) 134, 159–60, 188, 257, 295–6, 364, 379
 *heiva purae* 167–8
 *heiva Peretane* (British entertainment) 324–5
 *heiva ra'a* (sacred *heiva*) renamed *upaupa* 373
Henry, Teuira 188, 195
Henshaw, John 46
Hewitt (surgeon's mate) 322–3
Heywood, Henry 403
Heywood, James Modiford 397, 398, 401, 402
Heywood, Nessy
 support of brother Peter 239–40, 397–406, 414–17, *399*, 433
Heywood, Peter (midshipman) 114–15, *399*
 and Fletcher Christian 210, 228–9, 233, 241, 248, 251–2, 433

and mutiny 176–7, 317
character testimonials from
    shipmates 412, 415
court martial, statement of defence
    411–12
family and legal support in England
    239–40, 397–406, 414–17
in Tahiti after mutiny 258–9,
    267–8, 399–400
in Tahiti with Bligh 149, 158, 163,
    176–8
journey to Tahiti with Bligh 127,
    128, 130
pardoned 414, 416, 433
poem about Tahiti 403–4
religious faith 404, 415–16
surrender in Tahiti 291–2
*taio* of Te Pau 262
Hikiau sacred site, Hawai'i 22, 23, 25,
    26, 28–9, 32
Hiro (god) 145, 162, 379, 386
Hiterire (chief) 246, 249–50
Hitihiti 75–6, *76*, 134–7
and Bligh 152, 155–7, 163, 182,
    191, 194, 200
and *Bounty*'s men 245, 252, 262,
    276–7, 292
and Edwards 287, 292, 299–300,
    354
desire to go to England 136
war exploits 270–1, 276–7
Hiva 253
Hodges, Joseph 305–6
Holwell, Colonel James 239
Home, Alexander 43, 85, 93, 96
Homer 19, 20
Hood, Lord Samuel 121, 332, 402,
    404–7, *406*, 414
horses 53, 72, *73*, 84, 88, 89, 134, 137,
    140, 203, 281
hostage and potential hostage
    situations 35–7, 65, 90, 92–4,
    145–6, 176, 178, 207, 217, 250, 257,
    277, 291, 292, 372–3, 483n
houses
    *ari'i rahi* 147
    *'arioi* 75, 326
    at Aitutaki 421
    built for Pomare II 364–5
    burnt or destroyed in attacks 85,
        87, 146, 275, 276, 357, 360
    *fare atua* (god-houses) *170*, 275,
        *278, 284, 367, 368, 377*
    *Fare no Peretane* built for Bligh
        449
    *fare noa* (profane, unrestricted
        houses) 197
    *fare ra'a* (sacred house) 262
    Ma'i's house at Huahine 88, 203,
        498n
    on Pitcairn's Island 344
    on Tupua'i 254
    'The House for the Men of
        England' 318
    Tu's house at Pare 366
'House of Lono' *24*
Howe, Lord 102, 113, 119–20, 446
Howell, Rev. William 415–17, 433
Huahine 88–91, 94, 203–4, 243,
    281, 299
Huggan, Thomas ('Teronu', surgeon)
    116, 126, 130, 131, 162, 165–6,
    170, 255
human sacrifices *80*, 503n

and investiture of Pomare II
    285–5
eaten by gods 184
in peacemaking rituals 83, 368–9
offered as sign of atonement
    390–1
offered for success in war 79–81
offered in apology 374, 386
on Tupua'i 254
view of Europeans 373
*Hunter* 46
Hunter, Captain John 117–18, 340,
    436
hurricane season 161, 171, 179
Hydrographic Office 41, 67–8, 106,
    452
hygiene
    on ships 122–3, 128, 129, 341, 388
    Tahitians 174

'ihi ari'i ceremony 196
Ikaifou (chief) 217
illness *see* sickness and disease
'inasi ceremony 67, 67, 303
Indian Ocean 47, 53–4, 312
infanticide 74, 143, 153, 166, 192,
    203, 373
investiture ceremony (Pomare II)
    281–6
*Invincible* 457
'Irihonu pass (To'ofaroa)
Irish Sea 46
*Irresistible* 452
'Isabella' (Mauatua, partner of
    Christian) 245, 250, 251, 258, 344,
    345, 346
*Isis* 451
Isle of Man 46, 101, 102, 103–5, 113,
    114, 128, 229, 414
Isle of Wight 119–21, 235
'Itia (Tu's wife) 135
    and Bligh's *Bounty* visit 141–8,
        153–4, 158–60, 162, 164–5, 169,
        184–201
    and Bligh's *Providence* visit 351–95
    and *Bounty*'s men 266–7, 281–2
    and her children 147–8, 197,
        363–4, 381, 383, 390
    and *Mercury* visit 255–6
    and Vancouver's visit 320–30, 352
    astute and capable 135, 143, 255,
        256
    'Great Woman' 135, 267
    *taio* of Tobin 352

Jamaica 429
*Jenny* 350, 388
'Jenny' (Te'ehuteatuaonoa) 245, 250,
    251, 342, 344
Jervis, Sir John 449
Jewell (boatswain, *Warrior*) 454–5
Johnson, Samuel 18
Johnstone, Lieutenant George
    (*Warrior*) 454–5
Johnstone, Major George 462–3,
    465–6
Johnstone, J. 327, 329

Ka'awaloa 26, 30, 33, 35–40, 482n
Kahura (chief) 57–9, *58*
Kalani'opu'u (high chief) 25–37, *26*
Kalimu (chief) 37, 41, 482n, 483n
Kamakaia (chief) 420
Kamchatka 43, 96, 107

Kamehameha 25, 26, 31
Kandavu 423
Kanekapolei 37
Kanina 23
Kao 205
*kapu* (sacred) 25, 28, 30, 32, 481n
Kaua'i 96
Ka'u'u (high priest) 26, 29, 40
Kealakekua Bay, Hawai'i 22–44, *30*,
    96, 107
Keate, George 238, 439, 440
Keith, Admiral 447
Keli'ikea 28–9, 32, 40, 482n
*Kentish Register* 432
Kerguelen 47, 54
Kermadec Islands 133
Kew Gardens 107, 108, 200, 201, 376,
    393, 448, 488n
kidnapping 261, 342, 344–5
King George's Sound Company 332
*King George* 332
King, James 50
    in Hawai'i 28–44
    in New Zealand 59
    in Tahiti 71, 82
    in Tonga 63–4, 66–8
King, John 97, 99–101, 109
King, Governor Philip Gidley 457
King William's Sound 314
'Knights of Otaheite' 177–8, 201–11,
    258
Koa 152, 203, 281
Ko'a'a (priest) 23–4, 30, 31
Koho (chief) 37
Kotu 64
Ku (god of war) 25, 26, 29
Kualelo 315, 328–9
Kupang 226–8, 424–5

La Pérouse 304–5, 423
*Lady Penryhn* 110, 133–7, 138, 143,
    161, 284, 482n
Lake Vaihiria 267
Lamb, Edward 105
Lamb, Robert (butcher) 173, 212,
    215, 240
Lambeth 109, 469, 471, 472
language, bad 178, 354, 376, 444,
    454, 456
language and communication
    in Hawai'ian 314
    in Tahitian
        Bligh 169, 174, 193, 388
        Gibson 69
        Heywood 404, 405, 416
        Peckover 131
        sailors learning Tahitian 266
        Stewart 405
        Tobin 373
    in English 193, 356, 323, 354
    in Spanish 154
    mixed languages 358
    sign language 140
    Tupua'ians with Tahitians 420
Lanyon, William 29, 38–9, 43, 50, 57,
    100, 482n, 483n
Larkham, Lieutenant John (*Pandora*)
    290, 296, 303, 307–10, 398, 410–11
Lau Islands 343
Laycock, Lieutenant 462
Lebogue, Lawrence (sailmaker) 114
    and Bligh after mutiny 218, 241,
        333
    and mutiny 212, 437, 439, 440, 441

in Tahiti 163, 436
Ledward, Thomas (surgeon's
    assistant) 116, 372
    and Bligh 116, 129, 230, 240
    and mutiny 212
    death on homeward journey 240
    in East Indies 231–2
Ledward, Thomas (surgeon's mate)
    116, 129, 212, 230, 231–2, 240, 372
Ledyard, John
    in Hawai'i 23, 25, 29–30, 31–2, 33
    in Tahiti 75
Leith Harbour 445
Lifuka 63–4, 63
light and dark see Te Ao; Te Po
Lima 71, 72, 74, 138, 154
Lind, Andrew (Matilda) 350, 392, 449
Lind, James 122–3
lineage linking 26, 142, 327, 365
Linkletter, Peter (quartermaster)
    116, 240
logs and journals 14, 42, 43, 47–9,
    64, 95, 100, 101, 109, 213, 215, 238,
    426–7, 483n, 491n
London Missionary Society 433,
    449, 497n
London visited by Ma'i 334–5
Lono (god of fertility, peace and
    plenty) 24, 25, 26
Lono (high priest) 33–4, 36
Lono (Kalani'opu'u, chief) 26, 29
Losh, James 437
Lynx 104

Macarthur, John 460–3, 465, 471
McCoy, William (able seaman) 208
    and Christian after mutiny 245,
        248, 258
    and 'Mary' (Te'o) 245, 258, 344
    at Pitcairn's Island 343–7
    child 344
    death 347
    during mutiny 211–12
McIntosh, Thomas (carpenter's mate)
    acquitted of mutiny 413, 414
    and 'Mary' 294, 317, 352, 371, 372
    and mutiny events 212, 214, 215,
        408, 409, 410, 413, 437, 414
    at Tupua'i and Tahiti after mutiny
        242, 258, 262, 264, 269–70, 273,
        280, 283, 285, 287, 371
    capture at Tahiti 294
    on Pandora 294, 296, 305, 307
McIntosh, Elizabeth 371
Macquarie, Governor Lachlan 463
Maealiuaki (Tu'i Ha'atakalaua) 62
Mahaiatea marae 276, 282, 287, 289
Mahau (high chief at Mo'orea)
    and Bounty's men 268, 279–80
    and Cook 86–8
    and Pandora's visit 296
    and Tu 135
    and Vancouver's visit 320, 321–2
    conflict with Mahine 78–9, 85–7
    death 325–6
    illness 320, 322
    threats to power 270–1
Mahau (named after high chief) 363
Mahine (high chief of Mo'orea)
    and Cook 85–7
    attack on Pare 134, 143, 144,
        146–7, 154
    attack on Tu's forces at Matavai
        Bay 135

conflict with Mahau 78–9, 85–7
    killed in battle 135, 162, 174, 380
mahu (man who lives as a woman)
    80–1
Ma'i (Te Tupai Ma'i, 'Omai') 17, 47,
    48, 53, 73, 77
    and Joseph Banks 334–5
    back in Society Islands after visit to
        England 71–91, 134, 155–6, 281
    battle dress 73, 281
    death 134, 139, 152, 156, 203, 281,
        299
    in Cook Islands 60–1
    in England 77, 77, 199, 334–5
    in New Zealand 57–9
    in Tasmania 55
    in Tonga 62–7
    gifts from England 281
    Māori attendants 59, 152, 203, 281
    married 498n
    pet monkey 88, 203
    relationship with Cook 91
    social status 72, 156, 281
Ma'iriri 271
Maititi
    and Bligh's Providence visit 351,
        352, 355, 374
    and Fletcher Christian 419
    death in England 431
    journey on Providence 389–90,
        393, 394, 419–20, 425, 428–9,
        430
Makaha'a 67
Makahiki festival 24, 27, 28, 28
malaria 316, 337, 425
Manby, Thomas 315–16, 321, 330
mana (ancestral power)
    'arioi 166, 168
    babies 192
    bark-cloth wrapping to intensify
        mana 135, 159
    Bligh 159, 351, 376
    ceremony combining mana of Tu,
        Cook and Bligh 159
    Cook 23, 59, 84, 125, 131–2, 135
    European god 195, 284
    Pomare II 284
    sacred relics 80, 81, 135, 284–5
    Tu 388
Manari'i 261, 345, 346
Manby, Thomas 315, 321, 330
Mangaia 60
Manu'a 304
Manua'e 61
Māori 55–60, 88
maps 106, 214, 219, 224–5, 238, 333
    see also charting
Mapu 368
marae
    at Pitcairn's Island 344
    Farero'i 157
    Mahaiatea 276, 282, 287, 289
    Taputapuatea see Taputapuatea
        marae
    Taraho'i 170, 172, 180, 278, 368,
        391
    'Utu-'ai-mahurau 79, 157
Mareva 345
Mari'ia 377, 378
Marion du Fresne, Marc Joseph 47
maro 'ura (red feather girdle) 74,
    79–81, 275, 281, 283–7, 321, 367,
    368–9, 391, 503n
Marquesa Islands 60, 253

marriage ceremony 365
marriage practices 380
Marsden, Samuel 459
Marsden, William 444
Marshall (first mate on Matilda) 349,
    355, 375
Martin, Isaac (able seaman) 178, 186,
    210–14, 258, 344, 346
'Mary' (Te'o) 245, 294, 317
masks 167
massage 157, 371, 380
Matahiapo (chief) 275
Matahiti (First Fruits) celebration
    160, 162, 169, 181, 183, 187, 317
Matavai Bay 139
    attacked by Pare 350–1, 354–5,
        360, 365
    Bligh made ari'i 167–8
    Bligh's memorial 472
    'Paradise of the World' 17, 20,
        149, 205, 232–3, 375–6, 395, 425
Matavy 293, 297, 301–3, 309, 310
Matilda 349
Matilda's whaleboat 349–50, 387, 389,
    393, 394
Matra, James 238
Mauatua ('Isabella', partner of
    Christian) 245, 250, 251, 258, 344,
    345, 346
Maui (island) 30–1
Maurua 300
Meares, Captain John 237, 500n
Me'eti'a 131, 198, 254, 347–8, 349
Menzies, Archibald 315, 316
    in Tahiti 319–20, 321–2, 324–5,
        328–9
merchant navy 332–3, 444
Mercury (Gustavus III) 254–7, 264
Millard (with Monarch) 452
Mills, John (gunner's mate)
    and Fletcher Christian 177, 242,
        258, 346
    and mutiny 177, 211
    and 'Prudence' (Vahineatua) 258,
        344
    child 344
    death 346
    on Pitcairn's Island 344, 346
Mills, Peter (Warrior) 455
Millward, John (able seaman) 163,
    318
    address to fellow sailors before
        hanging 418
    and mutiny 212–13, 407, 408–10,
        414, 418
    capture and voyage home 294–5,
        306–7, 352
    court martial evidence 414
    desertion attempt at Tahiti 175–6,
        182–3, 186–7
    in Tahiti after mutiny 258–9,
        263–4, 268, 269, 277, 280, 283,
        285, 287
    in Tahiti with Bligh 179, 182
    hung 414, 417–18, 444
mirrors 94, 333
mission house at Tautira 71
missionaries 74–5, 334–5, 395, 433,
    449, 494n
Mitford, Mary Russell 466
Moana (high chief)
    and Bligh's Bounty visit 82, 140,
        144, 145, 149, 157, 161–72,
        175–6, 179, 180, 182, 186

and Bligh's *Providence* visit 351, 375, 376, 384, 384
and *Bounty*'s men 283
and Cook 82
and *Lady Penryhn* visit 133–4
political ambitions 82
Monarch 452
money 166–7, 350, 356, 359–60, 367, 368, 372–3, 375
Monmouth 45
*monoi* oil 89, 272, 274, 280
Montague, Captain (*Hector*) 401, 416
Monuafe 67
moon 68, 167, 191
Mo'orea 78, 85–8, *86*
Mopiha 300
Morrison, James (boatswain's mate) 116
and Bligh 124, 130, 168, 202, 208
and Fletcher Christian 177–8, 242, 244, 251–4
and Tahitian women 140
consolation in religion 308, 404
during mutiny 212–13, 215, 433–7
in Tahiti after mutiny 258–9, 263, 264–93
and construction of *Resolution* (schooner) 264–5, 269, 272–3
and Teri'irere 282, 283, 285, 287–9
and Tu 271–2
on *Pandora* 295, 305–7
on Tupua'i after mutiny 251–4
pardoned 414, 416, 433
religious faith 404
return to England 308–11
shipwrecked 305–8
surrender 289, 293
testimony at court martial 412–13
written account of mutiny 404, 416, 417, 433, 434–5
Mortimer, Lieutenant 255–7
Mota 221
Mothe (Sunday Island) 223–4, 422
Motu Au 364
Mou'aroa (chief) 148, 193, 353–4, 377, 494n
Mouat, Alexander 92, 94, 233
Moulter, William 306, 307
Mount Tetufera 267
Murray Islands 423–4
music
Europeans 26, 27, 28, 65, 78, 428
Tahitians 90, 148, 188, 266, 364, 373
Tongans 62, 63
muskets, guns
desired by Tahitians 84, 148, 152, 256
stolen from *Matilda* 350, 356, 359–60, 367, 368, 372–3, 375
tally among districts in Tahiti 361
musketoons 259, 266
Muspratt, William (cook's assistant) 163
and mutiny 40, 409, 410, 414
at Tahiti after mutiny 258–9, 262, 269–70, 276, 277, 279, 287
capture at Tahiti 294
court martial 405, 407, 414, 436
desertion attempt at Tahiti 175–6, 182–3, 186–7
flogged for neglect of duty 173

shipwrecked on *Pandora* 305–7
stay of execution, pardoned 416
mutineers on *Bounty* 233–4, 241
arrival back in England 401–2
at Pitcairn's Island 342, 343–8, 464–5, 466–8, *467*, 470–1, 472–3
at Tahiti 244–5, 254–94
absorbing Tahitian ways 286–7
Captain Edwards' search 287–311
construction of *Resolution* 264–5, 269, 272–3
dispersal to different districts 262, 268, 269–70
division into two groups 258–9
lies told to Tahitians about Bligh's whereabouts 256, 259, 318, 336
stealing from each other 268–9, 271
surrender and capture 287–94
at Tupua'i, Fort George 242–4, 245–54
Bligh's condemnation 228–9, 233–4, 239, 395, 435
characterised as pirates, wretches and villains 213, 228, 229, 223–4, 237–8, 291, 342, 352, 395
court martial proceedings 406–18
descendants 472–3
in-fighting 242, 248, 251, 270
listed and described 233–4
on *Hector* awaiting trial 401
on *Pandora* 294–308
return to England 308–11
search for mutineers
by Edwards 289, 291–304
by Vancouver 312–30
mutinies
against Captain John Meares 237, 500n
in Naval fleet 446–7
on *Bounty* 20–1, 208–15, 232–4, 235–41
accounts 232–4, 237–40, 241, 310, 397–418
court martial evidence 406–17
Edward Christian's defence 434–41
factors leading to mutiny summarised 443–4
fictional poetic account in verse 466, 468
political context 21, 235–6, 444
on *Defiance* 445–6
mutinous behaviour 294
Charles Christian 120
under Bligh 163–4, 176–9, 230–1
under Christian 242
under Cook 22, 59
under Edwards 289–9
under Vancouver 316
*see also* desertion and potential desertion
mythic projections of Europeans 17–21, 297–8

Nagiti (chief) 207–8, 217
Nairai 221
names
changes 361
exchanges 25–6, 85, 141–2, 189–90, 246, 322, 352–3

Narcissus 289–90
navigation
ancestors of Polynesians 60
Bligh 68, 215, 219, 222–3, 237, 452
Cook 53–4
Finau 62, 301
Nelson, David (gardener, botanist) 20, 50, 341, 488n
and mutiny 212, 213, 243
at Adventure Bay 130
at Bruny Island 341
death in East Indies 228
illness 225, 228
in Tahiti 138–9, 141, 149, 153, 168–9, 200, 357
in Tonga 206–7, 362
preparation for breadfruit voyage 110–11, 115–16, 117
view of Bligh 124
with Bligh after mutiny 223, 224, 225, 241
Nelson, Horatio 448, 450–2
'Nelson's Hill' 341
neo-Classical themes 17–21
Nepean, Sir Evan 333–4, 444
Neptune 339
Netherlands 119, 447–8
*nevaneva* (crazy) 359
New Guinea 110, 161, 305
New Hebrides 393, 423
New South Wales 109, 110, 114, 117–18, 133, 340, 436, 456–64, 497n
New Zealand 21, 47, 55–60, 67, 108, 110, 130, 152, 245, 281, 317, 341, 473
New Year's Day 321
Ngau ('Paradise Island') 221, 422
Niau 261, 346
Nichols (with *Providence*) 424
Ni'ihau 96
Niue ('Savage Island') 204, 421
*noa* (ordinary, profane) 166, 192, 197
Nomuka 62–4, 205–8, 217, 256, 299, 302, 303, 304
Nootka Sound 96, 237, 314, 315
Nore off Sheerness 446–7
Norfolk Island 336, 340, 472
Norman, Charles (carpenter's mate) acquitted of mutiny 413, 414
and mutiny events 214–15, 371, 407–10, 413, 414
at Tahiti after mutiny 258–9, 262, 264, 268–9, 283, 287–9
return to England 308–11
shipwrecked 305–8
surrender 289, 293
Norris (surgeon on *Matilda*) 349–52, 354, 356–7, 362, 374, 375
North Sea 445–6
'Northwest Passage' 17, 43, 47, 94, 312, 314, 487n
Norton, John (quartermaster) 144, 163, 215–18, 241, 303
death in Tonga 217–18
Norton Sound 96
Nu'a (chief) 25, 38, 482n
Nuku'alofa Harbour 65
Nukunonu 301

O'Connell, Lieutenant Colonel 463
Odysseus 20
*Odyssey* 21
Oha 258, 345
Oliver, William 297, 301–2, 309, 401

'One Tree Hill' (Tahara'a)  138, 170, 175, 262, 354, 366, 379
Ono-i-lau Islands  302
Onslow, Admiral  447
Ori (chief)  88
Oroho (Tu's son)  363, 383
'Oro (god of fertility and war)  73, 74, 78–9, 184
'Oro worship  74, 195
    see also gods
Orohena Mountain  198, 371–2
Orsmond, John  74–5, 166, 494n, 496n
Otaheiti  see Tahiti

Paine, Tom  444
Palea  23, 30, 33–5, 314, 483n
Palliser, Sir Hugh  50, 54
Palmerston Island  61, 299, 300
Pandora  287, 288, 289–311, 397
    'Pandora's box' (prison)  293, 294, 296, 305–7
    shipwrecked  305–7, 306
'Pandora Passage'  305
Pantassey River  425
Papeno'o River  370–1
Papeno'o Valley  370
Papeto'ai Bay, Mo'orea  85, 86, 279, 320
Paradise  17, 18, 20, 149, 205, 232–3, 297, 375–6, 395, 425
Paradise after the Fall  396
Parker, Admiral Sir Hyde  101, 449–52
Pascoe, Lieutenant William  454
Pasley, Commodore Thomas (Vengeance)  333, 397, 398, 401, 402–3, 405, 406, 432, 510n
Passmore (mate)  307
Pateama'i ('Itia's sister)  266
Patiri  271–2
Paulaho  205, 207, 216, 217
Paupo  357
    death in Jamaica  431
    journey on Providence as stowaway  419–20, 423–31
Peace of Amiens  452
Peace of Paris  332
peace-making  83, 190, 209, 246, 249, 250, 277–8, 365, 367
Pearce, Jane (Bligh's mother)  45, 46, 484n
Pearce, Lieutenant (Providence)  353, 357, 360, 385, 392
pearl-shell  26, 167, 181, 204, 243, 250, 342, 420, 422
Peckover, William (gunner)  116, 176, 489n
    and Bligh after mutiny  241, 333, 402, 408, 409, 412, 435, 437, 441
    during mutiny  209–13
    evidence at court martial  409
    in Tahiti with Bligh  131, 138–9, 149
Pele (goddess of volcanoes)  33
penal colonies
    at Botany Bay  109, 110, 114, 117–18, 133, 340, 436, 488n
    at Port Jackson  133, 308, 311, 331, 336, 340
Peretane/Peretani (Britiain)  88, 133, 138, 172
Pereue ('arioi house)
Peru  71, 72, 74, 138, 154
Phillips, Molesworth  36–44, 50, 81, 416, 443, 482n

Pi-'a-roa pool  169, 362
pigs  145, 156
Pipon, Captain (Tagus)  470, 471
Pirates, or, the Calamities of Capt. Bligh, The (play)  237–8
pistols  194, 361, 407
Pitcairn's Island (Hiti-au-rereva)  342, 343–8, 464–5, 466–8, 467, 470–1, 472–3
Pitt, Hon. Thomas  315, 316, 326–7
plantations  108, 109, 110, 191, 429, 470, 495n
    see also gardens
Pleiades (Mata'ari)  150, 153, 154, 157, 167
Plymouth  45, 51, 446
Poe'e'eno (chief of Matavai Bay)
    and Bounty's men  264–6, 270, 273
    and Matilda's muskets and money  350, 356, 359–60, 367, 368, 372–3, 375
    and Mercury visit  255, 256
    and Pomare II  350
    and Vancouver's visit  322, 323
    district attacked  350–1, 354–5
    exiled  376
    taio of Bligh  82, 140–1, 149, 157, 165, 168, 169, 172, 179, 182
    taio of Morrison  259–60, 263
Pohuetea (chief)
    and Bligh  154, 180
    and Bounty's men  279, 287, 289
    and Cook  79
    island politics  154, 273–8, 387
Pohuetea Ti'i (chief)  374
Poiatua  91–3, 92, 152
Point 'Utuha'iha'i  377
Point Venus (Te Aurora)
    and Bounty's men  267
    and Cook  75, 81, 140–1
    Bligh's memorial  472–3
    Bligh's visits  140, 149–50, 355, 356, 357–8, 360, 385–6, 392
    breadfruit plants  173
    Vancouver's visit  321, 322–3, 324, 326, 327–8
Pomare I  see Tu
Pomare II (paramount chief)  184, 202, 387, 494n
    and Bligh  146, 147–8, 174–5, 197, 353, 360, 361, 363, 376, 390, 392–3, 394
    and Bounty's men  262–3, 268, 273–6, 285–6, 287
    at human sacrifice ceremony  390–1
    betrothed  374
    Chatham's and Discovery's visit  317, 318, 319, 327
    described  319
    differing views on authority  272, 277, 283, 284, 286, 329, 388
    gifts presented by Europeans  365, 394
    investiture at Taputapuatea marae  281–6
    sacred relics returned to Pare  275–8
Pomona  264
Porapora  61, 88, 92, 93–4, 95, 155, 299–300
Porpoise  457–8, 463
Port Jackson  133, 308, 311, 331, 336, 340

Port Palliser  54
Port Royal Harbour  429
Port Venus  133
Portlock, Nathaniel  332, 333, 337 40
    in Tahiti  347–87 passim
    praised by Bligh  386
    promotion  432
Price, Dr Richard  235, 236
priests  79, 154, 157, 167, 169, 252, 273, 274, 281–4, 368–9, 391
    installation of Pomare II  284–5
    Vaita's prophecy  60–1, 286
Princess Amelia  102
Prince William Sound  96
prophecy of European advent in the Pacific  60–1, 286
Providence  332–3, 337
    breadfruit expedition under Bligh  332–96, 419–31
    officers tainted by Bligh's reputation  436
'Prudence' (Vahineatua)  258, 344
Puarai  344
Puget, Peter  316, 325, 328
Puni (paramount chief of Borabora)  93, 94, 155, 299–300
punishment
    in Hawai'i  29, 33
    in Tahiti  87–8, 90, 91, 178, 194, 266, 355, 376, 377
    in Tonga  63, 65
    on Pitcairn's Island  345
    over-harsh  65, 90, 178
    sailors  59, 90, 94
    see also floggings
Purahi  74
Purcell, William (carpenter)  116, 129, 163–4, 209–10, 437
    arrested  231
    defying authority  224
    illness  225
    imprisoned  230
    insolence  224
    mutinous behaviour  163–4, 230
    punished for flouting orders  129, 240
    reprimanded in England  240
    role in mutiny  212–14, 402, 408, 409, 411, 412, 435, 441
    testimony at court martial  409
    with Bligh after mutiny  217, 223, 224, 225, 230–1, 240, 289
Purea ('Queen of Otaheiti')  18, 80, 193, 286
Purutea  342
Putland, Lieutenant John  452, 457–8, 462
Putuputua  64

Queen Charlotte Sound  55–9, 67
Quintal, Matthew (able seaman)  125–6, 163, 207
    during mutiny  210–14, 407, 408, 414
    punished for insolence and contempt  125–6
    with Christian after mutiny  248, 258, 344–7

ra'a (sacredness, ancestral power)  147, 192, 202, 282, 285, 361, 365, 497n
rahui (sacred restriction)  198

Ra'iatea  60–1, 91–4, 193, 253, 285–6,
    299, 498n
    see also Taputapuatea marae
Rainbow (sacred canoe)  278
rainbows  147
rampages  87–8, 134, 170
Ranger  46
Ranswell, William (Warrior)  455
Rarotonga  342–3
rats  85, 89, 117, 163, 249
Raymond (in St Helena)  428–9
red, sacred colour  196, 391, 428
red bunting from the Dolphin  80, 275,
    284, 369, 391
red feather girdle (maro 'ura)  74,
    79–81, 275, 281, 283–7, 321, 367,
    368–9, 391, 503n
red feathers as gifts and for barter
    71–4, 81, 136
religion
    Christianity see Christianity
    'Oro worship  73, 74, 78–9, 184,
        195
    see also gods
Renouard (midshipman)  302
Reo (chief)  91–4
Resolution  52
    Banks's modifications  111–12
    Bligh master on Cook's 1776
        voyage  22–96
    damaged  31, 68
    poor condition  51
Resolution (schooner, constructed by
    mutineers)
    building and preparing  264–5,
        269, 273, 274–5, 279
    renamed Matavy  293
    sailed  279–80
    sold  310
    stripped by Teri'irere's men  288
Resource  228, 230–1, 336
Restoration Island  223
Reynolds, Joshua  48, 77
Rickman, John  101
    in Hawai'i  22, 37, 40, 41
    in Society Islands  81, 96
Rights of Man, The (Paine)  444
Rio de Janeiro  291, 463
Riou, Edward  59, 234–5, 450–1
Roberts, Henry  36, 38, 39, 44, 50, 54,
    55, 67, 100, 105–7, 109, 314, 482n
Rodger, N.A.M.  443
Rodríguez, Máximo ('Matimo')  71,
    72, 95
Rohutu-no'ano'a  188, 192
Roman and Greek mythology see
    European mythic projections
Romantic poets  466, 514n
Romilly, Samuel  437
Rotuma  304
Rousseau, Jean-Jacques  236
Royal Gazette  336
Royal Navy
    attack on Danish fleet  450–2
    attack on Dutch fleet  447–8
    Channel Fleet  332, 446
    'Floating Republic'  447
    mutinies at poor conditions  444,
        446–7
Royal Navy Hydrographic
    Department  452
Royal Society  18, 102, 107, 452
Royal William  240
Ruahatu (sea god)  385

rum  54, 122, 123, 129, 173, 214, 219,
    220, 222, 292, 321, 380, 410, 445,
    459, 463
Rum Rebellion in New South Wales
    459–63, 465–6
Rurutu  253
Russia  43, 96, 332, 450

sacred drums  80, 284, 368, 503n
sacred relics from Taputapuatea
    79–81, 193, 275–7, 286, 367–9
sacred restrictions  32, 144, 180, 192,
    364, 395
sacrifices, human see human sacrifices
Sahlins, Marshall  21
St Helena  425–6, 427–8, 448–9
St Jago  338
St Vincent  429
Samoan archipelago  60, 164, 301–2,
    304
Samuel, John (captain's clerk)  198,
    209, 212–13
Samwell, David  25, 27, 31, 38, 75–6,
    78–9, 84, 85, 482n, 484n
Sandwich  446–7
Sandwich, Lord
    and Banks  112
    and Bligh  51, 101–2, 105, 109,
        117–18
    and Cook  49, 98–9
    and Ma'i  90–1, 335
    publication of Cook's Voyage
        101–2, 105, 109
Sandwich Islands  107
'Sarah' (Tevarua)  345
Savai'i  301
scurvy  117, 122–3, 127–8, 129, 130,
    131, 133, 136, 341, 435, 455
Season of Plenty (Matari'i-i-ni'a)
    150–1, 153, 157, 159–60, 169,
    317, 326
Season of Scarcity (Matari'i-i-raro)
    72, 138, 144, 355, 379, 385, 386, 388
Season of the High Seas (te tau miti
    rahi)  164, 323
Selkirk, Lord  102, 117–18
Semarang  231–2, 302
Sever, Captain William (Lady
    Penrhyn)  133–7, 139
Sevill (midshipman)  300
sexual behaviour
    age of first activity  203
    chiefs  359, 382
    in public as part of rituals or
        festivals  74
    mahu (man living as a woman)
        180–1
    prohibitions on sailors  173, 319,
        326–7, 347
    rape by sailors  57, 267
    same-sex relationships  31, 180
    sex in bartering see barter
    sexual tolerance  382
    sexually transmitted diseases see
        venereal disease
    Tahitian view of adultery  180,
        203
    Tahitian view of sex  74, 382
shaddocks  78, 88, 141, 169, 206, 214,
    262, 362, 375, 380
sharks  174, 503n
shark-teeth  92, 165, 914–5, 208, 325,
    365, 389, 393
Shaw, Thomas  92

Shillibeer, Lieutenant (Briton)  470
shipwrecks
    Matilda  349
    Pandora  305–7
shooting and killing of islanders
    in Cook Islands  342
    in Dungeness and Warrior islands
        424
    in Hawai'i  37–41, 52
    in Murray Islands  423
    in New Zealand  57–8
    in Samoa  301
    in Tahiti  267, 270, 280, 293–4, 354,
        385
    in Tonga  303
    on Pitcairn's Island  345–6
    on Tupua'i  243–4, 246, 253
Short, Captain  458
sickness and disease
    among Europeans  150, 156, 425
    among Tahitians  69, 132, 162,
        192, 195, 297–8, 322, 352, 374,
        497n
    at Tupua'i  243–4
    scurvy and scurvy prevention see
        scurvy
    Tahitian interpretations of illness
        150, 195, 383
    venereal disease see venereal
        disease
    see also specific diseases
Simpson, George (quartermaster's
    mate)  212, 216
singing  19, 23, 24, 251, 273
Sirius  340
Skinner, Richard (able seaman)  163,
    352
    drowned  305–6
    in Tahiti after mutiny  258–9, 260,
        276, 287
    on Pandora  292, 293, 294–5
    red hair  391, 502n, 503n
skits  90, 149, 169, 257, 375, 379
skulls  29, 158, 271–2, 314, 377, 277,
    496
slashing the head or body
    in celebration  75, 365
    in grief or distress  92, 165, 194,
        195, 208, 249, 295, 325, 381, 389,
        393
slaves in West Indies  108–9, 110, 429
smallpox  104, 121, 428, 431
Smith, Alexander (John Adams, able
    seaman)  152
    and 'Jenny' (Te'ehuteatuaonoa)
        245, 250, 251, 342, 344
    and Puarai  344
    at Pitcairn's Island  343–8, 465,
        470–1
    at Tahiti after mutiny  245, 250–1
    during mutiny  211–12
    hostage on Tapua'i  250
    punished for allowing theft  151–2
    'romantic hero'  471
Smith, Christopher (botanist–
    gardener)  333, 419, 425,
Smith, John (Bligh's servant)  163,
    214, 226–7, 333, 410, 414, 437,
    439–41
Smyth, Bowes  134, 136, 137
social structure in Tahiti  156, 192,
    194, 380
    ari'i (chief)  156
    ari'i rahi (paramount chief)  156

manahune (commoner) 156, 192, 196, 281
ra'atira (landowner) 156, 196
ta'ata mauri (middling class) 156, 194
ta'ata tu'au (baron) 156
teuteu (servant) 144, 156, 192, 380
Society Islands
  Bligh's visits 138–201, 347–96
  Cook's Resolution visit 60, 69–97
  see also Tahiti
Society for the Encouragement of Arts, Manufactures and Commerce 436
Solander, Dr Daniel ('Torano') 53, 108, 139, 335, 366
soundings 55, 62, 305
South America 60
'South Sea' (Te Moana-nui-a-Kiwa) 60
South Seas 17–19
Spain 69, 71–2, 74, 132, 291
Spikerman, Captain 226–7, 231
Spithead 119, 311, 337, 446
Staines, Captain Thomas (Briton) 470
stars 27, 60, 160, 167, 178, 191
Stewart, George (midshipman) 114, 130, 176–8, 233
  and Bligh 193, 195–6, 228–9, 233
  and Fletcher Christian 241–2, 244, 245, 251, 258, 260–1
  and mutiny 210, 215, 258, 317
  and 'Peggy' 245, 262, 294–5, 317–18, 324, 327, 329, 330, 360–1
  daughter Charlotte 294, 317, 318, 324, 329, 360
  killed in shipwreck 306, 317
  on Pandora 293–5, 306
  on Tahiti after mutiny 262, 269, 287, 400
  surrender 287, 291
Stewart, Keith 102, 118
storms at sea
  Chatham 317
  endured by Bligh 162, 164, 220–1, 222, 225–6, 300, 341
  endured by Cook 22, 31, 55, 61, 126–7
  Rembang 308–9, 319
  shipwreck of Pandora 300, 305–7
storms on land 317
stowaways 200, 245, 252, 392, 419
stripping to the waist in respect 262, 265
Stuart, Charles 315, 316
sugar cane 22, 153, 192, 342, 365, 429
summer solstice 169, 170
Sumner, John (able seaman)
  and mutiny 211–12, 215, 407
  at Tahiti after mutiny 248, 259, 260, 264, 269, 276, 287
  captured 294
  flogged for neglect of duty 204
  killed in shipwreck 306
  on Pandora 294, 306
sun 60, 67, 191
Sunday Island 223–4, 422
Surabaya 230–1, 302
surfing 162
'Susannah' (Teraura) 344
Sutter, Captain (Jenny) 350
Swallow 343
syphilis 163, 198

Ta'apuna 156–7, 253, 276–7
Ta'aroa (god) 73, 184
Ta'aroahine (Auo's daughter) 374
Ta'aroamiva (Tetahiti) 251, 252, 253, 254, 258, 345–6
Ta'aroatohoa (chief) 246–54
Tagus 470
Taha'a 92, 94, 299
Tahamaitua (Tu's daughter) 197, 363, 381, 495n
Tahara'a Hill ('One Tree Hill') 138, 170, 175, 262, 354, 366, 379
Tahatu (chief) 299–300
Tahiti (Otaheite) 70
  Afa'ahiti district 283
  Atehuru alliance 185, 276, 367–8, 387
  Atimaono district 387
  district alliances 387, 504n
  Fa'a'a district (Tetaha) 156, 158, 182, 273–5
  Ha'apaino'o (Papeno'o) district 253, 370
  Ha'apape district 82, 140, 158, 172, 366
  Hitia'a district 145, 182, 253, 283, 374, 387, 504n
  Mahaena district 387
  Matavai district 253, 274, 275
  Pa'ea district 156–7, 161, 185, 275–6, 387
  Papara district see Teri'irere
  Pare district 144, 146–7, 171–201, 253, 269, 281–6
  Patere district 387
  'Paradise' 17, 18, 20, 149, 205, 232–3, 297, 375–6, 395, 425
  political geography of island 387
  population decline 195
  Tahiti-iti / Tai'arapu (southern Tahiti) 69, 70, 161, 185, 263, 269, 283, 374
  Tahiti-nui 70
  Tautira district 71, 268, 271–2, 498–9n, 504n
  Te Porionu'u (Te 'Aharoa) alliance 253, 276, 283, 387, 388, 504n
  Teahupo'o district 268, 373, 387
  Teva-i-tai alliance (Tai'arapu) 387
  Teva-i-uta alliance 387
  Ti'arei district 387, 504n
  Vaiari district 282–3, 387, 504n
  Vai'uriri district 387, 504n
Tahiti visited by European ships
  Bounty under Bligh 138–201
  Bounty under mutineers 244–5, 254, 258–62
  Discovery and Chatham under Vancouver 312–30
  Lady Penryhn 133–7
  Matilda's shipwrecked men 349–51, 92
  Mercury 254–7
  Pandora under Edwards 289–98
  Providence and Assistant under Bligh 347–96
  Resolution and Discovery under Cook 69–96
Tahitians
  adoption of European symbols of power 195
  at Pitcairn's Island 243–8
  criticised by Bligh 395
  desire for European support and

  protection 82–4, 154, 194, 351, 352
  disenchantment with the British 330
  despoliation by Europeans 69–70, 132–3, 163, 195, 358, 375–6
  European mythic projections 17–21, 297–8
  irresistibility of Tahitian women to sailors 93–4, 95–6, 176–7, 232–3, 330
  morality appraised by Europeans 335, 382, 395, 396, 403
  relieved at Bligh's departure 392
  social structure see social structure in Tahiti
tahu'a (priests) 157, 368
Tahuhuatama (chief) 246–54
Tai Aiva 321, 370–1
Taieri 156
taio (bond friend) 25–6, 142, 154, 172–3, 353
Taipipi ('Cockroach Point') 273, 274, 276, 281, 364, 367
Tamatoa (chief) 152, 246, 248, 253
Tane (god) 147, 184, 272
Tapa (chief) 63, 205–8
Tapairu (Moana's son) 181
  and Bounty's men in Tahiti 260, 291, 292
  and Bounty's men at Tupua'i 253–4
  and Chatham visit 318
  and Matilda's muskets and money 350–1, 356, 359–60, 370, 372–3, 374, 375
  and Pomare II 350
  and Providence visit 370–1
  assistance with desertion 175, 179, 180, 318
  attack on Matavai Bay 354–5
tapu (sacred) 286
  ari'i rahi 262, 394
  birth 145, 192
  death 325–6
  food 144
  head 285, 391
  tapu-raising 180
  words 147, 361
Taputapuatea marae (at Rai'atea) 60–1, 74, 152, 202, 275, 278
  ravaged by Porapora warriors 283–6
  sacred relics 79–81, 193, 275–6, 277, 286, 367–9
Taputapuatea marae (at Pare) 283–6, 325, 368, 377, 390
Taputapuatea portable marae 275, 278, 367
Taraho'i marae 170, 172, 180, 278, 368, 377–8, 391
Tararo 261, 345
Taravao isthmus 283, 288
Tareu 146
Taro 366, 373
taro 168, 187, 191, 204, 246, 253, 342–3, 496n
Tasman, Abel 65, 221, 422
Tasmania 19, 55, 100, 129–30, 341
tattoo
  'arioi 75, 377
  at Aitutaki 420
  at Huahine 203
  Fletcher Christian 233

'Knights of Otaheiti' 178, 233–4, 258
Porapora warriors 300
sailors 116, 136, 178, 213, 233–4, 260, 286, 397, 405, 413
sailor's partner 245
*taumi* (warrior's breastplate) 190, 213, 327, 354
Te Ao (realm of the people) 74, 157, 167
Te Auroa *see* Point Venus
Te Matangi ('Lagoon Island') 347
Te Moana-nui-a-Kiwa 60
Te Pau (chief)
 and Bligh 158, 182, 184, 188, 191, 194, 353
 and *Bounty*'s men 262, 267, 269, 295
 illness and death 184, 194, 353
 *taio* of Peter Heywood 262
Te Po (realm of the gods) 74, 81, 84, 157, 167, 184, 192
Te Ra'i-puatata (red feather girdle) 74, 79–81, 275, 281, 283–7, 321, 367, 368–9, 391, 503n
Te Ri'itaria (chief) 88
*te tau miti rahi* (season of the high seas) 164, 323
Te Wai Pounamu 281
Te Weherua 152, 156, 203, 281
Teano (Vaiareti) 281
Tearamoana Pass 242, 245–6, 248
Te'ehuteatuaonoa ('Jenny') 245, 250, 251, 342, 344
Teimua 346
Temua 261
Tenani'a 281
Tenerife 122, 291, 316, 337
Te'o ('Mary' Burkett) 245, 294, 317
Terano (Te Pau's wife) 353
Teraura ('Susannah') 344, 346
Teria ('Peggy') 245, 262, 294–5, 317–18, 324, 327, 329, 330, 360–1
Teri'i-na-vaha-roa (Tu's daughter) 197, 388
Teri'irere 80, 263, 275–6, 387–8, 449
 allegiance to Pomare II 282–3
 and Bligh's books 389
 and use of *Bounty*'s men 263–93 *passim*, 320, 359–60, 361
 illness 378, 388
Teri'itapunui (Tu's son) 197, 363, 374, 388, 494n
Teri'itaria (Ori's son) 88
Terra Australis 313
*Teta'i* (season of weeping) 174
Teti'aroa 175, 180, 181, 182–3, 186–7, 196, 203
Teto'ofa (grandson of 'the Admiral') 387
Teto'ofa (son of 'the Admiral') 273–8
Teto'ofa ('the Admiral') 79, 83, 84, 85, 134, 140, 146, 276
Tetuanui (Mahau's son) 363
Tetua-teahama'i 77
Tetumu 60–1, 74, 159, 188, 286
Tetupaia (Tu's mother) 152, 285
 and Bligh 160–1, 162, 165, 170, 193, 198, 372, 389, 393–4
 and *Bounty*'s men 267–8
 and Cook 77, 78, 84, 321
 and *Mercury*'s visit 257
 and Tamatoa 152, 253
Teu (Tu's father) 77, 81

and Bligh 140, 141, 149, 162, 190, 193, 198, 200, 358, 359, 364, 389, 390, 392, 393
and *Bounty*'s men 273, 275
and Vancouver 321
 death 497n
teuteu (servant) 144, 156, 192, 380, 438
thanksgiving ceremony (*otai*) 171–2
theft
 animals 63, 65–6, 86–8, 266
 cleaver 173
 cloth, bed linen 193–4, 374, 376
 clothing 57, 266, 301, 303, 326, 327–8, 350, 355, 372, 386–7, 389
 cutter 35–7, 175–6, 314
 flag 282
 from boats or ships 140, 145–6, 151–2, 162, 198, 207, 243, 257, 266, 304, 317
 from shore camps 193, 198, 327–8, 385, 386
 handkerchief 366
 iron, nails and tools 33–4, 63, 91, 206
 money 359–60, 367, 368, 372–3, 375
 Tahitians warned not to steal 172, 173, 193
 technical instruments 89–90, 193–4
 weapons 66, 175–6, 266, 349–50, 359–60, 372
 writing equipment 280–1
thirst 226, 302, 307, 308, 399, 424
Thompson, Matthew (able seaman)
 and Fletcher Christian 248
 and mutiny 211–12, 398, 399, 409, 411–12
 flogged for insolence and disobedience 164
 in Tahiti after mutiny 259–72
 killed 271, 283, 291, 369–70, 377
 murderous attack on Tahitians 267–8
 punished for insolence 164
thunder and lightning interpretation 392
*ti'i* (carved poles) 148, 184, 377, *378*
Ti'itorea 161, 268
Timor 226–34, *227*, 308–11
Tinafanaea 345
Tinarou (chief) 245–6, 249–53, 371, 419
Tinkler, Robert (midshipman) 214–15, 217, 451
To'aroa Harbour 157, 170, 171, 194, 202, 278
Tobin, George 332–3
 and Bligh 129–30, 340, 341
 in Tahiti 347–94 *passim*
 journey to West Indies with breadfruit plants 419–31
 summation of Bligh's character 472
*to 'erau maeha 'a* (Westerly Twins) 188
Tofua 20, 208, 210, 215–18, 227, 303–4, 393, 398–9
Toga 221
Toipoi 374
Tolaga Bay 55
Tollen, Samuel (stowaway) 392

Toma 374
Tongan archipelago ('Friendly Isles') 20, 62–8, 205–18, 227, 256, 299, 302–4, 343, 393, 398–9, 421–2
Tongatapu 65, 67–8, 304, 343
Tongaware (chief) 420
*to'o* (god images) 188, 365
To'ofaiti 345
tools, European 116, 132, 140, 143, 154, 163, 179, 201, 269, 373
*Topaz* 464
Torres Islands 221
Torres Straits 225–6, 423
trade *see* barter
trees 18, 297, 422
 damaged by animals 249
 destroyed in raids 85, 146, 276, 357, 362
 felled for ship-building 264, 265
 New Zealand trees in England 108
 on ships 342–3
 planted by Europeans 78, 88, 130, 318, 341, 362, 380, 381
 sacred 79, 157
Trevenen, James 39, 42, 86, 104, 314
tricks 91, 145–6, 162, 207, 257, 264–5, 250, 280, 368, 377
*Triumph* 345
Tu (paramount chief) 20, 72–4, 134
 and Bligh's *Bounty* visit 141–201
 and Bligh's *Providence* visit 351–95, 449
 and *Bounty*'s men 263, 264, 268–76, 283, 295
 and *Discovery* visit under Vancouver 320–2, 324–30
 and Fletcher Christian 244–5
 and *Lady Penrhyn* visit 134–7
 and *Mercury* visit 255–7
 and *Pandora*'s visit 292–7
 attached to European visitors 136–7
 attacked by Mahine 135
 contrasted with his brothers 384–5
 death 497n
 desire for items from England 84, 136–7, 148, 152, 256
 desire to go to England 184, 194, 200, 296, 389
 marginalised politically 388
 regaining power in Pare-'Arue 174–5
 *taio* of Bligh 20, 141–2, 144–5, 154, 156, 158–9, 189–90, 351, 358–9, 388, 395
 *taio* of Cook 73–88, 94, 134, 141–2, 158–9, 286, 320, 388
 veneration of Cook 141, 158–9
 vulnerable because of closeness with Europeans 185
 wives 320, 359
Tuamotu Islands 60, 291, 347
Tuauru River 78, 164, 293, 317, 324–5, 355, 357, 362, 371, 383
Tuauru Valley 168, 360
tuberculosis 35, 51, 83–4, 96, 109, 192, 194–5, 297–8, 322
Tu'i Ha'atakalaua 62
Tu'i Kanokupolu 62
Tu'i Tonga 62–7
*tupapa'u* (funerary biers) 157, 166, 192, 381, 384
Tupaia (high chief, high priest) 80, 156, 193, 198, 275, 285

Tupoulagi (chief) 62, 205–6, 303–4
Tupua'i 68, 93, 242–4, 245–54, *247*, 399
Turtle Island 225
Tutaha (chief) *see* Ha'amanimani
Tutuila 301–2, 304
Tuvan-i-ra 302

Union Jack 133, 226, 243, 249, 252, 264, 282, 285, 324
*'unu* boards 325, 368, 377, 378, 503n
*upaupa* (formerly known as *heiva*) 373
'Upolu 301
Uru-pou 156
Utopia 17–18, 69, 235–6, 419, 471
*utu* (equivalent return) 59
*utu* (offering) 265
'Utu-'ai-mahurau *marae* 79, 157

Vaetua (Tu's brother) 76–7, 141, 385, 388, 502n
 and Bligh's *Bounty* visit 144, 351, 363, 385, 395
 and Bligh's *Providence* visit 351, 353, 363, 371–3, 380–1, 384, 385
 and *Bounty*'s men 259–61, 295
 and Pomare II 350–1, 388
 and Vancouver's visit 321–9
 attack on Matavai Bay 350–1, 354–5
 beautiful wife 370–1, 380–1
 fondness for *'ava* 154, 162, 384, 385
 hatred of Bligh 395
 killer of Mahine 135, 174, 380
 skirmish at Fa'a'a 274–5
 *taio* of Hayward 154, 175, 183, 186, 261, 289, 293, 295, 321, 351
 war on Matavai Bay 350, 354
Vahine Metua 196–7, 295, 364, 374
Vahineatua ('Prudence') 258, 344
Vai'are Bay 279–80
Vaiaotea 268, 271
Vaiareti (Teano, 'Itia's sister)
 and Bligh 324–5, 328, 358–9, 363, 366, 371, 374, 382, 384, 393
 and Edwards 292
 affair with Ari'ipaea 359
 dislike of Bligh 391, 395
 Tu's wife 281, 320
 Vehiatua III's widow 281
 'wanton display' 382
Vaiava stream 371
Vaio'opo'o River 151
Vai'otaha *marae* 271–2
Vaita (priest) 60–1, 286
Vaitepiha Bay 17, 19, 71–2, 144
Valentine, James (able seaman) 130, 163
Van Diemen's Land *56*
Van Este, Governor 226, 228, 231
Vanavana 349
Vancouver, George 34, 312–16, *313*
 brutal commander 316, 443
 illness 316
 in Hawai'i with Cook 34–5, 312–14

in New Zealand 317
 search for mutineers in Tahiti 312–30
 offending Tahitians 327, 351, 352, 376, 351
Vanikoro 304
Varari 320
Vava'u 304
Vehiatua II 71, 72
Vehiatua III 72, 73–4, 77, 263, 267–8, 359
 succeeded by Charles Churchill 269, 322
venereal disease 69, 72, 94, 131, 136, 140, 144, 162, 163, 173, 174, 195, 197–8, 206, 239–40, 297–8, 347, 385
*Vengeance* 397
Venus (Bligh's dog) 272
'Venus' (washerwoman) 394
Venus/Aphrodite (goddess) 17, 90
*vi* (Tahitian apples) 133, 198, 272
Virgil 19
Viti Levu 221
*Vlydt* 234
Voltaire 236
*Vreedenberg* 310–11
*Vrijheid* 448

Waiaka 251
Wales, William (astronomer) 114, 313
Walker, John 49
Wallis, Captain Samuel (*Dolphin*) 69, 80, 143
Wallis Island 304
Walpole, Horace 69, 335
Wana (chief) 374
Wanjon, Governor 226, 308, 334, 425
War of Independence 46, 51, 103, 109, 132
war with Netherlands 119, 447–8
war with Russia 332
*Warrior* 453–6
Warrior Island 424
water rockets 63–4
waterspouts 204, 221, 423
Watman, William 28
Watt, Sir James 316
Watts, Lieutenant John ('Tona') 37–8, 41, 133–7, 139, 141, 143, 284, 327
weapons
 as gifts 90, 394
 European weapons desired 84, 148, 152, 256
 stolen 66, 175–6, 266, 349–50, 359–60, 372
 weapon displays 82, 137
Weatherhead, Captain Matthew (*Matilda*) 349
Webber, John 17, 19, 20, 59, 83, 84, 134, 141, 152, 158, 201, 320
Welsh, William
West Indies 20, 46, 104, 108–9, 427–30
whalers 349–50
Whareunga Bay ('Grass Cove') killings 57–9, 67

Whyte (surgeon's mate) 366
Wilberforce, William 334, 416, 437
Wiles, James (botanist–gardener) 333, 357, 419, 425, 429
Williams, John (able seaman)
 and Fa'ahotu 344–5
 and mutiny 211, 212
 at Pitcairn's Island 343, 344–6
 at Tahiti after mutiny 258
 flogged for neglect of duty 128
 murdered 346
Williams, John (missionary) 342–3
Williamson, John
 commander of *Agincourt* 448
 court martialled 448
 in Hawai'i 35–44
 abandonment of Cook 38–9, 105, 484n
 in Society Islands 67, 74, 81, 87–8, 94, 95, 160
 in Tonga 66–7
 unpopular 39, 53, 81
Wilson, Captain (*Duff*) 449
wind 60, 126, 161–2, 164, 188, 496n
Windham, William 42–3, 238
Windward Islands 221
winter solstice 386
women
 *'arioi see 'arioi*
 at Pitcairn's Island 343–8
 convicts 133
 eating separately from men 144, 197, 357, 386
 'English women' 152, 160, 255–6
 'Great Women' of Tahiti 135, 143, 193, 267
 irresistibility of Tahitian women 93–4, 95–6, 176–7, 232–3, 330
 kidnapped by Christian 261, 342, 344–5
 partners of mutineers 294–5, 317–18, 344–8, 501n
 wrestlers 155, 191
Wordsworth, Captain John 437
Wordsworth, William 113, 236, 437
wrapping in bark cloth *see* bark cloth
wrestling 19
 in Hawai'i 24, 27, 28, 29
 in Tahiti 95, 154–5, 162–3, 181, 183, 190, 191, 266, 282, 375, 386, 390

yams 168
Yarmouth 447
yaws 162, 174, 184, 197–8, 206, 345, 372
yellow fever 428
Yonge, Sir George 114, 117
Young, Edward ('Ned', midshipman) 114, 176–7, 178, 208, 234, 241, 258, 344–7

Zimmerman, Heinrich 101
Zoffany, John 260
*Zwan* 398